ORNAMENTATION IN
BAROQUE AND POST-BAROQUE MUSIC

With Special Emphasis on J. S. Bach

Frederick Neumann

Ornamentation in Baroque

and Post-Baroque

Music

With Special Emphasis
on J. S. Bach

Princeton University Press

Published by Princeton University Press, Princeton, New Jersey
In the United Kingdom: Princeton University Press, Guildford, Surrey

Library of Congress Cataloging in Publication Data
will be found on the last printed page of this book

Publication of this book has been aided by
the John Simon Guggenheim Memorial Foundation and
the Windsor Foundation

This book has been composed in Linotype Baskerville

Printed in the United States of America
by Princeton University Press, Princeton, New Jersey

To Margaretta

Preface

The first impulse for writing this book came from intuitive misgivings about the prevailing theories of baroque ornamentation. My doubts became more tangible when I started probing into the matter and now appear fully vindicated in the light of continued research. The results of this research are embodied in the present volume.

Briefly, these are some of the doctrines I questioned: all principal small graces such as the appoggiatura, the slide, the mordent, must start exactly on the beat, taking their value from the following note, and must carry a metric-dynamic emphasis; the trill must start with the upper auxiliary which also must strike the beat and retain its metrical prominence in the manner of a "repeated appoggiatura." Considering that all other graces were to be similarly treated, the effect of these restrictive rulings has been far-reaching indeed in a style in which ornaments played an immense role.

The beliefs in question have been held by so many for so long that they have become quasi-articles of faith. It was the rigidifying effect of these principles that aroused my suspicion. Rigidity is out of place in any aspect of artistic performance, but nowhere is it more incongruous than with ornaments, whose function has been at all times, and in every field of art, to add grace, to relieve austerity, to soften rigidity, to round angularity. Clearly something must have gone amiss. It turned out that mistakes had been made in the crucial matter of evidence, its selection, its application. Since similar questionable procedures have affected other aspects of historic research as well, a reexamination is due for many theories in the whole domain of performance practice.

The purpose of this study is to attempt such reexamination in the field of baroque and post-baroque ornamentation with a strong emphasis on the music of J. S. Bach. This focus on Bach's music explains certain features of outline and presentation. Thus, for instance, the whole body of English ornamentation was left out because it has no traceable bearing on Bach—nor even on Handel. The omission is regrettable but should not affect the principal aim of the study.

The attempt to revise firmly established ideas required much evidence to build a convincing case. The mass of the needed material could discourage readers who are interested in the subject but do not care to be involved in overly detailed discussions. In an effort to reconcile the divergent concerns of scholarship and pragmatism, I resorted to the use of two sizes of type, the large one of which can be read *alone* without loss of continuity. The *large type* contains the main narrative, the most important theoretical and musical documentation and the basic conclusions. The *small type* serves to corroborate the evidence by supportive documentation and discussion. Hence those readers who want to probe into the soundness of my conclusions will need to read the complete text.

The voluminous material that contradicts the prevailing doctrines (much of which is unknown so far) might create in some minds the impression of an unbalanced presentation. However, I am confident that the open-minded reader will find in this study not the substitution of a new dogmatism for an old one, but the establishment of far greater freedoms for historically authentic ornament interpretation. Within these freedoms I never deny the important, rightful place to the on-the-beat and related designs of modern doctrine; I only deny them their claim to monopoly.

NOTATION and clefs were modernized except for original features of special interest.

Acknowledgments

In the course of the roughly ten years which it took me to research and write this book, I received generous help and encouragement from so many that an attempt to acknowledge them all would extend this tribute to forbidding length. Regretfully, I shall therefore have to limit myself to name those persons and institutions whose assistance was truly crucial, while at the same time extending my heartfelt thanks to the unnamed, but not fogotten many, in the hope that they will accept, understand, and forgive this seemingly ungracious collective gesture.

First I want to acknowledge with gratefulness those organizations without whose financial assistance the book could not have been written. I tender my thanks to my own institution, the University of Richmond, for numerous research grants over the years; to the John Simon Guggenheim Memorial Foundation for a fellowship (1967-1968); to Princeton University for a Senior Fellowship of its Council of the Humanities (1970-1971); to the American Philosophical Society for a Grant-in-Aid; to the American Council of Learned Societies for three Grants-in-Aid. Moreover, I am indebted for publication subsidies to the Windsor Foundation in Richmond and the John Simon Guggenheim Memorial Foundation.

Among colleagues who read parts or all of the manuscript and helped me with invaluable advice and constructive criticism were Professors Arthur Mendel (who made me rethink and rewrite many a section), Howard M. Brown (with an analogous impact), William S. Newman, Robert Donington, Eva and Paul Badura Skoda and my brother Karl Neumann. Kern Holoman, Richard Sherr, William Drabkin, and George Bozarth, members of a seminar I conducted during my Princeton fellowship year, by their keen questioning helped me reformulate a number of arguments. Professors John Hsu, Gordon J. Kinney, David Fuller, and the late Walter Emery assisted me with expert answers to specific questions. I also feel obliged for the support and encouragement received from Professors Edward E. Lowinsky, Paul Henry Lang, John R. White, and Hans-Peter Schmitz.

I am indebted to the staffs of: the Music Division of the Library of Congress; the Music Division of the New York Public Library; the British Museum; the Bibliothèque Nationale, Département de la Musique (in particular to M. François Lesure); the Deutsche Staatsbibliothek in East Berlin (in particular to Frl. Eveline Bartlitz); the Deutsche Staatsbibliothek, Preussischer Kulturbesitz in West Berlin; the Deutsches Musikgeschichtliches Archiv in Cassel; the Gesellschaft der Musikfreunde in Vienna (in particular Frau Dr. Mittringer); the library of the Conservatorio in Bologna (in particular Sig. Sergio Paganelli); the library of the Conservatorio "Giuseppe Verdi" in Milan; the Biblioteca Nazionale in Turin. I also wish to thank Professor Vincent Duckles, Director of the Berkeley Music Collection, Miss Paula Morgan, Music Librarian of Princeton University, and Frau Dr. Ortrun Landmann from the RISM staff for East Germany, for their great helpfulness in securing important materials for me. To Dr. Alfred Dürr I am indebted for placing at my disposal the resources of the J. S. Bach Institute in Göttingen, and similarly, to Professor Walter Gerstenberg for the free use of the Musicological Institute at the University of Tübingen.

Acknowledgments

———

x

I am grateful to Mrs. Joanna Hitchcock, Managing Editor of the Princeton University Press, for her confidence in the merits of my manuscript; to my editor, Mrs. Eve Hanle, for her devoted and successful efforts in anglicizing and simplifying my involuted style; to Mr. Bruce Stevens for laying the solid foundation of the index and for many valuable suggestions regarding the text; to Mr. David Woolard for expert proofreading; to Mr. Michael Simpson for his very efficient help in completing the index. Finally, a word of deep appreciation to my wife Margaretta for her patient suffering, and for her wise counsel in soft-pedaling polemics and pruning excess verbiage; moreover, I owe her thanks for significantly expediting the last crucial stage of readying the material for the publisher through her exceptional gift for planning and organizing.

Contents

Contents

xii

List of Abbreviations

I

ABB	*Andreas Bach Buch*	Gio.	Collection Giordano of the Biblioteca Nazionale, Turin
AmB	Amalien Bibliothek		
AM	*Acta Musicologica*	GMF	Gesellschaft der Musikfreunde, Vienna
aut.	autograph		
Berk.	Italian MS collection, Music Library, University of California, Berkeley	*HHA*	*Hallesche Händel Ausgabe*
		HdM	*Handbuch der Musikwissenschaft* (ed. Bücken)
BB	Deutsche Staatsbibliothek, Berlin		
BB (PK)	Staatsbibliothek, Preussischer Kulturbesitz (at present Berlin-Dahlem)	*KB*	*Kritischer Bericht* (of *NBA*)
		LC	Library of Congress
		M&L	*Music & Letters*
BG	*Bach Gesellschaft* edition (Leipzig, 1851-1899)	*MGG*	*Musik in Geschichte und Gegenwart*
BJ	*Bach Jahrbuch*	MS(s)	manuscript(s)
BM	British Museum	*MMB*	*Monumenta Musicae Belgicae*
BN	Bibliothèque Nationale	*MQ*	*Musical Quarterly*
Bol.	Biblioteca del Conservatorio, Bologna	Nos.	Collection Noseda, Biblioteca del Conservatorio, Milan
BWV	Wolfgang Schmieder, *Bach-Werke-Verzeichnis* (Leipzig, 1950)	*NBA*	*Neue Bach Ausgabe*
		Opéra	Bibliothèque de l'Opéra, Paris
CAMB	*Clavier-Büchlein* for Anna Magdalena Bach	P 00	BB (or BB PK) Mus. MS Bach P 00
CdLF	*Corpus des Luthistes Français*	*SIMG*	*Sammelbände der Internationalen Musikgesellschaft*
CEKM	*Corpus of Early Keyboard Music*		
CWFB	*Clavierbüchlein* for W. F. Bach	St 00	BB (or BB PK) Mus. MS Bach St 00
DDT	*Denkmäler Deutscher Tonkunst*	Thomana	Bach MS Collection of the Thomas School, Leipzig
DTB	*Denkmäler der Tonkunst in Bayern*	*VfMw*	*Vierteljahrsschrift für Musikwissenschaft*
DTÖ	*Denkmäler der Tonkunst in Österreich*	*WC*	*Well-Tempered Clavier*
Foà	Collection Foà of the Biblioteca Nazionale, Turin		

II

For the following secondary sources which are frequently quoted, the last name of the author alone is used as an abbreviated reference.

Beyschlag, Adolf	*Die Ornamentik der Musik* (Leipzig, 1908)
Bodky, Erwin	*The Interpretation of Bach's Keyboard Works* (Cambridge, Mass., 1960)
Dannreuther, Edward	*Musical Ornamentation* (London, 1893-1895)
Dolmetsch, Arnold	*The Interpretation of the Music of the 17th and 18th Centuries* (London [1915])

Donington, Robert   *The Interpretation of Early Music*, New Version (London and New York, 1974)

Emery, Walter   *Bach's Ornaments* (London, 1953)

Haas, Robert M.   *Aufführungspraxis der Musik, HdM* (Wildpark-Potsdam, 1931)

Kreutz, Alfred   *Die Ornamentik in J. S. Bach's Klavierwerken* (Frankfurt, 1950) (annex to the Peters Urtext edition of the English Suites)

Landshoff, Ludwig   *Revisions-Bericht zur Urtextausgabe von J. S. Bach Inventionen und Sinfonien* (Leipzig, 1933)

Schmitz, Hans-Peter   *Die Kunst der Verzierung im 18. Jahrhundert* (Cassel and Basel, 1955)

PART I
INTRODUCTION

Ornament and Structure

In all the fields of baroque art, ornamentation played a conspicuous role. In architecture, sculpture, and painting "baroque exuberance"—a combination of passionate expression, luxuriant design, and abundant decorative elements— became the antithesis of classical balance, restraint, and simplicity (as embodied, for example, in the earlier style of the High Renaissance). The musical baroque received, in part at least, its designation because its creations were animated by a similar anticlassical fervor, and because the rich melismas of their meandering melodies and the wealth of their decorative figurations formed a fitting counterpart to the prevailing style in the visual arts.

Though no one denies the immense importance of ornamentation in baroque music, not all will agree about what constitutes an ornament and how it can be set apart from the non-ornamental structural elements of the musical fabric. The problem of definition is admittedly difficult and not fully solvable, but it must be faced because of its practical relevance for historically correct performances.

In music, as well as in the visual arts, an ornament is generally conceived as an addition to structure, in the sense that structure embodies what is of the artistic or—if this overworked term may be excused—of the expressive essence. An ornament serves to set off the structural elements to greater aesthetic advantage, most typically by imparting to them more grace, elegance, smoothness, or variety. Ornament and structure thus conceived are complementary. Either can, at least theoretically, appear in its pure state: structure per se in no need of additions and ornament as a wholly decorative accessory that can be omitted with little loss. In practice, however, the two elements will often combine into mixtures that defy clear separation, as is the case when florid designs that *could* be pure decoration become, to varying degrees, part of the expressive essence. However, the fact that a dividing line often cannot be clearly drawn does not invalidate the antithetical character of the two categories.

A modern school of thought denies that certain parts of the musical fabric can be definitely assigned to structure, others to ornament. It advocates instead the idea that the relationship between the two categories is constantly shifting, depending on the time-span involved.[1] The same note that is structural ("ornamented") over, say, the time-span of a quarter-note, can become "ornamental" over the time-span of a whole-note. Then, by widening the focus, the note that is structural over the time-span of a whole-note can become ornamental over the time-span of several measures, and so on until—in a tonal composition—over the time-span of the whole work, the structural element can be reduced to a few chord progressions, if not to the tonic chord alone.

Without denying the logical consistency of this concept or its usefulness as a tool of formal analysis, it is unhelpful for our own, merely historical purpose because its principle of relativity tends to efface what is paramount to our

---

[1] I owe the explanation of this concept to Professor J. K. Randall of Princeton University.

inquiry: the hierarchy among the various elements of the musical texture, the differences in their absolute degree of musical significance, or as we shall refer to it, in their *specific weight* within the musical fabric.

Therefore, instead of pursuing this concept of relativity (which is only one among several that have been produced by modern scholarship), we find a historically more appropriate approach to the ornament-structure dichotomy in the perspective of 17th- and 18th-century musicians. Baroque theorists had in fact given a direct and concrete answer to the problem with their theory of "affects" (*Affectenlehre*) which interpreted music as the communication of feelings to the listener. They likened this communication to that of an orator, "affecting" the feelings of his audience. Pursuing this idea, they arrived at a system of rhetorical "figures" (*Figurenlehre*) and elaborated a contrast, clearly analogous to that of structure and ornament, between *figurae fundamentales* and *figurae superficiales*.[2] According to this concept, the hard core of the musical matter, containing both melodic and harmonic progressions and sufficient in itself to convey the basic "affect," would correspond to structure, whereas any additions would represent ornaments of varying specific weights. Those ornaments whose function is strictly decorative, not admitting any artistically significant communication, would belong to the outermost layer of near weightlessness.[3]

From this theoretical basis we can now try to approach the practical aspect of the problem: the diagnostic task of identifying the two categories. Such identification is of considerable importance because the difference between the categories involves two significant interpretative principles. One, flowing from the lighter weight of ornament, implies that it should not be rendered with the intensity, solidity, or gravity appropriate for the weighty, structural elements. Accordingly, ornaments will as a rule call for a more flowing tempo and easier dynamics. The second principle derives from the improvisatory heritage of musical ornaments and suggests for their rendition a touch of spontaneity, of rhythmic freedom, and of imaginative nuance—all earmarks of inspired improvisation. Both principles are, of course, dependent in their application on the varying specific weight of a given ornament.

The task of recognizing ornament or structure for what they are is not always easy. In certain phases of the baroque era, the contrast between the two categories was made fully explicit by the notational habit of composers to write down only what was to them of the musical essence and to leave ornamental elaboration to the performer; in such instances there remains little room for ambiguity. The same can be said, by and large, for ornaments indicated by symbol. Hence the problem of identification is centered on those ornaments that are spelled out in

[2] Bernhard, *Ausführlicher Bericht vom Gebrauche der Con- und Dissonantien*, chaps. 10-22 of MS (from after 1669). See also Stierlein, *Trifolium Musicale . . .* , p. 18; Samber, *Continuatio ad manuductionem organicam*, p. 219; Walther, *Praecepta der musikalischen Composition*, p. 152. (For complete citations of sources, see the Bibliography on p. 601.)

[3] A clear characterization of such lightweight ornaments was once given by the French gambist-composer Marin Marais. Speaking of groups of little unmetrical notes, he says they stand for "certain *coulades* [i.e. slurred and usually scalewise figurations] which one may or may not do without altering the piece, and which I have written down solely for the sake of variety" (". . . certaines coulades que l'on peut faire ou ne pas faire sans alterer la piece, et que j'ai marquées seulement pour une varieté d'expression"). The stated fact that these *coulades* would not be missed confirms their pure ornamental nature. *Pieces a une et a deux violes* (1686), Preface.

regular notation, because in this guise they are outwardly indistinguishable from structural elements.

Even there diagnosis may be simple if the melody is first presented in a plain and later in a more elaborate version. However, a comparison of two such versions has its pitfalls: the simple version may not necessarily be all structural, and the second one may exceed the scope of ornament and become, partly or entirely, a free variation.[4]

A similar situation obtains when the melody is known from other sources in its simple unadorned form, though the composer presents it only in an elaborate version. We find such cases frequently in chorale figurations which are by definition ornamental.

Identification of ornaments is harder when we encounter melismas without any direct clue as to a hidden basic melody. In such cases we have to "decolor" the melody, i.e. reduce it into a simpler form, in order to find out whether the substance of its thought stands unimpaired.

Many are the instances where knowledge about the performance practices of a given style can be of help. We know for instance that arias in the Italian style and slow movements of concertos and sonatas required florid embellishments. Though they were mostly left to the performer's improvisation, Bach wrote them out as a matter of principle, and other masters did so from time to time and to various degrees. Thus, if we find florid passages in a setting of Bach's Italianate arias or instrumental adagios, there is a strong presumption for their ornamental nature. If, in addition, these figurations start after a tie, occur as 32nd-notes,[5] move largely stepwise or by broken chords, and have a legato articulation either marked or implied, then the presumption gathers weight, because the just mentioned qualities are all typical attributes of melismatic ornaments. If, to give an example, we find the first adagio movements of Bach's Sonatas in G minor or A minor for Unaccompanied Violin, which are patterned after the Italian-style *sonata da chiesa*, filled with this very kind of melisma, we can be reasonably certain that we have to do with ornaments. Moreover, ornaments of this type, which other composers would not have entered into the score at all, are by this very fact likely to be of light specific weight.[6] In other contexts, such as some of Bach's chorale preludes where lightweight florid ornaments are not a stylistic hallmark, similar figurations, though ornamental in origin, might well partake of the melodic essence.

[4] The two notions, ornament and variation, are related as a narrower to a wider concept. Any ornamental addition is a variation, but not every variation is an ornament. Whether a change is to be classed as ornament or as non-ornamental variation will depend chiefly on whether most of the structural notes remain in place while a number of intervening tones are added. If they do remain, it is an ornament. On the other hand, if many structural notes are changed, or if no increase in the number of notes takes place, we have to do with a non-ornamental variation. There are, of course, the inevitable borderline cases which will arise, for instance, when an ornamental melisma temporarily loses its close rapport with the basic melody.

[5] Up to Bach's time and beyond, there still prevailed a definite link between meter and tempo and, therefore, between relative and absolute note values: a quarter-note could never be very fast nor a 16th-note very slow.

[6] The failure of some modern performers to recognize the essentially decorative, rather than deeply meaningful, character of these coloraturas frequently leads to misrepresentation. Many modern violinists play such a movement too slowly, often changing the bow two or three times within one coloratura, in order to extract the maximum resonance and expressiveness from every single note. With lightweight ornaments thus impersonating structure, such rendition is wrongly focused and misses the forest for the trees.

What is true of the many-toned ornaments applies to the brief and briefest graces as well. Those of purely decorative character and especially those whose sole function lies in smoothly connecting structural notes have to be rendered with the lightness and unobtrusiveness fitting their small specific weight. On the other hand, certain pitches that enrich the harmony on the strong beats or enrich the rhythm can appear weighty, but their ornamental nature will often manifest itself in their need for dynamic and rhythmic flexibility.

With regard to such very brief graces a troublesome problem, touching on the ornament-structure contrast, arises frequently from the fact that many composers wrote what *could* be the same ornament sometimes with regular notes, sometimes with symbols. The question then arises whether the difference in notation was intentional or accidental, whether it did or did not convey a difference of execution. For Bach in particular the question is difficult because he was inconsistent in many matters of notation. A key that would solve all such puzzling cases can hardly be found, but an attempt to sketch at least an outline of an answer will be made below in ch. 16 (dealing with Bach's one-note ornaments); further references to this problem will be made in other places as well.

PERFORMERS have often overlooked the ornament-structure dichotomy when analyzing a work with a view to its proper interpretation. This neglect ought to be remedied, because the identification of ornaments and the consequent assessment of their respective specific weight may hold the key to questions of nuance and phrasing, of tempo, rhythm, and dynamics, and at times, indeed, to the true spirit and character of a composition.

The Categories of Musical
Ornaments

The present study will deal primarily with ornaments of one or more pitches that are inserted between the written notes and are either indicated by symbol (including the unmetrical little notes) or not indicated at all. In addition to the above types, the survey will include the arpeggio and the vibrato. Excluded will be rhythmic manipulations of the written notes, such as premature or delayed entries, which a few writers count among the embellishments.

For the purpose of this study it is necessary to establish a working terminology. In the following, certain basic categories that apply to the whole field of ornaments will be defined and assigned terms, some of which are new. A similar working terminology for specific ornaments will be given at the start of the respective chapters.[1]

When discussing the *melodic design* of ornaments, we shall distinguish two pairs of contrasting categories: the first, *small* and *large* and, the second, *melic* and *repercussive*. With regard to the *small* and *large* ornaments, the two adjectives refer not to the actual length of the ornaments but to the number of pitches involved. In this respect the difference between small and large is crucial. An ornament that contains very few pitches, from one to three or four, can develop only a limited number of patterns, which thus lend themselves to being typed, labeled, and expressed by symbols. Beyond four or five notes the possibilities of tonal combination increase at a rate that makes the difference of degree turn into a difference of kind. *Repercussive* ornaments consist of trills and mordents in which two neighbor tones are alternated, or the same note repeated. *Melic* will be the term used for all other designs, ranging from a single pitch inserted into a melodic context to a long row of irregular tone sequences. Thus, while the repercussive ornaments are always "small," the melic ones can be either "small" or "large."

The *rhythmic* relationship of an ornament to the principal note or notes yields important categories. For want of a better word, "beat" will be used here in the sense of the notated *starting point* of the principal note, a point which of course can fall on any subdivision of the beat as well. According to this definition, ornaments that start *on* the beat will be called *onbeat* graces. By displacing the starting point of the principal note they are meant to embellish, they cause the note to enter with a delay.

Ornaments that start *off* the beat will be called *offbeat* graces. They are inserted in a way that leaves the starting points of their principal notes in place. They can be of three types: *prebeat* (or *anticipated*) graces when they precede their principal note and are slurred to the latter; *afterbeat* graces when they follow and are slurred to their principal note; *interbeat* graces when they are equally linked to both neighbor notes and inserted between their starting points.

[1] In the case of uncertainty the reader is referred to the Glossary of Terms on p. 577.

With regard to the *musical function* of ornaments, two groups of categories will be distinguished. The first contrasts *connective* and *intensifying* ornaments, the second *melodic* and *harmonic* ones.

Connective and intensifying ornaments. Ornaments that are attached to a single note as their principal note and are relating to it for the sake of coloring or emphasizing it will be called *intensifying*. Characteristic examples are most trills or mordents, onbeat *Vorschläge* or slides, and generally any ornament at the start of a phrase. Other ornaments, instead of resting on one tone alone, have the function of gracing the link between two neighbor tones. Such ornaments will be referred to as *connective*. They can range from a single tone to a multinote coloratura.

Melodic and harmonic ornaments. We shall call ornaments *melodic* when their impulse in embellishing a phrase is predominantly linear. If small, they find their natural place between two neighboring beats as prebeat, interbeat, or afterbeat graces. If too large to be accommodated in such limited space, they may have to cross one or more beats. We shall call ornaments *harmonic* when a vertical impulse places them on a beat, *provided* that by this placement they change a consonance into a dissonance or a milder dissonance into a stronger one. This important qualification sets off the harmonic ornaments from the wider category of onbeat graces. An ornament which is susceptible of becoming harmonic can, by straddling the beat, mix the characteristics of the contrasting melodic and harmonic types in many different ratios.

It should be added that a rhythmic element can also enter into the question of musical function when the most pronounced effect of an ornament is rhythmic invigoration rather than melodic or harmonic enrichment. Position in the measure has a decisive bearing not only on harmonic and melodic, but also on rhythmic, perception. Thus, e.g. the iambic or anapestic pattern is rhythmically inconspicuous if the short note or notes are *before*, the long one *on* the beat. The same patterns can assume strong rhythmic prominence when the short notes are placed *on* the beat.

Though many more categories could be and have been formulated,[2] the above listed ones are indispensable for this study.

[2] One of the most detailed tabulations of ornament categories by an old theoretician can be found in Marpurg's *Der critische Musicus an der Spree*, vol. 1, pp. 56-57, 80-81.

Historical Performance and
the Problem of Method

———— ◆•◆ ————

Concern with historical performance is of surprisingly recent date.[1] Roughly speaking, the 17th and 18th centuries were not interested in old music; the 19th century was the first to cultivate systematically old, mainly 18th-century, music, but not in its historical setting. Interest in historical performance emerged just before the turn of the 20th century, with Arnold Dolmetsch as its chief pioneer. Since then, this interest has grown to reach a spectacular height in our present day. However, the growth of this interest and the ensuing proliferation of literature on the subject were not paralleled by a needed refinement of research methods. The problem of method is complex, and questionable or outright erroneous procedures are so varied that we must limit ourselves here to a brief discussion of two types that are of special relevance to ornaments. One is the application of historical documents outside their legitimate pertinence through unjustified generalizations; the other is the too literal application of the verbal or musical text of such documents.[2]

Concerning unjustified generalizations, many researchers perpetuate the pioneer's assumption of a European "common practice" of the 17th and 18th centuries. On the strength of this purely hypothetical assumption they feel justified in making sweeping generalizations of rules found in theoretical documents which they project across the whole European landscape, as well as backward and forward in time. However, a "common practice" in either the 17th or the 18th centuries across simultaneous personal, regional, national styles and across such drastic stylistic watersheds as separate the late baroque from the *galant* style is an unrealistic assumption, and any inference based on it has to be viewed with the utmost skepticism. It is revealing to note that so far no one has postulated a "common practice" for the 20th or even for the 19th century; it seems only our spotty knowledge of earlier times can explain the vogue of such a chimerical assumption for the 18th, the 17th, and earlier centuries.

The second point, the too literal interpretation of a theoretical document and in particular of ornament tables, has led to similar fallacious results. Notation is at all times an unavoidable oversimplification that only a pedestrian performer takes on face value. Truly artistic performance is replete with delicate nuances, subtle inflexions, and tantalizing rhythmical irregularities which the score cannot begin to indicate. This is still true today, though notation has made great strides in refining its methods of conveying the composer's intentions. But the further we go back in time the more fragmentary the notation, the greater the gap between score and desired sound, the more demanding the responsibility of the artist-performer to fill the gap by using his insight, taste, and imagination.

---

[1] So is, with very few exceptions, concern with stylistic consistency and historical authenticity in all the arts.

[2] For a more detailed discussion of this matter as it relates to theoretical documents, see Neumann, "The Use of Baroque Treatises on Musical Performance."

He has to have, as Marpurg said, "the greatest sensitivity and the most felicitous gift of divination."[3] Couperin put it still more strikingly: "Just as there is a great distance between grammar and rhetorical delivery, there is also an infinitely great distance between musical notation and artistic performance."[4] Thus literalness in performance is not a virtue but a vice which grows in proportion to the age of the music. This is true even of the most solidly structural elements. The implications of this fact are raised to the second power with regard to ornaments that are predestined by their very nature for improvisatory flexibility.

If we move from graces in a composition to those ornament tables with which composers or theorists tried to clarify the meaning of an ornamental symbol, the oversimplification is raised to the third power, because the models, referring to any and all contexts rather than to a specific one, must be extremely abstract. Ornament tables are thus thrice removed from the reality of desirable execution: first by the general shortcomings of musical notation, second by the capricious nature of ornaments, and third by the abstract nature of any general model. The model is the Platonic idea, as it were, of the grace in question, its conceptual essence, which in reality has countless concrete embodiments that differ from one another through innumerable variations of nonessential elements. The gifted music student of those bygone ages who had heard countless embodiments of this idea had no difficulty in distinguishing what in this model was of the conceptual essence and what was not. There was little danger that he might mistake the model for a pattern to be reproduced mechanically. Many modern researchers, however, separated by centuries from the live experience of the times, have fallen victim to this very danger of mistaking the models of ornament tables as strict norms, as dies from which they must cast ever-identical coins. This fatal misunderstanding has resulted in a distorted picture of historical ornamentation, by enthroning a rigid discipline that contradicts the very nature of ornaments.

The idea that ornaments are too free to be tamed into regularity and to be taught by book goes like a red thread through the literature of two centuries. The following few select quotations should suffice to make the point.

Peri, in 1600, speaks of embellishments "which cannot be written, and if we do write them, cannot be learned from the writings."[5]

The 17th-century lutenist Jean-Baptiste Bésard explains why he does not deal with ornaments: "If it were possible to prescribe how to play sweet ornaments and trills on the lute, I would make some remarks about this here; since they cannot be explained, however, either orally or in writing, it will have to suffice for you to imitate someone who can play them well or to learn them by yourself."[6] L'Affilard, who presents in 1694 an ornamentation table, cautions that in dealing with ornaments he tries only to "give a general idea . . . not believing in the need of giving a more detailed explanation, and convinced that one can learn them much better by the example given by singing than by any dissertation that one could write on the subject."[7]

[3] Marpurg, *Crit. Musicus*, p. 216: "Ein Musicus muss also die grösste Empfindlichkeit und die glücklichste Errathungskraft haben."

[4] François Couperin, *L'art de toucher le clavecin*, Preface. "Comme il y a une grande distance de la Grammaire à la Déclamation; il y en a aussi une infinie entre la Tablature, et la façon de bien-jouer."

[5] Peri, *Euridice*, Preface: ". . . e vaghezze, e leggiadrie, che non si possono scrivere, e scrivendole non s'imparano dagli scritti."

[6] Quoted by Julia Sutton, "The Lute Instructions of Jean-Baptiste Bésard," *MQ*, vol. 51 (1965), pp. 345-368.

[7] L'Affilard, *Principes très faciles pour bien apprendre la musique*, p. 19: ". . . donner une idée générale . . . ne croyant pas qu'il soit necessaire d'en donner une explication plus ample, convaincu qu'on pourra beaucoup mieux les apprendre par l'Exemple que l'on en donnera en chantant, que par aucune dissertation que l'on pût faire sur ce sujet. . . ."

Saint Lambert in 1702 carries the freedom of ornaments to a point where the composer's prescriptions may be ignored and other ornaments substituted for those specified.[8] In 1736, Montéclair prefaces his chapter on the *agréments* with an apology for attempting such a discussion in print: "It is almost impossible to teach in writing how to execute well these ornaments since the live demonstration of an experienced master is hardly sufficient to do this. However . . . I shall try to explain [them] the least badly I am able to."[9]

Rameau stresses the need for spontaneity as opposed to pure imitation: "Let an ornament be as well rendered as possible, it will still lack a certain indescribable something which constitutes its whole merit if it is not guided by feeling: too much or too little, too early or too late, too long or not long enough in suspensions, in swelling or diminishing, in the repercussions of trills; finally, when it lacks precisely what expression and context require, any ornament becomes insipid . . . ; taste flows from feeling, it adopts what is good, rejects what is bad. Guided by such feeling one finds the true way of rendering the ornaments which it dictates. All the master can do is provide the means of executing the ornaments well and demonstrate them if he can do so . . . it will be by example and never by rules that he [the master] can show the man of taste how to use his fine talents as a performer. . . ." And again: "I give no examples of *roulades*, trills and *ports de voix*, because youth needs a teacher in all these matters."[10]

Duval, in 1775, writes concerning ornaments: "We can indicate only very tentatively the principal rules, because the fine points of the art are infinite, very hidden and difficult to explain. They can be learned only by listening to the best singers, or, more properly speaking, they issue from taste and feeling. What are compared to this all the rules of the world?"[11]

In Germany, Hermann Finck, devotes a chapter in his treatise of 1556 to "Graceful Singing," a term synonymous with the art of free ornamentation. This art, he says "cannot be mastered by rules alone . . . but rather by usage, practice and much experience."[12]

Johann Caspar Lange, speaking of ornaments in 1688, says that one could give rules for them, "but because the graces are variable, and can be best taught and learned *viva voce*, the following few observations . . . will suffice."[13]

In the early 18th century, Johann Beer, whose writings were highly esteemed by Mattheson, asks the question whether ornaments ought to be precisely defined and answers in the negative. Among his reasons is the fact that ornaments change from day to day. Music, he says, is so wedded to freedom that it won't put up with any prescription, let alone with any compulsion. The teaching [of ornaments] can proceed only by singing demonstration. "All ornaments exist *quantitate intrinseca*. And *quantitas intrinseca* can not be indicated by any outward symbol."[14] The last sentence means that the subtleties of ornaments defy notation.

[8] Saint Lambert, *Principes du clavecin*, p. 57.

[9] Montéclair, *Principes de musique*, p. 78: "il est presque impossible d'enseigner par écrit, la maniere de bien former ces agréments, puisque la vive voix d'un Maitre experimenté, est à peine suffisante pour cela; cependant . . . je vais tâcher de l'expliquer le moins mal qu'il me sera possible."

[10] Rameau, *Code de musique pratique*, p. 13: ". . . qu'un agrément soit aussi bien rendu qu'il le puisse, il y manquera toujours ce certain je ne sais quoi qui en fait tout le mérite, s'il n'est guidé par le sentiment: trop ou trop peu, trop tôt ou trop tard, plus ou moins longtemps dans des suspensions, dans des sons ou enflés ou diminués, dans des battemens de *trils*, dits *cadences*, enfin cette juste précision que demande l'expression, la situation, manquant une fois tout agrément devient insipide . . . ce ne sera que par des exemples, & jamais par des règles, qu'il [i.e. le maître] pourra faire sentir à l'homme de Goût l'usage qu'il doit faire de ses heureuses facultés dans l'exécution . . ."; p. 19: "Je ne donne aucun exemple de roulades, trils & ports de voix, parceque la jeunesse a besoin de Maîtres dans tous les cas de la méthode."

[11] Duval, *Méthode agréable*, p. 5.

[12] Finck, *Practica musica*, ch. 5 (no pagin.): "Ars recte & bene canendi, non solis praeceptis . . . sed verius usu, multa tractatione, longaque experientia comparatur."

[13] *Methodus nova*, pp. 44-45.

[14] Beer, *Musicalische Discurse*, p. 136: "Alle Manieren . . . bestehen *quantitate intrinseca*. Die *quantitas intrinseca* kann durch kein äusserliches Zeichen gewiesen werden." Mattheson, in *Der brauchbare Virtuoso*, Preface, calls Beer "A man of special erudition, who has published a number of good treatises that might serve as touchstone . . . to our concertmasters to test them whether or not they are equal to their job. . . ."

Mattheson again and again heaps scorn on pedants who worship rules as the supreme law of music. In 1713 he writes, "Concerning such would-be luminaries who believe that music has to follow their rules, when in truth their rules have to follow the music, one can rightly say: *Faciunt intelligendo ut nihil intelligant*" (they manage their thinking to understand nothing).[15]

In a later book he says, "rules are valid as long as I consider it well and sensible to abide by them. They are valid no longer than that."[16] And elsewhere more brusquely yet: "Rules are what I like and as long as I like it." Quoting approvingly Beer's statement that the ear determines rules and not vice versa, Mattheson says: "The rule of nature is, in music, nothing but the ear."[17]

Mattheson also quotes both Finck and Heinichen (1728) to show the agreement, two hundred years apart, of old and modern writers on the idea that in matters of ornaments, experience and judgment are more important than rules.[18] Later in the chapter, when describing a leaping *Vorschlag* (Sprung-Accent), he illustrates "approximately" how it ought to be done. "I say *approximately*, because ornaments cannot properly be indicated by notes; the live voice of the teacher must always play the most important role."[19]

The list of quotations just presented could be extended at will. Whether the writers stress the impossibility of teaching ornaments by book, or whether they stress the questionable character of rules, the implications are the same: descriptions of an ornament, whether by words or notes, are only rough outlines. This conclusion has far-reaching consequences for the procedures to be adopted in historical research. Chief among them is the realization that there simply is no "definitive" solution to any given ornament in any given situation. Instead, the basic question ought to be reformulated and the investigation directed toward an approximate solution, one that circumscribes an area within which a basic design could be varied. In some cases this area will permit a wider, in others, a narrower scope of variation, but the area will not shrink to a point where the ornament becomes rigid. It follows that nothing is more untrue historically and at the same time nothing more unartistic than those specimens of metrically measured trills or their counterparts in other ornaments that have often been presented as allegedly "definitive" models of historical authenticity.

In attempting to answer the reformulated questions, the theoretical documents, if carefully treated and flexibly interpreted with awareness of their limitations, can provide valuable information about certain procedures that were followed by some, at some time, somewhere. If, however, we try to apply this information to a specific composer, it will have to be clarified, focused, and sifted by musical evidence. Such musical evidence can be external or internal: external if derived from distinctive features of notation, internal if derived from musical logic, i.e. where the context either suggests or else excludes a certain solution. An example of external evidence would be the writing of a grace symbol before the bar line, indicating clearly its prebeat start. Internal evidence can be extracted from almost any aspect of music through the logic of melody, harmony, counterpoint, rhythm, meter, diction, or phrasing.

Considering the myriads of notes written at any period, the resources of musical

---

[15] Mattheson, *Das neu-eröffnete Orchestre*, p. 3: "Von solchen *praetendirten luminibus Mundi*, die da meinen/ es müsse sich die Music nach ihren Reguln/ und sich nicht vielmehr ihre Reguln nach der *Music* richten/ mag man wol mit Recht sagen: *Faciunt intelligendo ut nihil intelligant.*"

[16] *Critica musica*, I, 302.

[17] Ibid., p. 338, footnote Z.

[18] *Der vollkommene Capellmeister*, pt. 2, ch. 3, pars. 18-19.

[19] Ibid., par. 25. The same passage reappears almost verbatim in Kürzinger, *Getreuer Unterricht*, p. 34.

evidence are practically unlimited, and the prospect of their gradual exploitation offers the brightest hope for progress in the field. However, such exploitation is fraught with dangers as great as those attending the use of treatises; here too, the greatest risk lies in the temptation to deduce general laws from too few individual pieces of evidence. We are apt to be too anxious to discover laws and our zeal prompts us to jump prematurely to sweeping conclusions.

Other dangers can derive from deceptive analogies. If, as mentioned above, a prebar notation of a grace indicates the prebeat start, it will be shown that the notation *after* the bar line does not necessarily indicate downbeat rendition, because small notes or abstract symbols were usually written very close to the parent note regardless of rhythmic intention; many such cases will be shown where either explicit directives or internal evidence require prebeat execution. Vertical alignment can be a telling clue of rhythmic relationships but only if it is clear that the alignment was intended and not the result of chance. Parallel passages, simultaneous voices, and different versions can sometimes yield legitimate evidence, but inferences can often be treacherous and great care is needed to avoid the many pitfalls.[20]

With regard to internal evidence, musical logic will yield inferences of varying cogency. Occasionally they will be unquestionable and absolute; more often they will be relative and indicate no more than a likely solution. Caution must then be applied to prevent excessive claims.

As an illustration of the problematic persuasiveness of internal evidence, a brief look will be taken here at the case of *forbidden parallels*—the most frequently used type of internal evidence, and in the field of ornaments probably the most important one.

The prohibition of parallel fifths and octaves may well be the most durable and universal rule in musical history, since it extended its jurisdiction over the whole Western musical world from the Middle Ages to the 19th century. As with any rule in art, its observance was based on a conviction of merit. Not that it was not broken from time to time, but the remarkable thing is that the violations were few and that in all these centuries not one composer chose to disregard the rule as a matter of principle. In Bach's time the rule was still at the height of its authority. Bach himself transgressed it from time to time, more often in his youth than in his later years, and it is significant that when he revised an earlier work, he manifested a conscious effort to eliminate parallels. This in turn permits us to assume that he would have found the same parallels objectionable when they occurred as the result of ornament execution. Yet, there can be no doubt that parallels did occur plentifully in actual performance along with many other untoward accidents. Finck, in the mid-16th century, mentions parallels produced by diminutions and finds them tolerable provided they are very brief. Telemann mentions instances where parallels resulted either from improvised ornaments or from makeshift arrangements that replace a missing voice by one that is an octave higher or lower and thereby turn parallel fourths into fifths.[21] Such occurrences

20 See on this question Neumann, "External Evidence and Uneven Notes."

21 Finck, *Practica musica*; Telemann, *Vorbericht zu musicalisches Lob Gottes* (no pagin.).

Worse things than parallels must have frequently happened in many of the slipshod performances of the time. In Bach's Leipzig church music for instance, the instrumental component, for all we know, may have never

do not sanction parallels for our use nor do they eliminate their evidence value for ornament execution since it is not the historical occurrence (undesired by the composer) that counts but the composer's intentions. Nothing else makes sense as a guide to today's performances.

It is on the basis of these principles that we are generally entitled to see in the avoidance of parallels an important clue to the rendition of certain ornaments, but we must be aware that the clues vary in force according to circumstances. During the baroque period there were lively debates about the degree of strictness with which the rules against parallels ought to be implemented. Some writers, Werckmeister and Mizler for instance, were intransigent and demanded an unconditional ban. Others, Kircher and Ahle for instance, were more flexible and applied a musical, rather than a dogmatic, yardstick. Their attitude gave rise to the subsequently much repeated differentiation between "ear fifths" and "eye fifths" with the obvious implication that only those parallels should be avoided which are offensive to the ear. In the sense of this distinction parallels can range all the way from impossible to permissible.

In principle one can say that parallels are the more objectionable the slower they are; the fewer voices are involved; the stricter the form and the more careful the part-writing in other respects; the more homogeneous the tone color and dynamics of the two voices involved. Parallels are also more obtrusive when they are open rather than hidden; when they occur between the outer voices or between basic progressions; and when the second of a pair falls on a strong beat.

Whenever parallels produced by a specific ornamental rendition reach a degree of offensiveness which could not have been gladly tolerated by the composer, we are entitled to assume that he had in mind a different execution.[22] Thus, the example of the parallels can demonstrate the potential of musical evidence as an important tool of historical investigation and the need for its thoughtful and flexible application.

In the course of the study, I shall quote theoretical documents abundantly, but an equally strong emphasis will be placed on the evidence of the musical

————

been rehearsed. That none of the original performance parts seems to show a single rehearsal memento is perhaps a common phenomenon of the time. But it is more surprising and revealing that even essential corrections were not made in instances where whole measures were left out of some of the parts. Dr. Alfred Dürr describes a particularly striking case with regard to Cantata No. 45 in NBA, I, 18. *KB*, p. 217.

Revealing in this connection is Telemann's picturesque expression *Hundetakte* [dog's measures] for the chaotic opening bars of an ensemble; he obviously did not like what he was forced to tolerate. (Quoted by Petri, *Anleitung zur praktischen Musik*, p. 45; 2nd ed., p. 171.)

22 Robert Donington, writing in *AM*, vol. 17 (1970), pp. 253-255 (and again in his recent book *A Performer's Guide to Baroque Music* [New York, 1973], p. 218), tries to downgrade forbidden parallels as evidence for ornament execution: "When one of the notes moving in parallel fifths is an accented passing note, re-solving before the other note has changed, the progression is not only correct but excellent." This, he adds in the *Guide*, applies also to long appoggiaturas. He has learned this rule in Oxford; yet I have never found anything remotely resembling it in any primary source. The tolerance shown by some of these sources is invariably hedged in by provisos such as passing by so fast as to be barely perceptible, whereas the Oxford rule will in many a context occasion highly conspicuous, hence genuinely offensive, "ear-fifths." Donington is inconsistent in ignoring on the one hand C.P.E. Bach's clear injunction that ornament execution must never produce forbidden parallels (see below ch. 34 at Ex. 34.11) while on the other hand looking upon all of that author's other directives as definitive rules for the whole 18th century. Moreover, passing notes are not the only ones that can be affected by ornament execution. Also, the 20th-century "Oxford rule" does not seem to apply to parallel octaves.

works themselves. I shall try for constant awareness of the dangers that imperil the proper treatment of evidence in the hope of avoiding such pitfalls as mentioned above and irrelevant reasoning inspired by wishful thinking and preconceived opinions. However, since it is always easier to detect other people's mistakes than one's own, I can only hope not to have stumbled into too many of these traps in my own discussions.

PART II
BAROQUE TRENDS OF
ORNAMENTATION

Introduction

The history of ornamentation is presumably as old as song itself. The urge to toy with musical materials, to manipulate a melody playfully by changing its inner rhythm or by adding new tones must spring from a deep-seated human instinct because we find its manifestations in all ages and cultures. Today it may not be much in evidence in art music because it is repressed by our prevailing conventions of performance. But the instinct is alive as ever, and where the restrictions are lifted, as in jazz, it manifests itself with undiminished vigor. Leopold Mozart spoke of a force of nature which compels us to ornament; even a peasant, he said, cannot help but adorn his peasant song with graces.

For the Middle Ages, documentation on improvised embellishment is fragmentary, but from the available bits of evidence several researchers, especially Ernest Ferand and Robert Haas, have succeeded in piecing together the broad outline of the picture. As early as the 13th and 14th centuries impromptu ornamentation was being practiced under two distinct forms. On the one hand musicians improvised diminutions, which are embellishments of a written melody whereby the melody is broken up ("diminished") into smaller note values. On the other, they sang *déchant sur le livre*, also known as *contrapunto alla mente*, in which an entirely new voice part was added *ex tempore*.

The second volume of Zacconi's famous *Prattica di musica* of 1622 devotes considerable space to this practice.[1] Thirty years later a very brief discussion, possibly the last, and limited to simple parallel motions, is contained in a treatise by Herbst.[2] How long the vocal practice survived is uncertain, but its importance seems to have decreased in the course of the 17th century to judge—precariously—from the apparent lack of theoretical mention. In instrumental music a species of *contrapunto alla mente* survived throughout the 18th century in thorough bass practice at the hand of players who realized the accompaniment in an impromptu polyphonic rather than chordal style.

The art of diminutions reached its first climax toward the end of the 16th century. In the meantime, out of the diminutions there had gradually crystallized a number of small graces ("small" in the sense of our previous definitions) whose smallness permitted them to assume characteristic designs. The story of the relationships between the "small" and the "large" graces varied from country to country, and these differences played a large part in shaping the divergent national styles of ornament usage. The next three chapters will attempt to bring these divergencies into clearer relief by sketching in broadest outline the evolution of ornamentation in Italy, France, and Germany from about 1600 to the threshold of the classical era. This sketch will be followed by a chapter attempt-

---

[1] Zacconi, *Prattica di musica, Seconda parte.* Zacconi tells (p. 127) how Willaert ("il grand' Adriano") made mistakes when he improvised a third part to a duo at sight, but corrected them on repeat; whereupon he used to say to bystanders, "now I have done it right"

("hora io l'ho fatto bene"), "indicating, so Zacconi comments, that one can make mistakes (*dell'indecentie*) in improvising, but to repeat them is reprehensible.

[2] Herbst, *Arte prattica et poëtica*, pp. 39-42.

ing to show how Bach's ideas on the subject were influenced by, and fitted into, the overall European picture of the age. Together, these chapters are intended to provide background and historical perspective for the detailed study of individual ornaments that forms the main part of this study.

Part II. Baroque Trends
of Ornamentation

20

By the end of the 16th century, the Italians had developed the practice of diminutions to a high point of refinement and virtuosity. Our chief sources for this practice are a number of pedagogical works that discuss its nature and in several cases demonstrate the application of the techniques to contemporary music—mostly motets and madrigals.[1]

The earliest known treatise on diminutions, Ganassi's *Opera intitulata Fontegara* of 1535, is perhaps the most remarkable of all. Basically it is a flute treatise, but the greatest part of the book is devoted to diminutions which are presented as the essence of skillful and artistic performance. The book teaches this skill first on a simple, then on a more advanced level, and on this latter the author manages with the help of such proportions as 3/2, 4/3, and 7/4, set against a background of either *tempus perfectum*: O or *tempus imperfectum*: C , to give a graphic suggestion of astounding rhythmic freedom and tantalizing rubato effects. Such freedom was certainly at the heart of artistic diminutions at all times, but Ganassi's ingenuity in conveying it on paper is a truly remarkable feat that was not matched by any later author.

Two foreign sources which follow in the mid-16th century appear to be related to Italian practice. Ortiz's *Trattado de glosas sobre clausulas* addresses itself to viol players, and most of the work concerns itself with presenting a series of embellishments of cadential formulas. Finck, the German theorist, devotes the last chapter of his *Practica musica* to the art of diminutions. Interesting is his opinion that all the voices, including the bass, ought to embellish their parts, but that they should take turns doing so, in order not to get in each other's way.

Toward the end of the century, Italian treatises began to appear in clusters, and with the writings of Dalla Casa, Bassano, Diruta, and Bovicelli we meet a group of texts which first show diminution patterns for various intervals and cadential formulas, then demonstrate how to embellish actual compositions of the leading masters of the day.[2] Of these books, Dalla Casa's and Bassano's concern themselves with all media, vocal as well as instrumental, Diruta's with keyboard instruments, Bovicelli's with singers. Before the turn of the century this group is joined by Richardo Rogniono, whose two books deal almost entirely with abstract patterns for "any kind of instrument," supplemented by only

---

[1] Composers' wishes regarding embellishments will be difficult to ascertain and must have changed with time as well as with individuals. Zacconi states that in the generation of De Rore and Willaert, vocal ornaments were not in use. He gives as his source old singers who in their youth had heard famous singers and important composers sing their music exactly as written without adding the smallest graces (". . . famosi cantori di quel tempo, & compositori d'importanza que cantauano le cantilene come le stauano scritte sopra de libri, senza porgerli pur un minimo accento, ò darli qualque poco di vaghezza"). *Prattica*, I, f. 7v. It may not be easy to reconcile such textual fidelity with the above reported practice of improvised counterpoint or with the elaborate diminution technique reported by Ganassi for the recorder in 1535. For his own time, Zacconi considers added embellishments a necessity but also tells of composers who preferred not to be performed

rather than risk having their works distorted by rich embellishments. They want, he says, only small and simple ornamental additions ("accenti schietti e semplici") that would not obscure the artistry of the composition (ibid., f. 64v).

[2] Dalla Casa, *Il vero modo di diminuir*; Bassano, *Ricercate, passaggi et cadentie*; Diruta, *Il Transilvano*; Bovicelli, *Regole, passaggi di musica*.

A canzona by Mortaro with diminutions by Diruta and a motet by Palestrina with diminutions by Bassano are reprinted in Beyschlag, *Die Ornamentik der Musik*, pp. 34-40. A madrigal by De Rore with diminutions by Dalla Casa and another one by the same composer with diminutions by both Dalla Casa and Bassano are reproduced in Ferand, *Die Improvisation*, pp. 57-74; also a motet by Finck with written-out diminutions, pp. 57-79. Illuminating illustrations and comments are given in Brown, *Embellishing Sixteenth-Century Music*.

two vocal models; Conforto, with a little book of abstract patterns only; and Zacconi, who devotes to this subject several chapters in the first volume of his treatise. After 1600, Banchieri makes contributions to the field; in 1615 Francesco Severi presents an interesting demonstration of the "Roman manner" of embellishing *falsi bordoni* with diminutions. In 1620, the son of Richardo Rogniono, Francesco Rognoni [*sic*] Taegio, published what was probably the last Italian treatise on diminutions.[3]

Zacconi points out that the composers set only the notes necessary to establish the "harmonic" (i.e. the contrapuntal) relationships, and that the singer is obligated to supplement them according to the meaning of the words. These are things, he says, that nature itself teaches. So much does he consider them a matter of course that he apologizes for discussing the subject at length. He felt compelled to do so, he says, because he has seen students graduate from music schools who have not mastered the art of graceful embellishments (*vaghezze & accenti*).[4]

Like Finck, Zacconi says that all voices including the bass should be ornamented (not all agree on this point: Banchieri[5] for instance advises against bass diminutions). Noteworthy is Zacconi's stress on word-meaning as a guide to embellishment. Of interest also is his description of agogic manipulations as a form of ornamentation. He speaks of notes that "are attended by some *accenti* produced by the slowing down and sustaining of the voice, and realized by taking a particle from one note and adding it to another one."[6] Since rhythmic alteration can affect contrapuntal relationships and blur an imitative intent, Zacconi issues the significant warning not to use such rubato technique *nor any embellishments* for *fughe* or *fantasie*; one must not break and spoil the logic of imitation, but let the *fughe* have their due.[7] (The term *fuga* referred at the time to any subject treated in imitative counterpoint.) However, even where these procedures of diminutions and rubato are admissible, Zacconi recommends moderation.

Bovicelli in 1594 stresses more strongly than Zacconi the importance of the text for choice and execution of ornament. His book contains some new departures, one of which refers to the treatment of final cadences. Whereas all the other authors mentioned let the diminutions, however florid, come unfailingly to rest on the final cadential note without impinging on its value, Bovicelli often lets them spill over onto this last note. A rider, he says, will not stop his galloping mount with abruptness, but let it slow down gradually. He considers it equally unnatural to bring the *élan* of an extended *passaggio* to a sudden stop. It is obvious from this explanation alone that the motivation for this carry-over design is strictly linear, and usually the effect will remain fully within the domain of melodic ornamentation. On occasion, however, Bovicelli combines the trespassing into the final note with another, more portentous innovation—an onbeat dissonance pattern. More about this shortly.

Among the small ornaments, trill-like graces were probably the first to receive attention. Ganassi in 1535 describes no less than four types of trills and marks them with different symbols. It was not, however, until the end of the 16th century that certain patterns of small melic graces began to be systematically singled out, described, and named. More importantly, they were, along with the trilled graces, assigned functions that differed from those of the *passaggi*.

Zacconi may have been among the first to segregate *accenti e trilli* from the *passaggi*.

---

[3] Conforto, *Breve et facile maniera . . . a far passaggi*; Richardo Rogniono, *Passaggi per potersi essercitare nel diminuire*; Zacconi, *Prattica*, I, bk. 1, chs. 63, 66; Banchieri, *Cartella overo regole utilissime*; Severi, *Salmi passaggiati*; Francesco Rognoni Taegio, *Selva de varii passaggi*.

[4] *Prattica*, I, bk. 1, ch. 63, ff. 56r-57r.

[5] *Cartella overo regole*, pp. 56-57: "The bass as the foundation of music must be steadfast, precise and quite black" ("saldo, & giusto e ben nero"). Banchieri even outlaws small graces for the bass: the *accenti*, which he recommends as substitutes to those who are not qualified to invent *fioretti* [i.e *passaggi*], "may

be used in all parts, except the bass" ("Gli accenti si possono fare in tutte le parti eccetto il Basso").

[6] *Prattica*, I, f. 56r: ". . . le dette figure s'accompagnano con alcuni accenti causati d'alcune rittardanze & sustentamenti di uoce che si fanno col torre una particella d'una figura & attriburla all'altra."

[7] Ibid., f. 56v: ". . . cantandosi alcune sorte di fughe, ouero fantasie per non rompere et guastar quei bei ordini d'immitatione di non ritardar veruna figura: ma cantarle equale, secondo que vagliano *senza veruno adornamento*; accioche esse fughe habbino il suo douere . . ." (italics mine).

The term *accenti* is used by Zacconi and by many other theorists and composers to designate a variety of small melic ornaments of from one to roughly four or five tones.[8] The *trilli* encompass all essentially repercussive graces. The difference between the group of the *accenti* and *trilli*, and that of the *passaggi* is a close counterpart to the distinction made above between "small" and "large" ornaments.

An important innovation in matters of the small ornaments was Bovicelli's introduction, in 1594, of onbeat dissonance patterns for *Vorschläge*. This may well be the first theoretical appearance of the harmony-enriching appoggiatura, since nothing comparable is to be found in any of the other contemporary treatises. The growing role of dissonance in the nascent baroque style was an unquestionable factor in this development. Example 4.1*a* gives two illustrations in abstract form; Ex. *b* shows a cadential appoggiatura in the embellishments of a Palestrina motet.

Ex. 4.1. Bovicelli (1594)

These patterns represent a definite landmark in the history of ornamentation. Their subsequent progress in Italy, though, is not easy to trace. To all appearances, the prebeat or (to use Hugo Goldschmidt's term) the "iambic" *Vorschlag* retained its ascendancy for most if not all of the 17th century. On the other hand, the onbeat *Vorschlag* gradually gained ground, because at the end of the century it did play a substantial role.

The emerging small graces received a powerful impulse from the dramatic change from renaissance polyphony to early baroque recitative, monody, and thorough bass—from the *stile antico* to the *stile moderno*. These changes, which had their roots in the relationship of words to music, were bound to have a deep effect on ornamentation.

Whenever music is wedded to words—and until 1600 most of it was—there arises the problem of reconciling two heterogeneous elements. An ideal balance between words and music, in which the discrepant dynamic tendencies of each are resolved in a perfect union, is very rare. More frequently, one of the two mates in the word-music combination usurps a domineering role at the other's expense. Historically, the pendulum has swung back and forth, but in the long run music has proved to be the stronger partner of the two. Polyphonic construction by itself, as well as ornamentation in all its forms, springs from purely musical impulses that have often relegated the word to mere insignificance.

The musical revolution which took place about 1600 constituted a pendulum swing of unprecedented scope in favor of the word. In the dramatic recitative, the focal center of the new style, music was assigned the comparatively subservient role of enhancing rhetorical declamation and of deepening the emotional impact, the "affect" of the words, by melodic inflection and chordal coloring. It was a natural consequence of this reorientation that polyphony was rejected and florid ornamentation outlawed, or at least restricted.

---

[8] Zacconi's flexible use of the term included even the substance of Riemann's "agogic accent" as shown in the above quoted passage (see n. 6 above) concerning the rubato.

Probably the earliest formulations of these demands are found in Count Bardi's *Discorso . . . sopra la musica antica* of c. 1580, and in Vincenzo Galileo's polemic *Dialogo della musica antica e della moderna* of 1581. The key sentence of Bardi's essay follows: ". . . the noblest function a singer can perform is that of giving proper and exact expression to the *canzone* as set down by the composer, not imitating those who aim only at being thought clever (a ridiculous pretension) and who so spoil a madrigal with their ill-ordered passages that even the composer himself would not recognize it as his creation."[9]

Peri, one of the founding fathers of the new style, in the preface to his opera *Euridice* (1600) credits Cavalieri with being the first to put "our [kind of] music on the stage" with his *Rappresentatione di anima et di corpo* (Rome, 1600). In the preface to this work (by his spokesman Guidotti) Cavalieri prohibits *passaggi* because, he says, they would get in the way of true declamation and could falsify the affective message. Instead, he demands expressive singing, dynamic shadings, and good declamation accompanied by appropriate gestures, so that the total effect will *muovere l'affetto*. This "stirring of the emotions" became the battle cry of the new style. Understandably, the impersonal brilliance of extended *passaggi* that well up from a purely musical fountainhead was out of place in the new scheme of things.

To fill in some of the bareness created by the lack of diminutions, Cavalieri introduces four small graces and a symbol for each, which he explains in what may well be the first genuine table of ornaments (Ex. 4.2). It is true that Diruta,

Ex. 4.2. Cavalieri (1600)

Conforto, Dalla Casa, Zacconi, and others had shown and explained various types of small ornaments, but they were meant to be inserted strictly at the performer's discretion and hence were not identified by symbol. Cavalieri's, by contrast, are no longer a demonstration of what *may* be done on unspecified occasions, but an explanation of what *is* to be done when the respective symbol appears in print.

Another important Roman voice echoing similar feelings is that of Viadana in the introduction to his *Cento concerti ecclesiastici* of 1602: ". . . such concerts must be sung sensitively with discretion and grace, using small ornaments (*accenti*) with judgment, and *passaggi* with restraint and in their proper places: above all, nothing must be added to what is printed because nowadays there are certain singers who, favored by nature with some vocal facility, never sing the songs the way they are written, without realizing that today such procedures are no longer welcome, indeed are held in very low esteem, especially in Rome where the true manner of good singing flourishes."[10] The passage seems on first sight to

9 Quoted in Strunk, *Source Readings*, p. 299. Excerpts from Galileo's treatise, ibid., pp. 302-322.

10 ". . . questa sorte di Concerti deve cantarsi gentilmente con discretione, & leggiadria, usando gli accenti con ragione, & passaggi con misura, & à suoi lochi: sopra tutto non aggiungendo alcuna cosa piu di quello che in loro se ritrova stampato, perciochè vi sono tal hora certi Cantanti, i quali, perchè si trovano favo-

be self-contradictory since with the same breath it appears first to permit, then to prohibit, ornamental additions. Yet the contradiction is not real. When Italians of this era speak of music "as it is written," they do not mean this in the modern sense of literal accuracy. The explanation of the apparent contradiction can be found in the two levels of ornamentation: on the lower level were the *accenti* and *trilli*, on the higher the *passaggi*. The *accenti* and *trilli* were basic requirements that one took for granted. The *passaggi* were a sophistication appropriate for certain occasions, out of place for others. When Viadana and others who remain to be quoted ask the performers to sing as printed, they ask them to refrain from *passaggi* but not from the *accenti* and *trilli*. In some spots like final cadences, even moderate *passaggi* (such as Viadana mentions) may be necessary. This explanation would seem to resolve Viadana's apparent contradictions with a principle that has a wide application throughout the 17th century.

In 1602, Caccini reaffirms, in the name of the Florentine Camerata, the ban against extensive diminutions.[11] Being a virtuoso singer himself, he found it difficult to renounce all opportunities of display, and understandably his rulings were more flexible than Cavalieri's. Caccini does condemn *passaggi*, those "long gyrations of the voice" ("lunghi giri di voce") that serve only to "tickle the ear" ("una titilatione a gli orecchi") since nothing could be more contrary to the communication of an affect. However, he admits brief ones up to a quarter or half of the beat for the sake of added grace, inasmuch as they pass quickly and also because considered judgment imposes exceptions to every rule ("perche il judicio speciale fa ad ogni regola patire qualche eccezione"). Final cadences seem to be exempt from any restrictions, as can be gathered from many examples in his music, of which a sample is shown in Ex. 4.3.

Ex. 4.3. Caccini (1602), Fortunato Angellino (*Nuove musiche*, p. 22), final cadence

Caccini lists two small ornamental types by name: the *trillo* and the *groppo*. The *trillo* in Florentine usage was a gradually accelerated tone repetition without any change of pitch. The *groppo* is a design related to both the trill and the turn, starting on a slightly prolonged main note. Example 4.4 shows Caccini's models.

riti dalla natura d'un poco di gargante, mai cantano nella maniera che stanno i Canti, non si accorgendo essi, che hoggidi questi tali non sono grati, anzi sono pochissimo stimati, parti-

colarmente in Roma, dove fiorisce la vera professione del cantar bene."

11 Caccini, *Le nuove musiche*, Preface.

Caccini mentions another small grace—the frequent sliding into the starting note from a third below. Often, he says, this manner does not fit into the harmony and therefore should not be used. Where it does fit, Caccini disapproves of the "widespread" style of leaning on the first tone (a style almost routinely used by Bovicelli). Instead, Caccini says, this tone should be touched only lightly; even so, he tolerates this only reluctantly and prefers to start on the pitch proper, letting the sound grow in intensity.

Trillo   *Groppo*

Ex. 4.4. Caccini

Very interesting are a series of illustrations in which Caccini shows how the affective power of certain melodic figures can be increased by rhythmic manipulation. The resulting rubato effect is related to that described by Zacconi.[12]

Marco da Gagliano in the preface to the opera *Dafne* (1608) asks singers to limit their *gruppi, trilli, passaggi et esclamazioni* to those places where the words permit their logical or innocuous use and to refrain from using them everywhere else. He likens a singer's indiscriminate use of ornaments to a painter who paints cypresses well and therefore crams them into every picture.[13] He seems to sum up the attitude of many monodists toward ornamental additions, including the *passaggi*: some are permissible as long as they do not conflict with the demands of good declamation.

Monteverdi, who had joined the ranks of the monodists, wrote out many elaborate figurations (see Ex. 47.2a below). The original print of *Orfeo* shows the hero's third act aria ("Possente spirto") in both simple and lavishly embellished form. Nowhere, however, could there be found a better dramatic justification for coloraturas since Orfeo in this scene exercises the magic power of his song to charm Charon into letting him pass to Hades.

Though monody was a product of secular vocal development, it had a powerful impact on the overall stylistic situation. It made almost immediate inroads into church music, where sacred monodies began to appear in ever growing numbers.

Banchieri in his *Gemelli armonici* of 1609, a sacred work for two voices and continuo, specifies that it is written "in the new style" ("Sotto moderno istile & inventione"). In the preface he asks for a broad beat, solid sound, and abstention from additional embellishments or diminutions. The concerti, he says, should be rendered "strictly as they are printed."[14] In a postscript to his *Vezzo di perle musicale* of 1610 he makes a nearly identical statement banning diminutions and other embellishments.[15] In 1610 Giovanni Paolo Cima begs his singers to perform his *Concerti ecclesiastici* "as written," with the utmost of expression, and if they wish to add anything, to limit themselves to *accenti* and *trilli*.[16]

[12] Caccini's models are reproduced in Dannreuther, *Musical Ornamentation*, I, 35-36; they are also in Strunk, *Source Readings*, p. 385.
[13] The whole preface is reproduced in Emil Vogel, "Marco da Gagliano," *VfMw*, v, 429ff. and 558ff.
[14] "Per ultimo ricercasi in questi Concerti, battuta larga, stabilmente suonati, & cantati

senza altre gorghe, o passaggi, ma puramente come vengono impressi. . . ."
[15] ". . . suonando & cantando senza diminutioni & gorghe."
[16] ". . . mi facciate gratia di cantarli come stanno, con quello maggiore affetto, che sia possibile. Et se pure alli leggiadri cantanti piacesse d'accrescerli qualche cosa: per cortesia

The doctrinaire stance taken by the founding fathers of monody with regard to the primacy of the word could not last very long. Being the stronger partner, music soon rebelled against its subjugation to the word. Melodic blossoms began to spring up in arioso passages to relieve the dryness of endless recitative, and the places multiplied where appropriate textual clues were taken as occasions for ornamental passages. Though for a while both types of musical happening remained in the service of dramatic projection, they nevertheless paved the way for the emancipation of both pure, singable melody and pure, playful ornament. This emancipation is largely realized in the so-called *bel canto* style of the mid-17th century at the hands of such masters as Cavalli, Carissimi, Cesti, and Stradella. In this style the occasional melodic buds of monody expanded into the full bloom of arias, imbued with that sensually beguiling melodiousness, the Italian *dolcezza*, that was to enchant the world for centuries to come. Hand in hand went the gradual liberation of free ornaments, a development which proceeded faster in the north of Italy than in the south. In the Rome of Carissimi, according to the testimony of Christoph Bernhard, the small graces, the *accenti e trilli*, were still preferred to the *passaggi*. The *bel canto* era, however, produced virtuoso singers and saw castrati rise to the forefront of musical prominence and power. They then used this power to arrogate the right to lavish embellishment without the need of a declamatory pretext.

Instruments are not involved in the word-music antagonism, and Caccini is only consistent when he declares that "diminutions are more appropriate for winds and strings than they are for the voices. . . ."[17] Therefore, the shock waves emanating from the monodic revolution affected instrumental ornamentation only indirectly through the overall change of style.[18]

The keyboard as a solo instrument stood farthest away from the stylistic break, and we need only to look at Frescobaldi's music to realize that his keyboard style developed in an unbroken line from his 16th-century predecessors and thus, incidentally, secured a continuity of polyphonic writing in an era which had allegedly discarded it. This is especially true of works, like the *ricercare*, written in the strict style. The toccatas, on the other hand, with their rhythmic freedom and declamatory style elements, had a kinship with the recitative.

Frescobaldi's ornamental figuration is written out in regular notation as was that of Merulo, Trabaci, and other keyboard masters of the late 16th and early 17th centuries.

———————

lo faccino solo negli accenti e trilli. . . ." See also the preface to Ottavio Durante, *Arie devote . . .* (Rome, 1608).

An amusing triple choice is offered by Bartolomeo Barbarino in his second book of motets (Venice, 1614). Throughout, the vocal line is printed in two versions: simple and with *passaggi*. The simple version serves a double purpose: it may be sung as printed by those who are not inclined to sing diminutions, or it may be used by those who have both inclination and contrapuntal skill to invent their own diminutions. Finally, the written-out *passaggi* are for the benefit of those who like to sing *passaggi* but do not know how to invent correct ones.

[17] *Nuove musiche*, Preface.
[18] The relationship of vocal and instrumental ornaments has given rise to a controversy in which Hugo Goldschmidt pleaded the case of instrumental, Max Kuhn the case of vocal primacy. The dispute, like the one about the hen and the egg, is unprofitable. Both types of ornamentation have always coexisted and can be assumed to have inter-influenced one another, though each medium developed ornamental characteristics of its own in line with its idiomatic needs and potentials. For centuries, however, instrumental teachers kept exhorting their disciples to "sing on their instruments," whereas vocal teachers have not been known to recommend instrumental styles as models to emulate. It is likely, therefore, that in the ornamental give-and-take the vocal style has given more than it has taken.

The ornamental nature of these figurations would itself suggest that they be played with rhythmic freedom, even if we had not received specific instructions to this effect in the famous preface to the first book of Frescobaldi's Toccatas.[19] It is unlikely that the addition of further diminutions in works that contain written-out florid figurations was welcomed by these masters; it is more likely that *accenti* and *trilli* were to be added in appropriate places. In this connection it may be revealing that Diruta in presenting, in the first book of *Il Transilvano*, a number of toccatas by various masters does not add any new ornaments. When, in the second volume, he demonstrates the free addition of ornaments he chooses a canzona with slow-moving notes.

Between vocal and string ornamentation there was understandably a greater parallelism. The violin, born in the first half of the 16th century, did not come into its own as an independent solo instrument until the 17th century was well on its way. Its literature developed around the two focal points of the sonata and the concerto, both of which comprised in their styles currents that were eminently sympathetic to the nature of the instrument: the lively rhythms of the dance and the songfulness of the *bel canto*. Thus, as could be expected, the lively dance-derived movements adopted ornaments that increased animation and brilliance, the slow movements those that added grace and elegance. When the sonata, followed later by the concerto, grew into maturity after the middle of the 17th century, *bel canto* and the *da capo* aria had regrown the clipped wings of the *passaggi*. Now the violin masters, taking their cue from the voice, expected the performer to add diminutions to slow movements and small graces (*accenti* and *trilli*) almost anywhere. The resulting performance manner remained alive until late into the 18th century.

This second flowering of the *passaggi* came to full development at a time when such large-scale embellishments had gone out of fashion in France, where principles akin to those of the monody were enthroned by the formidable Lully. Hence from that time on, generous improvised embellishment of skeletal melodies became associated with the Italian style as contrasted to the French style, in which ornamental additions' were generally limited to small graces only.

The newly gained freedom, like any freedom, engendered abuse, and the never-too-rare species of performers who are vain and lacking in intelligence must often have indulged in tasteless exaggerations that distorted many a composition.

In 1672 Gio. Maria Bononcini pleads with his performers to leave the music as it stands and not to disfigure it. Though his appeal is contained in an instrumental work, it is addressed to singers at the same time. He gave as his reason: "because today there are some [performers] so little informed of that art of tasteful embellishment that in singing or in playing they want with their disorderly and indiscreet extravagances of bow or of voice to change, indeed to deform, the compositions (even though these were written with every care and conscientiousness) in such a manner that the authors have no alternative but to beg those singers and players to content themselves with rendering the works plainly and purely as they are written. . . ."[20]

But the few lonely voices that were raised in agreement with Bononcini were incapable of stemming a still-rising tide; the high point of the virtuoso singer's power was not to be reached until the early part of the 18th century. From this latter period we hear another

[19] *Toccate e partite*, bk. 1, Preface.

[20] Bononcini, *Sonate da chiesa a due violini*, Preface: ". . . perchè oggidi sono alcuni così poco intelligenti di quest'arte che ò cantando, ò sonando vogliono sempre co' loro sregolati & indiscreti capricci d'arco, ò di Voce, alterare, anzi deformare le Composizioni (quantunque fatte con tutto studio e applicazione) in modo che gli autori sono arrivati à dover pregare gli medesimi Cantanti e Sonatori, acciò si contentino di dire e di fare le cose schiettamente e puramente come per appunto stanno. . . ."

outcry from a composer who clothed his distress in satirical garb. Benedetto Marcello (1686-1739), in his famous lampoon on operatic abuses, *Il teatro alla moda*, had briefly illuminated the lowly station of the composer in the musical pecking order: "In walking with singers," he writes, "especially *castrati*, the composer will always place himself at their left and keep one step behind, hat in hand. . . ."[21] The same master writes in the preface to solo cantatas and two madrigals: ". . . in the adagio they [i.e. the *castrati*] sing with coloraturas, which they call of good taste and good style, that ruin in this manner the regular notes of the counterpoint and create unbearable effects. That happens again at the end of the madrigal where . . . they all join in making diminutions that create the most dissonant results with one another. Such abuses are the reason why the counterpoint does not produce the good effect it is supposed to produce, and the music directors as a consequence are rather martyrs of the *castrati*."[22]

Thus within less than two generations the pendulum of the word-music conflict has swung back to where music has regained much of the lost territory. In the vocal field, it did so by means of a compromise that created, as it were, two separate spheres of influence: the recitative was allotted to the dominion of the word, the aria to that of music. But the solution was only temporary. Extravagances by star singers sparked a resumption of the tug of war through operatic reforms that were launched on behalf of the word. The pendulum resumed its swing and it has kept swinging to the present day.

The temporary eclipse of the diminutions during the era of monody raised the small graces to a position of prominence when they were called upon to relieve the austerity of pure declamation. Though they now had to share the limelight with the returning *passaggi*, the small graces remained in the foreground from this time on.

Except for the trill, which was occasionally indicated by symbol, the small ornaments, during the 17th century, were either written out in regular notation or, like the *passaggi*, left to the discretion of the performer. It was not until about 1710 that more and more Italian masters began to write small graces with the little notes they had adopted from the French.

Regrettably, we have for the greater part of the 17th century and for the beginning of the 18th century practically no Italian theoretical sources that discuss ornamentation. Thus we are incompletely informed about the prevailing style of the *passaggi*, while, with regard to the small graces, the silence of their theorists may not prove, but strongly suggests, that definite rules did not exist. Some preferred practices did develop, though with considerable regional differences, and we know something about them from several sources. One is represented by the many instances in which composers wrote some graces in regular notation. A second important source is provided by a number of German theorists who studied and described Italian manners of vocal performance. Finally, after 1710 when the Italians adopted the French use of little notes, we have reason to assume that the new notation did not mirror a new fashion but represented only the clarification of something that had existed before. This assump-

21 Quoted in Strunk, *Source Readings*, p. 527.
22 Bol. ms GG 144: "Nel adagio cantano con passi que loro chiamano di buon gusto e belle maniere, guastando in tal forma le note regolari del contrapunto e formandone insopportabili effetti. Ciò si rileva parimente nel chiudere del Madrigale, dove . . . gareggiano tutte in diminuire, riuscendo in tal forma dissonantissima trà di loro. Dal quale abuso deriva poi que li Contrapunti non producono quel buon effetto que produr dovrebbero, e li Mastri di Capella sono per conseguenza più Martiri de Castrati medesimi."

tion is borne out by Pier Francesco Tosi, a well-known castrato singer who, writing a treatise in his old age on the art of singing, deplores the new-fangled ways of specifying the use of appoggiaturas.[23] He considers this an insult to singers, who should be credited with enough taste and judgment to know when to apply those graces without the benefit of a prompter.

When Italy in the early decades of the 18th century gave birth to the *galant* style, its light, essentially homophonic texture permitted and encouraged appoggiaturas to proliferate and to extend in length. The prebeat *Vorschlag* may now have lost the prominent position it had held throughout the 17th century and the early years of the 18th, but it still played a large role during the rest of the 18th century, supplementing and complementing the long appoggiatura forms. Not only in matters of the *Vorschlag*, but also with regard to all the other small graces, the age-old Italian freedom and flexibility remained fully alive well beyond the mid-18th century.

[23] Tosi, *Opinioni de' cantori*, p. 23.

French Developments

The roots of French 17th-century ornamentation are difficult to trace because only a few sources for 16th-century practices seem to have come to light. The most important sources are Attaignant's keyboard transcriptions of chansons with written-out diminutions. It can be readily assumed that singers practiced similar methods of embroidery: the complex diminutions in the early 17th-century *airs de cour* for which we do have documentation cannot have come into being from a vacuum; they must have had their antecedents in the preceding generations.

The first detailed report about these early 17th-century practices may be the one by Mersenne. In his *Harmonie universelle* he devotes several chapters to questions of ornamentation and includes another one, written by Basset, on lute ornaments; in the latter a number of small graces are described along with their symbols.[1]

We owe to Mersenne also an interesting example of an *air de cour*, as written and as sung; an excerpt of it is given in Ex. 5.1. It shows the characteristic two couplets of which the second was sung in diminutions.

Ex. 5.1. *Air de cour* by Boësset as sung by Moulinié

[1] Mersenne, *Harmonie universelle*, vocal ornaments: *Traitez des consonances, des disso-* nances . . . , pp. 354ff.; lute ornaments: *Traité des instrumens à chordes*, pp. 79-82.

Though Mersenne does not say so, it is clear that the song was never meant to be sung in its original bareness. For the two couplets we see three versions. The richly ornamented third version is meant for the second couplet as indicated by the title, hence the second version, the one equipped with *ports de voix*, must have been intended for the first couplet. The *ports de voix* then correspond interestingly to the Italian *accenti e trilli*, the small graces whose addition was taken for granted even where the composer asked that his music be performed "as written."

This manner of vocal embellishment continued through the better part of the 17th century, though in the process it underwent an evolution toward greater refinement and elegance as well as increased sensitivity to the demands of diction. The airs of Michel Lambert, Bénigne de Bacilly, and D'Ambruis, published after 1660 with written-out second-couplet diminutions, are characteristic of this later, exquisitely suave and polished ornamental style. Example 5.2 gives an illustration from an air by Lambert and the first measures of one by Bacilly. The latter example shows the suggestion of rhythmic freedom through unmetrical notation of the embellished version. (For further illustrations see below Exx. 45.1 and 45.2.)

a. Air de cour by Michel Lambert (*Les airs de M. Lambert*, Paris, 1666), with 2nd couplet diminutions

b. Air de cour by Bénigne de Bacilly (Paris, 1668)

Ex. 5.2.

The songs of these masters are of special interest to us because they show, as Mersenne's examples had before, the predominantly prebeat character of the small graces, especially the *Vorschlag* types of the *ports de voix* and *coulés*.

Lambert was the most famous singer of his time and the father-in-law of Lully. Lully himself was opposed to the practice of free diminutions and is said to have tolerated in his operas only those second-couplet embellishments that were prepared by Lambert.[2] Lully's rejection of willful embroidery, which he called nonsensical, was rooted in his ideal of truthful dramatic declamation; and it is interesting to note that he made this style prominent in France at a time when it was being eclipsed in Italy.

There is little doubt that Lully's strictures against arbitrary ornaments were, like those of the monodists, directed against large diminutions and *not against small graces* whose addition here, too, seems to have been expected. The scores of his works that were printed in his lifetime show only austere melody lines for both voice and instruments. The only symbols we find in them are those for trills; others were not yet in common use.[3] When after Lully's death the use of the symbols spread, several second editions of his works and a few posthumous first ones show ornamental additions mainly of the *port de voix* and slide type.

Lully's rejection of the large diminutions was unquestionably a weighty factor in the subsequent decline of this practice in French performance. However, he could not have singlehandedly brought about such a profound change if the rejec-

[2] Mattheson quotes—in *Critica musica*, II, 50—the anonymous author of *Tome II de l'histoire de la musique*, pp. 23-24, as saying that Lully made use of *roulements* [i.e. of embroidery] at the most three to four times in any opera, and when occasionally he had to use a *double* as a favor to one or the other singer, he asked Lambert to prepare it. Some of these diminutions for Lully's airs that were presumably written by Lambert are accessible in modern editions, for instance in Lully's *Oeuvres complètes* (Paris, 1933), II, 182-183. Additional documentation will be found in ch. 46 below.

[3] Unfortunately none of Lully's autographs, which might have given us further clues, has been preserved.

tion of the diminutions had not been supported by the growing wave of rationalism that had begun to sweep the nation. This rationalism not only favored the word in its conflict with music but went so far as to find the ultimate justification of music in its literary or pictorial associations. Dominance of the word implies, of course, opposition to lavish embroidery. The rejection of diminutions led inevitably to a proliferation of the small ornaments, the so-called *agréments*. This was analogous to the emphasis on *accenti* and *trilli* when the *passaggi* were frowned upon by the monodists. But in France, in contrast to Italy, the small graces managed to retain henceforth their newly won ascendancy on the ornamental scene.[4]

Although performers were now denied the right to insert large ornaments, they were still at liberty to add at their discretion a great variety of small graces. However, in this realm, too, composers now began to attempt greater control by introducing symbols for many small ornamental designs. Most important among the new symbols was the appearance, during the last third of the 17th century, of the little notes called *notes perdues* or *notes postiches* that were not included in the metrical count of the measure.

Nivers in his *Livre d'orgue* of 1665 used little notes in the preface to show the designs of trills and mordents, but he did not use them in the main text. The first examples of such use within the score may have been the ornamental, extrametrical letters in lute tablatures (see for instance Ex. 35.1a below), and passing notes of smaller value that were inserted in some unmeasured preludes for keyboard instruments. Example 5.3a, from Le Bègue, shows one of numerous instances where 16th-notes and 8th-notes are placed between the beats. Similar ornamental interbeat insertions can also be found once in a while in the metrically measured music of this master. Example *b* shows an unmetrical interbeat *port de voix* and Ex. *c* an analogous interbeat *coulé* where the 16th-note is placed before the metrically aligned dot of the preceding half-note. In Ex. *d* we find three-note slides that, preceded by a 16th-note rest, fill a whole surplus beat in the measure. The pattern occurs several times in the course of the piece, with the obvious meaning that the three notes are to be played as an upbeat to the chord.

Ex. 5.3. Le Bègue

[4] Diminutions did not completely vanish, though they became rare and did shrink considerably in size. Some modest *passages* continue to be listed in a few treatises as one of the *agréments*.

It is possible that the little notes were first written by the gambists. Marais uses them in his first book of *Pièces de viole* (1686) for all manner of ornamental designs with a degree of refinement and sophistication that suggests a history of previous practice.

The clavier players showed at first a distinct preference for abstract symbols, inherited from the lutenists, whose meaning was not more or less self-explanatory as was that of the little notes. The significance of these abstract symbols had to be explained. Nivers, as has been mentioned, gave explanatory illustrations. Chambonnières in 1670 had a short table of ornaments, so did Le Bègue, Boyvin, and Raison soon thereafter. All of these tables and similar ones by other masters were outdistanced by D'Anglebert who in 1689 prefaced his book of harpsichord pieces with a table containing no less than 29 ornamental symbols and their notational translations.

The role played by the ornament tables in forming the misconceptions about the true nature of the graces involved has been discussed previously at sufficient length. The frequently heard references to the crystallization of the French *agréments* into definitive, rigid patterns would seem to be an analogous misunderstanding. True, the French ornaments were disciplined into smaller shapes, but within their narrower ranges they maintained throughout a vital measure of liberty and flexibility.

The adoption of the symbols by no means spelled the end of free ornamental additions. Composers differed greatly in the degree of completeness with which they prescribed the necessary graces. Some kept, or at least tried to keep, a tight rein on the performer by giving very detailed ornamental instructions. Couperin, for instance, bitterly complains about those performers who do not honor all of his ornamental prescriptions and demands that no ornament he indicated be left out and none be added.[5] He did take great care in marking all ornaments, and the great density of their occurrence leaves no room for sensible additions. Other masters were far less explicit, used symbols more sparingly, and relied on the performer to supply other ornaments at appropriate places. Because of this state of affairs, we still find many late 18th-century treatises preoccupied not only with explaining the ornamental designs, their symbols and their execution, but also with explaining the contexts in which certain ornaments could, or should, or should not, be used.

The right of the performer to use his judgment in matters of the *agréments* had an eloquent advocate in the eminent theorist Saint Lambert, author of the first known harpsichord treatise.[6] In diametric opposition to Couperin's attitude, he stresses the complete freedom of the small ornaments and claims for the performer the right not only to add new ones but to leave out those that are prescribed or to substitute others in their stead.

The introduction of symbols had proceeded at random and had led to wide divergences in choice of signs, meaning, and terminology. This bewildering disarray gives an exaggerated picture of disunity, because in spite of the outward confusion there was on the whole, especially within a specific medium, a certain measure of agreement on the basic shapes of the most important graces. Yet such

[5] *Troisième livre de pièces de clavecin,* Preface.   [6] *Principes du clavecin,* p. 57.

agreement was never complete and certainly far removed from the Utopian picture which Eugène Borrel painted of a complete unity of all French performance practices, allegedly persisting throughout the whole 18th century. Quite apart from the chaos of symbols and terms, there were coexisting divergences in substance and there were, of course, changes with time. Concerning these latter changes it can be said in broadest outline that there was a gradual trend from the preponderant prebeat character of the *agréments* in the 17th century to growing onbeat tendencies in the 18th century. This trend generally paralleled that occurring in Italy and Germany. Increased communication between the three countries and a consequent leveling of their stylistic differences were factors that promoted this parallelism. The motivations for this international trend toward the growing role of onbeat graces were closely linked to the new homophonic preclassical style whose impoverished texture was in need of the harmonic or rhythmic enrichment that the onbeat graces could bestow.

However, prebeat and onbeat styles continued to coexist in the second half of the century in France as well as in the other two countries. This fact will emerge not only from subsequent specific documentation but can in a preliminary fashion be gathered from a statement made by Jean Jacques Rousseau who, speaking of the *notes perdues*, says that they are "marked by little notes that do not count in the measure, whose very short value is taken from the preceding or from the following note."[7] That means, of course, they are either prebeat or onbeat graces.

THE elegant and sophisticated art of the French *agréments* had reached its fullest bloom in the first half of the 18th century and achieved its classical expression in the finely chiseled and infinitely graceful works of Couperin. The inevitable decadence set in around the middle of the century and paralleled the gradual disintegration of the formerly sovereign French style into the international musical language of the preclassical era with its strong Italian overtones. The French harpsichord school, which had emitted the strongest radiations in ornamentation practice throughout the musical world, was by now in full decline, the overture and ballet suite were rapidly falling out of fashion, and after Rameau's death even the French opera had to call on foreigners to keep its great traditions alive. Under these circumstances it is not surprising that the creativity had gone out of the field of ornamentation and that the French, who had achieved so much in this domain, now had little new to add to it.

[7] *Dictionnaire de musique*, s.v. *notes de Goût*: "Les autres Notes de goût . . . se marquent seulement avec de petites Notes qui ne se comptent pas dans la Mesure, & dont la durée très-rapide se prend sur la Note qui précède ou sur celle qui suit."

Germany presented a more complicated picture. It is hard and dangerous to generalize in any circumstance, but it is harder and more dangerous to do so with regard to the Germany of the baroque, an empire on paper only, a country split up religiously, fragmented politically, and completely decentralized culturally. Important musical establishments were dominated or influenced by foreigners, many by Italians, some by the French. Individual foreign artists, including a number of eminent English instrumentalists, found adherents, created schools, and thereby injected new ingredients into a most varied and complex situation. We find accordingly a kaleidoscopic coexistence of indigenous German, of Italian, and French styles, with a sprinkling of English elements, as well as all kinds of mixtures and crosscurrents. In Bach's time the picture became still more complicated by the rise of the new *galant* stylistic trends with their countless shadings, radiations, and interactions. To think under these conditions in terms of "unified practices," be it in matters of composition or of performance, is completely unrealistic. Any general statement can only be understood as something that applies "by and large."

"By and large," then, it can be said that German ornamentation of the 17th century was patterned on Italian models. It is not surprising that this should have been the case. The musical baroque was an Italian phenomenon that burst on the musical firmament of Europe with dazzling brilliance. All those changes of styles and forms that are summarized by the label "baroque" were wrought by Italian musicians: recitative, monody, thorough bass, opera, oratorio, cantata, toccata, sonata, concerto. Small wonder that this brilliant display of creativeness and innovation made a formidable impression on all the musical nations of Europe. Nowhere was the impression stronger than in Germany. To German musicians the Italy of the 17th century had become the Mecca of music, and those among them who could not make the actual pilgrimage made their obeisance in its direction.

The Italian impact was strongest in the Catholic south where Italian influence became domineering. With countless Italian masters appointed to key positions, and most native composers eager to follow their example, south Germany and Austria became practically musical satellites of Italy. But the radiations from Italy extended into the Protestant north, and in the field of ornaments it is significant that some of the most eminent Protestant masters, among them Praetorius, Schütz, and Schein, became ardent advocates and efficient propagators of the Italian singing style, including its ornamental practices. Caspar Kittel, too, is reported to have planned a treatise on this subject that unfortunately did not materialize.

Praetorius, to his sorrow, had never been to Italy, but he tells his readers that he derived his knowledge of Italian methods from treatises, from prefaces to compositions, from Italian masters he met personally, and from German musicians well acquainted with Italian practices. Praetorius's books were widely disseminated and his chapters on the Italian styles of singing and ornamenting were relayed to later generations of German musicians by Crüger and by Herbst who, in their respective treatises, quoted him almost verbatim. Praetorius's plan for a detailed monograph on diminutions was unhappily frustrated by his death. Schütz, of course, acquired his knowledge firsthand during his Venetian studies and refreshed it later by continuing Italian contacts. His Italian-oriented ideas were effectively disseminated by his student Christoph Bernhard, who himself spent a considerable time in Rome, where he was probably closely associated with Carissimi. Through Bernhard's widely read treatises this important Schütz-Bernhard stream of Italian-oriented influence can be traced up to the first half of the 18th century through Mylius, Feyertag, Fuhrmann, and Walther.

It would be, of course, an exaggeration to say that in the 17th century all of Germany followed Italian models. There were certainly German masters who went their own indigenous ways or who absorbed what they heard or learned from France, Holland, or England. But Italian influence was very strong indeed; and in the field of vocal ornament it was dominant—so dominant that it is not possible to distinguish a German 17th-century ornamental practice from the Italian. Therefore, the practices that were current in the Germany of that age will be referred to as "Italo-German." They represent one of the two great tributaries that shaped the ornamental situation in the Germany of Bach's time. The other, which joined later but with telling impact, was French.

Though a few German musicians like Froberger and Muffat[1] had gone to France in the 17th century as well as to Italy, it was not until the early part of the 18th century that French ornament practices became known and imitated in Germany. When they finally did, their influence spread so rapidly that they soon assumed a role equal to, and in keyboard music probably superior to, that of the Italians. The growing international popularity of the French overture and ballet suite, as well as the Germans' admiration of the standards and style of French instrumental (notably keyboard) performance were responsible for the eagerness with which the Germans absorbed French ornament practices after 1700.

After French influence had thus strongly asserted itself, German musicians were expected to be conversant with both the Italian and French *Geschmack*, i.e. style of performance, and, in particular, style of ornamentation.

This confluence on German territory of the Italian and French streams of ornament practice took place largely in Bach's lifetime, in the first half of the 18th century. It led to a mingling of far from unified French procedures with the Italo-German ones that were in matters of diminutions licentiously free, and in matters of small ornaments diversified and in a state of constant flux. The result, as could have been foreseen, was an extremely fluid situation. The confusion was heightened by the above mentioned momentous development in matters of style: the emergence in the first half of the 18th century of the *style galant* alongside and in competition with the late baroque. The sharp turnabout in musical aesthetics—from the contrapuntal to the homophonic, from free, unsystematic linear rhythm to metrical regularity, from (as seen by the spokes-

[1] Georg Muffat, though born in Savoy of English-Scotch-French ancestry, seems to have considered himself a German musician.

men of the new music) a dry constructivism, a music of the brain, to a music of sentiment that spoke to the heart—this dramatic change, not unlike the events around 1600, was bound to have a deep influence on the function and nature of ornaments. Most significant was the basically international shift from predominantly melodic to much more frequent harmonic ornamentation. In particular, appoggiaturas and related onbeat graces, following the Italian lead, now proliferated and expanded in size.

It was not until midcentury that the turbulence in matters of ornamentation began to subside and settle to a measure of regularity. The clash of styles had by then been resolved with the demise of the baroque, leaving the *galant* style in uncontested control. Moreover, the confusion created by the collision of Italian and French ornament practices had gradually sorted itself out and yielded to the somewhat more unified ways that are reflected in a greater measure of agreement in the treatises of the period. Ornamentation was now divided into the "arbitrary" (*willkürliche*) and the "essential" (*wesentliche*) graces. The former were the Italian-type diminutions, the latter the small graces that were mostly indicated by French-derived symbols.

The German synthesis of the "essential" ornaments produced what could be called the first distinctly German school of ornamentation. Its headquarters was the Berlin of C.P.E. Bach, Marpurg, and Agricola, and—to a much lesser degree—of Quantz. Possibly influenced by the *genius loci* of Prussian militarism, these authors tried to regiment ornamentation into far more definite patterns than had ever before been envisioned. We search in vain for the counterpart to the French, and earlier German, apologies for the inadequacies of printed explanations and gain on the contrary the impression that the new ornament tables mean what they say in a more literal sense than all the preceding ones. Unquestionably what we witness here is a manneristic hardening that is regrettable because it contradicts the nature and function of ornament itself. One of the aspects of this rigidity was the new manner of regulating the precise rhythmical shapes of ornaments, especially the length of appoggiaturas, by writing the little-note symbols in the exact values they were supposed to represent. However, the full measure of the new rigidity is only reached with C.P.E. Bach's unyielding insistence on the onbeat start of *every* small, symbol-prescribed ornament, regardless of its musical function or harmonic implications. The onbeat start as such had now become an absolute musical value and, in the name of the Berlin School, was proclaimed a categorical imperative of ornamental ethics.

Such extremism could not help but meet with objections. Quantz, for one, older and more cosmopolitan than his Berlin colleagues, was not in sympathy with such one-sided rigidity. In matters of ornaments he took a much more flexible, more truly artistic, attitude than his colleagues, though he shared with them a common allegiance to the *galant* style. Even C.P.E. Bach's chief disciples, Marpurg and Agricola, though endorsing the onbeat doctrine in principle, nevertheless inserted into the ornamental fabric interbeat graces in the guise of *Nachschläge*. Leopold Mozart, as could be expected from his Italian ties, took a flexible stand that was akin to Quantz's. Incidentally, when C.P.E. Bach speaks deprecatingly of interbeat graces as those "ugly *Nachschläge* . . . which are so extraordinarily fashionable," he thereby documents the great frequency of their midcentury use.[2] It is rather amusing that he himself could not help but stress the need for *Nachschläge* after trills, evidently unaware of the implicit contradiction to his own pronouncements. There is other evidence, too, that the unquestionable hardening process did not degenerate into complete ossification. Doubtless, C.P.E. Bach was not as rigid about ornaments in practice as he appears to be in theory. Not only was he too great an artist to have turned into a drill sergeant, but he himself says while speaking of certain ornaments that their rendition requires "a liberty which avoids everything slavish and machine-like."[3] Be this as it may, there is no denying the rigidifying, coarsening influence of this school on German ornament practices of its generation, since after midcentury its teachings were widely quoted, copied, and followed. However, these principles enjoyed their greatest triumph two hundred years later when modern researchers elevated them to a basic law for the whole 18th century, subjecting to their jurisdiction the masters of the late baroque along with those of the classical era for all the countries of Europe. Concerning the late baroque, and in particular J. S. Bach, the illogic of such extrapolation will be demonstrated in the course of this study. Regarding the classical era, which does not concern us here, there is a similar need for reexamination: Mozart and Haydn, too, have to be disengaged from the stranglehold of the onbeat monopoly.

[2] *Versuch über die wahre Art das Clavier zu spielen*, vol. 1, ch. 2, sec. 2, par. 25: "die hesslichen Nachschläge . . . die so gar ausserordentlich Mode sind. . . ."

[3] Ibid., ch. 3, par. 7: "Es gehört hiezu eine Freyheit, die alles sclavische und maschinenmässige ausschliesst."

The earliest stages of Bach's artistic career are enveloped in a darkness which only sensational new discoveries will dispel. We do not know whether he had any composition teacher at all; the instruction he received in Ohrdruf from his older brother, Johann Christoph—so Philipp Emanuel speculates in a letter to Forkel—may well have been limited to organ playing.[1] The famous obituary which was prepared by Philipp Emanuel and Agricola (one of Sebastian's students) tells us that Bach taught himself how to compose "chiefly by the observation of the works of the most famous and proficient composers of his day and by the fruits of his own reflection upon them."[2] The obituary mentions Bruhns, Reinken, Buxtehude, and "several good French organists" as masters whose music he studied. Philipp Emanuel, in response to a inquiry by Forkel, supplemented this information with the added names of Froberger, Kerll, Pachelbel, Frescobaldi, Fischer, Strunck, and Böhm.[3] The names of such masters as Grigny, Dieupart, and D'Anglebert, some of whose works he copied for himself, belong here, too, as well as those of other masters whom he transcribed, foremost among them Vivaldi.

In his ardent desire to learn, Bach selected for his educational nourishment whatever he could find that suited his needs. During his earliest period his surroundings probably offered chiefly German sustenance, presumably with the strong Italian admixtures that were to be expected at the time. The first portentous meeting with French style and French practices occurred in Celle during the years 1700 to 1703 where, as pointed out by the obituary, he acquired "a thorough grounding in the French taste." Further German infusions that are recorded came during the following years through visits in Lübeck and perhaps Hamburg. The Weimar period (1708-1717) finally witnessed the intake of a strong dose of Italian stylistic matter, this time in its pure and unalloyed state.

It was in Weimar that this remarkable process of self-education culminated in consummate mastery and the crystallization of Bach's personal style which by then had evolved as the synthesis of the international musical legacies from older masters, adapted, molded, transformed by his artistic ideals and strivings, or as the obituary put it, by "his reflection upon them."

The style he thus evolved at the age of about thirty underwent no significant changes for the rest of his life and those that did occur, tended toward conservatism, not modernity.[4] Thus, when in the 1720's he witnessed the emergence of the *style galant* and saw it engulf ever wider areas of the musical landscape, he remained essentially impervious to its blandishments. With remarkable stead-

[1] David and Mendel, *The Bach Reader*, rev. ed., p. 278.

[2] Ibid., pp. 216-217.

[3] Ibid., p. 278.

[4] The revolution in the chronology of Bach's works that was effected in the 1950's by research of Alfred Dürr and Georg von Dadelsen, in the course of which many solidly established dates were found to be wrong by as much as twenty years, was obviously possible only against the background of a long-lasting basic unity of style. A similar upheaval for the works of, say, Haydn or Beethoven is hardly thinkable.

fastness he remained rock-like among the rising floods of a style that must have seemed superficial and frivolous to him. "Berlin-Blue" (a color that faded) was his derisive term for the music of the royal Berlin establishment that included his son Philipp Emanuel. The older he became and the more he saw the structures of the baroque realm crumble under the onslaught of the stylistic revolution, the more he turned with profound absorption into the world of his spiritual ancestry. He consecrated this communion with his last unfinished work, the *Art of the Fugue*, a supreme document of baroque polyphony. The gap between the world of Bach and that of the *galant* composers had become so wide that little communication remained between the two. This fact is not contradicted by such decidedly un-baroque works as the "Coffee Cantata" (c. 1734) or the "Peasant Cantata" (1742) whose jocular folksiness was totally marginal to Bach's *oeuvre*. Even his occasional efforts to please a public or a patron with a bow toward a lighter and more "modern" style had no lasting impact on his artistic credo, as attested by the contrapuntal complexities of all the major late works that preceded the *Art of the Fugue*, such as the *Well-Tempered Clavier* (II), the *Goldberg Variations* (its fluffy, *galant* "Aria," as Schering surmised, is most likely not by Bach), the *Canonic Variations*, and the *Musical Offering* (in spite of some understandable gestures toward the Berlin style in the slow movement of its Trio Sonata, a severe work that taxes the brain rather than "moves the heart"—the touchstone of a *galant* composition).

Not surprisingly, the story of Bach's style is paralleled by the story of his use of ornaments. He began with the adoption of multinational models, mostly French and Italian, which he then assimilated as an integral part of his musical idiom. Of greatest consequence is the fact that in this field of ornaments, too, his style was fully established sometime between 1710 and 1715 and showed no noticeable change thereafter. His immunity against the fashions of the *galant* style extended to ornamentation.

In speaking of Bach's style in both its general sense and in the special one concerning ornaments, we are dealing with a complex phenomenon. Bach was not an eclectic in the usual sense, and his adoption of models did not, therefore, proceed by accumulation and assembly into neatly separable units; instead, he synthesized what he adopted into a higher, uniquely Bachian entity. Hence Bach did not have three distinct styles in which he dwelled alternatingly, but essentially *one* style with different orientations and shadings, comparable to one organ with its multiple registrations. Though we can expect to find the German heritage more manifest in the stylistic "registration" of the chorale preludes and phantasies, the Italian in concertos and sonatas, the French in overtures and suites, we find nevertheless in many, perhaps in most, works different strands of Bach's musical heritage inextricably interwoven. Dense German polyphony permeates the Italian concerto; Italian concerto elements invade the French suite; both concerto and overture-suite intimately mingle with German chorale elaborations in Lutheran cantatas, oratorios, and passions.

What happened with regard to his style as a whole was again mirrored in the small world of ornaments. There is no question either that we find in French-oriented works, such as the keyboard suites, many French-derived *agréments* and many written-out Italian-inspired diminutions in the sonatas and concertos. In other words, a certain stylistic orientation favored congenial ornaments. Yet we find a profusion of both French and Italian ornaments in the supposedly arch-German chorale preludes and analogous cases of integration across stylistic border-lines almost anywhere. Obviously, Bach was not in the least concerned with pre-serving pure breeds of the various national ornaments and confining them to their proper habitats. Therefore the greatest skepticism is in order when we read, for instance, that certain types of Bach's works, because they were alleged to be written "in the French style" have to follow alleged "French rules" of perfor-mance. Whatever the national origin of the ornaments adopted by Bach, we can assume that he made them his own, giving in performance free rein to the impulse of the moment. These imponderables of artistic performance were cited before as the reasons why, not only for Bach but for all old masters, exact answers can-not be given and why approximations are the only realistic aim of historical research in matters of ornamentation.

In trying to approach this aim as far as Bach's usage is concerned, we can derive from the preceding discussions two main guiding principles. First, the early establishment and stabilization of Bach's ornamental practices require us to look for his models in the time of his youth, roughly from 1700 to 1710 if not before, and certainly no later than 1715. We must place the starting point of our inquiry upstream in those early sources from which Bach chose to draw, and not downstream in those which he chose to ignore. The importance of this point can hardly be overstressed inasmuch as this downstream procedure has been so over-whelmingly, and almost routinely, followed by researchers who let themselves be guided by the easy availability of sources rather than by their historical logic. Thus it happened that the *galant* treatises of the midcentury—notably those of C.P.E. Bach, Quantz, Marpurg, and Agricola—with their plethora of information, their numerous rules, and their methodical thoroughness were eagerly consulted concerning Bach performance, and their authority for such use taken for granted. The rationale for this attitude must have been that these treatises, published shortly after Bach's death, were assumed to reflect practices which were already current during Bach's later years. Though this assumption is correct, it proves little. Considering what has been said before about the vast difference in artistic orientation between Bach and the *galant* "moderns," contemporaneousness as such becomes a meaningless argument.

Second, it should have become clear that the early, upstream sources are not by themselves sufficient to enlighten us on Bach's practices. They inform us of the environmental situation by showing what designs were familiar to Bach dur-ing his youthful exploratory stages. The exploration of these data is clearly impor-tant and therefore constitutes the logical starting place for the proposed inquiry. However, in order to find out *what* Bach decided to select and what he did with it afterwards, we have to look for answers in Bach's music itself, the more so since we cannot expect to find them in Bach's own keyboard ornamentation table (the *Explication* from the *Clavierbüchlein vor Wilhelm Friedemann Bach*) which, as we shall see, has been much overrated and much misinterpreted.

PART III
ONE-NOTE GRACES

Introduction

Vorschlag, Nachschlag, Zwischenschlag, Zusammenschlag

———◆●◆———

Ornaments that consist of a single tone only will in the following be called *one-note graces*. Like any other ornament, a one-note grace cannot stand alone but has to be linked to a *principal* or *parent* note that it is meant to embellish. This note can be the one that precedes the grace or the one that follows it. The grace can also link—like a hyphen—the preceding and the following notes, thus serving two equal parent notes.

These functional relationships are reflected in instrumental articulation and in diction. Normally the grace is slurred to its single parent; in vocal music it shares the same syllable with the parent and is detached from its other neighbor. The "hyphenated" grace is encompassed in a slur linking both equal parent notes and shares with them the same syllable.

A one-note grace that precedes its parent note, ♩, will be called by the German generic term *Vorschlag* (plural: *Vorschläge*);[1] a grace which follows its parent, ♩, will be called *Nachschlag*; one that connects two equal parent notes, ♩, will be called *Zwischenschlag*.[2] A fourth type that is sounded simultaneously with its parent note, ♩, will be called *Zusammenschlag*.

The *Nachschlag*—to start with the least problematical grace of the set—will always take its value from its preceding principal note. This fact is noncontroversial.

The *Zwischenschlag* will also as a rule take its value from its preceding parent note. (Inconspicuous exceptions can occur when both parent notes fall within the same beat, e.g. ♩, in which case the exact rhythmic disposition of the grace can become irrelevant.) The basic interbeat character of the *Zwischenschlag* needs an explanation because it would seem more logical that a grace serving two parent notes on equal terms would be allotted equal values from both. The reason this is not so is of importance to ornament behavior in general. The explanation turns on the fact that what matters most in a musical phrase are the *starting points* of its constituent tones. This fact is most obvious with regard to all percussion and all plucked instruments, including the harpsichord and the piano. It is almost as obvious in all melodies rendered in staccato articulation regardless of medium. Yet even where tones are sustained, it is, as a rule, the start that matters most. The time after the start represents the phase in which the linear energy flow is decreased, occasionally to the point of near disappearance. This in essence is the reason why the *Zwischenschlag*, as well as ornaments

---

[1] It was necessary to replace the commonly used term "appoggiatura" because its connotation of "leaning" is too specific. The German term seems to offer the best alternative because it is neutral with regard to its melodic, rhythmic, and dynamic design.

[2] The term *Zwischenschlag* has been used by Leopold Mozart in a slightly different meaning for two-note interbeat graces which also served a purely connective function (see ch. 18 below).

of more than one tone whose function is the *purely connective* one of gracing the transition from one structural note to another, will spontaneously and naturally take their place in the time of the preceding note. By not interfering with the starting points of the principal notes, such connective graces do not impinge on the structural integrity of melody, rhythm, harmony, or counterpoint. The naturalness of this procedure accounts for its uninterrupted use through centuries to the present day, including, as will be seen, the whole of the 18th century.

For the reasons given, the *Nachschlag* or the *Zwischenschlag*, once they are selected as the proper solution, will offer few difficulties of execution. Both will be short and light and take their value as a rule from the preceding note.

There are specific problems of execution for *Vorschläge* which can run the whole gamut of rhythmic-dynamic designs. The *Vorschlag* can be short, long, soft, swelled, stressed; it can be placed before the metrical pulse, it can be placed most prominently on the beat, or straddle it in a variety of syncopated designs. Immensely variable, it can have the most diversified impact on melody, on harmony, and on counterpoint. As regards terminology, a brief and soft *prebeat Vorschlag* will be designated with the modern term of "grace note," while the term "appoggiatura" will be reserved for the accented or swelled *onbeat Vorschlag* regardless of its length.

The *Zusammenschlag* consists typically of the simultaneous striking and immediate release of, more often than not, the lower neighbor of the principal tone, . Although technically it is a one-note grace, functionally and historically the *Zusammenschlag* stands between the *Vorschlag* and the mordent and will be dealt with in an independent chapter (see Chapter 42 below).

Today this grace is best known under the name of *acciaccatura*. This term, however, is confusing because it stood for two different designs. One is the just described *Zusammenschlag*, the other is a *Zwischenschlag* linking two notes of an arpeggiated chord, . In this form the grace belongs functionally to the arpeggio and will be dealt with in connection with this ornament.

The French *Port de voix* and *Coulé*: Definition and Character

In France, throughout the 17th and 18th centuries, different symbols and terms often designated the same or a similar grace, while identical symbols and terms stood for different graces. As a working terminology for this study, it seemed best to adopt those names for each ornament that were sanctioned by majority use. Accordingly, the French one-note graces will be classed under the four headings of *port de voix*, *coulé*, *accent*, and *chûte*. The first two, which will be discussed first, are most often *Vorschläge*, sometimes *Zwischenschläge*. The *accent* and *chûte*, which are of lesser importance, are almost always *Nachschläge*.

THE *Port de voix*

The term *port de voix* will be used to designate a one-note grace that *ascends* to its parent note.

As the name indicates, its origin has been vocal and its primary meaning a connection of pitches by gradual gliding. As a designation for a specific grace, the term refers to an added note from which the gliding ascent of the voice is to start. In the transfer of this grace to the instrumental field, the glide was often impracticable; for strings, however, the *coulé de doigt* of the French gambists (a gentle sliding up of a finger from fret to fret) or Montéclair's *son glissé* were true equivalents of the vocal grace.

In its most typical melodic design the *port de voix* repeats the preceding note and rises stepwise to its following parent note. This principal melodic design is given in Ex. 8.1*a*. Other designs occur that are indicated in the same example under *b–f* (in this schematic illustration and in all similar ones to follow, parent notes are marked as unstemmed heads, ornamental notes as diamond-shaped heads).

Ex. 8.1.

The structural context most congenial to the insertion of a *port de voix* is a stepwise ascent to a note that is at least as long or longer than the first and placed on a strong beat. Such a pattern is shown at the beginning of Ex. 8.2 as the "simple" basis for the following models. The *port de voix* itself is susceptible of infinite rhythmic variations. For the purpose of this study the multitude of designs will be reduced to the four key types shown in Ex. 8.2, with the understanding that they represent only landmarks in a continuum of changing shapes.

Type 1 represents a purely melodic grace with little or no effect on either counterpoint or harmony.

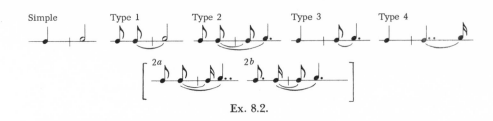

Ex. 8.2.

When the *port de voix* of Type 1 does not repeat the preceding note (e.g. in the designs of Exx. 8.1*b-d* and *f*), it can become a *Zwischenschlag* if it is slurred to the preceding as well as to the following note.

Types 3 and 4 not only reshape the melody but may strongly affect both harmony and counterpoint. Characteristically for these types, the parent note will fall on a consonant strong beat. The use of the *port de voix* then produces a dissonance prepared by its left neighbor and resolved by stepwise ascent into its delayed parent note.

In Type 2 a harmonic effect will be present but its impact blunted by partial anticipation. It will depend on several factors, such as speed, dynamics, distribution of the grace on either side of the beat, and whether this design is perceived horizontally as a rubato or vertically as a suspension-dissonance. Because of the ambivalence of this straddling pattern, its two faces have been distinguished in Ex. 8.2 as 2*a* for the horizontal-rubato type, 2*b* for the vertical-harmonic type.

The *port de voix* has a frequent sequel in a brief *pincé*: a mordent-like but normally unaccented inflexion made at the link of the grace proper with its parent note, ●—♪♪●. This sequel was so frequently, often almost routinely, associated with the *port de voix* that it must be discussed together with the latter. The sequel adds to the grace a new element of variability by assuming different rhythmic shapes that might adapt to the four basic types as indicated in Ex. 8.3.

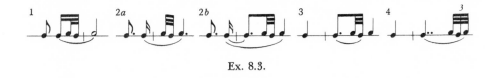

Ex. 8.3.

The *Coulé*

The term *coulé* will be used to designate a one-note grace that *descends* to its parent note.[1] In some respects, but not in all, it is a mirror image of the *port de voix*. Differences between the two stem from the different musical implications of rising and falling pitches. Thus, a melody which descends by thirds in notes of equal length became for the French a classical context for a procedure they called *couler les tierces*. It meant the insertion of graces for the purely connective purpose of smoothly gliding instead of leaping downward (see Ex. 8.4).

[1] *Couler* means "to flow" and the term *coulé*, "in a flowing manner," has been used in various connotations so that misunderstandings can easily result. A frequent meaning was that of a legato slur independent of any ornament. In the area of *agréments*, the term is predominantly used for the descending one-note grace. Another application is for a slide-like connection between two notes, usually a third apart, of which the first is held, ♩♪♪; this pattern is a subform of the arpeggio and will be discussed in ch. 44 below.

Ex. 8.4.

Much evidence that remains to be cited confirms this French interbeat style with either *Vorschlag* or *Zwischenschlag* character. On ascent the procedure was less frequent.

In its role as a genuine *Vorschlag*, the most frequent melodic designs of the *coulé* are those shown in Exx. 8.5a-c.

Ex. 8.5.

Concerning rhythmic dispositions, what has been said about the *port de voix* applies in close analogy to the *coulé*, and consequently we can formulate the corresponding four main types of designs—the prebeat, the straddling, the short-long, and the long-short onbeat—given in Ex. 8.6.

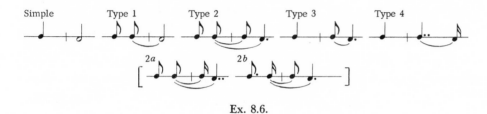

Ex. 8.6.

Port de voix and *Coulé* for
Voice and Melody Instruments
1636-1715

———◆◆———

THE SINGERS

Mersenne in 1636 illustrates the vocal *port de voix* as a prebeat grace (Ex. 9.1)
and gives a graphic description of the manner in which the voice gradually slides
into the principal note: "the voice passes flowingly from *re* to *mi* as if it pulled
the *re* along while continuing to fill the space of the whole interval."[1]

Ex. 9.1. Mersenne (1636)

From the early part of the 17th century we find many cases of similar prebeat
ports de voix and *coulés* written out in regular notation. Example 9.2 shows a
specimen from an *air de cour* by Antoine Boësset (1586-1643).[2]

qui com -men - es   qui com - men - es

Ex. 9.2. Boësset

Another of Boësset's airs as sung by Moulinié and reported by Mersenne was
excerpted above in Ex. 5.1. A striking feature in Mersenne's illustration is the
preponderance of prebeat *ports de voix* and *coulés*. The second and third versions
together contain two onbeat and twelve prebeat designs. As will be seen, the
predominance of anticipation sets the pattern for the vocal style of the entire
17th century and beyond.

A generation later, three important groups of sources—represented by the collection of airs with written-out second-couplet diminutions by Michel Lambert,
Bénigne de Bacilly (both in the 1660's) and D'Ambruis (1685)—emphatically
reconfirm the same usage. Small but typical excerpts from the first two of these
masters have been shown in Ex. 5.2 above. The prebeat designs exhibited therein
pervade the books of all three masters. These designs are the unquestionable rule,
the onbeat patterns the infrequent exception.

That the diminutions were free and sung with countless subtle rhythmic inflections
that carried the anticipated grace often across the bar line (changing rhythm Type 1 to

---

[1] *Harmonie universelle, Traitez des consonances . . .*, pp. 355-356: ". . . la voix se coule
& passe de *ré* à *mi* comme si elle tiroit le *ré*
après soy & qu'elle continuast à remplir tout

l'intervale. . . ."

[2] Example 9.2 is from BN Rés. Vma MS 854,
p. 255.

Type 2a) whenever meaning, diction, and musical line suggested it, is unquestionable and attested by documents that remain to be quoted. But such agogic manipulations do not detract from the essentially melodic prebeat character of the vast majority of these one-note graces. In general, only long syllables such as *mort* suit the strong musical emphasis of a harmonic onbeat *Vorschlag* with its stressed dissonance. Yet due to the smooth legato flow and the lack of distinct accents in French diction, even most of the long syllables can be placed just as naturally before or astride, as on, the beat.[3] The excerpt from D'Ambruis shown in Ex. 9.3 contains no less than three prebeat *coulés* in a single measure.[4]

For an illustration of a prebeat *coulé* and *port de voix* by Lully, see below Ex. 24.6b (the places marked by asterisks).

Ex. 9.3. D'Ambruis (1685)

Jean Millet's vocal treatise of 1666 has several original features of terminology and ornament design.[5] He calls *avant-son* a sound that "precedes the principal note" and *reste du son* one that follows it. The *avant-son*, which interests us here, can be taken on the pitch of the main note. This design, which (for a *Vorschlag*) seems to have no parallel in any other known treatise, is recommended by Millet for use at the start of a piece, after a rest, or after a leap. The grace may also be taken a step below or a step above the principal note, making it a *port de voix* or a *coulé* respectively. The *avant-son* is rendered before the beat, and though this important fact is not immediately apparent from the unmetrical notation in Ex. 9.4a, it is clarified in the further course of the book. Thus we see the *avant-son* between thirds in Ex. *b*, in combination with a *reste du son* (Ex. *c*), and find the *avant-son* tied to the principal note on the same pitch (Ex. *d*), which indi-

Ex. 9.4. Millet (1666)

[3] The characteristic sound quality of any language, its pattern of intonation, accentuation, and inflection, its slurred or detached articulation of words and phrases has doubtless influenced the musical style of that nation—including its style of ornamentation.

[4] D'Ambruis, *Livre d'airs*, p. 9.

[5] *La belle methode ou l'art de bien chanter.* Albert Cohen devoted an article to this interesting treatise: "L'art de bien chanter (1666) of Jean Millet," *MQ*, pp. 170-179. He points out that Millet's diminution style belongs to the older school of Moulinié and Boësset, not to that of his contemporaries Lambert and Bacilly. To underline the point, Dr. Cohen reproduces on pp. 178-179 an entire *air de cour* by Millet with second-couplet diminutions. In this ornamented version we find sixteen prebeat *ports de voix* and *coulés*, one brief onbeat *port de voix*, and four onbeat trill preparations (*appuis*).

cates that this pattern amounts to an anticipated entry—or else the slur would make no sense.

The most important vocal treatise of the period was written by the same Bénigne de Bacilly whose songs were mentioned and excerpted before.[6] The treatise is a substantial work that contains a long chapter on ornaments. Though on occasion obscure, the book bespeaks on every page the imaginative artist who presents rules and principles but also makes it clear that they are only guidelines that must yield in any individual case to dissenting artistic feelings; *goût*, a combination of musicianship, judgment, and imagination, is throughout declared the supreme authority.

Bacilly devotes a long section to the *port de voix*. He uses no symbol, hence the execution of the grace (unless indicated in regular notation) is a matter of improvisation. Unfortunately, his descriptions and classifications for the various types of this *agrément* are often vague, ambiguous, and inconsistent; therefore, some guesswork had to enter into the attempt to interpret Bacilly's thoughts and to transcribe his verbal explanations into musical examples. Despite the uncertainties about details, the one thing that emerges clearly from the text is the great flexibility conveyed by it that seems to permit the *port de voix* to range through all four rhythm types. Although its most common application is in the context of a stepwise rise, the grace may be applied to other rising intervals up to a sixth.

Bacilly establishes two main categories for this *agrément* which he calls *port de voix plein* or *véritable*, and *demi port de voix*; the latter has in turn two subspecies, the *port de voix glissé* or *coulé*, and the *port de voix perdu*. Common to all types seems to be the repetition of the preceding note which is split in two; this in turn implies the prebeat start of the grace.

In the *port de voix plein*, the voice, starting before the beat, sustains the lower note before moving up, but normally arrives at the upper parent note in the right time, whereupon it performs a *doublement du gosier* with a measure of firmness, then sustains the parent note to its end. What exactly is meant by *doublement du gosier* is not explained. Austin B. Caswell in his translation of the treatise renders and transcribes it as a tone-repetition; however, it seems more likely that it is simply the *pincé* sequel which, as several French authorities show, was at that time already almost routinely linked with the vocal *port de voix*. A tentative model of this species is given in Ex. 9.5a.

The *demi port de voix* appears to have as common denominator for its two subspecies an absence of an assertive *doublement*. It may have none or an extremely delicate one. The first subspecies, the *port de voix glissé* or *coulé*, implies a gentle sliding of the voice through the whole range of the interval, obviously in the same sense in which Mersenne

---

[6] *Remarques curieuses sur l'art de bien chanter* (1668). A second edition of 1679 was an unchanged reprint except for a new preface in answer to some criticisms. Bacilly was originally a priest from Brittany. Sébastien de Brossard concedes to him an admirable genius for the composition of French songs but adds the surprising information that Bacilly, for lack of theoretical training, needed an assistant to put his compositions down on paper (". . . comme il n'avait pas assez de Musique Prattique pour les notter et les mettre sur le papier, il était pour cela obligé de se servir de l'oreille et de la main d'autruy"). This comment is contained in an autograph catalogue of Brossard's personal library: *Catalogue de livres de musique.*

Bacilly's book contains no music examples and the author refers for illustrations to various song-books by himself and by Lambert, a circumstance which complicates the study of the work. This difficulty has now been largely overcome by the publication of an English edition of the book under the title *A Commentary upon the Art of Proper Singing*, tr. and ed. Austin B. Caswell. In it, the editor has inserted all the music examples that he could locate. Although this is very helpful, the reader must be aware that in many examples where a version labeled as "printed" is accompanied by one labeled "performed," this latter is strictly an editorial opinion and in many instances open to doubt.

had explained it. Bacilly stresses that in spite of this slide the entrance of the principal note must not be delayed ("et toutefois laissant la Note superieure dans sa valeur et dans sa quantité"). This implies full anticipation of the grace. The *doublement du gosier* is not mentioned. From the description, the model of the grace could be tentatively rendered as shown in Ex. *b*.

The *port de voix perdu* starts like the others, by splitting the preceding note, but instead of moving up to reach the higher note in its proper time, the lower note is sustained throughout almost all of the principal note's value, whereupon a *doublement du gosier* is performed with the utmost delicacy without letting the voice come to rest on the principal note at all. Its presumable execution is sketched in Ex. *c*.

Bacilly nowhere specifies an onbeat start of the grace, but once in a long while we find it written out in one of his own songs, which seems to justify the previous statement that his *ports de voix* cover the full range of rhyhmic variants.

Ex. 9.5. Bacilly (1668)

The need for flexibility in executing any of these types is emphasized in an interesting passage about ornamental straddling of the beat. Referring to a fragment from an air by Lambert (see Ex. 9.6*a*), Bacilly says that the word *mort* requires a *port de voix*, and although the *usual* procedure would be simply to split the quarter-note in two, in this case the *port de voix* must also borrow a little from the following note to add refinement to the grace[7] [i.e. approximately ♩♩♩♩♩]. Then, speaking of the same passage as it appears in the second couplet (Ex. *b*), where the *port de voix* is written out for *d'A-mour*, he says it would be "ridiculous" to sing it the way it is written. One has to "help the letter" and borrow from the following note [i.e. approximately ♩♩♩♩♩]. Thus, occasionally, where expression requires it, one "writes in one way and sings in another."[8] Bacilly's explanation simply confirms what has been pointed out before, that usually written-out ornaments must not be taken on face value and should yield to free rubato treatment. However, it would be a mistake to deduce from this passage that all *ports de voix* are to be stretched across the bar line. Bacilly only claims the legitimacy of such treatment where it is suggested by the contextual elements of word-meaning, diction, expression, or cadential emphasis. In many other cases pure anticipation makes better sense (after all, Bacilly speaks of anticipation as the "usual procedure"), but so will occasionally the pure onbeat start, or, as he expressly points out, no *port de voix* at all. The *goût* has to decide for each individual case.

Ex. 9.6. Bacilly (Lambert)

[7] P. 141: "Il ne faut pas seulement emprunter une Croche à cette syllabe precedente, mais il faut encore en emprunter par anticipation quelque peu de la valeur de la Notte superieure, pour joindre avec ce qui est déja emprunté, afin que le *Port de Voix* soit plus parfait. . . ."

[8] P. 143: "L'on marque sur le papier d'une maniere, & l'on chante d'une autre."

Another interesting vocal treatise was written in 1678 by the eminent gambist Jean Rousseau, whose second treatise about the gamba will be discussed later.[9] In the vocal treatise, which is far less detailed and elaborate than Bacilly's but luckily also far less obscure, Rousseau distinguishes two kinds of *port de voix*. The first is performed before the beat and is referred to as *port de voix par anticipation de valeur et de son*. It is to be used in stepwise ascents from a shorter note to a longer one (Ex. 9.7a) or to one of equal length, provided that long syllables are involved (Ex. b) and the execution of the *port de voix* does not interfere with meter and tempo (not "au prejudice de la valeur & du mouvement . . ."). A *port de voix* that follows a trill is also to be executed before the beat (Ex. c). Furthermore, anticipation is specified when the bass voice leaps a fourth or a fifth in cadences of airs or *récits* (Ex. d).

Ex. 9.7. J. Rousseau (1683,1691)

Rousseau's second type, which he calls *port de voix par anticipation de son seulement* is performed on the beat. It can be applied when ascending from a short note to one at least twice as long (Ex. 9.8).

Ex. 9.8. J. Rousseau

9 *Méthode claire, certaine et facile, pour apprendre à chanter la musique.* References in the following will be to the 2nd edition of 1683 unless otherwise stated.

Brossard (in the aforementioned catalogue of his library) gives Rousseau the following accolade: "Another master of the viol to whom we are indebted for the right and noble manner in which this instrument is played nowadays."

In his vocal treatise, Rousseau does not mention the *pincé* sequel to the *port de voix*, but he must have taken its frequent use for granted; for when he writes in his later viol treatise that the sequel is inseparable from the *port de voix*, he adds that the voice makes it spontaneously with "a small agitation of the throat" ("une petite agitation du gozier") on ending the *port de voix*, and that instruments ought to imitate it.[10]

So far the vocal *ports de voix* and *coulés* were either fully written out or left to the impromptu addition by the singer. D'Ambruis in his *Livre d'airs* of 1685 lists the vertical wedge ˅ for the *port de voix*. We find this same symbol in a vocal treatise by Pierre Berthet from the end of the century where the only illustration of a *port de voix* shows the prebeat character of the grace (Ex. 9.9).[11]

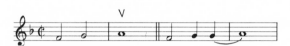

Ex. 9.9. Berthet (1695), *Port de voix*

In the motets of De La Lande, the little note of a *coulé* or *port de voix* is sometimes placed before, sometimes after the bar line.[12] This was done rather indiscriminately, as we find the two versions not only in parallel spots but also in simultaneous voice parts where a different rendition could not have been intended (see Ex. 9.10). Since prebeat notation clearly implies the upbeat, whereas postbar notation *may* imply it (as will emerge from numerous other pieces of evidence), there is little doubt about the anticipatory character of these graces. (Whether the notation was the original one of the autograph could not be established. If it is editorial, it is hardly less interesting, since it thereby reflects musical practices of the Rameau era.)

Ex. 9.10. De La Lande, *Judica me Deus*

In the early 18th century we frequently encounter in vocal music the same type of written-out prebeat *Vorschlag* of which much earlier specimens were shown above in Ex. 9.2. The illustrations from Clérambault and Campra in Exx. 9.11a-b are truly representative of this continuing vocal preference.[13]

[10] *Traité de la viole*, p. 87.
[11] *Lecons de musique*, 2nd ed., p. 47.
[12] *Motets de feu Mr. De La Lande*; the motets were written in the 1680's.

[13] Clérambault, *Cantates françaises à 1 et 2 voix, livre premier*; Campra, *Amarillis pastorale*.

a. Clérambault (1710), Cantata No. 2, *Récit.*

en vain sans doute il est ai-mé

b. Campra, *Amarillis*, Sc. 1

for-cée à fein - dre ver - tu cru - el - le

Ex. 9.11.

THE GAMBISTS AND FLUTISTS

Sainte Colombe was the famous head of a brilliant school of gambists that counted among its members Marin Marais, Jean Rousseau, and Danoville. The latter called Saint Colombe "the Orpheus of our time, the rarest genius ever to appear for this instrument." In Sainte Colombe's *Concerts à 2 violes* (BN Rés. Vma MS 866) we find innumerable written-out prebeat *ports de voix et pincés* of the kind shown in Ex. 9.12, where the *port de voix* falls before and the *pincé* on the beat (the cross signifies a *pincé*, the comma after a note a trill).

a. Le Tendre, p. 6

b. L'Emporté, p. 29

Ex. 9.12. Sainte Colombe

The gambist virtuoso Demachy explains the *port de voix* (in 1685) briefly and ambiguously, as being done "by anticipation of one note or [tablature-] letter to another" (["Le port de voix] se fait par anticipation d'une note ou d'une lettre a une autre")[14] and gives this symbol:

Jean Rousseau's gamba treatise describes the *port de voix* exclusively in its prebeat design.[15] This was no mere oversight, since even for those contexts for which, speaking of the voice, he had recommended the onbeat style, he specifies prebeat rendition for the instrument, as seen in Exx. 9.13*a-c*. He gives no symbol.

"as if written:"

Ex. 9.13. J. Rousseau (1687)

[14] *Pièces de violle*, pp. 9 and 13.   [15] *Traité*, ch. 6.

That occasionally the anticipation was carried in rubato style somewhat across the beat is more than likely, but undoubtedly these were only occasional variants of a basically anticipatory pattern. Moreover, the factor of diction, which prompted Bacilly's straddling designs, is irrelevant for instruments.

Rousseau deals with the *coulé* (under the term *cheute*) in a separate chapter, again with no symbol. Interestingly, for this grace too all of his numerous illustrations show the prebeat design. In addition, his verbal explanation of "touching passingly the grace with the second bowstroke" (p. 93, "on touche en passant du second coup d'Archet") leaves little doubt that the anticipation of our rhythm Type 1 was here, too, the fundamental design, though naturally subject to slight modifications.

Although it was introduced primarily as a grace to fill in descending thirds, Rousseau shows its versatile use in other contexts as well. Example 9.14 shows *tierces coulées* at letters A, B, D, and G, a repeated note at C, a chromatic ascent at E, a falling diminished fourth at F, and stepwise descent at H; at letter I we see how in a similar stepwise descent an *aspiration* (his term for *accent*) can be combined with the *coulé*.

Ex. 9.14. J. Rousseau

Danoville confirms the fundamental prebeat design for both the *port de voix* and *coulé* in a treatise that, as he expressly states, presents the ideas of his revered teacher Sainte Colombe. The *port de voix*, Danoville says, "is done by halving the note which precedes the one to which the grace is applied and by slurring the second half to the following note."[16] His illustration is shown in Ex. 9.15a; the execution according to his verbal instructions is shown under 9.15b. He adds: "You see by these examples that one writes it [i.e. the *port de voix*] by a little note, in order to leave the note that has to be divided in its entire length, the famous composers do not use any other method." This may be the first theoretical explanation of the little notes.

[16] *L'art de toucher*, p. 42: "Il se fait en coupant la moitié de la Note, qui precede celle sur laquelle on va porter la Voix, & prenant la derniere moitié on la lie avec celle qui suit."

Ex. 9.15. Danoville (1687)

A year before Rousseau's and Danoville's treatises, Marin Marais, the most famous of Sainte Colombe's students, published the first of his five books of gamba pieces.[17]

Apart from its great musical value, the volume is remarkable for the unprecedented editorial care with which the composer has indicated such matters as fingerings, bowings, ornaments, and other details of technical execution. The later volumes added further refinements of notation by indicating dynamic shadings, varieties of articulation, different manners of executing multiple stops, etc. Ornaments are given labels and symbols, some of which remained specifically associated with the gamba school. Most interesting is the fact that the little *notes perdues* abound everywhere, singly, in pairs, in larger groupings.

Like Danoville, Marais calls the *Vorschlag* (whether rising or falling) a *port de voix*. It is likely that Danoville's prebeat style applies generally also to Marais, though the latter does not specifically say so. Against the background of Danoville's statement that "the famous composers do not use any other method," of Rousseau's exclusive prebeat patterns for the gamba, and of Sainte Colombe's prebeat *ports de voix*, it is difficult to assume that Marais had a rendition in mind which opposed in principle that of his teacher and of his fellow students and did not avail himself in any of his five extensive prefaces of the opportunity to clarify this different intention.

Furthermore, there is corroborating evidence. Of the illustrations in Ex. 9.16 the first (*a*) shows a *port de voix* from a G to a G-sharp. The cross over the G-sharp stands for a mordent done with an F-sharp. In this context, only anticipation makes musical sense. In Exx. *b* and *c* technical necessity dictates anticipation (as Professor John Hsu, the eminent gambist from Cornell University confirms in a personal letter); in Ex. *d* onbeat rendition would be impossible (the symbol ·/. standing for *doigt couché*, i.e. keeping the finger down). In Exx. *e* and *f*, the "e" symbols, which indicate a swell, make sense only if the preceding *coulés* have unaccented prebeat character. In Ex. *g* the encompassing slur reveals the *Zwischenschlag* nature of the grace.

Ex. 9.16. M. Marais

[17] *Pieces a une et a deux violes,* dedicated to Lully, with whom Marais had studied composition. The bass accompaniments appeared separately.

Everything considered, we can assume that, on the whole, Marais's *ports de voix* and *coulés* followed the prebeat style of Rousseau and Danoville, with the usual qualifications of ornamental freedoms and with probable exceptions in analogy to certain vocal practices.

As regards the flutists, if we may judge from two eminent masters, De La Barre and Hotteterre, they too seemed to favor anticipation of the *port de voix* and *coulé*. De La Barre, in 1703, invariably writes those graces that belong to the first note in a measure *before* the bar line as shown in Exx. 9.17*a* and *b*.[18]

Ex. 9.17. De La Barre (1703)

Jacques Hotteterre, author of the first important flute treatise (1707), explains the *port de voix* as "anticipated articulation of the lower neighbor" ("coup de Langue anticipé d'un degré au dessous de la Note sur laquelle on le veut faire").[19] He says that the *coulé* (*coulement*), taken from one step above, is rarely used other than in descending thirds. He mentions that the *port de voix* is often followed by a *battement*, i.e. the usual *pincé* sequel.

His models from the treatise are shown in Ex. 9.18*a*. In his first book of flute pieces, Hotteterre uses the abstract symbols shown in Ex. *b*.[20] The fact that the little note is not a symbol, but the explanation of a symbol, suggests prebeat rather than onbeat meaning. Further confirmation of Hotteterre's prebeat style can be found in his trios for two flutes and bass in which, according to an early 18th-century manuscript, a great many *coulés* and *ports de voix* are written before the bar line.[21] Examples 9.18*c* and *d* give a few specimens.

Ex. 9.18. Hotteterre

THE GENERAL THEORISTS

Three important theorists—Loulié, L'Affilard, and Montéclair—did not focus their writings on one specific medium but dealt with matters common to all.

---

[18] *Pièces pour la flute traversière avec la basse-continue.* The same master's *Triots* [*sic*] for two flutes and bass (MS BN, 4° Vm 848) are equally filled with the same kind of prebar *ports de voix* and *coulés*.

[19] *Principes de la flute traversiere,* pp. 28-29; see also his *Méthode pour la musette,* p. 58.

[20] *Premier livre de pieces pour la flûte traversière.*

[21] *Sonata* [*sic*] *en Trio* (MS BN, 4° Vm 848).

Loulié's and L'Affilard's books were recommended by Rameau to those of his readers who needed information on elementary matters. Loulié, in 1696, defines an *agrément* as one, two, or more "little tones" (*petits sons*) interspersed with the "regular tones, to render the melody more agreeable."[22] The "little tone" is *weaker* and *shorter* than the "regular" one. Indicated by small notes or by symbols, the "little tone" is linked by slur to the regular note, is executed lightly, and is sounded sometimes *before*, sometimes *on* the beat.[23] The illustration given in Ex. 9.19a shows a *Vorschlag* in anticipation, one on the beat, and a *Nachschlag*.

Loulié's definition of the *port de voix* is that of a stepwise ascent from a short or weak tone to a regular one ("une Elevation de la Voix d'un Son d'une petite durée ou foible, à un Son ordinaire & plus haut d'un degré"). He uses as a symbol an oblique dash and, in keeping with what he had said about ornaments in general, his illustrations show that the same symbol can refer to either prebeat or onbeat execution (Ex. 9.19b); the choice is the performer's. Interesting also is Loulié's solution where a leap is involved: instead of repeating the preceding note and gliding up through the interval, the *port de voix* starts a half-step below the following note as seen in mm. 3 and 4 of Ex. *b.*

Ex. 9.19. Loulié (1696)

Loulié defines the *coulé* as ". . . an inflection of the voice from a small, or weak, or short tone, to a lower and stronger one" (". . . une Inflexion de la Voix d'un petit Son ou Son foible, ou d'une petite durée, à un Son plus bas & plus fort"). He uses as a symbol a comma above the staff and his illustrations show, significantly, anticipation in *every* one of ten illustrations, six of which are reproduced above in Ex. 9.19c. These illustrations also show two distinct versions for a *coulé* connecting a downward leap: the grace is placed either a step above the parent note (mm. 2-4) or on the level of the preceding note (mm. 5-6). Though Loulié mentions and illustrates the onbeat alternative (see Ex. 9.19a), the exclusively prebeat illustrations of the grace in the section specifically addressed to it suggest that anticipation was the favored design.

L'Affilard's treatise of 1694 carried (besides Rameau's recommendation) in its first edition an endorsement by De La Lande. L'Affilard provides an ornament table (cast in the form of a brief composition) which shows for the *port de voix*

[22] *Eléments ou principes de musique*, p. 66.
[23] Ibid.: "Elle [i.e. la petite note] se prend quelquefois sur la valleur de la Notte ordinaire qui la precede, quelquefois sur la valleur de la Notte ordinaire qui la suit. La Petite Notte se doit passer legerement."

the symbol and execution as given in Ex. 9.20a.[24] We find the same familiar sub-division of the preceding note and, possibly for the first time, the written-out *pincé* annex. It is probable that a *pincé* following a prebeat *port de voix* often occurred *on* the beat, but it is certain that on occasion the *pincé* was still rendered *before* the beat. L'Affilard documents this fact as shown below in Ch. 35 (Exx. 35.15a and *b*). The strength of the prebeat trend is further manifested when anticipation appears in a context where it is least expected, e.g. in a *port de voix* that follows the suffix to a trill (Ex. 9.21*b*).

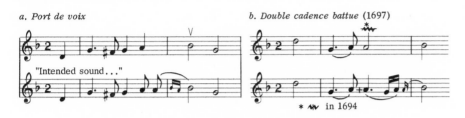

Ex. 9.20. L'Affilard (1694,1697)

Anticipation of the *coulé* is revealed in one of the musical illustrations that follow the theoretical part of L'Affilard's book: in the *Sarabande en Trio* (p. 45, 2nd ed. p. 57), the little 16th-notes symbolizing *coulés* are placed before the bar line every time they occur before the first beat (see Ex. 9.21*a*). With all these indications of prebeat predominance we can assume that L'Affilard intended pre-beat rendition for the *tierces coulées*, which he calls *coulements* and marks with small half-circles. (His model is given in Ex. 9.21*b*.)

Ex. 9.21. L'Affilard (1694,1697)

Montéclair (1667-1737), whose eminence as a theorist was enhanced by his prestige as a composer, wrote in 1709 the first of two important treatises. The second, which was published in his old age in 1736, represents an elaboration of the first, with no indications of a basic change of ideas.[25] We may be justified, therefore, in discussing the later, more important book, as well as the earlier one, in the context of pre-Couperin documents.

Montéclair laments the chaos in the terminology, symbols, and designs for all *agréments* and deplores in particular the discrepancies between the notational usages of the various media. He explains the *coulé* as "an ornament that sweetens the melody and smoothens it through the linking of sounds."[26] To Montéclair the *coulé* is still a grace that need not be marked but ought to be used as the

---

[24] *Principes*, 1st and 2nd eds., pp. 20-21.

[25] *Nouvelle méthode pour apprendre la musique; Principes de musique*. Montéclair was a bass player whose opera *Jephté* met with considerable success. He wrote a few more

treatises that were aimed at the elementary level and contain no new material.

[26] *Principes*, p. 78: "un agrément qui adou-cit le chant et qui le rend onctueux par la liaison des sons."

goût directs, though he mentions that some masters use the little notes as symbols. His illustration (see Ex. 9.22) shows how the *coulé* is to be applied impromptu to descending thirds, to steps, or to leaps of the melody. He explains the first *coulé* as a "little note A, which is linked to the strong note B, into which it glides" ("une petite notte, A, qui se lie avec la notte forte sur laquelle il faut couler B . . ."). At letter C he shows a slur-like mark that suggests the same execution. Failure to mention the downbeat, the lack of a symbol, the wording of the preceding quotation, the indicated function of smoothening and linking, all combine to support a basic prebeat character for the grace. Occasional exceptions can be taken for granted.

Ex. 9.22. Montéclair (1736), p. 78)

Further confirmation for the basic prebeat character of Montéclair's *coulé* can be found in the first treatise where in a demonstration of slurred note patterns (see Ex. 9.23) regular long-short dotted notes are mixed with short-long "Lombard" pairs and with *coulés* symbolized by little notes.[27] The only rationale for differentiating the "Lombard" notation from the *coulé* symbols would seem to be that of a different rendition through anticipation of the *coulés*.

Ex. 9.23. Montéclair (1709)

Montéclair describes the *port de voix* as the "inversion of the *coulé*" (p. 79) and sees its most fitting use where the melody rises stepwise, especially by a semitone, from a weaker to a stronger tone. Often left unmarked even where it may be required by *goût*, the *port de voix*, he says, is sometimes indicated by the little notes, sometimes by (L'Affilard's) ∨ symbol, sometimes by (Loulié's) oblique dash. Montéclair's explanation that the principal note to which the *port de voix* is slurred has to be rendered with greater loudness, suggests the prebeat style.[28] Besides this description, which excludes onbeat emphasis, we also find a number of prebar notations, such as the ones shown in Ex. 9.24, which clarify at least the prebeat *start* of the grace.

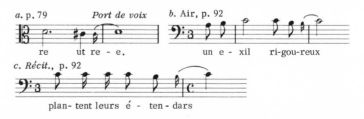

Ex. 9.24. Montéclair (1736)

[27] *Nouvelle méthode*, p. 41.
[28] *Principes*, p. 79: "[La Note postiche] qui prend le nom de la note forte, à laquelle elle se lie, et sur laquelle il faut elever la voix."

On the other hand, onbeat rendition is strongly suggested in Ex. 9.25, which illustrates Montéclair's statement that every *port de voix* is followed by a *pincé*.

Ex. 9.25. Montéclair, p. 84

Thus it seems that the position of Montéclair's *coulés* and *ports de voix* varied from prebeat to onbeat, with the center of gravity on the side of the former. This would represent simply the crystallization of the practices prevailing for voice and melody instruments throughout most of the period under consideration.

Port de voix and *Coulé* on
the Lute and the Keyboard
1615-1715

THE LUTE

French 17th-century keyboard, and in particular harpsichord, ornamentation owed much to the lute players who had by the earliest part of the century developed a very sophisticated embellishment practice that included several types of small *agréments* as well as the use of a number of symbols.

Nicolas Vallet may have been among the first to introduce ornament symbols into the lute tablature (in addition to fingerings for both left and right hands and signs that indicate the finger should be held down to sustain a note). In the preface to his *Secretum Musarum* (Amsterdam, 1615 and 1616; reedited as *Le Secret des Muses*, Amsterdam, 1618), he explains two ornaments without using terms for either grace: the *coulé*, marked with a comma after the letter (c,) and a trill-like repetition of the *coulé* "two or three times" for dotted quarter-notes or for half-notes. His illustration of the *coulé*, which places the ornamental note directly above the bass note graphically suggests onbeat execution.[1]

Basset, writing in Mersenne's *Harmonie universelle* of 1636, discusses lute ornaments and introduces seven symbols.[2] Among them are the comma (*virgule*) after the letter (a,) which stands for a trill with a whole tone, but can apparently also signify a very short *coulé*, presumably for small note values. A line above the comma (a̅,) indicates half-tone distance of the auxiliary. A dot before the comma (c.,) stands for the *accent plaintif*, i.e. a *port de voix*. Basset explains that one plucks the ornamental tone, then "after the sound of the string is half elapsed" ("apres que le son de la chorde est à demi passé") one drops the finger on the next fret. The explanation suggests a fairly long onbeat execution. Here too a line above the symbol (c.̅,) specifies half-tone distance.

Dufault (or Dufaut), who flourished c. 1630-1650, used various symbols whose meaning is not always clear, because their use in various sources is inconsistent. The hook under the letter (ḓ) is probably a *port de voix*, though often a very short one (André Souris transcribes it most often as a grace note:). The x after the letter (c x) may stand for a *coulé* or sometimes for a mordent.[3]

Ennemond (*Le vieux*) Gaultier (c. 1575-1651) used the hook under the letter (c̣) for a *port de voix* that apparently could vary from very short to long.[4] The rather infrequent symbol ʌ is interpreted by André Souris as a *coulé*, though this meaning is not definitely established. (Also, as will be presently shown, the symbol was used by Denis Gaultier to indicate a prebeat *port de voix*.) In at least one piece, the *Volte* (No. 51 of the *CdLF* edition), we find a multitude of unmetrical ornamental letters. Mostly they indicate short anticipated *coulés*; but there is also one *port de voix* preceding a mordent,

---

[1] The facsimile of the preface to the 1618 edition is reproduced in *Oeuvres de Nicolas Vallet pour luth seul*, *CdLF* (Paris, 1970).

[2] Mersenne, *Harmonie universelle, Traité des instrumens à chordes*, pp. 79-80.

[3] *Oeuvres de Dufaut*, *CdLF*, ed. André Souris (Paris, 1965).

[4] *Oeuvres du vieux Gautier*, *CdLF*, ed. André Souris (Paris, 1966).

and one anticipated mordent (concerning the latter see below Chapter 35 and Ex. 35.1*a*). As was mentioned in Chapter 5 above, such unmetrical letters were the predecessors of the little unmetrical *notes postiches* in the regular scores.

Very interesting is a publication by Perrine of 1680 (when the French lute school was nearing its extinction) in which he transcribed into regular notation pieces from both Gaultiers—Ennemond and Denis—for use on either lute or harpsichord.[5] Whenever in the works of Ennemond the tablature indicated a unison, with a hook representing a *port de voix* (and sometimes without such a symbol), Perrine usually interprets the grace on the beat: ♯♭ Whether such interpretation (as well as many rhythmic manipulations, including the dotting of originally even notes in the vein of the *notes inégales*) reflected Ennemond's performance style of fifty years earlier is not certain. However, all these specifications are of considerable interest, at least for the time in which they were written.

Denis (*le jeune*) Gaultier (c. 1600-1672), cousin of Ennemond, lists in two publications several symbols and gives explanations which unfortunately are not always clear.[6] The comma after the letter (c,) signifies a *coulé* for a short note, a trill-like repetition for a longer one. What he calls an *accent* and marks with the symbol ∧ is, to all appearances, a very brief, basically anticipated *port de voix*. He explains that one plucks the next lower note with a finger of the *left* hand then immediately drops this finger on the principal note, while plucking it with the *right* hand. The shortness of the ornament, in addition to the tendency of the principal note (plucked with the right hand) to be louder than the grace itself (plucked with the left), suggests anticipation of the ornament (this is how André Tessier, the modern editor, interprets and transcribes the grace).

Thomas Mace, an English representative of the French lute school, which during the 17th century exerted decisive influence in England, wrote the most thorough treatise on the instrument and deals with ornaments in considerable detail.[7] He describes the *coulé* (*back fall*) as a very short grace. The grace itself is plucked by the right hand, but the finger stopping it uses a left hand pizzicato "a kind of a Twitch" to give strength to the principal note (p. 104). The *port de voix* (half-fall), too, emerges from his explanation as a very short grace, always done from the half-tone below. Speaking of a half-fall into the *f* fret he explains that one plucks the *e* "but so soon as *e* has given its *perfect sound*, my next *Finger*, must fall *smartly* into *f*; so that *f* may *Sound* strongly, only by *That Fall . . .*" (p. 105).

On the lute the alternative of prebeat and onbeat can often become meaningless, unless we have to do with a distinctly long *Vorschlag*. Great freedom of rhythm, where rubato as well as arpeggiation often blurred the location of the beat, was the essence of the *style luthé*. The idea expressed by some modern writers that all lute graces have to fall on the beat because they alone were plucked and therefore had the natural accent that seeks the beat is not conclusive. Apart from the frequent vagueness of the beat, in a very short *port de voix* the upper finger striking the principal note can, by a hammer-like action, convey the impression of an accent, and in a *coulé* a gentle plucking with the right hand and a strong left-hand pizzicato can actually reverse the dynamics in favor of the principal note. Moreover, there is Denis Gaultier's technique of plucking the *port de voix* with the left, the principal note with the right hand. Thus, technical considerations alone did not dictate an exclusive rhythmic style for the lute *Vorschlag*. Both prebeat and onbeat execution were technically and musically possible and were certainly used whenever a distinct beat was present. Unquestionably the onbeat and straddling styles played a large role and can be assumed to have served as models for the analogous designs of later keyboard players.

[5] Perrine, *Pieces de luth en musique.*
[6] *Pieces de luth*, and *Livre de tablature des*
pieces de luth.
[7] *Musick's Monument*, ch. 22.

Beginning in the 1670's, a series of keyboard documents, mostly in the form of ornament tables, call for the onbeat start of both the *port de voix* and the *coulé*. An early case is the table in Chambonnières's first book of harpsichord pieces of 1670 in which the *port de voix* is explained in the following manner:[8]

We see in this model the familiar splitting of the lower note, except that the first of the two repeated notes is placed on the beat. Nineteen years later, in 1689, D'Anglebert models for the *port de voix* (*cheute en montant*) and for the *coulé* (*port de voix* or *cheute en descendant*) formulate, perhaps for the first time, the pattern of preparation, onbeat dissonance, and resolution as a standard design for these two graces (Exx. 10.1*a* and *b*).[9] The *port de voix et pincé* (Ex. *c*) follows the same principle. However, in his book we find numerous cases of written-out prebeat *Vorschläge* (see Exx. *d* and *e*).

Ex. 10.1. D'Anglebert (1689)

D'Anglebert's table greatly influenced the models of other masters such as Dieupart, Le Roux, Rameau, and above all Bach. Bach had copied for his own use the whole of D'Anglebert's table, along with one of this master's suites, and later borrowed from it for his own small ornament table, the *Explication*.

Boyvin offers a good illustration of the confusion of terms and of symbols inasmuch as he changes both in the course of his writings.

First he calls both graces *ports de voix* using the cross symbol for either. Later he introduces the term *coulé* in our sense, reserving for it the cross symbol, and using a comma symbol for the *port de voix*.

In his first organ book, he says the *coulé* should be subdued ("stifled") and barely held, but that it must "strike against the bass."[10] By contrast, the *port de voix et pincé* (*pincement*) starts with a long appoggiatura occupying, "in spite of its being dissonant," one-half of the length of the note (Ex. 10.2*b*). An exam-

---

[8] Chambonnières, *Les pieces de clavessin*, Livre premier.

[9] D'Anglebert, *Pieces de clavecin*, Preface.

[10] Boyvin, *Premier livre d'orgue . . .* , Preface.

ple from a later treatise shows such halving for a long binary note (Ex. *c*) but only a very short rendition of the *port de voix* in front of a dotted note.[11] (The comma-like appendix under the mordent sign stands for *port de voix*.)

10. *Port de voix* and
Coulé on Lute and Keyboard
1615-1715

———

69

Ex. 10.2. Boyvin

Gaspard Le Roux presents in his harpsichord pieces of 1705 a table in which the models for *port de voix*, *coulé*, and *port de voix et pincé* are precisely copied from those of D'Anglebert (see Exx. 10.1a-c).[12] In the preface Le Roux says that his table contains all symbols, except the "little notes." He uses the latter, however, quite frequently for certain *Vorschläge*, slides, and other graces. He feels no need to illustrate the meaning of the little notes, because at that time they were still considered self-explanatory. His own onbeat patterns, as well as those of D'Anglebert, Boyvin, and Dieupart, were all associated with abstract symbols. D'Anglebert and Boyvin hardly used the little notes, but Le Roux and Dieupart did so rather liberally, and internal evidence points to their interbeat meaning.

In the excerpts from Le Roux shown in Ex. 10.3, onbeat execution would cause questionable fifths in *a*, would make the two-voice notation meaningless in the third quarter of *b*, would be illogical in *c* in combination with the onbeat *agrément "séparez"*

and would be obviously incongruous in *d*. Written-out prebeat *coulés* can be found, among other places, in Suite III, Sarabande, mm. 6, 7, Gavotte, mm. 2, 14; Suite VI, Courante, m. 2, *La Favoritte*, mm. 8-9, 27; in *Pièces pour deux clavecins*, Gavotte, mm. 2, 6, 14. For an anticipated *port de voix et pincé*, see Suite III, Sarabande, m. 10.

Ex. 10.3. Le Roux (1705)

[11] Boyvin, *Traité abrégé de l'accompagnement*, 2nd ed., Preface.

[12] *Pièces de clavessin*, back of title page.

Charles Dieupart wrote his harpsichord suites in London, which explains the bilingual terms in the appended ornamentation table.[13]

Bach showed his respect for this master by copying out two of his suites. Also, the chief scribe of the *Möllersche Handschrift*, an important manuscript from the Bach circle, manifested his (or his employer's) interest in French ornamentation by filling an empty page with a copy of Dieupart's table, though most of the symbols had no bearing on any of the music contained in the manuscript.

Dieupart's table presents for *port de voix, coulé,* and *port de voix et pincé* the same onbeat patterns as did D'Anglebert's, the only difference being that the *coulé* (which he calls *cheute*) is sandwiched between thirds instead of repeating the preparatory note (see Ex. 10.4).

Ex. 10.4. Dieupart (c. 1702)

Like Le Roux, Dieupart did not include the small notes in his table and the presumption that he, too, uses them in interbeat meaning seems borne out by passages like those of Ex. 10.5. In the first of these (*a*) it would be difficult to explain the little note other than as a *Nachschlag* or a *Zwischenschlag*; in *b* interbeat meaning is obvious; in *c* the little note leaping up before the written-out long *port de voix* makes best musical sense as a grace note. (As will be seen below in Chapter 18, even C.P.E. Bach prohibits an onbeat *Vorschlag* on top of a written-out *port de voix*.)

Ex. 10.5. Dieupart

PREBEAT PATTERNS ON THE KEYBOARD

The onbeat patterns of D'Anglebert and his followers have been quoted so frequently that the dissent of other masters of the keyboard has received but little notice. Yet there were a number of important composers and teachers who preferred prebeat *Vorschläge*. Nivers, in his organ book of 1665, first explains the technique of legato playing, which he places midway between the "distinctiveness" of detached articulation and the "confusion" of blurring passages by holding keys down too long. Then he says that such legato (*coulement des notes*) is

[13] *Six suittes de clavessin.*

most frequently used in *ports de voix* and proceeds to illustrate them (Ex. 10.6a) and what he calls closely related passages (Ex. *b*). The small dashes indicate notes that are to be slurred "the most" ("qu'il faut le plus couler"). Anticipation for both *coulé* and *port de voix* is clearly spelled out. We see the exact prebeat mirror image of Chambonnières's onbeat pattern in both ascent and descent.[14]

10. *Port de voix* and
Coulé on Lute and Keyboard
1615-1715

71

Ex. 10.6. Nivers (1665)

André Raison, in the table of his organ book of 1688, gives one *Vorschlag* model only for the *coulé* (*port de voix*) and indicates prebeat rendition (Ex. 10.7a).[15] Since he used the single term of *port de voix*, it is reasonable to assume that the model was equally valid for the ascending type, the *port de voix* in the narrower sense. Lambert Chaumont, in his organ book of 1696, shows prebeat rendition for both the *coulé* and the *port de voix* (Ex. 10.7b).[16]

Ex. 10.7.

Gigault, too, is very specific regarding the anticipation of both the *coulé* and the *port de voix*. In an organ book of 1682 he presents "a diatonic piece in the form of an Allemande notated in simple form as well as with *ports de voix* in order to serve as guide and instruction how to form and how to adapt them [i.e. the *ports de voix*] to all sorts of pieces."[17] Example 10.8 shows the beginning of this instructional piece in both versions (*a* and *b*). The *ports de voix* are with the rarest exceptions all anticipated.

Three years later in another organ book Gigault announces that he has written out *ports de voix* in one of the pieces and that one can apply them to others as well.[18] The piece in question is the *Benedictus*, which contains a great number of prebeat *ports de voix* and *coulés*. The first few measures of this paradigmatic piece are given in Ex. 10.9.

Nicolas de Grigny's organ book of 1699 is one of the works which Bach, presumably while he was in Arnstadt, copied for study purposes.[19] Walther did so

[14] Nivers, *Livre d'orgue*, Preface.
[15] *Livre d'orgue*, Preface.
[16] *Pieces d'orgue sur les 8 tons*, Preface.
[17] *Livre de musique dédié à la très Ste. Vierge.* The unmetrical excess beams in Ex. 10.8*b* are authentic. Gigault tells his readers in the preface not to worry about them (occasionally he uses as many as eight and more!),

that they are simple 16th-notes.
[18] *Livre de musique pour l'orgue.*
[19] *Premier livre d'orgue contenant une messe et les hymnes . . .* (Paris, 1699). A second edition of 1711 is identical, obviously made from the same plates. Bach's copy is in the University Library of Frankfurt a. M.; Walther's copy BB (PK) Mus. MS 8550.

Ex. 10.8. Gigault (1682), *Allemande par fugue*

too, and both men's copies are noteworthy for their faithfulness to the details of the original. Among those details are many cases of ornaments written in small notes before the bar line, thus suggesting their prebeat nature. Most of these ornaments are various types of slides and turns, some of which will be quoted

Ex. 10.9. Gigault (1685), *Benedictus*, p. 34

later. Here and there one finds an occasional *port de voix* or *coulé* before the bar line, like the one shown in Ex. 10.10*a* (which is actually the anticipated auxiliary of a trill).

In other cases internal evidence points to anticipation. In Ex. *b* harmonic logic suggests the simultaneous anticipation of both *ports de voix* at the start of the second measure, in order to permit the dissonance instead of the consonance to strike on the beat. In Ex. *c* at the spot marked by an asterisk the simultaneousness of a plain *pincé* and a *port de voix et pincé* favors the anticipation of the *port de voix*.

Ex. 10.10. Grigny (1699)

In the important volume of manuscripts from the Bach circle, P 801, we find in the hand of (most likely) Walther a copy of a Minuet-Rondeau by Louis Marchand with a passage in the following telltale notation:

10. *Port de voix* and
Coulé on Lute and Keyboard
1615-1715

73

Ex. 10.11. Louis Marchand

The turn of the century witnessed the publication of the first French harpsichord treatise.[20] In general, according to Saint Lambert, the choice of ornaments on the harpsichord is "arbitrary" and subject only to the law of good taste. However, he declares certain graces such as trills, *pincés*, *arpégés*, and *coulés* to be essential and proceeds to discuss them in some detail. Interestingly, he reports and comments on the opinions of other masters as well.

His term *port de voix* stands for both the ascending and descending *Vorschläge*. He sees the essential feature of the *Vorschlag* from a step above or below the principal note in its repeat, in its being "touched twice instead of just once." Saint Lambert sees no difference of opinion in the matter of this repeat, but points to a controversy with regard to the alternative of prebeat versus onbeat: "It has not been agreed upon," he writes, "whether the second [sounding of the preceding note] should be done in the time of the principal or of the preceding note. According to D'Anglebert, it is taken in the time of the principal note, but I doubt that this is the best way of rendering the *port de voix* [or *coulé*] on the harpsichord. I know that this manner is appropriate for songs; but I find there are few occasions where it is appropriate for [clavier] pieces and that the manner of taking it on the preceding note is much more fitting."[21] Hence he proposes a correction of D'Anglebert's patterns, which he has reproduced earlier, to that of anticipation for all types of *ports de voix* and *coulés*, as shown in Ex. 10.12.

In this illustration he presents four types of "descending *ports de voix*" (i.e. our *coulé*) as given in Ex. 10.12*a*. First is the *port de voix simple*, an anticipated *coulé* in stepwise descent; second, an "alternate" form, where in a downward leap of a third the grace is struck twice; third, the *port de voix appuyé*, "done by striking three times the preceding note that is one step higher" (actually, though the note is heard three times, the grace itself is struck only twice as in the preceding model); the fourth design, called *demy port de voix* touches only once in the typical manner of the *tierce coulée*. For the "rising *port de voix*" he gives only the two designs of Ex. 10.12*b*: the *port de voix simple* and the *appuyé*, mirror images of the first and third descending designs of Ex. *a*. In explanation he observes that the rising *port de voix* is never done when the preceding note is two steps below (but excepts from this rule a *port de voix et pincé* combination). He prefers the rising *port de voix appuyé* to the descending type. Either one, he says, is suitable only in slow tempo when the preceding note has at least quarter-note value.

[20] Saint Lambert, *Principes du clavecin*, attests to great pedagogical insight.

[21] P. 49: ". . . il n'est pas bien décidé si c'est sur la valeur de la Note marquée que se doit prendre cette seconde [note] ou si c'est sur la valeur de la Note précédente. De la maniére dont Mr. d'Anglebert l'exprime, elle se prend sur la Note marquée; mais je doute que ce soit-là la meilleure maniére d'exprimer le Port de Voix dans les Piéces de Clavecin. Je sçais que cette maniére convient tout-à-fait aux Chansons; mais je trouve qu'il y a peu d'occasions où elle soit propre aus Piéces, & que celle qui prend cette seconde Note sur la précédente, est beaucoup plus convenable."

Ex. 10.12. Saint Lambert (1702)

Clérambault appears in agreement with Saint Lambert. In the unmeasured preludes in his book of harpsichord pieces of 1704,[22] he indicates the simultaneousness of certain main notes by dotted lines between the two staves; these lines indicate in every instance the prebeat character of the *coulé* and *port de voix*, as shown in Exx. 10.13*a* and *b*.

Ex. 10.13. Clérambault (1704)

For orchestral performance, a reference to onbeat style was found in the account of the German Georg Muffat. Thirty years after studying with Lully, Muffat published in his two *Florilegia* (1695 and 1698) a report on the "Lullian" ballet style. He illustrates the *port de voix* and the *coulé* (using the single term *port de voix* for either grace) with a short onbeat rendition (see Ex. 10.14) and marks each with Loulié's dash symbol.[23] It will be remembered that for Loulié this symbol had predominantly prebeat and only occasionally onbeat meaning. How reliably Muffat's memory served him after such a long lapse of time is impossible to know. At any rate, as far as could be ascertained, none of his symbols for ornaments—with the sole exception of Loulié's dash—were used by any other Frenchman. Hence in this particular field some reservations are in order concerning his testimony.

Ex. 10.14. G. Muffat (1698)

The well-known and widely quoted onbeat patterns of D'Anglebert and his followers were *not* representative of common keyboard practices of the era in question: those patterns were limited to certain masters. Demonstrably, some of these same masters used the prebeat side by side with the onbeat style, whereas other masters on principle preferred the prebeat design. Thus the two prototypes coexisted. It must also be borne in mind that all these models were of course subject to agogic variations.

[22] Clérambault, *1er livre de pièces de clavecin.*

[23] *Florilegium I* and *Florilegium II*, Prefaces.

Couperin's *Ports de voix*
and *Coulés*

The most famous and the most frequently quoted of all French authors on performance and in particular on ornamentation is François Couperin. This eminent composer's main pedagogical writings are embodied in an ornamentation table which accompanied his first book of harpsichord pieces (1713), in his treatise on the art of harpsichord playing (1716/1717), and in a few prefaces to compositions.[1]

Although Couperin's ornamentation table does not explain the *coulé*, it does present three species of the *port de voix* which are designated as *port de voix coulé*,[2] *simple*, and *double* (Ex. 11.1).

Ex. 11.1. Couperin (1713)

The illustration fails to offer an explanation for species one, and owing to the use of the unmetrical little notes, it is vague for species two and three. Three years later in his treatise he states that "the little note of a *coulé* or *port de voix* must strike with the harmony in the time of the following note."[3] This sentence has carried extraordinary weight as one of the key statements in support of the modern ideas regarding the obligatory onbeat start of all *Vorschläge*. It was also the chief pillar for the formulation of Brunold's equation given in Ex. 11.2.

Ex. 11.2. Brunold (1925)

Couperin's sentence seems to go further than the previous indications of onbeat treatment in the tables of D'Anglebert and his followers, who had linked and apparently limited the onbeat design to the specific context of stepwise approach in a preparation-dissonance resolution pattern.

---

[1] *Pièces de clavecin*, 1ᵉʳ livre; *L'art de toucher le clavecin*; a first edition of 1716 was shortly supplanted by one in 1717 that contained six additional pages dealing with fingering problems of the second book of harpsichord pieces. Couperin personally offered all owners an exchange of the new edition for the old one.

[2] The mixing of the terms is confusing. In the designation *port de voix coulé*, the term *coulé* indicates a slurred connection without the *pincé* sequel. The same term, *coulé*, occurs twice more in the table outside of its *Vorschlag* meaning.

[3] *L'art*, p. 22: "Il faut que la petite note perdue d'un port-de-voix ou d'un coulé, frape avec l'harmonie: c'est à dire dans le tems qu'on devrait toucher la note de valeur qui la suit."

The sweeping nature of Couperin's rule—as well as its conflict with a great deal of evidence (some of which still remains to be presented) that points to a substantive role in France of anticipated *Vorschläge* before, during, and after Couperin's time—warrants a closer look.

No more needs to be said about the danger of taking performance rules from treatises on face value—a danger that is great even with a careful, precise, and systematic author and magnified where these attributes are missing. Couperin's treatise, because written by a man of his stature and influence, would be fascinating to the reader, even if it did not contain its many points of significant information; but clear formulation and methodical organization are not among its notable virtues. It does not read like a work well planned and thoroughly thought through, but rather like the transcript of an impromptu lecture in which the speaker talks about matters of pedagogy, problems of technique, and questions of interpretation just as they happen to come to his mind. It is typical that our key sentence is sandwiched between a discussion of fingerings for the *port de voix* and the admonition to teach children how to trill with all the fingers.

It is then no surprise to find that his ornamentation table is unsystematic, ambiguous, and incomplete. Four of Couperin's symbols are not mentioned at all, including the *coulé* itself. Two other frequent ornaments are not explained: $\tilde{\;}$ and ⌐⌐ (the latter probably meaning a strong legato with overlapping of the notes, as explained in Foucquet's ornament table); neither is a fourth one that seems to occur only in one piece, *L'Enfantine* (7th *Ordre*): ⌒ .

The lack of coherence in the treatise, together with the lack of system in the table, are sufficient to arouse suspicion regarding the literal value of Couperin's onbeat rule; but by themselves they do not disprove it. The actual necessity to qualify the rule emerges only from an examination of musical evidence.

I have published such an examination which disclosed a considerable number of passages in Couperin's works where the logic of melody, harmony, rhythm, notation, and technical feasibility, either singly or in combination militates against applicability of the rule.[4] For reasons of space only a few of these illustrations (with a few new ones added) will be repeated here; the reader is referred to the earlier study for more complete documentation.

Couperin, who was scrupulously careful about his voice-leading, would hardly have condoned the kind of offensive parallels that would result from the onbeat execution of the *Vorschläge* in Exx. 11.3a-d.[5] In all these cases anticipation would seem the best answer.

In Ex. 11.4a the simultaneous *port de voix* in the bass and *coulé* in the second voice, both on the same scale tone, would make little harmonic sense *on* the beat. Anticipation of both seems the most graceful solution. In Ex. *b* the onbeat rendition of the *port de voix et pincé* on the third quarter would seem to make sense only against the G in the bass and not against the *coulé* A. The likely solution is

---

[4] "Couperin and the Downbeat Doctrine for Appoggiaturas," *AM*, vol. 41 (1969), pp. 71-85. See also answers to this article by Friedrich Neumann and Robert Donington, *AM*, vol. 42 (1970), pp. 252-255, and by Klaus Hofmann, *AM*, vol. 43 (1971), pp. 106-108.

[5] The Roman numerals in the music examples refer to the *Ordres* into which Couperin grouped his harpsichord pieces. I-V are in the

first book of 1713, VI-XII in the *Second livre de piéces de clavecin* (Paris, n.d.) [1716-1717, date of royal privilege 1713]; XIII-XIX in the *Troisiéme livre de piéces de clavecin* (Paris, 1722), and XX-XXVII in the *Quatriéme livre de piéces de clavecin* (Paris, 1730). The quoted preludes are from *L'art*. For further examples see IX, *Allemande à deux clavecins*, m. 7, and *Les Nations, L'Impériale, Sarabande*, m. 6.

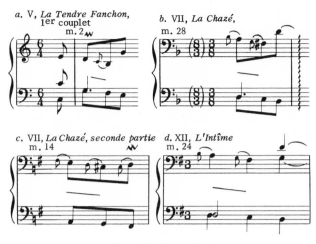

Ex. 11.3. Couperin

anticipation of the bass *coulé*. In Ex. *c* an onbeat *coulé* would be melodically, rhythmically, and technically incongruous.

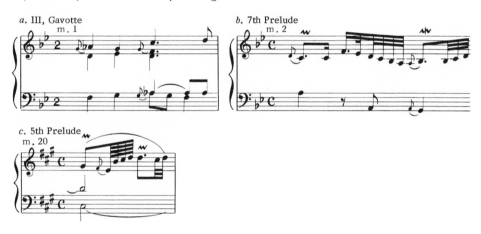

Ex. 11.4.

In Ex. 11.5*a* the rhythmic motive ⌐⌐⌐ in the alto part of the first measure would lose its identity on its repeat in the second measure unless the *port de voix* is anticipated. In Ex. *b* the onbeat execution of the little notes marked by an asterisk would be understood without the grace, therefore the only possible meaning is that of anticipation; this meaning is likely to extend spontaneously to the *tierces coulées* which precede them. Example *c* is another illustration of a similar case where onbeat interpretation would be pointless.

Ex. 11.5.

In Exx. 11.6a and b, where only one of two simultaneous mordents is preceded by a *port de voix*, the tendency to synchronize the mordents suggests anticipation of the *port de voix*. In Ex. *b*, moreover, it would be difficult to accommodate both the *port de voix* and the mordent within the span of a 16th-note. In Ex. *c* an onbeat *coulé* would deprive the mordent of its identity.

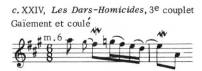

Ex. 11.6.

There are many cases where a grace—not only a *Vorschlag*—precedes a note that belongs in unison at the same time to another voice. In all these cases the melodic integrity of the unembellished voice can be assured only by anticipation. In Ex. 11.7 this consideration is further strengthened by the need to avoid a confusing clash with the simultaneous mordent in the bass. Other illustrations for the implications of a unison were seen in Ex. 11.4a in the bass and in Ex. 11.5a at the start of the second measure.[6]

Ex. 11.7.III, *Allemande la Ténébreuse*

The evidence produced here, supplemented by that in my previous study, should make it clear that Couperin's rule was *not* to be taken on face value and that in many cases the onbeat principle had to yield to demands of musical logic.

These findings complicate, of course, the interpretation problems of Couperin's works. We can no longer apply to his *Vorschläge* a ready-made formula à la

[6] Kenneth Gilbert, in his new edition of Couperin's harpsichord works (Paris, *Le Pupitre* Collection) discusses in his preface to the first volume (1972) contexts for prebeat *coulés* and points to the internal evidence in the passage from VI, *Les Moissonneurs*, m. 10, "in which the unison sign, a vertical line, renders any other interpretation out of the question." See also XVIII, *La Verneüilléte*, start of m. 14.

Brunold. Each case has to be decided on its own individual merits. General directives can be given only in the broadest terms and with the proverbial grains of salt. With such proviso it can be said that the onbeat rule is most likely to apply to *coulés* and *ports de voix* in the upper voice or voices that strike a dissonance against the bass on strong metrical beats; and that the *coulés* in these circumstances will tend to be short and will rarely reach the length of Brunold's formula. On the other hand, the *port de voix*, especially in the *port de voix et pincé* combination, may have a slightly wider scope of rhythmic freedom. Anticipation is most likely to occur on weak beats (especially on feminine endings), at the start of a piece or a phrase, between descending thirds, in the bass line, in an unaccompanied voice, where anticipation clarifies two or more simultaneous ornaments, and where onbeat rendition would impoverish the harmony, interfere with a rhythm pattern of structural importance, or infringe on the integrity of a second voice that coincides with the embellished note.

The last word, of course, belongs always to the *goût*; and it too decides when and how the two principles of prebeat and onbeat are to be combined in the mixed breeds that straddle the beat.

Port de Voix and *Coulé*

1715-1775

Rameau wrote volume after volume on questions of musical theory and several essays on keyboard technique but devoted, unfortunately, only a few chance remarks to matters of musical performance. With regard to the *agréments* we must therefore content ourselves with his two ornament tables for the keyboard, supplemented, however, by the significant passage in which he stressed the need for imaginative treatment of all graces, lest they become "insipid."[1]

A short table in Rameau's youthful first book of harpsichord pieces (1706) shows the *port de voix* in symbol and execution modeled on D'Anglebert (Ex. 12.1a).[2] Eighteen years later, in 1724, the *port de voix* is the same: the tied-over note is simply a more precise indication of a legato slur.[3] The "*coulez*" shows, besides the usual stepwise descent, a leap of a fourth (Ex. b).

Ex. 12.1. Rameau

Even if we did not know of Rameau's strictures against the academic execution of ornaments, many indications in his own music would make the same point. Though probably most of Rameau's *Vorschläge* were intended for the beat, the following illustrations suggest the need for flexibility—and occasional anticipation.

In Ex. 12.2a from his early harpsichord book, the E minor context identifies the *coulé* marked by an asterisk as an f sharp. Onbeat placement would produce objectional fifths, hence anticipation seems logical. Example *b* offers an illustration of the fairly frequent coincidence of a simple *pincé* and a *port de voix et pincé* (marked by asterisks) where the probable synchronization of the *pincés* suggests prebeat *ports de voix*. In Ex. *c* we see three ornamental clusters (marked by asterisks). The first, a *port de voix* written by a little note against a trill, the second, a *coulé* against a *pincé*, the third, a prepared trill (with support) against a *port de voix et pincé*. The dangers of untidiness and indiscernibility inherent in such ornamental collisions will usually call for a flexible mutual adjustment, often involving the anticipation of one or the other of the graces in question. In this particular case a prebeat rendition of the *Vorschläge* would seem to suggest itself. In Ex. *d* the *Zwischenschlag* character of the first little note is underscored by the slur to both neighbor notes; its obvious transfer to the echo in the bass is confirmed on its

---

[1] See above, ch. 3, n. 10.
[2] Rameau, *Premier livre de pièces de clavecin.*

[3] *Pièces de clavecin avec une méthode pour la mécanique des doigts.*

second occurrence, where the little note in the bass is slurred to its predecessor. In Ex. *e* the onbeat start of the *coulé* in the middle voice would result in open fifths with the bass. Most revealing of all, perhaps, Ex. *f* shows a violin *coulé* in *L'Agaçante* from the 2nd *Concert* and its written-out anticipation in Rameau's transcription of the piece for harpsichord solo.

Ex. 12.2. Rameau

Rameau's operas, the center of his creative output, present yet a different problem. That his keyboard tables might not be automatically applicable could be inferred alone from the use of a different set of symbols as shown in the tabulation of Ex. 12.3. (Note the reverse use of the trill and mordent symbols for some operas as compared to Couperin or Bach.) We can assume that all operatic ornaments had to be treated with *goût*-directed freedom and that onbeat design, though predominant, was not a pervasive obligation.

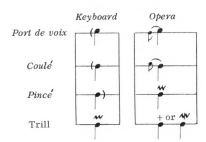

Ex. 12.3. Rameau's symbols

Nicolas Siret, organist of the Troyes Cathedral, provides evidence for anticipated *ports de voix.*[4]

4 Siret, *Pièces de clavecin,* dédiées à M. Couperin (Paris [1716]); *Second livre de pièces de clavecin* (Paris, 1719).

In Exx. 12.4*a* and *b* the upbeat start is clearly marked. In Ex. *c* where the small note is written in its more usual place (next to its parent note), the context suggests anticipation, because a downbeat start would interfere with the second voice in 16th-notes. Example *d* shows the identical prebeat design three times, written out in regular notes.

a. Pièces de clavecin (1716), Courante, p. 20 *b. Pièces de clavecin*, Sarabande, p. 24, final cadence *c. 2e livre* (1719), Sarabande, p. 12

d. Pièces de clavecin, Sarabande grave

Ex. 12.4. Siret

In Ex. 12.5*a*, from the works of the violinist Jacques Aubert, an onbeat *coulé* would produce unpleasant fifths, with analogous spots in mm. 5, 19, 23 of the same movement; anticipation is likely. The same is true of Ex. *b* from Cupis, where the slow tempo adds to the force of the evidence.[5]

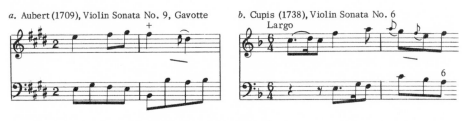

a. Aubert (1709), Violin Sonata No. 9, Gavotte *b.* Cupis (1738), Violin Sonata No. 6
Largo

Ex. 12.5.

Dandrieu's ornament tables of 1724 and 1739 provide evidence for anticipation of the *port de voix* in combination with the *pincé* (Ex. 12.6). Fiocco and Van Helmont, the Belgian, French-oriented masters, adopted this model—along with all the rest of Dandrieu's models—in their own respective ornament tables.[6] The tendency for a small note in the *realization* of a symbol to have interbeat meaning is strengthened here by the metrical equivalence of the regular notes in model and transcription.

Pincé et port de voix

Ex. 12.6. Dandrieu (1724, 1739),
Fiocco (1730),
Van Helmont (1739)

[5] Aubert, *Sonates à violon seul et basse continue*, livre 1 (Paris, n.d. [1719]). J. B. Cupis, *Sonates pour le violon*, Op. 2 (Paris, n.d. [date of privil., 1738]).

[6] Dandrieu, *Premier livre de pièces de clavecin* (1724); *Premier livre d'orgue* (1739). Fiocco, *Pièces de clavecin*; Van Helmont, *Pièces de clavecin*.

David, in his treatise of 1737, presents the onbeat *port de voix* in the usual stepwise ascent and adds a graphic representation of its dynamic treatment with a crescendo-decrescendo on the principal note, hence without emphasis on the *port de voix* proper (Ex. 12.7*a*). David also illustrates a leaping *Vorschlag* (twice on the beat, once probably before the beat), which he feels is "too bizarre" (*trop gothique*) and tolerates only on unspecified occasions (Ex. *b*). We receive another reminder not to take tables at face value when David, while illustrating the *cadence coulée*, transcribes the *port de voix* symbol affixed to the whole note in full anticipation (Ex. *c*).

Ex. 12.7. David (1737)

David's *coulé* is to all appearances anticipated. This is borne out first by the verbal explanation of the grace as one or more *notes supposées* a term at that time generally designating stepwise-moving notes inserted *between* the consonant notes of a melody; and second by the notation in unmetrical little notes in contrast to the written-out values of his onbeat *ports de voix* (see Ex. 12.8).[7]

Ex. 12.8. David, *coulé*

Michel Corrette (1709-1795), was a successful composer and prolific author of more than a dozen treatises dealing with almost all conceivable media of performance. On musical matters his books are largely repetitious and, with regard to the *port de voix* and *coulé*, not very revealing. In his vocal treatise he refers to the *coulé* as a "small inflection of the voice," done when descending by thirds

[7] David, *Méthode nouvelle*, pp. 135-136. Concerning the term *notes supposées*, see Brossard, *Dictionnaire*, s.v. *supposition*. Walther, commenting in his *Lexicon*, s.v. *supposition*, on Brossard's explanation equates a one-note insertion (where two notes are set against one in the bass) with *transitus regularis*, i.e. a dissonant passing note between two consonances, hence, in our case an interbeat grace. Other theorists extend the meaning of *supposition* to onbeat dissonances as well.

and marked by a small note.[8] This seems to indicate an unstressed grace and therefore most likely a basically anticipated one. The same might apply to the plain *port de voix* for which no new explanation is given. Speaking of what is frequently called the *port de voix feint*, the long onbeat tapering into the mordent, he indicates its Italian origin by calling it in his first flute treatise of 1735 a *martellement à la manière Italienne* and illustrates it as shown in Ex. 12.9. In Corrette's harpsichord method the little notes are all unslurred, a fact which, in the complete absence of any onbeat directives, would seem to reinforce the pictorial symbolism of interbeat meaning in that they could be *Nachschläge* or *Zwischenschläge* as well as *Vorschläge*.[9]

Martellement à la manière Italienne

Ex. 12.9. Corrette (1735)

Villeneuve (1677-1756), in a treatise first published in 1733, offers a musical sequence as foil for demonstrating ornaments.[10] Both the sequence and the demonstration are a quasi-plagiarism of L'Affilard's explanation of ornaments, with but a few minor changes and a shift of the passage from minor to major. Since Villeneuve was a musician of note whose compositions were performed on important occasions, his all too literal endorsement of L'Affilard's teachings is significant in itself. Along with a reedition of L'Affilard's treatise in 1747, sixty years after its first publication, Villeneuve's adoption of it in 1733 and again in a later edition of 1756 testifies to a continued viability of the older master's principles. Thus we find in Villeneuve a reconfirmation of the anticipated *port de voix* and *port de voix double* (the slide) as seen in Ex. 12.10. The mordent sequel to the *port de voix* is not shown, but Villeneuve mentions it in the verbal explanation

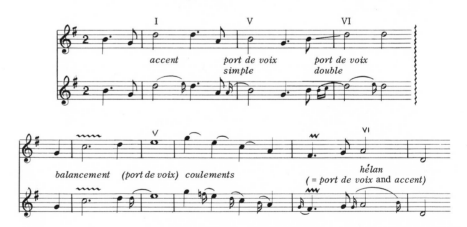

Ex. 12.10. Villeneuve (1733,1756)

[8] Corrette, *Le parfait maître*, p. 49.
[9] *Méthode pour apprendre aisément à joüer de la flute traversière*, p. 35; harpsichord: *Les amusements du Parnasse.*

[10] Villeneuve, *Nouvelle méthode.* Compare its p. 38 with L'Affilard, *Principes*, 1st and 2nd eds., pp. 20-21.

with which he supplements the musical example (p. 39). For the *coulé*, the pictorial evidence of the Villeneuve-L'Affilard model is less conclusive, but, as the reader may remember, the anticipation of L'Affilard's *coulé* was revealed later in his treatise. Villeneuve clearly suggests the same by his explanation: "the *coulé* is done by descending three notes and passing through the one in the middle gracefully and lightly."[11]

Daquin (1694-1772) shows an interesting variant in the design of the *port de voix et pincé* in his harpsichord book of 1735 where he describes and illustrates an afterbeat entrance of the ornamental note (Ex. 12.11).[12]

Ex. 12.11. Daquin (1735)

La Chapelle, in 1736, demonstrates the *port de voix* and *coulé* as shown in Ex. 12.12. (The syllables represent the French solfège system of "naming" notes: each note being named separately when detached, the principal note only in the case of a slurred ornament.) Since the example is meant to illustrate the realization of the graces ("démonstration pour en concevoir l'exécution"), it is clear that *b* is the realization of *c*, *f* that of *g* and that therefore both the *port de voix* and *coulé* are anticipated.[13]

Ex. 12.12. La Chapelle (1737)

Denis, in 1747 and 1762, illustrates the various *agréments* in a musical passage where each grace is named as it occurs.[14] He clarifies the prebeat nature of the *coulé*, leaving the design of the *port de voix* undetermined, as shown in Ex. 12.13.

Ex. 12.13. Denis (1747,1762)

[11] Villeneuve, *Nouvelle méthode*, p. 39: "Les coulements se font en descendant de trois notes, passant par celle du milieu gracieùsement, sans la marquer trop."

[12] Daquin, *1er Livre de pièces de clavecin*.

[13] La Chapelle, *Les vrais principes*, vol. 2, p.

14. Little is known about this writer.

[14] Denis, *Nouveau système*, p. 45; 2nd ed. under title *Nouvelle méthode*, p. 44. Denis was the translator of Tartini's *Regole* . . . (see below ch. 17, n. 30).

In a collection of ensemble pieces, Luc Marchand writes both *ports de voix* and *coulés* often before the bar line and sometimes in an analogous context after the line.[15] As shown in Ex. 12.14 the prebar spelling (marked by asterisks) indicates anticipation and reflects equally on the prebeat phrasing of the other little notes, including those written after the bar line.

Ex. 12.14. Luc Marchand (1748)

In 1755 the opera singer Bérard published a vocal treatise[16] and was immediately accused of plagiarism by Blanchet. A year later Blanchet brought out an almost identical book.[17] Their explanation of the *port de voix* is identical and not very specific. In the simple *port de voix* the principal note (not the grace itself) is sustained or even swelled; the rhythmical shape of the actual grace is not clarified. The *port de voix feint* is explained in the usual way of a long prepared appoggiatura, on which the tone is swelled, followed by a gentle upward resolution to the last note which is softly touched ("qu'on escamotte moelleusement"). No mention is made of the final *pincé*. The *coulé* is described by both authors as a stepwise-descending, small, and very gentle inflection of the voice ("une petite inflexion de voix très douce") that marks it as a *Zwischenschlag*.[18]

Saint Sévin, better known as L'Abbé le Fils, published in 1761 the first substantial French violin method. In it he describes two kinds of *ports de voix*, both of which take the beat.[19] One is the *port de voix feint*, which he calls "*port de voix* followed by a weak sound"; it starts with dynamic emphasis and tapers without the usual mordent sequel. The other kind, which he calls "*port de voix* followed by a full sound with mordent," reverses the dynamic pattern—it starts softly and swells to the principal note (Ex. 12.15).

For the *coulé*, L'Abbé le Fils makes an interesting distinction for the respective use of the onbeat and the prebeat type. The onbeat type he calls "sustained" (*soûtenu*), though his example (our Ex. 12.16a) shows it in a context where there is no room for actual sustaining; the meaning of *soûtenu*, additionally clarified

15 Luc Marchand, *Pièces de clavecin avec accomp't de violon, hautbois, violoncelle ou viole* (Paris [1748]).

16 Bérard, *L'art du chant.*

17 Blanchet, *L'art ou les principes philosophiques du chant.* It called itself "second edition," obviously with reference to Bérard's book as the first. According to Marpurg

(*Kritische Briefe über die Tonkunst*, vol. 2, pt. 3, p. 292), Blanchet sold the manuscript to Bérard who failed to pay for it, whereupon Blanchet sued for embezzlement.

18 Bérard, pp. 117-119, 129-132, Blanchet, pp. 115-116, 120, 124-125, 132.

19 L'Abbé le Fils, *Principes du violon*, pp. 15-16.

Ex. 12.15. L'Abbé le Fils (1761)

by the dynamic symbol, is simply that of an accented onbeat grace. This form of the *coulé* is used when it leads to a weak sound ("lorsqu'il mène à un son feint"). By contrast, the *coulé* is short—and clearly anticipated—when it leads to a *son soûtenu*, i.e. to an accented principal note. There is, he continues, no need for different symbols, since the *goût* decides which type to use. In Ex. *b* (which is only a brief excerpt of a lengthy passage laden with "short" *coulés*), the graces preceding the triplets in the first and third measures disclose their prebeat character because onbeat rendition would deprive the following note of its *soûtenu* character in every conceivable meaning of the term.

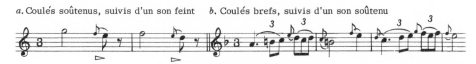

Ex. 12.16. L'Abbé le Fils

Jean Jacques Rousseau in his musical dictionary of 1768 shows the prebeat pattern for the *coulé* (Ex. 12.17*a*) and the onbeat pattern for the *port de voix* (Ex. *b*) and for what he calls the *port de voix jetté* (Ex. *c*), which corresponds to the *port de voix feint* (both designs given with *pincé* annex).[20]

Ex. 12.17. Jean Jacques Rousseau (1768)

Le Menu de Saint Philbert speaks only of the *coulé* and describes it clearly as a *Zwischenschlag*: "[the *coulé* being] always placed between two principal notes, one must only very lightly touch it ['il en faut effleurer le son'] . . . as its serves only to descend more tenderly to the lower note."[21]

L'abbé Duval illustrates in 1764 the *port de voix* as the apparent onbeat type with *pincé* annex of Ex. 12.18*a*. His *port de voix feint* is of the usual kind (Ex. *b*) also followed by a *pincé*. In addition he also describes what he calls *martellement*,

[20] Jean Jacques Rosseau, *Dictionnaire*, Planche B, fig. 13.

[21] Le Menu de Saint Philbert, *Principes de musique*, p. 14.

a syncopated variant of the *port de voix et pincé* that is not limited to stepwise ascent (Ex. *c*). Duval's *coulé* is not clearly defined but seems to lean to interbeat character.[22]

Ex. 12.18. L'abbé Duval (1764)

In 1766 Lacassagne wrote a vocal treatise that received at the time critical acclaim in France and Germany. He distinguishes a *port de voix réel* and *feint* as shown in Ex. 12.19. In the *réel* (Ex. *a*), the three little notes which comprise the *pincé* annex were light and unaccented, as can be gathered from their description as a "small wavering" (*petite ondulation*) of the voice. The pattern of Ex. *b*, still under the label of *réel*, shows the leapwise ascent in a design almost identical with the *martellement* of L'abbé Duval. The *port de voix feint* (Ex. *c*) is of the usual type.

Ex. 12.19. Lacassagne (1766)

Lacassagne's *coulé* is likely to have *Zwischenschlag* character, to judge from the author's stress on "connecting notes" ("pour donner de la liaison aux notes") as well as from the fact that the little notes remain unchanged in their various resolutions.[23]

Lécuyer in 1769 distinguishes three types of the *port de voix*: the *feint*, the *appuyé*, and the *achevé*. As shown in Ex. 12.20, the *feint* is as usual of Type 4, the *appuyé* of Type 3, and the *achevé* of undetermined rhythm. All three, he says, end in a *pincé*. Lécuyer compares the *feint* to a comma, the *appuyé* to a colon, the *achevé* to a period. He does not mention the *coulé*.[24]

Ex. 12.20. Lécuyer (1769)

22 L'abbé Duval, *Principes de la musique pratique*, pp. 56-58.

23 Lacassagne, *Traité général des élémens du chant*, pp. 65-69. The book was supposedly written in the 1740's.

24 Lécuyer, *Principes de l'art du chant*, pp. 14-16.

Duval in 1775 shows both the *port de voix* and the *coulé* with onbeat start (Exx. 12.21a-c); then, however, he presents with the same symbol a seemingly anticipated *port de voix et pincé* as well as a *Schneller* under the term of *flatté* (Ex. *d*).[25]

Ex. 12.21. Duval (1775)

Francoeur ("neveu"), the nephew of François Francoeur, in autograph additions to his treatise on wind instruments of 1772, shows both the *coulé* and the *port de voix* on the beat; the former short, the latter long (with *pincé* annex), as seen in Exx. 12.22a and *b*. In the strangely unmetrical Ex. *b* the *coulé* is ambiguous in rhythm.[26]

Ex. 12.22. Francoeur ("neveu") (1772)

Levesque and Bêche, presumably around the same time, preface their collection of *Solfèges d'Italie* with a tabulation of thoroughly French ornaments; their listings for the *coulé* are given in Ex. 12.23.[27] Model *a* shows clear anticipation, but *b* is puzzling. On

Ex. 12.23. Levesque and Bêche

[25] Duval, *Méthode agréable*, p. 11. Bornet l'aîné points to the double meaning of the little notes in his *Nouvelle méthode de violon et de musique* (1786), p. 18: "The little notes . . . are generally rendered very fast and almost always slurred to the following note. There are [however] instances where taste requires the little note to be long, in which case one borrows from the value of the following note ('pour lors on emprunte sur la valeur de la Note qui suit'). . . ." The explicit limitation of the onbeat requirement to the long execution suggests grace-note character for the "very fast" little notes.

[26] Francoeur ("neveu"), *Diapason général de tous les instruments à vent.*

[27] Levesque and Bêche, *Solfèges d'Italie*, p. 6. The book contains didactic works of Leo, Durante, Scarlatti, Hasse, Porpora, etc.

the face of it, the Lombard pattern written above was to be resolved as a prebeat grace. On the other hand, it is not impossible that the two lines were reversed.

Marcou (a writer of undetermined qualifications) presents in the 1780's an interbeat *coulé*, an onbeat *port de voix achevé*, and the usual *feint* which he calls *jetté* (see Ex. 12.24).[28] Except for the different articulation of the *coulé*, the illustrations and terms are identical with those of J. J. Rousseau's *Dictionnaire* (see above Ex. 12.17).

Ex. 12.24. Marcou (1782)

Borghese, in 1786, describes the *port de voix* in terms of anticipation only, by saying that the little note standing for the *port de voix* "indicates by its value the portion that is to be taken from the *do* in order to carry it to the *re* and similarly with the others." He adds that such anticipated *ports de voix* can take place also by leaps.[29]

Choquel makes a revealing comment in a treatise of 1762. He stresses the need to execute both the *port de voix* and the *coulé* very softly (*à demi voix*) and in a "quasi syncopated manner," which is "absolutely necessary" to do justice to these graces.[30] Clearly he refers to the free rhythmic manipulation that carries the ornaments across the beat. One hundred years earlier, Bacilly had described the same procedure as an artistic necessity in certain circumstances. The two statements, one hundred years apart, fittingly frame a period during which such practices were a common feature of artistic performance.

PERHAPS the most striking feature of the period under consideration is its fundamental resemblance to its predecessor with regard to the treatment of *Vorschläge*. True, the onbeat style made headway, but its progress was largely limited to the *port de voix*, whereas the *coulé*, especially in the context of descending thirds, continued predominantly in the orbit of anticipation.

As an appropriate postscript to this chapter we might quote an eminent foreign observer who in midcentury characterizes the anticipation of *coulés* as the typically French style of execution. Quantz, in his famous treatise on the flute, points to the first two of the models shown in Exx. 12.25a and b and tells us that their small notes especially in slow tempi must *not* be played on the beat; "otherwise it sounds as if they had been written out in regular notes. . . . But this would not only be contrary to the intention of the composer, but also to the French manner of execution from which these *Vorschläge* originate. For *the small notes belong in the time of the preceding note* and must not, as shown in the second example [i.e. Exx. *c* and *d*], be played in the time of the following note" [italics mine].[31]

[28] Marcou, *Elémens théoriques et pratiques de musique*, p. 53.
[29] Borghese, *L'art musical*, p. 80.

[30] Choquel, *La musique rendue sensible par la méchanique*, pp. 161ff.
[31] Quantz, *Versuch einer Anweisung die*

Ex. 12.25. Quantz (1752)

Flöte traversiere zu spielen, ch. 17, sec. 2, par. 20: ". . . diese [kurzen Vorschläge] . . . dürfen nicht angehalten werden, zumal im langsamen Tempo: sonst klingt es, als wenn sie mit ordentlichen Noten ausgedrücket wären, wie Fig. 38.39 [our Exx. 12.25 *c* and *d*] zu ersehen ist. Dieses aber würde nicht nur dem Sinne des Componisten, sondern auch der französischen Art zu spielen, von welcher diese Vorschläge doch ihren Ursprung haben, zuwider seyn. Denn die kleinen Noten gehören noch in die Zeit der vorhergehenden Note, und dürfen also nicht, wie bey dem zweyten Exempel steht [our Exx. 12.25 *c* and *d*] in die Zeit der folgenden kommen."

Another French-oriented document on anticipated graces can be found in the Dutchman's Gerhardus Havingha's *VIII Suites . . . voor de Clavecymbal off Spinet* (Amsterdam, n.d. [c. 1725]), reprinted in *MMB*, vol. 7 (1951). The collection contains (p. 29) an air "with ornaments" (*met d'Agrements*) where we find several prebar notations of little notes, including *Vorschläge* and slides.

Compared to the *port de voix* and *coulé*, the *accent* and *chûte* are less important graces. Fortunately, there is, on the whole, more agreement on the nature of these graces and on their names and symbols.

What is by most called *accent* is called by some *aspiration*, and what is by most called *chûte* is called *plainte* by a few. Confusion can enter largely because some masters use the term *chûte* to designate other ornaments. D'Anglebert and Le Roux applied it to the prepared onbeat *port de voix* and *coulé*. Moreover, one has to take care not to confuse the French *accent*, which is a *Nachschlag*, with the Italian *accento* or the German *Accent*, which are used mainly to designate *Vorschläge*.

What we shall, in accord with majority usage, call the *accent* is a small sound, slurred briefly and delicately to the very end of a tone. Though it belongs to the preceding note (as do all *Nachschläge*), it also serves a connective purpose by making the transition to the following neighbor smoother. The borrowed note will usually be the diatonic upper neighbor, and the most characteristic designs are those indicated in Exx. 13.1*a-c*, where the following neighbor note descends or remains on the level of the parent note, involving therefore a change of direction. Such is the *accent* pattern *par excellence*.

Variants remain within a fairly narrow range. Examples *d* and *e* show cases where an *accent* to a long note is not added at the end, but before the end, like a rudimentary trill. Example *f* shows the downward instead of upward inflection (the inversion of Ex. *a*); Exx. *g* and *h* show the *accent* without change in direction in a chiefly connective function. The variant of Ex. *i* is rather rare. In vocal music the types involving reversal of direction must have often used inflections of such subtlety that they consisted of microtones rather than of whole or half-steps.

Ex. 13.1. *Accent*

The *chûte*, too, is tied to the preceding note and, as its name indicates (chûte meaning "fall"), moves downward to anticipate most typically the pitch of the following note, as shown in Exx. 13.2*a-c*. Exx. *d* and *e* represent less frequent variants.

Ex. 13.2. *Chûte*

The symbols vary somewhat. The oldest one for the *accent* seems to be the vertical slash above the note (not to be confused with a staccato sign). We find it in D'Ambruis in 1685, who speaks of *accent* or *plainte*, and somewhat later in L'Affilard and Loulié. The sign was used by some until the middle of the 18th century when it became obsolete. Here and there we find ∧ or ∨ but, from Couperin on, the little note is the most common symbol. Often, of course, the grace was not indicated at all and was improvised in fitting spots. For the *chûte*, the only symbol other than the little note may have been an oblique descending dash above and between the notes involved (as seen below in Ex. 13.5).

Bacilly (1668) is among the first to describe the grace, which he calls *accent* or *aspiration*, and mentions that some call it *plainte*. He recommends the use of the grace for long syllables only and preferably for tones followed by a note on the same pitch or a step lower. The *accent*, he says, is "very delicate, very lightly touched, and quasi-imperceptible."[1]

Jean Rousseau in his gamba treatise calls the grace *aspiration* and shows its typical design (see Ex. 13.3*a*) without introducing a symbol.[2] L'Affilard illustrates the grace (see Ex. *b*) in the sense of Bacilly's description and uses the symbol of the vertical slash.[3]

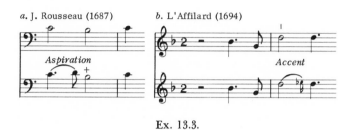

Ex. 13.3.

Loulié explains the *accent* as a stepwise elevation from a strong to a small and weak sound.[4] His illustration (Ex. 13.4), which uses the vertical slash as a symbol, shows the characteristic reversal of motion except for the second measure which corresponds to our model in Ex. 13.1*g*.

Ex. 13.4. Loulié (1696), *Accent*

Montéclair (1736), fully concurring with Loulié's opinion, uses the same symbol and mentions the "dolorous" quality of the grace[5] (a quality that obviously prompted the alternate term of *plainte*).

The *chûte* is defined by Loulié as a downward inflection of the voice from a strong or regular note ("son fort ou ordinaire") to a small sound. Using an oblique descending slash as symbol, the illustration (Ex. 13.5) shows that the grace can bridge any interval and falls to the pitch of the following note. Here too Montéclair is in full agreement and adds that the voice, after having held the

---

[1] *Remarques*, pp. 189-191.
[2] *Traité*, pp. 90-93.
[3] *Principes*, 1st and 2nd eds., pp. 20-21.

[4] *Éléments*, pp. 68-69.
[5] *Principes*, *accent*, p. 80; *chûte*, pp. 79-80.

Ex. 13.5. Loulié, *Chûte*

previous tone for some time, falls "like dying" to the lower tone without holding it.

Corrette (1758) shows for the *accent* the usual reversal of motion. For our above pattern Ex. 13.1c—the following neighbor note on the level of the preceding one—he uses the name of *flaté* and demands for it an "almost unnoticeable inflection of the voice," a wording suggestive of microtones.[6] For symbols he uses the little notes.

David's examples (1737) all belong to the pattern of Ex. 13.1c, with the return to the same pitch, and so does Jean Jacques Rousseau's model of 1768. By describing the grace as an inflection that is "quasi-cut off" (*entrecoupée*), David seems to imply a short interruption before the following note, underlining its *Nachschlag* character. His terms are either *plainte* or *aspiration*.[7] Denis (1747) and Villeneuve (1733, 1756) with the vertical slash and La Chapelle (1737) with the little-note symbol all follow Loulié's standard pattern.[8]

L'Abbé le Fils (1761) notes that the *accent* helps both to distinguish and to connect the two neighbor notes. Using the little notes as symbol, he shows the rise and fall of the patterns given in Exx. 13.1a and b while also indicating the tapering of the sound on the preceding note. He deviates from the usual pattern in one illustration where the accent rises a third instead of a second.[9]

There are, by and large, only two noteworthy kinds of deviations from the common pattern of stepwise rise and subsequent fall. One is its mirror image of stepwise fall and subsequent rise, the other is an *accent* that repeats the preceding parent note.

Saint Lambert's *accent*, which he calls *aspiration*, can move in either direction.[10] In keeping with his idea of devising graphically suggestive symbols, he uses here an upright caret ∧ for the ascending *accent* and a downward one for the descending type, as shown in Ex. 13.6.

Ex. 13.6. Saint Lambert (1702), *Aspiration*

[6] *Le Parfait maître*, p. 50.

[7] David, *Méthode nouvelle*, p. 136; Rousseau, *Dictionnaire*, Planche B.

[8] Denis, *Nouveau système*, pp. 12, 45. In the 2nd ed. (*Nouvelle méthode*, pp. 11, 44), he specifies that the *accent* moves only upward. La Chapelle, *Vrais principes*, vol. 2, p. 14; Villeneuve, *Nouvelle méthode*, pp. 38-39.

[9] *Principes du violon*, p. 15.

[10] *Principes du clavecin*, pp. 56-57.

Hotteterre's *accent,* as seen in Ex. 13.7, is also two-directional.[11]

Ex. 13.7. Hotteterre (1707), *Accent*

Fifty years later, Lécuyer questions the correctness of the directive that the *accent* must rise or fall one step. Instead, he writes, it ought to be only the echo of the previous sound.[12] He sees the need for such an *accent* at the end of every held-out or swelled-and-tapered tone ("son tenu ou filé").

Duval seems to share Lécuyer's idea about the nature of the *accent* when he speaks of a slight inflection ("un léger coup de gozier") that repeats the relinquished sound at the end of a long-held tone.[13] His illustration is given in Ex. 13.8.

Ex. 13.8. Duval (1775), *Accent*

Lacassagne indicates a wider than usual expressive range for the *accent* by referring to it as a more or less tender, or lively, vocal inflection that serves to end a note with art and grace.[14] His *accent* can consist of either two notes or the usual one; it can rise or fall, as shown in Ex. 13.9.

Ex. 13.9. Lacassagne (1766), *Accent*

L'abbé Duval's (1764) *accent,* for which he uses no symbol, is probably related to Lacassagne's descending two-note *accent.* In the absence of an illustration, his description of the grace as a lower passing note followed by the repeat of the original sound would permit either of these designs:[15]

Dard specifies downward inflection for the *accent,* which he marks with a caret. He spells out a pattern that places the grace near the end of the parent note, as shown in Ex. 13.10.[16] The effect of this design will probably resemble that of Lacassagne's two-note suffix.

Choquel records the demise of the old slash symbols for both *accent* and *chûte* which, he says, are now marked only with little notes.[17] His explanation and examples for the *accent* are in the tradition of Loulié with the one exception of an *accent* that—like our Ex. 13.1*i*—rises a fourth to reach above the following

---

[11] *Principes de la flute,* p. 29.

[12] *Principes,* p. 16: "[L'accent] n'est que la répercussion du Son déjà donné."

[13] *Méthode agréable,* p. 11.

[14] *Traité,* p. 65.

[15] *Principes,* p. 59.

[16] *Nouveaux principes,* p. 17.

[17] *La musique,* p. 65.

Ex. 13.10. Dard (c. 1769), *Accent*

note (see Ex. 13.11*a*). His description of the *chûte* is also in line with Loulié, except that his examples show a slur of the grace to the following, identical note instead of to the preceding one, suggesting premature entry for the grace (Ex. *b*). This unorthodox notation is confirmed in the text, hence no misprint is involved.

Ex. 13.11. Choquel (1762)

OF THE TWO graces under consideration, the *accent*, with its characteristic change of direction, is quite typically French. Its occasional parallels abroad, such as Ganassi's *accento* and an Italo-German *Nachschlag* called *superjectio*, could not match in importance the place of the *accent* in the French ornamental scheme where its improvised use far exceeded its prescription by symbols. The *chûte* had more nearly an international complexion with its partial counterpart in the Italo-German *anticipatione della nota*. In parenthesis, it might be noted that among the German disciples of French ornamental practices, Walther was fond of the *accent* and used it very frequently, whereas Bach, as far as we can judge from notational evidence, used it hardly at all. This contrast, incidentally, provides us with yet another commentary on the myth of "common practice."

Italian One-Note Graces

1590-1710

One-note graces, the smallest type of diminution, conformed to the overall tradition of interbeat design. Except for Bovicelli who, as noted before, occasionally placed a one-note grace on the beat, all other sources invariably show offbeat designs. Richardo Rogniono offers the representative tabulation given in Ex. 14.1.[1] In it we see under Exx. *a* and *b* the first diminution patterns as *Nachschlag* types; under Exx. *c* and *d* we find, both rising and falling, the characteristic *Zwischenschläge* of the *tierces coulées*.

Ex. 14.1. R. Rogniono (1592)

Zacconi discusses an *accento* that fills the leap of a third and gives the illustration of Ex. 14.2*a*. He says that one should tarry on the first semibreve, but not longer than a semiminim's worth (♩), then, while rising, sound approximately a semichroma (♬).[2]

Chrysander was justified in interpreting the combined evidence in the manner shown in Ex. *c*, with a rubato delay of the offbeat connective grace. Zacconi also discusses the leap of a fourth or fifth and gives the example shown in Ex. *b*; his comments point to anticipation rather than retardation ("la detta Chroma puntata & la Semichroma si pronuntia sempre su la prima figura"). Here too Chrysander's interpretation as a prebeat *Vorschlag* (Ex. *d*) seems fitting.[3]

Diruta in 1609 illustrates, under the name of *accenti*, a series of *Nachschläge* (Ex. *e*) that rises one step prior to falling, in the style of the French *accent*. As can be seen, the principal notes are all consonant.[4]

[1] Richardo Rogniono, *Il vero modo*, pp. 17, 18, 20, 22.

[2] Zacconi, *Prattica*, I, bk. 1, ch. 63, f. 56r: ". . . su la prima si ha alquanto di ritardare: la qual ritardanza, non ha da esser di più spatio che d'una Semiminima: Onde non solo si deve questa Semiminima dalla secunda figura torre, & darla all'altra: ma anco nel trattenersi, & ascendere alla compagna, si fa in mezzo (fuggendo) sentire come una Semichroma. . . ."

[3] Chrysander, "L. Zacconi als Lehrer des Kunstgesanges," pp. 249-310.

[4] Diruta, *Transilvano*, vol. 2, p. 13.

a. Zacconi (1592) f. 56r   b. Zacconi, f. 56r

c. Chrysander's interpretation   d. Chrysander's interpretation

e. Diruta (1609)

Accenti

Ex. 14.2.

Bovicelli's innovative onbeat designs were discussed before (Chapter 4) and illustrated in Ex. 4.1. It might be added that these significant models occur, in both the abstract and concrete examples of Bovicelli's book, only in stepwise rise, not in descent and not when larger intervals are involved. The one specimen shown for a rising third, given in Ex. 14.3 side by side with the anticipated pattern, is dependent on a prebeat preparation and remains therefore within the domain of stepwise rise.[5]

Ex. 14.3.

About 1620, a long silence, which lasted more than one hundred years, settled on Italian ornamentation theory. During this period we are dependent for information largely on musical evidence, supplemented by what German theorists had to say about Italian practices. For *musical* evidence concerning one-note graces, we must rely on specimens written out in regular notation, because symbols were not yet in use. Fortunately, we find that Italian vocal composers wrote out the *Vorschlag* innumerable times, and the record thus created from the start of the 17th to the early years of the 18th century points to predominant, indeed overwhelming, prebeat usage. Hugo Goldschmidt has stressed this fact in his important study on vocal ornamentation and illustrated it with examples, which the reader may wish to consult in addition to the ones offered here.[6] It is interesting to note that even on final cadences the *Vorschlag* was most typically anticipated. The form of this grace was called the *anticipatione della syllaba*. Since this prebeat *Vorschlag* was motivated melodically, it occurred in the most varied harmonic contexts. In some spots it could be viewed as resolving a preceding dissonance, in others it may repeat either a dissonance or a consonance, or may, as a passing note, connect two consonances. All these possibilities will be represented in the following illustrations.

5 Bovicelli, *Regole*, pp. 17, 18.
6 Goldschmidt, *Die Lehre von der vokalen*   *Ornamentik*. Music examples in Appendix, pp. 14ff.

The prebeat *Vorschlag*, generally applying to the last unaccented syllable of a word, was ubiquitous, but it had no monopoly. Occasionally on final cadences, but also in the middle of phrases, we encounter the long appoggiatura, usually on accented syllables of words that carry strong affective meaning. However, throughout most of the 17th century, the incidence of the notated onbeat *Vorschlag* remains small; and, as Goldschmidt pointed out, such *Vorschläge* occurred often as a consonance, hence without harmonic implications. We cannot know, of course, exactly what the Italians did in improvised additions to the score. However, as will be documented in the next chapter, the German theorists fully support the reasonable assumption that, as far as the ratio of the two rhythmic styles is concerned, improvisation mirrored the pattern of notation.

In the early part of the 17th century the rising prebeat *Vorschlag* was more frequent than the descending one.

The first two excerpts in Ex. 14.4 from Peri's *Flora* show a rising and a falling prebeat *Vorschlag* (Exx. a and b). Examples c-g are from Monteverdi. Example c shows a prebeat type from below, Ex. d from above; Exx. e and f present appoggiaturas on stressed syllables, one rising, one falling; Ex. g has two very short prebeat *coulés* in close succession, the second of which falls on an accented syllable.[7]

Domenico Mazzocchi's prebeat *Vorschläge* are overwhelmingly of the ascending species. One such specimen is shown in Ex. 14.5a from *La catena d'Adone*. In this opera—which is literally filled with this design, notably in cadences—there may be no more than three or four instances of descending prebeat *Vorschläge*, one of which is given in Ex. b.

Ex. 14.4.

[7] Peri, *Flora*, Act II; Claudio Monteverdi, *L'incoronazione di Poppea* (1642); *Il ritorno d'Ulisse* (1640).

The descending type gradually becomes more frequent and by midcentury achieves approximate equality with the ascending one. But for both types, the prebeat design continues to be favored by all contemporary masters, and the few further specimens shown here are truly examples of an all-pervasive style.

Examples 14.5 *c-f* are from Cavalli. In Ex. *c* the rising prebeat *Vorschlag* resolves a suspension; in Ex. *d* the descending *Vorschlag* connects two consonances; in Ex. *e* an upward leap precedes the descending prebeat *Vorschlag*; Ex. *f* shows an appoggiatura.[8]

Ex. 14.5.

Pietro Cesti presents the same picture of extensive anticipation and an occasional appoggiatura. Example 14.6a shows a stepwise descending, prebeat *Vorschlag*, Ex. *b* a downward leaping one (a remarkably frequent design with this master); in Ex. *c* we find an appoggiatura.[9] Luigi Rossi, Stradella, Legrenzi, and a number of other contemporary composers whose works were examined confirm these usages in the same approximate distribution.

Ex. 14.6. Cesti

True, the appoggiatura designs are mostly connected with accented syllables and the prebeat graces with unaccented ones; true too that harmonically the ascending prebeat graces often, but not always, fulfill the function of resolving a dissonance, frequently in a 4-3 sequence. But by being slurred to the following

[8] Mazzocchi, *La catena d'Adone* (Venice, 1626) (facs., Bologna, 1969); Cavalli, *Didone abbandonata* (1641); *Serse* (1654).

[9] Cesti, *L'Orontea* (1649); *Il pomo d'oro* (1666).

syllable, their character as prebeat *Vorschläge* is clearly established. The frequent descending prebeat *Vorschläge* that connect consonances in the fashion of *tierces coulées*, or leap downward, speak for themselves. The same designs continued into the early years of the 18th century, as can be gathered by numerous passages from many different masters.

Example 14.7a shows an ever-recurring pattern in Alessandro Scarlatti's *Concerti sacri*; Ex. *b* gives a specimen from a Steffani recitative; in Ex. *c*, from the same work, we see a consonant, hence unharmonic, onbeat *Vorschlag* on *sol* and, perhaps, an unmarked appoggiatura on *affligge*.[10]

a. A. Scarlatti (c. 1700), *Concerti sacri*

a - ma - re   a - ma - vit

b. Steffani, *Tassilone* (1709), I, 7   *c.* Steffani, *Tassilone*, I, 7
m. 25

soc - cor - so al pet - to   me sol aff - flig - ge

Ex. 14.7.

Around that time a different style for recitative cadences was gaining ground. It involved a design that placed the last accented syllable (the penultimate in a feminine, the ultimate in a masculine ending) on the beat; this beat in turn was probably often taken by an appoggiatura, sometimes unwritten but implied, sometimes spelled out in regular notes. In operatic recitative the Italians often compressed the bass cadence and let its dominant clash with the tonic of the voice. During the late 17th century and the early part of the 18th, these clashes were real (though generally softened by a 4-3 harmonization of the continuo). The prevailing modern idea that the clashes were resolved by a delayed cadence of the continuo is a questionable, retroactive application of a postbaroque convention. Alessandro Scarlatti, in his operas, used this type of compressed formula, and so did Handel. The two chief models of this pattern are shown in Ex. 14.8. The first of these (Ex. *a*) has the unwritten but perhaps frequently implied stepwise appoggiatura (which would in this case create questionable fifths!); the second (Ex. *b*) has the downward leap of a fourth which Scarlatti often, perhaps always, wrote out as actually sung, whereas later composers often chose to write the same design in the form given in Ex. *c*.

a   *b*   *c*

par - ti - te   Ad - di - o

6   ♯

Ex. 14.8. A. Scarlatti, *Laodicea* (1701)

[10] A. Scarlatti, *Concerti sacri*, Op. 2 (Amsterdam, n.d. [c. 1700]). His opera *Amor non vuol inganni* is full of prebeat *Vorschläge* at the end of recitatives. Agostino Steffani, *Tassilone* (1709).

The spread of this recitative fashion is symptomatic of a generally wider use of the appoggiatura that, at the turn of the century, led to a more balanced distribution of the two rhythmic styles. The written-out prebeat *Vorschlag* becomes less frequent after 1700, especially following the introduction into Italy—after 1700—of the little unmetrical notes. However, the prebeat style as such continued to be widely used throughout the 18th century side by side with the appoggiatura, as will be borne out by evidence presented later.

German One-Note Graces
1620-1715

THEORETICAL SOURCES

The third volume of Michael Praetorius's (1571-1621) great theoretical work of 1619 deals with the new type of Italian ornamentation.[1] The last chapter of the volume is titled, ". . . How boys who like to sing ought to be informed and instructed in the current Italian manner."[2] For this new Italian manner of singing, Praetorius names Caccini and Bovicelli as his chief mentors.

Under the term *accentus*, Praetorius, like Bovicelli, lists a number of small graces, including the *Vorschlag*. Almost all of the models for the *accenti* were taken from Bovicelli's tables of interval diminutions. From these tables Praetorius selected only the first, and simplest, patterns that involve no more than three or four ornamental tones. For the table of the ascending third, for instance, Praetorius selected only 5 patterns out of Bovicelli's 28. It is important to note that among the patterns selected are, side by side, Bovicelli's prebeat and onbeat patterns for *Vorschläge*. Example 15.1 gives all of Praetorius's models for one-note graces.

Those for the rising second (Ex. *a*) comprise two *Nachschläge* and an onbeat *Vorschlag*; for the rising third (Ex. *b*), the prebeat *Vorschlag* (or *Zwischenschlag*) and the prepared onbeat *Vorschlag*; for the descending second (Ex. *c*), only a *Nachschlag* pattern of a type later called *anticipatione della nota*; and for the descending third (Ex. *d*), only one *Zwischenschlag* pattern of the *tierces coulées* type. Then we see two onbeat models (Ex. *e*) not contained in Bovicelli for two notes on the same pitch. The description "nota initialis & finalis in Unisono" makes it clear that the pattern was meant to be read as shown in Ex. *f*.

Ex. 15.1. Praetorius (1619); also Herbst (1642,1658)

The Protestant theologian and cantor Johann Crüger (1598-1662) was a highly esteemed composer who wrote several treatises on composition, thorough bass,

---

[1] *Syntagma musicum.*

[2] Ch. 9: "Instructio pro Symphoniacis: Wie die Knaben, so vor andern sonderbare Lust und Liebe zum singen tragen, uff jetzige Italianische Manier zu informiren, und zu unterrichten seyn."

and the art of singing.[3] Crüger follows Praetorius's lead concerning ornaments; the term *accento* is still used in the sense of small-scale diminutions, and Crüger's models for such *accenti* are taken mainly from the older master's book.

We find for the "unison" one-note grace the onbeat pattern of Ex. 15.2*a*. No models are given for the interval of a second; for both rising and falling thirds, Crüger gives only the prebeat patterns of Ex. *b*, leaving out Praetorius's prepared onbeat design. Other one-note graces are given among models of *accenti* for ascending and descending scales; these are shown (Ex. *c*) in the version of 1654. Number 1 is related to the French *accent*, 2 and 5 are *Nachschläge* of the type *anticipatione della nota*, 3 is an onbeat *Vorschlag*, and 4 is a delayed *Vorschlag* whose interbeat placement neutralizes its harmonic effect. It is interesting, and possibly significant, that in the 1660 version the onbeat-appoggiatura pattern alone is omitted, the other four retained. For the descending scale, both versions contained *Nachschlag* patterns only. (The omission of all slur marks in the 1660 edition was unquestionably only a printing deficiency.)

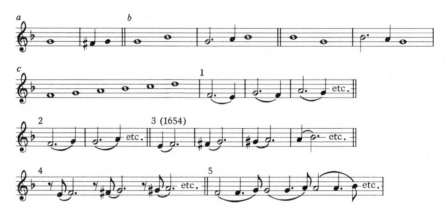

Ex. 15.2. Crüger (1654,1660)

In a treatise published in 1642, with a second enlarged edition in 1658, Johann Andreas Herbst (1588-1666) follows Praetorius quite literally in matters of the *accenti* and other small ornaments.[4] (In the preface Herbst admits that he often cites Praetorius verbatim.) All of Praetorius's one-note graces shown above in Ex. 15.1, as well as Crüger's scale embellishments of Ex. 15.2*c*, are presented here.

Christoph Bernhard (1628-1692), a student of Schütz and highly esteemed by him, wrote three treatises (hereafter referred to as I, II, and III) which are considered to be a faithful reflection of Schütz's own ideas. The first of these essays is devoted entirely to the art of vocal ornamentation, the second is a substantial work on composition, the third, written much later, is essentially a brief résumé of the second.[5] Though these writings were not published, they circulated in many copies and were studied by important musicians (Kuhnau was among those

[3] *Praecepta musicae practicae figuralis* (1625); *Synopsis musica* (1654); the latter's section two on ornamentation was later incorporated into *Musicae practicae praecepta brevia* (1660).

[4] *Musica practica* (1642). Even the subtitle, "Instructio pro Symphoniacis, . . . Wie die Knaben . . ." is taken verbatim from the title of Praetorius's chapter 9 (see n. 2 above). A second edition under the title *Musica moderna prattica . . .* (1658) contains all the material of the first with some corrections (missing ties supplied) and minor changes. Newly added are diminution patterns by Frid. Helwig (pp. 8-12) and cadential diminutions presumably by Herbst (pp. 47-62).

[5] I, *Von der Singe-Kunst oder Manier*; II, *Tractatus compositionis augmentatus*; III, *Ausführlicher Bericht vom Gebrauche der Con- und Dissonantien*.

who copied them); their principles were further disseminated in a widely read treatise by Bernhard's student Mylius. It is not surprising, therefore, that we can trace Bernhard's influence through the rest of the 17th and well into the 18th century to Walther, Mattheson, and some lesser masters and teachers.

The brief treatise on ornamentation is of special significance because it reflects Bernhard's firsthand knowledge of Italian practices acquired during two sojourns in Italy. Bernhard's first treatise must be considered the single most important theoretical source on Italian ornamentation practices in mid-17th century. As such it deserves to be dealt with in detail.

Bernhard distinguishes three Italian singing styles: the Roman, the Neapolitan and the Lombard. Of these, only the Lombard style deviates strongly from the written score and emphasizes the use of the *passaggi*. The Neapolitan style is distinguished by *cantar d'affetto*, the domination of musical expression by the affects, the emotional implications of the words. Such yielding adaptation, which he refers to as *moderiren*, involves changes of dynamics, of tempo, and of articulation (I, pars. 31-33). The Roman style is the *cantar sodo*, the "simple or even" singing which refrains from *passaggi* but ornaments the notes individually. This means that ornamentation is by and large—with unquestionable exceptions—limited to the small graces, comparable to the *accenti e trilli* of the monodists. Bernhard lists nine such Roman graces: 1) *fermo*, 2) *forte*, 3) *piano*, 4) *trillo*, 5) *accento*, 6) *anticipatione della syllaba*, 7) *anticipatione della nota*, 8) *cercar della nota*, 9) *ardire*.[6] No less than four of these (numbers 5-8) refer to one-note graces and all four are presented as interbeat designs.

The *accento* is identified as a *Nachschlag*; it is related to the French *accent* and formed "at the end of a note with a quasi-appended tonal inflection."[7]

Bernhard says that it is a mistake to use a "powerfully ejected exultation" ("einen stark herausgestossenen Jauchzer"), which fills the listeners with disgust, instead of a "gentle *accento*." The *accento* is not illustrated in the first treatise, but its *Nachschlag* nature, though obvious enough from the definition, is further confirmed in the second essay (II, ch. 22). There the *accento* (which Bernhard now calls *accentus*) is equated with *superjectio*, defined as an added tone a step above, and illustrated as shown in Ex. 15.3. (See also III, ch. 14.)

Ex. 15.3. Bernhard (c. 1660), *superjectio* or *accentus*

The *anticipatione della syllaba* is a prebeat *Vorschlag* for which Bernhard proposes the symbol *S*. He defines it as "a grace which assigns to the preceding note a part of the syllable that belongs to the following one,"[8] and illustrates it as shown in Ex. 15.4a.

---

[6] *Fermo*, stands for a steady unwavering sound, *ardire* for the opposite, a *tremolo* that is admitted only in rare cases (I, pars. 6,25).
[7] I, par. 15: "*Accento* . . . bey Endigung einer Note mit einem gleichsam nur anhenk-

kenden Nachklange geformiret. . . ."
[8] I, par. 19: ". . . ein solch Kunststück, welches die zu der folgenden Note gehörende *Syllabe* auch der Vorhergehenden in etwas zutheilet."

He sees its most common use where the melody rises one step. It is rarer for rising or falling thirds or larger intervals (see Exx. *b*, *c*, and *d*). In Ex. *c* he demonstrates for the fall of a fifth the insertion of a second ornamental note to achieve a more elegant connection. He says the pattern of Ex. *d*, the rise of a larger interval, is very rare, but that it occurs nevertheless in the form shown.

Ex. 15.4. Bernhard, *anticipatione della syllaba*

The *cercar della nota* extends the domain of the prebeat *Vorschlag* even further; though it partly overlaps syllabic anticipation, it covers much new territory. In conformance with the term, which means "to search for the note," the grace always approaches the following tone stepwise from either below or from above, and always before the beat. The symbol listed is *C*. As can be gathered from the illustrations of Ex. 15.5, it appeared in two forms, mostly as prebeat *Vorschläge* sung on the following syllable, occasionally as *Nachschläge* sung on the preceding one.

The *Vorschlag* type can occur at the beginning of a phrase, between notes of the same pitch, or for various intervals as shown in Exx. 15.5 *a-d*. The *Nachschlag* type of the *cercar* is demonstrated in the filling of both rising and falling thirds (Ex. *e*) in the manner of *tierces coulées*.

The *anticipatione della nota* is a grace described as having "the first note divided and its latter part drawn to the pitch of the following one."[9] Its symbol is *N* and it is used in stepwise progressions in either direction, as demonstrated in Ex. 15.6.

In his second and third treatises Bernhard returns to these and similar ornaments, now classing them as rhetorical figures and giving them Latin names which are, alas, not always the exact equivalent of the Italian ones. The discrepancies are minor but nevertheless create some terminological complications. It will be helpful to list these new terms because important German theorists who perpetuated the doctrine of the figures (*Figurenlehre*) used them until almost the middle of the 18th century.

The identity of *superjectio* and *accento* was noted above. *Quaesitio notae* (II, ch. 33) is the same as *cercar*; the *anticipatio notae* (II, ch. 23) is obviously the same as *anticipatione della nota*. The *anticipatio notae* in Ex. 15.7 is marked by an asterisk; here the

[9] I, pars. 21-22: ". . . wird die erste Nothe getheilet, und der letzte Theil derselben in den *Tonum* der nachfolgenden gezogen. . . ."

Ex. 15.5. Bernhard, *cercar della nota*

Ex. 15.6. Bernhard, *anticipatione della nota*

anticipated pitch is tied to the principal note, resulting in a premature entry rather than in the more usual repeated articulation.

The formidable terms *subsumtio praepositiva* and *subsumtio postpositiva*, which appear only in the third, late, treatise (III, ch. 15), have no exact Italian equivalents. The first of these is an anticipated *Vorschlag*, generally of the *cercar* type; the *postpositiva*, as the name indicates, is a *Nachschlag*.

Ex. 15.7. Bernhard, *anticipatio notae*

The remarkable fact that Bernhard fails to list a single onbeat pattern does not necessarily mean that he did not know them or that he disapproved of them, but it certainly shows that in his mind they can have played at best a minor role. In this circumstance we can find an important confirmation of the previously ventured hypothesis that the strong preponderance of the prebeat over the onbeat *Vorschläge*, found in the notation of 17th-century Italian music, must have had its full counterpart in the field of improvisation, because it is the latter that Bernhard is writing about.

That all these graces *alla Romana*, though fundamentally derived from the singing style, were applicable to the instruments is spelled out by Bernhard when he writes that they ought to be used by all musicians, "singers as well as instrumentalists" (I, par. 25).

Wolfgang Mylius (1636-1712), a student of Bernhard's, published a treatise (1685) which was widely disseminated and frequently quoted half a century later in Walther's *Lexicon*; later still it was praised by Adlung as "one of the most useful texts for schools."[10] Mylius declares that his discussion of ornaments is based on his teacher's principles. He contrasts this modern orientation with the ideas of Herbst, which he subtly intimates were by now (1685) outdated. Mylius brings a few interesting additions and modifications to the substance of Bernhard's teachings. Regarding the one-note graces, the most notable difference concerns the *accento*. According to Bernhard's text, it was a simple *Nachschlag*; with Mylius (who calls it *Accent*), it still can be a *Nachschlag*, but primarily he introduces it as a *Vorschlag* and, interestingly, as one that can be performed *on* as well as before the beat. Mylius describes the execution of the *accento* as a gentle *portamento* in muted, unstressed stepwise movement ("mit einer gedämpfften and sanfften Stimme . . . gelinde und ohne grossen Stoss des Halses gezogen und gemacht"). It is to be used only on stressed syllables and occasionally on final ones. In the first of two illustrations (shown in Ex. 15.8 with halved note values and added bar lines), the first two *accenti*, on *vi-* and *mo-*, are on the beat, the

Ex. 15.8. Mylius (1685), *Accent*

third, on *re* before the beat. Mylius does not comment on this dualism; the choice between the two styles was clearly a matter of musical judgment. It should be kept in mind that at the time the difference between the prebeat and onbeat *Vorschlag* was not as sharp as it became in the course of the 18th century. Judging from several descriptions of the grace (including Mylius's), the onbeat versions were usually just as short and gentle as their prebeat counterparts, and the two types could in many an instance become indistinguishable.

Mylius's second illustration of the *Accent* (given in Ex. 15.9 with addition of bar lines and correction of obvious misprints) contains five specimens (marked *a.*).

---

[10] *Rudimenta Musices* has no pagination; ornaments are discussed in the fifth chapter entitled "Von der lieblichen, artigen und zier- lichen Sing-Art." Jacob Adlung's praise is in *Anleitung zu der musikalischen Gelahrtheit*, p. 613, n. "y."

This time all of them are *Vorschläge* and *all* of them are anticipated, including the two on the accented syllable *Wort*.[11]

The other graces are those familiar from Bernhard, the *anticipatione della syllaba*, the *cercar della nota*, and the *anticipatione della nota*. For all three of these, Mylius's definitions are either entirely or practically identical to those of Bernhard and need not be repeated. Suffice it to note that *all* are, without exception, *interbeat* graces.

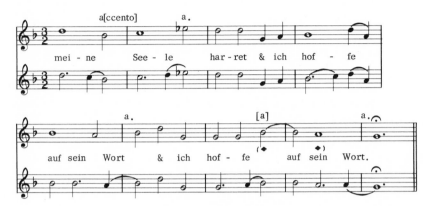

Ex. 15.9. Mylius, *Accent*

Mylius, mentioning the close intermeshing of their categories, points to the near identity of the *anticipatione della syllaba* and the *cercar*, and the close link between *cercar* and *accento*.

Mylius illustrates the *anticipatione della syllaba* (as shown in Exx. 15.10a and b) in the preferred stepwise progression—with anticipation on stressed syllables—and in the filling of thirds (the *S* is Bernhard's symbol for this grace, whereas the *C* over the syllable *-um* is probably one of the many misprints in this book).

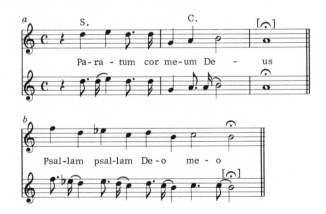

Ex. 15.10. Mylius, *anticipatione della syllaba*

Mylius's *cercar*, like Bernhard's, can occur at the start of a phrase as well as in the middle of it. Its use at the start is linked with the more specialized problem

---

[11] The blackened semibreves indicate simply the straddling of the beat in the barless notation. Mylius himself expressly writes that the value of the blackened notes is identical with that of the white ones.

of how to begin a song in general. Mylius says that the Italians won't be bound by any rules in this respect; some start on the written tone, some a half-tone, a whole-tone, a third, or a fourth from either below or above. Mylius recommends starting with a semitone below, drawing the voice up in a "semi-muted, elegant manner."[12]

The *cercar*, he continues, can hardly be distinguished from the *Accent*, "except that the *Accent* is used mostly at the beginning or the end of a note, whereas [the *cercar*] can be used also in polysyllabic words."[13] The meaning of this sentence is rather obscure, yet Walther was later to take it over verbatim into both of his treatises without trying to clarify it. (Probably one should substitute "word" for "note," meaning that the *Accent* is used at the beginning or end of a word, whereas the *cercar* can also be used in the middle.)

Of the two illustrations for the *cercar* (Ex. 15.11), the first (Ex. *a*) shows its use at the start of a phrase. In the second illustration (Ex. *b*) the slur marks, perhaps owing to the printer's carelessness, are inconsistent and most of them seem to indicate a *Nachschlag* rather than *Vorschlag* character of the grace, which would not be in line with the grace's assigned function of preparing or "seeking out" the following note.

Ex. 15.11. Mylius, *cercar della nota*

The *anticipatione della nota* (Ex. 15.12) is the same as Bernhard's, a gently gliding *Nachschlag* to the pitch of the following note.

Ex. 15.12. Mylius, *anticipatione della nota*

The considerable overlapping of the categories is confusing, and the following brief summary of Mylius's principles might be helpful: the *anticipatione della syllaba* is a prebeat *Vorschlag*; the *anticipatione della nota* is a *Nachschlag*; the *cercar della nota* can be a prebeat *Vorschlag* or a *Nachschlag*; the *Accent* can be either a *Nachschlag*, a prebeat, or an onbeat *Vorschlag*.

[12] *Rudimenta*, ch. 5. See on this question ch. 4 regarding Caccini's opinions, and Francesco Rognoni's example (Ex. 47.1*f* below).

[13] ". . . nur dass der Accent meist im Anfang und Ende einer Noten gebraucht, dieser aber sonst in Viel-Syllbigten Wörtern kan angebracht werden."

Mylius showed in one illustration the onbeat potential of the *Accent*. However, the exclusively interbeat character of the three other graces, the remark that the *Accent* is practically indistinguishable from the *cercar*, and the clear majority presentation of the prebeat pattern for the *Accent* itself point again to the conclusion that the anticipated designs were, in Mylius's eyes, the more important ones.

Wolfgang Caspar Printz (1641-1717), a theorist of note, published in the last third of the century a number of treatises (many more books of his remained unpublished). With regard to ornaments, he follows in the line of Praetorius and Herbst and shows no sign of an acquaintance with Bernhard nor, in his later works, with Mylius.

One-note graces are not systematically dealt with in any of his books; they are shown under different headings and *accentus* is the only term used.[14] In *Phrynis* of 1676/1677 he describes the *accentus* as a very gentle gliding of the voice stepwise up or down (ch. 9, par. 9) and illustrates it as a variant of a semibreve (Ex. 15.13). The patterns shown in this example contain onbeat *Vorschläge*, *Nachschläge*, and *Zwischenschlag*-related designs in the middle of a note.

Ex. 15.13. Printz (1677)

In the *Musica modulatoria* we find (p. 45) the illustration of Ex. 15.14 where we recognize three successive *Nachschläge*, an onbeat *Vorschlag* on -*ru*-, and a prebeat *Vorschlag* at the end. Under the heading of *groppo* (par. 14), we find the interbeat graces shown in Ex. *b*.

Ex. 15.14. Printz (1678)

In the *Compendium* of 1689 little new is to be found, nor do various later editions bring any changes in substance. No symbols are introduced, and since we find again the coexistence of the two rhythmic designs without further directives, we must assume that it was up to the performer to decide which to use.

The Vice-Capellmeister at the Ducal Court of Würtemberg, Johann Christoph Stierlein (?-1693), published a treatise in 1691.[15] His *accentus*, defined as stepwise

14 Printz's treatises dealing with ornaments are *Phrynis mitilenaeus oder satyrischer Componist*, Part II (1677), ch. 9, no pagin.; *Musica modulatoria vocalis* (1678), ch. 10; *Compen-* *dium musicae signatoriae & modulatoriae* (1689), ch. 5.

15 *Trifolium musicale*.

sliding up or down (p. 16), is also called *superjectio* (Bernhard's term for the *Nachschlag-accento*) and presented in both *Vorschlag* and *Nachschlag* form. In the illustrations given in Exx. 15.15a and b, the *accent* at the start of the first example is apparently anticipated, patterned after the Bernhard-Mylius *cercar*. The *accent* in Ex. b is the French type of stepwise rise at the end of a note that is described as dynamically tapered. However, the fact that Stierlein, like Mylius, viewed the *accent* also as *Vorschlag* in the dual role of either onbeat or prebeat design is incidentally revealed in an example that demonstrates diminutions over various intervals. Among those shown for the ascending third (Ex. c), we find side by side an onbeat and a prebeat *Vorschlag* pattern for the same syllable, each labeled as *accent* (p. 19; the *trem[ulus]* is a trill).

Ex. 15.15. Stierlein (1691)

Under the term *subsumptio postpositiva*, Stierlein demonstrates the usual *Nachschlag* pattern of the *anticipatione della nota* (p. 16). While discussing the various musico-rhetorical figures, he shows under the title of *retardatio* an interesting illustration (Ex. 15.16) where delayed upward resolution produces a long ascending appoggiatura (p. 20).

Ex. 15.16. Stierlein

A further noteworthy feature of Stierlein's treatise is the use of little notes as ornamental symbols, possibly the earliest instance in a German treatise and certainly among the earliest in Germany anywhere.

Moritz Feyertag, music director in Duderstadt, published a treatise in 1695 that agrees in principle with Bernhard-Mylius regarding one-note graces, though it differs partly in terminology.[16] The *anticipatio syllabae* (p. 211) conforms to the usual pattern and its prebeat design is shown in Ex. 15.17a. The *accentus*—both *intendens* (rising) and *remittens* (falling)—is illustrated in a form (Ex. b) which suggests anticipation (p. 205).

[16] *Syntaxis minor zur Sing-Kunst.*

Ex. 15.17. Feyertag (1695)

The prebeat character of the *accentus* is further clarified by a later comment which refers to this one-note *accentus* as well as to a two-note *accentus circumflexus* to be described later. In mentioning the unmetrical notation, Feyertag explains that he had notated the *accentus* not for the sake of the measure but only *ad rei notitiam*, i.e. to take note of its presence. He says that if it were to be taken as part of the measure, then it would not be an *accentus* but "a real and complete syncopation."[17] Hence, he says, both types of *accenti* must be played as fast and as gracefully (*manierlich*) as possible in order not to take anything away from the measure ("dass er dem Tackte nichts entziehe"). The "syncopation" he wants to avoid obviously refers to the result of an onbeat execution that, moreover, would take something "away from the measure."

In 1701 the Bohemian Thomas Balthasar Janowka, organist in a Prague church, wrote one of the early musical lexica[18] (two years before Brossard's). It is quoted a few times in Walther's *Lexicon* of 1732 but hardly mentioned anywhere else.

In his discussion of one-note graces, Janowka describes under the word *Einfall* a rising or falling *Vorschlag*, symbolized by Kuhnau's dashes: / or \ . It is described as falling on the beat and taking half of the note's value. (Walther, in his *Lexicon*, s. v. *accento*, mentions Janowka's rule and applies it to short note values only.) The descending type is said to be most appropriate before trills and on longer notes. This may well be the first definite German rule about the long appoggiatura. However, Janowka's reference to Kuhnau's partitas and his use of the dash symbol suggest the need to qualify Janowka's rule. As will be shown presently, Kuhnau's dash symbol could not have been consistently interpreted according to Janowka's formula. Janowka describes, somewhat unclearly, another unnamed grace which is nevertheless definitely anticipated. Symbolized by two vertical dashes ‖ , it appears to be the equivalent of the *anticipatione della nota*.

Johann Samuel Beyer, cantor and music director in Freiberg, published a vocal treatise in 1703 (2nd ed. 1730).[19] In a chapter on the *Musica ornata seu colorata* Beyer first takes up the *Accent* and declares it to be almost identical with ("fast nichts anderes als . . .") the Italian *anticipatione*, or *retardatione della syllaba* or *della nota*. The *anticipatione della syllaba* is the prebeat *Vorschlag*, the *retarda-*

17 Ibid., p. 208: ". . . hätte ich dir den gesetzt, wie es dem Tackt gemäss wäre, so wäre fürwar kein Accent zu vermuten sondern eine rechte und vollkommene Syncopation."
18 *Clavis ad thesaurum magnae artis musicae.*
19 *Primae lineae musicae vocalis.*

tione a short onbeat *Vorschlag*; for the first of these he gives the expected pattern shown in Ex. 15.18.

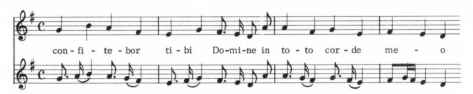

Ex. 15.18. Beyer (1703,1730), *anticipatione della syllaba*

For the *retardatione* the second edition (pp. 32-33) supplements the missing illustration of the first. The example is very interesting, as Beyer gives three ornamented versions (Exx. 15.19*b-d*). He approves of the first anticipated one (Ex. *b*) and of the second brief onbeat version, the—unnamed—*retardatione*, but not of the third, using a *Nachschlag*, in which the grace is attached to the preceding instead of to the following syllable.

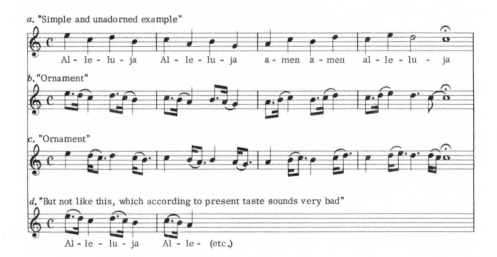

Ex. 15.19. Beyer (1730)

For the *anticipatione della nota*, Beyer follows the Bernhard-Mylius definition and illustration, as shown in Ex. 15.20.

Ex. 15.20. Beyer, *anticipatione della nota*

Kerll's eminent student, Franz Xaver Anton Murschhauser (1663-1738), presents in 1703 a brief ornament table which includes a short onbeat *Vorschlag* with the symbol ⌄ to indicate a start from below, and the symbol > a start from above (Ex. 15.21).[20]

Ex. 15.21. Murschhauser (1703)

While most of the treatises discussed in this chapter were concerned with the voice, two essays, written in 1704 and 1709, by Johann Baptist Samber (1654-1717), organist at the Salzburg Cathedral, address themselves to the organist. They also offer much information of general musical interest.[21]

Of his one-note graces, the *accentus* is of the French type, the stepwise rising before the fall (Ex. 15.22a). For the *Vorschlag* and *Nachschlag* he uses Bernhard's terms of *subsumptio praepositiva* and *postpositiva* (pp. 219-220). The latter overlaps with the *accentus,* and his illustration (Ex. *b*) shows simply an inverted pattern of stepwise fall prior to rise (p. 220). For the *praepositiva,* he gives one example (Ex. *c*) which shows a downbeat *Vorschlag* forming a dissonance; but interestingly, Samber calls it "rare." Another illustration of the *praepositiva* is the *Nachschlag* of the *anticipatione della nota* type (Ex. *d*).

Ex. 15.22. Samber (1709)

Martin Heinrich Fuhrmann (1669-1745)—a Lutheran cantor, eminent theorist, and colorful personality who spiced his writings with an earthy humor—is of special interest to us because of his apparently close spiritual affinity to Bach. He communicated his ideas on ornaments chiefly in two treatises of 1706 and 1715 (hereafter referred to as I and II) which were paid the compliment of being plagiarized.[22]

[20] *Prototypon longo breve organicum,* pt. 1, *DDT* ed., p. 122.

[21] *Manuductio ad organum; Continuatio ad manuductionem organicam.* Both volumes deal with ornamentation, but only the second one refers to one-note graces, pp. 219-220.

[22] *Musikalischer Trichter* (1706) appeared anonymously; *Musica vocalis in nuce* (1715). Martin Ruhnke, in his article on Fuhrmann in *MGG* declares him to be closer to the world of Bach than either of the two antagonists Mattheson and Buttstedt. Fuhrmann was one of

Fuhrmann explains the *accento* as a "partitioning of the note, whereby the voice gently and fast rises or falls into the second or third." (In the second treatise only stepwise motion is mentioned, the leap to the third omitted.) The *Accent*, he says, is used mostly at the beginning and the end of a note (I, p. 24), which would imply that the term could be used for either *Vorschlag* or *Nachschlag*. His example shows only a fast onbeat *Vorschlag* (Ex. 15.23a). Like Printz, he lists interbeat graces under the category of *groppo* (II, p. 46) as shown in Ex. *b*, and more importantly still, he endorses the Bernhard-Mylius *anticipatione della syllaba* and *della nota* (Exx. *c* and *d*); the former, he says, is best suited for rising or falling thirds.

Ex. 15.23. Fuhrmann (1706,1715)

Two things are noteworthy in Fuhrmann's work: first, the persisting rhythmic dualism of prebeat and onbeat types, and second, the shortness of the grace when it does occur on the beat.

Although the last few cited authors flourished during Bach's childhood and youth, with Johann Gottfried Walther (1684-1748), we move much closer to Bach. Walther was a close relative of Bach, his exact contemporary, and at least during the years of Bach's second stay in Weimar (1708-1717) the two became friends and were closely associated in many musical pursuits.

Walther wrote two important treatises. The first, *Praecepta der musicalischen Composition* (1708), remained in manuscript until its recent publication in 1955; the second, the famous *Musicalisches Lexicon*, was published in 1732.[23] The first of these is of special interest because it reflects Walther's ideas at the very start

the first admirers of Bach's music, not just of his organ virtuosity. One of the plagiarists was Johann Ludwig Steiner, with his *Kurz- leicht- und gründtliches Noten-Büchlein* (1728).

[23] All references to the *Praecepta* will be to the pages of the modern edition (ed. Benary). In this treatise, ornaments are dealt with on pp. 37-39, 120-121, and 152-156.

of his ten-year association with Bach. The next few paragraphs will refer to the *Praecepta* alone. There the Italo-German tradition concerning ornaments is still clearly dominant, though a few French elements are already discernible.

Walther leans strongly on Mylius for his discussion of one-note graces and agrees with him regarding the basically anticipatory nature of these ornaments, but deviates in the use of some terms.

The *Accent* (or *accentus, accentuatio, accento*) is first defined as "the manner of singing or playing in which prior to rendering the written note . . . its upper or lower neighbor is sounded so unobtrusively as to make both notes seem to be but one."[24] As symbols Walther lists ╱ or ⌒ for the ascending, ╲ or ⌣ for the descending type. They are, he says, usually marked for the keyboard but rarely for vocal works where they are left to the singer's discretion (p. 39). His significant illustration, given in Ex. 15.24*a*, shows the anticipatory nature of the grace and reveals the prebeat meaning of both his dash and hook symbols. The text furthermore implies that the unmarked, improvised *accenti* of the singers were of the same nature. (The terms *major* and *minor* in the legend refer to whole-step and half-step intervals of the grace.) However, by reproducing on p. 152 of the *Praecepta* the starting measures of Mylius's two illustrations (our Exx. 15.8 and 15.9), with their two onbeat and six prebeat *accenti*, he reveals the onbeat potential of this grace.

Ex. 15.24. Walther (1708)

Walther proceeds to explain another interbeat type of *Accent*, the *gedoppelter Accent*, a *Nachschlag* of the *anticipatione della nota* species, marked with Janowka's symbol of two vertical dashes (Ex. 15.24*b*). Then, referring to both the single and the "double" *accents*, both of which had just been shown to be of interbeat design, he makes the revealing statement that "the French indicate such *accents* in their printed vocal and instrumental works with very small notes placed next to the large ones."[25] This remark adds another significant confirmation for the interbeat meaning ascribed at the time to the French little notes. Walther adds that the *accents* must be rendered so gently and softly that one can hardly hear them. Such style is, of course, fully consistent with their purely melodic-connective function.

[24] "Es ist aber ein *Accent*, diejenige Art zu singen oder zu spielen, dass, ehe und bevor man die auf dem Papier vorhandene Note . . . *exprimiret*, die nächste entweder drüber oder drunter folgende Note dergestalt, *submisse* gehöret wird, dass es scheinet, als wenn beyde Noten nur eine zusammen wären," *Praecepta*, p. 38.

[25] Ibid., p. 39: "Diese *Accentuationes* pflegen die Frantzosen in ihren im Druck vorhandenen *Vocal-* und *Instrumental Sachen*, mit gantz kleinen, neben die andern grössern Noten, gesetzten ♪ zu *exprimiren*."

The other one-note graces are all listed under the term *subsumtio*, which in turn is equated with the always anticipatory *cercar della nota*. As subdivisions of these generic terms Walther lists the *anticipatione della syllaba* and *anticipatione della nota*. The former is the familiar pattern and he illustrates it with both of Mylius's models shown above in Ex. 15.10. The latter term, the *anticipatione della nota*, is not used in the same sense as it was by Bernhard, Mylius, Beyer, and others who referred with this term to prebeat pitch anticipation. As mentioned earlier, Walther called prebeat pitch anticipation *gedoppelter Accent*. What Walther calls and illustrates as *anticipatione della nota* (Ex. 15.25*a*) might confuse the terminology, but it commands our interest by offering evidence of a different kind. Since the term *anticipatione* obviously does not refer here to pitch, it can only refer to the value of the note, or else it would make no sense in this model. The French little notes which he uses in his illustration are therefore for the second time confirmed as anticipatory in character. A third confirmation is offered in the illustration of a mordent (Ex. *b*), the only other instance where the French little notes appear in this treatise. Not only would an onbeat execution be impractical in the given rhythm pattern, it would destroy the identity of the mordent for the first two graces which would bear no resemblance to the third, unembellished one.

Anticipatione della nota

Ex. 15.25. Walther (1708)

Between the *Praecepta* and the Bernhard-Mylius principles we thus find some divergencies of terminology, but agreement in substance. In the *Praecepta*, with the exception of the *accentus* which was first explained in anticipation but later incidentally revealed as being susceptible of occasional onbeat rendition, all the other one-note graces—including such *Vorschläge* as were written by little notes— were assigned to interbeat placement.

The twenty-four years which elapsed before the publication of the *Lexicon* in 1732 witnessed the main influx of French practices. During that time, too, certain other ornamental fashions had changed, and one of these changes was the growing popularity of the onbeat *Vorschlag*. This trend is reflected in the *Lexicon* when Walther writes in the article *Accento* that a long note following an *accento* loses only a little, whereas short notes may lose as much as half of their value. This, of course, implies an onbeat design but eliminates any extended rendition on long notes. In Table I, Figure 2, Walther gives as illustration three types of symbols, the hook, the little note, the little dash, and their onbeat resolution (Ex. 15.26).

a. [*Accentus*] *descendens, minor, simplex*   *b. Ascendens, major, simplex*

Ex. 15.26. Walther (1732)

This particular article has been quoted by various modern writers in support of the idea that onbeat rendition of the *Vorschlag* was the rule for Bach and his contemporaries. However, such a conclusion is fallacious. In addition to the *Praecepta* documents, the

Lexicon itself contains many more references to one-note graces under the following headings: *accento doppio, anticipatione della nota, anticipatione della syllaba, aspiration, cercar della nota, coulé, port de voix, superjectio*; and every one of these deals either exclusively or partially with interbeat placement. Of these graces, the *accento doppio* is the *gedoppelter Accent* of the *Praecepta* whose model (see above Ex. 15.24*b*) serves again as illustration in Table I, Figure 3 of the *Lexicon. Anticipatione della nota*, now in line with majority use, is described as the same type of *Nachschlag*, anticipating the sound of the following note, except that it can move only stepwise. It is illustrated in Table I, Figure 6 in the sense of Bernhard and Mylius. *Aspiration* is shown as the French *Nachschlag accent*, both rising and falling, with Saint Lambert's model (see above Ex. 13.6) reproduced in Table I, Figure 8. *Superjectio* is a rising *Nachschlag*, which Walther, in the article on *Accento doppio*, equates with Loulié's interbeat *accent* (see above Ex. 13.4). Walther shows Loulié's model in Table I, Figure 3. Janowka's similar *Nachschlag* design is referred to in the article *Einfall. Anticipatione della syllaba* follows the customary prebeat *Vorschlag* design, and Table I, Figure 7 reprints Mylius's two examples (see above Ex. 15.10) which had previously been reproduced in the *Praecepta*. Walther intimates that the grace might on occasion be detrimental to proper prosody, but Bach, as will be seen, did not share this concern. The *cercar della nota* refers to Mylius's anticipatory concept and repeats the statement that this grace is practically indistinguishable from the *accent*, thus conferring upon certain types of *accents* the prebeat character of the *cercar*.

The article dealing with the *coulé* refers impartially to D'Anglebert's onbeat model as well as to Saint Lambert's and Loulié's prebeat patterns, all of which are reproduced in Table X, Figure 2.

The *port de voix* is treated in the same way; the analogous conflicting patterns are explained and illustrated in Table XVIII, Figures 17 and 18.

The complete picture gained from the sum of these articles reflects the persisting ambivalence, the "Janus face," of the *Vorschlag* and the related graces: the onbeat design has made headway, but the interbeat designs in the form of both *Nachschläge* and anticipated *Vorschläge* are still very much alive. As far as Walther himself is concerned, this latter fact will be confirmed presently with musical evidence from his compositions.

MUSICAL EVIDENCE

Johann Pachelbel (1653-1706), uses very few ornament symbols except for the trill and has no signs for *Vorschläge, Nachschläge*, or slides. He writes out innumerable prebeat *Vorschläge* but practically none of the Lombard type. Thirds, either rising or falling, are almost routinely filled in between the beat, thereby revealing a distinct ornamental preference. Example 15.27 gives one representative illustration.[26]

Ex. 15.27. Pachelbel, 32nd Suite, Sarabande

Johann Kuhnau (1660-1722) discusses ornaments briefly in the preface to his *Neuer Clavier-Übung Erster Theil*.[27] The *accentus*, he says, is marked with a little oblique dash that can either follow or precede a note. If it follows, it is obviously

[26] Example from *Hexachordum Apollinis, DDT*, 2nd ser., vol. 2, pt. 2.

[27] *Neuer Clavier-Übung Erster Theil* (1689); *Neuer Clavier-Übung Andrer Theil* (1692).

a *Nachschlag*, and Kuhnau illustrates it by referring to the start of Piece No. 21 shown in Ex. 15.28, where it is marked by an asterisk.

Ex. 15.28. Kuhnau (1689), Sarabande

Kuhnau offers no illustration of the dash that precedes a note and signifies a *Vorschlag*. His verbal explanation of it is not clear, and the translation can only be tentative: "These [*accents*] touch very delicately and softly upon the tone of the second, above or below, depending on whether the [principal] note rises or falls and [they may touch] quasi-twice, in which case they could also result in a type of ornament in which the note, despite the fact that a different one immediately follows, will thus be heard a little longer and hence more pleasingly."[28] What seems to be implied are two alternatives (indicated by the words "could also result"). One is a simple *Vorschlag*, the other a double one: Kuhnau does not mention it, but the direction of the dash certainly indicates rise or fall of the grace. It is likely that Kuhnau's *Vorschläge* conformed with the dominant usage of the time, that is, of being susceptible of both prebeat and onbeat designs. Karl Päsler, who edited the *Clavier-Übung* for the *DDT*, sees, with good reason, both possibilities.

Apart from environmental considerations, several more reasons speak for the frequent, probably predominant, anticipation. In Kuhnau's lifetime, Walther interpreted the dash symbol on the upbeat. Also, the great frequency of occurrence militates against a regular onbeat rendition considering the latter's strong "spice" value. In Ex. 15.29, for instance, insistent onbeat placement would be for these very reasons musically unsatisfactory. The effect would be ungraceful, indeed clumsy, and weaken the driving force of the dotted rhythm. By contrast, anticipation would add brilliance without damaging the rhythm. Moreover, we see how the very first *accentus*, here as well as in many other cases, is ambiguous: it is impossible to decide whether it belongs as *Nachschlag* to the preceding or as *Vorschlag* to the following note. Such ambiguity did not matter as long as the *Vorschläge* were anticipated.

Ex. 15.29. Kuhnau, *Partie II*, Allemande

In a concurrence of mordent and *Vorschlag* such as the one shown in Ex. 15.30, the likeliest solution is their successive rendition with anticipation of the *Vorschlag*.

---

28 "Diese touchieren die Secunde vorher entweder drüber oder drunter nach dem die Note auf oder niedergestiegen fein sachte, und gleichsam zweymal, woraus auch diese Manier folgen kann, dass der gleichen Note, ungeachtet eine andere gleiche folget, etwas länger und also angenehmer gehöret werde." *Neuer Clavier-Übung Erster Theil*, Preface.

In the keyboard works written after the two parts of the *Clavier-Übung,* Kuhnau limits himself again to indicating trills. In the preface to *Frische Clavier Früchte* (1696) he tells the reader that in his previous works [meaning the *Clavier-Übung*] he had shown how to use the other ornaments. Now he leaves it to the performer to use his own judgment in applying them and in choosing their fitting designs.

Ex. 15.30. Kuhnau, *Partie II*, Bourrée

Additional evidence about the anticipation of Kuhnau's *Vorschläge* can be found in the *Andreas Bach Buch*, a very important manuscript from Bach's inner circle.[29] This manuscript contains a few of Kuhnau's Biblical Sonatas with some added ornaments. In the three excerpts shown in Ex. 15.31 the placement of the *Vorschlag* notes before the bar line in both stepwise and leaping designs establishes their upbeat meaning. It should be noted that these Kuhnau works were written by the chief scribe of the *ABB* (Bernhard Bach?) in a calligraphic copy. This is not conclusive proof about Kuhnau's own ideas, since it was not he who wrote in this manner, but it is important evidence about ornamental practices in the inner circle of Bach's family.

a. 2nd Sonata *(ABB)*   *b.* 5th Sonata *(ABB)*

c. 5th Sonata *(ABB)*

Ex. 15.31. Kuhnau

The written-out *anticipatione della syllaba* was perhaps as common in Germany during the 17th century as it was in Italy. Example 15.32 shows sample specimens from the century's end, taken from Erlebach (Ex. *a*) and Bruhns (Ex. *b*).

Reinhard Keiser (1674-1739) may have been, along with Bach and Walther, among the early users of the little notes in Germany. In *Adonis* of 1697, his oldest preserved opera, the autograph (contrary to Goldschmidt's belief), contains no ornaments at all, not even trills.[30] In his opera *Janus* of 1698 there are no little notes either (with the exception of

---

29 Spitta (*Bach,* I, 795, n. 18) explains why the *Andreas Bach Buch* was presumably written by Bach's nephew Bernhard Bach while he studied with Johann Sebastian between 1715 and 1717. The manuscript contains fourteen works by Johann Sebastian, in addition to a number of compositions by fifteen identified masters, including Kuhnau, Böhm, Buxtehude, Pachelbel, Marais, Fischer, and a few

unidentified ones. After Bernhard's death the book passed into the possession of his brother Andreas who wrote his name on the title page but had nothing to do with its contents.

30 *Adonis,* aut. BB Mus. MS 11488; *Janus,* aut. BB, Mus. MS 11481; Goldschmidt claims that all of Keiser's written-out *Vorschläge* were "iambic," meaning anticipated.

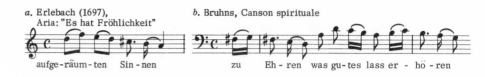

a. Erlebach (1697),
Aria: "Es hat Fröhlichkeit"

aufge-räum-ten Sin-nen

b. Bruhns, Canson spirituale

zu Eh-ren was gu-tes lass er - hö-ren

Ex. 15.32.

Julia's aria in the third act which, however, is an insert in a different hand). For the rest, we find in this work, and in all other operas that could be inspected, a multitude of written-out cases of the *anticipatione della syllaba*, like the three in one measure shown in Ex. 15.33, the second of which falls on the accented syllable *Won-*.

du mei - ner See - len Won - ne

Ex. 15.33. Keiser, *Janus*, III, 5

The autograph of *Circe* (1702) used a fair amount of little notes (BB Mus. MS autogr. Keiser 1), *Massaniello Furioso* of 1706 many more. Surprisingly, the later *Fredegunda* (1715) contains no ornaments except one solitary slide.

Keiser wrote the little notes mostly as 16th-notes, occasionally as 32nds and 8ths, with no discernible pattern or consistency. The short values suggest brevity and, considering the prevailing fashions in the early years of the century as well as Keiser's innumerable written-out prebeat *Vorschläge*, it is likely that many of his little *Vorschlag* notes were meant to be anticipated.

In Walther's music many passages point to the prebeat character of some of the little notes.[31] There are many cases of the *Nachschlag* in the French *accent* design with its characteristic rise before the fall and its slur to the preceding note (Ex. 15.34a). There are also instances where the slur is omitted but the identical character is unmistakable (Ex. *b*), or where the slur to the preceding note simply indicates interbeat rendition as *Zwischenschlag* in such contexts as rising or falling thirds (Ex. *c*). In Ex. *d* the prebar notation clarifies the anticipation of what is musically unquestionably a *Vorschlag* and not a *Nachschlag*; Ex. *e* shows the anticipation of leaping *Vorschläge*; Ex. *f* exhibits an unusual notation that joins the graces to the main notes, ingeniously indicating that the latter must remain in place. Though the first of these is written as *Vorschlag*, the second as *Nach-schlag*, their musical function is the identical one of interbeat *tierces coulées*. Example *g* shows Walther's use of the hook symbol in what is quite certainly an appoggiatura.

To SUMMARIZE briefly, we find that the rhythmic dualism of the *Vorschlag* as formulated by Praetorius (after Bovicelli) runs like a leitmotiv through the whole period and that its decisive presence could be documented in the inner circle of J. S. Bach during the crucial years of his stylistic development.

[31] All examples from *Gesammelte Werke für Orgel, DDT*, 1st ser., vols. 26-27, ed. Max Seiffert, new ed. Wiesbaden-Graz, 1958, crit. rev. H. J. Moser.

Ex. 15.34. Walther

A good part of the story of Bach's one-note graces has already been written in those chapters which outline the picture of the environmental situation in France, Italy, and Germany during Bach's youthful years (1695-1710). In that period we have found in all three countries a widespread use of *Nachschläge* and *Zwischenschläge*, and a variety of *Vorschläge* in their double-faced prebeat and onbeat shapes.

Given this environmental situation and Bach's previously described multinational studies, we have reason to speculate that he availed himself of a variety of existent designs. The study of Bach's music confirms this speculation and reveals that he did use what he found among his models of those years throughout his lifetime. As far as the *Vorschläge* are concerned, his use appears to have ranged approximately as indicated in the tabulation of Ex. 16.1, that is, from the anticipated "grace note" to an appoggiatura that can take from short binary notes (8th-notes and less frequently quarter-notes) up to about half their value, and from ternary notes up to about one-third of their value. What is labeled in the tabulation as "overlong" designs, such as one-half of a long binary note (half-note or more) or two-thirds of a ternary note, was generally not intended. Exceptions always occur, but they must have been rare. The "overlong" interpretations were mostly later developments brought to the fore by the *galant* style. Musical evidence will confirm their inappropriateness for Bach's music.

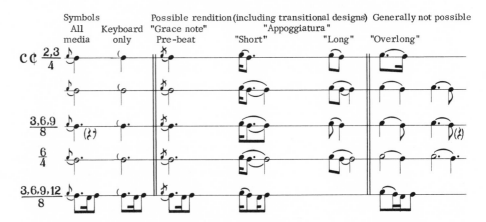

Ex. 16.1. Approximate Range of Meanings for Bach's Most Important *Vorschlag* Symbols

For the symbol-indicated *Vorschläge*, the appoggiaturas—especially in vocal music—most likely outnumber the grace notes, but the latter do play a substantial role. Contrary to widely held opinion, there are for Bach no rules that present us with easy solutions for the realization of his symbols, and a measure of orientation can be achieved only by analyzing musical evidence.

To designate one-note graces, Bach used the French little note for all media, most frequently in the form of an 8th-note, fairly often in the form of a 16th, rarely of a quarter, never of a half-note.[1] Often Bach slurs the little note to the following note: ♪ thus identifying the grace as a *Vorschlag*; sometimes the little note is encompassed within a slur that comprises both adjoining notes: ♪♪ thus clarifying its *Zwischenschlag* character; very rarely does he slur the little note to the left neighbor: ♪♪ to designate it as a *Nachschlag* (in contrast to Walther who did so very frequently). Very often, in fact far more often than would appear from modern editions, the little note is left unslurred. In many of these cases we have to do with a *Vorschlag*, and the omission of the slur, due either to haste or to indifference, has no specific significance. In cases, however, where such an unattached little note has *Zwischenschlag* or *Nachschlag* character, the omission of the slur to the following note *alone* was logical and doubtless purposive.[2]

The values of the little notes have no literal meaning. That Bach's rare little quarter-note, for instance, has no direct meaning can be gathered from almost every case in which it appears. In Cantata 69, the original voice part, written by Bach's copyist under his supervision (St 68), has the same phrase (Ex. 16.2) written twice with quarter-notes and a third time with 8th-notes; in the instrumental parts this same phrase is written with 8th-notes more than twenty times. On the other hand, when Bach goes to the trouble of writing a 16th-note grace, he most likely had brevity in mind. Quantz, who did *not* use the literal correlation of his Berlin colleagues, was still to note this meaning of the 16th, as contrasted to the 8th-note denomination (as will be seen below).

Ex. 16.2. BWV 69, 5 (St 68)

Bach's other symbol, the hook with or without a slur mark: ♪ is limited exclusively to the keyboard.[3] Here, the duality of *Vorschlag* symbols,

[1] There are even fewer quarter-note symbols than would appear on the first inspection of the autographs. What may look like a quarter-note and has been taken as such by Bach's copyists is frequently an 8th with an atrophied flag. As regards the few half-note symbols which once in a while appear in modern editions, they derive from unreliable sources and are unauthentic. A case can be found in *NBA*, IV, vol. 6, p. 54 at the end of the Organ Prelude in G major (BWV 568) whose primary source is a 19th-century copy.

[2] Unfortunately, the *NBA* has made it a principle of editorial policy—as the *BG* had mostly done before—to slur every little note to the note that follows it without identifying the editorial addition as such by different print or parentheses. This is being done on the mistaken premise that every single little note is a *Vorschlag* and that Bach's omission of the slur was simply due to an oversight which ought to be remedied. This editorial policy disregards

the fact that not infrequently the little note stands for a *Zwischenschlag* or even a *Nachschlag*, in which cases the editorial addition misrepresents Bach's intentions. Such "reconstruction" is particularly incongruous in those cases where the little note is encompassed in a larger slur that extends to the preceding note: ♪♪ because it results in a pattern totally foreign to Bach's usage, since he never wrote a slur within a slur, except to indicate a tie. Several examples of such illegitimate reconstructions will be given in the course of this chapter. Though many of these additions used to be listed in the *Kritische Bericht*, not all of them were; at best they were cumbersome to sift out, besides being inaccessible to non-German-speaking readers. But beginning with the publication in 1969 of Volume I 40, even this practice was discontinued.

[3] This statement may bewilder those who have seen countless hooks in the vocal works as they appear in the *BG* edition and other

hooks or little notes, might suggest a differentiation of meaning such as that found in Dieupart or Le Roux. However, there is no evidence to support such an assumption for Bach. All indications point to the essential identity of meaning for the two types of symbols. In parallel spots, in different copies of the same piece, the two symbols are frequently interchanged with complete indifference. Example 16.3, showing the start of the Loure from the 5th French Suite in the autograph from the "Note Book" of Anna Magdalena, provides a characteristic illustration. There a little note is written for the theme, a hook for its imitation in the bass.

Ex. 16.3. BWV 816, 6 (aut. P 224), Loure

There may be only one case on record, in the Sarabande from the 5th Partita, mm. 20 and 22, where Bach used hooks and little notes simultaneously with seemingly different meaning. The case is, however, not authenticated by an autograph, the primary source being the original, rather poor, print of 1731. Assuming the authenticity of the text, a differentiation between the two symbols would be necessary in m. 22 (see Ex. 16.4) where identical execution would produce objectionable parallels. One possible solution would be anticipation of the hook and short onbeat rendition of the little notes.[4]

Ex. 16.4. BWV 829, 4, Sarabande

THE EXPLICATION

Every discussion of Bach's ornaments has to come to terms with the famous *Explicatio* (an "n" was added later, possibly by Bach, to make the word read *Explication*), the small table of ornaments which Bach wrote in 1720 along with other elementary explanations at the beginning of the *Clavierbüchlein vor Wilhelm Friedemann Bach*, his first-born son, then ten years old. This table, far from being a ready and easy key to Bach's ornamental usages, has proved more of a hindrance than a help; the respect for its autograph authenticity has

———

publications based on it. However, as the editor Wilhelm Rust explained in the preface to Volume XII, the hooks were strictly an editorial device to indicate a little note that was absent in the autograph score but present in the original performance parts. While this procedure provided a ready insight into an interesting source situation, it gave a misleading impression about Bach's use of the hook symbol in non-keyboard works.

[4] Hans Bischoff in his Steingräber edition was bewildered by this spot with its combination of hooks and small notes and speculated that the hooks may stand for a mordent. However, Bach never used a hook as a mordent symbol, while some French masters who did placed it after not before the note.

prompted scholars and performing musicians alike to take its models at face value and has prevented them from seeing its limitations. Example 16.5 shows the models for the *Vorschlag* (*accent*).

Ex. 16.5. *Explication*

Several comments need to be made to place this document into a better perspective. First, everything said before about ornament tables and their limitations applies to this one. Second, Bach's descriptive title reads: "Explication unterschiedlicher Zeichen, so gewisse manieren artig zu spielen, andeuten" (Explanation of various signs, intimating the way of gracefully rendering certain ornaments). The word *andeuten*, meaning to intimate, to hint, emphasizes the approximate nature of the models. Third, the table was written as a first introduction for a child, hence in a situation that more than any other calls for oversimplification. Fourth, the models were basically excerpted from the much larger table of D'Anglebert to provide a first introduction to certain French practices which an aspiring clavier player needed to learn; the models were not qualified to do justice to Bach's own much broader and more diversified needs. The casualness of this table is further disclosed by its incompleteness, notably the failure to include the most important symbol of all, the little note; also missing is the *custos* symbol for the slide: .

There is another qualifying factor which seems to have been overlooked so far, namely the fact that all the symbols of the *Explication* are strictly limited to the keyboard. Among all the signs, only the turn: occurs once in a while in late vocal works, and seemingly never in orchestral and chamber music. The appearance of any of the other symbols in non-keyboard music is very rare and probably is inadvertent.[5]

All things considered, the table tells us that the graces in question *may* have the shapes indicated, but not that they *must* have these shapes which, as will be shown, are often disqualified by musical evidence.

THE main problem regarding Bach's one-note graces—as with those of most 18th-century composers—is their rhythmic-dynamic disposition. Modern doctrine for the greatest part—a few exceptions will be quoted—fails to recognize the prebeat-onbeat dualism, the "Janus-face," of Bach's *Vorschläge* and limits the *Vorschläge* to the onbeat design. Moreover, most modern researchers apply to Bach the "overlong" patterns that were derived from the midcentury treatises. Our tabulation at the outset of the chapter was intended to point up the need to revise these ideas.

[5] In the very early Cantata 106 (*Actus Tragicus*), the sign **W** is used for trills, but it is probably unauthentic; no autograph exists and the earliest source is a MS of 1768.

It is true that certain long *Vorschlag* interpretations had existed before Bach's time. The French in their *vocal* music had occasionally used the *port de voix feint* (of Type 4), though only very rarely its descending counterpart. The *coulé*, except as a trill preparation in the *tremblement feint*, appears in most, if not all, theoretical sources in short designs only that do not exceed an 8th-note. In the Italo-German tradition, the *accenti*, both rising and falling, whether taken on or before the beat, were all basically short. The theoretical documents that have been presented—from Bovicelli through Praetorius, Herbst, Crüger, and Printz, and from Bernhard through Mylius, Feyertag, Murschhauser, Fuhrmann, and Beyer to Walther—bear out this fact and, as remains to be shown, so will documentation on several masters and theoreticians who flourished well into the middle of the 18th century. C.P.E. Bach, in midcentury, confirms the newness of the long designs and their association with the "new" (i.e. the *galant*) style in a passage that will be quoted below. Quantz, in another passage yet to be quoted, affirms the same link by stressing the need in *galant airs* for long appoggiaturas to relieve the monotony of their "simpleminded melodies." The *galant* style with its simple texture and slow harmonic rhythm not only needed these designs, as Quantz so pointedly remarked, but could easily accommodate them: there was harmony to be enriched and no polyphony to be disturbed. The opposite was the case with the polyphonic style of the late baroque masters, and in particular with Bach's more than commonly dense and complex textures and his fast-moving harmonic rhythm. Here "overlong" *Vorschlag* interpretations not only constituted a menace to polyphony but were far less needed for enrichment of an already exceptionally rich harmony. Whenever Bach wanted an appoggiatura of more than 8th-note length, he *had* to write it out in regular notes because such desired interpretation would not have been understood from the symbol. (The *galant* masters who used such long interpretations had to introduce new symbols that would clarify their meaning.) Very often Bach wrote out in regular notation 8th-, 16th-, and even 32nd-note appoggiaturas, though such interpretation *could* have been meant by the symbol. The implications of these notational choices will be discussed later, after a number of pertinent illustrations have been shown.

If to all these historical and stylistic considerations are added the following facts—that in many cases the overlong interpretation leads to musical incongruities; that the overlong rendition is often hard to reconcile with Bach's bass figuring; that Bach's editorial casualness in adding *Vorschlag* symbols to the performance parts without adding the same graces in all unison parts is understandable only if the graces were innocuously short—then the case is strong indeed for the thesis that the "overlong" formulas were anachronistic for Bach's ornament style and that consequently there is no historical justification for applying them in those instances where they happen to be musically possible.

Concerning the formula for dotted notes, examples abound to show that is neither nor

Only a few cases can be given here. In Ex. 16.6*a* from Cantata 89, such execution would be musically incongruous in that an appoggiatura of 8th-note length on g' would, after its harsh clash with the f' sharp of the harmony, "resolve" to another major seventh (the f' sharp with the g in the bass). Therefore, the *Vorschlag* has to be shorter than an 8th-note.

In Ex. *b* from Cantata 210, approximate synchronization of the graces in voice and instruments within the brief unison confluence of the two parts makes best musical sense; the second instrumental grace before the even 16th-notes was most likely intended for anticipation, which would reflect an analogous approximate *tierces coulées* treatment of the first one. Surely the overlong formula cannot be applied to the dotted quarter-note on *Brust*. In Ex. *c* from the Gigue of the French Overture, the second measure shows that the *Vorschlag* cannot have quarter-note or dotted quarter-note duration, which means that in m. 1 it cannot have been thus intended either, though here such length is musically possible. The formula is clearly inapplicable in countless other passages, which any interested reader can easily find. Moreover, in the many cases listed below where a *Vorschlag* before a dotted note would, on the beat, create parallels, a long and overlong execution would strongly enhance their offensiveness (see for instance Exx. 16.15*a*, 16.17*a*, *b*, *g*).

Ex. 16.6.

It has been argued (by Arthur Mendel in a personal communication) that in the violin obbligato of the alto aria "Erbarme dich" from the *St. Matthew Passion*, the "overlong" i.e. 2:1, interpretation of the *Vorschlag* before the prevailing siciliano pattern in m. 3 (Ex. 16.7*a*)—and in presumable analogy also in mm. 11, 12, 17, 18, 25, 28, 29, 31, 34-36, 41, and 42—finds support (an "echo") in the violin figure of m. 16 (Ex. *b*). Professor Mendel finds the "bittersweet" clash of such appoggiaturas (in m. 3) with the main notes in the *tutti* in accord with the affect of the piece. The argument is unconvincing. Several reasons speak against the equivalence of the pattern in m. 16 with that of the *Vorschlag*-siciliano design of m. 17 (given in the same Ex. *b*). It is hardly a coincidence that the pattern of m. 16 recurs in mm. 40-41 in an exact parallel spot (Ex. *c*) where the voice rests on a long note, whereas in the following measure, as before, little *Vorschlag* notes are written when the dotted notes of the violin coincide in quasi-unison with the voice. In other words, the two styles of *Vorschlag* notation occur in completely different musical contexts. The interpretation based on the "echo" theory, as given in Ex. *d* for mm. 16-17, is questionable also for its notational illogic. The methodical difference of spelling suggests a difference of execution, the more so since the notation in m. 17  is more troublesome to write than ⟦figure⟧ It is difficult to assume that Bach went to *greater* trouble to be *less* specific, and risk a different interpretation, when he wanted "overlong" identity with the "echo." If we further add that an "echo" rendition would obliterate the pervasive siciliano rhythm, which appears to be of the rhythmic essence, the conclusion seems inevitable that mm. 16 and 40 provide an argument *against* not *for* the overlong interpretation.

*In the autograph written as a″, presumably by mistake.

Ex. 16.7. BWV 244, 47 (aut. P 25)

The other type of "overlong" interpretation that is not connected with a dotted but with a tied binary note ⟦figure⟧ = ⟦figure⟧ is linked to Bach even more precariously.

It was apparently unknown in France where none of the numerous 17th- and 18th-century ornament tables I consulted mentions the design. In Italy, where theoretical sources are scarce, it *may* have come into use toward the middle of the 18th century, but neither Tartini nor Geminiani mentions it. The first appearance that I could trace is in the books of C.P.E. Bach, Leopold Mozart, and Agricola, all of whom, however, indicate the length of the *Vorschlag* in these patterns by the denomination of the symbol. The pattern is not mentioned by Quantz and Marpurg. Considering these circumstances, as well as what was said before about the illogic of such "overlong" symbol interpretation for a polyphonic master, it should not be necessary to give more than a few illustrations to show the incongruousness of an interpretation that assigns to the *Vorschlag* the full values of the principal note and resolves the latter on the tied note.

In Ex. 16.8*a* from the B minor Flute-Clavier Sonata, 8th-note, and in Ex. *b* not only 8th- but even 16th-note, meaning is musically impossible. In the 2nd Bourrée of the French Overture the overlong (here a half-note) interpretation happens to be possible in m. 1 as well as in mm. 2, 21, and 22, but it is revealed as incorrect in m. 24 (Ex. *c*).

Ex. 16.8.

In addition to all the foregoing, there is further evidence against the overlong pattern in the bass figuring, especially for *Vorschläge* that would under these formulas exceed the length of an 8th-note. Wilhelm Rust had, at least in rough outline, gained this insight a hundred years ago when he pointed out that Bach's figuring, which follows, as he put it, the smallest inflections of all voices, never acknowledges the *Vorschlag*. "From this we can gather," he writes, "that this [i.e. Bach's] *Vorschlag* must not through arbitrary lengthening disturb either the purity of the harmony or the voice leading."[6] The statement must be strongly qualified inasmuch as fast-moving notes cannot be reflected in the figures and often even longer notes, and among them many a written-out appoggiatura, do not show up in Bach's figures (see e.g. the "Domine Deus" of the *B minor Mass*, mm. 2, 13, etc.). However, the fact that very many of Bach's written-out *Vorschläge are* reflected in the figures, whereas none of those indicated by symbol are (if there should be exceptions they must be extremely rare), provides a contrast so striking that it can hardly be explained other than by the basic shortness of Bach's symbolized appoggiaturas.

[6] *BG*, vol. 7, p. xiv.

Illustrations confirming the basic shortness of Bach's symbol-indicated *Vorschläge* are so many that they could fill a book; only a few samples will be shown here. In Ex. 16.9a from Cantata 97, diction suggests onbeat rendition, but an 8th-note duration would result in offensive fifths. In Ex. *b* from Cantata 201, penetrating fifths would result from an analogous execution in mm. 24, 25, and 72. In Ex. *c* from the same work a rather unthinkable unison would be created by the same style.[7]

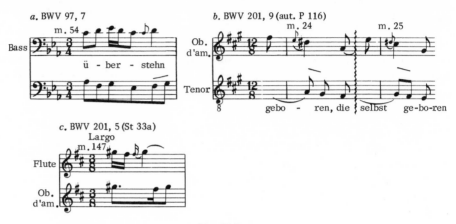

Ex. 16.9.

Beyschlag, like Rust, stresses the basic shortness of Bach's *Vorschläge* and gives a number of good examples on pp. 122-127 of *Die Ornamentik der Musik*. Bodky, though accepting the prevalent textbook formulas as basically valid, demonstrates the need for exceptions in his "Appoggiatura Table" (pp. 378-381 of *The Interpretation of Bach's Keyboard Works*) where every single one of the seventeen examples illustrates the incongruity of these very formulas.

VERY SHORT AND ANTICIPATED DESIGNS

It is difficult to separate completely the very short onbeat and the anticipated designs, because there are many cases in which the musical evidence points to extreme shortness of the *Vorschlag* without limiting it to one rhythmic style alone. The other point is this: whereas on the dynamically inflexible baroque keyboard (except the clavichord) the difference between prebeat and onbeat rendition will be quite clear whenever a distinct beat is present in another voice, it will be less clear in concerted music when the graces in question are sung or played by an instrument capable of dynamic nuance. In these cases, given the agogic accents of artistic execution and the greater natural flexibilities and inaccuracies of ensemble performance, the on- or prebeat alternative of a very short grace can become a moot point. In such circumstances a distinction between very short *Vorschlag* categories resides more in their dynamic alternative of being or not being accented. If accented, the grace will be heard as appoggiatura; if unaccented, as grace note regardless of whether either of them happens to fall on or before the beat. In the following discussion no attempt is made to formulate

---

[7] The *Vorschlag* was added in the original flute part (St 33a). For a few more examples where ♪ cannot be ♪ or ♪ not ♪ see Cantata 2,5, mm. 5 and 61; 8,4, m. 18; 27,1, mm. 14, 15, and 20; 47,4, m. 34; 51,3, m. 20; 77,3, m. 21; 97,2, mm. 68 and 70; 210,8, m. 39; *Christmas Oratorio*, 29, m. 5.

rules; I am simply trying to indicate tendencies of various degrees of urgency which have to be assessed on their individual merit.

The prebeat *Vorschlag* of the type called *anticipatione della syllaba* was, as will be remembered, lavishly used by the Italians and Germans throughout the 17th century and was described by many German theorists from Bernhard to Walther. Bach's occasional use of it, in written-out form, is one of many signs showing the 17th-century roots of his ornamental style. Illustrations of this use are given in Ex. 16.10.

The first example (*a*) is from the early Cantata No. 131 (1707), the second (*b*) from Cantata 84 (see also mm. 68, 75, and 93, each time with different words). Interesting is the prebeat phrasing of the accented syllable—*gnügt* which elsewhere in this movement, for instance in mm. 34 and 35, is placed on the beat. Examples *c* from Cantata 169, *d* from Cantata 172, and *e* from Cantata 100 provide further llustrations, the first two for a descending, the last for an ascending *Vorschlag* (see also below Ex. 16.26*b* from the *St. Matthew Passion* and Ex. 21.1*d* from Cantata 84). The purpose of these examples is to show that Bach was not averse to the sound of a prebeat *Vorschlag* even where it is not overly congenial to diction.

Ex. 16.10.

Interesting *external evidence* that hooks can stand for anticipation as easily as the little notes is found in an important early source for the French Suites (P 418). According to von Dadelsen, the manuscript, which dates from approximately 1723, was written by one of Bach's students.[8] In it the many hooks are written close to notes that occur in the middle of a measure, but when the hooks occur at the start of a bar, there is an unmistakable attempt throughout the manuscript

[8] *NBA*, V, 3, p. X; Landshoff (p. 20) had previously assumed that the scribe belonged to Bach's inner circle. He is the same scribe who wrote the earliest known source of the English Suites (P 1072) and a very early copy of the Inventions and Sinfonias (P 219) which was in the possession of Wilhelm Friedemann Bach.

to shift them across, or at least place them astride, the bar line. This happens consistently, even when there was much space available (see Exx. 16.11a and b). Prebar and crossbar hooks in the P 219 manuscript of the G minor Sinfonia (Ex. c) seem equally suggestive of prebeat intention. In the recently discovered manuscript of the French Suites written by the devoted Bach student Heinrich Nicolaus Gerber, we find a number of clear prebeat notations of hooks, three of which—suggesting an anticipated auxiliary to a trill—are given in Exx. d, e, and f.

In this connection it is of additional significance that Gerber—in an autograph collection of his own compositions (Princeton University Library, AM 16915) dated 17 July 1727—while still in Leipzig, repeatedly uses the clearly intentional prebar notation of the hook symbol. In Ex. 16.11g this is shown as anticipated coulés, in Ex. h as a prebeat port de voix before a pincé at the start of m. 2 of the example and as an anticipated auxiliary of a trill at the start of m. 4 (reflecting the identical meaning for the trill in the first measure); and again as prebeat port de voix in Ex. i.

Ex. 16.11.

Another revealing document from Bach's innermost circle, the prebar notation of little Vorschlag notes in the Andreas Bach Buch, was reported in the preceding chapter and illustrated above in Exx. 15.31a-c.

Another type of external evidence can be found in the Canonic Variations of 1748. In the Canon per augmentationem (Variation 4), the Vorschläge in mm. 2, 10, and 21 (Ex. 16.12a) as they appear in the original print are ignored in the augmentations of mm. 4, 19, and 41 respectively (Ex. b). Only a very short, and more likely a prebeat, grace could have been thus omitted in the otherwise mathematically precise augmentation. In Bach's late autograph (P 271) the second of the three *Vorschläge* is left out, which would further seem to confirm its intended inconspicuousness.

Ex. 16.12. BWV 769 (orig. print), Variation 4

Two main principles of what could be called *contrapuntal logic* can provide guidance for ornament execution. One is the need to avoid *offensive* parallels, the other is the desirability not to impinge on the polyphonic relationship of the voices.

The avoidance of parallels will almost always require shortness and often anticipation. A striking case is presented by the passages from the *Art of the Fugue* of 1749-1750 given in Exx. 16.13a and b. In the first place, the *Vorschlag* precedes a written-out appoggiatura. When Quantz formulated the rule that a *Vorschlag* before a written-out appoggiatura must be anticipated,[9] he expressed a principle of musical common sense that transcends a single age and style. Here, moreover, the appoggiatura is prepared, and onbeat rendition of the *Vorschlag* would obliterate the dissonant suspension by sounding the empty octave. This by itself is sufficient to require the prebeat execution. Besides, the onbeat style would produce hidden octaves which are particularly disturbing when the same passage appears in inversion (Ex. *b*). It was pointed out in Chapter 3 that not every parallel is noticeable enough to make its impact felt on the design of ornaments. Here, however, there can be little doubt about their implications. In this supreme manifesto of the art of voice-leading, and in the strictest possible setting of a two-part canon, the octaves that would result from the onbeat execution cannot have been intended.

Ex. 16.13. BWV 1080, 14 (aut. P 200), Canon per Augmentationem in contrario motu

Scarcely less convincing are some passages from the equally late (1748) *Canonic Variations*, shown in Ex. 16.14. In the first of these (Ex. *a*) the tie of the two c's across the beat (in both the autograph P 271 and the original print) is in itself sufficient indication that the little note d′ is a *Zwischenschlag*; furthermore, onbeat execution here would destroy the suspension effect and create open octaves. In Ex. *b* the prebeat execution is needed to avoid objectionable fifths. It is a fair assumption that most little notes in Variation 3 (*Canone alla Settima*)

[9] *Versuch*, ch. 8, par. 6.

are interbeat graces (except the one on the final note, and perhaps the two in m. 9).

Ex. 16.14. BWV 769, Variation 3

Fifths probably also rule out the onbeat style in Ex. 16.15a from the 6th Organ Sonata. In Ex. b from the Sarabande of the 6th Partita, onbeat execution with its ensuing open fifths is hardly possible. Anticipation of the grace and an addition of a mordent on the following note seem indicated. In Ex. c from the Organ Fantasy in C minor, onbeat performance would create fifths between the two graces; anticipation of one of the two seems the best way to avoid the parallels. In Ex. d from the Harpsichord Suite in E flat major, the hooks in the first measure could be played before, straddling, or on the beat (shorter than 8th-notes); the hook in the second measure would produce on-the-beat fifths that favor anticipation while definitely requiring great brevity. The whole piece is actually filled with hooks for which anticipation often seems the best solution.

The Toccata in G minor contains in its principal source (written by Preller in Bach's lifetime) the passage given in Ex. e. The little note will have to be anticipated to avoid open octaves. (The fingerings are from the manuscript and give every indication of having been written by the original scribe.) Example f from the G sharp minor Fugue (WC II) suggests the need for anticipation of the grace to avoid disagreeable hidden octaves.

Ex. 16.15.

Bodky (p. 179) points to the 13th of the *Goldberg Variations* where the prebeat *Vorschlag* is needed to avoid "very ugly parallel octaves" in m. 17, and "equally bad parallel fifths" in mm. 25 and 26 (Exx. 16.16a-c). Emery, too, refers to m. 17 and considers prebeat rendition obligatory (p. 77, Ex. 158).

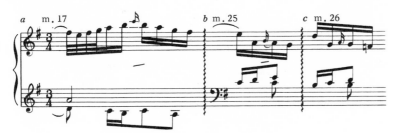

Ex. 16.16. BWV 988, Variation 13

Outside of the keyboard literature there are many more instances of similar evidence provided by parallels, and the following examples show only a few specimens.

Onbeat rendition would produce fifths in Ex. 16.17a from the Flute Sonata in E major; fifths also would occur in Ex. *b* from the 6th Violin-Clavier Sonata.

In Ex. *c* from the *A major Mass*, onbeat style would result in fifths between soprano (reinforced by the first violins) and alto (reinforced by second violins). Examples *d* from Cantata 210 and *e* from Cantata 137 present an interesting situation in which onbeat execution would produce not just one but two pairs of parallel fifths in succession—in the first example between oboe and soprano, in the second between soprano and bass.[10] Both examples are surpassed by the passage from Cantata 215,9 (Ex. *f*) where no less than three pairs of parallel fifths in a row would result unless the *tierces coulées* are played before the beats. In the next example (*g*) from Cantata 134, the *Vorschlag* was presumably added to the oboes to fill in as *Zwischenschlag* the leap of a third and make them, slightly ahead of the beat, smoothly join the unison with the violins.

It stands to reason that in linear music the execution of an ornament ought not to interfere with the basic relationships of the voices. Hence the degree of freedom with which, say, a *Vorschlag* can be manipulated—especially with regard to its length—will depend on the complexity of the texture and on the speed of the harmonic or the polyphonic rhythm. The term "polyphonic rhythm" will be used to signify the speed with which the single notes of the fastest moving melodic line succeed each other. What matters here is the sequence of structural linear impulses, not the succession of notes that simply break a chord in arpeggio fashion or are purely ornamental. Because a *Vorschlag* or any other inserted grace could strongly affect the linear relationships if it were to outlast two or more linear impulses in another voice, only a short grace can prevent such interference.

While Bach was occasionally casual about some aspects of notation that did not greatly matter, he was on the whole very particular about the concordance of polyphonic lines and consequently wrote out most *Vorschläge* or other ornaments that were contrapuntally sensitive and whose length therefore had to be properly apportioned.

From such considerations we can gain this general directive: the thinner the polyphonic texture and the slower the harmonic or the polyphonic rhythm, the

10 The second of these parallels can be presumed, because the onbeat *Vorschlag* could not, in view of a harmonic rhythm that moves in 8th-notes, exceed the length of such an 8th.

Ex. 16.17.

greater the latitude in the treatment of the *Vorschläge* (or other small graces); the more complex the texture and the faster the polyphonic rhythm, the more the treatment is restricted to great brevity or anticipation. For this reason, in the 1st English Suite great shortness for the double *Vorschläge* (less than a 16th if taken on the beat) is advisable to avoid interference with the bass line (see Ex. 16.18).

Ex. 16.18. BWV 806, Sarabande

Consideration of what could be called *melodic logic* will yield several further clues for ornament rendition. Probably the most important aspect of melodic logic concerns graces whose function is the strictly connective one of smoothly linking the elements of a melody by rounding its corners or by filling spaces between intervals. Such graces are pure lubricants that should not aspire to melodic-rhythmic prominence. Their logical place is *between* rather than *on* the beats, unless they are inconspicuously short.

The *tierces coulées* are the prime examples of this type of grace. The naturalness of their interbeat design is reflected in diminution tables of three centuries where this very design is usually the only one-note pattern given for the gracing of a descending third. In Bach too the context of a *tierce coulée* often creates a strong presumption for such interpretation, as we have seen in several examples given above. In Bach's works this tendency is also manifested in second versions, in transcriptions, or in parodies, because some of these are more embellished than the original; and when the intervals of thirds are filled in in regular notation, it is mostly done between the beats.

Example 16.19*a* compares a passage from the 4th Brandenburg Concerto with its transcription as a clavier concerto; Ex. *b*, Cantata 210a, is compared with its parody, Cantata 210.[11]

Ex. 16.19.

An interesting indication for the interbeat meaning of the little notes in such connective situations can be found in the Clavier Concerto in F minor. In the autograph, Bach wrote this movement first in a simple pattern of 16th-notes (Ex. 16.20*a*, top), undoubtedly copying it from a lost violin concerto which must have served as model also for the Sinfonia of Cantata 156. As in other analogous instances of violin-clavier transcriptions, Bach had some second thoughts about the ornamentation needed to compensate for the loss of the violin's sustaining power and expressive nuance. Thus he inserted throughout the movement additional notes, resolving in diminution fashion many 16th-notes into running 32nd's (bottom line). In m. 7 (Ex. *b*) he obviously intended to follow the pattern set in the fourth beat of m. 4 (given in Ex. *a*), but these notes happened to be written so

Ex. 16.20. BWV 1056 (aut. P 234)

[11] See also the "Agnus Dei" from the *B minor Mass* as compared with Cantata 11,4, mm. 1, 2, etc. Although the parody dependence is not entirely clear, it does not affect the point at issue since both versions are expressions of the same melodic idea, one embellished, one plain.

closely together that they permitted no insertion of regular notes; consequently, he wrote little notes instead, which could just barely be squeezed in and achieved the identical effect with *Zwischenschläge*.

Part III.
One-Note Graces

140

Another telling indication for prebeat usage in the Bach household can be found in Ex. 16.21, giving on top a measure from Couperin's *Les Bergeries* (6th *Ordre*). This piece was entered by Anna Magdalena into her "Note Book" of 1725, and in copying it she simplified the notation and wrote out several ornaments. The bottom line shows her written-out interbeat *tierces coulées*.

Copy of A.M. Bach in her "Note Book":

Ex. 16.21. Couperin, *Les Bergeries*

A piece of evidence from the vocal medium that is sufficiently revealing to deserve detailed analysis can be gained from the comparison of a passage in Cantata No. 34 with its secular model Cantata 34a (*O ewiges Feuer*). In the fifth movement of Cantata 34a we find the passage of Ex. 16.22a; the corresponding passage in Cantata 34 is given in Ex. *b*. At the spot designated by an asterisk, Bach had copied at first in the autograph of Cantata 34 (AmB 39) the three 8th-notes that in Cantata 34a were set against the pattern of the violins in near-melodic unison. For the word *Jacob* in Cantata 34a this was perfect diction, adapted to the syllable *-cob* with its short vowel and its sharply clipped consonant ending. By contrast, the syllable *-er-* from *ausersehn* in the parody (Ex. *b*) is longer, quasi-diphthonged, without a clear consonant ending. Hence, there was no reason for this syllable to skip the *tierce coulée* of the unison violin melody, the less so since throughout the movement in the many repeats of the word *ausersehn*, the syllable *-er-* is invariably set with two 16th-notes. Two illustrations of this are given in Ex. *c*. There can be hardly any doubt that, after mechanically copying the three 8th-notes from its model, Bach wanted to change them to ♪♫♪ and not to ♪♪♫
                                          aus- er - sehn   aus- er - sehn
However, having written the 8ths (with their downward stems in alto clef) so close together that he could not squeeze in another regular note, he therefore inserted the little note, with the obvious meaning shown in brackets in Ex. *b*. Here, then, the little note is a genuine *Nachschlag*, slurred with the same syllable to the preceding note.[12]

Two very revealing examples are found in Altnikol's 1755 copy of the *WC* I. (Altnikol was Bach's student and son-in-law.) In the E flat minor Prelude, a hook of Bach's autograph (P 415), as shown in Ex. 16.23a, is expressed by Altnikol as a *Nachschlag* slurred to the preceding note (Ex. *b*), hence in unmistakable prebeat meaning. In the C sharp minor Prelude, Altnikol fills in a descending third that Bach had left vacant with a grace before the bar line, again clarifying its prebeat nature (Ex. *c*).

So compelling is the musical tendency toward interbeat rendition in genuine *tierces coulées* contexts that a number of modern researchers, among them Dannreuther, Beyschlag, Dolmetsch, Emery, and Kreutz, have acknowledged and demonstrated this need for Bach's music. A few of their illustrations are shown in Ex. 16.24. Both Dannreuther and Emery speak in terms of *Nachschläge* when-

---

12 The *NBA*, I, 13 (in keeping with its above mentioned editorial policy) slurs the little note here with its right neighbor and thereby misrepresents the *Nachschlag* as a *Vorschlag*.

Ex. 16.22.

Ex. 16.23.

ever the prebeat rendition is indicated, whereas Dolmetsch and Beyschlag more realistically acknowledge the existence of an anticipated *Vorschlag*.

Among Dannreuther's examples is a passage from the Organ Chorale *Allein Gott* (Ex. *a*). Dannreuther sees confirmation of prebeat rendition in m. 26 where appoggiatura treatment would result in "cacophony." Some of his other illustrations are from the Flute Sonata in E major (Ex. *b*), from the Air of the *Goldberg Variations* (Ex. *c*), and from the 1st Gamba-Clavier Sonata (Ex. *d*). Dannreuther's examples, given in Exx. 16.22*a* and *b*, are also offered by Emery (his Exx. 20 and 105) as instances where prebeat execution is necessary. He also finds confirmation of prebeat rendition in m. 26 of the organ chorale (Emery's Ex. 201) where, "appoggiatura interpretation is harmonically highly improbable" (p. 94). He gives a similar prebeat *tierce coulée* passage (his Ex. 205) from the Courante (mm. 93-94) of the Violin-Clavier Suite in A major (BWV 1025, of uncertain authenticity). Dolmetsch (p. 152) gives prebeat interpretation to the *tierces coulées* (Ex. *e*) in the B major prelude (*WC* II). Emery considers this solution reasonable, provided the autograph slide (which Dolmetsch had omitted) is also done before the beat, a proviso that makes both melodic and rhythmic sense.

Beyschlag gives an interesting example (p. 121, his Ex. *e*) of an anticipated *Vorschlag* from the *Christmas Oratorio* (No. 42, m. 13), which will be quoted below (Ex. 29.54) in connection with the anticipated auxiliary for trills; this same passage is also reproduced as Emery's Ex. 209. Landshoff points out (p. 65) that in the D major Two-Part Invention the "*Nachschlag*" b′ in m. 45 is written out in the autograph (Friedemann's *Clavier-büchlein*) of 1720 (Ex. *f*) whereas it is marked with a hook in the autograph of 1723 (P 610; Ex. *g*). In its preceding parallel spot in m. 3, the grace is marked with a hook in the 1720 autograph and with a little note in the 1723 source, as shown in Exx. *f* and *g*. Kreutz, too, believes that Bach's *tierces coulées* are mainly anticipated ("Bei Bach sind sie meistens als Durchgänge gedacht," p. 3).

Ex. 16.24.

Diction can often identify the purely connective character of a one-note grace. If, for instance, such a grace appears in the middle of a syllable, it is unlikely to have a meaning other than that of a *Zwischenschlag*, since either a *Vorschlag* or a *Nachschlag* would make little sense in the middle of an uninterrupted vowel.

Not that it greatly matters exactly how the singer will place such *Zwischenschläge* rhythmically: we have to do here usually with a second subdivision of a weak beat, and it will make little difference whether they are made to fall before, on, or after such a mathematical point. What does matter is that they are not accented and that they are slurred to *both* of their parent notes. The same consideration applies, of course, to all similar situations.

In the passage from Cantata 140 (Ex. 16.25*a*), diction alone will identify the first unslurred little note as a *Zwischenschlag*. This interpretation is reinforced by the notation: on the first recurrence of the same passage (Ex. *b*), a slur links the grace logically to both of its adjoining notes; secondly, there are four written-out 16th-notes at the start of m. 33 (Ex. *c*). In Ex. *d* from the *St. Matthew Passion*, the second grace can hardly be a detached, let alone an accented, *Vorschlag* in the middle of *den*.

In the autograph score of the soprano aria, "Nur ein Wink" from the *Christmas Oratorio* (No. 57), the little note in m. 41 is encompassed both within the same syllable and within a slur (Ex. *e*), thereby making the *Zwischenschlag* character unmistakable; furthermore, it could logically be transferred to the instrumental parallel spots in mm. 25, 43, and 81. (Though the slur of the autograph starts above the little note, it is not the small, dainty curve Bach used for such graces; rather, it is the thick, heavy one he used to link principal notes which often falls short of reaching both note heads. Alfred Dürr in his edition [*NBA*, II, 6, p. 281] without question interpreted the slur as belonging to both principal notes, then added, as usual, the mistaken second slur linking the grace to its following note.) Example *f* from Cantata 210 is a counterpart to Ex. *d*: here too the second grace in midsyllable is a *Zwischenschlag*, and Bach's failure to link it to the following note by a slur (in his autograph soprano part) was dictated by logic; its routine "reconstruction" in the *NBA* (I, 40, p. 49) was prompted by the usual misunderstanding. Further specimens are shown in Exx. *g* and *h* from Cantata 100. The grace in the middle of the word *Gift* (Ex. *g*) and the grace (f sharp) in the middle of *auf* (Ex. *h*) are certainly *Zwischenschläge*.

It is hardly surprising that in spite of diligent search I could not find a single case where a one-note grace, written by Bach in the middle of a syllable, was slurred by him to the following note *only*. They were either left unslurred or encompassed in a larger slur.

Where the grace is placed *before* an unaccented syllable and between the beats (as shown in Ex. *i* from Cantata 16), an accented appoggiatura is obviously out of place. It may be that this particular grace was meant as a *Nachschlag* to be sung with *Schät-* rather than as unaccented and presumably anticipated *Vorschlag* to *-zen*. The written-out *tierces coulées* in the sequential phrase of the next measure offer some support to the first of these alternatives (though such "echo" arguments are never fully conclusive).

Ex. 16.25.

Even without the clue of diction, a grace placed within a slur that encompasses both adjoining regular notes—in vocal as well as in instrumental music—will usually by this fact alone be identified as a *Zwischenschlag*.

The start of the violin solo in the aria "Erbarme dich" from the *St. Matthew Passion* offers an interesting illustration. The first measure of this solo was written in the autograph score as shown in Ex. 16.26a. Its articulation, with the third 8th-note of the measure tied to the fourth dotted one, corresponds exactly to the melodic design of the beginning of the voice part (Ex. *b*) in which the third 8th-note is also sustained through the first syllable. In the original part for the solo violin (St 110), as written by the chief scribe of the set under Bach's supervision with certain autograph additions, there is a little note added above the tie (see Ex. *c*). This notation alone, of the grace at the seam of a tie, establishes its *Zwischenschlag* character. Neither in the score, nor in the part, nor in the analogous voice passage are the two neighbors of the little grace conceived as separate notes; hence, the second of them cannot support a *Vorschlag*. To misconceive it as such, let alone as a long appoggiatura, would sever the continuity of the note and strongly alter the melodic physiognomy of the phrase. The logical solution is a gentle touching of the grace while the bow continues its uninterrupted flow as suggested in Ex. *d*. (See the identical interpretation of this little note in Emery, Ex. 27 and in Dannreuther, I, 186.)

Other such *Zwischenschläge* are revealed by the notation, for instance in the 1st Gamba-Clavier Sonata and in the Flute Sonata in E major. The first of these passages is shown in Ex. 16.27a as it appears in the autograph. In all the extant sources of the flute sonata,

Ex. 16.26.

the little notes (in the characteristic motive shown in Ex. *b*) are, on their every return, embedded in a tie of their neighbors, hence their *Zwischenschlag* character is unmistakable. Again both *BG* and *NBA*, in accord with their editorial policies, give a misleading text by substituting for the tie a slur connecting the little note with the following note only.

Ex. 16.27.

A further clue of melodic logic can be found in certain unison passages. When one voice, say a solo instrument, has *Vorschläge* where a *stronger* voice or combination of voices proceeds in unison and has none, anticipation of the *Vorschlag* will probably be the intended solution, because the *main* note will be attracted to the beat by the sympathetic pull of the stronger force. Moreover, an *acciaccatura*-like clash would be ineffectual in such a situation: the weakness of the dissonant sound would make it appear as an accident rather than an intended ornament. For example, in Cantata 7 the solo violin often plays in unison with the whole violin section plus the two oboes but has in these passages added *Vorschläge*. Under these circumstances, they would be barely audible and make little sense as appoggiaturas. Since the main function of the *Vorschläge* is to put the solo part in plastic relief, grace notes are admirably suited to fulfill such a task. Example 16.28 shows the first two measures, but identical patterns occur another 32 times in the movement.[13]

* The first grace not in part but occurs in all parallel spots.

Ex. 16.28. BWV 7, 1 (Thomana)

Clashes that under such circumstances would be produced by onbeat execution are generally far more fitting where the ornamented part is strong enough to be perceived clearly. In the third measure of the above cited violin solo from "Erbarme dich" (Ex. 16.29*a*), the *Vorschlag* would clash on the beat with the *ripieno* violins. If the "ripienists"

---

[13] For other examples see Cantata 96,5, mm. 2, 3, 7; Orchestra Suite in B minor (BWV 1067), Sarabande, mm. 4, 6, 8, 11, 14, etc.; Polonaise, mm. 1, 6, 11; Clavier Concerto in A (BWV 1055,3), mm. 2, 3, 10, 11, and especially mm. 60-64 against the staccato unison of the violins.

play piano and the solo violin forte, as Bach prescribed, an appoggiatura of about 8th-note length will make a very good effect. If, however, the section overpowers the soloist, the same clash would be less satisfactory. By contrast, when in the same aria the solo violin has *Vorschläge* before a note sung unembellished by the alto voice (Ex. *b*), the weaker violin will do well to get the *Vorschläge* out of the voice's way—by shortness or, preferably, by anticipation—to insure that the graces will be heard. (Beyschlag, p. 122, Ex. 3, had quoted the same passage to prove the shortness of the *Vorschläge*.)

Ex. 16.29. BWV 244, 47 (aut. P 25)

Clues can be derived from various aspects of *harmonic logic*. One of these is the fact that the main purpose of onbeat execution is the enrichment of the harmony and that onbeat rendition may be purposeless where no enrichment takes place and outright incongruous where impoverishment results. Impoverishment happens when the *Vorschlag* either turns a dissonance into a consonance or enfeebles the harmonic impact of a written-out dissonance by preventing it from striking on the beat. In Ex. 16.30*a* from the Organ Prelude in B minor, a written-out, long suspension-appoggiatura first creates then resolves a dissonance on the heavy beat of midmeasure against the c sharp of the upper voice. If the *Vorschlag* before this upper voice is taken on the beat as an 8th-note (Ex. *b*), the dissonance is obliterated; if the *Vorschlag* is taken on the beat as a 16th-note (Ex. *c*), the solution is slightly better, but the dissonance would still be emasculated—the c sharp would be perceived not vertically as a dissonance produced by the written suspension-appoggiatura but horizontally as if it were passing between two consonances. Moreover, such rendition would weaken the characteristic rhythm combination of the two voices. Only extreme shortness that in absence of a distinct beat in another voice makes on- or prebeat placement indistinguishable on the organ can guarantee this passage its full harmonic-rhythmic meaning. In the second measure the situation is repeated with the roles of the voices reversed; consequently the same considerations apply.

There are other factors that argue against the "overlong" interpretation of the *Vorschlag* symbols in this piece (not to mention the previous arguments against their validity for Bach). It is hardly a coincidence that the little notes are used all four times the siciliano rhythm occurs in this piece. In all these cases they are consonant with the simultaneously written-out suspension-appoggiatura, whereas in the many cases of a *Vorschlag* that is either outright dissonant (as in mm. 3, 9, 11, 29, 42, 53, 85, etc.) or functionally so (as for instance the fourth-third progression of m. 2 or the $\begin{smallmatrix}6 & 5\\ 4 & 3\end{smallmatrix}$ of m. 7, or analogous progressions in mm. 33 and 65), the 8th-note *Vorschlag* is written out in regular notes. The juxtaposition of the two styles of notation is particularly striking in the first three measures (Ex. 16.30*a*). Also, it is probably no coincidence that in the two closely related two-measure phrases of Ex. 16.30*d* the little *Vorschlag* note e' in m. 9 is consonant with the suspension on c sharp (which has to be read as shown in Ex. *e*), whereas at the start of m. 11 the appoggiatura on a', which is dissonant with the suspension on d" sharp, is written out as an 8th-note. True, the first *Vorschlag* (of m. 9), though consonant with the suspension, is dissonant with the bass, but the dissonance is much milder than the one generated by the principal note on the beat; hence 8th-note rendition would impoverish the harmony, and 16th-note meaning is excluded by parallel octaves with the upper voice. The only other remaining small-note *Vorschläge* in this piece are the ones in the bass line (mm. 8 and 10 of Ex. *d*). They occur in isolation and therefore are neither harmonically nor polyphonically sensitive. Shortness seems indicated here again—with a length not exceeding an 8th-note and probably best limited to a 16th or less—in order to sound the main note before the upper voice sets in.

Ex. 16.30. BWV 544

Vorschläge in the bass part are rather infrequent in Bach's music. When they do occur there is generally a presumption for their shortness because as the foundation of the harmony, the principal note can rarely be missed more than fleetingly on the beat, especially in a context of fast-moving harmonic or polyphonic rhythm. The argument gains weight when the harmony as such is a dissonance and the onbeat *Vorschlag* would dilute it. Such would be the case in Ex. 16.31*a* from the *Musical Offering* (Trio Sonata). For another example see Prelude 4, m. 3 (*WC* II).

When a *Vorschlag* precedes a note that establishes a new harmonic progression, the clarification of this change is particularly urgent when the new harmony is a dissonance and when one or more of the other voices are tied over the beat; in such a case the clarification can best be achieved by undelayed entrance of the principal note, hence by anticipation of the *Vorschlag*. An illustration is offered from the Organ Fantasy in C minor (Ex. *b*) for the *Vorschlag* at the start of m. 3.

Ex. 16.31.

Considerations of *rhythmic logic* can provide further guidance. Rhythm patterns that have definite motivic importance, or display a pervasive regularity, or have a sharp, characteristic contour are likely to resist a marked ornamental disturbance. Consequently they create a strong presumption for anticipated or short, unaccented treatment, because these alone insure rhythmical non-interference. For example, the Organ Chorale *Wachet auf* has ♫♩ as the rhythmic-motivic nucleus. The notes are unadorned in the original version of the chorale (the fourth movement of Cantata 140), but in the organ version (the first of the Schübler Chorales) many of these patterns are preceded by *Vorschläge* (Ex. 16.32). To safeguard the motivic integrity, anticipation seems to be the best choice.

Ex. 16.32. BWV 645

In the Loure from the G major French Suite (Ex. 16.3), extreme shortness and preferably anticipation of the *Vorschläge* are suggested by the facts that a Loure always opens with the rhythm: ♪♩ | ♩. ♪♩ (here divided between the two hands) and that, being a slow French Gigue, it is characterized by the prevalence of the dotted patterns ♩. ♪♩ . The frequently heard "overlong" rendition of the *Vorschläge* in the first measure ♫♩ obliterates at the very start the rhythm which is the essence of the Loure.

Pervasive rhythmic regularity is, of course, extremely frequent in the music of the baroque and is in fact one of its stylistic hallmarks. To take a random example, the 17th of the *Goldberg Variations* is almost throughout written in running 16th-notes. For this reason alone, the two lone graces in m. 14 (Ex. 16.33*a*) will best be anticipated. In addition, these graces are written as 16th-notes and represent *Vorschläge* before written-out appoggiaturas (the nature of the latter clarified by slurs that are very rare in Bach's clavier works). The regularity of running triplets, exemplified in a passage from the E major Flute Sonata (Ex. *b*) will for the same reasons tend to relegate the *Vorschläge* into prebeat space. When in such contexts the *Vorschläge* are placed on the beat, they disturb the unity of rhythm. Contrarily, prebeat rendition adds brilliance without impinging on this unity.

Ex. 16.33.

Another principle of rhythmic logic concerns *Vorschläge* that are placed before notes of such shortness that there is no reasonable time left for onbeat placement. An attempt to squeeze the *Vorschlag* into such crowded quarters will usually make for rhythmic-melodic awkwardness if not outright unintelligibility. The obvious solution is anticipation. Thus, in the passage from the E major Clavier Concerto (Ex. 16.34a), an onbeat *Vorschlag* would be senseless harmonically, melodically, rhythmically, and even technically. Anticipation is also indicated in Ex. *b* from the Flute-Harpsichord Sonata in B minor for both graces and for the first *Vorschlag* in Ex. *c* from the 25th *Goldberg Variation*.

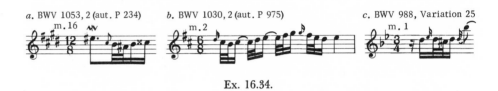

Ex. 16.34.

In the often discussed *aria a doi cori* from the *St. Matthew Passion* (Ex. 16.35), the flute graces, whose purely decorative character is evidenced by their absence in the voice parts, should be unaccented and short. As quarter-notes they would be anachronistic; as 8th-notes they would undo the polyphonic relationships; as 16th-notes they would mar the characteristic rhythmic interplay of the two voices and be unnecessarily different from the vocal line.

Ex. 16.35. BWV 244, 33 (aut. P 25)

Guidance can also be gained from considerations of ornamental logic. One of these considerations involves the principle of saturation in the sense that certain musical passages can profitably absorb only a limited amount of ornamental matter. Since this amount is the product of quantity times weight, ornaments that congregate in great density will often profit from being lightened. The way to do so is, singly or in combination, to shorten them, to render them softly, or to place them between the beats. For instance, in the violin passage from the E major Clavier Concerto (Ex. 16.36), unaccented brevity will prevent heavy-handedness. (In an ever-recurring simile, old theorists compare ornaments to spices which improve a dish by moderate use and spoil it by an overdose.)

Vns. I

Ex. 16.36. BWV 1053, 2 (aut. P 234)

Another principle of ornamental logic is the desirability that a grace be clearly audible. A grace that cannot be heard might as well not have been added. Where ornaments are bunched in clusters, they should not get into each other's way; in such cases it will often be advisable to separate them sufficiently to permit each to be heard. In the Organ Fantasy in C minor (see above Ex. 16.31*b*), the cluster at the start of m. 2 finds its simplest solution by anticipation of the *Vorschlag*.

Even in cases where the cluster consists of two or more *Vorschläge*, the effect of these graces will often be enhanced by differentiated treatment. In the passage from the Aria of the *Goldberg Variations* (Ex. 16.37*a*), both synchronized anticipation and synchronized onbeat execution are unsatisfactory. A good solution may be to treat the middle voice as anticipated *tierce coulée*, the upper voice as appoggiatura (Ex. *b*).

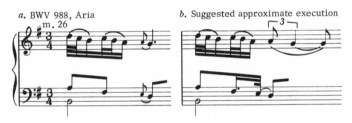

a. BWV 988, Aria
b. Suggested approximate execution

Ex. 16.37.

One might speak of a logic of articulation, which suggests anticipation when a *Vorschlag* is placed before short staccato notes. An onbeat *Vorschlag* before such a note would detract from, if not obliterate, its staccato character. In Ex. 16.38 from the Organ Chorale *Vater unser*, the evenness of the triplet pattern dovetailed between the two upper voices reinforces the case for anticipation.

Ex. 16.38. BWV 682

In the foregoing discussion we have found cases that required anticipation; in addition, we met with many contexts that simply called for great brevity without limiting the execution to one rhythmic style alone.

Among the one-note graces, only the *Vorschlag* qualifies for a decisive onbeat design. In Bach's music all available onbeat designs are present, from the short to the long and overlong one, but only some of these are conveyed by symbol. Type 4, which lasts for the greater part of the principal note's value, always had to be written out in regular notes. Type 3, lasting up to approximately one-half of a binary or one-third of a ternary note, is very frequently written out, but it *can* be indicated by a symbol before relatively short notes.[14] Type 2, the short onbeat pattern, is probably frequently understood by Bach's *Vorschlag* symbol, regardless of the value of the principal note.

The solo keyboard is generally in the best position to accommodate relatively long appoggiaturas in the middle of a phrase, because the experienced player can tell at a glance from the score whether the context both suggests and permits such a solution. Outside of the keyboard literature, notably in vocal music, the appoggiatura was very frequent indeed, but generally short.

In order to gain some orientation about the circumstances demanding or favoring the onbeat start, it will be helpful to separate those *Vorschläge* which aim at a heightened expression and must be slow enough to make such an impact felt from those which are very short and are either meant to provide greater rhythmic vitality or are the frequent possible alternatives to prebeat execution. Whether a passage calls for one or the other type of *Vorschlag* will depend on various factors such as tempo, basic affect, harmonic, polyphonic, or metric context, and in vocal music on word-meaning and diction.

In instrumental music, the first (harmonic) type will generally find the following circumstances particularly congenial (without being limited to them by any means): a move from a shorter preceding note on a neighboring pitch to a longer principal note on a strong beat where the *Vorschlag* strengthens the harmony. In such contexts the appoggiatura is akin to a suspension. An illustration is given in Ex. 16.39 from Prelude 18 (*WC* II), where the hooks stand for suspension-appoggiaturas and should have the approximate length of 8th-notes in accord with the model of the *Explication* (the same design recurs in mm. 4, 17, 31, and 42). Interestingly, in mm. 44 and 45, where the appoggiaturas do not repeat the preceding notes, they are written out in regular notation.

Ex. 16.39. BWV 887 (aut. BM)

The C sharp minor Prelude of *WC* II (for which the autograph is unfortunately missing) is filled with *Vorschläge*, most of which appear to be fairly long appoggiaturas. In the first of the two Altnikol manuscripts (P 430 of 1744) they are mostly marked by little

[14] For the written-out Type 3, which is frequent, see Cantata 13,5, mm. 4-5, 24-25, etc. or the Toccata from the 6th Partita (BWV 830,1) that is filled with them. The "overlong" one is less frequent but does occur from time to time; see, for instance, Cantatas 21,3 and 154,1 throughout; the final chorus of the *St. Matthew Passion*, m. 10 and parallel spots; the C minor Organ Prelude and Fugue (BWV 537,2), last measure.

notes, in the second (P 402 of 1755), mostly by hooks. In a few instances (e.g. in mm. 16 and 17) these manuscripts have written-out 8th-notes (Ex. 16.40*a*) where other sources, among them Kirnberger's manuscript, have small-note symbols (Ex. *b*). We find the same notational differences between manuscripts in a few other spots of the same piece as well. This does not by any means imply 8th-note value for *all* the *Vorschläge* in the prelude: in cases where the main note is strongly dissonant, great shortness is indicated (see Ex. *c* and also mm. 6 and 41).

Ex. 16.40. BWV 873

In Ex. 16.41*a* from the Aria of the *Goldberg Variations* there are two *ports de voix* in one measure on the same pitch. The first of these graces (written as a 16th), before a note barely longer than its preparation, will best be very short, perhaps anticipated; the second one, before the half-note, should be long, but slightly shorter than an 8th-note in order not to collide with the tenor part. If both graces were to be played in the same manner, their effect would be marred by repetitiousness. A few measures later (Ex. *b*) the *coulé* (again written as a 16th-note) will best be very short or anticipated, the *port de voix* again rather long, slightly shorter than an 8th-note. The same applies to a similar place in m. 24.

Ex. 16.41. BWV 988, Aria

In the Sarabande from the 1st English Suite, the prepared *port de voix* of Ex. 16.42*a* can, in view of the slower polyphonic rhythm, be longer (perhaps like a dotted 16th-note) than the similar graces of the same piece that were quoted above in Ex. 16.18. The same is the case with the analogous *Vorschläge* in mm. 28, 29, and 30, though it will be advisable to vary their lengths to avoid monotony.

The *coulé* of Ex. *b* from the *Orgelbüchlein: Das alte Jahr* is likely to be a harmonic grace of approximate 16th-note length.

A much discussed case for harmonic appoggiaturas concerns the *Sinfonia* (Three-Part Invention) in E flat. Bach wrote it first in simple, fairly austere style in the autographs of 1720 (Friedemann's *Clavierbüchlein*) and 1723 (P 610). Then he subsequently entered in the latter autograph copy a large number of graces.[15] Many of these are unquestion-

[15] The first version can be found in the main volume of Ludwig Landshoff's edition (Peters), the ornamented one in Annex I; see also *NBA*, V, 3 (ed. von Dadelsen).

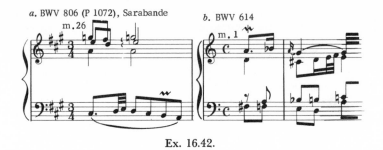

Ex. 16.42.

ably harmonic appoggiaturas; but probably there are not as many of them nor are they as long as usually assumed. For reasons previously discussed, it is most unlikely that these *Vorschläge* were meant to be played as quarter-notes (as suggested among others by Landshoff in his distinguished *Revisionsbericht*). Apart from being anachronistic, this solution is incongruous in some instances, producing, as Bodky (p. 180) pointed out, impossible fifths in m. 20; moreover, it would obliterate the cadential intensification by the genuine quarter-note appoggiaturas which Bach had written out in mm. 22-24. Also, the relentless massing of the same type of *Vorschläge* would create a tedium that would be only slightly lessened by Bodky's solution of playing all *Vorschläge* as 8th-notes. As usual, a mechanical formula is out of place. It will be better to vary *Vorschlag* types and lengths, ranging from anticipation (especially for some of the leaping *Vorschläge*) through straddling to lengthy onbeat renditions up to the approximate value of an 8th-note. The resulting variety will be truly ornamental.

Another case in which researchers and performers yielded to the temptation of applying the anachronistic overlong formula, because it happens to be musically possible, occurs in the E flat Prelude (*WC* II) in mm. 2, 4, and 62 (Ex. 16.43*a*). There are more reasons than the ones already given to reject the *galant* formula for this piece. True, it does not sound bad, but it does not fit the affect of the sparkling and lively piece with the driving energy of a Gigue and without the slightest touch of sentiment. By comparing the beginning with mm. 17-20 (Ex. *b*), where the same rhythmic pattern recurs without graces, one realizes that the overlong appoggiatura-sigh is out of character. A brief rendition that, if taken on the beat, is finished before the bass enters might make the best effect; slight lengthening beyond an (onbeat) 8th-note is possible but seems less satisfactory; a quarter-note or a dotted quarter (the latter the common favorite) is simply an un-Bachian misreading of the symbol.

Ex. 16.43. BWV 876 (aut. BM)

Even in those cases where the *Vorschlag* symbol precedes a cadential dominant chord, with or without notated trill and where many German and Italian contemporaries would have understood a very long appoggiatura, Bach's harmonic

Vorschlag will, as his figures usually reveal, be fairly short. One characteristic illustration is the final cadence in the first movement of the Trio Sonata from the *Musical Offering* (Ex. 16.44). Here the authentic figures do not favor the intention of a long appoggiatura, inasmuch as in the countless instances of written-out long cadential appoggiaturas on the dominant, the figures, if given, invariably reflect the harmonic progression.

Ex. 16.44. BWV 1079, 8

An interesting and quite rare parallelism is to be found in Cantata 172 which exists in three versions. In these three sources, all autograph, we find the same passage written as shown in Ex. 16.45; in one version (Ex. *a*) a *Vorschlag* is written by symbol, in the other two (Exx. *b* and *c*) it is written out as an 8th-note appoggiatura, long enough to enhance expression without interfering with the counterpoint (the 16ths in the bass are more chordal than linear). Clearly, the same approximate solution was expected for the symbol.

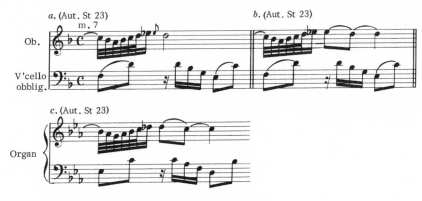

Ex. 16.45. BWV 172, 5

On the ultimate note of a cadence a *Vorschlag* most likely will be long, provided all voices have come to rest. The same will be the case, with the same proviso, before a hold in the middle of a piece. Example 16.46 from the B minor Prelude (*WC* II) offers a typical illustration.

Ex. 16.46. BWV 893, 1

In vocal music a *Vorschlag* on a strong beat before a long and accented syllable will lean toward appoggiatura treatment. Examples abound everywhere and only a few illustrations need to be given.

In the passages from Cantata 177 (Ex. 16.47a), diction calls for onbeat execution of all four *Vorschläge* whose length might best be varied from one-fourth to one-half the value of their principal notes. In Ex. *b* from the *St. John Passion* the demands of diction seem underscored by the parallelism of symbol-indicated and written-out appoggiaturas. The same is the case in Ex. *c* from Cantata 54.

Ex. 16.47.

Whereas there is limited scope for varying the length of a harmonic appoggiatura before an 8th-note, matters are different when a longer principal note is involved. Here a similar parallelism of symbolized and written-out *Vorschlag* can be deceptive. In Ex. 16.48 from Cantata 19, we have *Vorschläge* marked by symbol on the words *nah* and *fern* at the start of the first and third measures, and find appoggiaturas of 8th-note length written out twice for *nah*, once for *fern*. It so happens that for both symbolized graces, especially the second one, a shorter-than-8th-note duration is more satisfactory. It appears that the difference in notation is not purely accidental.

The short onbeat *Vorschlag* in Bach's music was not as rigid as it was to become later as the "invariable" short and accented *Vorschlag* of the Berlin School. In Bach's music the short appoggiatura was most likely a flexible type that, standing halfway between anticipation and the longer harmonically active type, could move in either direction and thus be susceptible of infinite transitional shapes.

Ex. 16.48. BWV 19, 3 (P 45 and St 25)

Dynamic nuances can also add a new dimension to this variety by deviating from the usual pattern that combines onbeat with accent and prebeat with softness.

In its accented form—or on the baroque keyboard, in its *decisive* onbeat form—this grace usually has the strongest impact on rhythm. In this form it can be expected to find a sympathetic context in energetic, brilliant, and lively pieces that have a pronounced metrical beat. Example 16.49*a* offers such an illustration from the Overture to the 4th Partita where the descending *Vorschlag* might best be executed quite short, on the beat (between a 32nd and a 16th), and accented on a modern piano.

For another related example, short, onbeat execution of the two graces in the first measure of Ex. *b* from the *French Overture* seems called for by the ceremonial splendor of the piece, though anticipation cannot be excluded. Of the three *Vorschläge* in mm. 7 and 8 of the same example, each might perhaps profit from a different treatment. The first could be done approximately as an onbeat 16th, the second in anticipation, the third again on the beat, perhaps slightly longer, as a triplet 8th.

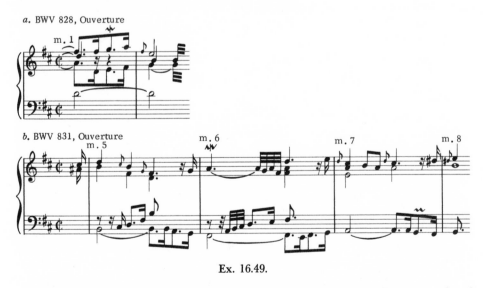

Ex. 16.49.

The possibility cannot be dismissed that on occasion Bach may have rendered a short onbeat *Vorschlag* on the keyboard in the form of a *Zusammenschlag*, i.e. by simultaneous striking and immediate release: ♩ = ♩ though we have no direct evidence to that effect.

Bach's infrequent *Vorschläge* that leap to their parent note by a third or more almost always repeat the preceding note and generally represent a distinct species.[16] They cannot enrich the harmony, since a dissonance has to be resolved stepwise, and whenever taken on the beat they have to remain within the harmony of the principal note. They are therefore by nature essentially melodic graces regardless of their place in the measure.

The downward leap taken slowly on the beat has a special application in recitatives and related contexts and will be discussed presently. There is no reason why the upward leap should be routinely accented on the beat. Such rendition will often counteract the ornament's implied homing impulse which calls for a soft start and a dynamic rise toward the goal (as evidenced most patently in a singer's *portamento*). Where Bach intended an onbeat emphasis for rhythmic or melodic reasons, he usually wrote it out to avoid a misunderstanding. (The pattern is rare in his music and its best known specimens are probably those in the slow movement of the *Italian Concerto*.) Naturally, we shall find cases where the onbeat designs seem either preferable or an equivalent alternative, and many instances where straddling would add variety. But by and large it is probable that the upward leaps lean to unaccented shortness or anticipation.[17]

In the passage from the *Musical Offering* shown in Ex. 16.50 there are several spots which suggest great brevity and probable anticipation of the leaping *Vorschlag*. Both leaps—that of the violin at the start of the measure and that of the flute in the middle—are set against a pattern of two slurred 16th-notes that pervades the whole movement as a melodic-rhythmic motive, frequently in the form of a prepared appoggiatura. Set against this written-out pattern, onbeat meaning for the *Vorschlag* is unlikely in terms of harmony, counterpoint, and notation. Notation is mentioned because of Bach's only infrequently relaxed care with regard to the proper combination of polyphonic voices. In a situation where the interplay of the voices is as fine-meshed as it is here, Bach can be expected to have resorted to rhythmic specification had he had anything else in mind except extreme shortness or anticipation.

Ex. 16.50. BWV 1079, 8

[16] The leap of a third is very rare in Bach, and it is probable that the few instances where a modern edition presents it in works for which no autograph survived may be due to misinterpretation. Bach's symbol for the slide was frequently misread by his own copyists for a little 8th-note grace when the tiny teeth of the *custos* were so closely written as to resemble a note head. The slide, not the *Vorschlag*, was for Bach the indicated choice whenever a grace was to a start a third below the principal note. Thus, the leaping *Vorschläge* of the oboe d'amore in Cantata 8,2, mm. 1 and 2 and the many parallel spots (as they appear in the *BG* edition) are almost certainly misread slide symbols. In the voice part the analogous graces appear far more logically all as slides. The same is most likely also the case with the leaping thirds in the siciliano from the E major Flute Sonata (BWV 1035,3), a work whose earliest known source is a 19th-century copy made by a scribe who probably was unfamiliar with the *custos* symbol for the slide.

[17] When Mattheson discusses leaping *Vorschläge* (*Sprung-Accenten* [*Capellmeister*, pt. 2, ch. 3, par. 23]) that fall on the beat but were not marked by symbol, he refers to them as the "newest" fashion for expressing scorn, effrontery, harshness, or arrogance.

In the course of this chapter, the dualism of *Vorschläge* indicated by symbols and those that were written out in regular notes was touched upon on various occasions. In trying to answer the obvious question of whether there is a specific meaning in Bach's use of either form of notation, it will be well to discuss briefly what conclusions can be drawn from the scrutiny of different musical contexts. We are dealing at the moment only with *Vorschläge*, but the same questions and presumably the same answers, which are tentatively sketched here, would apply to other ornaments as well.

After what has been said before, there is no need to repeat that the problem focuses only on those types of graces which in Bach's usage could be understood by a symbol; more specifically in matters of *Vorschläge*, on those within the range indicated in the tabulation of Ex. 16.1 above.

The problem, like so many others in the field of Bach interpretation, stems from his occasional inconsistency in notation. However, by examining his notational usage in this particular matter, three different categories will emerge.

One is that of plain arbitrariness, where Bach used symbols and regular notes with carefree indifference for the identical or near-identical meaning. This seems to occur most frequently in the case of an approximately 16th-note appoggiatura in the setting: 🎵 = 🎵 as we have seen in Ex. 16.47*c*; sometimes we find it for appoggiaturas of approximately 8th-note meaning, as we have seen in Exx. 16.45*a-c*; or in a recitative formula as given below in Ex. 16.54*a* when compared to Ex. *c*.

In the second category, Bach, to all appearances, uses regular notes, either to insure onbeat instead of prebeat rendition (once in a while vice versa), or where he wishes to specify the intended length of an appoggiatura. Thus, e.g. in m. 11 of the D minor Organ Toccata (see below Ex. 29.24*b*), he writes out a prebeat *Vorschlag* (before a trill) which, if written by symbol, would have probably been interpreted as an appoggiatura (see also the specimens of *anticipatione della syllaba* of Ex. 16.10 above). On the other hand, in m. 7 of the Chorale Prelude *O Mensch, bewein* (see below Ex. 29.24*c*), a 32nd-note appoggiatura preceding a trill is written out, presumably to prevent the prebeat interpretation that a symbol could have called for. In m. 18 of the same work, a 16th-note appoggiatura is written out before a half-cadential trill to insure polyphonic coordination. In many, perhaps most, cases of written-out appoggiaturas, Bach appears to have used this procedure to safeguard the integrity of his polyphonic intentions.

A third category can be discerned in those contexts where Bach uses both notational types in a pattern that indicates, or strongly suggests, intentional differentiation. We have encountered and discussed such contexts in Exx. 16.7*b* and *c* from the *St. Matthew Passion*, in Ex. 16.30 from the B minor Organ Prelude, and with lesser clarity in Ex. 16.48 from Cantata 19. Whenever we are satisfied that we can discern a *method* in the distinction, we are entitled to assume that the difference in notation reflects a difference of intent, most frequently involving shortness or anticipation of the symbol as contrasted to the longer written-out appoggiaturas.

These three categories present only a rough outline of ways in which this difficult question can be approached. Admittedly, more thoroughgoing analysis is needed to shed a clearer light on this complicated matter.

In Bach's time, certain aspects of recitative performance pertaining to the addition of unwritten appoggiaturas had become formalized into more or less widely applied conventions that presumably originated in Italian opera and sacred music. In Chapter 14 above, the conventions were referred to in connection with A. Scarlatti's—and later Handel's—compressed operatic cadences with their tonic-dominant clash. With Bach such cadential clashes are extremely rare. Practically always he waits for the singer to end on the tonic before writing the cadence for continuo or, in accompanied recitatives, for orchestra.

As usual, there are exceptions. Examples 16.51*a* and *b* show two such illustrations from Cantatas 27 and 35. Assuming that simultaneity was intended, possible solutions are indicated below each excerpt.[18] The rarity of such occurrences might suggest that among Bach's performers delay of such cadences was not a routine procedure, though rhythmic freedom in recitatives certainly was. The reality of many of these clashes, as was pointed out in Chapter 14, is supported by much evidence. However, Telemann, who is one of the sources to confirm this fact for operas, nevertheless contrasts this practice with "cantatas" where, as he writes, the cadence is delayed.[19]

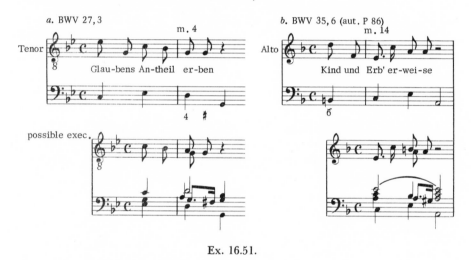

Ex. 16.51.

The most important procedures for the addition of appoggiaturas concern the fall of the fourth from 8 to 5 on the tonic and the fall of either a third or a second. Example 16.52 shows their notation and execution for both masculine and feminine endings, according to an illustration by Telemann.[20]

Ex. 16.52. Telemann's Recitative Formulas

[18] See also Cantatas 81,2, m. 10; 92,2, m. 8; 111,3, m. 11.

[19] Georg Philipp Telemann, *Singe- Spiel- und Generalbass-Übungen* (Hamburg, 1733-1735), ed. M. Seiffert (Berlin, 1914), p. 41.

[20] The convention is explained by Telemann in the preface to *Harmonischer Gottesdienst. . . .* (Hamburg, 1725). His illustrations are reproduced and commented upon in Spitta, II, 141ff.

It seems, however, that the convention was far more general with regard to the falling fourth than with regard to the insertion of a stepwise descending appoggiatura. Agricola, who confirms in 1757 the falling-fourth appoggiatura as a definite requirement, speaks by contrast of the appoggiatura inserted for a falling third or second as something that is done "occasionally" (*zuweilen*), then proceeds to show how in these very contexts (including those of tone repetition) a "mordent" can be inserted in a manner (given in Ex. 16.53) which proves that *no* appoggiatura had been used.[21] This is significant because for both types of formulas the Telemann resolutions have thus far been considered to be binding conventions for the whole 18th century.

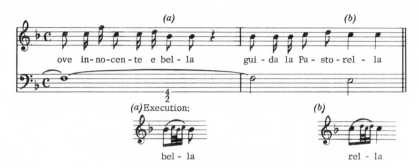

Ex. 16.53. Agricola's Variants

As so often, Bach went his own way and chose not to rely on the convention regarding the falling fourth. In the innumerable cases in which he desired such a falling appoggiatura, he seems to have always indicated it. He did so mostly in regular notes, but once in a while, in a masculine ending, he used little notes that unquestionably had the same meaning. Examples 16.54*a-c* show both styles of notation: the regular notes for masculine and feminine endings (Exx. *a* and *b* from the *St. Matthew Passion*) and the use of the symbol (Ex. *c* from Cantata 210). I could not find a single case where Bach had, in a feminine ending, written the patterns of Ex. 16.52*c* above. This unusual consistency suggests that in the rare instances of a straight downward leap of a fourth in a masculine ending, no appoggiatura insertion was intended. Thus, Ex. *d* from the *St. John Passion* was probably meant to be sung as written, especially in view of the sharp-edged diction of the word *Rock*.

Matters were different with the stepwise descending appoggiatura in recitative cadences. Bach hardly ever wrote this type of appoggiatura in regular notation. However, he frequently indicated it by little notes as shown in Ex. 16.55 from Cantata 30.[22]

---

[21] *Anleitung* (1755), pp. 154-156. Marpurg offers further documentation against a binding convention of inserting an appoggiatura in the context of a falling third. Speaking of feminine recitative cadences, he says that in the secular style the falling fourth:

is more frequent than the repeated note ("mit dem wiederholten Einklange"):

He unmistakably speaks of sound, not of notation, and immediately thereafter inveighs against the habit of some to write the falling fourth like this:

"because one ought to write the way one sings." (*Kritische Briefe über die Tonkunst*, vol. 2 [Berlin, 1763], p. 352.)

[22] Analogous cases for such notation in masculine endings can be found a.o. in Cantatas 45,2, m. 11; 48,2, m. 10; 58,2, m. 5; 61,4, m. 9; 62,3, m. 3; 66,4, mm. 12 and 14; 94,3, m. 49; 107,2, mm. 8 and 15; 210,5, m. 14; *St. John Passion*, 57, m. 14, etc.

Ex. 16.54.

Ex. 16.55. BWV 30, 2

For feminine endings, the use of the symbol in Cantata 60 (Ex. 16.56) and in several analogous occurrences (e.g. in Cantata 45,2, m. 8 and Cantata 181,4, last measure) suggests an appoggiatura that differs from Telemann's formula in that it is resolved within the first syllable. Its probable design is approximately

.[23]

Ex. 16.56. BWV 60, 4

More often than not, the fall of a third or of a second is left unmarked by Bach, and the problem then arises whether to add or not to add an appoggiatura. Whenever such an addition would improve the musical declamation without interfering with other legitimate considerations, it will probably be advisable to make it. Example 16.57 from Cantata 90 shows an instance where an appoggiatura seems welcome.[24]

There are, however, many cases of a falling third where for various reasons the addition of an appoggiatura seems inappropriate. The reasons may have to do with the relationship to other voices, with demands of diction, with word-meaning

[23] The latter interpretation, given in Haydn's famous letter of 1768 regarding the *Applausus* Cantata, reflects *galant* practices.

[24] For other examples see Cantatas 34,4, m. 23; 58,4, m. 4; 65,5, m. 7; 75,4, m. 7; *Christmas Oratorio*, 22, m. 6.

Ex. 16.57. BWV 90, 4

and "affect," and possibly some other factors as well; after all, according to Agricola, who wrote at the heyday of the long appoggiatura, this convention applied only from time to time.

In the Duo Recitative from Cantata 62 (Ex. 16.58), an added appoggiatura in the soprano would produce a very awkward combination with the alto part; moreover, it is unlikely that Bach would have spelled out the appoggiatura of a falling fourth in the alto and would have left a simultaneous appoggiatura in the soprano unmarked.

Ex. 16.58. BWV 62, 5 (aut. P 877)

In Ex. 16.59a from the *St. John Passion*, the abrupt shortness of the syllable -*ab* (from *her-ab*) would resist any ornamental intrusion. Moreover, the inherent symbolism of the descent from the cross would be weakened. In Ex. *b* from Cantata 75 such an appoggiatura would produce parallel fifths with the first violins. In the illustration from Cantata 28 (Ex. *c*), with its feminine ending, an appoggiatura would also create bad fifths and therefore was presumably not intended.[25]

All considered, the conclusion is inevitable that for Bach's recitatives we cannot rely on the standard formulas. The chief problem centers on the fall of a third where an appoggiatura not indicated by symbol may or may not be understood. The decision has to be made individually for each case; and in making it, it will be well to follow Spitta's wise counsel of considering *first* whether there may not be positive reasons why a passage ought not to be sung as written "and frequently such reasons will be found."[26]

THE most noteworthy finding of this complex chapter on Bach's one-note graces is the impossibility of giving positive rules. Negatively, it can be said with a degree of assurance that the long interpretations lasting for a quarter-note or more are generally out of place and that the "overlong" formulas for dotted notes or

25 For other cases where adding an appoggiatura to feminine endings would produce fifths that are probably disturbing enough to discourage the addition, see Cantatas 28,4, mm. 6 and 11; 33,4, m. 12; 117,5, m. 5; 168,2, mm.

5-6; 174,3, m. 5; 187,6, m. 9. In Cantata 18,3, m. 4 an added appoggiatura would produce incongruous frictions with the accompanying four violas.

26 *Bach*, II, 148.

a. BWV 245, 66

Tenor

nahm den Leich-nam Je - su her-ab

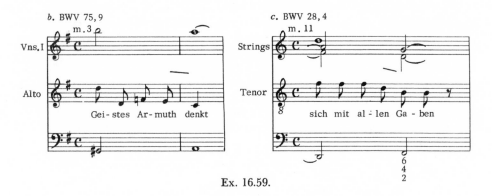

b. BWV 75, 9

Vns. I

Alto

Gei - stes Ar - muth denkt

c. BWV 28, 4

Strings

Tenor

sich mit al - len Ga - ben

Ex. 16.59.

for tied notes were foreign to Bach's usage. Apart from that, within the ranges indicated in the tabulation of Ex. 16.1, any of the solutions and all transitional patterns are possible—including, of course, the use of varied dynamic nuances. The performer has to give up the crutch of ready-made solutions and suffer the "embarrassment of riches," with a wide choice and a commensurately wide artistic responsibility. To provide at least some measure of orientation, the following tentative guidelines are extracted from the preceding discussion.

Anticipation is favored when the *Vorschlag* symbol is placed *before*: (1) short notes such as 16ths or smaller; (2) a written-out appoggiatura; (3) triplets; (4) a dissonant note on a strong beat; (5) a rhythm pattern of structural importance whose integrity ought to be preserved; (6) an unaccented syllable on a weak beat or between beats; (7) a bass note that carries a structural progression; (8) a short note with a staccato dot or dash.

Moreover, a *Vorschlag* will tend to anticipation *whenever*: (1) its onbeat placement would produce obtrusive parallels or other unpleasant voice-leading; (2) it links thirds in a clearly connective function; (3) at least one other voice moves in fast polyphonic rhythm; (4) it is encompassed within a slur (or a tie) linking both neighbor notes, or in analogous *Zwischenschlag* functions; (5) it is set against a stronger, unadorned unison part; (6) it occurs within a cluster of ornaments, and must be made audible.

In a few of the just listed contexts, anticipation alone will be satisfactory; in others, a short, unaccented onbeat execution will be an equivalent alternative (especially in concerted music).

The very short and accented, rhythm-reinforcing onbeat type will on the whole be best fitted for lively, energetic, or festive pieces before note values of an 8th or longer that are placed on a beat. The harmony-enhancing appoggiatura will usually be required in recitatives and related textures, before final notes, and before a hold; in vocal music, before an accented, not too short syllable that is placed on a beat. It will often be favored in its instrumental counterpart on principal beats where it strengthens the harmony for note values of an 8th or longer; the tendency is reinforced where the principal note is preceded by a shorter one, especially if the latter is on the pitch of the *Vorschlag*. The length of the harmonic appoggiatura will vary with the context. It will tend to be long on final notes, before holds, in recitatives, and can often be long in homophonic and quasi-homophonic settings. The denser the texture, the faster either the harmonic or polyphonic rhythm, the better it will be to limit the length in order not to disturb other clearly indicated musical intents.

After all this is said, the performer's taste and judgment, tempered by the framework staked out by our historic investigation and enlightened by stylistic insight, must have the final word here as everywhere else in the field of performance.

—◆◆◆—

MUSICAL EVIDENCE

About 1710, Italian composers began to adopt the French unmetrical little notes to indicate one-note graces, slides, and occasionally, turns. During the same period, Italian and German ornamental practices began to diverge. From this time on it is therefore advisable to make a distinction between the Italians and Italianate Germans on the one hand, and those Germans on the other, who mixed French and Italian styles to achieve a measure of national or personal independence.

It may never be possible to establish when the Italians started to use the little notes. None have been found among the major composers before 1710. Caldara includes them in a cantata collection of 1712. However, neither Vivaldi's opera *Orlando* (1714) nor his *Incoronazione di Dario* (1717) contains a single little note, whereas his dated operas and vocal works of the late 1720's and 1730's are filled with them. There were none in his concerti up to and including Op. 7, but they made a first sporadic appearance in his Op. 8 that was composed around 1725. Vivaldi, then, evidently started to use little notes some time in the early 1720's.

The denomination of the little notes varied from composer to composer and sometimes from work to work, or from one copyist to another. Many masters, among them Vivaldi, Vinci, Leo, and Tartini, limit themselves mostly to 8th-notes, which do duty for all forms of *Vorschläge* from the prebeat to long onbeat. Occasionally 16ths and 32nds are used, usually to suggest either brevity or prebeat performance. A few masters and copyists prefer quarter-notes, using them even in front of 16ths and 32nds.[1] Others relate the denomination of the symbol to the length of the principal note. In Caldara, for instance, we usually find the following relationships: ♪ ♪ ♪ ♩Later in the century, G. B. Sammartini—who in his early works exclusively used 8th-notes—also fits the symbols to the note values, but uses the following slightly different scheme: ♪ ♪ ♪ ♩

These varied note values were not meant to be interpreted literally as was the case in music by members of the Berlin School. This fact is borne out by passages from Caldara of the kind shown in Ex. 17.1, where the graces were undoubtedly synchronized in spite of their routinely different face values.[2]

a. I Disingannati (1729)   *b. Temistocle* (1739)

Ex. 17.1. Caldara

The little notes in Italy also had a "Janus-face" character in that they could stand for prebeat *Vorschläge* or for appoggiaturas of varying lengths. By and large, it seems that in the vocal medium appoggiatura meaning of the little notes

[1] Thus we find in a contemporary MS copy of *Solfeggi* by Leonardo Leo (Bol. GG 97) in the first 57 folio leaves all *Vorschläge*, including those preceding 16th- and 32nd-notes, written in quarter-note form; in the subsequent pages a new scribe had taken over and now all *Vorschläge* are written as 8th-notes.

[2] Aut. GMF No. 393.

predominated. This, however, does not necessarily imply quantitative preponderance in actual performance, because the less conspicuous prebeat *Vorschläge* continued to be left to a greater extent to the singer's initiative. On the other hand, in instrumental music, and particularly in keyboard works, prebeat and onbeat meaning of the little notes is more evenly balanced, as can be deduced from both musical and theoretical evidence.

In Ex. 17.2a from Pergolesi's *L'Olimpiade*, the "affect" indicated by the term *amoroso*, the length of the principal notes which permit a true "leaning" *Vorschlag*, their place in the measure, and the homophonic setting all combine to favor the long type in all four instances. One of the innumerable cadential appoggiaturas is shown in Ex. *b* from Leonardo Leo.

Ex. 17.2.

In Ex. 17.3a from Caldara, the appoggiatura must be shorter than a dotted quarter-note to avoid bad octaves. In Ex. *b*, the *Vorschlag* on *-dar* has to be fairly short; 8th-note value is unsatisfactory, quarter-note value impossible because of open octaves. The grace here and in many other similar passages was perhaps intended as a brief, unaccented inflection whose exact metrical position, whether on, before, or between the beat, may have been largely immaterial.

Ex. 17.3. Caldara

In Ex. 17.4 from a Veracini sonata, 8th-note duration is impossible for all four graces. Indeed, the sequence of suspensions in the bass requires great shortness. From the preceding and many similar passages, we can gather that the "overlong" appoggiatura designs,

which became current in the 1730's and '40's cannot be routinely applied to the early decades of the century.

Ex. 17.4. Veracini, Op. 1, Sonata 2 (c. 1720)

A study of the music also reveals the widespread use of anticipation of many little notes, in addition to their repeatedly attested improvised insertion.

Musical evidence can be found in passages where onbeat execution is illogical because the principal note is too short to support an appoggiatura. The case for anticipation is strengthened if the little note occurs off the beat (an incongruous location for an appoggiatura) or is encompassed in the telltale slur with both the preceding and the following note, indicating *Zwischenschlag* character.

A few examples will clarify these points. In Ex. 17.5a, there is hardly an alternative to anticipation and the same is true of Ex. *b* with its embellished Lombard snaps. In Ex. *c* (from the same aria) the offbeat grace is clearly identified as a *Zwischenschlag*, and the same is true of Ex. *d*. In Ex. *e*, the third grace, off the beat, is again a *Zwischenschlag*, and all four graces are presumably anticipated.[3]

Ex. 17.5.

Johann Adolf Hasse, the completely Italianized German, was extremely fond of the Lombard rhythm and, like most of his Italian contemporaries, wrote out with meticulous care innumerable patterns of ♫. ‖ ♫ ‖ ♫. ‖etc. This notational custom suggests anticipation in Ex. 17.6a; Ex. *b* is self-explanatory.[4]

Ex. 17.6.

Perhaps the most characteristic case of anticipation before short notes is the typically Italian form of the mordent preceded by the grace note. The Italians had no symbol for the mordent.[5] On the other hand, the formula 🎵 occurs with such regularity and frequency in the Italian music of this period that it has the character of a standard ornament. In this formula, the dynamic stress is always placed on the principal note, a fact underlined by Tartini's later-to-be-quoted explanation that whenever tempo and time permit, the emphasis is strengthened by the addition of a trill: 🎵 (See below Ex. 17.23*d*.)

---

[3] L. Vinci, *Artaserre*, MS BN, D 14258; Vivaldi, *L'Usignuolo*, Foà 28; L. Leo, *Toccate per cembalo*, Nos. M. 47-6.

[4] Hasse inserted the aria for the famous castrato Farinelli (MS Gio. 36).

[5] Geminiani in midcentury introduced for the multiple mordent the English-derived symbol 𝄽 which, outside of his didactic works, was hardly used by himself nor apparently adopted by any other Italian composer of note. The French keyboard symbol: ⌁ does not seem to have been used until the later part of the century, for instance by Manfredini in 1775 (see below Ex. 39.6).

Onbeat emphasis on the little note would produce a turn; however, an intended turn was written  .

Following are a few samples from a limitless supply. Examples 17.7a-d show specimens from Vivaldi,[6] Leo, Locatelli, and Somis. Example *e* from a Vivaldi concerto is especially illuminating because onbeat rendition of the *Vorschläge* in the 2nd violins would be incongruous in relation to the figures of the 1st violins.

Ex. 17.7.

Sometimes the little notes occur in such profusion that their quantity alone suggests anticipation to avoid awkward heaviness. Giambattista Martini uses them so often in all of his instrumental and most of his vocal works that consistent onbeat rendition would make them insufferable. The three passages of Ex. 17.8 are truly typical[7] (with particularly telling offbeat locations in the second measure of Ex. *b*).

Voice-leading will often clarify the need for anticipation. Example 17.9a from Vivaldi shows a progression—repeated two measures later—where onbeat execu-

Ex. 17.8. G. B. Martini

---

[6] Foà 28.

[7] The examples are from his *Sonate d'inta-* *volatura per l'organo, e'l cembalo* (Amsterdam [1742]).

tion would produce unlikely octaves.[8] And in Ex. *b* from a Porpora cantata, anticipation seems advisable not only to avoid parallel fifths, but because of the appoggiatura character of the principal note g.[9] Example *c*, from a much later period, shows the need for the prebeat in the last measure.[10]

Ex. 17.9.

In Domenico Scarlatti's sonatas we find *Vorschläge* that were clearly intended to add a spark of vitality and seem to call for prebeat performance. In some of these instances, anticipation is further suggested by the need to avoid unpleasant parallels. Thus, in Ex. 17.10*a*, onbeat performance would lead to obtrusive fifths, repeated in analogous passages in mm. 19 and 74. The same is true in Ex. *b*; octaves would result in Ex. *c*, and fifths in Ex. *d*.[11]

Ex. 17.10. D. Scarlatti

[8] The autograph of this concerto for "violini d'accordature diverse" (Gio. 28, fols. 96ff.) is interesting because Vivaldi made several mistakes in the notation of the scordatura (he hardly ever used it) and corrected them through fingerings.

[9] Ms Bol. EE 22. [10] Ms Bol. C 205.

[11] The "K" numbers refer to Ralph Kirkpatrick's chronological catalogue. K 1-30 are from *Essercizi per gravicembalo* (London, 1738); *Complete Keyboard Works* in facs. from the manuscript and printed sources, ed. Ralph Kirkpatrick, 18 vols. (Johnson Reprint Co., New York, 1972).

Once in a while we find anticipation graphically expressed by prebar notation of the grace. In Ex. 17.11a from a sonata by Porpora, a mere engraver's error is excluded inasmuch as the grace a″ sharp is the last note on the line; the next measure appears on a new system. (See also below Exx. 30.36a, c, and d.) Example b from Vivaldi is taken from its primary source, a contemporary manuscript.[12] The repeat of the notational pattern, which was not due to lack of space, adds to its evidence value.

Ex. 17.11.

In Ex. 17.12 from a Vivaldi concerto, the unadorned entrance of the second voice in parallel thirds makes best harmonic sense if the grace in the first voice is anticipated.[13]

Ex. 17.12. Vivaldi, Concerto for two violins in C minor

In Ex. 17.13a from Giambattista Sammartini, harmonic logic favors the onbeat entrance of the dissonance in the 1st violins in order to clarify the suspensions of the seconds; this in turn implies anticipation or extreme unaccented shortness of the graces. In Ex. b the prebeat character of the graces is spelled out by the notation as *Nachschläge*.[14]

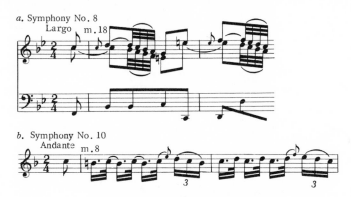

Ex. 17.13. G. B. Sammartini

The execution of ornaments should not interfere with a characteristic and prominent rhythmic design. An inserted grace that displaces the principal note from a syncopation, for example, actually distorts the rhythmic disposition. In

---

[12] Foà 29, f. 126. [13] Gio. 28, f. 200. gin. They are derived from primary, partly
[14] I owe these examples to Dr. Bathia Chur- autograph, sources, at the BN.

Ex. 17.14*a*, the syncopated notes of the tenor interlock rhythmically with the violins playing on the main beats. All graces in both parts have to be anticipated to clarify this rhythmic disposition.[15]

a. Leo, *La morte di Abelle*
Gravoso é Orvido

Vns.

Tenor

non spe - ro pie - tà

b. Vivaldi, Violin Concerto in B flat
Allegro mà poco

c. Vivaldi, Violin Concerto in D minor

"guardate la legatur[a]"

Ex. 17.14.

The Lombard snap ♫. is another rhythmic pattern whose characteristic physiognomy must not be blurred by an inserted grace. If the pattern in Ex. 17.14*b* were to be rendered as 𝄐, its characteristic shape would be erased.[16] Only anticipation 𝄐 can prevent this from happening. In another concerto, Vivaldi in fact writes out this resolution in regular notation (Ex. *c*) with the apparently autograph comment, "guardate la legatur[a]," to insure the same articulation that was indicated in Ex. *b* and thereby bring the Lombard rhythm into still sharper relief.[17]

The common dotted pattern might not be as distinctive as the Lombard snap, but when it pervades a lively composition, imparting to it a sense of rhythmic energy and brilliance, onbeat graces should not be permitted to emasculate this effect. That such brilliance and energy is intended in the first movement of Vivaldi's Cello Concerto in G is evident from the brief fragment of Ex. 17.15.[18] While anticipation of all the graces adds to its verve, onbeat rendition would blunt the sharply chiseled profile of the driving theme. If the solo cellist were to play the embellished patterns like ♫ or even like ♫, a limping effect would replace the dashing *élan*.[19]

Vns.

Cello
Solo

Ex. 17.15. Vivaldi, Cello Concerto in G major

15 Ms Bol. GG 97. 16 Foà 31, f. 39. 19 See for further illustrations D. Scarlatti's
17 Foà 30, f. 202. Sonatas, K 12, mm. 4-6; K 24, mm. 7-10; K 159,
18 Foà 29, f. 227. mm. 7-12, 26-33.

Other distinctive elements in the rhythmic design, such as contrast between successive figures or rhythmic interplay between voices, should not be effaced by ornaments. In Ex. 17.16, the contrast between the embellished dactyl at the beginning of the measure and the ensuing triplets is an attractive and recurring feature of the theme.[20] The grace had best be anticipated to clarify this contrast; onbeat execution would practically erase the rhythmic diversity.

Ex. 17.16. Vivaldi, Concerto for *violino in tromba*

Articulation and technical feasibility provide further clues. In Ex. 17.17*a*, the staccato dashes over all descending notes, including the first one, make sense only if the *Vorschlag* is anticipated.[21] The same is true of Tartini's staccato dashes in Ex. *b*.[22] In Ex. *c*, onbeat execution would be technically forbiddingly awkward for the solo violin.[23]

Ex. 17.17.

By way of appendix, we must, under the heading of the Italian school, also consider Handel's use of the one-note graces. This is in no way meant as a commitment in the complex question of Handel's musical citizenship but simply as an acknowledgment of the unmistakable Italian vintage of Handel's ornamentation (with but a few minor exceptions in his harpsichord works that show distinct traces of French influence).[24]

Like the Italians, Handel left to the performer both the freedom and the responsibility of adorning slow movements and *da capo* arias with diminutions and cadential improvisations. This freedom extends of course to small ornaments as well.

As to the *Vorschlag*, the long appoggiatura is occasionally written out, especially in the cadential appoggiatura-trill combination, but often left to the discretion of the performer. Often a little note will denote a long appoggiatura; not infrequently, however, the little note stands for a very brief grace.

---

[20] Foà 29, f. 94. The *violino in tromba* has not yet been identified. It may have been a violin with a bell-mouth attachment. In Rinaldi's catalogue of Vivaldi's works this concerto and its companion work are incorrectly listed as concerti for violin *con tromba*. There is no trumpet in the score.

[21] Ms AmB 273/2.
[22] Aut. BN MS 9793.
[23] Berk. No. 60.
[24] For a penetrating analysis of this matter, the reader is referred to Paul Henry Lang's *Georg Frideric Handel* (New York, 1966).

In his operas, oratorios, cantatas, and anthems, the little ornamental notes are very rare. Several oratorios do not contain a single one. One of the very few to be found, e.g. in *Judas Maccabaeus*, must be a grace note since onbeat execution with its unmitigated fifths is hardly thinkable (see Ex. 17.18a). In Ex. *b*, the unfailing consistency of the distinction between the little 16th-notes and the written-out Lombard rhythm leaves little doubt that a difference of execution was intended.[25] There seems to be no sensible alternative to anticipation. An analogous case of rhythmic variety is shown in Ex. *c*, from the Concerto Grosso in C major for two oboes and strings, where the same reasons call for anticipation. Here too the notation is not accidental; it is repeated exactly a second time, and the grace omitted altogether a third time:  .

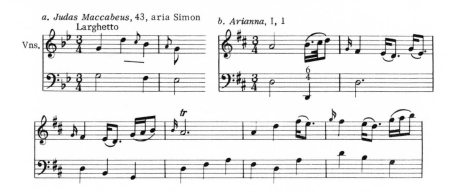

a. Judas Maccabaeus, 43, aria Simon   *b. Arianna*, I, 1

c. Concerto Grosso in C major for two oboes and two violins

Ex. 17.18. Handel

That at least some of Handel's little notes had interbeat meaning even for one of the early onbeat advocates is shown in a transcription which Theophil Muffat (Georg's son) made of Handel's Harpsichord Suites in 1739.[26] In it some of Handel's little notes are written out in metrical notation; many other ornaments are added, and Muffat's own symbol for the onbeat appoggiatura used so lavishly that one has to doubt its uncompromising onbeat meaning for Muffat himself. Example 17.19, taken from this manuscript, gives the transcriptions of Handel's original print.[27]

Ex. 17.19. Handel, Clavier Suite No. 2

[25] Aut. BM RM 20a6.

[26] The manuscript of this transcription, probably autograph, is in the BB (PK) Mus. MS 9160. It is entitled *Suites des pièces pour le clavecin composées par G. F. Händel et mises dans une autre applicature pour la facilité de la main. Par Theophile Muffat 1736.* In the upper right corner are the words *ex libris Theophili Muffat.*

[27] Published by Walsh (London n.d. [c. 1724]).

These, along with many other examples that could be shown, permit us to say that whenever a short interbeat rendition of a little note seems to make musical sense in Handel's works, it is likely to have been thus intended. Here too context and "affect" can give a clue whether an appoggiatura or a grace note is preferable.

As a final word on the preceding discussion of the musical evidence regarding Italian one-note graces, it might be added that the disparity between the relatively small space allotted to the discussion of the appoggiatura as contrasted to the grace-note style must not be misunderstood as a reflection of their respective importance; it is simply a reflection of their respective controversialism.

THEORETICAL SOURCES

Pierfrancesco Tosi (1647-1727), composer and castrato singer, wrote the previously mentioned treatise that was widely acclaimed as the authority with regard to the most admired vocal culture of the time. Unfortunately, the original contains no music examples, and many of Tosi's directives about ornaments are vague or ambiguous. This is notably the case with the *Vorschlag (appoggiatura)*.[28] According to him, this is easy to learn and easy to teach, but he does not tell us anything specific about it except to enumerate the degrees of the scale on which it can be used. Instead, he goes into a tirade against the "foreign puerility" with which modern composers indicate the *Vorschlag* in the score. He sees in this procedure an unpardonable encroachment on the singer's traditional privileges and views with horror the prospect that one day composers might even indicate the coloraturas!

Francesco Geminiani (1679-1762), a student of Corelli and a distinguished violinist-composer, had taken up residence in England and published in that country, as well as in France, a series of pedagogical works of which the most important are *A Treatise of Good Taste in the Art of Musick* (1749) and *The Art of Playing on the Violin* (1751). The theoretical discussion of ornaments is identical in both of these treatises. In addition to these essays and their musical materials, important insights into his style of ornamentation can be gained from several sonata volumes which he published with added diminutions in small print.

Geminiani distinguishes the descending type of *Vorschlag*, which he calls the *superior apogiatura* [sic], from the ascending, the *inferior apogiatura*. The former, he says, "is supposed to express love, affection, pleasure, etc. It should be made pretty long, giving it more than half the length of the note it belongs to, observing to swell the Sound by Degrees, and toward the End to force the Bow a little. If it be made short, it will lose much of the aforesaid Qualities; but will always have a pleasing Effect, and it may be added to any Note you will."[29] The *inferior apogiatura* has the same qualities, but its use is limited to spots where the melody rises one or two steps. It should always be followed by a mordent (the French *port de voix et pincé*).

Geminiani's instructions are cryptic regarding the short *Vorschlag*, but circumstantial evidence favors anticipation. When Geminiani says that it loses much of

[28] Tosi, *Opinioni*, ch. "Del' Appoggiatura," pp. 19-23.

[29] Prefaces to *The Art* and *Treatise*.

its expressive potential but will be pleasing and can be added to any note, the characterization, especially its unlimited applicability, fits the prebeat more than the onbeat type. Musical evidence will add confirmation and so will Tartini's explicit directives.

Whereas Geminiani lists ♪ as the symbol for the long appoggiatura, he uses ♪ and occasionally ♪ to signify the short, presumably anticipated one.

In Ex. 17.20a from the violin treatise, the 16th-note form of the grace adds support to the violinistic instinct which favors anticipation. A desire for a Lombard pattern in the same piece is indicated by Geminiani in regular notation as shown in m. 18 (Ex. b). In Ex. c, the first and third *Vorschläge* make best musical sense in anticipation. The first in 32nd-form is written as *Zwischenschlag* within a slur, before a weak beat; the third precedes a written-out appoggiatura. Only the second one could musically be a long type, yet the notation in 16th-notes indicates a different intention. Anticipation is also unmistakable in Ex. d: only by anticipation and sharp, short accentuation of the main note can a staccato effect be achieved.

Ex. 17.20. Geminiani, *The Art*

Giuseppe Tartini (1692-1770), the eminent violinist, composer, and teacher, wrote, presumably around 1750, a treatise that deals almost exclusively with ornamentation.[30] Tartini sees two main categories of *Vorschläge*: the long or sustained and the short or passing types (*appoggiatura lunga ossia sostentata*, and the *appoggiatura breve ossia di passaggio*).

The long appoggiatura, Tartini says, takes one-half of the value of the principal (binary) note and two-thirds of the value of a dotted note, as shown in Ex. 17.21. He explains why composers do not write them out in regular notes by referring to a difference in execution: as a regular note the first 8th would carry the normal metrical accent and be in need of a short trill to further underline it; as an appoggiatura it should start softly, then swell and diminish before it falls onto the main note. This style of execution agrees with that advocated by Geminiani, and, as will be seen, by Quantz and Leopold Mozart.

Tartini considerably limits the use of the long appoggiatura. It belongs only

[30] *Regole per arrivare a saper ben suonar il violino.* The original version, which had not been published, seemed for a long time to have survived only in a French translation by Pierre Denis (author of the previously cited *Nouvelle méthode*) under the title *Traité des agréments* . . . (Paris [1771]). In 1957, by unusual coincidence, two manuscript copies of the Italian original were discovered, one complete, one incomplete. In 1961 Erwin R. Jacobi published (Celle & New York) the French version of the treatise in a trilingual edition—German, French, and English—to which is attached as a supplement a facsimile of the complete Italian manuscript written by Tartini's student G. F. Nicolai. A comparison reveals that the French version, apart from the omission of the first chapter, on occasion takes considerable liberties with the original. Hence the Italian manuscript has to be consulted as the primary source.

Ex. 17.21. Tartini, *Regole*

to the heavy beat, he says, and is generally proper only for pieces in a slow tempo; the long species would dim the brilliance of faster pieces and weaken their liveliness. (For unspecified reasons Tartini admits exceptions for ¾ meter.) Very significant is Tartini's principle that the long appoggiatura is out of place within a setting of equal notes, because, he says, it would then prejudice the intended effect of evenness. This principle is to apply to any note values in any tempo.[31] It relates, of course, to what was referred to repeatedly as one of the aspects of rhythmic logic: non-interference, without compelling reasons, with a characteristic rhythm pattern. When, according to Tartini, the evenness of successive notes must be safeguarded, then *a fortiori* a far more striking rhythmic idea such as syncopation must not be similarly compromised.

Tartini sees the natural location of long appoggiaturas among notes of unequal length when the note carrying the grace is longer than the one that follows:

He dislikes a long ascending appoggiatura that forms a dissonance, because a dissonance ought to be resolved downward. He proposes to remedy the flaw by inserting two little notes, as shown in Ex. 17.22 where Ex. *a* is performed as Ex. *b*, to insure a correct downward resolution. Where a long appoggiatura is in order, Tartini continues, it can be applied by leaps—in which case it will not form a dissonance (see Ex. *c*).

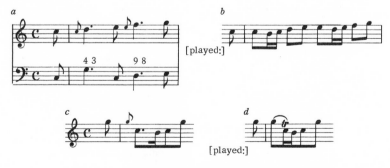

Ex. 17.22. Tartini, *Regole*

31 *Regole*, facs. ed., p. 5: ". . . date Note equali per serie, l'Appoggiature lunghe naturalmente non hanno loco sennon con pregiudizio del sentimento scritto, e ciò è vero in qualunque valore di Nota, ed in qualunque tempo. . . ."

What Geminiani failed to specify concerning the *appoggiatura breve*, Tartini makes very clear: this species is an anticipated grace. He speaks of its "fleeting" expression (*espressione sfuggita*), then, in keeping with this character, explains that the accent falls not on the *Vorschlag* but on the principal note: "these *Vorschläge* must be done quickly in such a manner that the [principal] note is always stronger than the *Vorschlag* and therefore the emphasis of the bowing or of the voice must always fall directly on the parent note, not at all on the *Vorschlag*."[32] The longer the principal note, the faster the *Vorschlag* seems to be, and in front of half-notes the *Vorschlag* "must be done so fast that it is almost unnoticeable" ("que appena si senta").

If the use of the long appoggiatura is considerably hedged in, the "passing" *Vorschlag*, in accord with Geminiani, can range over a much wider field. Tartini says that its most natural place is "among equal notes of many kinds and of any place."[33] As particularly favorable contexts, Tartini lists descending thirds among equally long notes (Ex. 17.23a); descending scales in quarter- or 8th-notes (Ex. b). For a rising ascending scale pattern, he gives an illustration (Ex. c) which clarifies the anticipation if such clarification were still needed. Almost equally explicit in this respect is a model of a descending pattern with a trilled variant (Ex. d) where an onbeat attempt, notably for the 8th-note model, would be absurd. The effect of these graces, Tartini says, is one of vivacity and spirit; they are not generally appropriate for very slow tempi, sad or melancholy expression, but are more at home in allegros or such intermediate speeds as an andante cantabile. Example e from Tartini shows an application of his rules concerning prebeat *Vorschläge* among even note values.[34]

Ex. 17.23. Tartini

[32] Ibid., facs. ed., p. 7: ". . . queste Appoggiature devono esser veloci in tal modo, che si senta sempre più la Nota, che l'Appoggiatura, e però la forza dell'Arcata, ossia della Voce, deve cader immediatamente sopra la Nota, non mai sopra l'Appoggiatura."

[33] Ibid., facs. ed., p. 7: ". . . di loro natura hanno luoco nelle Note equali in molti modi, ed in qualunque sito."

[34] Ms BN MS 9796.

The "Janus face" of the *Vorschlag* with its two polarities, the long appoggiatura and the grace note, is clearly drawn in Tartini's treatise which thus provides conclusive theoretical confirmation of the inferences drawn from musical evidence. In particular, Tartini's principles also throw light on the much more vaguely formulated ideas of Geminiani and make it clear that the latter's "short appoggiatura," which he said could be applied to any note, was indeed the anticipated grace. It is interesting to note that Tartini, like Geminiani, presents only the two contrasting types, the anticipation and the long onbeat, and that no mention is made of the short, accented onbeat *Vorschlag*.

In his discussion of the long appoggiatura, Tartini's principles show the trend to a greater length of the grace than that which applied to Bach or Handel, and also to greater regularization of its length. In both these respects we can see a link to German *galant* practices as well as an indication of its Italian origin. Concerning the other end of the pole, the prominent role which Tartini assigns to the prebeat *Vorschlag* permits interesting inferences with regard to the countless foreign masters who looked for guidance to Italy rather than to Berlin.

18

German One-Note Graces

1715-1765

The *galant* style, which emerged in Italy between 1715 and 1720, largely out of the ingratiating tunefulness and popular stance of the Opera Buffa, found its way into Germany almost immediately. There it soon grew into a powerful movement that set out to reform music by abolishing all polyphonic complexities in favor of an art that unashamedly appealed to the senses. Because German masters had pursued and continued to pursue the intricacies of counterpoint to far greater lengths than any foreigners had done, the impact of the reorientation was more strongly felt in that country than anywhere else. Moreover, in Germany the stylistic upheaval was dramatized by the ideological militancy with which the spokesmen of the "new" music attacked the protagonists of the "old," i.e. the late baroque, music for indulging in sterile constructivism and for addressing themselves solely to the rational mind while failing completely to "flatter the ear" and "speak to the heart." Soon the battle lines were clearly drawn and for some thirty odd years the country was split between the old and the new by a "generation gap" as deep as perhaps any in the history of music.

As was briefly sketched in Chapter 6 above, the stylistic revolution brought with it a change in ornamental fashion. Within the family of one-note graces the main change concerned frequency and length of the appoggiatura. Its long and especially its "overlong" forms, which were inconsonant with the linear music of the baroque, were now not only free to proliferate but were constantly needed, as Quantz put it, to enrich the new "simple-minded" melodies and to relieve the tedium of too much consonance.

Johann David Heinichen (1683-1729), though steeped in baroque tradition as student of Kuhnau's in Leipzig, became one of the earliest converts and eloquent advocates of the new aesthetics. He wrote two treatises on the thorough bass.[1]

---

[1] The first (in the following pages referred to as I), is entitled *Neu erfundene & gründliche Anweisung . . . zu vollkommener Erlernung des General Basses* (1711); the second (referred to as II) is a much enlarged and revised edition of the first, entitled *Der Generalbass in der Composition* (1728). In this second treatise of 1728 he leaves no doubt about his new allegiance when he unleashes a blistering attack on contrapuntal artifacts (fn. on pp. 1-5). He satirizes the old composers who indulge in would-be learned speculative manipulations, putting "innocent notes" on a torture rack, stretching, pulling, reversing, repeating, exchanging them, fabricating useless counterpoint, concerned not with the sound of the notes but with their appearance on paper. By contrast, he says, the *new* music reestablishes the supremacy of the ear and relegates reason to the role of a subordinate adviser. Admitting to have lost his erstwhile enthusiasm for counterpoint, he now tolerates it only in sacred music and otherwise sees a legitimate place for it in beginner's training in composition. But he warns against studying it too long for fear that the student will become as big a pedant as his teacher. He abhors, he says, its excessive use and the very idea of "papernotes" posing as the last word in nobility and artistry. He points his accusing finger unmistakably at the Germans as the people most inclined to indulge in such intricate musical nonsense (*Tiff-taff*). He suggests as the best stylistic solution one that would wed Italian *dolcezza* with French *vivacité*; thus he became, halfway between Georg Muffat and Quantz, another advocate of a mixed style for Germany, but the first, however, whose mixture had a definitely *galant* taste. There is, of course, a direct line from Heinichen's belligerent manifesto over Scheibe's notorious attack on Bach's turgidity to the preface in Quantz's treatise in which the latter expressed similar feelings albeit in more reserved and diplomatic terms.

In both of them he discusses ornaments that are used in accompaniment while pointing to the difficulty of a written explanation and to the superiority of personal demonstration. What matters, he says, are not rules but experience and judgment, and therefore he presents only *prima principia* (I, p. 175; II, pp. 521f.).

The two treatises show interesting differences regarding one-note graces which reflect the changing fashion. In 1711 two one-note graces are listed, both of which are of the interbeat type. One is the *transitus* or *Durchgang* into the third, an anticipated *tierce coulée*; the other is the *superjectio* or *Überschlag* in its usual meaning as *Nachschlag* in the manner of the French *accent*. Example 18.1a shows (for the top voice only) the *transitus* before the bar line and the *superjectio* on the second quarter of the complete measure.

In 1728 the *transitus* is still listed but is characterized as making generally a poor effect on the clavier unless the notes are fairly slow or graced with a trill. The *superjectio* is replaced by the *Vorschlag* (symbol ⌣) that can rise or fall in any interval but is most frequently used when the melody moves stepwise or by thirds. As Heinichen's examples show, the *Vorschlag* is now basically a long appoggiatura; yet in specifying *ohngefähr* (roughly), he underlines its variability. Interesting to note is the differentiation he makes between vocal and instrumental rendition, with the instruments briefly anticipating the appoggiatura (Ex. 18.1b). The long appoggiatura is shown only in connection with a quarter-note and then still subject to modification by "experience and judgment."

Ex. 18.1. Heinichen (1711)

Theophil (Gottlieb) Muffat (1690-1770), the son of Georg, did not turn his back on the baroque heritage that was handed to him from both his father and his revered teacher Fux. But Theophil, having assimilated both Italian and French stylistic influences, had at the same time absorbed many elements of the new stylistic currents; these are revealed in lighter polyphonic textures, the wider use of homophony, and the simple song-like nature of many of his themes. His ornamentation shows strong indebtedness to his father, but more still to D'Anglebert. A first ornamentation table of his appeared in 1726 and a much more detailed one about 1736.[2] Both show only onbeat patterns and those from the latter work that refer to the *Vorschlag* are given in Ex. 18.2a. No doubt we find here an important tributary to the later exclusive onbeat patterns of C.P.E. Bach. However, in spite of the tables, such exclusivity was not practiced by Th. Muffat. Some of his interbeat interpretations have been shown with his version of Handel's Harpsichord Suites (see above Ex. 17.19a). His use of the prebeat *Vorschlag* is revealed by a few cases of prebar notation in the original edition of the *Componimenti* (no manuscript survived), such as the passages of Exx. b and c.

---

[2] *Versetl sammt 12 Toccaten* (1726); *Componimenti musicali* (c. 1736).

Moreover, when Muffat uses a much shorter than usual denomination for the *Vorschlag*, such as the 32nd of Ex. *d* or the 16ths of Ex. *e*, the likelihood is strong that either extreme shortness or anticipation was intended.

Ex. 18.2. Th. Muffat, *Componimenti musicali* (c. 1736)

The composer Johann Mattheson (1681-1764) was an eminent critic and theoretician. Though he published volume after volume about every conceivable aspect of music, he was strangely reticent about ornaments, to which he devotes only a few chance remarks here and there and a few not overly revealing paragraphs in one treatise.[3] The reason for this neglect can be found in his previously quoted idea that usage and experience matter more in this field than theoretical discussions and rules. However, he feels that Heinichen went too far in licensing everyone's personal taste and experience for the fashioning of ornaments (footnote to par. 19). What Mattheson does suggest is that the performer follow, more or less, the best Italians "without compulsion and without exaggeration" (par. 18). Then he sets out to describe a few ornaments which he says are still widely used (par. 20).

With such reservations, Mattheson proceeds to discuss the *Accent*; unfortunately his exposition is partly obscure. First he speaks of touching very softly, very fast, and "quasitwice" the upper or lower neighbor. Although this explanation, with its combination of "very fast" and "very softly," suggests the prebeat, the next paragraph implies the onbeat. In it Mattheson distinguishes two types, the simple and the double *Accent*; the simple, he says, takes only very little from the value of the following note, the double, in which the grace is repeated, takes half (pars. 20-21).

[3] *Capellmeister* (1739). Ornaments are discussed in pt. 2, ch. 3, entitled "On the Art of graceful Singing and Playing." The following references will be to paragraphs of this chapter.

Matteson then turns to the leaping *Vorschläge* and mentions the frequent use, in recitatives, of those that descend by a fourth or fifth (par. 24). They can also rise, he says, and be done "approximately," as shown in Ex. 18.3a. The improvised use of a downward leaping appoggiatura is shown in Ex. *b*. In addition to such appoggiaturas, Matteson also mentions *Ueberschläge* (par. 26) which are *Nachschläge* of the French *accent* type (see Ex. *c*).

Ex. 18.3. Matteson (1739)

Matteson mentions no symbols and speaks only of improvised additions. Though his few remarks reflect the growing tendency toward the onbeat *Vorschlag*, his failure to mention the prebeat style explicitly within his cursory discussion permits no inference of non-use. Considering his highly flexible attitude toward ornaments in general and his contempt for binding rules, it is hard to believe that he wished to ban the prebeat style for *any* grace.

Franz Anton Maichelbeck (1702-1750), an Italian-trained keyboard composer and organist at the Freiburg Cathedral, published in 1738 a clavier treatise.[4] In it he calls the *Vorschlag* a *Mordant*, and he too speaks of unmarked, hence improvised, ornaments. Prebeat interpretation is likely for the first grace in Ex. 18.4a, as a *cercar della nota* (cf. above Exx. 15.5a and 15.11a); it is also probable for the first three graces in Ex. *b* and is quite certain for what he calls doubling (*Dopplierung*), where the *Vorschlag* is sounded twice (Ex. *c*). Further confirmation comes from the notation at the end of Ex. *c* where the first of the repeated *Vorschlag* notes is stemmed together with the preceding 8th-note.

Ex. 18.4. Maichelbeck (1738)

In his treatise of 1745, Meinrad Spiess (1683-1761) echoes Heinichen's derisive tirades against counterpoint and surpasses them in violence of invective.[5] In contrast to his modern aesthetics, his ornamental teachings appear still retrospective. To define the *accentus musicus*, or *Stimm-Einfall*, he borrows Walther's defini-

---

[4] *Die auf dem Clavier lehrende Caecilia.* The treatise deserves attention for its advanced keyboard fingerings that stress liberal use of the thumb and fairly modern patterns for the scales. The *Vorschlag* is discussed on pp! 38f.
[5] *Tractatus musicus.* Although born two years before Bach, Spiess bestows on the polyphonic masters such epithets as "old quacks," "antiquarian pedants," "enemies of the ear," "contrapuntal bigwigs who excel in paper artifacts and witchcraft."

tion of lightly touching the neighbor tone before sounding the principal note. No mention is made of its rhythmic disposition, which is still meant to be flexible but obviously could not include a *long* appoggiatura. As symbol he uses a little quarter-note and mentions the dash as an alternative.

Georg Friedrich Kauffmann (1679-1735), a composer of the old school, lavishly ornamented his chorale preludes.[6] All his slides, and most of his *Vorschläge*, appear to be anticipated. Example 18.5a shows French-style *accents*, an anticipated slide, and a *Schneller*. In Ex. *b* anticipation is obvious.

Ex. 18.5. Kauffmann (1733)

Georg Philipp Telemann (1681-1767), like Mattheson, was a transitional figure who bridged the "generation gap" between the baroque and the *galant* style. His ornamentation is largely Italian oriented with some French admixtures. His *Vorschläge* seem to have had the full Italian range from the grace note to the long appoggiatura. He is inconsistent regarding symbols: in some works he used only the little quarter-notes (e.g. the "Table Music" of Ex. 18.6), in others he used 8ths and 16ths, in many he writes no symbols at all.

Ex. 18.6. Telemann, *Musique de Table*, II (1733)

The "Mannheimer" Johann Stamitz (1717-1757) was one of the "moderns." In the passage shown in Ex. 18.7, he used the *Vorschlag* unmistakably in prebeat meaning.

Ex. 18.7. Stamitz, Op. 8ᵛ

Christoph Graupner (1683-1760), in a clavier work of 1738, writes *tierces coulées* (Ex. 18.8a) which must be anticipated, because their onbeat execution would produce serious parallels.[7]

Ex. 18.8. Graupner, Partita 8, Sarabande

[6] *Harmonische Seelenlust* (Leipzig, 1733) was accessible in BB Mus. MSS 11419, 11420, written by J. C. Kittel.

[7] *Partien auf das Clavier . . .* (Darmstadt, 1738); MS copy Yale University, Lowell Mason 4981.

In several of his operas, Carl Heinrich Graun (1703-1759), court composer of Frederick II, followed the Italian practice of correlating the values of the little notes and the big notes: ♩♪ ♪♩ ♪♩ ♩·♪ ♩·♪.
Graun's practice might represent an intermediate stage on the road to exact metrical meaning of the little notes assumed by C.P.E. Bach and his followers.

It seems that Graun did not yet use the half-, or whole, or dotted note as symbol; the quarter-notes, on the other hand, often had literal meaning, as can be seen in Ex. 18.9a where the same quarter-note appoggiatura is written out in big notes for the horns, in little ones for the voices. The 8th-note symbol, too, seems to represent generally an appoggiatura of about 8th-note length. However, the little 16th-note seems to stand occasionally for anticipation. In Ex. b, contrary to the usual correlation, he writes 16th- instead of 8th-notes; this fact, combined with the *tierces coulées* and the great frequency with which Graun everywhere spells out the Lombard rhythms, would seem to favor a prebeat rather than Lombard interpretation of these graces. In Ex. c, anticipation avoids the encroachment of one appoggiatura on top of another one; in Ex. d, the prebeat meaning is inescapable.[8]

Ex. 18.9. Graun

THE BERLIN SCHOOL

Graun takes us to Berlin where his own, largely Italian-bred practices may have had a good part in shaping the new ornamental fashions associated with that city. These fashions crystallized in the teachings of a number of eminent authors who became identified as the "Berlin School." The word "crystallized" is singularly evocative of what happened here: the hardening of a fluid mass into solid and rigid shapes.

Quantz and C.P.E. Bach were unquestionably the commanding personalities among the city's composer-theorists. However, the two men disagreed on many important matters, and when we think of the Berlin School in terms of a more or less unified doctrine, Quantz can be included under that label only with considerable qualifications.

Johann Sebastian's second son, Carl Philipp Emanuel (1714-1788), published his celebrated essay on the art of clavier playing in two parts, of which the first deals with solo performance, the second with accompaniment.[9] His famous onbeat rule

[8] *Le feste galante* (1747), MS AmB 195; *Adriano* (1746), MS AmB 193; *Montezuma* (1755), *DDT*, I, vol. 15.

[9] *Versuch*, pt. 1, 1753; pt. 2, 1762.
Ornaments are discussed in both parts; most important for our present purpose is pt. 1,

is formulated in bk. 1, ch. 2, sec. 1, par. 23, where he categorically states that all ornaments indicated by little notes have to be played in the time of the following note, "consequently the preceding note must never lose any of its value while the value of the little notes has to be subtracted from the following note." At the same time, he acknowledges that this rule is frequently violated: "This remark is the more necessary, the more one sins against it" ("Diese Anmerckung ist um so viel nöthiger, je mehr gemeiniglich hierwider gefehlt wird . . .").

Bach distinguishes two types of *Vorschläge*: those of variable length (*veränderliche*) and those that are invariably short (*unveränderliche*). He then makes a statement that must be quoted in full: "Because of the former circumstance [i.e. the variable value of some *Vorschläge*], one has *not so long ago* started to indicate the *Vorschläge* according to their value, instead of marking all of them with 8th-notes. *Before that, Vorschläge of such variable length were not yet introduced.* However, in today's style, unable to rely on rules about their length, we cannot do without such exact indication, since all kinds [of lengths] occur with all kinds of notes"[10] [italics mine].

This paragraph is extremely revealing. In it Philipp Emanuel contrasts "today's," i.e. the *galant* style, in which the new symbolism was introduced "not so long ago," with the older style, where the 8th-note symbol was adequate because *Vorschläge* of such varying length did not exist, which of course implies their essential shortness. Since J. S. Bach did not belong to "today's style" but represented what was practiced "before," we have here a clear statement by Philipp Emanuel himself that his rules do not apply to the music of his father. It further confirms that Johann Sebastian's *Vorschläge* were basically short and adds weighty support to our characterization of the "overlong" Berlin formulas as "un-Bachian" and anachronistic.

With the length of the *Vorschlag* indicated through the symbol, the rhythmic problem of the long appoggiatura is largely solved. In general, binary notes lose one-half (Ex. 18.10*a*), ternary two-thirds (Ex. *b*), of their value to the *Vorschlag* (par. 11). A note extended by a tie loses its full value, be it binary (Ex. *c*) or ternary (Ex. *d*), and so does a note followed by a rest (Ex. *e*).

Among other noteworthy principles, Bach states that the *Vorschlag* is always stronger than the following note, that the long, "variable" appoggiatura is best on heavy beats (par. 9), that the short, "invariable," one must be played so short that the loss of value to the following note is barely noticeable (par. 13). On the whole, he stipulates the use of the short *Vorschlag* in all those instances where, in the music of J. S. Bach, anticipation was favored: before triplets, for filling in descending thirds, and for consonances before dissonances. *Vorschläge* that fill descending thirds in an Adagio should be slightly less short to allow tenderness of expression (par. 14).

---

ch. 2, sec. 2 (pp. 62-70), which is entirely devoted to the *Vorschlag*, and unless otherwise stated, all the references in the following pages will be to paragraphs in that specific section.

[10] Par. 5: "Vermöge des ersten Umstandes hat man seit nicht gar langer Zeit angefangen, diese Vorschläge nach ihrer wahren Geltung anzudeuten, anstatt dass man vor diesem alle Vorschläge durch Acht-Theile zu bezeichnen pflegte, ... Damahls waren die Vorschläge von so verschiedener Geltung noch nicht eingeführet; bey unserm heutigen Geschmacke hingegen können wir um so viel weniger ohne die genaue Andeutung derselben fortkommen, je weniger alle Regeln über ihre Geltung hinlänglich sind, weil allerley Arten bey allerley Noten vorkommen können."

Ex. 18.10. C.P.E. Bach

Philipp Emanuel tolerates a descending short *Vorschlag* on top of another that is written out in regular notation, provided the preceding note is repeated and it is not done on a final note. (As will be seen, Agricola has more reservations, and Quantz rejects such a design entirely.) Written-out rising appoggiaturas do not, however, suffer any additional *Vorschläge* (par. 23). *Vorschläge* must not interfere with the purity of voice-leading; therefore *parallels must be avoided*, as he demonstrates with two such undesirable examples (par. 17). Finally, Bach warns once more against anticipation which creates those "ugly *Nachschläge*" which he significantly admits to be "extremely fashionable" (par. 25). Thus he finds the *Nachschläge* of Ex. 18.11a objectionable in a singing passage and corrects them with onbeat *Vorschläge* (Ex. *b*). It is interesting that W. A. Mozart did not share this aesthetic judgment: much of the first movement of his D major String Quintet (K 593) is based on the very motive which C.P.E. Bach found so reprehensible (Ex. *c*).

Ex. 18.11.

Marpurg was the highly regarded author of several treatises and an editor of musical journals. His first detailed discussion of ornaments was published in 1749. The next treatment in depth appeared in 1755, with additional documentation in 1762.[11]

There are striking differences between the two presentations of 1749 and 1755. The first shows strong indebtedness to the French in symbols and in execution. Notable in it is the absence of a long (one-note) appoggiatura. By contrast, the second discussion (1755), two years after the publication of C.P.E. Bach's treatise, shows that Marpurg has now—with a few exceptions—by and large fallen in line with the new leader's ideas. The process of conversion may have been

11 *Crit. Musicus.* The articles on ornaments appeared in 1749, pp. 48ff. The most important of his treatises dealing with ornaments are the *Anleitung zum Clavierspielen* (referred to hereafter as 1755) and *Die Kunst das Clavier zu spielen*, 4th ed. (referred to hereafter as 1762); the first edition of 1750 does not discuss ornaments.

started in 1749 by a pamphlet of Agricola's; under the pseudonym of "Olibrio," Agricola violently attacked Marpurg's ornament models as well as his ideas on meter, measure, and time beating.[12] Agricola charged that Marpurg, writing for Germans, did not take German masters as his models when discussing ornaments. He declared several of Marpurg's terms and symbols to be completely wrong, several of his designs to be in bad taste or falsely taught. This attack reveals an attitude of intolerance in matters of ornaments never before known in this field.

One of Agricola's criticisms makes it significantly clear that he speaks of the *new* ornamentation and not of anything he may have learned from J. S. Bach (whose student he once was, and who at the time of the pamphlet was still living). He berates Marpurg for not knowing that the short symbols for trills and mordents with only two waggles (⌇⌇) stand only for the short variety, whereas long trills and mordents have to be indicated by three waggles (⌇⌇). This, as will be shown, does not at all apply to J. S. Bach who used the short symbols indiscriminately for trills or mordents of all lengths.

In 1749 Marpurg still calls the *Vorschlag "Accent,"* uses the hook symbol, and gives the short onbeat solution of Ex. 18.12a. The *Accent,* he writes, consists in *gently* touching the borrowed tone before playing the principal note.[13] The "gentle touching," like Mattheson's similar expression, is more akin to an interbeat than an accented onbeat *Vorschlag.*

Marpurg's *Doppelaccent* (Ex. *b*) resembles Chambonnières's *port de voix* and is one of the models that aroused Agricola's ire. It is tasteless, he says; no German or Italian singer or instrumentalist would use it in this manner and, he adds, even Heinichen's similar pattern, with the first of the repeated notes in anticipation, has been out of fashion for twenty years.

Under the name of *Rückschlag,* Marpurg then gives the French *accent* design in both directions (Ex. *c*).

Ex. 18.12. Marpurg (1749)

The treatise of 1755 already goes a long way to meet C.P.E.'s principles, including the rule that the *Vorschlag* must always fall on the beat.[14] The adaptation is almost complete in 1762; now the "invariable" *Vorschläge* are, in accord with the new procedures, marked as ♪ or ♫ ; the long, "variables" as ♪♩ ♩ , indicating their exact values.

Marpurg deviates from Philipp Emanuel in a pattern (Ex. 18.13) where a *Vorschlag* before a pair of 16th-notes turns the latter into a triplet (1762, p. 22).

---

[12] [J. F. Agricola], *Schreiben an Herrn. . . .* The tone of the pamphlet is very sharp and personal. It refers to Marpurg sarcastically as "chief art expert" and contains repeated insinuations of bad taste and ignorance. Yet the two men must have made up, for Marpurg later welcomed Agricola's contributions to his second, more successful journal, the *Historisch-*

kritische Berichte zur Aufnahme der Musik (1754-1762).

[13] *Crit. Musicus,* p. 66: "Der Accent . . . besteht darinn, dass bevor man die Hauptnote anschlägt, man [den] . . . entlehnten Thon kurz zuvor gelinde berührt."

[14] 1755, p. 48; 1762, p. 22.

This solution is illogical, and it is hard to imagine that any composer wanting the effect of a triplet would choose to write it: C.P.E. Bach's implied solution:  will often be awkward but will at least leave the binary character intact.

Ex. 18.13. Marpurg (1762)

Far more significant is another deviation in which Marpurg in 1755 not only presents the "ugly" *Nachschlag* but uses a little note with inverted flag ♩ to signify an interbeat grace. In Ex. 18.14*a*, we see the new symbol indicating a French *accent* (as an alternative to Saint Lambert's caret sign); in Ex. *b* it competes with a dash symbol to signify *anticipatione della nota*, whereas in Ex. *c* it stands only for an anticipated *Vorschlag* (1755, p. 50).

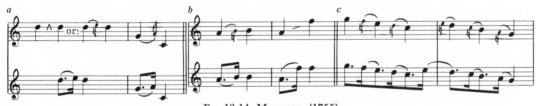

Ex. 18.14. Marpurg (1755)

In 1757, Johann Friedrich Agricola (1720-1774) presented his ideas in extensive annotations to his translation of Tosi's previously cited treatise.[15] Agricola goes into great detail in supplementing Tosi's vague ideas about the *Vorschlag*, and his lengthy presentation largely agrees with Philipp Emanuel.

Agricola lists four functions for the *Vorschlag*: 1) to better connect the melody, 2) to fill apparent voids, 3) to enrich the harmony, and 4) to give vivacity and luster to the melody. Onbeat start is again demanded for both long and short *Vorschläge*. For the long ones, Agricola stresses their harmonic aspect, saying that they mostly form a dissonance with the bass (p. 68). In turn, he links their dissonance function with the need to place them solely on the heavy metrical beats (p. 71). Consequently, he says, *Vorschläge* on light beats are always short. However, since harmony enrichment is not the only function, they may occasionally occur on consonances when they help to "fill a void" (p. 69).

Concerning the length of the "variable" *Vorschläge* and their new mode of literal symbolization, Agricola agrees with C.P.E. Bach. *Vorschläge*, Agricola says, may rise or fall by step or by leap, but rising ones must always repeat the preceding note whereas falling ones may, with certain limitations, sound a new note. Like C.P.E. Bach, Agricola cautions against faulty voice-leading, but, with regard to octaves only, limits his prohibition to such parallels as are "all too noticeable" (p. 77, "allzudeutliche verbotene Oktavenfolgen"). His *Vorschläge*, like Philipp Emanuel's, carry the dynamic stress (p. 64). Agricola says that the short *Vorschläge*, even though they take the beat, have no harmonic func-

15 *Anleitung zur Singkunst*, tr. from P. Tosi's *Opinioni*.

tion; rather, they serve the purpose of either connecting notes or of adding brilliance (p. 66). In the frequent pattern of Ex. 18.15*a*, the *Vorschlag* must be sounded not as a 16th-note (Ex. *b*) but as a 32nd (Ex. *c*). Furthermore, a *Vorschlag* must never transform a binary into a ternary rhythm, nor a ternary into a binary rhythm (as Marpurg had done); hence Ex. *d* is not to be rendered as Ex. *e*, nor Ex. *f* as Ex. *g* (p. 77).

Ex. 18.15. Agricola (1757)

Like Marpurg, who opened the door for prebeat *Vorschläge*, Agricola too departs from the onbeat-only rule in two significant instances. First, he tells us that "several famous performers" will play *Vorschläge* between descending thirds "in the manner of the French in the time of the preceding note . . ." (p. 68) and will render Ex. 18.16*a* like Ex. *b*; "other famous performers," however, prefer to play those very *Vorschläge* as all others—on the beat and in an Adagio not too fast (Ex. *c*).

Ex. 18.16. Agricola

The second deviation concerns *Nachschläge* which, Agricola says, are often necessary to connect and fill in the melody (p. 81). He distinguishes simple and double *Nachschläge*, consisting of one and two notes respectively. The double ones, he says, are written out by the composer, the single ones *never*, but are added freely (p. 81). Whereas Philipp Emanuel had acknowledged the widespread use of such interbeat graces and deplored it, Agricola reaffirms their frequent improvised use and recognizes their musical justification.

In 1752 Johann Joachim Quantz (1697-1773) published his justly famous treatise.[16]

The differences that separated Quantz from his Berlin colleagues in matters of the *Vorschlag* have often been overlooked because some of his frequently quoted rules about the long types were fully in accord with C.P.E. Bach, whereas the principles that contradicted Bach were scattered in different chapters of his treatise, and some were conveyed by indirection only.

In the very first paragraph of Chapter 8, Quantz establishes the *raison d'être* for the [long] *Vorschlag*—the enrichment of the harmony through dissonance.

[16] *Versuch.* Quantz was flute instructor of Frederick II of Prussia and leader of the court's musical establishment. His book far exceeds the scope of a flute treatise; its greatest part deals with questions of performance that are of universal interest. The *Vorschlag* is dealt with chiefly, but not solely, in ch. 8 and, unless otherwise specified, all references in the following paragraphs will be to this chapter.

Such enrichment, he writes, is a "necessary thing" to prevent a melody from sounding "meager and simple-minded" ("sehr mager und einfältig") and to relieve the monotony of too many consonances which are, he says, usually associated with a *galant* air. The paragraph is very significant because it reaffirms the link between the long and "overlong" appoggiatura (of which he speaks) and *galant* homophony. Who could argue that J. S. Bach's music was in need of added long appoggiaturas to relieve the monotony of consonances and lend a helping hand to meager and simple-minded melodies?

There are, Quantz says, "two types of *Vorschläge*. Some are rendered on the beat, others rendered as passing notes, or on the upbeat ('im Aufheben des Tactes'). One could call the former *anschlagende*, the other *durchgehende Vorschläge*" (par. 5). The two types are not differentiated by symbol. They share the little 8th-note sign, which can stand for anything from an anticipated *Vorschlag* to the longest appoggiatura. On the other hand, Quantz says, the little 16th-note is reserved only for very short *Vorschläge*. Quantz did not adopt the new fashion of indicating the exact length of the appoggiatura through the denomination of the symbol. In this respect, too, he shows his greater flexibility.

Speaking first of the onbeat *Vorschlag*, Quantz writes that one should start it softly (*weich anstossen*) and, time permitting, let it swell and glide into the next note which is to be played "a little softer." Like Tartini, Quantz does not think of an accented start, but rather of a gently emphasized one, and he acknowledges the Italian origin of this execution.

Quantz does not divide the onbeat *Vorschlag* into the long variable and the short invariable species. His onbeat *Vorschlag*, like Tartini's, seems to have been basically long.

The only mention of what appears to be a very short onbeat *Vorschlag* is made in a statement that involves a certain contradiction (par. 2). Quantz speaks of 16th-note symbols in front of such notes "which must not be deprived of any of their value" ("denen an ihrem Zeitmaasse nichts abgebrochen werden darf"). Though only anticipation could safeguard their full value, Quantz adds that these notes are rendered very fast and articulated in the place of the principal note, on the beat ("ganz kurz ausgedrücket, und anstatt der Hauptnoten im Niederschlage angestossen . . ."). The only example he gives for this execution consists of long repeated notes (Ex. 18.17).

Ex. 18.17. Quantz (1752)

For the long appoggiatura, Quantz gives a set of rules that was repeated in many treatises that were published during the rest of the century. They are in essence the same as Tartini's and Philipp Emanuel's. Thus, a *Vorschlag* before a binary note takes one-half, before a ternary note two-thirds, of the principal note's value (par. 7), as shown in Exx. 18.18a and b. In 6/8 or 6/4 meter the *Vorschlag* takes the full value of a dotted note that is prolonged by a tie (Ex. c). A *Vorschlag* can also take the full written value of a note followed by a rest, in which case the rest has to accommodate the displaced principal note (Ex. d).

Quantz's presentation of the prebeat *Vorschläge* is not very systematic and paragraph 6, in which they are introduced, gives by itself only a very incomplete

Ex. 18.18. Quantz

picture of their real scope. In that paragraph Quantz seems at first to limit the grace notes to descending thirds alone. However, his illustration, given in Ex. 18.19a, immediately widens the scope, since two of the four *Vorschläge* do not link descending thirds. Quantz cautions the performer not to play the notational pattern of Ex. *a* like that of Ex. *b* (i.e. as short appoggiaturas) nor like that of Ex. *c* [i.e. as long appoggiaturas]. He says that although the pattern of Ex. *b* is melodically almost the same, it nevertheless produces an altogether different expression: one of boldness and vivacity ("frech und lebhaft"); the correct rendition calls for caressing smoothness ("einen schmeichelnden Ausdruck").

Ex. 18.19. Quantz

When a long appoggiatura is written out in regular notes and is preceded by another *Vorschlag* indicated by a little note, the latter, Quantz says (par. 6), has to be played *before* the beat, as shown in Ex. 18.20. This rule makes excellent musical sense. The onbeat start of the appoggiatura is meant to enrich the harmony. A second appoggiatura, displacing the first from the beat, will drain from the first the better part of its power to enrich and often create an awkward melodic-rhythmic design. That J. S. Bach used Quantz's solution was shown above in Ex. 16.13.

Ex. 18.20. Quantz

Another extremely important application of the prebeat *Vorschlag* by Quantz was shown above in connection with his characterization of the prebeat design as the typically French style of performance. His arresting illustration was reproduced in Ex. 12.25 which showed that even in the pattern ♪ ♫ ♪ ♫ the *Vorschlag* must be played in anticipation and not resolved into four equal 16th-notes (as we do it almost routinely today for all 18th-century music), nor, as Agricola prescribes, rendered with a Lombard snap. This significant piece of information was given incidentally in a chapter on the *ripieno* violinists, which shows that the enumeration of contexts for the prebeat style was never meant to be exclusive.

Quantz's Chapters 13 and 14, which deal with diminutions, are a treasure trove for anticipated *Vorschläge*. Only two of many illustrations will be given here. In Chapter 13 (par. 30) Quantz writes that in certain passages little notes can be added to make them more songful. Among the illustrations is that given in Ex. 18.21a which, he says, is to be rendered like Ex. *b*; Ex. *c* is to be rendered like Ex. *d*. In Chapter 14 (par. 30) the interpretive instructions for the passage given in Ex. *e* read: "the first [8th-] note strong, the second weak, the little note weak, and the others like the first two." This unmistakably implies grace-note treatment.

Ex. 18.21. Quantz

To Quantz, the term *Vorschlag* can always mean either of the two types into which he divided the term, the long onbeat and the prebeat type. In the absence of any guidance from the symbol itself, which is the same for both types, selection depends on the performer, though Quantz had staked out certain contexts favoring one or the other. Except for the graces before long, repeated notes, no mention is made of the short, Lombard-style onbeat type. Most probably, Quantz, as did Tartini, used the prebeat *Vorschlag* in many, if not most, contexts in which Philipp Emanuel, inhibited by his onbeat rule, could resort only to the short, "invariable" appoggiatura.

Leopold Mozart (1717-1787) published in 1756 a violin treatise[17] that ranks in importance with the great works of Quantz and C.P.E. Bach. Like the treatises of his two predecessors, Mozart's book has more than historical importance and contains a great deal of profound musical insight and violinistic wisdom that even after 200 years is far from outdated.

Mozart certainly knew and learned from both Berlin treatises. In many questions of aesthetics he is in close rapport with Philipp Emanuel; but in matters of ornaments, Mozart's ideas are far closer to those of Quantz and still nearer to those of Tartini, whom Mozart never mentions by name though he echoes many of his ideas and reproduces many of his illustrations.[18]

[17] *Versuch einer gründlichen Violinschule.* Unless otherwise specified, all references in the following paragraphs will be to ch. 9.

[18] In the last paragraph of ch. 10, Mozart gives two excerpts from Tartini's works and says they are taken "from the pieces of one of

Mozart distinguishes the falling and the rising *Vorschläge*, and each of these in turn can be *anschlagend* or *durchgehend* (par. 2; Mozart uses Quantz's terms for onbeat and prebeat *Vorschläge*).

For the ascending onbeat type, Mozart borrows (in F instead of C) Tartini's illustration (see above Exx. 17.22*a* and *b*) that inserts a little slide-like two-note grace (Mozart calls it *Zwischenschlag*) to permit a correct downward resolution of the dissonance. It is interesting to compare this Tartini-Mozart pattern with the French *port de voix et pincé*:

The descending *Vorschläge* which Mozart, like Tartini, calls the "most natural ones" (par. 7) can be either "long" or "short." Though Mozart does not expressly say so, subsequent explanations suggest that only the "long" ones were intended for the onbeat, the "short" ones for the prebeat, style. The term "long" is used in a relative sense to denote such *Vorschläge* that take one-half of the principal note's value, even if the latter is as short as a 16th and the *Vorschlag* therefore not longer than a 32nd. This "long" type is illustrated in Ex. 18.22.

Ex. 18.22. L. Mozart (1756)

The *Vorschlag* is "overlong" (*länger*) if it takes more than half of the principal note's value, for instance two-thirds, three-quarters, or all of it. The two-thirds extension applies mainly to dotted notes; if they are followed by their small companion, the characteristic dotted 3:1 rhythm, endangered by the intrusion of the long grace, is restored by its compression into smaller space (Ex. 18.23*a*). A *Vorschlag* before a half-note can under circumstances extend to three-fourths of the latter (Ex. *b*).

In agreement with Philipp Emanuel, Tartini, and Quantz, Mozart shows how the entire written note value can be taken over by the *Vorschlag* when a note is extended by a tie (Exx. *c* and *d*).

Ex. 18.23. L. Mozart

_____

the most famous violinists of our time." Other than this remark, Mozart does not acknowl-edge that he has borrowed many examples and ideas from Tartini's treatise.

When Mozart turns in paragraph 9 to the "short" descending *Vorschlag*, his description points to the prebeat *Vorschlag*, which he discusses later in the chapter. "There are," he writes, "also short *Vorschläge* where the accent falls not on the *Vorschlag* but on the principal note. The short *Vorschlag* is done as fast as possible and touched not strongly but very weakly." This is, of course, the exact opposite of the short "invariable" *Vorschlag* of the Berlin School, with its sharp accent. Nothing is said about playing this short *Vorschlag* on the beat, and there is no reason to do so. The accent on the principal note is as spontaneously attracted to the beat as the softness of such a short *Vorschlag* is to the prebeat space. If anyone should place the fast and soft *Vorschlag* on, instead of before, the beat, the effect would be that of a grace note, agogically delayed, and not that of an appoggiatura.[19]

The fact that Mozart speaks separately first of the "short" and later of the "passing" species has little significance considering his general inconsistency of outline and terminology. This is not the only place where identical or closely related matters are haphazardly disconnected in the book. Far more revealing than the physical separation or the difference in terminology is the identity of definition for the two types: the unquestionably anticipated "passing" (*durchgehende*) *Vorschläge* are characterized *solely* by what is listed as the chief criterion of the "short" species, namely the fact that the accent falls on the principal note: "Now we come to speak of the passing *Vorschläge*, *Zwischenschläge*, and other related graces which have the accent fall on the principal note and which are rarely or not at all indicated by the composer"; the violinist, he says, has to apply them in the right places according to his "sound judgment" (par. 16). Moreover, there are overlapping contexts that are presented as being favorable to either of the two types. Descending thirds and descending scales are listed for both types, and the first example of either is one of *tierces coulées* (Ex. 18.24*a*). Other situations listed as favoring the short type are *Vorschläge* preceding a series of half-notes (Ex. *b*), imitative textures where the long rendition would interfere with the counterpoint, and generally any passage where the long species would be too dull (par. 9).

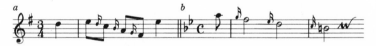

Ex. 18.24. L. Mozart, "short *Vorschläge*"

In paragraph 17 Mozart states that the *durchgehende Vorschläge* belong in the time of the preceding note. If, he continues, the composer wishes to indicate them, he can use the little notes but might as well write them out in regular notes. Mozart's illustrations (Ex. 18.25) show the notation of scale passages without and with symbols and their style of performance.

The given preferred contexts for the passing *Vorschläge* are, of course, not limited; by handing over to the performer the improvised use of these graces, he opens the door to their widest application.

[19] Beyschlag, commenting on this paragraph, convincingly argues that an onbeat rendition in such a case makes no sense and is impractical to boot. The listener, he says, would not understand it because he associates the accent with the start of the measure and the performer would spontaneously let beat and accent coincide. In fast tempo, he would hardly have a choice in this respect (p. 169). Beyschlag is unquestionably right in this reasoning, but is probably wrong in assuming that Mozart had onbeat execution in mind. Mozart never said so and had he wanted it, it would have been doubly necessary to say so because of its unnaturalness as a general principle in such a context.

Ex. 18.25. L. Mozart, "passing *Vorschläge*"

From Mozart's text it appears that, in analogy to Tartini and probably also to Quantz, his *Vorschläge* are either long or anticipated. If he also used the short, accented onbeat *Vorschlag*, the "invariable" one of the Berlin School—which well he might—he too failed to mention its existence.

A Danish student of Walther's, Carl August Thielo, published in 1753 a treatise that was focused mainly on the clavier.[20] In it he explains the *Vorschlag* with the familiar formula of briefly touching the neighbor note "so that the lower or upper second will be heard a little beforehand" (p. 52). No mention is made of the rhythmic disposition, and it is probable that the prebeat style applies to what he calls the "very short" (*ganz kurze*) *Vorschläge* which are systematically written without a slur mark. The long onbeat *Vorschläge* are called *schleifende* [i.e. slurred] *Vorschläge* and indicated by a slur mark (p. 58). Some of his illustrations for the "very short" *Vorschläge* are shown in Exs. 18.26a-d; some for the long, the "slurred" *Vorschläge*, appear in Ex. *e*. For certain illustrations, e.g. Ex. *c*, anticipation is certain, for several others very likely. Improvised additions of descending, and presumably anticipated, *Vorschläge* are recommended for notes that follow each other on the same pitch, or that move scalewise either up or down.

Ex. 18.26. Thielo

An important fascicle of manuscripts in the possession of the BB (P 803) contains on pages 19ff. a discussion of ornaments, including an illustrative table. Paul Kast assigned the penmanship of this section to an unknown writer of the second half of the 18th century, and so did Hermann Zietz.[21] Actually, the pages must have been written at the very end of the century, because they are excerpts from Löhlein's *Clavier-Schule* and more specifically from its fourth edition of 1782.[22] Only about one-half of Löhlein's table is reproduced in

20 *Grund-Regeln.*
21 Kast, *Die Bachhandschriften der Berliner Staatsbibliothek*, p. 48; Zietz, *Quellenkritische Untersuchungen*, p. 106, speaks of "scribe 4" leaning on Türk.
22 Löhlein was a very influential theorist.

His clavier treatise continued to be published under new editorship until well into the 19th century, and his violin treatise was re-edited by Reichardt eleven years after Löhlein's death.

the manuscript and only fragments of the text; but whatever was reproduced was done with utmost literal accuracy so that there can be no doubt about its derivation. One model and one sentence of the manuscript (both of which will be quoted presently) make their first appearance in the fourth edition of Löhlein's treatise, which establishes the year of 1782 as date *post quem* for the ornamentation table of P 803. An unknown copyist simply made an extract from Löhlein's fourth edition. Example 18.27 gives Löhlein's *Vorschlag* patterns in his *Clavier-Schule*, where he shows how, in the tradition of the Berlin School, the principal note may lose one-half (Ex. *a*), two-thirds (Ex. *b*), or all of its written value (Ex. *c*).

Ex. 18.27. Löhlein, *Clavier-Schule* (4th ed. 1782) and P 803

Then in the fourth edition we find this addition to the text (which is included in P 803): "the little notes that in a fast tempo are placed before 8th- or 16th-notes are rendered short so that the principal note loses little or nothing" (Ex. *d*).[23] "Or nothing" implies anticipation. Anticipation is further suggested by Löhlein's failure to give a transcription of this pattern: onbeat rendition would have called for such. More explicit documentation on the prebeat nature of such *Vorschläge* can be found in Löhlein's violin treatise of 1774.[24] There, after presenting models for the long appoggiatura that match those given above for the clavier, Löhlein writes with reference to Ex. 18.28: "There is also a *fast type of Vorschläge* that is irrelevant to the measure. They either take the upper neighbor (d) or they repeat the preceding note (e) or fill the empty space between two notes (f). They are slurred very fast to the following note."[25] [The letter references are from the original.]

Ex. 18.28. Löhlein, violin treatise (1774)

[23] Fourth edition, p. 14: "Die kleinen Noten, so im geschwinden Zeitmaasse vor Achteln oder Sechzehntheilen stehen, werden kurz abgefertigt; so dass die Hauptnote wenig oder nichts verliert (d)."
[24] *Anweisung zum Violinspielen*, p. 44.
[25] Ibid.: "Man hat auch eine *geschwinde Art Vorschläge*, die in Ansehung des Tacktes in keine Betrachtung kommen. Sie nehmen entweder den in der Höhe zunächst anliegenden Ton d) oder sie wiederhohlen die vorhergehende Note e), oder füllen den leeren Raum zwischen zweyen Tönen aus f). Sie werden sehr geschwind an die folgende Note geschleift."

Rhythmic anticipation is fully revealed in the illustration (Ex. 18.29) accompanying the next sentence: "sometimes they also fill in leaps of a third (g); also simple stepwise progressions (h)."[26]

Ex. 18.29. Löhlein

Since these latter passing *Vorschläge* belong, according to Löhlein, to the category of the "fast" *Vorschläge*, they illuminate the prebeat design of Ex. 18.28, including, presumably, that of the slide (f).

Most of the German treatises in the second half of the century show C.P.E. Bach's influence, though few follow him to the extreme of banishing all interbeat graces, including the *Nachschlag*. Johann Samuel Petri (1738-1808) in a treatise of 1767, as well as in its much enlarged second edition of 1782, follows Bach's rules for the long appoggiatura.[27] He calls it *Vorhalt* to distinguish it from the short *Vorschlag*. (This terminological distinction of unknown origin became henceforth widely accepted in Germany.) Like Bach and Agricola, Petri stresses the greater loudness of the *Vorschläge*.

While following C.P.E. Bach's *Vorschlag* doctrines, Petri recognizes *Nachschläge*, characterizes them as "passing notes," and adopts for them Marpurg's symbol of the reversed flag: ♪ . In the second edition (p. 151) he has one of these *Nachschlag* symbols slurred to the *following* note, whereas he usually leaves them unslurred (Ex. 18.30). Unless a misprint, it indicates an anticipated *Vorschlag*.

Ex. 18.30. Petri, *Nachschläge*

The eminent theorist Georg Joseph Vogler (1749-1814) describes and illustrates in 1778 *Zwischenschläge*, appoggiaturas, grace notes, and *Nachschläge*. The *Zwischenschläge* (*Zwischenklänge*) fill in spaces between consonant notes (Ex. 18.31a); the appoggiaturas (*grosse Vorschläge*) create dissonances and take one-half of a binary, two-thirds of a ternary note (Ex. b); the grace notes (*kleine Vorschläge*) "do not lessen the value of the following note and are therefore always notated with smaller than half-value denomination" ("Die kleinen Vorschläge mindern den Werth der folgenden Not nicht, und werden deswegen

---

[26] Ibid., p. 44: "Auch füllen sie manchmal Terzensprünge g); auch wohl nur Secunden aus h)."

[27] *Anleitung zur praktischen Musik*, 1st ed., pp. 28-29; 2nd ed., pp. 150-151.

immer geringer, als im halben Werthe angezeigt"). His illustration (Ex. *c*) was not transcribed, but its meaning is clear from the text.[28]

Ex. 18.31. Vogler (1778)

The organist Michael Johann Friedrich Wiedeburg, in a three-volume treatise, deals little with ornaments, but speaks of the filling in of rising or falling thirds "to better connect the melody." This can be done either before or on the beat ("beydes kann angehen"), though anticipation is most common ("die gewöhnlichste Art ist, dass es der vorhergegangenen Note angehänget wird . . ."). Either style can be used for the bass.[29]

In both of his main treatises, Johann Adam Hiller (1728-1804) follows C.P.E. Bach's *Vorschlag* rules very closely.[30] New is his comment that the following patterns:  are reprehensible (*verwerflich*) though, he says, we meet with them not infrequently. He gives no reason for his censure, but we can probably find the explanation in the unavoidable grace-note character of such little notes. However, Hiller does admit *Nachschläge* which, he says, have "a certain resemblance with the *Vorschlag*" (1780, p. 46). With the French, he says, they are still very common; the Italians and Germans either write them out in regular notes or leave their insertion to the singer's fancy (ibid.). His examples show what he calls *Nachschläge* in the connective function of *Zwischenschläge* (see Ex. 18.32).

Ex. 18.32. Hiller

A number of treatises in the latter decades of the 18th century are essentially derivative. Among them is one by Albrecht in 1761, who by his own admission takes Marpurg as his model in matters of ornaments. Tubel in 1766, Laag in 1774, Rigler in 1779, Petschke in 1785, E. W. Wolf in 1788, and G. F. Wolf in 1789 all follow C.P.E. Bach's lead fairly faithfully, though a few among them, G. F. Wolf for instance, admit *Nachschläge*, while Petschke gives a strong indication of grace-note use.[31] Tromlitz in his flute treatise of

---

[28] Vogler, *Kuhrpfälzische Tonschule*, p. 21, and *Gründe der Kuhrpfälzischen Tonschule in Beispielen*, Table 6. Vogler, teacher of Weber and Meyerbeer, is hailed by *MGG* as a key figure of music history.

[29] *Der sich selbst informirende Clavierspieler*, vol. 2, pp. 117-118, 128, 184. Wiedeburg (spelled Wideburg in the second and third volumes) was organist at the "Great Lutheran church in Norden, Ostfriessland." The first volume was devastatingly criticized in the *Wöchentliche Nachrichten und Anmerkungen die Musik betreffend*, vol. 3, 1st quarter (Leipzig, 1768), p. 28. The anonymous critic (possibly J. A. Hiller) castigates the "nauseating chatter," the "endless repetition," "falsehoods," etc. Such criticism is uncalled for and

the very violence of the attack arouses suspicion about its objectivity. Actually, the book is written with intelligence, obvious knowledge, and common sense.

[30] *Anweisung zum musikalisch-richtigen Gesange* (referred to hereafter as 1774), pp. 165ff. *Anweisung zum musikalisch-zierlichen Gesange* (referred to as 1780), pp. 40ff.

[31] Albrecht, *Gründliche Einleitung in die Anfangslehren der Tonkunst*, pp. 69ff.; Tubel, *Kurzer Unterricht von der Music*, p. 20; Laag, *Anfangsgründe zum Clavier-spielen*, p. 22; Rigler, *Anleitung zum Klavier*, p. 31; E. W. Wolf, *Musikalischer Unterricht*, pp. 32f.; G. F. Wolf, *Unterricht im Klavierspielen*, 3rd ed., vol. 1, pp. 67ff. In his *Versuch eines Unterrichts zum Klavierspielen*, p. 33, Petschke

1791 is understandably indebted chiefly to Quantz, whose treatise had just been republished unchanged in a third edition in 1789. Accordingly, Tromlitz lists the *durchgehende* along with the *anschlagende Vorschläge*.[32]

A few words should be said about Türk's important clavier treatise of 1789, though the date carries us beyond the proposed limits of this study.[33] The principles he stipulates for the *Vorschlag* are generally faithfully patterned after C.P.E. Bach's rules and include accordingly the duration-indicating symbols. However, the apparent rigidity of doctrine is considerably tempered by various remarks in the text.

At the very outset of the *Vorschlag* chapter, Türk says that *Vorschläge* are largely a matter of taste and therefore general rules can be formulated only "with great difficulty" because taste varies strongly, at least in minor matters (*Nebendingen*). Then he makes a statement that has significance for the whole field of interpretation. Clear decisions in controversial issues, of which, he writes, there are many in matters of the *Vorschläge*, could be made only on condition that the greatest masters would write in the identical "taste" [meaning "style"]. However, "that this [i.e. identical style] has not come to pass in music is common knowledge. For certainly the same taste does not prevail in the works of [C.P.E.] Bach, Haydn, Mozart, etc."[34] However, Türk continues, even if such identical taste were to animate all great composers of each nation, "this would still not imply that all would have to agree upon the smallest matters." No better or clearer case could be made against the literal application of the rules of any treatise to any master.

Another interesting point concerns the descending thirds. Though here too Türk endorses C.P.E. Bach's onbeat pattern, he mentions that other teachers want these thirds to be played before the beat "in the manner of the French" (par. 23).

Anticipation is actually implied in another passage where Türk discusses the question whether the rule that the *Vorschlag* is to carry the dynamic accent is to apply also to the short, "unchangeable" *Vorschlag*. He mentions that C.P.E. Bach, Agricola, and Marpurg answer the question in the affirmative, whereas L. Mozart dissents. Türk says that since these *Vorschläge* are mostly passing (*durchgehend*) and often even appear before a written-out appoggiatura, he himself prefers to play them gently, "flatteringly" rather than too strongly, leaving the emphasis on the following note. As was pointed out on several occasions, this dynamic pattern instinctively produces anticipation. It is no coincidence either that the term "flatteringly" was Quantz's characterization for the prebeat *durchgehende Vorschläge*.[35]

---

speaks, in contrast to the "usual" *Vorschläge*, of "short" ones (*kurze Vorschläge*), which occur mostly before short notes, repeated pitches, syncopations, slurred notes, and triplets. He adds that "the nature of these [principal] notes must not be altered by the *Vorschläge*, since the latter have to be rendered as fast as possible." The stress on the integrity of the principal notes suggests anticipation of the graces.

[32] Tromlitz, *Ausführlicher und gründlicher Unterricht die Flöte zu spielen*, pp. 240ff.

[33] Türk, *Klavierschule*. Türk devotes his long third chapter entirely to *Vorschläge* and *Nachschläge*. All the present references are to this chapter.

[34] Sec. 1, par. 2: "Sollte man in streitigen Fällen—deren es in Ansehung der Vorschläge viele giebt—sicher entscheiden können, so müssten wenigstens die grössten Meister einerley Geschmack haben. Dass es aber in der Musik noch nicht so weit gekommen ist, lehrt die Erfahrung. Denn gewiss herrscht in den Werken eines [C.P.E.] Bach, Haydn, Mozart, etc. nicht einerley Geschmack."

[35] See also below ch. 43.

Moreover, like most other theorists, Türk does not go along with Philipp Emanuel's ban on *Nachschläge* and devotes to it the fourth section of his third chapter (pp. 230-235).

Viewed in the light of all these reservations, Türk's endorsement of Philipp Emanuel's principles appears considerably qualified and in part, especially with regard to the short *Vorschläge*, actually reversed.

UNTIL about the middle of the century, the treatment of the *Vorschlag* was largely dependent on stylistic leanings. For the masters upholding the baroque polyphonic traditions (some of whom like J. S. Bach and Walther were dealt with in previous chapters), the prebeat type continued to play a large role as a carry-over from its 17th-century predominance, while the onbeat type, though it had considerably gained in importance, remained basically short. By contrast, the German masters who rallied to the new *galant* style, which around 1715 to 1720 had begun to invade Germany, were naturally receptive to its concomitant ornamental fashions, which meant more and longer and more varied appoggiaturas. However, the interbeat graces never ceased to flourish. Imported from both Italy and France as well as home grown by the irrepressible natural impulse to melodic ornamentation, they were immune to the ban which Philipp Emanuel had hurled against them. As long as this master based his principles on certain current practices, even though he adapted them with a heavy hand, his great prestige in Germany assured him a strong following, notably among keyboard players. But when he turned into an arbitrary lawmaker and tried to legislate his ban of all interbeat graces in defiance of widespread practices (which he himself acknowledged) and of musical nature itself, he was clearly ineffectual. Even his most faithful disciples refused to follow him on that path; practically all of them recognized and legitimized the use of *Nachschläge*. Such eminent authorities as Quantz and L. Mozart, in full accord with both Italian and French practices of the day, assigned a wide berth to the prebeat *Vorschläge* as well, while Türk implied the prebeat nature of all short *Vorschläge*. The way in which modern doctrine mistook a mid-18th-century abortive attempt at legislation for a law actually in effect and internationally enforced during the whole of the century is one of the more striking illustrations of unjustified generalization.

PART IV
THE SLIDE

Introduction
Two-Note Graces and the
Nature of the Slide

———•◆•———

Graces that consist of two ornamental notes ("two-note graces") have, in analogy to the one-note graces, either the character of a *Vorschlag*, a *Zwischenschlag*, or a *Nachschlag*. They have *Vorschlag* character when the two notes are more or less clearly detached from the preceding note and slurred to the following regular note; they have *Nachschlag* character when they are slurred to the preceding note and detached from the following one; they have *Zwischenschlag* character when they are slurred to both neighbor notes, linking the two on an equal basis.

Among the two-note graces of the *Nachschlag* or *Zwischenschlag* types, only those that rise or fall stepwise can be considered standard ornaments. Within the two-note *Nachschlag* category, the best known and most important species is the characteristic suffix to a trill: —♪♫— The same pattern can, of course, be used without a trill, or it can be inverted. Though such a *Nachschlag* may occasionally end a phrase, more commonly it will lead to another tone, and there is hardly any pitch that could not follow such two-note graces.

Generally, these two-note *Nachschläge*, when clearly identifiable as such, present no special interpretive problems. Their unstressed rendition at the end of the preceding note's value is not controversial. (Some special questions relating to the suffix of a trill will be dealt with in a later chapter.)

When the two little notes are assigned *Zwischenschlag* function by either an encompassing slur ♪♫♪ or by the logic of the context, there is rarely any question that interbeat rendition, in analogy to a one-note *Zwischenschlag*, is in order.

The chief problems are again centered on the *Vorschlag*-related patterns. A few of these patterns have become standardized in the framework of larger ornamental families. Thus the design ♫♪ called the *Schneller* or, by some, the inverted mordent, is a miniature trill; its mirror image ♫♪ is a one-alternation mordent. Both of these will be discussed together with their respective families. A third one, the *Anschlag* ♫♪ , in which the two ornamental notes are a third or more apart and frame the principal note, will be dealt with in a special chapter. Among the *Vorschlag* types, the only remaining two-note grace that played a prominent part in the baroque era and beyond is the slide, which will be the subject of the following five chapters.

The term "slide" is most commonly applied to a two-note ornament whose tones rise diatonically to the principal note and are slurred to it. Its melic design is shown in Ex. IV.1*a* (for the meaning of the notation see Ex. 8.1 above). Less frequent are the descending types of Ex. *b* and those of Exx. *c* and *d* that consist of three instead of two ornamental notes. In all these forms, continuity of direction is essential to the slide character. Four, five, or more notes can also form such an ornamental scale-like design. These multitone patterns (called *tirata* by

Italians, *coulade* by Frenchmen, and *Pfeil* by Germans) are generally *Zwischenschlag* types and belong more properly to the diminutions.

Ex. IV.1.

For the standard slide, the rhythmic dispositions are manifold, and we shall distinguish the three basic designs of Ex. IV.2 to represent, as usual, landmarks in a continuum of gradual transition. Type 1 will be referred to as anapestic, Type 2 as Lombard, Type 3 as dactylic.

Ex. IV.2.

The usual dynamic treatment for the anapestic pattern will be softness of the grace and accentuation of the principal note; for the Lombard type, a distinct accent on the first ornamental note, sharper in faster, milder in slower tempi; for the dactyl, a gentle emphasis on the first note.

An anapest that is shifted astride and across the beat, retains its typical dynamic profile and also its fundamental prebeat character. If we hear, for example, the following three versions:

we shall perceive all three designs as the identical pattern in varying degrees of delay. Thus the pattern of *c*, far removed from the Lombard type, is simply an anapest rendered with a touch of rubato. By the same token, the Lombard pattern: does not lose its character by being started either slightly before or slightly after the beat. Hence, if we hear   or   it will be felt not as an upbeat, but as an agogically shifted downbeat.

The dactyl can vary the ratio between the long and the short notes from a near equality: to a dotted pattern: .

With regard to the rhythmic disposition, it is very important to realize that, in contrast to the one-note *Vorschlag*, onbeat rendition of the slide cannot enrich the harmony. The first note of an onbeat slide will normally have to be consonant since as dissonance it would have no satisfactory resolution. (For this very reason Caccini had rejected a slide with a dissonant start.) Hence the onbeat pattern for the slide can spring only from melodic and rhythmic but not from harmonic motivation.

The French Slide
1689-1776

The French theorists paid little attention to the slide. French composers started to indicate it by symbol in the last quarter of the 17th century. Little notes slurred to their parent became the most frequently used symbol, although a few masters of the early period also used a dash before the principal note. We find various terms, among them the generic *coulé* or *coulade*, but for the two-note ascending slide the more commonly used one was *port de voix double* (or *doublé*).

D'Anglebert may have been the first to explain the slide in his extensive ornament table.[1] Using a crescent shaped symbol which starts on the line or space of the slide's start, he presents three types (Ex. 19.1); two (Exx. *a* and *c*) begin on the beat, one (Ex. *b*) before the beat. The models given in Exx. *a* and *c* may be the only French reference to onbeat rendition. All other theoretical sources that could be found either specify or imply anticipation, and so does a great deal of evidence gained from the music.

Ex. 19.1. D'Anglebert (1689)

In Marin Marais we find many spots like the two shown in Exx. 19.2*a* and *b* where the swell on the principal note prescribed by the symbol *e* clarifies the anapestic character of the slide.

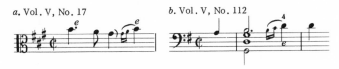

Ex. 19.2. Marais (1725)

Boyvin uses the slide as shown in Ex. 19.3.[2] At first he indicates it with two little notes, then continues to mark it with a dash. He explains neither symbol in any of his prefaces, but this does not favor the onbeat style since the little notes (as contrasted to abstract symbols) had preponderantly interbeat meaning at this time.

[1] *Pieces de clavecin* (Paris, 1689).

[2] Boyvin, *Second livre d'orgue* (Paris, 1700).

Ex. 19.3. Boyvin, Organ Book 2, *Fugue 6ᵉ ton*

In L'Affilard's treatise of 1694 the slide is called *port de voix doublé*, and the dash symbol, though written *after* the bar line, is, in its illustration, clearly spelled out in anticipation (Ex. 19.4), shedding thereby some light on Boyvin's intentions in this respect.[3]

Ex. 19.4. L'Affilard (1694), *Port de voix doublé*

In Loulié's treatise of 1696 the slide is presented under the overall category of *coulade*, which is defined as "two or more conjunct small sounds or little notes placed between two distant tones in order to connect them more pleasingly."[4]

He uses no special symbol, but says that the grace is expressed and illustrated as shown in Exx. 19.5*a* and *b*. The definition of the slide as a means of providing a smooth connection, the alternate slurring to the preceding and to the following note, and the company of the many-toned *coulades* which obviously belong into interbeat space all point to the prebeat nature of the two-note slide. The supposition is strengthened by the fourth and sixth models of descending slides that are split in articulation. Only in anticipation can such separated parts of the slide still be perceived as *one* ornament rather than as two different ones. Moreover, in a synoptic tabulation of all ornaments at the end of Loulié's book, the sole representative of the *coulade* shows its interbeat character by its slur to the preceding note (Ex. *c*). Undoubtedly Loulié's slide, like L'Affilard's, was basically anticipated.

a. Coulade (rising)

b. Coulade (falling)

c. Coulade [synopsis]

Ex. 19.5. Loulié (1696)

3 *Principes*, 1st and 2nd eds., pp. 20-21; 5th ed., pp. 26-27.

4 *Éléments*, p. 74: ". . . deux ou plusieurs petits Sons ou petites Nottes par degrez conjoints . . . que l'on met entre deux sons eloignez, pour passer de l'un a l'autre avec plus d'agrément."

Grigny's anticipated slides are of special interest because, as mentioned before, Bach, as well as Walther, had copied the Frenchman's first organ book of 1699 with great care.[5] Examples 19.6a-c show a few of the places in that book where prebar notation of the slide clarifies its rhythmic disposition. In Ex. *d* Grigny wrote the slide *after* the bar line, but Bach placed it *before*. Even when Grigny occasionally failed to write the slide before the bar line, the meaning emerges from examples like *e* and *f* where onbeat performance would produce offensive octaves.

Anticipated descending slides are shown in Exx. *g* and *h,* and a characteristic variant of the downward slide in which the first note is touched twice is given in Ex. *i.* This variant occurs many times in the book and is written without exception before the bar line.

Ex. 19.6. Grigny

Saint Lambert, in 1702, uses for the slide the symbol of a dash whose beginning and end on a specific line or space indicate the desired ornamental notes.[6] He does not indicate the rhythmic disposition. In light of his decided advocacy of the prebeat style for all *Vorschläge,* the failure to mention the downbeat favors the supposition that here too a prebeat rendition was probably intended.

Ex. 19.7. Saint Lambert

The same seems to be the case with Hotteterre. In his first book of flute pieces the slide is called *port de voix doublé,* and the symbol of a dash is explained as shown in Ex. 19.8a.[7] The little notes here are not symbol but resolution and as such more likely to be under-

[5] Nicolas de Grigny, *Premier livre d'orgue* (Paris, 1699).

[6] *Principes,* p. 53.
[7] *Premier livre,* Preface.

stood in anticipation—the more so since it would have been easy to indicate an intended onbeat execution. In Ex. *b* we find the anticipation of a downward slide clarified in prebar notation.[8]

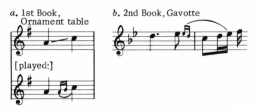

Ex. 19.8. Hotteterre

Montéclair, following again the lead of Loulié, illustrates the slide as belonging to the species of *coulade*, a scale-like connective grace with an indetermined number of notes.[9] Since the multinote variety is invariably done between beats, the two-note slide, as a member of the larger group, is likely to follow the same principle.

Jean-Ferry Rebel's 7th sonata of 1720 has a fifth movement called *Tombeau de M. de Lully*. Its theme is shown in Ex. 19.9*a*. In a contemporary manuscript of the bass alone, we find the notation given in Ex. *b*.[10]

Ex. 19.9. J. F. Rebel, 7th Sonata

Couperin uses the slide fairly often and writes it with little notes. He never mentions it as an independent *agrément* and musical evidence points to its prebeat character. In Ex. 19.10*a* the change from the G sharp of the slide to the G natural below the principal note obviously precludes onbeat interpretation. In Exx. *b* and *c*, onbeat rendition would result in bad octaves. Occasional prebar notation of a three-note slide, as shown in Ex. *d*, clarifies its expected rhythm.[11]

After Couperin, references remain sparse but those that could be found all specify or suggest anticipation. In the passage from Nicolas Siret (Ex. 19.11*a*), the fact that the two little notes are slurred across the bar line identifies them as an anticipated slide rather than as a suffix to a trill. The slide in Ex. *b* has to be anticipated because of the coincidence of voices. Most logically both the slide and the mordent could be synchronized before the beat, as indicated in Ex. *c*. Example *d* shows D'Agincour's prebar notation of a slide.[12]

[8] *Deuxieme livre de pieces pour la flûte traversière*, Op. 5 (Paris, 1715).

[9] *Principes*, p. 87.

[10] The documentation is from L. de La Laurencie, "Une dynastie de musiciens aux XVIIᵉ et XVIIIᵉ siècles: les Rebels," *IMG*, VII (1905-1906), 253-307.

[11] Von Dadelsen in his article "Verzierun-

gen" in *MGG*, p. 1,541, points out that the contexts of Couperin's two- and three-note slides often indicate their prebeat nature.

[12] Siret's passages are from his first book, *Pièces de clavecin* (Paris [1716]); D'Agincour's example is from *Pièces de clavecin, Premier Livre* (Paris, 1833), Iᵉʳ Ordre. It should be noted here that a modern edition (*Le Pupitre*

a. XIII, *Les Folies Françoises*, 11th couplet

b. VII, *L'Adolescente*, 1st couplet

c. XII, *L'Intîme*

d. I, Menuet *(Double)*

Ex. 19.10. Couperin

a. Siret (1716), Courante

b. Siret (1716), Allemande, *Le Bouquet*

c. Suggested execution

d. D'Agincour, *La pressante Angélique*

Ex. 19.11.

Michel Corrette mentions the *port de voix double* briefly in his voice treatise as a grace done by quickly singing two little ascending notes with the same breath.[13] The explanation is indefinite, but his illustration (Ex. 19.12*a*), with the grace on the lightest beat, seems to favor and certainly does not exclude the anapest.

La Chapelle explains the *port de voix double*, as shown in Ex. *b*, under the title: "Demonstration how to understand the execution [of various ornaments]." The prebeat implication is clear.[14]

Denis invites the same implication by his syllabification of written-out prebeat slides (the "naming" of the principal note only), as given in Ex. *c*.[15]

Luc Marchand in his previously cited chamber music work of 1748 writes the slide always before the bar line as shown in Ex. *d*.[16]

Azaïs, in a practice composition in his treatise of 1776, writes the two passages of Ex. *e*. In the first, a prebeat rendition of the slide is necessary to avoid unacceptable octaves; in the second, the slide is notated before the bar line.[17]

series [Paris, n.d.]) edited by Howard Ferguson contains an ornament table that is unauthentic and misleading. Its editorial character is not indicated.

[13] *Le parfait maître*, p. 49: "Le Port de Voix double se fait en montant subitement deux petites notes d'un seul coup de gosier."

[14] *Vrais principes*, II, 14.

[15] *Nouveau système*, p. 45; *Nouvelle méthode*, p. 44.

[16] *Pieces de clavecin*.

[17] Azaïs, *Méthode de musique*, p. 63.

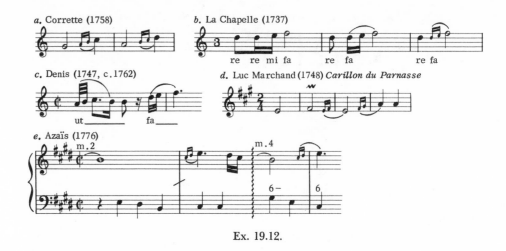

Ex. 19.12.

Finally, the reader is reminded of the previously presented illustration (Ex. 12.10) from Villeneuve's treatise (1733 and 1756) where, in accord with his model from L'Affilard, *the port de voix double* is marked with a dash before and an inverted caret sign above the principal note, while the resolution places the slide before the bar line:[18]

UNDOUBTEDLY, the French symbol-indicated slide was predominantly anticipated. The one, partial dissent from D'Anglebert—which was only an alternative to the prebeat type—may not have found any followers with regard to either symbol or execution. (A related ornament that was often done *on* the beat and usually marked with an oblique dash between the interval of a third: will be discussed in a later chapter.)

18 *Nouvelle méthode*, p. 38.

The Italo-German Slide

1600-1715

Slides or slide-like patterns were common in improvised diminutions. Ganassi has many quasi-slides within his more extensive diminution patterns;[1] Ex. 20.1a gives one such illustration. Ortiz's first diminution patterns for ascending fourths and ascending seconds show the prebeat slides of Ex. *b*.[2]

Ex. 20.1.

Richardo Rogniono offers a number of slides in analogy to the prebeat one-note graces previously shown (cf. Ex. 14.1). A few of his slide patterns are given in Ex. 20.2; many more, both rising and falling ones, are contained in his treatise, *all* of which are anticipated.[3]

Ex. 20.2. R. Rogniono (1592)

Bovicelli presents as his first patterns for the rising fourth both an anticipated and an onbeat slide (Ex. 20.3a); for the descending leap, however, the corresponding two patterns are both anticipated.[4]

The onbeat slide, starting a third below the written note, is his favorite way of beginning a piece, and the excerpt shown in Ex. *b* from Bovicelli's embellishments of a Palestrina motet shows this pattern both at the start and in the middle of a phrase in the third measure on *las-*. The initial pattern is the type of *intonazione* which Caccini mentions a few years later as being in common use. He did not favor it; as was pointed out above, he objected most to the extension of the first note; if this slide pattern is to be used at all, he says, the first note, a third under the principal note, should be touched only lightly. Caccini's preferred choice was to begin with the principal note itself.

Banchieri offers specimens of onbeat slides (Ex. *c*) under the heading of *accenti*. Diruta, using the term *clamatione*, presents a model of the dotted onbeat slide

[1] *Fontegara.*
[2] *Trattado*, reprint 1961, pp. 42 and 46.
[3] *Il vero modo*, pp. 7, 11, 25, 26, 29, 30.
[4] *Regole*, pp. 19, 24.

that understandably starts on a consonance (Ex. *d*). In his embellishments of a canzona by A. Mortaro, he uses, in addition to a few of these dactylic slides, the prebeat type of Ex. *e*; both types are indicated by the same symbol: C.[5]

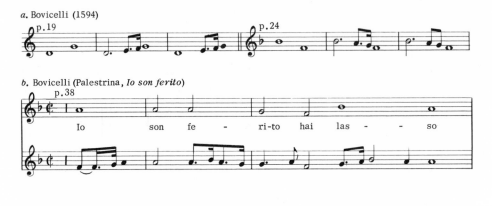

Ex. 20.3.

In Germany, Praetorius reproduced Bovicelli's patterns of both prebeat and onbeat slides for the interval of a rising fourth, and the prebeat type only for the falling fourth (Ex. 20.4*a*).

Crüger and Herbst again follow Praetorius very closely. Crüger's slide patterns are given in Ex. *b*. Herbst's models, derived from Praetorius, appear in Ex. *c*. Herbst then reproduces, with due credit, Francesco Rognoni's prebeat slides (which are analogous to those of his father Richardo given above, Ex. 20.2). He also writes, under his own initials, slides as diminution patterns for rising and falling fourths that are all anticipated. Illustrations for the rising models are given in Ex. *d*; the falling models are analogous.[6]

Falck, who had in 1688 adopted Praetorius's onbeat as well as prebeat *accentus*, presents within his diminution patterns only anticipated slides (Ex. *e*). Stierlein's diminutions, with slides filling in rising and falling fourths, are all of the prebeat type.[7] The first of his illustrations, given in Ex. *f*, is perhaps slightly irregular in that the slide is divided between the two syllables (in a manner akin to Loulié's models with divided articulation). However, the prebeat design of the slide remains unmistakable.

One of the first, if not *the* first, to introduce a symbol for the slide may have been Johann Kuhnau, who used ⌣⌢ for the ascending and ⌢⌣ for the descend-

[5] Caccini, *Nuove musiche*, p. 3; Banchieri, *Cartella overo regole*, p. 58; Diruta, *Transilvano*, pt. 2, bk. 1, pp. 13 and 18. Analogous patterns are also to be found in Pedro Cerone, *El melopeo y maestro*, p. 542, and in Francesco Rognoni's *Selva*, I, 1.

[6] Praetorius, *Syntagma*, III, 234; Crüger, *Synopsis*, p. 193; Herbst, *Musica prattica* (1658), pp. 4, 20, 23, 25, 28-29.

[7] Falck, *Idea boni cantoris*, p. 94; Stierlein, *Trifolium*, p. 19.

a. Praetorius (1619)

b. Crüger (1654, 1660)

c. Herbst (1642, 1658)

d. Herbst (1658)

e. Falck (1688)

Lae - ta   Lae - ta   Do - na

f. Stierlein (1691)   *tril.*   *trem.*

De - us   De - us   Om - nes   gen - tes

Ex. 20.4.

ing slide (*Schleiffer*). His explanation tells us only that they are "drawn into the following note from either the third below or the third above."[8] He refers for an illustration to "measures 4, 5, and 6 of Number 6," of which mm. 4 and 5 are shown in Ex. 20.5*a*.

The illustration raises more questions than it answers. It shows one pattern repeated five times, with a slide of the Lombard type on the weak part of the beat, preceded by a dotted note-pair of which the first note is a step below and the second, short one on the pitch of the first slide note. How much of this pattern belongs to the slide? Is the anticipation of the first slide note part of the ornament? Should we assume that in the context given in Ex. *b* the slide would be performed as in Ex. *c*? Beyschlag (p. 69) considers this likely and he may well be right. Yet Kuhnau's slides do not always occur in this specific metric-intervallic context, and in the second measure of Ex. *a*, Kuhnau writes a *custos* symbol before the full beat, and the above pattern does not fit. The very fact that the *custos* appears here in the middle of a cluster of written-out Lombard slides makes it doubtful that the symbol meant the same thing. Furthermore, an example like the one given in Ex. *d* (from the 7th *Partie*), where onbeat execution would create penetrating octaves with the tenor, indicates the need for occasional anticipation. Clearly, his slide was as flexible and adaptable as his *Vorschlag*. Beyschlag is again probably justified in pointing out that Kuhnau's *custos* before a full beat may have either Lombard or anapestic meaning.

Nicolaus Bruhns (1665-1697) may have used the *custos* symbol (with prebeat meaning) in the Organ Chorale *Nun komm der Heiden Heiland*, according to its principal source, a mid-18th-century copy whose writer has been identified as J. F. Agricola.[9] We find at the start of the piece the fugal theme given in Ex. 20.6*a*. In its answer in m. 5 and thereafter in every repeat of the theme, the slide is written out in anticipation (Ex. *b*).

The manuscript is replete with ornamental symbols, but practically all of them (in particular the little French *Vorschlag* notes or the signs for compound trills and mordents)

---

[8] *Clavier-Übung*, I, *Preface*: ". . . aus der Tertia entweder drunter oder drüber in die   nachgesätzte Note . . . trainiret werden."   [9] BB (PK) Mus. MS 2681/1.

a. No. 6, Allemande

m.4

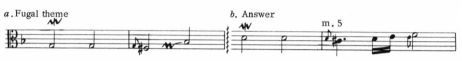

b.   *c.*   *d. Partie* 7, Allemande

Ex. 20.5. Kuhnau

a. Fugal theme   *b.* Answer   m. 5

Ex. 20.6. Bruhns

are clearly unauthentic additions by the copyist, because they were anachronistic for Bruhns's Germany. However, the slide symbol may be genuine. Not only was it a German symbol already extant at the time of the composition, but it happened to be one which Agricola did *not* use for his own slides. Moreover, it makes perfect musical sense. In fact, if it were not written (which is possible), a slide would have to be inserted, because it is unlikely that the theme would have been written with the naked leap of a diminished fourth when in every subsequent appearance the interval was filled in. That the symbol should be used only in the first statement of the theme is understandable, because in this measure alone the exact rhythmical shape of this passage matters less; the polyphonic context of all later appearances calls for a more precise fixation.

Reinhard Keiser indicated slides in his opera scores by the little notes, writing them sometimes in 16ths, more often in 32nds, as shown in Exx. 20.7a and *b*.[10] Keiser was very fond of the Lombard rhythm, and its written-out patterns, including those for the Lombard slide, appear frequently in his scores. This fact makes it likely that the slides written with little notes, in analogy to his many prebeat *Vorschläge*, were meant to be basically anapestic.

a. Circe, I, 5 (aut.)

b. Massaniello, II, aria Mariana

Ex. 20.7. Keiser

In his brief ornamentation table, F.X.A. Murschhauser has a Lombard-type slide for which he uses the letter "c" as symbol (Ex. 20.8).[11]

---

[10] *Circe* (1702), aut. BB Mus. MS autogr.   MS autogr. Keiser 6.
Keiser 1; *Massaniello furioso* (1706), BB Mus.   [11] *Prototypon*, I.

Ex. 20.8. Murschhauser (1703)

Thomas Balthasar Janowka describes in 1701 a grace that is a mixture of slide and turn. He calls it *circuitus* and uses a small letter "c," followed by a high or low dot, to indicate whether the grace is rising or falling. His illustration (Ex. 20.9) marks the design as fully anticipated. The value of the grace, he says, has to be taken from the preceding note so that the following one can enter exactly on time.[12]

Ex. 20.9. Janowka (1701)

Walther seconds Janowka on the *circuitus*, adopting the Bohemian theorist's term, symbol, and description.[13] But much more importantly, Walther illustrates the meaning of the *custos* symbol for both the rising and falling slide (*Schleiffer*) in complete anticipation. His model from the *Praecepta* (p. 37) is given in Ex. 20.10.

Ex. 20.10. Walther (1708)

In the *Andreas Bach Buch* we find revealing evidence regarding the anticipation of the slide. Among the items contained in this manuscript are three sonatas by Kuhnau who, as mentioned before, had left the ornamentation of these works to the discretion of the performer. Bernhard Bach, the presumable scribe of the manuscript,[14] indicated by symbols many of these desired graces. When he added the *custos* symbol for the slide at the start of a measure, he most often placed it either before or astride the bar line. Neither lack of space nor carelessness is involved, and in this calligraphically written manuscript the repeatedly anticipated placement of the symbol is unmistakably intentional. This manner of notation is shown in Exx. 20.11*a-d* in passages from Kuhnau's 2nd and 5th Sonatas. Moreover, there is a spot in the 5th Sonata (which in the manuscript is mistakenly

[12] *Clavis,* s.v. *circuitus.* The passage in question gains considerable added interest because it reveals the anticipatory meaning of the French little notes. After having explained the principle of anticipation for the *circuitus,* Janowka declares it to be the same that underlies the meaning of the "Gauls'" little notes: "Solet autem in simili accipiendo modo aliqua

mora temporis a priori nota . . . rapi, ut debito tempore ad sequentem notam pervenire possit; et huic similes modos Galli, ut in eorum Operis expresse videre est, per notulas minori ad distinctionem substantialium notarum typo, apponere solent."

[13] *Praecepta,* p. 37.

[14] See ch. 15, n. 29 above.

marked as the 6th) where an onbeat rendition of the slide would lead to double parallels: open octaves with the middle voice, plus hidden ones with the bass (Ex. *e*). This could not have been intended and the cumulative evidence is unmistakable. That such anticipated slides would have met with Kuhnau's approval is very likely, but much more important for us is the implicit revelation about the use of this style in the inner Bach circle.

Ex. 20.11. Kuhnau (according to *ABB*)

SUMMARIZING the period, we see for Italy and Germany a picture of both prebeat and onbeat designs, with the prebeat types apparently predominating and, through Walther and Bernhard Bach, traced into Johann Sebastian's immediate circle.

J. S. Bach's Slide

Bach uses two distinct symbols to indicate the slide. One is Kuhnau's *custos:* the other is the French two little notes:.[1] Though in many, perhaps in most, instances the two symbols have the same meaning, they are not fully identical in that the *custos,* but not the little notes, can occasionally stand for the dactylic type. Bach used both symbols for all media. Neither was contained in the *Explication,* Bach's ornament table.

Bach wrote out in full notation many slide patterns of all three types, the anapest, the Lombard, and the dactyl, and thereby revealed certain rhythmic leanings that are of sufficient interest to warrant a closer look. Illustrations of the anapestic pattern are given in Ex. 21.1.[2]

Ex. 21.1.

Slides of three or more notes, which through their anticipatory *élan* highlight the principal note, are not frequent but do occur in a few places like those shown in Ex. 21.2, of which Ex. *a* is from Cantata 92 in a movement filled with similar thrusting figures of

[1] Bach writes the little notes mostly as 16ths: but once in a while as 32nds: —e.g. in the autograph (P 109) of Cantata 48,4, where the copyist of some of the original parts (St 53) reduced the three beams of Bach's symbols to two.

The little notes appear less frequently in autographs than in the prints derived from the *BG* edition which occasionally arbitrarily substituted the little notes for the *custos.*

[2] Example *a* is from the *St. Matthew Passion*; Ex. *b* from the Violin-Harpsichord Sonata in C minor; Ex. *c* from the Violin-Continuo Sonata in E minor; Exx. *d*, *e*, and *f* from Cantatas 84, 129, and 97. For further specimens see Cantatas 13,5, mm. 3-4; 108,5, mm. 1, 10-11, 14, 17; 129,2, mm. 29ff.; 146,3, mm. 2, 12; Gamba-Clavier Sonata in G minor, 1st movement, mm. 30-34, 82-94.

varied length (not all of which are exactly reproduced in the *NBA*, I, 7). In Ex. *b* from Cantata 155 the *tirata* is written in as an afterthought with different ink but in Bach's hand; in Ex. *c*, from Cantata 173a, a similar *tirata* occurs three times, written in unmetrical little notes.

Ex. 21.2.

The written-out Lombard form, illustrations of which are given in Ex. 21.3, seems to occur frequently in affect-filled passages where the onbeat placement on the strong part of the measure produces a sigh-like quality of pain, sorrow, or similar emotion.

In accord with such expression, the tempi lean to slowness. Both Ex. *a* from the aria "Erbarme dich" (Have mercy on me) of the *St. Matthew Passion* and Ex. *b* from the *St. John Passion*, with the words "Melt, Oh my heart in floods of tears," were in no need of tempo directives. Example *c* from Cantata 97 is marked largo; Ex. *d*. from Cantata 179 is marked adagio for its parody in the *G major Mass* (BWV 236).[3]

Ex. 21.3.

There are, of course, cases where the Lombard slide is written out in fast tempi, but they occur less frequently on the heaviest beats and generally seem to be less typical. We do find many of them in Cantata 11 throughout the first movement and also a good number in the first movement of the A minor Violin Concerto (BWV 1041).

The descending slide of the Lombard design is fairly frequent too, and one of its loveliest applications is the soaring sequence of the solo violin in the "Laudamus te" from the *B minor Mass* (mm. 5-6) with its anapestic counterpart in Cantata 13,5, m. 7.

It is interesting and significant that in none of the cases where the Lombard slide is part of a recurring theme is the full notation ever replaced by either of the symbols. Thus, the slide in Ex. 21.3*b* is written out 30-odd times, not count-

[3] For analogous passages see Cantatas 179,3 and 188,3 and the Violin-Clavier Sonata in G major, 4th movement.

ing the doublings; in Ex. 21.3*d* from Cantata 179 (as well as in its parody in the *G major Mass*) the slide is written out 28 times, and we can find this same phenomenon in all analogous situations. If, as it is usually assumed, both slide symbols stand for this very Lombard-style design, it is difficult to understand why in these and numerous similar cases Bach did not once avail himself of the symbol's shorthand convenience. It is true that Bach was less concerned with labor-saving devices than were some of his copyists. Yet, his consistency in avoiding the symbol in such situations can hardly be explained as being entirely accidental. Would it not be more plausible to assume that Bach never used the symbol as a notational aid in such circumstances because it did not *have* to mean a Lombard slide?

The dactylic pattern, derived from the Italians, was one of Bach's favorite melodic figures. It appears countless times in full notation of which Ex. 21.4*a* from Cantata 94 is a representative model. In all of these cases the dactyl is repeated many times and not once replaced by a symbol.[4] Generally, the dactylic pattern is more typically at home on unaccented beats or subdivisions, just as the Lombard type was more attracted by the heavier beat. But, as always, there are exceptions and Ex. *b* from Cantata 75 shows the dactyl on the downbeat in a pattern that is repeated 32 times in oboe and soprano.

Ex. 21.4.

The written-out slide-type patterns are interesting because they reveal all three types as part of Bach's melodic vocabulary; yet because of their overlapping contexts, they cannot provide definite clues for deciphering Bach's symbols, and we must therefore turn to other musical evidence.

THE ANAPEST

Prevailing doctrine for the most part rejects the anapest, ignores the dactyl, and limits Bach's slides generally to the Lombard type. Our first effort will aim at showing evidence for Bach's use of the anticipated, the anapestic pattern.

Bach's slide appears often, marked by either symbol, in the setting of an upbeat

that leaps to a siciliano rhythm:

This pattern occurs in Cantatas 8,1; 62,2; 82,1; 115,2; and 140,3; in the violin obbligato of "Erbarme dich" from the *St. Matthew Passion*; and in the second movement of the 6th Organ Sonata. In almost every one of these examples we find one or two instances where the onbeat rendition leads to the kind of objectionable parallels which were not likely to have been intended.

[4] For other specimens see Cantatas 87,3, m. 11; 75,5, mm. 1 and 5; 76,3; 94,7; 98,5; 101,6; 208,4.

Among the illustrations given in Ex. 21.5, the first, Ex. *a* from Cantata 140, with its parallel octaves is particularly persuasive, because the two voices, except for the continuo realization, are completely open and alone. Almost as open and just about as objectionable are two passages from the *St. Matthew Passion* (Exx. *b* and *c*) where the perfect octaves of the solo violin with the bass would hardly be veiled by the piano chord of the *ripieno* strings. In Ex. *d* from Cantata 8, the onbeat octaves between voice and bass are slightly camouflaged by the presence of an upper voice; however, they are still improbable and prompted Beyschlag, who quotes this measure, to see in it one of the exceptions to what he too believed to be the general rule of the onbeat for the slide. When—in the transition to m. 83 of the same movement—the oboe, according to the *BG* edition, has a *Vorschlag* leaping up a third (as shown in Ex. *e*), this *Vorschlag* is almost certainly a misread *custos* symbol and ought to be corrected as indicated in brackets in the same example.[5] Whether we have to do with a *Vorschlag* or slide, the octaves return to the outer voices and onbeat rendition would be objectionable in either case. In Ex. *f* from Cantata 62 the onbeat slide would produce an unlikely unison between 1st and 2nd violins in a constellation which occurs three more times in mm. 53, 61, and 115 and can be no oversight. In m. 53, the faulty voice-leading would be still more conspicuous because oboes reinforce the 1st and 2nd violins respectively. In Ex. *g* from Cantata 82,1, a unison between oboe and viola would be questionable. In Ex. *h* from Cantata 69 (as in Ex. *a* above), the octaves between bass and continuo would be entirely open. In Ex. *i* from Cantata 115, the unison between the top voices is aggravated by the simultaneous, hidden octaves with the bass. The same situation recurs in mm. 53 and 95.[6]

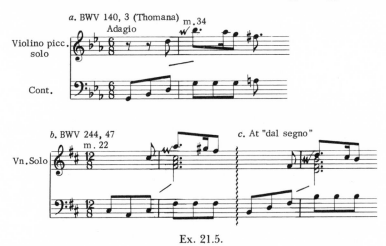

Ex. 21.5.

[5] Bach's writing of the *custos* is often hard to distinguish from a little 8th-note, especially when the two waggles are so close that they seem to merge. There are quite a few cases where his *custos* in a score has been misread by a copyist for an 8th-note grace. This has happened even when the autograph *custos* was very clear; in Cantata 215,9, for example, an unmistakable *custos* in the autograph score (P 139) finds itself transformed in the original part (St 77) into a leaping *Vorschlag*. Another case is that of Prelude 23, m. 23 (*WC* II), where the London autograph has an unmistakable *custos*, and Kirnberger's copy (P 209) a leaping *Vorschlag*.

[6] For further examples see Cantatas 16,5, m. 33: undiluted open fifths between tenor and continuo; 82,1, m. 168: unison of oboe and viola; 122,3, m. 11: hidden fifths between soprano and bass (somewhat diluted by upper voices); 125,2, m. 12: hidden but bothersome octaves between flute and continuo; 152,6, m. 19: hidden octaves between bass voice and continuo; 164,3, m. 9: similar questionable octaves between outer voice and continuo; 167,1, m. 13: hidden octaves between tenor voice and continuo; 182,5, m. 40: open fifths between flute and alto voice; *St. Matthew Passion* (BWV 244), 75, mm. 10 and 12: unison of voice and viola.

The above listed passage from Cantata 16,5, m. 33 is another case where a leaping *Vorschlag* was erroneously substituted in the *BG* for the original *custos* (aut. part St 44). The *NBA*, I, 4, p. 125 has the correct reading. See also Cantata 20,5 (oboe I in m. 4 and parallel spots): *custodes* in original Thomana parts, leaping *Vorschläge* in *BG*.

Ex. 21.5 *cont.*

Inasmuch as keyboard parallels are always more conspicuous than those between various media, the following examples give even stronger suggestions of anticipation. In Ex. 21.6a from the 5th Partita, onbeat execution would produce open fifths in the outer voices. Particularly striking is Ex. *b*, from the early Capriccio of 1704, where the slow tempo intensifies the need for the anapest to avoid fifths unmitigated by any audible middle voice. In Ex. *c* from the 6th Organ Sonata and Ex. *d* from the French Overture, the octaves, though hidden, would be very disturbing in the transparency of two-part writing.

Ex. 21.6.

There is more evidence for anticipation. Example 21.7a gives an excerpt from the *Aria Variata* of 1709 as it appeared in its primary source, the *ABB*. We find two slides in close succession; the first of them, however, is improperly placed: a step, instead of a third, below the principal note. It may possibly stand for a three-note grace: 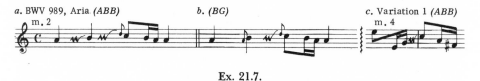 but most likely it was a slip of the pen or the misreading of a little *Vorschlag* note for a *custos*; the *BG* has corrected it as shown in Ex. *b*. More important for our case is the second *custos* which can hardly be a slip of the pen, and which *had* to be anticipated, however one wishes to interpret the following *Vorschlag* note d″. The anticipated reading for the slide is confirmed in Variation 1, m. 4, where the *ABB* places the *custos*—without problem of space—clearly and completely before the bar line (see Ex. *c*), in the identical manner noted above, in the same document, for slides inserted into Kuhnau's sonatas.

a. BWV 989, Aria *(ABB)*   *b.* *(BG)*   *c.* Variation 1 *(ABB)*

Ex. 21.7.

The onbeat solution is often eliminated by the demand of "polyphonic logic." A case in point is the excerpt from the 6th Organ Sonata shown in Ex. 21.8a where the onbeat descending slide is written out in the upper voice against a *custos* symbol in the middle part, as well as in m. 28 (Ex. *b*) where the pattern is reversed between the two upper voices. Not only would there be a triple unison on the empty B, but it is unlikely that Bach would have left the synchronization of two simultaneous slides to chance. The only solution that would not interfere with the combination of voices seems to be anticipation.

Ex. 21.8. BWV 530, 2

When we take into account the evidence produced, the naturalness of the anapest when employed in a purely connective function, and its widespread international use that was traced into Bach's immediate circle, it should become clear that both slide symbols could and many times did stand for the anapest.

THE LOMBARD

The first movement of the E major Clavier Concerto (a transcription from a lost violin concerto) contains intriguing specimens of the slide. One of these, which seems to speak for the Lombard style, invites a closer look.

The characteristic fragment of the theme (Ex. 21.9a) occurs for the solo clavier five times in the first part of the movement. All of these instances recur in a *da capo* which Bach understandably did not write out in the autograph. Each of the five times there is a slight deviation. In the first occurrence (Ex. *a*) the *custos* appears both in the clavier and the unison violins, and the latter have staccato dots. The second time (Ex. *b*) a Lombard slide pattern is written out for the clavier. The third time (Ex. *c*) there are dots over the first four 8th-notes of the clavier and a trill over the fifth 8th-note. The unison violins have neither slide nor trill symbol. The fourth time (Ex. *d*) the slide is again limited to the clavier; here, a small melodic variant at the start of the measure avoids the hidden octaves that would result if the measure were to start with the D sharp. The fifth time (Ex. *e*) there are no dots and both unison parts agree on the trill and the lack of the slide.

Ex. 21.9. BWV 1053, 1 (aut. P 234)

Each time there is a certain change in the complexion of the theme-fragment. Though some of these variants may be, and probably are, due to a casual disregard for detail, the need for a measure of variety is understandable in a theme that recurs ten times. It is the second incident (Ex. *b*) of the written-out Lombard design that might be taken as the key to the interpretation of the slide symbol in this piece. However, several reasons speak against such an assumption.

1. The Lombard design is used the only time the violins are *not* in unison with the clavier. Had the Lombard design appeared simultaneously with a symbol in the unison part, the evidence for the Lombard meaning would be far more convincing.

2. The onbeat design is used where anticipation would produce noticeable parallel octaves with the violas; hence it combines improvement of voice-leading with relief from monotony.

3. In the passage given in Ex. *c*, the dots over the four notes, including the one with the slide, would seem to favor anticipation, because onbeat execution would blunt the staccato effect. (The written-out Lombard slide of Ex. *b* carries no dot; only the note following the slide has the staccato mark.)

4. If Bach was using the demonstration-*segue* technique for ornaments, the written-out Lombard slide as explanation for the symbol would have been used logically the first, not the second, time. However, as was pointed out, whenever Bach called for the repeated Lombard slide, he always wrote it out.

These reasons alone make it appear more likely that the notational difference bespoke an intended difference in execution. A confirmation of this reasoning can be found in Cantata 169,1 whose introductory Sinfonia is a sister work of this same E major Clavier Concerto movement in that it is parodied from the same lost model. This cantata movement, standing visibly closer to the original, has no slide symbols at all, yet m. 14 (which, because of an omitted measure, corresponds to m. 15 in the clavier version) has the same Lombard figure; hence the latter is revealed as a free variant.

In the 2nd Gamba Sonata, the theme of Ex. 21.10 occurs seven times in various keys but in the identical rhythm and invariably in the identical notational pattern: a written-out onbeat slide on a subdivision of the beat and, in midmeasure, a *custos* symbol before the siciliano pattern on a strong beat. Given the difference in the rhythmic and metric setting, the symbol is unlikely to represent a counterpart to the preceding onbeat slide. Moreover, the whole phrase would hardly have always appeared in the exact same notation, nor would the very same onbeat pattern be written out 24 times in the movement if both notational versions had the same meaning. The indication is very strong that the two versions correspond here to different meanings.

Ex. 21.10. BWV 1028, 3

So far no evidence has been found that unequivocally *requires* Lombard interpretation of certain of Bach's slide symbols. However, in view of the many Lombard slides written out in regular notation, we can assume that such interpretation is justified whenever the context favors its specific qualities.

THE DACTYL

There is evidence that the *custos* could stand for dactylic rendition. Example 21.11 from the *Trauerode* shows a configuration where the *custos* in the sopranos is matched by the dactyl in the oboe d'amore. It is an intriguing passage, with its melodic unison and rhythmic discrepancy. Because of the latter, one could argue that a rhythmic difference was intended for the execution of the slide, and certainly the case for the dactylic identity would have been stronger had there been throughout a complete melodic-rhythmic congruence. However, the motivation for the rhythmic discrepancy of the 16th-notes was the anti-vocal character of a long-sustained dotted pattern.[7] By contrast, for the slide, the dactyl is not less but more singable than its alternatives and is appropriate on the weak subdivision of a beat, in keeping with Bach's preferential usage. We may therefore assume that here the dactyl was intended.

An interesting clue for dactylic meaning, again on an unaccented beat, is contained in the Organ Chorale Fantasia *Super Schmücke dich* (Ex. 21.12). In the early Weimar version we find in m. 123 the *custos* (Ex. *a*), in the late Leipzig version the written-out dactyl (Ex. *b*).

[7] Mattheson, in *Capellmeister*, pt. 2, ch. 12, par. 20, discusses the characteristic differences between vocal and instrumental writing and notes that the vocal melody does not admit of the same sharp dotted style as do the instruments ("dass die Vocal-Melodie kein solches reissendes punctirtes Wesen zulasse, als die Instrumente").

Ex. 21.11. BWV 198, 1

Ex. 21.12.

Conclusive evidence about the occasional dactylic meaning of Bach's *custos* symbol can be found in the alto aria "Saget mir geschwinde" from the *Easter Oratorio*. In the autograph score the alto part has in m. 15 the written-out dactyl of Ex. 21.13*a*. Shortly thereafter, in m. 21, we find the somewhat bewildering combination of Ex. *b*: for the identical melody (except for its being shifted by two beats) in the alto part, the previous dactyl is now indicated by the *custos* symbol, the otherwise unison oboe sounds only the main note, and the 1st violins have, for the fourth quarter, the written-out dactyl a third below the voice. The dactylic meaning of the *custos* in the alto part of the score is definitely confirmed in the autograph alto solo part, where m. 21 reads as shown in Ex. *c*. In the oboe part, written by one of Bach's copyists but revised by Bach himself, Bach added the *custos* to the originally unornamented note to make the part conform with the alto and the violins (Ex. *d*).

The puzzling inconsistency in the notation of m. 21 in the score can perhaps be explained as follows. The *Easter Oratorio* is a parody of the so-called Schäfer Cantata, for which the text is preserved but the music lost. It is very likely that the original melody of this passage, whenever it occurred, contained no slide of any kind. It was written to the words "hauche mit dem Westenwinde," and the short syllable *West-* is not conducive to a dactylic slide. In the parody version, the first syllable of *Jesum*, which takes the place of *West-*, invites the tender inflection of this grace. This assumption would explain why in m. 3 of the aria—which Bach copied in semi-automatic haste from the model—the violins and the oboe have no ornament symbol in the score of P 34 (Ex. *e*). It was in m. 15 that Bach presumably first modified for the voice the original melody by the insertion of the dactyl for *Jes*um; in m. 21 (Ex. *b*) Bach probably started again to copy the unornamented original for the alto and the oboe; then, remembering the dactylic modification, he may have inserted the *custos* for the voice and perhaps next wrote out the dactyl for the 1st violins. In the original parts, the same dactyl in m. 21 is then likewise indicated for the oboe by the *custos* (Ex. *d*) and, in analogy, in m. 3 for both oboe and 1st violins (Ex. *f*, first and second systems). In this measure, however, Bach forgot a corresponding adjustment in the 2nd violin part (Ex. *f* third system) which as things stand now, would move in an unlikely unison. It would seem advisable to make the forgotten adjustment here, as well as in the parallel spot of m. 38, by maintaining the parallel thirds of the original notation for the dactylic revision of the melody, as suggested in Ex. *g*.

A few more passages suggest a link between the *custos* and the dactylic pattern. In Ex. 21.14*a* from Cantata 87, the *custos* of m. 7 becomes in the autograph score a dactyl in m. 41 (Ex. *b*). In Ex. *c* from Cantata 36c, the oboe d'amore has, according to the autograph score, a dactyl in the first measure, while the unison violins have only the principal

Ex. 21.13. BWV 249, 9

note; in m. 8 both oboe d'amore and violins have the *custos*. In a parody of the work (Cantata 36b) the flute, substituting for the oboe d'amore, has, according to the autograph part, the *custos* in the same first measure (Ex. *d*).

The case of Couperin's two little slide notes which were transcribed by Anna Magdalena as a dactyl (see above Ex. 16.21) slightly confuses the issue. It is unlikely that Bach ever indicated an intended dactyl by evenly written little notes; to do so would have been

Ex. 21.14.

incongruous and misleading. It is probable that the following association caused this puzzling transcription: the two little notes signify a slide and the slide *may* be a dactyl.

Bach's association of the dactyl with the *custos* and not with the little notes makes not only notational but also historical sense. The little notes came from France where the slide was almost always anapestic and always even. By contrast, the *custos* is a German symbol, and the dactyl, a product of Italo-German traditions, goes back at least to the dotted slide patterns of Bovicelli that were adopted by Praetorius. Its currency in early-18th-century Germany is attested to by Heinichen. In midcentury the pattern will be seen with Tartini and will appear in the Berlin School as a subspecies of the slide, marked by a dotted pair of little notes: ♩♪♩ .

For a final illustration let us return to the *St. Matthew Passion* and the aria "Erbarme dich" with its many slides. (Samples of those that were written out in either anapestic or Lombard style were given above in Exx. 21.1*a* and 21.3*a*.) In addition, the *custos* appears repeatedly in the parts of the alto voice, the solo violin, and the *ripieno* violins.[8] Anticipation of these slides is indicated for a number of reasons, two of which were pointed out above in connection with Exx. 21.5*b* and *c*, where onbeat execution would produce bad octaves in sensitive spots. Another clue is provided by the interesting concordance between voice and solo violin shown in Ex. 21.15*a*, where the anticipation is spelled out for the violin against a *custos* in the voice. Beyschlag also refers to this spot, and he too favors anticipation in this aria. Other considerations reinforce the clues given by the notation. Example *b* shows the start of the alto melody as it appears in both score and voice part. This corresponds to the solo violin as it was written in the autograph score (Ex. *c*), whereas in the solo violin part (St 110) the two ornaments were added, as given in Ex. *d*.

The anticipation of the slide in the violin would parallel a small *portamento* with which a singer could bridge the interval smoothly and idiomatically in the manner of a *cercar della nota*. On the other hand, an accented onbeat start of the slide would alter the contour of the melody and blur its identity with the vocal line. Also, anticipation imparts more unity to the phrase with its written-out prebeat slides in mm. 2, 3, and 4 that give it its pleading, submissive character.[9]

Ex. 21.15. BWV 244, 47

[8] The symbols for voice and *ripieno* were contained in the autograph score, those of the solo violin only in the original part that, though not written by Bach, was revised by him so that the added ornaments—some of which are autograph—are authentic.

[9] An interesting detail is the fact that Bach wrote in the autograph score (P 25) at the start of the first measure of the solo violin a b′ of unknown denomination which he corrected to the d″. Though the score is a very carefully written fair copy, a slip of the pen is of course possible. If, on the other hand, the b′ may have been the intended first note of a written-out Lombard or dactylic slide, Bach discarded the idea almost the moment it was conceived and substituted for it on the beat the unadorned principal note. If Bach actually first considered then rejected the onbeat style, it would make a further point for the anapest interpretation of the subsequently added *custos*.

The Altnikol copy (published in facsimile by the *NBA*, II, 5a) that predates P 25 is in accord with the latter concerning the d″ on the downbeat.

FROM THE presented evidence, one conclusion is certain: there is no simple, routine solution to Bach's slide symbols. The French little notes can stand for the anapest or the Lombard design; the *custos*, in addition, can also stand for the dactyl. Several considerations may help us in making a sensible choice. In vocal music, diction and word-meaning are most important. By and large, a sharp initial accent will attract the Lombard type, an unaccented or only gently emphasized syllable the dactyl, a crescendo-implying syllable the anapest. In all media, the anapest, due to its neutral nature, can fit any place in the measure, whereas the dactyl is more congenial to weak beats, the Lombard to strong ones. Often the most important element will be the "affect" of a given passage, as well as the relationship to other voices. Whenever these and other considerations of musical logic do not point to a clear preference, it will probably not greatly matter which design is chosen. Aware of the alternatives, the performer must make the choice.

The Italian Slide
1710-1760

In the early part of the 18th century the patterns of the so-called Lombard rhythm: ♪♩. ♫♩. became favorite formulas in Italy and are found countless times in their written-out versions. Therefore, when composers used the newly introduced little notes: ♪♪● the difference in notation suggests a difference in meaning, because a notational advance is logically used for the sake of greater precision, not greater ambiguity. It makes more historical sense to assume that the little notes expressed something that had previously been left to improvisation—to wit, anticipated slides—rather than that they expressed vaguely what had been expressed precisely a thousand times by regular notes. Internal evidence will bear this out.

There are many cases where anticipation is unavoidable because onbeat execution would be rhythmically incongruous or impossible or both. Illustrations of such contexts are given in Ex. 22.1 from sonatas by Geminiani, Locatelli, and Alberghi.[1]

a. Geminiani (1739), Op. 1, Sonata No. 2   *b.* Locatelli (1746), Op. 6, Sonata No. 2   *c.* Alberghi, Sonata No. 6

Ex. 22.1.

A great number of instances can be found where considerations of voice-leading indicate the prebeat meaning of the two little slide notes. Example 22.2 gives a few representative examples of cases where onbeat execution would produce objectionable parallels.[2]

In the first known work written for pianoforte, Giustini's sonatas of 1732, we find numerous instances of slides that could not be meant for the beat. A few specimens are given in Ex. 22.3. They are set off by some Lombard slides written out in regular notation.[3]

[1] Francesco Geminiani, *Le prime sonate à violino è basso*, new ed. with added graces (London, 1739); Pietro Locatelli, *XII Sonate à violino solo è basso*, Op. 6 (Amsterdam, 1746); Paolo Alberghi, Sonata No. 6, MS Berk.

[2] The sources of the illustrations are: Ex. *a*, Locatelli, *Sonate à flauto traversiere solo è basso*, Op. 2 (Paris, n.d. [1732]); Ex. *b*, Francesco Durante, *Sonate per cembalo*, MS Bol. EE 173; Ex. *c*, Antonio Vivaldi, Concerto for *violino in tromba*, Foà 29, fols. 94ff. (concerning the *violino in tromba*, see above, ch. 17, n. 20); Ex. *d*, Nicola Antonio Porpora [*XII Cantate*] (London, 1735); Exx. *e-g*, Giovanni Battista Martini, *Cantata latina sopra la passione* (1745), aut. Bol. HH 66; Ex. *h*, Lorenzo Somis, *Sonate da camera* (Paris, n.d. [1740]); Ex. *i*, Carlo Tessarini, *Trattenimenti à violino è basso*, Op. 4 (n.p., n.d.) (Urbino?, dedication 1742); Ex. *j*, Alessandro Besozzi, MS Berk. No. 72; Ex. *k*, Giuseppe Tartini, *Sonata*, MS Berk.; Ex. *l*, Tartini, *Concerto*, MS BN MS 9793; Ex. *m*, Tartini, *Sinfonia à violino solo*, aut. BN MS 9796; Ex. *n*, Geminiani, *Sonate à violino è basso*, Op. 4 (London, 1739).

[3] Lodovico Giustini, Op. 1. *Sonate da cimbalo di piano e forte detto volgarmente di marteletti* (Florence, 1732).

Ex. 22.2.

Such musical evidence, uncontradicted by any known theoretical rule for the period in question, makes it clear that in the case of the Italian slide an automatic application of the onbeat principle is uncalled for. On the contrary, the probability is high that in Italy a slide, written by two equal little notes, was mostly anticipated.

What is true of the Italians applies equally to Handel's none-too-frequent slide

Ex. 22.3. Giustini (1732), Sonata 3

symbol of two equal little notes. As was shown before (Ex. 17.19), even Theophil Muffat gave Handel's slides a prebeat interpretation.

It is another matter when, once in a while, we find the slide symbol written in unequal notes, indicating a dactylic rhythm. In Ex. 22.4a from a Porpora cantata, the onbeat intention is unmistakable. This is also true of Ex. b from Geminiani's *Pièces de clavecin*. Example c, an extremely rare case for Vivaldi, is found in very clear writing in a contemporary manuscript (though not autograph) source.[4] The complete dactyl is written in little notes which here can hardly be intended for the downbeat since the allegro tempo does not leave sufficient time to execute them. The context suggests at least partial anticipation.

Ex. 22.4.

To summarize briefly, in Italy, slides of all kinds were improvised and therefore left no traces. Those slides that were more and more frequently marked by little notes were largely, probably overwhelmingly, of the anapestic type. The dactyl, when desired, was indicated by the Italian innovation (unknown in France) of a small dotted note-pair. The Lombard slide was written out in regular notation with such frequency that it probably played no more than a very minor role in the rendition of slides indicated by little notes.

[4] Porpora, see n. 2 above; Geminiani, *Pièces de clavecin* (London, 1743) (the pieces are all transcriptions by the composer from works in different media); Vivaldi, Gio. 35, fols. 222ff.

Heinichen mentions the dactylic slide in his early treatise of 1711, but amplifies the matter in his later work of 1728.[1] He distinguishes two types. The plain dactyl without preparation is to be used in vocal music (Ex. 23.1*a*); in instrumental performance one "anticipates with a little note," thereby changing the patterns of Ex. *a* to those of Ex. *b*. In both cases the slide proper is anchored on the beat. For a symbol he uses a slanted cross placed on the spot where the slide is to start. His adverb *ohngefähr* (approximately) implies flexibility.

Ex. 23.1. Heinichen (1728)

In his ornament table of c. 1736, Theophil Muffat gives the Lombard pattern of Ex. 23.2 as an example of the slide.[2] The symbol is one that his father had used to signify either straddling or anticipation of the beat.

Ex. 23.2. Th. Muffat (c. 1736)

The eminent German flutist Johann Christian Schickhardt (1680-1762) published a treatise sometime between 1720 and 1730 in which we find many slides written in little notes that are placed before the bar line.[3] Example 23.3 gives but one illustration which illuminates the prebeat rendition of other such slides, regardless of their place in the measure.

Ex. 23.3. Schickhardt (c. 1720-1730)

[1] *Anweisung*, p. 174; *Generalbass*, p. 528.
[2] *Componimenti*, Appendix.
[3] Schickhardt, *Principes de la flûte*, p. 3. According to Carl Ferdinand Becker's *Darstellung der musikalischen Literatur*, Schickhardt's book came out approximately in 1730. *MGG* does not attempt to date it but expresses the supposition that most of Schickhardt's works were published before 1720.

In Ex. 23.4a from Georg Friedrich Kauffmann's collection of chorale preludes, anticipation of the slide would seem to assure better coordination of the moving parts.[4] More conclusively, a prebar slide of his was given above in Ex. 18.5a.

Thielo, Walther's student, indicates the anapestic character of his slides, as shown in Ex. 23.4b, by his explanation for the ascending type. He says that one strikes e, f, g quickly, "but in such a manner that the g sounds strongest at the end."[5] He indicates that the descending slide is to be done in an analogous manner.

Van Blankenburg uses a new symbol resembling a check mark,[6] and his resolution by means of little notes is rhythmically noncommittal (Ex. c).

Ex. 23.4.

In the Berlin School we find the first clear distinction between the even slide and the dactylic one. The even or "fast" slide is most often illustrated as Lombard type. However, we shall find exceptions in theory which were probably outstripped in practice.

Marpurg, in 1749, calls the slide *Schleiffer* or *coulé* and uses the dash from note to note as a symbol for the Lombard solution of Ex. 23.5a. In his table of 1755, he adds to the dash symbol the little notes and the *custos*; all three signs have the identical Lombard meaning (Ex. b). He also introduces now the dactylic slide with the illustration of Ex. c.[7] However, in 1763 he presents under the heading of *Nachschlag* the pattern of Ex. d. The term implies interbeat execution.[8]

Ex. 23.5. Marpurg

[4] *Harmonische Seelenlust.*
[5] *Grund-Regeln*, p. 52.
[6] Van Blankenburg, *Clavicimbel-en Orgelboek*, Preface.

[7] *Crit. Musicus*, p. 67, Table 2, fig. 23; *Anleitung zum Clav.*, p. 52, Table 4, figs. 14-21.
[8] *Anleitung zur Musik*, p. 153.

C.P.E. Bach, as expected, recognizes only the onbeat types of the Lombard and the dactylic slide.[9] He sees no problems in the Lombard slide, for which he offers only the symbols given in Ex. 23.6a and the remark that occasionally its execution is written out in regular notes as shown in Ex. b. The usual symbol, he says, is two small, even 32nd-notes (or 16th-notes in alla breve). He lists also the *custos* with identical meaning, but omits Marpurg's dash symbol. This (Lombard) type, he says, always occurs in a leap whose interval it fills (par. 4).

Ex. 23.6. C.P.E. Bach (1753)

On the other hand, he says, the dactylic slide presents a real problem because its execution can be "more varied than that of any other ornament."[10] This statement was repeated many times by later writers. The symbol for this species is a dotted pair of little notes: . The note with the dot is always played loudly, the second tone of the slide together with the principal note, softly.

The variable element is the length of the first ornamental note which will often be long enough to relegate the two dactylic partners to the very end of the time allotted to the principal note (see Ex. 23.7a). However, occasionally the first note usurps the entire length of the principal note, in which case the two partners have to find their place in the time of the following note, as seen in the second alternative of Ex. b.

When the slide occurs before a dotted note-pair, such as a dotted quarter followed by an 8th, this dotted relationship is compressed in proportion to the shortening of the principal note as shown in Exx. c and d.

Ex. 23.7. C.P.E. Bach

Though this dactylic slide is a direct descendant of those used by J. S. Bach and older masters, it appears not only with a new symbol—the dotted little notes of Italian origin—but also in a new design embodying an extreme disproportion between the first note and the two junior partners. Such design, in analogy to the overlong appoggiatura, represents a new fashion of the *galant* era.

Agricola makes the same distinction between the two-note slides that are either equal and fast or dotted and slow.[11] As far as the dotted slide is concerned, Agri-

[9] *Versuch*, I, ch. 2, sec. 7 is devoted to the slide and all references will be to this section. Bk. II, ch. 28 deals with the problems of accompaniment for the dactylic slide.

[10] Par. 11: "Seine Eintheilung ist so verschieden als bey keiner andern Manier."
[11] *Anleitung*, pp. 87-91.

cola follows C.P.E. Bach's presentation closely, at times almost literally (pp. 88-90).

As far as the "even" or "fast" slide is concerned, however, Agricola takes an independent attitude which commands attention. The fast slides, he says, can precede either a strong or a weak *Tactglied*,[12] adding that composers often write them out when they fall on the strong beats. This manner, he thinks, has given rise to the characteristic three-note figure of the Lombard style, for which he offers the model of Ex. 23.8.

C'io par - to reo

Ex. 23.8. Agricola (1757)

"Now," he continues, "there is this difference, that the two short notes in this [Lombard] figure are performed very loudly: whereas a slide which fills in a leap and falls truly within the weak *Tactglied* will be performed softer."[13] This type of slide, he cautions, should be used only sparingly so as not to dull and enfeeble ("lahm und matt machen") each and every leap. And only on rarest occasion should it be used where no leap is involved. Clearly, we have to do here with a slide that is not of the Lombard type. Türk, 35 years later, expressed his bewilderment over this passage which, he says, only few will be able to understand.[14] Türk assumed that Agricola wanted to limit slides that fill a leap to weak beats only, and such limitation would indeed make little sense. This, however, is certainly not what Agricola had in mind. His text, not too clear on that point, becomes meaningful if we interpret the reference to the weak *Tactglied* in the sense of a slide placed *before* a strong, hence *in* a weak, *Tactglied*. This interpretation, which reveals the anapestic character of the slide in question, is fully in line with Agricola's concept of *anschlagende* and *durchgehende Tactglieder* and his wording that the slide itself falls within the weak *Tactglied*. The interpretation finds itself doubly corroborated: first, by Agricola's directive that, in contrast to the Lombard style, here the two little notes are to be rendered "more weakly"; and second, by his remark that this type of slide can "enfeeble" or "dull" a leap. The weaker rendition of the two little notes is of course a mark of the anapest and the enfeebling effect is certainly incompatible with a Lombard phrasing.

It is not surprising that Agricola, speaking as he does from the singer's point of view, should have made these comments regarding the anapest, because in the vocal style the expressive gliding into a note, the *cercar della nota*, is a spontaneous gesture of the sensitive throat. To perform purely connective ornaments

[12] In Agricola's terminology, which he explains on p. 73, the *Tactglied* represents the secondary subdivision of a measure below the primary one of the *Tacttheil*. Thus in a C meter, two half-notes represent *Tacttheile*, the quarter-notes *Tactglieder*. The first and third of the latter are *anschlagend* the second and fourth *durchgehend*. This polarization between *anschlagend* and *durchgehend*, or *gut* and *schlimm* (i.e. "good" and "bad" notes) extends down the line through all smaller subdivisions of 8ths, 16ths, etc.

[13] "Nur ist dabey der Unterschied, dass die zwo kurzen Noten in dieser Figur mehr stark vorgetragen werden: dahingegen ein Schleifer der einen Sprung ausfüllet, und eigentlich auf das schlimme Tactglied fällt, schwächer ausgeführet wird."

[14] *Klavierschule*, ch. 4, sec. 2, par. 20.

immutably accented on the beat is pedantic enough for the keyboard but runs counter to the very essence of the vocal impulse. Moreover, Agricola mentions two-note *Nachschläge* which, as he says, are only rarely indicated in notation, hence simply added *ex abrupto*. They have to be very short, he says, and slurred to the preceding note, as shown in Ex. 23.9.

Ex. 23.9. Agricola

Quantz does not deal with the slide in a systematic fashion but mentions it incidentally in a few spots in his treatise. One reference to the dotted slide occurs in the section of the book dealing with the responsibilities of the *ripieno* violinist.[15] There he explains and illustrates the execution of the dotted symbol in slow tempo.

The principal note of his model (Ex. 23.10*a*) happens to be dotted also, and this dotted relationship is not only reproduced in proportion as it was with C.P.E. Bach and Agricola, but sharpened to a double dot in accord with Quantz's principles that dotted rhythms ought to be sharpened when they would sound too dull in their literal rendition (Ex. *b*).

Quantz adds that these ornamental notes have to be played with much expression ("mit viel Affect"); that one should take the first double-dotted note on the downbow and let it swell, then slur and diminish to a piano the following two notes, and then emphasize the last short one again with the upbow. Example *c* is an attempt to transcribe Quantz's verbal directives into notation.

Later Quantz speaks of the even slide and shows its symbol of the two little 16th-notes. He says that these notes are more usual in the French than the Italian style and in contrast to the dotted ones must be played very fast, as illustrated in Ex. *d*.

Ex. 23.10. Quantz (1752)

That the even slide was not limited to an onbeat start is revealed in an illustration from Chapter 13 of Quantz's work which deals with improvised ornamentation. In paragraph 42 of that chapter, Quantz shows how leaps between long notes may be filled with the scale notes that lie between them rather than with meandering diminutions. To demonstrate the procedure, Quantz gives first the structural leaps (Ex. 23.11*a*), then writes the notes that belong to the chord as quarter-notes and the "passing notes" as little 8ths and 16ths, as shown in Ex. *b*. Finally, he spells out their meaning in regular notation (Ex. *c*), which reveals complete anticipation of all the scale-like passages. Although the example is not meant to demonstrate the meaning of the little notes, it provides further intelligence that anticipation was compatible with the slide symbol of two equal little notes.

15 *Versuch*, ch. 17, sec. 2, par. 21; Table 22, fig. 40.

Ex. 23.11. Quantz

Leopold Mozart mentions only briefly the dactylic slide, which he sees as a variant of the long *Vorschlag*—namely one that leaps from a third below. He points to the somewhat long-held first note ("etwas länger halten") to which the second and principal notes are softly and very gently slurred ("ohne Nachdruck des Bogens ganz gelind daran schleifen").[16]

In the second edition of his treatise,[17] he adds an illustration (Ex. 23.12) showing what he calls *Nachschläge*, which he defines as "a few [or: a pair of] fast notes, appended to the principal note." The graces are more in the nature of *Zwischenschläge* than *Nachschläge*.

Ex. 23.12. L. Mozart (1770)

Petri, in 1767 and 1782, does not mention the dactylic form; his even slide pattern occurs, he says, "like the *Vorschlag* and *Nachschlag*, sometimes before, sometimes after the note," as shown in Ex. 23.13a.[18] In the second edition of his book an example that is meant to show the combination of *Nachschläge* (with reversed flag) and *Vorschläge* incidentally documents the anticipation of a slide that is placed ahead of the bar line (Ex. *b*).

Ex. 23.13. Petri (1767, 1782)

Hiller, though in matters of ornamentation a disciple of C.P.E. Bach, failed to follow him in the condemnation of *Nachschläge*. Specifically, he describes a *doppelter Nachschlag* which, he says, greatly resembles the slide ("dem Schleifer sehr ähnlich"), and he sees as the only difference "its rendition in the time of the preceding instead of the following note. It serves to connect two principal notes, to give them life and luster" ("macht sie

[16] *Violinschule*, ch. 9, par. 11.
[17] Published in 1770, ch. 9, par. 30.

[18] *Anleitung*, 1st ed., pp. 30-31; 2nd ed., pp. 151, 153.

lebhafter und schimmernder").[19] His illustration is shown in Ex. 23.14. Hiller's specification that the two little notes have to be very short and firmly connect with the following note ("dass sie sich fest an die darauf folgende Note anschliessen") points to their *Zwischenschlag* function.

Ex. 23.14. Hiller (1780)

Türk follows C.P.E. Bach in juxtaposing the fast, even slide in Lombard style and the slow dotted one as principal models.[20] Yet, he too qualifies the one-sidedness of such limitation when (ch. 3, sec. 4, par. 27) he points to the *Nachschläge* where a pattern like the one of Ex. 23.15a, especially in absence of a slur, can be interpreted either in terms of a *Vorschlag* (Ex. b) or a *Nachschlag* (Ex. c). He actually criticizes (in a footnote to the same par. 27) C.P.E. Bach for having overlooked the *Nachschlag* potential of the little notes. C.P.E. did not overlook it, he expressly condemned it.

Ex. 23.15. Türk (1789)

It would seem clear from the garnered evidence that during the second third of the 18th century the slide continued to flourish in Germany in all of its three main species: the dactyl, the Lombard, and the anapest. Of these three, the dactyl underwent some changes in application and design. Instead of J. S. Bach's simpler pattern and his preferred use on the weak parts of the measure, it found in the music of the *galant* style a more frequent application on the heavy beat in slow movements where its first note was often extended to the limit, to increase its expressive potential, thus forming a fitting pendant to the long appoggiatura sigh.

The Lombard style gained prominence in theory and presumably in practice. The anapest, like its cousin the prebeat *Vorschlag*, easily survived C.P.E. Bach's theoretical ban. The musical need for a slide that could unobtrusively connect notes without obscuring the principal tone assured the continued use of the anapest. Regardless of doctrinaire prohibitions, an ornament rarely fails to respond to the summons of musical demand.

Symbols were changing; the *custos* and dash gradually disappeared, leaving in the end only the two little notes. For the dactyl, the dotted pair of little notes was imported from Italy, but this new symbol in turn had a limited life span. Not only for J. S. Bach, but for the masters of the *galant* and preclassical style (with the exception of C.P.E. Bach), there is no reason to avoid the anapest whenever it appears to make better musical sense.

[19] *Anweisung* (1780), p. 48.   [20] *Klavierschule*, ch. 4, sec. 2, pars. 18-23.

PART V
THE TRILL

Introduction
Designs and Terms

The trill involves a whole family of graces in which the basic pattern is the rapid alternation of a tone with its upper neighbor. The family history is complex and controversial, hence its chronicle must be considerably detailed.

There are three main types of trills: 1) the simple trill, consisting only of two pitches—the principal note alternating with its upper auxiliary; 2) the simple trill followed by a suffix of one or two notes, involving a third pitch—the lower neighbor of the principal note; 3) the compound trill that is preceded by a turn, a slide, or a mordent, each of which adds the same third pitch. The simple trill and the simple trill with suffix will be discussed together; the compound trill will be treated separately.

The simple trill has two melic designs. One starts with the main note, as in Fig. *a*, the other with the auxiliary, as in Fig. *b*. 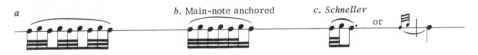 In either case the trill ends with the main note. This ending on the main note is inherent in the nature of the trill. An ending on the upper note could convert the trill into a mordent.[1]

In order to discuss the rhythmic disposition of the two melic designs, we must introduce a working terminology to help us cope with the usual chaos of symbols and terms. The trill that starts with the main note will be called a main-note trill (Ex. V.1*a*). If the main note continues to be emphasized, the trill will be referred to as being main-note anchored (Ex. *b*). A main-note trill with only one alternation will be called a *Schneller* (Ex. *c*), a term coined by C.P.E. Bach.

Ex. V.1. Main-note trill

A trill that starts with the upper note, on the beat, will be called an appoggiatura trill, because a distinct onbeat entrance with the upper note has the effect of a short appoggiatura (Ex. V.2*a*). If the emphasis on the auxiliary continues, the trill will be referred to as being upper-note anchored (Ex. *b*). The appoggiatura effect is extended for the length of this anchor, and the trill assumes the nature of an ornamented appoggiatura.

Ex. V.2. Appoggiatura trill

[1] Exceptions are often more apparent than real. In a case like the following: the last upper note of the trill is more properly a *Nachschlag* or *Zwischenschlag* connecting the trill with the following note:

The lengthening of the first trill note, be it the main or the upper note, will be called "support" (for the French trill, *appui*), and a trill thus started a supported trill.

The supported main-note trill may have main-note anchor (Ex. V.3*a*), or upper-note anchor (Ex. *b*), or may be neutral (Ex. *c*). Observe that an upper-note anchor following a main-note support does not produce an appoggiatura effect, because the latter depends on onbeat entrance of the auxiliary.

Ex. V.3. Supported main-note trill

The supported appoggiatura trill is in fact a long appoggiatura whose resolution is ornamented by the trill proper. The alternations may be anchored on the upper note (Ex. V.4*a*), on the main note (Ex. *b*), or be neutral (Ex. *c*).

Ex. V.4. Supported appoggiatura trill

A trill with the auxiliary before the beat and the main note on it will be called grace-note trill, because the anticipated upper note will have the function of a grace note. The alternations will usually be main-note anchored (Ex. V.5*a*) or be neutral (Ex. *b*). An upper-note anchor is hardly possible. A variant of this type dwells, after the prebeat auxiliary, on the main note before starting the alternations (Ex. *c*).

Ex. V.5. Grace-note trill

If the alternations are taking place in the time of the preceding note, we shall speak of an anticipated trill (Exx. V.6*a-c*). We shall call the trill straddling when the alternations are divided between the preceding and the principal note (Exx. *d* and *e*).

Ex. V.6. Anticipated and straddling trills

Trills often stop their alternations before the end of the trilled note. Such stopping will be referred to as the rest point (Couperin's *point d'arrêt*) (Exx. V.7*a-b*).

Ex. V.7. Trill with rest point

These varied patterns still do not represent all trill designs of the period, even if we take into account the fact that the number of alternations and the length of supports and rest points were variable. Further elements of flexibility and nuance resided in the fastness, slowness, acceleration, or retardation of the alternations, in dynamic nuances, and in subtle and gradual changes of the rhythmic anchor from the upper to neutral, from neutral to main note, or vice versa.

Not every composer used all these possibilities. But by and large there was in use a far wider range of designs than modern research has tended to acknowledge. Thus, many modern writers believe that the only authentic type for the period was the appoggiatura trill, in accord with Marpurg's often quoted definition of a trill as a "series of descending appoggiaturas." The trill, so the argument goes, was like the *Vorschlag*, a "harmonic ornament," and therefore had to stress the auxiliary to enrich the harmony by its dissonance (the argument overlooked the many instances where the main note, not the auxiliary, was dissonant). Prevalent doctrine rejects all main-note trills as unhistorical and, strangely, completely ignores the grace-note trill, unaware apparently of its very existence in spite of the prominent role it played in all three countries. The following chapters will establish the need to revise substantially the prevailing ideas about the use of the trill in the 17th and 18th centuries.

The French Trill

1630-1715

EARLY SOURCES

We do not have much specific information about the French trill before Marin Mersenne (1636). However, seventy years earlier, in 1565, a Spaniard, Tomás de Santa Maria wrote a truly remarkable book about the art of clavichord playing in which he deals most interestingly with various ornaments, including the trill.[1] Santa Maria distinguishes the regular or "reiterated trill" (*quiebro reyterado*) and the "simple trill" (*quiebro senzillo*), as seen in Ex. 24.1 (in modern notation the note values ought to be at least halved).

Ex. 24.1. Santa Maria (1565)

The regular or "reiterated trill" starts on the main note (Ex. *a*); the two forms of the "simple trill" are the *Schneller* (Ex. *b*) and the mordent (Ex. *c*). However, following this illustration, Santa Maria reports on a "new fashion" of starting the regular trill (on note values long enough to accommodate multiple alternations) not with the main note but with the upper note, whereby this upper "first note has to be sounded alone, and the second note has to fall on the consonance [i.e. the harmony] to which it belongs."[2] In other words, the auxiliary has to be anticipated. It is very interesting and probably very significant, too, that the emerging convention of starting the trill with the auxiliary is linked to its anticipation.

In the first part of the 17th century, Marin Mersenne presents us with an object lesson on how not to take ornament tables at face value. In the *Harmonie universelle* of 1636 he explains the trill with the illustration of Ex. 24.2, adding that to execute it "in all perfection, one must double the note that has

---

[1] *Libro llamado arte.* Its discussion of keyboard technique and the fine points of touch could benefit many a keyboard player today; its section on fingerings was far ahead of its time, with the basically modern use of the thumb that had to be rediscovered by J. S. Bach more than 150 years later. The trilled graces are discussed in ch. 19, ff. 46v ff.

There seems to be a link to French practices which appears not only in Santa Maria's treatment of the trill but also in his description of *inégalité* which corresponds closely to one found in Loys Bourgeois's *Le droict chemin de musique* of 1550.

[2] Ibid., f. 48r: "Ha se mucho de notar . . . que agora se usa, començar el Redoble [meaning here a type of compound trill] y el Quiebro reyterado [i.e. the regular trill] de Minimas, desde un punto mas alto de donde fenece, y de mas desto, el primer punto del sobrediche Redoble y Quiebro ha de herir solo, y el segundo punto ha de herir en la Consonancia que entonces se diere." Reference is made to the minims (corresponding in modern notation to quarter- if not 8th-notes), as the shortest note values to accommodate a regular trill with more than the two alternations of a *Schneller.*

a dot on top and do so with utmost delicacy attended by an extraordinary softening."[3]

Ex. 24.2. Mersenne (1636)

This special manner of ending a trill may not be described again, but the metrical start of the trill with the upper auxiliary on the beat became almost standard practice for keyboard ornament tables in the 150 years to come. It is interesting and very revealing to put Mersenne's trill model (and implicitly those that were to follow) into the right perspective by comparing it with an illustration of diminutions in which all trills are written out. In this illustration almost all of the trills start not with an upper note but with a somewhat sustained main note on the beat. Excerpts from the passage are shown in Ex. 24.3.[4]

In the places marked *b* and *c*, the main-note start is the one that makes the best melodic sense, since a start with the upper auxiliary on the beat would obscure the underlying melodic progression. However, the case of *a* is perhaps most remarkable because here the stressed main note usurps the place of a suspension on the auxiliary. It will be well to keep in mind this instructive conflict between ornament-table theory and demonstrated practice.

Ex. 24.3. Mersenne

[3] *Harmonie universelle, Traitez des conso-nances . . .* , p. 355. In the same section Mersenne makes the interesting statement that

"one does not use the [Italian] *trillo* in France" (p. 328).
[4] Ibid., *Traité des instrumens à chordes*, pp. 186, 188.

Jean Millet goes into great detail in his treatise, illustrating many kinds of small and large ornaments, but he hesitates when he comes to the trill. He feels it defies description and can be learned only by imitation. Nevertheless, he tries to put it down on paper "as far as it is possible,"[5] as given in Ex. 24.4.

Ex. 24.4. Millet (1666)

Several things are noteworthy in this reluctant model. The characteristic beams show that the trill was anchored on the main note which in turn clarifies the iambic, prebeat nature of the upper auxiliary  at the trill's start. This is in keeping with Santa Maria's description one hundred years earlier. The second point of interest is the way in which the trill combines with the Italian type of *trillo* that is based on tone repetition, then comes to a rest and leads with anticipated *port de voix* to the next note. This is a highly sophisticated mixture of ornamental elements, and it is not surprising that the author hesitated to present a model that can give nothing but a rough idea at best.

For Lully, the trill seems to have been the only ornament he marked (he did so either with the Italian *t* or the French cross: +).[6] In the scores that were printed during his lifetime, we often find the long appoggiatura trill written out as shown in Ex. 24.5*a*. Also interesting are numerous instances where a trill is prepared on the main note, e.g. the specimens of Exx. *b* and *c*.

Ex. 24.5. Lully, *Armide* (1686)

Example 24.6*a* from *Alceste*, which shows a similar measure-long main-note preparation, received in the second edition of 1708 an editorial insert of two little notes, indicating a slight anticipation of the alternations. Example *b* from *Psyché* (1678) shows a partially anticipated trill on the word *des* in the third full measure. The first edition of the work from which the example is taken was not published until 1720, hence editorial hands may have been at work here too; yet the example remains interesting, whether pertinent to Lully or to the age of Rameau.

[5] *La belle méthode*, p. 10.
[6] In the scores that were printed during Lully's lifetime, no other symbols were found, though the little notes appear in scores published shortly after his death.

a. Alceste (2nd ed. 1708), Ariette Céphise

la vic - toi - - - - re

b. Psyché (1678, 1st ed. 1720), Prologue, 1

Des - cen - dez Des - cen - dez ___ Mè - re ___ des ___ A - mours

Ex. 24.6. Lully

In the *airs de cour* of Michel Lambert, Bacilly, and D'Ambruis, we find countless examples of a trill with an anticipated auxiliary written out as a prebeat *coulé*, numerous main-note supported trills, and many cases of a combination of the two: grace-note start then main-note support leading to the trill proper. There are also instances of supported appoggiatura trills, but they are much less frequent.[7]

In the illustrations of Ex. 24.7, all of which are taken from the ornamented second couplets of these masters, the anticipated auxiliary (grace-note trill) is shown in Exx. I *a,b,c,* and *d,* Exx. III *b* (three in two measures), *c* (two), *d,* and *e.* The anticipated *coulé* plus main-note support appears in Exx. II *a* and *b,* and Exx. III *a* and *f* (2nd measure). The supported appoggiatura trill is given in Exx. I *e* (two) and III *f* (1st measure); Ex. I *f* shows the main-note start with long *appui* at the beginning of the measure (the wavy line stands for a *double cadence*) and an anticipated main-note start at the end of the measure.

I. Bacilly
a. Second livre d'airs (1664), p. 6   *b*   *c.* p.14

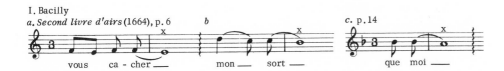

vous ca - cher ___   mon ___ sort ___   que moi ___

d   *e.* p.15

in - ter di - - re ___   veux ___ rien ___ di - - re

f. Les trois livres d'airs, I, p.12

di - - - re

Ex. 24.7.

[7] Lambert, *Les airs de M. Lambert* (Paris, 1666); Bacilly, *Second livre d'airs* (Paris, 1664); Bacilly, *Les trois livres d'airs,* reprinted in 2 vols., augmented with new airs, and with *Ornemens pour la méthode de chanter,* 1st pt. (Paris, 1668); D'Ambruis, *Livre d'airs* (Paris, 1685).

Ex. 24.7. *cont.*

The conclusion is inescapable that among the various trill forms used in the vocal style of Lully's age, the start with the anticipated auxiliary was the most frequent one, followed at some distance by the supported main-note trill, with the supported appoggiatura trills that are found mostly, but not exclusively, in final cadences left far behind.

D'Ambruis introduced in his song-book of 1685 the following trill symbols: *cadence ou tremblement appuyé*: ẋ *cadence ou tremblement en l'air*: × *double cadence*: ⌒⌒⌒

Judging from the contexts in which it appears, the *cadence en l'air*, the unprepared trill, is usually a main-note trill. It is used every time when preceded by a written-out onbeat or prebeat *Vorschlag*. The *double cadence* is presumably the trill with two-note suffix.

Bacilly, like most other theorists after him, distinguishes in his treatise various types of trills.[8] His term for a trill is either *cadence* or *tremblement*. His basic form would seem to be one that has a preparation ("anticipation ou soutien de voix"), then the actual alternations, and finally a liaison with the following note, in form of "a note most delicately touched"—a regular *Nachschlag* to all appearances.[9] In his own and his fellow songmaster's music, the preparation occurs before or on the beat and more frequently the former.

Very interesting and significant is the ensuing passage (on pp. 178-179) in which Bacilly excoriates the pedants who insist on strict observance of rules, and who consequently would not think of singing a trill without "preparing" it. Yet,

[8] *Remarques curieuses*, pp. 167, 178.
[9] A more positive statement is not possible because here too the presentation is not sys-

tematic, at times obscure, and not helped by lack of illustrations.

as Bacilly tells us, this *soutien* is omitted "very often and very fittingly in a thousand places." He continues: "Those who fancy themselves as great experts of the vocal art ('de grands Docteurs dans le chant') would not for anything in the world omit that preparation of the trill (of which I just spoke), as if it were of its essence, even in the case of the shortest trills. They consider it a crime to do otherwise and thereby render the performance dull and monotonous without realizing that the most universal rules have exceptions which often produce more pleasing results than the rules themselves. There are even cases of cadential trills where the preparation is inappropriate and where one plunges immediately into the alternations *starting them upward* ('Il y a mesme des Cadences finales, ou cette preparation sied mal, & dans lesquelles on se jette d'abord sur les Tremble-mens de bas en haut') . . . and after all these observations it would be naïve to try establishing rules where such [preparation] fits and where it does not fit; good taste alone has to be the judge" (italics mine).

The passage is significant for its clear formulation of main-note trills, even on occasional final cadences; for the eloquent attack on the tyranny of rules, and for the enthronement of the *goût* as highest authority in matters of performance, a principle that will recur like a leitmotiv for the next 150 years of French musical interpretation.

From these explanations alone one can gather that there are many ways to start a trill. This impression is confirmed by the evidence found in the above quoted musical examples.

Besides this basic form of the trill, Bacilly speaks of a *tremblement étouffé* or *demi tremblement* which, if I interpret the description correctly, is the prototype of what later writers called the *tremblement feint*: a trace of a trill appended at the extreme end of a long appoggiatura, forming approximately the following design:
As can be seen, it is related to the *port de voix feint*.

Furthermore, Bacilly describes a *double cadence* but in terms so obscure that any attempt to elucidate it would be only a guessing game. Bacilly himself says that this type of trill belongs more to practice than to theory. The only thing we can be sure of is that this type, whatever it is, further widens the variety with which the trill idea could be expressed.

Jean Rousseau may serve again as a natural link between vocal and instrumental music. Speaking in his vocal treatise of the trill (his term: *cadence*, his symbol: +), he distinguishes two basic forms: "with preparation" (*avec support* [in later editions replaced by *appuy*]) and "without preparation" (*sans support*).[10] Though the English term "support" is the literal translation of both *support* or *appuy*, "preparation" is here a better equivalent because we have reserved the term "support" for extended onbeat emphasis. Rousseau's *support* or *appuy*, which involves the upper note, can be either anticipated, forming a grace-note trill, or on the beat, forming a lightly supported appoggiatura trill. Rousseau describes the prebeat type as a preparation "by anticipation of note value and sound"; he refers to the onbeat type as "anticipation of sound only." The unprepared trill, the *cadence simple* or cadence *sans appuy*, is a main-note trill, done "on the natural tone of the note simply by agitation of the voice."[11] He illustrates

---

[10] *Méthode*, pp. 54ff. The references will again be to the second edition of 1683 unless otherwise stated.

[11] Ibid., pp. 54-55: "La Cadence avec un Sup-

port se fait ou par Anticipation de valeur & de son, nommant une Note sur une partie de la valeur de celle qui la precede, & sur le son de celle dont la sçituation est immediatement

the grace-note trill, the *anticipation de valeur et de son,* as shown in Ex. 24.8a;
the supported appoggiatura trill appears in Ex. *b.*

Ex. 24.8. J. Rousseau (1683, 1691)

Rousseau discusses in great detail the contexts that call for the use of the three types
of trills. The main principles are these. The grace-note trill is to be used in descending
to a note of equal length or from a shorter to a longer note. The supported appoggiatura
trill is to be used when descending from a short note to one more than twice its length,
e.g. from an 8th-note to dotted quarters or from a 16th to a quarter-note. The main-note
trill (*cadence simple*) is to be used in ascending, or—somewhat surprisingly perhaps—on
the same pitch, or even in descending, especially for leaps of a fourth or more. Moreover,
this main-note trill is to be used anywhere ("en toutes rencontres") in gay pieces such as
minuets, and any preparation one might wish to add has to be extremely light.

In addition to the three types mentioned, Rousseau also introduces for certain
long notes a trill with main-note support. Speaking of a whole note in common
time that is to be trilled, he mentions the possibility of an appoggiatura support,
but only on the triple condition (1) that it be a perfect cadence, (2) that the
singer be a soloist, and (3) that the note be either on the same pitch or be reached
by descent. However, if such a note occurs outside of a cadence or in a harmony
part, or if it is reached by ascent, then one must start by sustaining the main note
and trill it only for the second half of its value.[12] He illustrates this directive with
the patterns reproduced in Ex. 24.9.

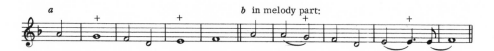

Ex. 24.9. J. Rousseau (1683)

au dessus d'elle, ou seulement par Anticipation de son; Et la Cadence simple se fait sur le
son naturel de la Note par la seule agitation
de la Voix."

12 Ibid., p. 58. The importance of this passage warrants its full quotation. "Il faut observer que si la Note Cadencée vaut Quatre temps
en descendant ou sur le mesme degré, on peut
en Mélodie, c'est à dire quand on chante seul,
faire le Support par Anticipation de son, pour-
veu que ce soit une Cadence parfaite; mais en
Harmonie, c'est à dire quand on chante en
Parties, et mesme en Mélodie hors la Cadence
parfaite, & lors que la Note Cadencée monte,
il faut prendre le son naturel de la Note, &
trembler simplement la seconde moitié de sa
valeur." See also on p. 52 an identical realization of such a trill within an example showing
anticipated *ports de voix.*

Important too is the further remark that all trills under a slur must be sung without preparation, hence as main-note trills.

In the next pages (59ff.) Rousseau gives detailed directives as to when trills that have not been prescribed may or even must be introduced. There is no need to report all the complicated instructions. Suffice it to say that many trills may or ought to be improvised where they add variety without obtrusiveness.

One last quotation from the vocal treatise may be in order to remove any possible doubt about the main-note nature of Rousseau's *cadence simple*. In the third and fourth editions of the treatise (see above Chapter 9, n. 9) the author has appended a question and answer series in which the fourteenth question is: "Why do you call *cadence simple* a trill that is done in an upward motion without preparation ('en montant sans appuy') when the term *cadence* signifies descent and something done in falling?" He answers: "I use the term *cadence* to designate the unprepared trill which is done upwards ('qui se fait en montant') because one does not use a distinctive sign to differentiate it from the trill that is made downwards (*en descendant*) and with preparation: because in all music books either of these trills is marked by a *t* or by a +. However, one ought to distinguish between them or else students are often deceived, and by seeing them marked in the same way they perform them in identical manner."

Rousseau's important treatise on the gamba confirms by and large all the principles about the trill presented in the vocal treatise.[13] There are many more illustrations of "prepared" trills; one sample is presented in Ex. 24.10 in which the first five measures show anticipation, the following four, onbeat preparation.

Ex. 24.10. J. Rousseau (viol) (1687)

The wide scope given the main-note trill is reaffirmed and its nature once more clarified by the instruction (on p. 83) that this trill is to be done like the prepared ones, "with the preparation cut off" ("en retranchant l'appuy"). Also restated is the principle of main-note support lasting half the value of a long note (p. 84).

Rousseau's discussion of the trill matches in importance that of the *port de voix* and *coulé*. His dual reports confirm the freedom and variety of design reflected in the *airs de cour* and in Bacilly's treatise; they show the wide currency of the grace-note trill and make it clear that a *support* can be done *before* as well as *on* the beat. His works give a systematic foundation to Bacilly's description of the main-note trill and describe and illustrate the main-note supported pattern

---

[13] *Traité*, pp. 76-84.

seen earlier in Mersenne's diminutions. Above all, the agreement between vocal and gamba treatise on all those matters is one more among many indications that there was close communication between the ornament practices of the voice and those of melody instruments. This is not surprising, since the latter have always looked to artistic singing as the guiding light for their own style.

Sainte Colombe, Rousseau's teacher, uses the lutenists' comma after the note (♪') as trill symbol.[14] In addition, we find many trills and trill-like figurations written out in a unique system of crisscrossing stems and flags that suggests their non-metrical nature. (Whenever a figure of short notes was meant to be metrically rendered, he beams them together in the conventional way.) The written-out trills start with either the upper or the main note. Example 24.11a shows a combination of both types in which the unmetrical element is clearly in evidence, as a synchronization would make no musical sense. Example b shows written-out grace-note trills, Rousseau's "anticipation of sound and value."

a. L'Empressé

b. L'Égal

Ex. 24.11. Sainte Colombe, *Concerts à 2 violes*

Marin Marais, despite all his carefully edited and annotated music, is unfortunately reticent about the nature of the trill, which he takes for granted. He calls it *tremblement* and marks it with a comma-like hook after the note (♪).[15] There are a few cases where he writes out what appear to be trills that start and are anchored on the auxiliary. As will be shown below in Chapter 41, these figurations are not genuine trills; they are, as no trill would be, played with detached articulation and are a species of the turn family.[16]

There is evidence that the many trills indicated by symbols were played with a variety of designs adapted to the occasion, including frequent main-note starts. One of a number of cases of trills with main-note support and suffix is shown in Ex. 24.12a; another, shown in Ex. b, is in accord with Rousseau's rule about trills on whole notes.

Marais (like Lully) wrote out many an *appui* for cadential trills as shown in Ex. 24.13a. It is quite certain that occasionally he used such an *appui* for a trill without such specific notation. But Dolmetsch's argument that all of Marais's shakes "must be prepared by

---

[14] *Concerts à 2 violes*, BN Rés. Vma MS 866.
[15] *Pieces à violes*, vol. 1, p. 4; Caix d'Hervelois does the same in his *Premier livre de pièces de viole* (Paris, n.d.).

[16] A few specimens are given below in Ex. 41.10. See also Jean Rousseau's explanation and illustration of this design as a form of the *double cadence* (Ex. 41.9).

a. IV, *La Plainte* (1717)

b. V, *Grand Rondeau* (1725)

Ex. 24.12. Marais

appoggiature of half their value" is erroneous.[17] He bases his claim on a spot from the 2nd Suite for two viols (Ex. *b*), arguing that the figure 4 in the bass calls for the realization given in Ex. *c*, clearly requiring a quarter-note appoggiatura for both solo viols. Now, the figure 4 in Marais normally stood for $\frac{5}{4}$ not $\frac{6}{4}$; nevertheless, it is perfectly possible that in this particular case $\frac{6}{4}$ was actually intended. It does make better sense and would suggest an *appui* for both trills, though not necessarily the length of a full quarter-note. (The incomplete figuring finds an easy explanation in the fact that the work came out in part books of which the bass appeared three years after the solo edition.) But accepting the $\frac{6}{4}$ meaning, all the example proves is that the simple trill symbol *could* imply an *appui*. Yet, two measures earlier in Dolmetsch's example, the figuring for a similar trill gives no indication of any kind of supported appoggiatura, nor does, more significantly, the figuring for the final cadential trill of the same piece. The next paragraphs will bring a few samples from a mass of evidence for a wide range of trill designs in Marais's works.

a. IV, Suite 4, Prelude

b. I, Suite 2 for two viols

Ex. 24.13. Marais

Example 24.14*a* shows a cadential trill that can have no preparation and where, moreover, the $\frac{5\ 5}{4\ 3}$ sequence, so characteristic of many of Marais's cadential trills, had to be spelled out exactly because of the way in which it follows a $\frac{6}{4}$ chord.[18] This trill

---

[17] Dolmetsch, pp. 99-101. See also Donington, p. 316, Ex. 173.

[18] In this example the dots over the fingering numbers denote second or third string re-

spectively; the *e* stands for a swell or dynamic emphasis; the oblique bar symbols indicate arpeggiation string by string.

ought to start with the main note, because the boldly arched run, gathering momentum with the fall, ought to hit its target, the trilled note, with uninterrupted élan; and also, because, as Gordon J. Kinney writes, a start of the trill with the auxiliary would, in view of Marais's fingering, be of forbidding technical awkwardness.[19]

For the following three examples (*b, c,* and *d*) I am indebted to the eminent gambist, Professor John Hsu of Cornell University. In Ex. *b*, the V-shaped symbol, signifying *coulé de doigt*, i.e. a gentle upward sliding of the finger to achieve a glissando effect (in this case the sliding of the second finger from A to A sharp), makes the main-note start of the trill a necessity. As to Exx. *c* and *d*, "one cannot help but begin the trill on the main note. To begin it on the upper note would require time to prepare the hand position. In the first example [i.e. our Ex. *c*], this means lifting the fourth finger off the "d" string, placing it on the "a" string, then placing the third finger on the "e" string, with both fingers on the same fret. All these movements require more time than the eighth of a Courante provides. Similarly, in the second example [Ex. *d*] one has to lift the fingers off the fingerboard before the bar line, change the hand position, then place the third finger on the "a" string and the second finger on the "e" string, both on the same fret, before starting the trill. This certainly takes more than a sixteenth-note in an Allemande to accomplish. *These are irrefutable examples.*"[20]

Ex. 24.14. Marais

Finally, of two interesting illustrations from Marais's opera *Semelé* (Ex. 24.15), the first, Ex. *a*, shows the start of the trill on the second half of a long-held note as described by Rousseau. (For the vocal medium Marais uses the customary cross symbol to indicate a trill.) The second, Ex. *b*, shows a main-note trill for two flutes that was written out for the obvious purpose of insuring exact coordination.

Danoville says the trill "is done through supposition; supposition means to anticipate on the note that precedes the one on which the trill is to be done: for instance, if a trill

---

[19] Personal letter. Such a start would involve a jump from the last note of the run in the fourth position on the third string to the trill in first position on the second string.

For further persuasive illustrations see also Kinney's article, "Problems of Melodic Ornamentation in French Viol Music," *Jl. of the Viola da Gamba Soc. of America*, Vol. 6 (1968), pp. 34-50.

[20] Personal letter from John Hsu.

Ex. 24.15. Marais, *Semelé* (1709) Prologue

is marked on the *mi* you anticipate on the *fa....*"[21] He adds that the alternations should be even and accelerate toward the end. He also demands, for the sake of better tone quality, a clear firm percussion of the finger and firmness of bow pressure.

Demachy, a gambist rival of Rousseau's, uses Sainte Colombe's symbol for the *tremblement*; he also introduces a smaller comma for the *petit tremblement* and a comma above or below the note for *tremblement sans appuyer*.[22] About the *tremblement* he says only that one should prepare it *(appuyer)* according to the length of the note and play it with evenness. The *petit tremblement* is a short trill whose alternations come to a quick end. According to the description, the *tremblement sans appuyer* is the two-finger vibrato of the French gambists (see below Chapter 45).[23] The *battement* is probably a main-note trill (eighty years later, Jean Jacques Rousseau and Mercadier de Belesta were to use the term in this sense), though it might be a multiple mordent starting on the auxiliary: "[It] is started with the finger lifted and continued like a trill" (["Le battement] doit etre commencé ayant le doigt levé et continué comme un tremblement").

Georg Muffat may be mentioned here again, though as was said above, his value as a French source is somewhat problematic. He speaks of three types of trills, all of which start with the upper note on the beat in accord with the tables of the clavecinists whom we will meet presently.[24] He illustrates the "simple" trill (symbols: *t*, + , ⁓) as shown in Ex. 24.16*a* and the *tremblement réfléchissant* in Ex. *b* (the term refers to the "reflexive" bending of the design through the suffix), and thirdly a *tremblement roulant* that does not come to a rest on the main note but moves directly into the next note (Ex. *c*). The names and symbols of the last two types seem to belong entirely to Muffat and have not been found in any other French source, a further indication that Muffat's presentation contains many personal elements.

a. Tremblement simple   b. Tremblement réfléchissant   c. Tremblement roulant

Ex. 24.16. G. Muffat (1698)

In Ex. 24.17 from Campra's *Télémaque*, the symbol of the small cross can stand only for a main-note trill with no possible stress on the auxiliary.[25] (The last measure shows again one of the ubiquitous prebeat *coulés*.)

[21] *L'art de toucher*, pp. 39-40. "[Le tremblement] se pratique par le moyen de la Supposition; Supposition est anticiper sur la Note qui precede celle sur laquelle se doit faire le Tremblement: Par Exemple s'il y a un Tremblement marqué sur le Mi, vous anticiperez sur le Fa." The term *supposition* refers to the stepwise use of a non-harmonic note, some-

times on, more frequently off, the beat. See above ch. 12, n. 7.

[22] Demachy, *Pièces de violle*, pp. 8-9, 13.

[23] "Press one finger against the other while touching the string only lightly" ("sans appuyer que fort peu sur la corde").

[24] *Florilegium II*, Preface.

[25] Contemporary MS *Opéra A 65*.

sur les hu - mi - des plai - nes

Ex. 24.17. Campra (1704), *Télémaque*

The main-note supported trills described by Jean Rousseau for long notes are shown in a motet by De La Lande (Ex. 24.18).[26]

Et la - bo - re po - pu - lo - rum

Ex. 24.18. De La Lande (c. 1680)

THE GENERAL THEORISTS

Loulié distinguishes two types of trills, the regular *tremblement* (+) and the *tremblement appuyé* (+̂). He describes the former as "a *coulé* repeated two or more times which moves from a small sound to a regular sound one step below."[27] He illustrates it as shown in Ex. 24.19.

Tremblement
simple   double   triple

Ex. 24.19. Loulié (1696)

As was pointed out above (Chapter 9), Loulié defined the *coulé* as "an inflection of the voice from a small, or weak, or short tone to a lower and stronger one," and his illustrations demonstrated its anticipatory nature. Hence the definition of a trill as a series of such iambic *coulés* imparts to the trill an iambic character that is antithetic to the trochaic one implied in Marpurg's definition of the trill as a series of descending appoggiaturas. In the iambic trill the emphasis is on the main note, the "lower and stronger one," and this emphasis has an important bearing on the relationship of the trill to the beat. If the trill starts on the upper note (as Loulié's does), but the emphasis is on the lower one

then the starting auxiliary is bound to acquire prebeat character since the accent on the lower note will be attracted by the beat. Thus, the basic shape of Loulié's trill is undoubtedly that of the grace-note species (with possible occasional exceptions).

---

[26] Cf. ch. 9, n. 12. The above example is from vol. 7, p. 24.

[27] *Éléments*, p. 70: ". . . un coulé repeté deux ou plusieurs fois d'un petit Son à un Son ordinaire, & d'un degré plus bas."

The *tremblement appuyé* is defined as one where the voice dwells on the first *coulé*; its illustration is given in Exx. 24.20a and *b*. In Ex. *a* the *appui* falls on the beat as genuine appoggiatura, while the notation of the alternations again suggests their iambic, main-note anchored character. However, Ex. *b* shows for the same trill pattern, again in metrical accuracy, the *appui* in complete anticipation.

Ex. 24.20. Loulié

It may be added that Loulié objects to the use of the term *cadence* for the obvious reason that a cadence is the ending of a phrase and that there are cadences without trills and many trills outside of cadences. Though many writers were aware of this incongruity and echoed Loulié's criticism, the term *cadence* for trill continued to be used in France along with the term *tremblement* throughout the 18th century.

L'Affilard illustrates several types of trills, as shown in Ex. 24.21, but fails to give any verbal explanations. He places the cross symbol before as well as above or below the note, and uses for the sustained appoggiatura trill, the *cadence soutenue*, the same symbol as did Loulié ($\widehat{+}$).[28]

The *tremblement subit* of Ex. *a* is an unprepared trill, which is all that can be gathered from the model. The *cadence soutenue* (Ex. *b*) consisted, as L'Affilard spells out, 1) of the *appui* on the auxiliary taking half the note's value, 2) the alternations, and 3) a "closing" note, a suffix. An illustration demonstrating the *cadence coupée* (Ex. *c*) shows an *appui*, two-thirds the length of a dotted note, then incidentally and interestingly, a grace-note trill at the end of the example. What L'Affilard called *double cadence coupée* is not a trill but a turn, whereas the *double cadence battue* (Ex. *d*) is a trill with a two-note suffix (the wavy line in this example is replaced in the 1705 edition by a cross: +).

a. *Tremblement subit*   b. *Cadence soutenue*: *appuyée, battue & fermée*

c. *Cadence coupée avec une Note, martellement avec deux Notes*   d. *Double cadence battue*

Ex. 24.21. L'Affilard (1694, 1697)

28 *Principes*, pp. 20-21.

Montéclair, in his treatise of 1709 does not describe any ornaments, but a music example given in Ex. 24.22 shows at *a* a trill with main-note support and anticipated auxiliary; at *b* the same with written-out prebeat start of the alternations; at *c* within the frame of a *tour de gozier*, a very brief grace-note trill: shortness of time leaves no other alternative, and the obvious anticipation of the *coulé* suggests its identical meaning in the settings of *a* and *b*.[29]

Ex. 24.22. Montéclair (1709), p. 41

In a small treatise addressed to children (c. 1710), Montéclair says this about the trill: "It is almost impossible to teach in writing its proper execution, it is learned by imitation."[30]

In 1736, Montéclair explains and illustrates the trill, in accord with Loulié, as series of *coulés*.[31] To him, the *coulé* implies a descent from a weak to a strong note, a circumstance brought out graphically by writing the little *notes postiches* of the *coulés* in 16th-note values. This clue seems to point to the grace-note trill as the basic shape of this ornament. This basic shape is the one he most likely had in mind for the *tremblement subit* which is to be done without *appui* and for which he reserves the symbol +. It is, he says, particularly frequent in recitatives. The *tremblement appuyé* (symbol: *t*) starts with a long appoggiatura support. The *tremblement feint* (⋏⋏) has an unusual symbol, but the standard shape of an overlong appoggiatura with, at its extreme end, a little *coup de gozier* (meaning here a tiny *Schneller*) that is "almost unnoticeable." The end of the trill connects with the next note, either with a *chûte* (Bacilly's *liaison*) when descending, or a *tour de gozier*, the common two-note suffix, when rising to its neighbor tone:

Neither L'Affilard nor Loulié nor Montéclair gives any indication that the basic shape of their trill resembled the onbeat, auxiliary-anchored pattern of modern doctrine. Loulié and Montéclair, though apparently favoring the start with the auxiliary, just as apparently favor anticipation. If ♫♫ is what they had in mind, why go to the trouble of a more complicated graphic design that at the time many, perhaps most, performers would not have interpreted in the above sense. If the trill were that simple, why refuse to explain it to children?

THE KEYBOARD BEFORE COUPERIN

Nivers in his *Livre d'orgue* of 1665 distinguishes three types of *cadences* or *tremblements* (see Ex. 24.23): The *agrément* ♪ , the *cadence* ♪ , and the

29 *Nouvelle méthode*, p. 41.
30 *Petite méthode*, p. 11.

31 *Principes*; trills are dealt with on pp. 80-83.

double cadence . In explanation he says that "all these little notes serve only to show the shake, the big note alone is being counted and on it as the principal note one comes to a brief rest after the alternations."[32]

Agrément   *Cadence*   *Double cadence*

Ex. 24.23. Nivers (1665)

Four years later, we find the metrical model of Ex. 24.24 in Chambonnières's first book of harpsichord pieces.[33]

Ex. 24.24.
Chambonnières (1670), *Cadence*

It shows the auxiliary starting on the beat and remaining in its metrically leading position. (A generation before, Mersenne had presented a similar appoggiatura trill model, and it was shown how he himself deviated from it.) Now, beginning with Chambonnières, this model becomes a standard fixture of keyboard ornamentation tables. For the basic trill pattern, whether called *tremblement* or *cadence*, we find it in identical form, as shown in Ex. 24.25, with Le Bègue (1677), Raison (1688), D'Anglebert (1689), Chaumont (1696), Saint Lambert (1702), Le Roux (1705), and Dieupart (c. 1702).[34] Many later composers adopted the same pattern for the keyboard.

D'Anglebert lists in addition to the simple trill a *tremblement appuyé* (Ex. *d*) and a *tremblement et pincé*, a trill with suffix (Ex. *e*). Le Roux has basically the identical *tremblement appuyé* (Ex. *h*) and Dieupart has a similar trill with suffix: *tremblement pincé* or "shake beat" in an unmetrical pattern (Ex. *j*).

The agreement on the keyboard trill model with its onbeat start on the auxiliary is certainly impressive. However, in the following, a few illustrations will show in some cases the likelihood, in others the certainty, of deviating trill patterns. The likelihood is strong in innumerable instances where the trilled note coincides with a second voice and where literal application of the model would make this second voice unintelligible. In such a context the main note will have to strike on the beat to affirm the identity with the second voice; and considering

[32] *Livre d'orgue*, p. 4: "Toutes ces petites notes ne sont que pour exprimer le tremblement, la grosse note seule étant comptée, et sur laquelle comme principale on demeure un peu après le battement."

[33] *Pieces de clavessin*, Preface.

[34] Le Bègue, *Les pieces de clavessin*; for the quoted works of Raison, D'Anglebert, Chaumont, Saint Lambert, Le Roux, and Dieupart, see above ch. 10, nn. 15, 9, 16, 20, 12, and 13, respectively.

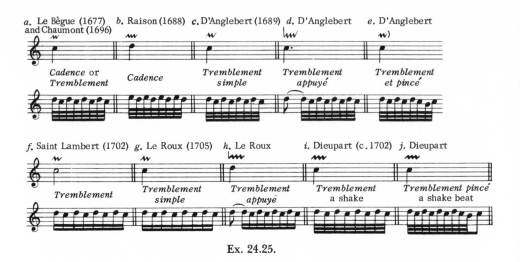

Ex. 24.25.

the preference of these keyboard masters for the start of the trill with the auxiliary, there are three possible ways to do so and yet prevent the second voice from being obscured if not effaced.

In Ex. 24.26 the three possibilities are shown—in descending order of clarity—as alternate renditions of a passage from Le Bègue. In Ex. *a* the whole trill is anticipated; in Ex. *b* the auxiliary alone is anticipated and the main note held while one or two alternations are made with the neighboring finger; in Ex. *c* a grace-note trill is played, which at least sounds the unison tone at the exact moment on the beat on which it is supposed to be pronounced. By holding the main note slightly before starting the alternation, the suggestion of the second voice will be strengthened.

Ex. 24.26. Le Bègue, 2nd Organ Book, *Agnus Dei*

Once in a while, a fourth alternative, a simple main-note trill or a *Schneller*, will be the likeliest solution. In Ex. 24.27, main-note start on the beat or an anticipated *Schneller* would seem to make good melodic sense and not obscure the second voice.[35]

Ex. 24.27. Le Bègue, *Pieces de clavessin*, II, Allemande

In D'Anglebert's works, a second voice descending from a trill is almost a stereotype. A specimen is shown in Ex. 24.28*a* for which the anticipation of the auxiliary would appear to be the logical solution. Similar patterns abound in Le Roux and Dieupart, as illustrated in Exx. *b* and *c*. In Dieupart's Allemande from the Suite in A major (Ex. *d*)—one of the pieces which Bach copied—we find the main-note prepared trill specified by regular notation.

[35] Le Bègue, *Second livre d'orgue* (Paris, n.d.); *Pièces de clavessin*, II (Paris, n.d.).

a. D'Anglebert, *Pièces de clavecin,* Allemande, p.4

b. Le Roux, *Pièces de clavessin,* Sarabande grave

c. Dieupart, Suite 1, Courante   d. Dieupart, Suite 1, Allemande

Ex. 24.28.

More direct evidence for the anticipated auxiliary can be derived from Chaumont's *Pièces d'orgue* of 1696. The prebeat execution of his *Vorschlag* symbol (∧) was shown above in Ex. 10.7*b*. Throughout the work, this symbol occurs innumerable times in front of the trill sign and very often for notes whose brevity excludes onbeat *appui* meaning—even if they were not rendered implausible by this master's prebeat *Vorschlag* style. Grace-note trill intention is hardly questionable. (The two illustrations of Exx. 24.29*a* and *b* are from the third and fourth pieces of the book.)

a. Duo   b. Trio

Ex. 24.29. Chaumont (1696)

Grigny was shown before to be partial to prebeat ornaments. In his *Premier livre d'orgue* of 1699 we find, as shown in Ex. 24.30*a*, the unmistakable notation of a grace-note trill (which incidentally was precisely copied by Bach). Example *b* shows a pattern where the auxiliary can be neither on the beat nor be emphasized. (The unusual tie from the 8th-note to the little note may be a misprint; Bach must have thought so because he left it out of his otherwise very exact copy.) An analogous case is shown in Ex. *c* where an anticipated downward slide to a main-note trill is the most logical solution, especially in view of Grigny's previously noted predilection for such anticipated slides.

a. *Ave Maris Stella*, p. 58   b. Dialogue, p. 25

c. Dialogue, p. 61

Ex. 24.30. Grigny (1699), *Premier livre d'orgue*

In Ex. 24.31a from Dieupart, the four-note grace leads into the trill and the fourth little note would seem to serve as the anticipated auxiliary. Its repeat on the beat (according to the tables) appears excluded by the slur. The same is true of the trill in Ex. *b* where the downward slide clearly belongs to and leads into the trill, suggesting its main-note start.

Ex. 24.31. Dieupart, Ouverture in B minor

A specimen of a grace-note trill by Jean Baptiste (John) Loeillet is given in Ex. 24.32, which also illuminates the prebeat nature of the preceding *coulé*.

Ex. 24.32. J. B. Loeillet (1709-1715),
Lessons for the harpsichord or Spinet, Gavot

GENERALLY, so it appears, the keyboard masters of this period preferred to start the trill with the auxiliary. It is far less obvious that their simple trill always had to start with the auxiliary on the beat—that, in other words, they knew nothing except the appoggiatura trill. Saint Lambert is the only one of the group and may be the only French writer (including those of the 18th century) who says that the start of the auxiliary should coincide with "the notes in the same or other hand."[36] Yet this single testimonial loses its force in the light of Saint Lambert's extraordinary permissiveness with regard to ornaments. His elaboration on the theme that "one is extremely free in the choice of *agréments*" was quoted above in Chapter 3.[37]

That onbeat placement plus upper-note anchor was often practiced is certain; that it was practiced always is most unlikely, and the quoted musical evidence to that effect should alone suffice to prove this point. As far as the non-keyboard players of the period are concerned, their preference for a start with the auxiliary was far less pronounced, and they ranged more freely over the whole field of trill design.

[36] *Principes*, p. 44.　　　　　　　　[37] Ibid., p. 57.

Couperin's Trill

Like all the other French keyboard players, Couperin says that every trill starts with the upper note.[1] He does not, however, say that this start should fall on the beat, though he does make such a specification for the *pincé* (the mordent) and, as we have seen, for the *coulés* and *ports de voix* that are marked by little notes. The omission of an analogous ruling for the trill is hardly due to an oversight, because it becomes apparent that the basic shape of Couperin's trill is one anchored on the main note with the auxiliary in anticipation—in other words, the grace-note trill. In his ornament table,[2] he illustrates the *tremblement continu* along with the *pincé continu*, the multiple mordent, as given in Ex. 25.1.

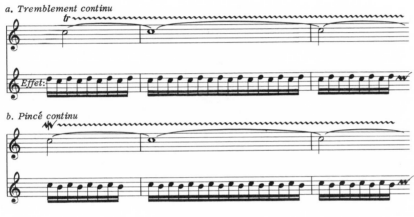

a. Tremblement continu

b. Pincé continu

Ex. 25.1.

Though this trill starts with the upper note, the second and third measures reveal unmistakably the rhythmic emphasis on the main note. The trill is the mirror image of the mordent, both anchored on the main note, the former alternating with the upper, the latter with the lower auxiliary. The only deviation from the mirror image is the first note of the trill, a surplus 16th for the time of a half-note, the only note that does not fit into the otherwise exact metrical pattern. There seems little doubt that this excess first note was meant to be played *before* and not *on* the beat as indicated in Ex. 25.2*a*. This solution is far simpler and more logical than an attempt to force it onto the beat, perhaps as shown in Ex. *b*, thus beginning the trill with an irregular, stumbling motion.

a   *b*

Ex. 25.2.

[1] *L'art,* p. 23.   [2] *Piéces de clavecin,* Premier Livre, p. 47.

Couperin himself rules out such irregularity when, three years later, he refers to this trill model in his treatise and says: "Although in the ornament table of my first book the alternations are notated in equal values, they must nevertheless start more slowly than they end, but the acceleration must be imperceptible."[3] The "equal value" as well as the "slower start" are incompatible with any quintuplet or similar absorption of the one excess note. There is further confirmation for the anticipation of the auxiliary. A striking case is offered by a passage given in Ex. 25.3 from the Sarabande, *La Majestueuse* from the first *Ordre* of harpsichord pieces. (As above, Roman numerals will indicate the *Ordres* in the four books of harpsichord pieces.) The last phrase of the piece is repeated in a *petite reprise* in which a few new ornaments are added. Thus, the passage given in Ex. *a* appears in the reprise as Ex. *b*.

Ex. 25.3. I, *La Majestueuse*

If we compare the *three* small notes in the bass at the end of the first measure in Ex. *a* with the *two* small notes in Ex. *b*, it becomes obvious that the missing third note is the *anticipated auxiliary* of the *tremblement continu* (the latter term is printed in the original).

The melodic logic of this interpretation is further supported by its harmonic logic. The e flat forms a strident dissonance which makes sense only on the beat. A start of the trill with f natural *on* the beat would not only obscure the meaning of the dissonance but intensify the latter to the point of irrationality.

Further evidence for the need of the anticipated auxiliary can be found in a passage from *La Reine des Coeurs* (see Ex. 32.8*b* below). In this excerpt we find that in mm. 17, 19, and 21 the auxiliary of the left-hand trill has to be anticipated to avoid unacceptable fifths.

In *Le Rossignol-en-Amour*, the *petite reprise* has a written-out *tremblement continu* with anticipated auxiliary, main-note anchored, and with rather fast acceleration (Ex. 25.4). It had to be written out to insure its slow start and the approximate and rather fast rate of gradual acceleration.

Ex. 25.4. XIV, *Le Rossignol-en-Amour*

When the trill is approached in fast movement from the upper neighbor, the trill will have to start with the main note and the preceding neighbor note will

---

[3] *L'art*, p. 23: "Quoique les tremblements soient marqués égaux, dans la table des agréments de mon premier livre, ils doivent cependant commencer plus lentement qu'ils ne finissent: mais cette gradation doit être imperceptible."

then often assume the character of an anticipated auxiliary, especially when the two are linked by a slur as in Exx. 25.5*a* and *b*.

Compare also *La Mézangére* which is full of trills with written-out anticipated auxiliaries and of *pincés* with anticipated *ports de voix*.

Such written-out specimens might not provide direct evidence about the interpretation of a symbol, but they add further confirmation that the grace-note type was part of Couperin's trill vocabulary.

Ex. 25.5.

A grace-note trill is presumably intended in Ex. 25.6, where an onbeat auxiliary would produce unlikely fifths.

Ex. 25.6. *Messe Solemnelle, Gloria*

Couperin's model and its implications clearly contradict the prevalent doctrine of onbeat start and upper-note emphasis, yet the doctrine is so influential that some researchers refused to acknowledge the Couperin document. Some (e.g. Dolmetsch and Donington) fail to mention it, though they reprint the companion model of the *pincé continu*. Others misrepresent Couperin's trill model by changing it to what they would like Couperin to have written. Thus, Brunold in his monograph on French harpsichord ornaments gives the wrong version of Ex. 25.7 for Couperin's *tremblement continu*:[4]

Ex. 25.7. Brunold's version (1925)

[4] Brunold, *Traité des signes et agréments*, p. 55. Faulty, too, is the reproduction of the model in the Oiseau Lyre edition of Couperin's works.

Germani follows suit and so does even Mellers;[5] both of them probably derived the model second hand from Brunold. Aldrich also presents a model in accord with Brunold's that, like the latter, is diametrically opposed to Couperin's illustration.[6]

The expurgated model of Brunold and his followers makes little sense because a *tremblement continu* on c would be identical with a *pincé continu* on d. Moreover, an emphasis on the upper note of a trill makes musical sense only as long as an appoggiatura stress on a dissonant note would be justified, and though an appoggiatura may on occasion be fairly long, it will rarely extend to the three measures of Couperin's model. However one looks at it, there is no avoiding the evidence that points to Couperin's basic trill pattern as being main-note centered with the auxiliary before the beat.

The appoggiatura enters for the supported trill. In his treatise, Couperin describes this design as consisting of three parts: first the *appuy*, that is the long appoggiatura, then the shake proper (*les batements*), and finally a *point d'arrest*, a rest on the main note, as shown in Ex. 25.8.

Ex. 25.8.

"Other trills are arbitrary," Couperin continues; "some have an *appuy*, others are so short that they have neither *appuy* nor *point d'arrest*.

Elsewhere, Couperin points to the inability of the harpsichord to sustain sounds, in contrast to string instruments. For the harpsichord, therefore, "it is imperative to sustain the alternations of trills as well as other ornaments, very long."[7] "The other ornaments" must be the *pincé continu*, the only other one that can be extended at will.

Ex. 25.9.

Returning to Couperin's ornament table, we find the interesting pattern of Ex. 25.9.

It is important to note that the quarter-notes in Exx. *b* and *c* are precisely lined

[5] Germani, *Metodo per organo*, vol. 3, p. 37; Mellers, *François Couperin*, p. 304.

[6] Aldrich, "The Principal Agréments," p. 208, referring to fig. 6 on p. 227.

[7] *Le Parnasse ou l'apothéose de Lully*, Preface: "Les instruments d'archet soutiennent les sons; & au contraire, le Clavecin ne pouvant le perpétuer, il faut de toute nécessité battre les cadences, ou treblements, & les autres agrémens, tres longtemps."

up and that the notes in small print, representing the trill proper, are clearly placed between the first and the second quarter-notes.[8]

Dannreuther already suspected that the *tremblement lié* of Ex. *b* was an anticipatory shake played in the time of the preceding note.[9] Several items support his thesis. To begin with, the exact alignment of the quarter-notes points to their identical start. For any other solution, this illustration would have been utterly misleading. Furthermore, Couperin's phrase, "sans être appuyé," would make no sense if the first note were to be held for its full value plus the increment of the tie. Such a trill, in accord with the pattern of Ex. *a*, would be very much *appuyé* indeed. In fact, to avoid any semblance of an *appui*, the alternations would have to start immediately. Also, the pattern of the *tremblement détaché* (Ex. *c*) is closely related. According to prevalent doctrine, this trill ought to be played:

Here, too, Couperin's clear spatial alignment contradicts such interpretation. Finally, there is no denying the melodic and rhythmic attractiveness of the anticipated design. The principle of anticipation for both of these trills can hardly be doubted. It can also be assumed that within the freedom of ornament rendition, such anticipation need not always be complete, but that the alternations may on appropriate occasions spill over into the next beat, forming transitional patterns of partial anticipation. It is interesting to see that sixty years later, at a time when onbeat start of trills and other *agréments* had become more widespread even in France, Engramelle gives the trills of Ex. 25.10, which closely correspond to Couperin's patterns in Exx. 25.9*b* and *c*, and has them rendered in anticipation.[10]

Ex. 25.10. Engramelle (Bedos de Celles) (1778)

Couperin's music reveals many other trill designs of which only a few can be shown here. As was mentioned on other occasions, Couperin frequently uses a combined trill-turn symbol ( ) which is not explained in his table. In these places the turn follows rather than precedes the trill. The symbol is invariably followed by a stepwise rise to the next note; hence, the difference between the combined grace and the simple trill must reside at the end of the alternations.

---

[8] The pictorial pattern of these examples has to be viewed in the light of Couperin's comment in the preface in which he extolls the intelligence and precision of the engraving, which was due to "extreme attention" and the lavish expenditure of his own time, effort, and money. Among the special assets of this great care he mentions the observation of the exact value of beats and notes in their *perpendicular alignment*. It is impossible, therefore, to argue that the alignment of the quarter-notes was accidental rather than intentional.

[9] *Ornamentation*, I, 104.

[10] Bedos de Celles, *L'art du facteur d'orgues*, vol. 4, plates 106 and 107. The chapter on the mechanical organ in this work was written by Père Engramelle, author of *La tonotechnie* (Paris, 1776). In Ex. 25.10*a* the notated model and the cylinder design are in complete agreement. In Ex. *b*, the cylinder design shows only partial anticipation of the trill.

It is probable that the symbol often implies a definite separation of the two ornaments through a brief rest point of the trill, provided there is time for it:

This rest point would distinguish the final turn from the two-note suffix, also frequently used by Couperin and, written with small 8th-notes, not limited to the pattern of stepwise ascent:

In Ex. 25.11a from *La Séduisante*, the bass has a trill starting with a main-note *appui*. This meaning is clear from the placement of the symbol exactly under the next half-beat. In Ex. *b* the meaning of the *coulé* is puzzling, but no misprint is involved because the same pattern of parallel trills in both hands, with but one *coulé*, recurs four times. Obviously, the trills need to be synchronized, and obviously they are to start differently. It is readily apparent that the grace cannot stand for a long appoggiatura preparation; neither can it stand for a short onbeat start, for if it did, how was the left hand to be played? It seems that the only solution that makes both notational and musical sense is anticipation of the *coulé* and main-note start of the left-hand trill.

a. IX, *La Séduisante*   *b.* IX, *La Princesse de Sens*

Ex. 25.11.

Example 25.12a from *Le Moucheron*, with its slurred alternation of trills and mordents, can only be done, and only makes sense, with the two graces as mirror images of one another—hence, with the trills starting on the main note. *Points d'arrêt* between the graces, however small, are essential; otherwise the ornaments will fuse and lose their identity. Anticipation of both trills and mordents would seem a distinct possibility worth exploring. A further case where an alternation of mordent and trill makes melodic, rhythmic, and ornamental sense only when the trill is started with the main note occurs in *La Favorite*, as shown in Ex. *b.* The same is true of *Allégresse des Vainqueurs* where a similar pattern abounds. In Ex. *c* from *La Raphaéle*, the trill in the bass has to start with the main note to honor the slur and has to start *on* the beat, or else there is no beat.

a. VI, *Le Moucheron*   *b.* III, *La Favorite*, 3e couplet

c. VII, *La Raphaéle*

Ex. 25.12.

For trills with anticipated main-note start see Exx. 25.13*a* and *b*; for further specimens see *La Visionaire* (XXV), mm. 27 and 32.

a. XXIII, *Les Gondoles de Délos*   *b.* XXI, *La Reine des Coeurs*

Ex. 25.13.

From the models in Couperin's ornament table, from his brief remarks in his treatise, and above all from the study of the musical evidence, we can glean a rich and so far unsuspected variety of trill design. Clearly, Couperin has exploited the potential of the trill idea in all dimensions, and the very thought of obliterating this rich variety is completely unjustified.

The French Trill

1715-1785

A wide assortment of trill designs remained in use after Couperin. Within this multiformity, certain trill types are unproblematical, others controversial. The first, unproblematical group comprises at least the following three types, which had been in use for a long time: 1) the supported appoggiatura trill, 2) a long appoggiatura with a token alternation at the end, and 3) the trill with suffix. In the second group, the controversial questions center mainly on the start of the trill—whether on or before the beat, on the main note or the auxiliary—or on such related matters as the treatment of the *tremblement lié*, the trill after a written-out appoggiatura.

THE NON-CONTROVERSIAL ASPECTS

In his tables of 1706 and 1724, Rameau (using D'Anglebert's symbol) illustrates the supported appoggiatura trill in the unmetrical models of Exx. 26.1*a* and *b* and calls it *cadence appuyée*. Dandrieu follows the same procedure in 1724 (see Ex. *c*).[1]

Ex. 26.1.

The qualifying term *appuyé* is used later again by Corrette, Buterne, Bérard, and Blanchet.[2]

Another term for the same trill is that of *cadence préparée*. It is used, among others, by David, Denis, L'abbé Duval, and Duval. Other semantic variants include Duval's alternatives of *cadence pleine*, or *parfaite*, Choquel's *cadence simple* and probably a number of others.[3]

On the other hand, when Lacassagne speaks of *cadence préparée*, the preparation, as will be shown below, is more often than not made on the main note rather than the auxiliary.[4]

Except for Rameau and Dandrieu, none of the authors mentioned introduced a special symbol for this pattern and left its rendition to the individual's judgment.

---

[1] Rameau, *Premier livre de pièces de clavecin* (1706); *Pièces de clavessin avec une méthode* (1724); Dandrieu, *Premier livre de pièces de clavecin* (1724).

[2] Corrette, *Le parfait maître*, p. 47; Buterne, *Méthode pour apprendre la musique*, p. 15; Bérard, *L'art*, p. 114; Blanchet, *L'art*, pp. 117-118.

[3] David, *Méthode nouvelle*, pp. 131, 133; Duval, *Méthode agréable*, p. 11; Denis, *Nouveau système* (1747), p. 11; L'abbé Duval, *Principes*, p. 62; Choquel, *La musique*, p. 166.

[4] Lacassagne, *Traité*, pp. 47-48.

The length of the preparation must have varied. Rameau's and Dandrieu's model, in accord with D'Anglebert, seems to suggest only a fairly modest duration. Other writers who discuss or illustrate the relative length of the appoggiatura usually stipulate for the *appui* one-half the length of a binary note; among them are David, Buterne, Bérard, Blanchet, and Corrette. As for a dotted ternary note, Bérard, Blanchet, and Choquel indicate a one-third length, Denis (Tartini's translator), probably under Italian influence, a two-thirds extension.

The long appoggiatura with a token alternation at the end is the mirror image

of the *port de voix feint* with its *pincé* ending:

The strong suggestion of a sigh prompted one writer to refer to it as *cadence sanglottée*. The vocal medium is its primary domicile; this explains why, after its early description by Bacilly, it was ignored by the purely instrumental masters, and why in the 18th century it was mentioned mostly in treatises that are all or in part related to the voice. Example 26.2 shows illustrations by L'abbé Duval, Lécuyer, and David.[5]

Ex. 26.2.

The most frequent term for this type of trill is *tremblement* (or *cadence*) *feint* (*e*). It was used by Duval, Denis, Corrette, L'abbé Duval, Bordier, Lacassagne, Lécuyer, Le Menu de Saint Philbert, and Brijon.[6] Some of these men mention alternate names; for instance, Denis: *sanglottée*; Corrette, Lécuyer, and Saint Philbert: *brisée*; Lacassagne: *coupée*. *Brisée* is the only term used by Buterne; *cadence coulée* is David's preference, and Bérard-Blanchet speak of *demi-cadence*. L'abbé Duval comments on the confusion of terms and the occasional mix-up with *martellement* and the *port de voix feint*. To add to the terminological chaos, Mercadier de Belesta, in speaking of *cadence brisée*, refers to something entirely different: a trill starting with the auxiliary as contrasted to the *cadence pleine* which starts on the main note.[7]

However, all these terms (except Mercadier's) signified the one basic pattern that was described above. It should be added that its execution characteristically entailed a *mesa di voce* effect on the preparation and a slurring of the rudimentary shake.

No special symbol was used to signify this design. (The little-known Saint Philbert may be the only one to claim the waggles **w** as such symbol in distinction to the cross for

[5] L'abbé Duval, *Principes*, p. 65; David, *Méthode nouvelle*, pp. 131, 133; Lécuyer, *Principes*, p. 12.

[6] Duval, *Méthode agréable*, p. 11; Denis, *Nouveau système*, p. 11; Corrette, *Le parfait maître*, p. 48; L'abbé Duval, *Principes*, p. 65;

Bordier, *Nouvelle méthode de musique*, p. 37; Lacassagne, *Traité*, p. 49; Lécuyer, *Principes*, p. 12; Saint Philbert, *Principes*, p. 20; Brijon, *L'Apollon moderne*, p. 51.

[7] Mercadier de Belesta, *Nouveau système de musique*, p. 214.

the regular trill.) This means, of course, that the performer, and in particular the singer, could on his own initiative interpret the regular trill sign and occasionally no sign at all with the pattern of the *tremblement feint*.

Again, as in the case of the *appuyé*, it will be advisable to speak of this particular grace only when the preparation is *not* written out in regular notation. When it is written out, for instance in what L'Abbé le Fils calls *cadence feinte preparée* and *cadence feinte jettée*, we have to do more properly with specimens of small anticipated trills that will be dealt with in their proper context.

The third of the non-problematical designs is the trill with the two-note suffix:

Couperin, using the little notes to mark it, had called it *tremblement ouvert* when it led upward, *tremblement fermé* when it led downward. Muffat spoke of *tremblement réfléchissant*. After Couperin, the most frequent term for the pattern is *double cadence*. Rameau and Dandrieu use it and both adopt (with slight modification) D'Anglebert's symbol. Bordet, Lacassagne, and Choquel use the same term but have no symbol. Both Duval and L'abbé Duval call it *cadence doublée*, while L'Abbé le Fils calls it *cadence tournée*. Again, so many words for the same thing. To complicate matters, *double cadence* is used by Bérard-Blanchet in the sense of what the Italians call *ribattuta*: a trill starting with a slow, main-note anchored dotted pattern that gradually evens out and speeds up.[8]

In relatively short trills the suffix has to follow the shake without a pause. In somewhat longer ones they may be separated by a rest point.

The trill with suffix is closely related to Couperin's trill-turn pattern (⚇). The two designs will overlap when the alternations fuse with either turn or suffix, whereas an inserted rest point will bring out the difference of the two designs. A pattern from Foucquet (Ex. 26.3) shows the clear separation of trill and turn.[9]

Cadence et redoublé

Ex. 26.3. Foucquet (c. 1750)

Since a number of models in Foucquet's extensive table are closely patterned after Couperin's, it is likely that this particular model is Foucquet's interpretation of Couperin's symbol.

THE CONTROVERSIAL ASPECTS

The preceding chapters have shown wide areas in which the alleged rule of the onbeat auxiliary did not apply. After Couperin a similar situation continued.

The Main-Note Trill

The principle of the start with the auxiliary had been proclaimed mainly for the keyboard where it unquestionably had the widest dissemination. It was not

[8] Bérard, *L'art*, p. 116; Blanchet, *L'art*, p. 119.

[9] Foucquet, *Les caractères de la paix*, con-tains on p. 5 *Méthode pour apprendre la manière de se servir des agréments. . . .* Fouc-quet was organist at St. Eustache in St. Honoré.

limited to the keyboard, but in other media, as shown, the start with the main note played a substantial role. The preference of the keyboard for the upper-note start continued after Couperin. Rameau, Dandrieu, and Corrette still present the well-known pattern for the simple trill (as shown in Ex. 26.4) though later this model is less and less in evidence.[10]

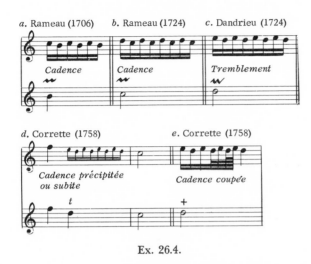

Ex. 26.4.

Rameau manifests outwardly the difference between various media by his divergent use of symbols (see Ex. 12.3 above). He reserves the *chevron* for the keyboard trill as other masters including Couperin had done before him and uses the cross for other media. However, confusion arises in some scores when he uses the *chevron* ($\wedge\!\wedge$) for a *pincé* and Couperin's *pincé* sign ($\wedge\!\!\wedge$) for a trill. The diversity of notation between keyboard and other media would not by itself imply a difference in execution, but evidence from the *Pièces de clavecin en concerts* (1747) does reveal such a difference. Rameau acknowledged that the start with the upper note was not understood by the strings, because when they play a trill in unison with the harpsichord, he routinely adds a little note to the string part to insure identical execution, as shown in the excerpts of Exx. 26.5*a-c*.

In none of these cases can it be argued that the little note stands for a long appoggiatura, because the symbol for the keyboard stands for a simple unprepared trill, not for the *appuyé* type. Obviously, if the addition of little notes is needed to elicit the same result, their absence would or could have produced a different one.

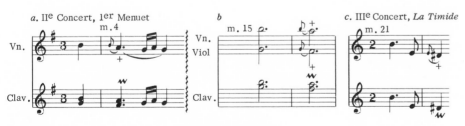

Ex. 26.5. Rameau

[10] See above, Ex. 24.25.

There are many spots in violin works where technical considerations make any but a main-note rendition of trills impractical. In the excerpt from Senaillé (Ex. 26.6), the asterisks mark the trills where an upper-note start within the legato slur would be violinistically incongruous.

Ex. 26.6. Senaillé, Op. 4, Sonata No. 1

In the two excerpts from Siret (Ex. 26.7), a main-note trill makes best musical sense. In Ex. *a* the second note of the prebeat grace represents the anticipated auxiliary. In Ex. *b* an onbeat auxiliary would be out of place for a trill following a mordent involving the same notes at the lively speed of a Gigue.

Ex. 26.7. Siret (1719)

In a model called *tremblement lié*, Dandrieu shows a special symbol to indicate the start of the trill with the main note on the beat (Ex. 26.8*a*). It applies, as the check mark—taking the place of a *guidon*—indicates, and as its frequent use confirms, in cases where the trill is preceded by its upper neighbor. However, this upper note rarely has the function of an appoggiatura. In some cases it takes the place of the anticipated auxiliary (Ex. *b*), in others it is simply a neighbor note without any closer functional relationship, as in Exx. *c* and *d*. The same is the case with the Belgian masters Fiocco and Van Helmont who adopted Dandrieu's model and usage.[11] Van Helmont, moreover, has his *Fuga Prima* followed by a version with written-out ornaments ("in Bewerking volgens de versierungen"). Its many trills start throughout with the supported main note, as shown in Ex. *e*.

Ex. 26.8.

[11] Dandrieu, *Premier livre de pièces de clavecin* (Paris, 1724); *Second livre de pièces de clavecin* (Paris, 1728); *Premier livre d'orgue* (Paris, 1739). For further examples see also my article "Misconceptions about the French Trill in the 17th and 18th Centuries," *MQ*, vol. 50 (1964), pp. 191ff. Regarding Fiocco and Van Helmont see above ch. 12, n. 6.

e. Van Helmont *Fuga prima*

Version with spelled-out ornaments:

Ex. 26.8 *cont.*

From now on, the theorists often refer to main-note start with such terms as *cadence jet(t)ée, subit(t)e, précipitée,* or *coupée.* The exact connotation of these terms varies somewhat from one writer to another, but all of the terms designate trills in which the alternations begin immediately, hence trills without *appui* and usually also without suffix.

To some theorists, for instance L'Abbé le Fils or Choquel, the terms *jetée* and *subite* (and probably *précipitée*) are synonyms. To others, for instance, Lécuyer and Duval, they designate different types. Others, like Lacassagne, use only one term which can accommodate varied designs. Some writers make it clear that one or the other of these terms implies, or can imply, a main-note start, others that it implies a grace-note trill, others again are noncommittal; hence caution is in order in interpreting these terms.

Among the writers who specify the main-note start, Buterne defines the *cadence subite* as one that starts with the note that carries the trill (literally: that gives rise to the trill).[12] Only the main note can be meant, especially since this trill type is contrasted to the *appuyé*, specifying the *son supérieur* as the one carrying the *appui.* Bérard and Blanchet, as usual in identical words, give an analogous directive for the *cadence précipitée*: "Throw the first alternation on the note on which the trill is to be made."[13]

L'abbé Duval in speaking of trills in general states first that they must always start with the upper note; however, two pages later he defines the *cadence subite* as one "which is never preceded by the sound of the upper note."[14] This *cadence,* he continues, is to be used when the trilled note is not a long one ("n'est pas d'une grande valeur") or when taste (*le goût*) requires it.[15]

La Chapelle uses the cross symbol (+) for the *cadence tremblée*, which he illustrates as an appoggiatura trill with gradual acceleration but without *appui* (Ex. 26.9*a*). He uses the *chevron* (w) for a *cadence coupée.*[16] The term *coupée* suggests something cut off, and the "something" is presumably the start with the auxiliary, inasmuch as the alternative *cadence tremblée* had a slow start but no support that could be cut off. La Chapelle does not explain the nature of the *coupée,* but main-note start is unmistakable in the model shown in Ex. 26.9*b*, with its slight anticipation indicated by the two little notes. In the next measure

[12] Buterne, *Méthode*, p. 15: "La Cadence subite est celle dont le tremblement doit commencer avec la Note qui l'ocasionne."

[13] Bérard, *L'art*, p. 115; Blanchet, *L'art*, p. 118: "Jettez le premier martellement sur la notte ou l'on doit battre cette cadence. . . ." The main-note meaning of the phrase "la notte ou l'on doit battre cette cadence" is further clarified by the definition of the *cadence appuyée* as one "[qui] se forme par un son soutenu majeur ou mineur, au-dessus de celui sur

lequel on la doit battre." Moreover, in the following chapter which deals with the physical aspect of ornament execution, the ascending start of the alternations is again confirmed: "La cadence précipitée demande qu'on fasse monter & descendre successivement le Larynx d'un degré. . . ."

[14] *Principes*, p. 63: "C'est celle qui n'est jamais précedée du son de la note supérieure."

[15] Ibid.

[16] *Vrais principes*, II, 14-15, 17.

the *coupée* is followed, as indicated by the cross symbol, by the *cadence tremblée*; apart from the telltale prefix, what else could account for the difference of symbol and term?

Ex. 26.9. La Chapelle (1737)

Denis distinguishes among the "unprepared" trills a *cadence subite*, a *jettée*, and a *cadence en l'air*, without explaining their differences.[17] From his illustration (Ex. 26.10a) we can gather that the *subite* is an upper-note trill; in the sole illustration for this type, a slight anticipation is written out by the preceding 32nd-notes. For the *jettée* (Exx. *c* and *d*), a main-note trill fits best in both cases and is the logical alternative for the contrasting term. The *cadence en l'air* is presumably also a main-note trill (in agreement with Jean Rousseau), differentiated from the *jettée* by its use in melodic ascent, whereas the latter occurs in melodic descent.

Ex. 26.10. Denis (1747)

Lacassagne has his *cadence jetée* start with either the upper note or with the main note, though his illustrations (Exx. 26.11a-d) show *only* the main-note type.[18] Very interesting is his analogous dualism for the *cadence préparée* which can start with a main-note support as well as with the more common support of the auxiliary, as given in Exx. *e-g*. Lacassagne does not like what he calls the *cadence pleine à progression* (another term for the *ribattuta*, the main-note anchored trill with dotted start and gradual acceleration), and in fact, he considers it outdated.

Ex. 26.11. Lacassagne (1766)

Duval distinguishes a *cadence subitte* and *cadence jettée*. Both have "neither preparation nor ending." Of these, the *subitte* is done downward ("se fait en descendant"), the *jettée* upward ("se fait en montant").[19] Their use is shown in

---

[17] *Nouveau système*, pp. 11, 45; 2nd ed., pp. 10, 44.

[18] *Traité*, pp. 47-48.

[19] *Méthode agréable*, p. 11.

Ex. 26.11 *cont.*

Ex. 26.12. "En descendant" and "en montant" cannot refer to rise or fall of the melodic line because the model of this *subitte* shows no descent of the melody. They can only refer to the trill's inner design. Hence it is clear that Duval's *subitte* is an upper-note, his *jettée* a main-note trill.

Ex. 26.12. Duval (1775)

Lécuyer, too, makes a distinction between the *cadence subite* and the *jettée*.[20] As usual, both have no "preparation." The *subite* (symbol: +), he says, is used when the melody descends and the *jettée* (symbol: ∓) when it rises, as shown in Ex. 26.13. (His *cadence double*, which has a suffix and rises to the following note, has no preparation either.) In agreement with Duval and other above quoted writers, Lécuyer seems to indicate upper-note start of the *subite* and main-note start of the *jettée*.

Ex. 26.13. Lécuyer (1769)

In one of the studies contained in L'Abbé le Fils's violin treatise, the pattern of a main-note supported trill occurs four times (Ex. 26.14).[21]

Ex. 26.14. L'Abbé le Fils (1761)

Choquel describes under the term *martellement* "a very short trill which is made after sustaining the sound of a tone" (symbol:〰)—hence a supported main-note trill. He gives this commentary on the f sharp in Ex. 26.15: "one must

20 *Principes*, pp. 11-13.   21 *Principes du violon*, p. 67.

sustain this tone for the duration of the quarter-note then trill lightly for the duration of the dot, thus forming the *martellement*."[22]

[The S is doubtless a misprint for ⟿.]

Ex. 26.15. Choquel (1762)

Saint Philbert describes the main-note start of the *cadence subite* when he says that "the note on which it [the little cross symbol] is placed is shaked as soon as it is sounded."[23]

Mercadier de Belesta distinguishes the *cadence pleine* and the *cadence brisée*. "The former starts the shake with the written note, the latter starts with the upper note."[24] He too, like Lacassagne, describes two types of prepared trills. The first of these sustains the upper note and is close to the *tremblement feint*; the other, which he calls *battement*, is prepared by the sustained main note ("Lorsque c'est la note écrite qui doit être soutenue, la cadence prend le nom de battement").

Jean Jacques Rousseau, like Mercadier, uses the term *battement* to signify a main-note trill. In his *Dictionnaire* of 1768 he explains the term as "A French vocal ornament which consists in shaking a trill upward from a note which one has started plain. The *Cadence* and the *Battement* differ in that the *Cadence* starts with the note above the one on which it is marked; whereupon one shakes alternatingly the upper and the true note: by contrast the *Battement* starts with the very note that is marked; whereupon one shakes alternatingly this note with the one above."[25]

Tarade in his violin treatise (c. 1774) gives examples of double trills in thirds starting either with their main notes or their upper notes. However, he characterizes the upper-note start as going out of fashion: "The French always prepare their trills; though these old preparations are still used in operas and old songs, they are not done any more in the modern music, and still less by other nations. . . . Today one does not even prepare final cadences." Since he sets his term *préparer* clearly apart from *appuyer*, the former refers quite certainly to the simple upper-note start.[26]

Père Engramelle in his *Tonotechnie* of 1776 explains his symbolic transcription of the various types of trills as well as of trills of varying lengths. In describing the trills of different lengths, from three "modules" up to ten, he alternates the start with the upper note "du dessus au dessous" with the start on the main note "du dessous au dessus."[27] In his examples of transcriptions for the mechanical organ, Engramelle generally favors

[22] *La musique*, p. 173: "Il faut appuyer sur cette note pendant la valeur de la noire, & cadencer légerement pendant la valeur du point, ce qui formera le martellement."

[23] *Principes*, p. 18: "La note sur laquelle elle [i.e. la croix] est mise se tremble aussitôt qu'on la prononce."

[24] *Nouveau systême*, p. 214: "La première se fait en commençant le tremblement de voix par la note écrite: la seconde, en la commençant par la note supérieure."

[25] *Dictionnaire*, s.v. *battement*: "Agrément du Chant François, qui consiste à élever &

battre un Trill sur une Note qu'on a commencée uniment. Il y a cette différence de la Cadence au *Battement*, que la Cadence commence par la Note supérieure à celle sur laquelle elle est marquée; après quoi l'on bat alternativement cette Note supérieure & la véritable: au lieu que le *Battement* commence par le son même de la Note qui le porte; après quoi l'on bat alternativement cette Note & celle qui est au-dessus."

[26] *Traité du violon*, pp. 45, 47-48.

[27] *La tonotechnie ou l'art de noter les cylindres*, pp. 47ff.

the start with the upper note, using the main-note start chiefly for trills preceded by the upper neighbor. On the other hand, he shows frequent, and occasionally lavish, use of the *Schneller*. The 24-measure Allemande (Table 5, No. 9) and the following 20-measure Marche (No. 10) have no less than fourteen *Schneller* each.

Brijon in 1780 shows *cadences jettées*, *cadences pleines*, and *cadences doublées* with models of main-note start (Ex. 26.16) that he adopted from Lacassagne.[28]

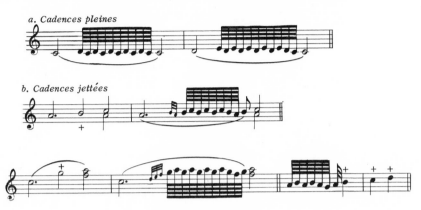

Ex. 26.16. Brijon (1780)

A further document pointing to the main-note start of the *cadence subite* or *jettée* can be found in the tables of Levesque and Bêche.[29] After explaining the *cadence parfaite* or *achevée* as one that is prepared by the upper note (Ex. 26.17a here also called *appuyée*), the authors show the *cadence brisée* (Ex. *b*), saying that "the preparation of the *cadence brisée* is less sustained than the foregoing." Finally, they say the "*cadence subite* is shaken immediately without preparation" ("La Cadence subite se bat d'abord sans être préparée"). This type, shown in Ex. *c*, is left without transcription, but it is hardly necessary; if the *brisée* is "prepared" and the *subite* is not, the difference can only lie in the omission of the starting auxiliary.

Ex. 26.17. Levesque and Bêche

A treatise by Dellain dated 1781, though not a valuable source, is nevertheless worth quoting as another document which reflects the relativity of rules. In defining the trill, the author first stipulates its start with the upper note. Then, a few pages later, he discusses *cadences lentes*, i.e. trills with a gradual acceleration of the alternations, and his illustrations, of which one is given in Ex. 26.18a, show the start with the sustained main

---

[28] *L'Apollon*, pp. 50-52.　　　　[29] *Solfèges*, p. 6.

note. (Here, as so often, the resolution precedes the model of the whole note with the symbol.) E. Roy, in his (undated) recorder treatise gives a similar main-note supported model for the standard trill (Ex. *b*).[30]

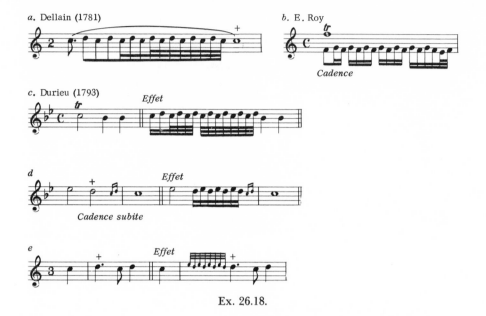

Ex. 26.18.

Still later in the century, in Durieu's vocal treatise of 1793, even the basic form of the trill as shown in Ex. *c* is main-note propelled, while his *cadences subites* start either with the main note (Ex. *d*) or the upper note (Ex. *e*)—the latter trill perhaps in part anticipated.[31] (See also Rodolphe's *cadence sans préparation*, Ex. 26.25*c* below.)

The preceding documentation was carried through to the end of the century to make the point that even in France, the chief domicile of the starting auxiliary, a strong undercurrent of main-note trills—with or without support—continued to flow incessantly from the 17th into the 19th century. The current was strongest in works for the voice and melody instruments. For the keyboard, a continued preference for the start with the upper note is possible, though for the second half of the century the evidence is meager. However, as will now be shown, this auxiliary start frequently took the form of anticipation.

The Grace-Note Trill

Example 26.19 from Rameau shows a written-out grace-note trill (unless one wishes to interpret it as a straddling main-note trill).

David presents a number of trill patterns that show interesting variants. The *cadence jettée* of Ex. 26.20*a* starts the alternations in rather obvious anticipation;

un coeur s'é lan - - - ce

Ex. 26.19. Rameau, *Achante et Céphise*, I, 2

[30] Dellain, *Nouveau manuel musical*, pp. 12 and 30; Roy, *Méthode complete pour le flageolet*, p. 4.

[31] *Nouvelle méthode de musique vocale*, pp. 61-62.

the *cadence subite* or *jettée en descendant* (Ex. *b*) has the auxiliary in presumable anticipation, before a sustained main note; the *cadence coulée* (Ex. *c*), is a main-note supported trill introduced by a downward slide.[32]

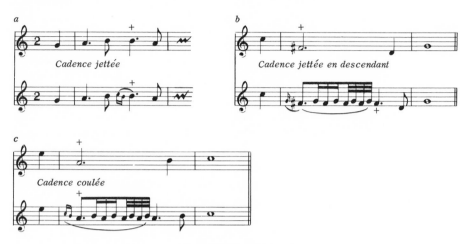

Ex. 26.20. David (1737)

Foucquet, in his table of ornaments, suggests the anticipation of the auxiliary and the main-note anchor of every trill pattern.[33] When he describes the *effet* of the trills shown in Exx. 26.21 *a-d* with the *notes postiches* as part of the resolution, the interpretation as anticipated *coulé* is the most likely one given the metrical precision of the regular notes. This seems to be most obvious in Exx. *c* and *d*, the delayed and the shortened patterns. His indebtedness to Couperin lends further weight to his grace-note intention.

For the *cadence ou tremblement jeté*, which he lists without transcribing it (see Ex. *e*), he takes the double precaution of writing the *notes postiches* as 16ths with the explanation that he is doing so to prevent them from being misunderstood as *appuis* and simply to show that these trills should always be prepared by the upper note.[34]

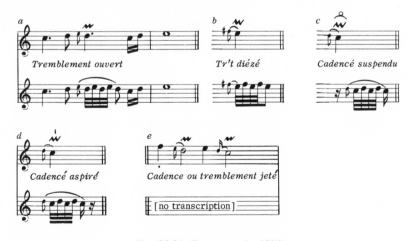

Ex. 26.21. Foucquet (c. 1750)

32 *Méthode*, pp. 131, 133.
33 *Les caractères*, p. 5.
34 Ibid.: ". . . je le marque par une petite note double croche afin qu'elle ne soit point appuyée mais toujours préparée de la note d'audessus."

Bordet gives the trill patterns shown in Exx. 26.22a and b and says: "To form a trill on any given note, one has to borrow the tone that lies above and that precedes the trilled note ('qui précède la dite note cadencée'); that is what is called to prepare a trill."[35] "Precedes the trilled note" probably admits anticipation.

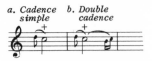

Ex. 26.22. Bordet (1755)

Revealing documentation on the grace-note trill is provided by L'Abbé le Fils in his violin treatise of 1761. He illustrates on page 14 the *cadence subite, ou jettée* as shown in Ex. 26.23a. The implication of the heavily inked notes cannot be misunderstood: the main note has the stress of the metrical accent and the auxiliary is anticipated.[36] Even without such an explanation it would be obvious that in the passage of Ex. *b* from the same treatise (p. 57) the auxiliary has to be anticipated.

L'Abbé le Fils's exercises for the study of the double trill (p. 65) confirm not only the main-note anchor of his basic trill pattern, but the main-note start for the actual trill symbol on the hold, as shown in Ex. *c*. Such main-note anchor, which was also revealed by Couperin and Foucquet, has clear implications for the *tremblement subit* that starts with immediate alternations: it leaves only the alternative of main-note start or anticipated auxiliary.

Ex. 26.23. L'Abbé le Fils (1761)

Lécuyer, explaining the *cadence parfaite* that has both an *appui* and a *terminaison* (i.e. a suffix), gives the unusual illustration shown in Ex. 26.24.[37] The model reveals the main-note anchor of the trill and the anticipation of the auxiliary, as well as the partial anticipation of the trill itself.

Ex. 26.24. Lécuyer (1769)

[35] *Méthode raisonnée pour apprendre la musique*, p. 6.

[36] *Principes du violon*, p. 14.
[37] *Principes*, p. 12.

Rodolphe gives the illustrations of Ex. 26.25.[38] The anticipation of the auxiliary is again suggested by the *effet* of Exx. *a* and *b*, especially in comparison with the *cadence brisée* of Ex. *d* that shows an appoggiatura trill and the obvious way of notating it.

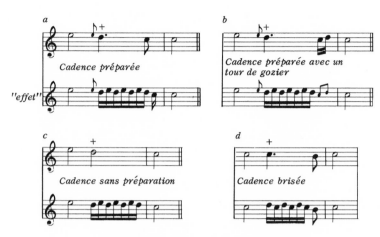

Ex. 26.25. Rodolphe (c. 1784)

The Tremblement Lié

Trills slurred to the preceding note offer problems when this note has the same pitch as the auxiliary. Prevalent doctrine requires the preceding note to merge with the first auxiliary in the manner of a suspension to insure the onbeat placement of the auxiliary:

There are only scant French sources for this suspension pattern. Corrette presents this model in several of his treatises in the form given in Ex. 26.26, and he may be the only Frenchman to do so.[39]

Ex. 26.26. Corrette (1741)

The main documentation in support of this pattern is not French but German, and from the second half of the century. There is no question that it was used in France. Why not? The design can be very appealing in a slow tempo, provided another voice articulates the beat over which the upper note is to be tied:

On the other hand, in the absence of a rhythmical support in another voice, the lengthening of the preceding note for the duration of a single trill particle might

---

[38] *Solfége ou nouvelle méthode de musique,* p. 36. Rodolphe (or Rudolph), opera composer and eminent horn virtuoso, was first hornist at the Paris Opera and professor at the Conserva-toire. He had studied with Traëtta and Jomelli; his theoretical works were greatly esteemed by his contemporaries.

[39] *Méthode pour le violoncelle,* p. 36.

satisfy the eye on paper as to the dutiful conformance with the "rule," but it can disorient the ear by obscuring the rhythm. Moreover, when the preceding note is short, for instance in a lively descending scale passage, the attempt to apply the suspension pattern becomes senseless.

Another possibility is the onbeat start with the main note. This is the obvious solution when the preceding note is short and unaccented, in which case this note will often take the place of an anticipated auxiliary. As was shown before (Ex. 26.8a), Dandrieu had a special symbol to indicate such a main-note start following the upper neighbor, and he *always* used it when the upper neighbor was short and frequently even when it was long, whether slurred or not.

For Rameau such a solution would be the logical sequence to his statement that "the note which is slurred to a trill or a mordent serves as a beginning to each of these ornaments."[40] The statement accompanies the illustrations of a slurred trill and a slurred *pincé* of which the former is given in Ex. 26.27. Since the preceding note is the "beginning," it takes the place of the starting upper note; hence, the alternations start with the main note—and there is no reason why they could not do so *on* the beat.[41]

Ex. 26.27. Rameau (1724)

Example 26.28 shows additional patterns from Dupuit (Ex. *a*) and J. J. Rousseau (Ex. *b*) which suggest onbeat start.[42] So did the above Ex. 26.25*c* of Rodolphe's *cadence sans préparation*.

a. Dupuit (1741)   *b*. Jean Jacques Rousseau (1768)

Cadence liée   *Cadence pleine*

Ex. 26.28.

Through his combination of small and big note heads, L'Abbé le Fils brings a very graphic and inescapable pictorial representation of the onbeat start (Ex. 26.29).[43] He refers to the model as *cadence appuyée*.

Cadence appuyée

Ex. 26.29. L'Abbé le Fils (1761)

The *tremblement lié* is closely related to the *tremblement appuyé* and overlaps with it in those instances where the preceding note has the harmonic function

[40] Ornament table in *Pièces de clavecin* (1724).

[41] The fact that Rameau gives only seven notes for the trill does not at all imply a suspension as Dannreuther has assumed. Rameau simply felt the need to end the trill with the main note. Besides, his example of the *cadence appuyée*: is similarly unmetrical, in keeping with the vagueness of such models.

[42] Dupuit, *Principes pour toucher de la viele*, p. III; Jean Jacques Rousseau, *Dictionnaire*, Planche B.

[43] *Principes du violon*, p. 14.

of a stressed *Vorschlag*, a genuine long appoggiatura. In such a case the *tremblement lié* is simply a spelled-out *appuyé*: the preceding note and the trill are both part of *a single ornament*, and this fact alone justifies, and often calls for, a free rhythmic treatment. Hence, the placement of the alternations can be free, be delayed in the suspension pattern, be placed on the beat, or be partially or totally anticipated.

Two specimens of such spelled-out *appuyés* from Rameau's harpsichord pieces are given in Ex. 26.30. The first (Ex. *a*) would seem to admit all three possibilities for the—presumably very brief—alternations: suspension, onbeat, or anticipation. In Ex. *b* suspension would make little sense in the absence of another voice to clarify the beat, and either anticipation or onbeat placement of a *Schneller*-type miniature trill would appear to be indicated.

Ex. 26.30. Rameau

When suspension is illogical, and onbeat treatment too square, the answer is *anticipation*. If we compare renditions *a* and *b*  it should be clear that *b* will occasionally be smoother, rounder, more elegant than *a*, yet give at the same time excellent rhythmic definition for the second beat where such is called for. Even if we did not have documentary confirmation, assets so easily achieved can be assumed to have been utilized. Actually this manner of anticipated trills, especially of small ones, is used countless times to the present day by many who are not even aware of what they are doing. Certainly it must have been done two hundred years ago.

The previously mentioned autograph additions to the wind instrument treatise of Francoeur ("neveu") show the illustration of an anticipated *cadence brise* [*sic*] *ou finte* [*sic*], given in Ex. 26.31*a*, as well as the *Schneller* (Ex. *b*) which he called—misleadingly—a *pincé* or *brissé* [*sic*]. In Ex. *a* the evidence is unequivocal; in Ex. *b* it is almost so. The little notes in their role not of symbol but of resolution can be assumed to have interbeat meaning in view of Francoeur's previously noted careful spelling out of onbeat graces.

In the preceding chapter, Couperin's model of the *tremblement lié sans être appuyé* (Ex. 25.9*b*) was shown to imply such anticipation, and its continued use

Ex. 26.31. Francoeur ("neveu") (1772)

was confirmed sixty years later in 1779 by Engramelle in a model reproduced above in Ex. 25.10.

Still later in the century Durieu gives an example of complete anticipation, at least for a *Schneller*. Speaking of a *cadence feinte*, which he notates as a *tremblement lié* (Ex. 26.32), he says: "The *cadence feinte* is done without preparation and ends with a little shake; that is, one puts two little notes *between the trilled note and the one which precedes it*." [Italics mine.][44]

Ex. 26.32. Durieu (1793)

Partial anticipation of the trill could also be simply inferred from the above mentioned ornamental unity between the appoggiatura and the trill proper. However, it did leave some distinct traces in both treatises and music, some of which have been shown previously (see a.o. Exx. 26.20*a* and 26.24).

Anticipation was not limited to the context of the *tremblement lié*. The reader will remember Couperin's model of the equally anticipated *tremblement détaché*, a pendant to the *lié* and its analogous reaffirmation by Engramelle (Exx. 25.9*c* and 25.10*b*).

From the latter part of the century a further document from Devienne distinguishes *cadences* (marked ⌇) that start with the upper note and have a suffix, and *trilles ou petites cadences* (marked *tr* , ⌇ , or +) that start with the main note.[45] The model with its little notes (Ex. 26.33) suggests anticipation, the more so since an onbeat intention would have been much easier to indicate.

Ex. 26.33. Devienne (1795)

SUMMING UP the second period for the French trill, it is possible to repeat almost verbatim what has been said of the first. A unified practice is again only a chimera. There were definite preferences, such as the start with the upper note on the keyboard—though it gradually waned, so it seems, in the later part of the century. No doubt there were some performers who kept their designs within self-imposed restrictions, but there is every reason to assume that many others exploited the full range of the trill's potential.

---

[44] *Nouvelle méthode*, p. 62: "La cadence feinte se fait sans preparation et se termine par un petit martellement c'est a dire qu'on met deux petites notes entre la note cadencée et celle qui la précède."

[45] *Nouvelle méthode pour la flute*, p. 18. Devienne was a composer and a brilliant flutist. His treatise was reprinted many times.

The Italian Trill

1590-1710

Though the trill is an age-old grace, it was probably not until the 16th century that Italian writers and composers started to describe and label its various shapes.

Vincenzo Capirola in his lute book, written about 1517, explains the execution of the trill and uses red dots as symbols to demonstrate proper contexts for its use. Ganassi in 1535 points to the trill as the simplest means of adding grace and elegance to any performance.[1] He distinguishes trills with thirds, whole tones, and half-tones. The intervals are subject to deviation in either direction, in other words, they may be played out of tune. The trill with a third is described as a lively ornament, the one with the half-tone as gentle and charming, and the whole-tone type as standing halfway in between. He introduces the symbols *t* for *tremolo*, *V* (*vivace*) for its lively variety, and *S* (*suave*) for the gentle trill. The trill with the third did not survive very long, and it seems that the only later references to such a trill condemned it as undesirable.

Toward the end of the 16th century a new species of trill emerges, and hereafter there existed side by side two distinct trill types. The first is the familiar oscillating variety, the trill proper. The other consisted of tone repetition. Strictly speaking, this type is not a trill in the sense in which this ornament was defined at the outset of Part V. However, its close link to the regular trill through many transitional and combination forms makes it advisable to treat it here as a member of the family.

The first type, the oscillating trill, is called *tremolo* by Ganassi, Diruta, Bovicelli, but *trillo* by Cavalieri, Frescobaldi, Trabaci, and others; *tremoletto* is Diruta's designation for a diminutive trill with only one or two alternations, including the *Schneller* type. An oscillating trill-related grace with slower and more distinct alternations, and ending with a turn of four notes is called *groppo* by Conforto, *groppolo* by Cavalieri, *gruppo* by Caccini.[2] The main patterns of these types, all of which start with the main note, are given in Ex. 27.1. Of these designs, Exx. *a* and *b* are Diruta's *tremoli*, which are main-note trills with a rest point; Exx. *c* and *d* are both specimens of Diruta's *tremoletti*, which, he says, were used frequently by Claudio Merulo. The first (Ex. *c*) demonstrates the *Schneller*, while the second (Ex. *d*) shows anticipation of the entire trill. Example *e* is Cavalieri's main-note trill; Exx. *f-i* are models belonging to the *groppo* family with the characteristic turn-suffix. They too start on the main note. In Cavalieri's *groppolo* (Ex. *f*), the alternations start immediately, whereas the main note is extended in a support in Conforto's *groppo* (Ex. *g*) and *mezzo groppo* (Ex. *h*), and Caccini's *gruppo* (Ex. *i*).

Bovicelli does not illustrate his *tremolo* which he says "is nothing but the trembling of the voice over one note" and requires a context of stepwise motion.[3] Using the symbol

---

[1] *Compositione di Meser Vincenzo Capirola*, ed. Otto Gombosi, p. lxxxviii. Ganassi, *Fontegara*, chaps. 24, 25.

[2] Of the previously quoted sources in this example, Diruta's work is addressed to organ and harpsichord, Cavalieri's, Bovicelli's and Caccini's to the voice, Conforto's to any medium.

[3] *Regole*, p. 12: "Il tremolo . . . que non è altro, que un tremar di uoce sopra ad una stessa nota, ricerca, que le note uadino sempre per grado. . . ."

Ex. 27.1.

∧ , he shows the application of the *tremolo* in embellishing the simple melody of the top line in Ex. 27.2. A short trill or *Schneller* seems the likeliest intention.

Ex. 27.2. Bovicelli (1594)

The second type of trill, the tone repetition, is called *trillo* by Caccini and illustrated in a pattern of acceleration, as shown in Ex. 27.3*a*. The execution of this grace must have ranged from a clear and sharp separation of its tones to smoothly connected dynamic stresses without a break of the breath. One could speak of *staccato* and *legato* style of execution (of which the latter is a form of intensity vibrato). Unquestionably, both styles were used. Documentation in the present chapter regarding this duality of style will be supplemented below in Chapters 28 and 45. Monteverdi, who used the tone repetition very frequently, gave in *Il Ritorno d'Ulisse* an example of staccato style. In the comic aria of Iro, the *trillo*, specifically so labeled, is used to portray the percussiveness of stylized laughter in a prescribed transition to "natural laughter" (*riso naturale*), as shown in Ex. *b*.

a. Caccini, *Trillo*

b. Monteverdi, *Il ritorno d'Ulisse*, III, 1   "Trillo"

ri - da ri - - - - -

"qui cade in riso naturale"

- - - - da del ghiot - to tri - on - far - -

Ex. 27.3.

The symbol of *t* or *tr* is used for both the regular trill and the tone repetition. However, when we find, as we often do, the symbol not on top of a note but *between* two notes of *equal* pitch:  we can assume that the composer intended a tone repetition (with oscillations *ad libitum*).

Conforto's pattern for the *trillo* (Ex. 27.4) is a mixed form: it starts like a main-note supported trill with one alternation only and ends with a suffix; the tone repetition is sandwiched between. We shall presently encounter related combination patterns on the keyboard.

3   [3]   3   3   [3]   *Mezzo*[*trillo*]
Trillo

Ex. 27.4. Conforto

As can be seen, the terminology is confused. What *tremolo* means is relatively clear; but what it means is also called *trillo* by some. The term *trillo* can stand for pure tone repetition, for pure oscillation, or for combination forms such as the one given by Conforto.

The terms *groppo* and variants such as *groppolo* or *groppetto* are also ambiguous. Usually they refer to a design that involves a trill-like oscillation with a turn-suffix, but the names of the *groppo* family are also used by Diruta, Bovicelli, and others for a wider range of designs that stand midway between a trill and florid diminutions. These designs are not limited to two or three tones but do not stray far afield; they most often move stepwise and usually contain some elements of oscillation. In this sense the passage of Ex. 27.5 is called *groppetto* by Bovicelli. Diruta uses the term *groppo* in the same meaning, and Caccini's use of the term is not limited either to his demonstrated trill-suffix design.

(Groppetto)

Ex. 27.5. Bovicelli, p. 12

In view of the terminological complexities, it will be best, once the facts have been stated for the record, to refer to the various trill designs according to our previously given working terminology, and to reserve the term *trillo* solely for Caccini's tone repetition.

In contrast to the theoretical models which apparently all started on the main note, some of the diminution treatises show as cadential formula a stereotyped trill-like six-to-eight-note figure consisting of two upper-note alternations plus a turn: . The figure that has the appearance of a brief appoggiatura trill with suffix was at the time not considered a trill but a turn, an ornate turn as it were. It was slower than a trill, more sharply articulated, and apparently rendered with a degree of metrical regularity. It was never classed as either *tremolo* or *trillo* but always as *groppo* or *groppetto*. The difference in identity is already obvious with Ganassi whose use of the eight-note formula is shown in Ex. 27.6a. When we compare this pattern with Ganassi's above recorded descriptions of the various species of *tremoli*, with their varying speeds and indefinite pitches, it is clear that we have to do with two different things. Bassano used the eight-note pattern almost routinely (Ex. *b*), Dalla Casa a similar six-note formula (Ex. *c*).

Ex. 27.6.

Praetorius, reporting on Italian practices, confirms the difference of character by informing us that the *groppi* are used in cadences and are to be more sharply articulated than the *tremoli*. More about this in the next chapter.[4] Whereas many *groppi* started on the main note (like the vast majority of the *tremoli*), it is quite likely that those cadential *groppi* which—like Bassano's eight-note formula—started on the upper note may have been the forerunners of the cadential appoggiatura trill. In late baroque music this trill also had an individuality of its own regarding both function and rendition.

Bovicelli, somewhat surprisingly, shows practically no cadential trill-like patterns in his examples of ornamented compositions. It almost seems that he studiously avoided them

---

[4] See ch. 28, n. 3 below.

in favor of figurations of more varied melodic-rhythmic designs. Only once in a while does he use Conforto's *mezzo groppo*, as shown in Ex. 27.7.[5]

Ex. 27.7. Bovicelli (motet by Victoria), p. 61

Another source for the shapes of trills and trill-related ornaments are compositions in which these graces are spelled out in regular notation. Luzzasco Luzzaschi, Frescobaldi's teacher, uses Bassano's eight-note formula as well as Conforto's *mezzo groppo* (see Ex. 27.8).[6]

Ex. 27.8. Luzzaschi, Madrigali (1601)

Giovanni Maria Trabaci, who uses the *t* symbol for *trillo*, which is a regular oscillating trill, introduces in 1603 the somewhat unusual pattern of Ex. 27.9. It starts with the leap of a third which frames the main note. In 1615 he introduces a special symbol for this figure: a *t* plus a cross (*t₊*). In the same work he also calls a trill with suffix a *trillo doppio*.[7]

Ex. 27.9. Trabaci (1603), Ricercate

Once in a while Frescobaldi uses the symbol *t* (for *trillo*) to indicate a fairly short main-note trill, but trills of some length he wrote out in regular notes. The vast majority start with the main note, including trills in cadential formulas, as illustrated in Exx. 27.10*a* and *b*. The closest he comes to the upper-note trill is

a. Book 2, Toccata 1

b. Book 1, Toccata 5

c. Book 1, Toccata 7

d. Cappriccio pastorale

Ex. 27.10. Frescobaldi

[5] *Regole*, p. 61.

[6] *Madrigali per cantare e sonare . . .* (Rome, 1601).

[7] *Ricercate, canzone Francese, capricci, canti fermi . . .*, bk. 1 (Naples, 1603); *Secondo libro de ricercare . . .* (Naples, 1615).

the occasional suspension pattern shown in Ex. *c*. Example *d* shows the beginning of a three-measure main-note trill reminiscent of Couperin's *tremblement continu*. Frescobaldi left us revealing instructions not to play his long written-out trills exactly as written but faster and freer, coming to a rest on the final tone.[8]

Michelangelo Rossi, Frescobaldi's student, follows closely in his master's footsteps with an equally decided preference for main-note trills. Example 27.11*a* shows one of his characteristic cadential formulas.[9] Tarquinio Merula uses a variety of trills of which Exx. *b-d* present a few specimens of upper-note and main-note designs.[10]

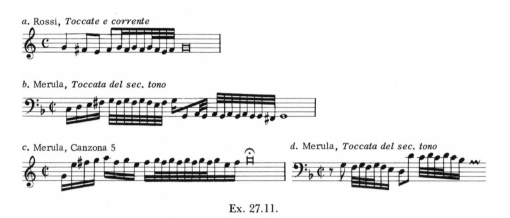

Ex. 27.11.

In 1672 we find a strangely mixed design, when Penna, in a treatise on the thorough bass, presents trills that contain elements of the tone repetition pattern shown in Ex. 27.12*a*.[11] We find similar designs with contemporary keyboard masters such as Gregorio Strozzi and Giovanni Salvatore. Example *b* gives such a mixed design from Strozzi's *Toccata prima (CEKM*, vol. 11, p. 54); Ex. *c* shows a plain-tone repetition by the same

Ex. 27.12.

[8] Example *a* is from *Il secondo libro di toccate, canzone, versi . . .* (Rome, 1637); Exx. *b-d* from *Toccate d'intavolatura di cimbalo et organo . . .* , bk. 1, 5th ed. (Rome, 1637); the instructions regarding the long trill appear in the Preface to *Toccate e partite d'intavolatura di cimbalo*, bk. 1 (Rome, 1615-1616).

[9] *Toccate e corrente per organo, o cemb.* (Rome, n.d.).

[10] *Monumenti di musica Italiana*, ed. Alan Curtis, Series 1, vol. 1.

[11] Penna, *Li primi albori musicali* (1672), III, 17; 5th ed. (1696), p. 152.

master (*CEKM*, vol. 11, p. 48). Salvatore, in a final cadence, given in Ex. *d*, labels a dotted alternation as *grup.[po]*, and a tone repetition as *trillo* (*CEKM*, vol. 3, p. 77). Even without this revealing nomenclature, the derivation of these patterns from the vocal *trillo* is quite clear and would seem to provide additional evidence that the *trillo* could involve sharply articulated tone repetition.

Example 27.13*a* from the end of the century shows an interesting pattern from Agostino Steffani: a diminutive trill at the end of a long main-note support.[12] From the same period, Ex. *b* shows a main-note trill in a final cadence written by Alessandro Poglietti.[13]

Ex. 27.13.

In a manuscript treatise this same Poglietti distinguishes *trilli gagliardi*, i.e. "robust" trills (Exx. 27.14*a* and *b*) from the *trillo* proper (Ex. *c*). The first of the *gagliardi* (Ex. *a*) seems related to the mordent; the second (Ex. *b*) is an appoggiatura trill with suffix, whereas the *trillo* pure and simple, is a main-note supported trill with turned ending.[14]

a. Trilli gagliardi

b. Trilli gagliardi   *c. Trillo*

Ex. 27.14. Poglietti

Bernardo Storace, an important keyboard master of the post-Frescobaldi era, prefers throughout the main-note trill and shows the strength of his preference by his willingness to pay the price of the awkward tone repetition of Ex. 27.15.[15]

Ex. 27.15. Storace, Ciaccona

[12] From the opera *Alessandro*, DDT, II, 12.
[13] From the canzona *Françoise Trommel*, Yale, MS E. B., 1688, p. 33. I am indebted for this reference to the late Earle Nettles.
[14] *Compendium oder kurtzer Begriff und*
Einführung zur Musica.
[15] *Selva di varie compositioni d'intavolatura per cimbalo ed organo . . .* (1664); reprint, Am. Inst. of Musicol. (1965), ed. B. Hudson.

The long silence of the theorists makes it hard to trace the story of the Italian trill in greater detail. It is difficult to ascertain where in Italy, or how long and how frequently the one-note *trillo* remained in improvised use. Most likely its use diminished in the course of the century, but several documents attest to its survival into the 18th century.

Quantz, reminiscing in his autobiography, speaks admiringly of Faustina's (Hasse's wife and Handel's prima donna) technical mastery and mentions her ability of tone repetition which he considered unique: "The passages may run or leap or consist of many fast notes on the same tone, she could articulate them in the fastest tempo with such a skill that it matches a rendition on an instrument. She is unquestionably the first to apply with finest success the mentioned [?] (*gedachten*) passages consisting of many notes on one tone."[16] Clearly, Quantz speaks here of true tone repetition. His obvious wonderment and the apparent fact that he had never heard this practice before shows that the art had but few practitioners left.

Faustina made her debut with Handel in London in his opera *Alessandro*, and it is hardly a coincidence that he wrote out *trilli* for her, such as the passage in Ex. 27.16*a*, besides those she improvised. There can be little doubt that actual tone repetition was involved here (*Andante e staccato*). The passage of Ex. *b*, from his 14th Organ Concerto in A major, which occurs two more times in different keys, is simply a *trillo* on the keyboard. The tone repetitions in Domenico Scarlatti's Sonata (K 96, mm. 33-40) may belong here too. A further document that strongly suggests actual tone repetition and not only a rhythmical vibrato is to be found in one of Benedetto Marcello's parodies (Ex. *c*). For this satire of the castrati's extravagances, Marcello may have introduced devices he considered in bad taste, but hardly any that had completely disappeared.[17]

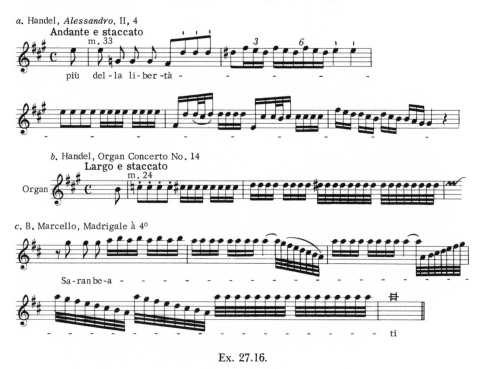

Ex. 27.16.

[16] Quantz's captivating autobiography in Marpurg's *Historisch-Kritische Beyträge zur Aufnahme der Musik*, vol. 1 (Berlin, 1754), pp. 197-250. The passage on Faustina is on pp. 240-241.

[17] *Madrigale secondo a 4°*, MS Bol. GG 144, p. 15. (The staccato tone repetitions in the Queen of the Night's second aria may possibly be late descendants of the Caccini-Monteverdi *trillo*.)

THE VERY absence of regulative treatises for the guidance of students, combined with the permissive Italian attitude toward ornamentation, strengthens the assumption that the Italian performer felt free to explore all rhythmic-melodic possibilities of the various trill designs.

The upper-note trill made occasional appearances, partly perhaps in response to French models, partly—especially in cadences—as an offshoot of the stereotyped eight-note formula derived from the *turn* family of graces. However, among the regular trills, the main-note pattern retained throughout the period under consideration its decisive predominance. This fact will find further confirmation from contemporary German sources that reflected Italian practices.

The German Trill

1615-1715

THEORETICAL SOURCES

Praetorius, writing in 1619 about the trill, continues to use Italian models. Explaining the *tremolo* or *tremulo* as a "trembling of the voice upon a note,"[1] he sounds the leitmotiv for the century by showing a straight main-note model for the trill, which he calls *tremulus ascendens* (Ex. 28.1a), side by side with its mirror image, the *tremulus descendens* (Ex. b), a multiple mordent which he considers inferior to the former. In either case, the semibreve is the note to be trilled and the respective resolutions show the alternations coming to an end in the second half of the note's value.

Ex. 28.1. Praetorius (1619)

Under the term *tremoletti,* Praetorius introduces miniature trills with one or two alternations (Ex. 28.2). The absence of symbols reveals that the trills here too are impromptu additions. The patterns of Exx. *b* and *d* are *Schneller;* the patterns of Exx. *c* and *e* are short main-note trills. Praetorius adds that all these trilled graces, including the *tremulo,* are more appropriate for the keyboard than for the human voice.[2]

Ex. 28.2. Praetorius, *Tremoletti*

Using the name of *gruppo* or *groppo,* Praetorious reproduces Caccini's main-note supported trill-like design with a turned ending (Exx. 28.3a and b). He says it is used in cadences and related clauses and ought to be rendered with greater sharpness than the *tremoli.*[3] The term *trillo,* we then are told, has a dou-

---

[1] *Syntagma,* III, 235-237: "ein Zittern der Stimme ober einer *Noten.*"

[2] Ibid.: "Und dieses ist mehr uff Orgeln und *Instrumenta pennata* gerichtet als uff Menschen Stimmen."

[3] Ibid.: "*Gruppo: vel Groppi* werden in den *Cadentiis* und *Clausulis formalibus* gerbraucht/ und müssen scherffer alss die *Tremoli* angeschlagen werden."

ble meaning (p. 237). One is Caccini's pattern: "when many rapid notes are repeated" ("Wann viel geschwinde Noten nacheinander repetiret werden"). This first type is illustrated in Exx. *c* and *d*; Praetorius refers to its use by Monteverdi. The second type of *trillo* can be learned only by live example. From several models for this second *trillo* species (of which two samples are given in Exx. *e* and *f*), we can gather that it was a brief melismatic figure that stayed close to the basic melody.

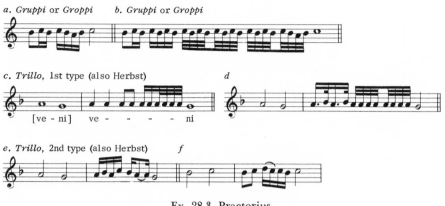

Ex. 28.3. Praetorius

Herbst in 1642 and 1658, as well as Crüger in 1654 and 1660, follow Praetorius very closely.[4]

Thus their patterns for the *tremulo* are literally taken over from the older master along with his declared preference for the ascending type (Ex. 28.4*a*). Their models for the *tremoletti* (Exx. *b* and *c*) show only slight modifications (except perhaps for Herbst's one-stroke mordents of Ex. *c*). Again, we find with both of these authors the *Schneller* as well as the brief main-note trill. Their models for the *gruppo* or *groppo* are identical to those of Praetorius that were shown above in Exx. 28.3*a* and *b*.

Their *trillo*, like Praetorius's, is presented in two guises: 1) the tone repetition and 2) the small melic patterns. Herbst's illustrations are identical with Praetorius's of Exx. 28.3*c*, *d*, *e*, and *f*. Crüger's slight variants are given in Ex. 28.4*d*.

Herbst and Crüger, by using Praetorius's text so freely, helped to transmit his Italian models to later German generations.

Christoph Bernhard (around 1660) speaks of *trillo* or *Trill*, which he says is the hardest but most graceful artifact, one that cannot be described but must be learned by ear.[5] Presumably Bernhard had the oscillating type in mind and recommends the use of the chest voice rather than the head voice. He cautions the performer not to let the trill degenerate into a bleat by "changing the voice" and urges moderation in adding trills to those already marked by a *t*.

Another type of the grace, a *trillo doppio*, is described as one way of introducing dynamic contrasts into lengthy trills (a crescendo being the other way). Bernhard's illustration of this grace, which is given in Ex. 28.5, is practically identical to Conforto's *trillo* (see above, Ex. 27.4): a combination of tone repetition, suffixes, and single alternations that could be viewed as *accenti*.

[4] Herbst, *Musica practica* (1642), pp. 7ff.; Crüger, *Synopsis*, pp. 197ff., and *Praecepta*

brevia, pp. 27ff.
[5] *Singe-Kunst*, pars. 12-14.

Ex. 28.4. Herbst (1642, 1658) and Crüger (1654, 1660)

Ex. 28.5. Bernhard (c. 1650), *Trillo doppio*

In 1685, Mylius, Bernhard's student, explains the term *trillo* as lovely wavering of the voice over one pitch ("ein liebliches Sausen, Zittern oder Wancken der Stimme über einer Noten").[6] He too says it is difficult to express in notes and has to be learned by ear. As shown in Exx. 28.6*a* and *b*, it can be done either upward ("the best and most agreeable") or downward ("also good" but dangerous for the steadiness of pitch). To demonstrate the introduction of dynamic nuances, Mylius gives an illustration (Ex. *c*) derived from Bernhard's *trillo doppio*. The example has to be read in the light of Mylius's previous remark that the change from forte to piano and vice versa should be gradual.

Mylius's *tremolo*, "mostly used by organists," has the two familiar forms of *ascendens* and *descendens* (the trill and mordent), the former again declared to be preferable. The illustration (Ex. *d*) shows half-steps in both of its forms. The *tremoletti*, like those of Praetorius and Herbst, are given only in their ascending species (Ex. *e*); they are small and very fast trills ("welche ganz geschwinde gemacht werden"). The *gruppi* (or *groppi*) are again set apart from the *tremoli* and *tremoletti* as sounding better and *sharper* and as being best suited for cadences. (See Exx. *f* and *g* for his two illustrations.)

[6] *Rudimenta,* ch. 5.

Ex. 28.6. Mylius (1685)

Stierlein in 1691 adds to the terminological confusion by reversing the terms *tremulus* and *trillo* and by giving a different definition to the term *gruppo*.[7]

Tremulus to him is the one-note repetition which he describes as "trembling in unison" ("Beben in unisono") and illustrates as shown in Ex. 28.7a. His definition of a "trembling"—rather than Praetorius's and Herbst's "repetition"—is more suggestive of an uninterrupted breath that would produce a vibrato-like effect. (The forte and piano marks in the illustrations are certainly meant to denote a swelling and tapering—as explained by Mylius—not a "terraced" abruptness.) What Stierlein calls the *gruppo* or *groppo* is more commonly called (by Herbst, for instance) a *ribattuta*, which leads into a trill, as shown in Ex. *b.*

Finally, the *trillo* or *trillet(t)o* is the usual two-note trill which Stierlein calls the most graceful of species. He advises the singer to open the mouth well, save breath, and apply legato smoothness; but he says nothing about the design. The exercises he gives for

[7] *Trifolium,* pp. 17-18.

Ex. 28.7. Stierlein (1691)

practice with various vowels, *a, e, i, o* (Ex. 28.8), show the start with the auxiliary *after* the beat. Such a start that misses the metrical emphasis assumes thereby the character of an anacrusis, not of an appoggiatura.

Ex. 28.8. Stierlein, trill exercise

Printz, in his various treatises covering a span of almost forty years (from 1678 to 1714), deals with the trill quite consistently with regard to design, less consistently with regard to terminology. In 1677 and 1696, he defines the *tremolo* as "a sharp trembling of the voice over a lengthy note touching the neighbor tone." The illustrations given in Exx. 28.9*a* and *b* show again the ever-recurring pattern of Praetorius's ascending and descending types, the latter again being a multiple mordent.[8] Each ascending figure probably ended on the main note:

which was difficult to notate metrically. The *Schneller* and its mirror image, the single mordent, are found under two guises: as *accentus* (Ex. *c*) and as *figura corta* (Ex. *d*); both are simple diminutions of a single note.[9] As a combination form of *tremolo* and *groppo*, Printz gives a main-note supported trill with turned ending (Ex. *e*).

a. Ascending *tremolo*

b. Descending *tremolo*

c. Accentus

d. Figura corta   *e. Groppo*

Ex. 28.9. Printz (1677, 1696)

8 *Phrynis*, II, ch. 9, pars. 13-18. The same patterns are shown in *Musica modulatoria*, p. 47, as well as (for quarter-note values) in the *Compendium*, ch. 5, par. 9.

9 Examples *d* and *e* are from the *Musica modulatoria*, pp. 45, 49-53, but occur in other treatises as well, e.g. in the *Compendium*, ch. 5, pars. 8 and 19.

Printz explains the (one-note) *trillo* as a "trembling of the voice in one pitch on a long note, with a somewhat sharp but pleasing and graceful articulation."[10] By contrast, the trembling of the *trilletto* is milder than that of the *trillo* and hardly articulated ("fast gar nicht angeschlagen wird"). Speaking of the "somewhat sharp" articulation of the *trillo*, Printz interestingly reveals actual tone repetition, whereas the *trilletto* which is "hardly articulated" leans to the vibrato effect. He thus confirms the dual staccato-legato style of execution mentioned before.

Falck in 1688 follows Praetorius with the *tremulus ascendens* and *descendens* (Exx. 28.10a and *b*), and with the *tremulo* and *groppo* of Ex. *c*. His *trillo in unisono* (Ex. *d*) "should flow mildly and gently from the throat and not sound like goats bleating" ("dass sie fein sanfft und lind aus dem Halse fliessen, und nicht, wie Gaisse mecklen, angestossen werden").[11]

Ex. 28.10. Falck (1688)

We find the same *tremulo* pair of main-note trill and multiple mordent with Feyertag in 1695, as shown in Exx. 28.11a and *b*.[12]

Feyertag's *tremoletti* are brief trills "which have to be done much faster than the *tremulo*." Their greater speed is indicated by the 32nd-values of Ex. *c*. Feyertag's *trillo* is still the tone repetition, defined as a "violent but graceful trembling and very fast wavering of the voice with a rather sharp articulation" which a pen cannot describe. It ends, he says, with a rising *accento* and, as the model (Ex. *d*) shows, also starts with one. Like Printz, he contrasts with the *trillo* a *trilletto* "with a very small wavering of the voice," the vibrato counterpart to tone repetition. Under *tremamento longo*, Feyertag shows a combination of various graces, notably one of a regular trill with a *trillo* (Ex. *e*).

Feyertag also presents the *Schneller*-(simple) mordent pair (Exx. *f* and *g*). He does so under the category of *accenti* and calls the *Schneller accentus circumflexo intendens*, the mordent *accentus circumflexo remittens* (p. 206).

Beyer, like Stierlein, reverses the terms *trillo* and *tremulo*. As seen in his illustrations (Ex. 28.12), the *trillo* is the main-note trill (*ascendens*) or the mordent (*descendens*), and the *tremulo* is the tone repetition.[13] Twenty-seven years later,

---

[10] Ibid., ch. 5, par. 22: "Trillo ist ein Zittern der Stimme in einer Clave über einer grossen Noten mit einem etwas scharffen, doch lieblichen und manierlichen Anschlagen."

[11] *Idea boni cantoris*, pp. 100-101, 103.
[12] *Syntaxis*, pp. 220-221.
[13] *Primae lineae* (1703), pp. 57ff.

Ex. 28.11. Feyertag (1695)

in 1730, Beyer still declares the *trillo ascendens*, i.e. the main-note trill, to be "the best and most agreeable" type but now adds that for *practice purposes only*, one should start with the upper note "whether it is written or not."[14] The limitation of this advice to practice use appears to imply the integrity of the original pattern for performance.

Ex. 28.12. Beyer (1703, 1730)

In 1703 Murschhauser still follows the traditional pattern of picturing the trill and mordent as each other's inversion. In his brief ornament table he transcribes the symbols as shown in Ex. 28.13.[15]

It is in the light of this traditional mirror-image dualism between the two trilled graces, the *tremulus ascendens* and *descendens*, that the verbal explanation

Ex. 28.13. Murschhauser (1703)

[14] Ibid. (1730), p. 36.   [15] *Prototypon*, pt. 1, Preface.

by Johann Adam Reinken in 1687, which was considered obscure by some, is fully clarified. This master wrote: "Should anyone be unaware of what is meant by the simple [symbol] × , he may know that it stands for a shake (*tremulus*) that touches [literally: hits] the note below: whereas the two dashes ‖ indicate a *tremulus* that touches the note above."[16] Clearly, the two types are each other's inversion and represent the longstanding dualism of main-note trill and multiple mordent.

Martin Heinrich Fuhrmann laments in his humorous way the disagreements among musicians whom he compares to Simson's horses who wanted to go off in different directions with their tails tied together. No one, he says, can find an accurate distinction between *trillo-trilletto* and *tremolo-tremoletto* that would meet with general agreement in Europe. Fuhrmann himself strikes out in a new direction with regard to terminology, though his designs are still the time honored ones we have met throughout the 17th century.[17]

His *trillo* (marked *tr*) is a main-note trill with a whole-step interval (Exx. 28.14*a* and *b*), the *trilletto* is the same grace with a half-step, as shown in Exx. *c* and *d*. The *tremolo* or *Mordant* (symbol: +) is defined as a trembling of the voice with the half-step under the note which is to be shaken. This definition clarifies the misprint in Ex. *e*: the half-note with the cross should be a d not a c sharp. (Adding to the confusion, the corresponding illustration in the 1715 treatise shows here a main-note trill instead of a mordent.) The *tremoletto*, finally, is the one-note shake, the "trembling of the voice in unison" illustrated in Ex. *f*. This grace is compared to the "tremolant register of the organ," and its essential vibrato character is revealed by a reference to the violin: "[the *tremoletto*] can be best demonstrated on the violin by leaving the finger on the string and shaking it a little and thus making the tone oscillate."[18] Fuhrmann also gives advice about where to apply unmarked trills and mentions, among others, dotted and syncopated notes, slow notes in the descant, and *penultima* and *antepenultima* in full and half-cadences (1715, p. 45).

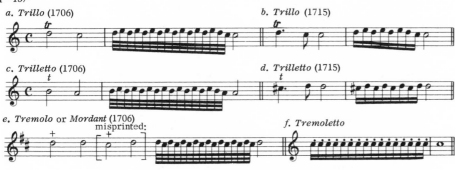

Ex. 28.14. Fuhrmann (1706, 1715)

Possibly the first German document that presents the appoggiatura trill is Johann Caspar Fischer's ornament table of 1696.[19] In it the French-oriented Fischer uses the French symbols and with them the trill model of Chambonnières and his followers, as shown in Ex. 28.15*a*. Johann Gottfried Walther in 1708, also

---

[16] *Hortus musicus*: "Si quis forte ignoraverit, quidnam simplex × sibi velit is sciat tremul.[um] significare, qui inferne tonum feriat: quemadmodum hae duae ‖ tremul. notant qui superne tonum contingit."

[17] The two treatises, which partly overlap, are the *Musicalischer Trichter* of 1706 and the *Musica vocalis* of 1715. They will again be dis-

tinguished by their dates; 1706, pp. 64-66; 1715, pp. 44-45.

[18] 1706, p. 66; 1715, p. 45: ". . . wie auf der Geige am besten zu zeigen, wenn man den Finger auf der Saite stehen lässt und selben doch mit Schütteln etwas bewegt und den Thon schwebend macht."

[19] *Musicalisches Blumen Büschlein.*

under French influence, presents the same trill pattern, for which he gives the symbols *t*, *tr*, and the *chevron*, as shown in Ex. 28.15*b*.[20]

Ex. 28.15.

This latter pattern, however, can hardly claim exclusivity for Walther, as will be presently seen in some musical evidence. But even his *Lexicon* of 1732 still reveals a plurality of trill designs. In the article s.v. *appuyé*, he defines this term as a trill that "is not started *ex abrupto* but prepared with the help of another tone."[21] This definition implies that a trill *ex abrupto* does not have the help of another tone for its start, hence, that it begins with the main note. Moreover, s.v. *tremolo*, he points to the double meaning of this term; it can stand for a trembling bowstroke over repeated notes, with the intent of imitating the *tremulant* effect of an organ; but it can also stand for a regular trill. For this latter meaning he quotes Printz and presents one of Printz's main-note trill patterns paired with the mordent (Ex. 28.16).

Ex. 28.16. Walther (1732, citing Printz), Table 22

The summary of the theoretical sources is rather straightforward. Dissensions have to do mostly with terms, not with the fundamental designs. There is throughout the 17th century and even beyond, a remarkable agreement about the main-note trill with or without support on the first note, with only the apparent exception of some of the *groppo* patterns that belong to a different category. With Fuhrmann and Printz this current can be traced to 1715. Also, we find until the end, the survival of the one-note oscillations. Not until we encounter the distinct French influx at the turn of the century do we meet—together with the French symbols—the first upper-note trill models. The musical evidence will underline the basic main-note character of the German trill during the whole period under consideration, with some qualifications only for its last few years.

[20] *Praecepta*, p. 38.
[21] *Lexicon*, s.v. *appuyé*: "wenn man ein *trillo* nicht *ex abrupto* anfängt, sondern vermittelst eines andern *Clavis*, erst die *praeparation* darzu machet."

The theoretical documents pointing to a near monopoly of the main-note trill during the 17th century are tellingly supported by evidence found in the music of German masters. Italian influences are easily traced with the two Frescobaldi students, Froberger and Kerll, who continue their teacher's manner of writing out in regular notes trills of a certain duration. Other German masters of the keyboard and in particular of the organ, among them Scherer, Lübeck, Pachelbel, and Buxtehude, adopted the same procedure. Evidently, these trills were written out to insure proper design and length, not metric regularity in the sense of Frescobaldi's above cited directives.

Froberger's keyboard works literally abound in main-note trills of different designs, with or without support, with or without suffix. Often they are written in complete regularity; other times an acceleration is indicated, as clearly as notation permitted it. We also find the *ribattuta* pattern of a dotted, invariably main-note anchored, start that glides into a trill; we find patterns of grace-note trills: main-note anchored with anticipated auxiliary; and only once in a long while do we find the appoggiatura trill.

Of the illustrations shown in Ex. 28.17, the first, Ex. *a*, represents the plain main-note trill; Ex. *b* a cadential main-note supported trill with indicated acceleration; Ex. *c* a main-note trill with suffix; Ex. *d* a *ribattuta*-prepared main-note trill with indicated acceleration and a transition from main-note to upper-note anchor; Ex. *e* a pattern that could be viewed as grace-note trill; Ex. *f* a short trill with anticipated auxiliary and suffix; Ex. *g* an interesting sequence of two main-note trills (the first introduced by *ribattuta*, the second upper-note anchored, starting with main-note suspension). Example *h* looks like an appoggiatura trill but can hardly be regarded as such because the upper note is consonant with the bass. It is not a trill, but a multiple mordent followed by a turn.[22]

Ex. 28.17. Froberger (c. 1645-1650)

[22] Froberger's examples are from *DTÖ*, IV, 1 (Ex. *a*); *DTÖ*, X, 2 (Exx. *b*, *c*); *Toccate, canzone, ricercate . . .* (Mainz, 1693) (Exx. *d*, *f*, *g*, *h*); BB Mus. MS 6711 (Ex. *e*).

Ex. 28.17 *cont.*

Main-note trills abound also in Johann Kaspar Kerll's (1627-1693) compositions. Moreover, in the many works that I examined, not a single appoggiatura
trill could be found.

A few characteristic illustrations are given in Ex. 28.18. Example *a* has one of this
master's favorite cadential formulas (Conforto's *mezzo groppo*) straight out of Frescobaldi's book. Example *b* shows a main-note supported and main-note anchored trill;
Ex. *c* a sequence of two main-note trills, both with suffix, the first plain, the second
with main-note support and upper-note anchor. Example *d* resorts to a tone repetition in

Ex. 28.18. Kerll (1627-1693)

order to start the trill with the main note; Ex. *e* is a cadential trill with indicated acceleration; Ex. *f* has a *ribattuta* start and a chain of two main-note trills for a cadence.[23]

A volume could be filled with similar illustrations, but only one more easily accessible example might be mentioned: the second toccata (*DTB*, II, 2), in which the last seventeen measures consist of an unbroken series of main-note trills.

We find analogous examples of main-note trills in the works of eminent organ masters from all parts of Germany—the north, the south, and the middle. They may occur with lesser density than with Froberger and Kerll, but they are frequent and not remotely approached by specimens of genuine appoggiatura trills.

Of the illustrations in Ex. 28.19, the first (Ex. *a*) from Vincent Lübeck (1654-1740) shows a supported, main-note trill; Ex. *b* from Johann Pachelbel (1653-1709) gives a simple main-note trill with suffix; Ex. *c* from Johann Speth (1664-1719) shows a cadential main-note trill. This master says in the preface to *Ars magna* that he leaves trills and other graces to the skill of the instructors and that only very few trills are actually marked. Example *d* from Georg Böhm (1661-1733) has a main-note trill, and Ex. *e* a main-note trill by Sebastian Anton Scherer (1631-1712); Ex. *f* gives one of this composer's occasional appoggiatura trills with suffix.[24]

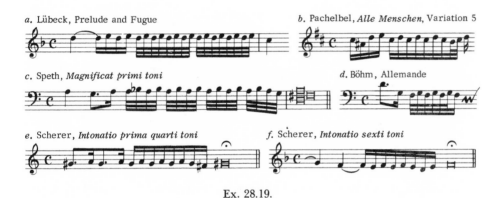

Ex. 28.19.

In Buxtehude, we find again frequent instances of written-out main-note trills as well as the usual near absence of the appoggiatura variety. As the musical evidence will show, the trill had an overwhelmingly main-note character for him.

Example 28.20*a* is of special interest because the instruction *trillo longo* (repeated later in the piece) provides additional proof that the written-out trill alternations were not meant to be taken on metrical face value; Ex. *b* has a main-note *ribattuta* pattern, and Ex. *c* a cadential main-note trill; Ex. *d* shows a main-note trill with *ribattuta* start and a wavy-line symbol at the beginning of the alternations, probably meant to underline their non-metrical execution.[25]

On occasion we find here, too, a design that looks at first glance like an appoggiatura trill but, e.g. in Ex. 28.21, turns out to be a multiple mordent with anticipated auxiliary, since the structural main note is the g sharp that is consonant

[23] Kerll's examples are from BB Mus. MS 40335 (Ex. *a*); Hintze MS, Yale (Ex. *b*); *DTB*, II, 2 (Ex. *c*); *Modulatio organica super Magnificat* . . . (Munich, 1668) (Exx. *d-f*).

[24] The illustrations are from Vincent Lübeck, *Musikalische Werke* (Klecken, 1921) (Ex. *a*); *DTB*, II, 1, *Hexacordum Apollonis* (Ex. *b*); *Ars magna consoni et dissoni* . . . (Augsburg,

1693) (Ex. *c*); *Möllersche Handschrift*, f. 39, also BB Mus. MS 2041/10 (Ex. *d*); Scherer, . . . *Tabulatura in cymbalo et organo* . . . (Ulm, 1664) (Exx. *e*, *f*).

[25] The illustrations of this example are from BB Mus. MS 2681/1, 2681, 2683 (Exx. *a*, *c*); BB Mus. MS 2684 (Ex. *b*); *Möllersche Handschrift* (Ex. *d*).

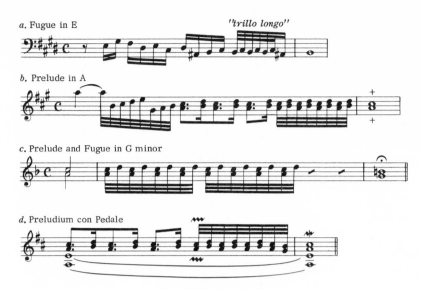

Ex. 28.20. Buxtehude

with the bass and not the f sharp that could hardly be conceived as the parent note of a trill.[26]

Ex. 28.21. Buxtehude, Prelude in F sharp minor

In many of Buxtehude's trills indicated by symbol, the placement of the auxiliary on the beat is excluded by objectionable parallels. A few specimens are given in Ex. 28.22 where such rendition would result in offensive parallel fifths (Exx. *a-d*) or octaves (Ex. *e*).[27]

Ex. 28.22. Buxtehude

[26] The illustrations are from *Orgelwerke*, ed. Spitta and Seiffert (Leipzig, 1903-1904).

[27] The illustrations are from *Orgelwerke*, ed. Spitta and Seiffert.

The French-derived start of the trill with the upper note was an entirely new fashion whose progress in Germany was gradual and spotty. It began to make inroads into the old main-note tradition, but the idea that at the start of the century it may have supplanted the latter in one stroke is completely unrealistic. Such happening would run counter to all historic and sociologic experience regarding the introduction and adoption of any innovation in any field. At this time, a composer had no reason to assume that the performer would interpret a trill symbol automatically in the French *keyboard* manner with the upper-note start. When the composer wished such a style for any of his trills, he needed to indicate it with the help of the equally new *Vorschlag* symbols. Therefore, if we encounter, say, with Walther, the combination of  or it may, and often does, stand simply for an unsupported upper-note start on or before the beat.

When Walther writes such *Vorschlag*, for instance in Ex. 28.23, the obvious need to synchronize the two trills on the dotted 8th-note leaves no simpler interpretation for the single *Vorschlag* in the upper voice than its anticipation and a main-note start for the lower trill.

Ex. 28.23. Walther, Chorale Prelude No. 82

If this example suggests the occasional main-note character of Walther's trills that are *not* preceded by a *Vorschlag* symbol, other contexts favor the same design. In the passage given in Ex. 28.24a, the trills occur in stepwise descent, the mordents in stepwise ascent. Considering that the contexts of one are the inversions of the other, both musical function and melodic logic will suggest the mutual mirror image of the two types in conformance with the dualistic tradition of the *tremulus ascendens* and *descendens*. Thus, if the single mordent design is used, the trill ought to be a *Schneller*. If the mordent can accommodate two or more alternations, the trill will do likewise.

In Ex. *b* we find in the second measure an indicated main-note trill that is slightly anticipated. The first measure, incidentally, offers another mirror-image situation where the main-note trill clarifies the melodic progression which an appoggiatura trill would obscure.[28]

a. Chorale Prelude No. 7, Verse 5
(Middle voice:)

b. Chorale Prelude No. 57, Verse 1

Ex. 28.24. Walther

As mentioned, Walther frequently uses the French combination symbol (, or when written below the note) which in France stood for a trill followed by a turn. Max Seiffert, who edited Walther's works for the *DDT*, claims that the symbol stands for a

[28] The illustrations are from *DDT*, I, 26/27.

main-note trill, but he does not substantiate this assertion.[29] It is unlikely that the meaning of Walther's symbol should have had no reference to its turn sign. There are, however, some puzzling instances, of which Ex. 28.25 gives two specimens, where this compound symbol is followed by a two-note suffix that would conflict with the original French

Ex. 28.25. Walther, Chorale Prelude No. 88

trill-plus-turn meaning. This incongruence may be due to inadvertence (only these two cases could be found), or else Walther may have used the symbol in the reverse order of a trill preceded by, instead of followed by, a turn. For this design Walther never used Bach's symbol: ⟨w .

It is no coincidence that so far all our illustrations have been taken from organists. Following an Italian tradition that goes back well beyond Frescobaldi to keyboard masters of the 16th century, most German organists were quite explicit in writing out florid ornamental figurations, including lengthy trill patterns. Occasionally we do find spelled-out main-note trills outside of the keyboard. An illustration is given in Ex. 28.26 from Graupner's opera *Dido* of 1707, where we find such trills throughout the same aria.[30]

Ex. 28.26. Graupner, *Dido*, aria Menalippe

Other designs certainly occurred, though they may not have left any visible traces in a period of fragmentary ornament notation. Yet once in a while one catches an interesting glimpse of such occurrences. Among them is a passage from the violinist Johann Jacob Walther (Ex. 28.27) where grace-note trills are unmistakably spelled out.[31]

Ex. 28.27. Johann Jacob Walther (1688), *Hortus Chelicus*

In some of Keiser's operas, indications abound of presumable grace-note trills. In the autograph of *Arsinoë* of 1710, for instance, we find the interesting trills of Ex. 28.28. Here too the upper-note start needed to be specified where desired. The two- or three-flagged little notes, interchangeably written, most likely suggest grace notes, rather than appoggiaturas.

Ex. 28.28. Keiser, *Arsinoë*, III, 2 (aut.), Aria con 2 Bassoni

29 Ibid., p. xxii.
30 Aut., BB Mus. MS Graupner autograph.
31 *Hortus Chelicus*, BB Mus. MS 22545.

MUSICAL EVIDENCE fully bears out the century-long theoretical agreement, from Praetorius to Fuhrmann, by demonstrating that in Germany the main-note start of the trill was by far the most commonly used design from Froberger and Kerll to Reinken, Murschhauser, and Buxtehude.

Not until about 1700 do we find the first indications of the upper-note trill in theory and its spreading fashion in practice. The progress of the new French upper-note trill types, which certainly included the grace-note and the anticipated trills, varied considerably from case to case, depending no doubt on the individual's contact and responsiveness to French performance styles.

Toward the end of the period, i.e. around 1715, the very recency of the clash between the long-established Italian and the freshly imported French procedures makes it more unreasonable than perhaps at any other time to try to postulate general rules about the rendition of the trill in Germany. It is far more realistic to assume that composers and performers who had old and new models to choose from (which by now in their combination included practically all known trill designs) helped themselves freely to what suited their purpose and fancy.

———— ◆◆◆ ————

Bach's trills must be viewed against the background of the practices he encountered in the earliest years of the 18th century. The salient environmental factor at that period was the coexistence and interpenetration of the old but still vigorous Italo-German main-note tradition with the wide spectrum of the newly introduced French models that included the full range of upper-note trills—from appoggiatura types through the grace-note design to full anticipation—as well as a substantial element of main-note trills, primarily from the media of the voice and the melody instruments.

In view of this situation alone, the prevalent modern doctrine which limits Bach's trills to the appoggiatura species, usually to one with continued upper-note emphasis, becomes highly suspect. Here too it is unrealistic to assume that Bach, in an environment offering the richness of a wide choice, would have confined himself to the poverty of a single design that is utterly inadequate to meet the needs of his infinitely varied musical contexts.

Again, much modern doctrine has fallen victim to the easy lure of the mid-18th-century "downstream" sources, combined with a far too literal interpretation of Bach's own ornament table, the previously discussed *Explication*. By contrast, it will be found that the expectations raised by the environmental factors favoring a much wider freedom of trill designs are borne out by musical evidence.

MODERN DOCTRINE

Modern doctrine about baroque trills in general, and Bach's trills in particular, is epitomized in this passage from Robert Donington: "The baroque trill proper is a harmonic ornament, and consequently starts, in all standard cases, from its upper (accessory) note, well accented to mark the ensuing modification of the harmony, and often to a greater or lesser extent prolonged so as to give this modification still greater prominence."[1] It should be noted that when modern writers speak of the trill's start with the upper note, they take it for granted that this start takes place *on* the beat, since none of them considered the possibility of a prebeat start. Arnold Dolmetsch, after presenting the upper-note-on-the-beat rule, says of Bach: "It is impossible, therefore, to justify any exception about the execution of shakes or other ornaments in his music."[2] For Putnam Aldrich, the upper-note start is part of any 18th-century trill's essence; it would not be a trill without it: ". . . it is certain, not because of any rule, but by definition, that the trill always begins with the note above the main note. . . ."[3] More specifically, speaking of Bach's organ trills, he says, "the truth is simpler than fiction; there are *no* exceptions, in Bach's music, to the rule that the trill begins with the note above the written note."[4] Ralph Kirkpatrick expressed his full agreement: "it cannot be too emphatically stated that the Bach trill *always begins with the upper* note . . . ," and adding later: "it should be noticed that the eighteenth century trill, beginning upon the upper auxiliary note, has an appoggiatura character in the accentuation of the dissonance which gives it quite

1 Donington, p. 239. The New Version adds: "The start takes the beat."

2 Dolmetsch, p. 168.

3 "On the Interpretation of Bach's Trills," p. 298.

4 Aldrich, *Ornamentation in J. S. Bach's Organ Works*, p. 32.

a different sense from the modern trill, which begins on the lower main note and has only the weaker character of a changing note."[5]

The same principle is endorsed by many other writers and implemented by many performing artists. Though practically all writers accept the auxiliary-on-the-beat rule as a basic law, not all of them recognize its sweeping claim that brooks no exception. Interestingly, we find more liberal attitudes among the older researchers. Beyschlag in 1908 may be actually the only important author who flatly denied that the rule had to apply to Bach.[6] Before him, Dannreuther (in 1889)—who *did* believe in the rule—nevertheless listed for Bach the following contexts in which the trill starts with the main note instead of with the auxiliary: 1) when the trill starts *ex abrupto*; 2) after a staccato note or after a rest; 3) on a repeated note when the repetition is thematic; 4) when the melody skips and the trill is part of a characteristic interval; 5) when melodic or harmonic outlines would be blurred, in particular where the movement of the bass would be weakened by the starting auxiliary; 6) whenever an appoggiatura from above would be out of place (Dannreuther credits Franz Kross with the formulation of this principle).[7] Dannreuther's exceptions were criticized by many writers, among them by Wanda Landowska who argued that Bach could not have been "so cruel" as to leave his performers in agonizing uncertainty about the rendition of the trill which would then cease to be an *agrément* and turn into "a trap" and "an ambush."[8]

Among recent researchers, Walter Emery affirms the rule for "the vast majority of Bach's plain shakes."[9] He counters Dannreuther's principle that the trill must not blur the harmonic or melodic outline by saying that the outlines were meant to be blurred (p. 42). Erwin Bodky believes in the rule and sees exceptions only as a makeshift where unpleasant parallels ought to be avoided.[10] Hermann Keller adopts two of Dannreuther's exceptions: main-note start for freely entering trills, and for characteristic intervals. He then adds his own exceptions: trills on organ-points in the bass, and the cases where tone repetition would result, i.e. where the trill is preceded by its upper neighbor.[11] Alfred Kreutz agrees with Dannreuther in calling for main-note support to avoid the blurring of characteristic intervals, and he adds long-held notes and organ-points.[12]

In spite of the exceptions and qualifications listed by a number of writers, there is no denying that the orthodox school, with its insistence on the onbeat-auxiliary rule, has made by far the stronger impact on today's Bach performance.

Written-Out Trills

Bach does not write out extended trills in regular notes in the manner of Kerll and Buxtehude. Once in a while we do find an exception when he either wanted to be more specific about the design, as was apparently the case in the passage from the Violin Sonata in E minor shown in Ex. 29.1*a* with its slightly supported main-note trill, or when he tried with the limited notational means at his disposal to convey the idea of a slow start and gradual acceleration by writing out the start of a trill in relatively longer note values followed by the trill symbol. This procedure is shown in Ex. *b* for the main-note trill of the Dorian Toccata; in Ex. *c* for the alto aria in Cantata 69; in Ex. *d* for the main-note supported trill from the Cello Suite in C major; and in Ex. *e* for a grace-note trill from the *praeludium & fuga pedaliter*, played unaccompanied at the start of a rhapsodic postlude to the fugue.

[5] Preface to edition of the *Goldberg Variations* (New York, 1938), pp. xiii and xiv.
[6] Beyschlag, p. 129.
[7] Dannreuther, I, 165-166.
[8] "Bach und die französische Klaviermusik,"
p. 43.
[9] Emery, p. 38.
[10] Bodky, pp. 150ff.
[11] *Die Klavierwerke Bachs*, p. 34.
[12] Kreutz, p. 6.

Ex. 29.1.

Shorter trill patterns are very frequently spelled out, such as the *Schneller* in Cantatas 208 (Ex. 29.2), 63,7, or 125,3.

Ex. 29.2. BWV 208, 2

SYMBOLS

In Bach's *Explication*, his much quoted ornament table,[13] we find, as shown in Ex. 29.3, the following trill symbols (excluding those for the compound trills that will be discussed later): Ex. *a*, the two-waggle *chevron* for the plain trill (*trillo*); Ex. *b*, the combination of *chevron* and mordent for the trill with suffix (*trillo und mordant*); Ex. *c*, the combination of hook and *chevron* for the supported appoggiatura trill (*accent und trillo*), and a synonymous symbol (Ex. *d*), in which the *chevron* is started by a longer vertical stroke.

These are all strictly keyboard symbols of French origin which Bach never used for other media except by rare oversight.[14] When he intentionally used a wavy line for the voice or melody instruments, it was usually a fairly long one that indicated not a trill but a vibrato (as will be shown in Chapter 45).

---

[13] See above ch. 16, Ex. 16.5.

[14] For examples of obvious oversight see, for instance, the Flute-Harpsichord Sonata in B minor (BWV 1030), first movement, m. 84 (aut. P 975) where Bach, following the keyboard pattern of mm. 82-83, used for the flute imitation the identical symbol. A few similar spots can be found also in the Flute-Continuo Sonata (BWV 1034). The exclusive use of the *chevron* for the trills in Cantata 106 has no evidence value, since the earliest source for this very early work (c. 1707) dates from 1768 (P 1018).

Ex. 29.3. *Explication*

The number of waggles in the *chevron* is only an incomplete indication of the trill's length. Whereas an extended wavy line of three or more waggles will usually denote a trill of some length, the short symbol of one and a half or two waggles, contrary to widespread belief, is not indicative of a very short trill only. It may also stand for a multialternation trill, as the *Explication* shows in Ex. *a,* and sometimes for a very long one (for instance, the unquestionably sustained two-measure trills in the G major Two-Part Invention, mm. 20, 22, and 24 which in the autograph [P 610] are marked with two waggles only). In writing the wavy line, Bach most often started from above with a downstroke; and if once in a while this downstroke was a little heavier than usual, it then becomes possible to confuse it with the symbol ⌐ for the *accent und trillo.*

In addition to all these exclusive keyboard symbols, Bach uses for all media, including the keyboard, the letter *t* either by itself or with an added stroke, a fragmentary *r*: ᵗ . Bach never indicates chromatic alterations of the auxiliary for any of his trill symbols; he relies on the performer's judgment in making the proper choice.

To indicate a lengthy trill, Bach will sometimes extend the ᵗ into a wavy line ᵗⱳ, as shown below in Ex. 29.15*a.* On other, very rare, occasions he combines the *t* symbol with a mordent to indicate a suffix as counterpart to the *trillo und mordant* of the keyboard: ᵗⱳ , as shown below in Ex. 29.16*c.* Once in a while he combines the *t* symbol with a slur sign ᵗ⌐when the trill is over a written-out appoggiatura that slurs with its resolution (see Ex. 29.4).

Ex. 29.4. BWV 1027, 2 (aut. P 226)

MULTIPLE DESIGNS

In our analysis of Bach's trills, the first effort will be to show that the monopoly of the onbeat-auxiliary rule (hereafter simply referred to as "the rule") cannot be justified.

In the following examples the execution of the trill according to the rule would produce extremely objectionable parallels. The passages given in Ex. 29.5 are from the Two-Part Inventions. By applying the rule for the trills, we would produce octaves in Ex. *a,* unison in Ex. *b,* and fifths in Ex. *c,* a situation aggravated by the openness of two part writing.

In all these cases the incongruousness of voice-leading would be topped by an

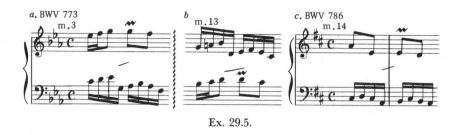

Ex. 29.5.

incongruousness of harmonic relationships. In these examples we recognize the characteristic "sigh motive": a written-out appoggiatura, prepared on the upbeat, creating a dissonance on the downbeat, and resolving to the tone below. A trill on the appoggiatura, performed according to the rule, would place a second appoggiatura on top of the first. The musical illogic of such procedure was discussed above for a situation where a *Vorschlag* symbol preceded the appoggiatura, and the argument need not be repeated here. Quantz, as will be remembered, spelled out the musically logical need for grace-note anticipation in such a context. The same reasoning applies to a trill that is to add brilliance to the appoggiatura, not emasculate it. Consequently, the main note of the trill which *is* the appoggiatura must sound on the beat. This requirement leaves three possible solutions for the trill: 1) a main-note trill with or without support; 2) a grace-note trill; 3) a fully anticipated trill. In Ex. 29.6 these three possibilities are demonstrated for the first passage of the preceding Ex. 29.5.

Ex. 29.6.

In the passages of Ex. 29.5, anticipation of the whole trill is, on the single keyboard for which it was intended, the more readily playable solution for Ex. *b*; in Exx. *a* and *c*, the grace-note trill may be the most attractive interpretation.

For the F minor Prelude (*WC* II), which is pervaded by the sigh motive, the autograph is unfortunately missing. The *BG* edition has no trills; however, the important Altnikol manuscript of 1744 has trill signs at the start (Ex. 29.7*a*) as well as in mm. 13 and 14 (Ex. *b*). In m. 13 the worst kind of fifths would result from applying the rule.[15]

Ex. 29.7. BWV 881 (P 430, Altnikol 1744)

[15] See also Cantata 93,6, mm. 2 and 31; Cantata 147,9, mm. 5 and 6; Flute Sonata in   B minor (BWV 1030,1), m. 36 (trill on a").

In Ex. 29.8 from Cantata 206, onbeat auxiliaries in the flutes would produce questionable clashes with the ornamented unison figuration of the violins.

Ex. 29.8. BWV 206, 1 (St 80)

In the F sharp major Fugue (*WC* II), several instances occur (in mm. 24, 25, 26, 73, and 75) where a similar trilled appoggiatura would yield parallels of different degrees of offensiveness, but the ones in m. 24 (Ex. 29.9*a*) would sound particularly unpleasant. Example *b* from the F minor Prelude (*WC* II) shows two cases of open fifths as results of onbeat auxiliaries. Here, in view of the involved leaps, a main-note start, perhaps with a slight dwelling on the first note, might be the best solution. However, regardless of the demands of correct voice-leading, harmonic logic alone requires for all occurrences of the sigh motive the same tripartite solution, provided we have to do with a genuine appoggiatura. Where such an appoggiatura is prepared on the same pitch, a grace-note trill will often be preferable, e.g. in the Gamba-Clavier Sonata in G, mm. 2 and 3, as shown in the above Ex. 29.4.

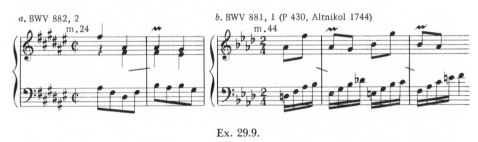

Ex. 29.9.

The next illustrations show cases other than the sigh motive where the rule is compromised by faulty voice-leading. The trill in the theme of the D minor Fugue (*WC* I) cannot be of the appoggiatura type because as such it would produce obtrusive fifths in mm. 12 and 22, as shown in Exx. 29.10*a* and *b*. The leap of the third might suggest the *tierces coulées* of an anticipated auxiliary, but the ever-recurring autograph dot over the quarter-note preceding the trill indicates an intended angularity of contour which probably favors a clear-cut main-note start of the trill. In Ex. *c* from the *Canonic Variations*, the first trill would form parallel octaves with the middle voice, the second trill parallel octaves with the bass. In Ex. *d* from the *Goldberg Variations*, the open fifths of the onbeat auxiliary between the two upper voices could hardly have been intended. Some editors have assumed an error and arbitrarily changed the simple trill symbol into one for a compound trill: ⟨⟨⟨. No error is involved; a grace-note trill solves the problem.

Ex. 29.10.

In the Chorale Prelude *Liebster Jesu*, two objectionable fifths would result in the passage of Ex. 29.11a; one between the two upper voices, the other between the second and third voice. The same passage is repeated exactly in mm. 9 and 10 and occurs, slightly varied but with the same parallels, in the version of BWV 634. Main-note or grace-note trills are indicated here, but whatever is chosen would have to be used consistently for all the trills in this piece since it is written throughout as canon in the fifth.

In Ex. *b* from *Nun danket Alle Gott*—one of the "18 Chorales," dating from Bach's last years and extant in autograph (P 271)—application of the rule would result in fifths for the trill in the second voice. Since the voices are in imitation, the rule is excluded for the first trill as well. The tone repetition of the trilled note is thematic in the chorale melody, and a good case can be made in Dannreuther's sense for a main-note start.

Ex. 29.11.

In Ex. 29.12a from the Capriccio in E major, a grace-note trill is probably preferable to a main-note trill in a passage where two-part writing would magnify the effect of open octaves. As will be seen presently, Erwin Bodky found three more cases of such rule-derived parallels in the same piece.

In Ex. *b* from the second movement of the first Gamba-Clavier Sonata, open octaves would result on the harpsichord; and in Ex. *c* from the first movement of the same work, the rule seems to be disqualified even for a cadential trill by the fifths between the two melody parts. In Ex. *d* from Cantata 63, a grace-note trill in the oboe will avoid an unpleasant unison in adagio.

Erwin Bodky offers in a "Trill Table" (pp. 375-377) no less than 24 examples of objectionable keyboard parallels produced by the rule. Since he was not aware

Ex. 29.12.

of the grace-note trill, these examples proved to him only the need for the occasional main-note start. A select few of Bodky's examples are shown in Ex. 29.13.[16]

Ex. 29.13. Excerpts from Bodky's "Trill Table"

MAIN-NOTE START

In the following paragraphs, examples will be shown where the start with the main note is either specified, or implied, or suggested for musical or technical considerations.

There are many cases where the notation clearly indicates that the main note should be sustained before the start of the alternations. We find such indications,

---

[16] They are taken from the Concerto for Two Claviers in C (Ex. *a*); the 1st French Suite (Ex. *b*); the Capriccio in E (Exx. *c-e*); the Organ Trio in D minor (Exx. *f* and *g*).

for instance, with ties, when the trill symbol is placed only on the second of the tied notes:

A very early specimen of this style is shown in Ex. 29.14*a* from the Chorale Variation *Sei gegrüsset* where the trill continues and intensifies the preceding note. Similar is the case of Ex. *b* from the Gamba-Clavier Sonata in G where the trill on the harpsichord sustains a sound that would otherwise have died out.

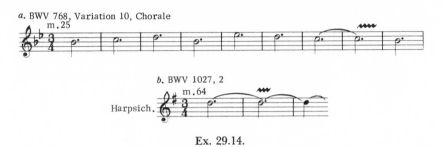

Ex. 29.14.

Certainly the trills in such cases must be anchored on the main note to avoid breaking the intended continuity, and for the same reason the alternations should start unobtrusively. The best means of achieving this effect would be to take 1) the auxiliary alone, or 2) the first complete alternation *before* the beat, or 3) to start shortly *after* the beat (the little notes in anticipation):

The need for main-note anchor is further underlined in such cases as shown in Ex. 29.15*a* from Cantata 42 where the main note of the trill is dissonant with the bass and has by itself appoggiatura function.[17]

When a trill tied to a main-note preparation is very short, as for instance in Exx. *b* and *c* from Cantatas 42 and 84, the grace-note type would seem to fit best, because the onbeat placement of the main note is necessary to secure the meaning of the tie that is to continue the sound into the trill.[18]

There are cases of dotted notes where Bach writes the trill symbol over the dot which itself is placed purposefully far away from the principal note. This indicates that the main note is first to be sounded alone and that the trill should be started with the dot—a classical case of a "supported main-note trill." In the autograph score of Cantata 102 (P 97) we find such a dot aligned, in the manner of the French, with the corresponding 16th-note of the bass, as shown in Ex. 29.16*a*. The same notational pattern occurs in "Cum Sancto Spiritu" from the *A major Mass* (the Darmstadt autograph) where it is repeated for several similar entrances of the theme in both tutti and solo passages (Ex. *b*). A similar case is that of Ex. *c* from Cantata 208 where the substantial shift of the symbol for the trill with suffix indicates an analogous intention.

[17] The same pattern recurs three measures later. These examples bring to mind the French practice of sustaining the main note in long trills for the first half of the note's duration and shaking only the second half.

[18] See also Cantata 97,7, mm. 15 and 75, and the Organ Chorale *Nun danket alle Gott* (BWV 657), m. 23.

Ex. 29.15.

Ex. 29.16.

Earlier in the chapter, passages were quoted in which a main-note trill was either written out (Ex. 29.1a) or the slow start of such a trill was spelled out and its faster continuation indicated by symbol. Of the passages given in Ex. 29.1, two (Exx. b and d) show a regular main-note trill, and one (Ex. c) a main-note supported trill; all of them have main-note anchor.

Moreover, there are many contexts where main-note start and anchor are dictated by musical logic. The purely linear-melodic character of certain trills often determines their main-note start. When a trill is used to sustain the sound of a note, be it as organ-point in the bass or in melody parts, it is that very main note that needs to be emphasized. Emphasis on the auxiliary in such contexts would make no sense because the resulting appoggiatura effect would falsify both harmony and melody. In many cases the best way to execute such lengthy trills will be to sound the main note alone for a while before starting the shake proper.

We find a characteristic example of trills whose purpose is to sustain the short-lived harpsichord tone in the G minor Prelude (*WC* I) with its long trills in mm. 1, 3, 7, and 9 (Ex. 29.17a). Franz Kroll in his *BG* edition of 1866 had already pointed out that "it is not to be assumed that the trills on such long held out notes ought to start with the auxiliary according to the general rule."[19] Cogent melodic reasons require a main-note start as well for the second trill in m. 3. The second measure introduces an important four-note motive, a species of a prebeat turn:  that pervades a good part of the prelude, with its thrust toward the fourth accented note as indicated in Ex. *b* by brackets. Melodic logic demands that on its fourth appearance in this measure, as in all its other occurrences in the piece, it maintain its motivic integrity by ending on the beat with the g′, i.e. with the main note of the trill (as shown in Ex. *c*), not with the auxiliary. In mm. 7 and 11 where the trill is in the bass, the need to stress the main note is still more vital; a pervading stress on the auxiliary would be incongruous, and even an appoggiatura start would be both melodically and harmonically pointless.

Ex. 29.17. BWV 861

Significant confirmation for the main-note anchor of Bach's long-held trills is contained in a copy of the Two-Part Inventions made in 1725 by Heinrich Nicolaus Gerber, Bach's devoted student. At the end of the E minor Invention, Gerber wrote out the ornamentation for m. 9. Example 29.18 shows on the top line the context of the measure according to the autograph (P 610) and Gerber's version on the line below.[20] The latter version reveals the main-note anchor of the continuous trill and shows, surprisingly, main-note anchor even for the cadential trill on c sharp.

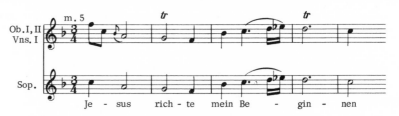

Ex. 29.18. BWV 778 (aut. P 610)

Example 29.19 from the *Christmas Oratorio* shows the purely melodic character of the two instrumental trills. Oboes and 1st violins add a *Vorschlag* and two trills to the chorale melody which is sung unadorned by the soprano; that the trill serves only to light up the main note and to underscore the linearity seems obvious.

Ob. I, II
Vns. I

Sop.

Je - sus rich - te mein Be - gin - nen

Ex. 29.19. BWV 248, 42, Chorale

[19] *BG*, XIV, 230. [20] Quoted by Landshoff, p. 69.

Bach's fugue themes are paragons of linearity which carry the whole fugue forward by their horizontal impulse. A "harmonic" trill is consequently misplaced in a fugue theme, where on its initial announcement there is no harmony to be enriched; in the answer and in all later appearances there is counterpoint to be disturbed by an emphasis on a note that is not part of the linear design.

In the D minor Fugue (*WC* I), the mistake of a "harmonic" rendition of the trill happens to be provable through the ensuing noxious parallels shown above in Ex. 29.10.

A famous example is the theme of the F sharp major Fugue (*WC* II) which starts with a trill on the leading tone (Ex. 29.20a). To start with the tonic as a would-be appoggiatura instead of the leading tone would destroy the suspense and the impulse toward the tonic. Dannreuther, Beyschlag, Keller, and Bodky all agree that main-note start is a necessity here.[21] Moreover, Bodky points out that in mm. 20 and 70 we encounter a stylized written-out form of this trill which clarifies the main-note start with its emphasis on the leading tone (see Exx. *b* and *c*).

Ex. 29.20. BWV 882, 2

Linear primacy is also logical when trills occur in a chromatic melody, whether singly or in chains. A chromatic progression has a sharply defined contour that is extremely vulnerable to the slightest alteration. Therefore, a trill within such a progression must not distort this contour. Thus, if we encounter a chromatically ascending trill, such as the one shown in Ex. 29.21a from the 2nd Organ Sonata, or a descending one like that given in Ex. *b* from the Gamba-Clavier Sonata in G, main-note start will be advisable—preferably with an ever so slight lingering on the first note to underscore the melodic line.

Ex. 29.21.

In a descending diatonic trill chain of the kind found in the second movement of the 4th Organ Sonata (Ex. 29.22a) or in the *Trio super Allein Gott in der Höh* (Ex. *b*), a main-note trill will be the best choice because it alone can at the same time embellish and clarify the melodic line. Dannreuther's principle upholding the clarity of the melodic line would seem to apply fully here. In Ex. *b*, main-note trills are needed because the sequence of suspensions and resolutions, with the dissonances on the first and third beats, requires for rhythmic-harmonic reasons the entrance of the resolutions exactly on the second and fourth beats.

[21] Dannreuther, I, 165; Beyschlag, p. 130; Keller, *Klavierwerke*, p. 235; Bodky, p. 158.

Appoggiatura trills stressing the upper note throughout would make harmonic nonsense out of the interplay of the two upper parts by forming, instead of the pattern of Ex. *c*, that of Ex. *d*.

Ex. 29.22.

Many are the cases where a trill follows its upper neighbor under a slur. If this upper neighbor happens to be a written-out appoggiatura, we have to do with the *tremblement lié* design that will be dealt with later. For the time being, we are concerned with an upper neighbor which is not an appoggiatura and does not fall on the heavy beat. This specific context is illustrated in Ex. 29.23 (Ex. *a* is from the Sonata in G minor for Unaccompanied Violin, Ex. *b* from Cantata 63).

In these cases and in countless others of a similar nature, a repetition of the preceding note for the rule's sake would be patently redundant—and often technically impracticable—besides breaking the slur intended by the composer. Main-note start is the obvious solution.

In the Chorale Prelude *Das alte Jahr*, there is a succession of two trills clearly marked in the autograph, as given in Ex. *c*. However the first of these trills is rendered, the second one has to be a main-note trill.

Ex. 29.23.

If no slur is written, the case is less clear-cut. Bach's original keyboard music (excepting transcriptions from other media) is almost entirely devoid of articulation marks. Even in the other media, which generally have more articulation markings, not all intended slurs are written; hence their absence per se is no proof of detached articulation. Therefore, whenever a trill follows its upper neighbor and a slur seems obviously intended, then main-note start is clearly desirable. Example 29.24a from the 3rd Partita and Ex. *b* from the D minor Organ Toccata provide good illustrations for such missing but intended slurs. (The first of these examples was one of Dannreuther's illustrations for main-note start.)

Interesting also is the case of Ex. *c* from the Chorale Prelude *O Mensch*. In the upper voice with its two trills a slur is implied at least for the syncopated figure of the first trill and its two neighbor notes. The note preceding the first trill, which spells out a quasi-appoggiatura, implies that the symbol itself stands for a main-note trill. The second trill is certainly not a replica of the first one with its written-out onbeat auxiliary. For the second trill there is again hardly a satisfactory alternative to main-note start.

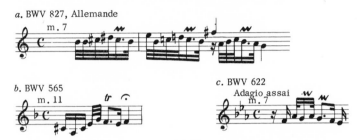

Ex. 29.24.

Where detached articulation from the preceding upper neighbor is likely or at least possible, the trill may be accessible to various designs. For instance, in Ex. 29.25 from the 1st Organ Sonata, the energetic concerto style of the movement favors an angularity of contour, hence detached articulation. Any trill type seems to be satisfactory here.

Ex. 29.25. BWV 525, 1

Other important clues can be derived from the nature and technique of an instrument. In Ex. 29.26a from the Sonata in D minor for Unaccompanied Violin, the only technically rational execution not involving anachronistic contortions is one that starts with the main note, which is sustained long enough to establish the idea of the g' as a held note, then uses the third finger after its release for the alternations. Example *b* from the same work is analogous, and the approximate rendition of both passages is sketched in Exx. *c* and *d*. (Today one might, in Ex. *a*, hold the g' with the third finger and trill with the fourth, but such Paganinian fingerings were not current in Bach's time.)

Ex. 29.26.

Similar spots are shown in Exx. 29.27*a* and *b* from the Suites in G major and D minor for Unaccompanied Violincello where the solutions suggested under Exx. *c* and *d* are the ones which Bach most likely had in mind. Nothing better proves the point made here than the outlandish acrobatics to which a famous modern editor resorts many times over to honor the alleged rule; his fingerings for Ex. *b* are given in Ex. *e*.

Ex. 29.27.

A main-note trill will also be desirable whenever harmonic logic calls for the entrance of the main note exactly on the beat. An illustration of this is presented in Ex. 29.28 from the F minor Fugue (*WC* I); during a tie in another voice, the trill alone articulates the beat, in the process changing a consonance into a dissonance. In this situation only a clear entrance of the g in the tenor *on* the beat, preferably slightly held, can clarify the harmonic-rhythmic scheme of the passage.[22]

Ex. 29.28. BWV 857, 2

Whenever a main-note trill is appropriate, and there is neither time nor need for more than one alternation, the *Schneller* can be used. A good illustration is

[22] Emery in "Is your Bach playing authentic—I," pp. 485-487, gives two examples where he says main-note start is required. One occurs in *Goldberg Variation* No. 12, which is a canon by inversion and where the trill in m. 29 has to be the mirror image of the mordent in m. 30. The other is in the Fugue from the C major Organ Toccata, m. 71, where an appoggiatura trill would form fifths with the alto and octaves with the tenor. Emery's first example is conclusive; his second one clearly disqualifies the appoggiatura trill, but a grace-note trill would be an alternative to the main-note type.

For other unquestionable cases of main-note trills, see below in ch. 38 the Emery-Kreutz argument regarding the Gigue of the 6th English Suite, illustrated in Ex. 38.4, as well as the three pairs of mirror-image trills and mordents in the two-voice canon in contrary motion from the *Musical Offering*.

the passage from the Organ Chorale *Christ lag* shown in Ex. 29.29*a*. At the start of this same chorale (Ex. *b*), the need for a *Schneller* is still more evident. Here the mordent and the trill are clearly used in their traditional counterparts as each other's inversion: the mordent when approached from below, the trill when reached on the same pitch or when approached from above. Inasmuch as there is hardly time for multiple alternations of either grace, the trill has to be a *Schneller*. Since both trill and mordent can on occasion be anticipated, this happens to be an auspicious occasion for such a design, since onbeat execution would obscure both rhythm and meter. Because the organ cannot counteract the weight of the graces on the offbeat by accents on the main beats, the meter cannot be understood and the ear perceives:

By contrast, the rendition suggested in Ex. *c* will not only easily absorb the multitude of graces but clarify the basic rhythmic design.

Ex. 29.29. BWV 718

THE GRACE-NOTE TRILL

Earlier in this chapter a few Bach excerpts were shown where this same prebeat design comes to the rescue for problems created by the school solutions.

Strangely enough, modern researchers have so far completely overlooked this important trill design. Only Dannreuther, with his remarkable musical instinct, though ignoring the principle in theory, acknowledged it in practice through a few well-chosen musical illustrations.[23] Some of the latter are shown in Ex. 29.30.

All these illustrations by Dannreuther can be unconditionally endorsed. In Ex. *a* from the 1st Partita, appoggiaturas on 32nd-notes in the weak part of the measure would make little sense. Beyschlag proposed here *Schneller*,[24] which fit very well, though Dannreuther's solution is just as good. Example *b* from the E flat Flute Sonata and Ex. *c* from the 3rd Partita shows similar cases where the trill occurs on a tone repetition. As always, each case has to be judged individually, but generally, tone repetition will favor grace-note use.

Dannreuther's Ex. *d* from the 2nd Violin-Harpsichord Sonata is also a felicitous choice. The trill occurs in the setting of a strict canon where the insertion of an appoggiatura would be improvident and also melodically untoward with its stress on the f sharp that precedes and immediately follows again. The unobtrusive grace note creates no redundancy and smoothens the connection.

[23] Dannreuther, I, 171.   [24] Beyschlag, p. 131.

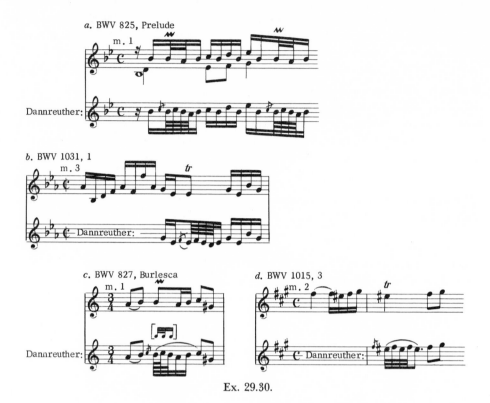

Ex. 29.30.

A fifth example of Dannreuther's, not reproduced here, shows the use of the grace-note trill plus suffix for the chromatic trill chains of the 2nd Organ Sonata, for which, in Ex. 29.21 above, the use of main-note trills was suggested.

Dannreuther offers interesting evidence for the grace-note trill in Bach. In the Organ Chorale *Nun komm, der Heiden Heiland*, Bach wrote m. 5 as shown in Ex. 29.31*a* and the parallel passage in m. 29 as given in Ex. *b*. The grace note in m. 5 gives a clue to the rhythmic design of the trill pattern in m. 29. As Dannreuther points out, the version of Ex. *a* is a trill substitute when time is too short to accommodate alternations.

Ex. 29.31. BWV 659

An actual written-out grace-note trill can be found in Cantata 140 as shown in Exx. 29.32*a* and *b*.

Ex. 29.32. BWV 140, 6 (*Thomana*)

The fully spelled-out grace-note start of a trill with a slow beginning and implied acceleration was shown above in Ex. 29.1*e*. In a passage from Prelude 13

(*WC* II), partially given in Ex. 29.33, each of the trilled notes is dissonant with the other voice and has to sound *on* the beat to prevent the counterpoint from being altered. Grace-note trills seem best here.

Ex. 29.33. BWV 882

Another context favoring the grace-note design are trills preceded on the upbeat by their tied main note. Since a genuine appoggiatura cannot be inserted within a tie, an appoggiatura trill would be equally out of place. Therefore, the choice is usually between a grace-note trill and an anticipated trill, though a delayed start of the alternations may on occasion be preferable. In Ex. 29.34*a* from the 3rd Organ Sonata, the first two alternatives are demonstrated in Ex. *b* and Ex. *c*.

Ex. 29.34.

A delayed start is also possible. Incidentally, an onbeat auxiliary is here excluded by the octaves it would produce with the bass. In Ex. *d* from the second movement of the same work, a pattern many times repeated can accommodate the grace-note trill (Ex. *e*) or delayed start (Ex. *f*).

Since both the main-note and the grace-note trill are more neutral than the more colorful appoggiatura trill, the two former will be more fitting when trills occur in quick succession where appoggiatura trills could soon become obtrusive. In Ex. 29.35 from the 6th English Suite, six trills follow one another in quick succession. Though appoggiatura trills could fit individually the second, third, fourth and fifth, and would not be overly objectionable on the first and sixth, some variety seems desirable. One acceptable solution among many would be to use main-note trills for numbers 1, 3, 5, and 6, with their stepwise descent, and grace-note trills for 2 and 4, with their tone repeat.[25]

[25] For another example, see the trill cluster in the 2nd Violin-Harpsichord Sonata (BWV 1015,1), mm. 24-26.

Ex. 29.35. BWV 811, Courante

The preceding illustrations were just a few samples, taken almost at random, of situations that strongly favor the grace-note trill. Its actual scope is extremely varied and wide because it offers an answer to the growing vogue of the upper-note start without interfering with either harmony or melody. Hence it will be the ideal solution where upper-note start seems desirable but where the melodic-harmonic alteration induced by the appoggiatura trill is either inappropriate or appears less satisfactory.

ANTICIPATION OF THE ALTERNATIONS

There have been a few previous references to the complete or partial anticipation of the trill's alternations. A few words remain to be added.

We cannot expect to find in Bach's music clear-cut evidence about the necessity of such anticipation; we can draw our conclusions only from the previously shown availability of the design and the musical logic of contexts that would favor its use. The best that can be said is probably this: whenever the start of the alterna-tions *on* the beat sounds awkward or stiff, either anticipation or delay should be considered; but where delay would weaken a desirable rhythmic definition, antici-pation alone will be the logical solution. In this sense a propitious context for anticipation will be presently shown to reside in the *tremblement lié*, where the trill sign is placed over the resolution of a written-out appoggiatura.

For an illustration of a different context, the trills in the 1st Two-Part Inven-tion (Ex. 29.36) may serve. An anticipated *Schneller*—or in slower tempo a double alternation—as shown in Exx. *b* and *c* provides here a sensible solution.

Ex. 29.36. BWV 772

THE APPOGGIATURA TRILL

Though the appoggiatura trill cannot claim its alleged monopoly, it did occupy an important place in Bach's music. As shown above in Ex. 29.3, Bach in the

Explication gave for the plain trill (*trillo*) the simple appoggiatura type in conformance with the usual French keyboard models; in addition, he gave two symbols with identical meaning for the supported appoggiatura trill (*accent und trillo*).

The limitations of Bach's models need not be reiterated, and the place for main-note and grace-note styles has been amply vindicated. One question remains: when is it proper to use the appoggiatura style in its simple and supported forms? For the simple type, the best answer is probably that whenever a short appoggiatura could be substituted for the trill to good advantage, the trill can fittingly start with the upper note on the beat. Frequent among such contexts are cadential trills, and two illustrations for innumerable others are given in Ex. 29.37 from the 5th English Suite and from the 3rd Two-Part Invention.

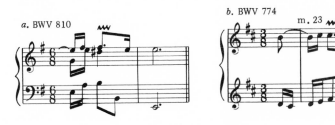

Ex. 29.37.

Whenever two trills follow each other in a cadence, it will rarely be advisable to render both in the same appoggiatura style. In Ex. 29.38a from the 7th Two-Part Invention, the first of the trills whose main note is dissonant will better be played as a main-note or grace-note type and only the second one as an appoggiatura trill. In Ex. *b* from the 6th English Suite, each of the three trills has an individuality of its own. The appoggiatura type would hardly fit the first of these on G sharp. Apart from the (harmless) hidden fifths, the harmonic dissonance of the main note would be transformed and the dissonant leap from the preceding note obscured. A main-note or grace-note trill will be preferable here. Of the two other trills which follow one another so closely, the last, the real cadential trill, suggests appoggiatura style; in turn, it will be set off more effectively by a more neutral physiognomy of the preceding one. For this latter, main-note design might be best.

Ex. 29.38.

Bach wrote innumerable supported appoggiatura trills with the appoggiatura spelled out in regular notes. He had to do so whenever the appoggiatura was too long to be understood by a symbol. For short ones he often did so to safeguard his melodic and polyphonic intentions, or without any conscious purpose as casual alternatives to a symbol. Such *tremblements liés* are illustrated for cadences in Ex. 29.39 from the *Christmas Oratorio* and below in Ex. 29.41a from Fugue 22 (*WC* II).

Ex. 29.39. BWV 248, 57

The two illustrations of Ex. 29.40 are fairly typical for situations other than cadences. (Ex. *a* is from the D minor Partita for Unaccompanied Violin; Ex. *b* is from the 4th Organ Sonata.)

Ex. 29.40.

The spelled-out notation still leaves some problems of execution. One is that of identifying as appoggiatura the preceding upper neighbor note whenever Bach did not mark the slur from appoggiatura to resolution. Appoggiatura function can usually be assumed when the preceding note occurs on the heavy beat and has a more complex harmony than that of the trilled note. Whether the slur is marked or implied, appoggiatura and trill belong together as part of *one* single ornament. Because of this ornamental unity, the metrical notation is only approximate. Its seeming dividing line does not divide and therefore will often better be ornamentally "blurred" to clarify, as it were, its non-existence. The trill should, especially in slow movements, grow out of its appoggiatura preparation organically without making an abrupt appearance.

In Ex. 29.41a, metrically precise rendition would seem rather unsatisfactory. Though such a solution, as indicated in Ex. *b*, may well be fitting on other occasions (such as faster, more rhythmic passages), there are three other alternatives which are preferable because they will do better justice to the ornamental oneness of this appoggiatura pattern. They are, with regard to the alternations, complete anticipation (Ex. *c*); a slight anticipation (Ex. *d*); a slight delay (Exx.

e or *f*). In this particular $\begin{smallmatrix}6&5\\4&3\end{smallmatrix}$ context, the solution of Ex. *e* might have a slight edge for its harmony-enriching brief suspension effect, without sacrificing the trill's main-note anchor. (The shortening of the last 8th-note is justified by its purely ornamental character as *Nachschlag*, and advisable for its preservation of the dotted rhythm. The same applies to countless analogous spots of a dotted trill plus one-note *Nachschlag*, where the alternations stop on the dot.)

Ex. 29.41. BWV 891, 2

The advocates of the "rule" recognize solely the delayed entrance in the form given under Ex. *f* with upper-note anchor. They object to the onbeat start of the alternations because such start suggests to them a main-note trill, which they consider to be unhistorical. They fail to realize that every one of the above three designs is a most emphatic form of the appoggiatura trill, one in which the onbeat start of the auxiliary is fully consummated by the written-out appoggiatura. It stands to reason that once the upper note has been sounded as part of the orna-ment, the alternations proper have to start with the main note. (By the same token, a main-note supported trill remains a main-note trill even though the alternations obviously have to start with the upper note.)

The delayed design was discussed above in connection with the French *tremble-ment lié*. Its undeniable assets were then pointed out together with its limitations. It can, as was said, be used to best advantage only where the beat at the trill's start is clearly marked in another voice. If, for instance, we were to render Ex. 29.40*a* from the Partita in D minor for Unaccompanied Violin as shown in 29.42*a*, the listener would not perceive the delay as upper-note-on-the-beat, because the beat has vanished and the impression will simply be one of rhythmic vagueness. The rule-oriented eye is satisfied, the ear confused.

A similar rendition of Ex. 29.40*b*, as indicated in Ex. 29.42*b*, is particularly pointless because it occurs in a strongly rhythmicized movement where every single beat is clearly marked and a blurring of the rhythm musically unjustified. A good execution for these and similar cases is the complete anticipation of the trill as shown in Ex. *c* for the Violin Partita and in Ex. *d* for the Organ Sonata. Such a solution not only avoids the vagueness of the delay and the awkward squareness of the onbeat alternation but offers an interpretation that is graceful and clarifies the beat.

Ex. 29.42.

THE TRILL WITH *Vorschlag* SYMBOLS

As mentioned above, Bach introduced in the *Explication* two keyboard symbols with identical meaning to indicate the supported appoggiatura trill: The first of these symbols is rare and limited to a handful of pieces. The second one is not quite so rare but still infrequent. In the Courante from the A minor Suite (BWV 818), we find one of the rare instances where either of these symbols occurs in a cadential setting (Ex. 29.43*a*) with probable appoggiatura meaning of about an 8th-note. Four measures earlier (Ex. *b*) we find the same symbol, and here the *Vorschlag*, if taken on the beat, has to be shorter than an 8th-note.

Ex. 29.43. BWV 818, Courante

In Exx. 16.11*a, c, d, e, f,* and *h* (from Chapter 16), the telltale prebar notation of the hooks in hook-*chevron* combinations in manuscripts from the inner Bach circle clarified anticipation of the *Vorschlag*, hence grace-note trills. The same design is indicated in Ex. 29.44*a* from the *Canonic Variations* (No. 4) where the symbol presents a trilled counterpart to the motive of Ex. *b* (from Variation 3) whose unquestionable anticipation was demonstrated before (see Ex. 16.11*b*). Moreover, apart from this analogy and apart from the appoggiatura character of the trilled notes (which alone calls for anticipation of the added *Vorschlag*), there would be two successive parallel octaves if the first hook were to be rendered on the beat and the next trill played as appoggiatura type.

The second symbol from the *Explication* (ᗧᴡ) also signifies simply a trill with a preceding *Vorschlag*. This *Vorschlag* can again range from anticipation to a

Ex. 29.44. BWV 769

supported appoggiatura. Bach uses the symbol only sporadically and rarely in cadences.

In Ex. 29.45a from Prelude 4 (*WC* I), the *Vorschlag* has to be shorter than an 8th-note in order to announce the harmony before the bass starts to move away.[26] Anticipation is a possibility here since it would help to clarify the harmonic progression against the tie in the bass. Such anticipation is recommended in Ex. *b* from the Organ Chorale *Allein Gott* in order to avoid open fifths.

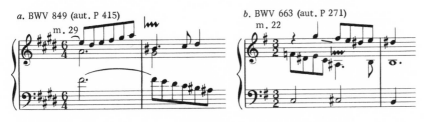

Ex. 29.45.

In Ex. 29.46a from the Organ Chorale *Komm, heiliger Geist*, several factors argue against long appoggiatura meaning for the symbol. One, pointed out by Walter Emery, is the "awkwardness" it would produce in such an "unlikely-looking" context.[27] Another is that the strong alteration of the melody implicit in a long appoggiatura would interfere with the logic of imitation in that for the four fugal entrances the symbol is attached only to the upper three voices but not to the bass. Thirdly, far from enriching the harmony, the alleged *raison d'être* of appoggiaturas, it would blur the harmonic outline and obscure the rhythmic interplay of the voices in m. 6 (Ex. *b*) and still more so in the fullness of four-part polyphony a few measures later. These reasons strongly suggest great brevity and possibly grace-note rendition.

In Ex. 29.47a from the Organ Chorale *An Wasserflüssen Babylon*, the syncopated entry of the second voice excludes a sustained appoggiatura interpretation

Ex. 29.46. BWV 652 (aut. P 271)

[26] In Altnikol's copy of 1755 (P 402) there is only a plain *chevron* without the initial dash, but the latter is clearly marked in the autograph (P 415).

[27] Emery, pp. 60-61.

of the vertical dash. In the Aria of the *Goldberg Variations* (Ex. *b*), Walter Emery also acknowledges the possibility of anticipation as an alternative to appoggiatura lengthening for the trill (Ex. *c*).[28] Anticipation is a very likely solution for this particular piece in which several *Zwischenschläge* of the *tierces coulées* type are contrasted with a number of written-out Lombard type appoggiaturas.

Ex. 29.47.

In Ex. 29.48 from the Organ Chorale *Nun komm, der Heiden Heiland,* the indicated appoggiatura will best be held for less than 8th-note length to resolve the dissonance before the middle part moves.

Ex. 29.48. BWV 660

In addition to the two keyboard symbols of the *Explication,* a third and much more frequent one, the trill sign preceded by the little *Vorschlag* note: is used for all media. The symbol, like its two keyboard companions, generally indicates the trill's upper-note start, and the little note, like the hook, could cover its whole normal range from anticipation to a mildly sustained appoggiatura.

Beyschlag found a spot in the *Christmas Oratorio* that shows anticipation for this symbol.[29] In a unison passage of oboe and violins, a *Vorschlag* before a trill is written by symbol for the violins and written out in anticipation for the oboe (Ex. 29.49).

Ex. 29.49. BWV 248, 42

[28] Ibid., p. 60.   [29] Beyschlag, p. 121.

In Ex. 29.50 from the D minor Concerto for Two Violins, grace-note interpretation best satisfies the melodic-harmonic demands of the situation. Bach wanted the *Vorschlag* for added brilliance and had to indicate it to insure its insertion. An accented onbeat *Vorschlag* would emasculate the melody; its bold ascent and dissonant leap into the leading tone would be transformed into a plain broken triad, the leading tone deprived of its tension, and its resolution anticlimactically anticipated. By contrast, the grace note with its unaccented little snap highlights the pungency of the accented leading tone.

Ex. 29.50. BWV 1043, 3

When Bach writes the symbol in 16th-note values before a relatively long note, extreme shortness will be his likely intention (see Exx. 29.51*a* and *b* from Cantatas 61 and 63). The second example shows an arresting threefold variation of the trill motive in a sequence that recurs several times in the same pattern.

Ex. 29.51.

In the Trio Sonata from the *Musical Offering*, we find the trill pattern of Ex. 29.52*a*. In spite of its slowness that might suggest a languorously long appoggiatura, and in spite of the fact that the piece was written at a late date (1747) for the Berlin musical establishment, the rendition according to the Berlin formula [symbol] is unlikely. In m. 5 (Ex. *b*) with the theme (though without a written trill) in the bass, extreme shortness of the *Vorschlag* seems to satisfy best the harmonic-rhythmic demands of the spot. Further evidence favoring actual anticipation can be found in the second part of the movement where the theme is inverted (Ex. *c*) as is the trill which starts from below. The three-note prefix, establishing the inversion of the trill, was definitely meant to be anticipated, because its onbeat start would produce impossible fifths three times in a row (see below Exx. 33.12*a-c*). The anticipated start of the trill in its mirror image suggests an analogous anticipation in the original form of the trill.

Problematic are those very rare cases where the symbol occurs for cadential trills, as it does at the end of both sections of the same movement (Ex. 29.53*a*). In Kirnberger's realization of the authentic bass (Ex. *b*), we see that the grace might admit an appoggiatura rendition of modest proportions, but not one of the Berlin style lasting the length of a quarter-note, as indicated by the apocryphal figures of the *BG* edition.

The question whether and when a supported appoggiatura trill may have been intended where only a regular trill sign is given (or no symbol is written but a

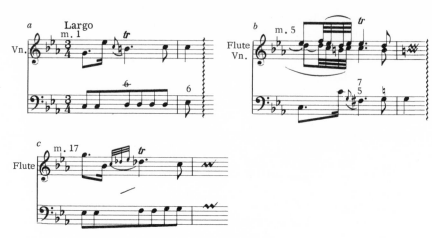

Ex. 29.52. BWV 1079

Ex. 29.53. BWV 1079

trill nevertheless expected) cannot receive a simple answer, because many are the instances where Bach probably had no exclusive preference in mind for one or the other design and where, as performer, he probably varied their use in a given spot. There is no genuine evidence for the modern idea that appoggiatura trills, plain or supported, are indispensable for Bach's cadences (any more than they were for Buxtehude's).

In Ex. 29.54 from the Ciaccona for Unaccompanied Violin, the cadential trill on e′ is not marked but understood. With the f′ forming an appoggiatura with a sharp suspension dissonance at the start of the measure, the immediate repeat of the same appoggiatura would be redundant. A grace-note or main-note trill would seem to provide here a better solution, the more so since the suspension on f′ functions as appoggiatura preparation for the cadential trill.

Ex. 29.54. BWV 1004, Ciaccona

The last example of the Ciaccona is typical of many a case where Bach did not write a trill symbol but where a trill was nevertheless understood. Mostly we shall find such cases in cadential or quasi-cadential settings, and Ex. 29.55 gives a sampling of different formulas which either demand or permit the addition of a trill. (The missing trill symbol is added in parentheses.)

Ex. 29.55.

THE ALTERNATIONS

In choosing the proper speed of the alternations, the chief consideration is the prevailing "affect" of the piece. In a slow tempo the speed of shaking should be not overly dashing. In a lively piece where the trills are meant to add brilliance, a faster shaking is appropriate. Other things being equal, trills in higher pitch range should be faster than those in a lower one. Also, in accord with Quantz's timeless remarks, the speed of the trill, as well as the tempo of a whole piece, has to be adapted to the acoustics of the locale: if the reverberations are strong, then a fast trill would be perceived only as a blur and therefore ought to be slowed down—as should the tempo in general. By contrast, in a dead acoustical setting the speed of both the trills and tempo of the piece should be taken somewhat faster to compensate for the dryness of the sound.[30] For longer trills, a slightly slower start and gradual acceleration, as recommended by Couperin, will often be pleasing; but this must not be done according to a mechanical formula. On instruments capable of dynamic nuance, shadings of loudness can add another element of variety.

Emphasizing either of the two notes can noticeably affect the trill's physiognomy. Thus, an appoggiatura trill with continuing emphasis on the upper note will for the length of this emphasis become an appoggiatura substitute. Therefore, such distinct upper-note emphasis will be appropriate only for as long as an appoggiatura would be in its place. By the same token, such continued emphasis will be pointless after a long written-out appoggiatura support that has already been held for the entire length intended for this grace, because at the point where this long appoggiatura resolves to its principal note, it is this principal note, i.e. the main note of the trill, which must be outlined. Hence, the alternation in such a *tremblement lié* should be main-note anchored to clarify the underlining

[30] *Versuch*, ch. 9, pars. 2 and 6; ch. 16, pars. 18-19.

design which a stress on the upper note would confuse. In all other related circumstances where the trill's function is strictly linear and not harmonic, it will better fulfill this function the clearer the emphasis on the main note can be perceived.

Where there is no musical reason for emphasizing either of the two tones, an equal distribution of weight will provide a very usable neutral pattern that, based on triplets, alternates the metrical placement of both notes:

A further question concerns the length of the alternations. Except in cases where continuing alternations are called for by obvious musical intent, they will often stop before the end of the note's value to form a "rest point." Its insertion and its length are matters of individual judgment. The rest point may last from an imperceptible hesitation to—in the case of an anticipated trill—the whole length of the written note.

THE SUFFIX

Many of Bach's trills end with a suffix of one or two notes. Very often it is notated, but often it should, or at least may be, added without specific indication.

For the keyboard only, as shown above in Ex. 29.3b, Bach uses the symbol ᨠᨠ to signify the trill with a suffix of two notes, as given in the *Explication* under the name *trillo und mordant*. Only very rarely did he use for its indication the two little notes which Couperin and other masters so frequently wrote.[31]

Neither did Bach use Couperin's trill-plus-turn symbol: ᨠ . Only one case authenticated by autograph could be found—in the 3rd Partita (in Anna Magdalena's Note Book)—that might be (and was, in Michel's copy P 643 and in the *NBA*, v, 4, p. 50) interpreted as signifying this combined symbol. However, the turn symbol is clearly written in front rather than on top of the *chevron* (Ex. 29.56) and was perhaps meant to be played as a separate ornament before and not after the trill. In the original print of the work the symbol looks approximately thus: ᨠ . Possibly the only case where this combination symbol truly occurs in Bach (Walther used it very frequently) is a spot in the "Little" Prelude (BWV 933). No autograph has survived, but the symbol recurs

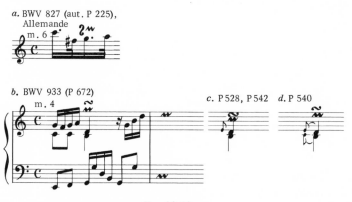

Ex. 29.56.

[31] One case can be found in the autograph (P 234) of the E major Clavier Concerto (BWV 1053,1), m. 63. Two other cases in the Fugue (BWV 903) of the Chromatic Fantasy and Fugue, mm. 13 and 23, are not authenticated by autograph. Others may well be found but certainly only a very few.

in several sources (P 672, P 528, P 542, and P 540) albeit with different *Vorschlag* patterns, as given in Exx. *b, c* and *d*. Being followed by a rest, the turn does not, as it always does with Couperin, connect with the following upper note.

Whereas Bach uses the keyboard symbol 〰 only rarely, he does write out the suffix for all media with such frequency that examples abound everywhere—from the shortest trills, such as the one in Ex. 29.57*a* from Cantata 114, to long ones as shown in Ex. *b* from the Organ Chorale *Nun komm, der Heiden Heiland.*

Bach's consistency is remarkable: he continues to write the troublesome pattern over and over again in identical contexts, even though the performers probably would have easily grasped the idea of the desired suffix after a few samples. A case in point is the first movement from the *Christmas Oratorio* and its model in Cantata 214, where in each of the autographs the pattern of Ex. *c* is written out in all parts 114 times with not a single omission. (In the cantata model, Bach often left out the trill sign but never the spelled-out suffix.)

Ex. 29.57.

In slow and moderate tempi, the suffix is most often written out in 32nd-notes; in faster tempi and often after a dotted quarter-note, it appears in 16th-notes. In very rare cases, the suffix is separated from the trill by a rest: e.g. in the French Overture, m. 8 and Prelude 10, m. 10 (*WC* I). In such instances the suffix assumes the additional function of a prebeat slide.

In soloistic music such written-out suffixes need not be taken on metrical face value. Provided we are satisfied that we have to do with a genuine ornament and not with a structural element of polyphony, the suffix could be treated as if it had been notated with two little unmetrical notes: , thereby often calling for a faster than written speed.

The familiar two-note suffix of the preceding paragraphs is the most important type, but there are other two-note suffixes that serve a similar function. The trills in the previously given passage from the 6th English Suite (Ex. 29.35) offer an illustration. Two of the four trills, the second and the fourth, have the regular suffix, the first and third a different type. Yet all seem to be *Nachschläge* and therefore may to good advantage be taken a little later than written.

Moreover, many written-out one-note *Nachschläge* that serve to smooth the transition to the following note will in view of their nature as ornaments often call for a lighter touch and a faster than literal rendition.

However often Bach may have written out the suffixes, there are many instances where he did not indicate them but where—sometimes probably, or even certainly—they were meant to be added. A suffix will usually *not* be called for 1) when the trill is tied to another beat (as shown in Ex. 29.58*a* from the A minor Violin Concerto); 2) when the trill is slurred to its lower neighbor within the same beat (Ex. *b* from the same work); 3) when the trill is followed by a suffix of one or more notes that have or may have *Nachschlag* function (Ex. *c* from the G minor Prelude [*WC* II], and Ex. *d* from the 6th English Suite); 4) when the trilled note is too short to admit a suffix without crowding (Ex. *e* from the same

English Suite). Also, a suffix would not be needed between a dotted note and its companion note or notes that complete the beat (Ex. *f* from the 2nd English Suite). These five points, to which others can be unquestionably added, are meant to be only tendencies with many exceptions.

Ex. 29.58.

As to the positive side, a suffix can be said to be appropriate whenever the straight trill would sound too angular or bare and when there is no apparent reason that such effect was intended. As always, the decision must be one of personal judgment. The point made here is simply that Bach's failure to write a suffix must not be interpreted as a rejection of this often desirable, sometimes indispensable, ornament.

In summarizing this chapter the following facts and ideas stand out. The alleged onbeat-auxiliary imperative was non-existent; hence, it is a misbelief that all of Bach's trills are "harmonic" ornaments. Probably the great majority of Bach's trills are of the "melodic" category that intensifies linearity without affecting harmony. It is a misbelief that all of Bach's trills have to start with the upper note. That Bach's trills frequently started on the main note is made probable through a powerful and longstanding Italo-German tradition (still fully operative in Buxtehude) and upheld by much musical evidence.

It is possible, though absolutely unprovable, that the greater part of Bach's trills, especially on the keyboard, started with the upper note; but it is likely that a large percentage of these trills was not of the appoggiatura but of the grace-note type.

There is good reason to assume that Bach's trills, far from being confined to one type only, ranged over the whole area of the trill's spectrum. Couperin had already thrown the door open to "arbitrary trills," yet the "anything goes" that is implied in this term was qualified for him by his definite preference for upper-note start (though often, perhaps mostly, before the beat). There were no such limitations for Bach, to whom the upper-note start whether on or off the beat was only one pattern among others.

The vast scope of possible trill interpretations creates problems that vary in difficulty and for which no ready-made solutions are available. The comparatively simplest case is the written-out long appoggiatura, the *tremblement lié*, where the only difficulty lies in the transition from appoggiatura to alternations. Here various options need to be considered whose priorities will change from case to case: exact onbeat start of the alternations, their slight delay, their slight anticipation, or the complete anticipation of the trill. One thing is quite certain —after the resolution of the appoggiatura, the alternations themselves should be main-note anchored.

The trills preceded by one of the three *Vorschlag* symbols (hook, vertical stroke before the *chevron* and the little notes) are the only ones for which the intended start with the upper note is obligatory. In many, perhaps in most, cases the purpose of these symbols was simply to specify the start with the upper note which was not automatically understood without it; and such start could be *on* as well as *before* the beat or could include a support of generally not more than moderate length. It is incorrect to assume that these symbols always stood for a supported appoggiatura trill and that this support had to be "overlong" according to Berlin formulas.

The plain trill symbols of either *chevron* or the various *t* signs can encompass every starting style of a trill: main-note or upper-note, support or non-support, full anticipation, grace-note, or appoggiatura trill (and even compound trills, as will be seen in the special chapter devoted to them).

The chief trill problem turns on the proper choice of these various starting styles in interpreting the simple trill symbol, and occasionally in the absence of any symbol at all. No rules can be given, but the following procedure is recommended in narrowing the choice and on occasion in making it. This procedure is predicated on the intimate closeness between an appoggiatura and an appoggiatura trill, a grace note and a grace-note trill. An appoggiatura trill is an ornamented appoggiatura of the combined length of the upper-note support, if any, plus the duration of a distinct upper-note emphasis of the alternations. Hence an appoggiatura trill will make musical sense only where an analogous appoggiatura as such would be apropos. The same can be said about a grace note and the grace-note trill: the latter starts with a grace note and will, therefore, be appropriate only where a grace note would be a fitting addition. The method consists in leaving out the trill and considering whether a *Vorschlag* could be properly added to the naked main note of the trill, and if so, what kind of *Vorschlag* (only those short *Vorschläge* that could be understood by Bach's symbols should be considered). If a fairly long appoggiatura seems indicated, so would its corresponding trill with support or with upper-note emphasis; if a short appoggiatura is pertinent, a plain appoggiatura trill without support or with a short one will be indicated or acceptable; where a grace note seems best, a grace-note trill will be the most desirable choice. Where no *Vorschlag* of any description will fit, the main-note trill will be in order; wherever main-note style is favored but the start of the alternation on the beat seems constrained or angular, anticipation of part or all the alternations will be fitting. Naturally, there will often be overlapping test results which simply indicate that more than one choice would be musically justified. An important asset of the suggested procedure is that the solutions are not rooted in abstract principles; rather they grow out of the live, individual situation. One danger, however, that can threaten the proper functioning of the proposed method is the deep-rooted belief in the onbeat-auxiliary doctrine. The choice of the best *Vorschlag* type can thus be affected by preconceived opinions unless we undertake the proposed tests with a completely open mind.

The many alternatives certainly tax the performer's musicianship, taste, and imagination, but the same is true of all aspects of performance. Here as elsewhere, "instant authenticity" in the form of a simple all-embracing rule is only a chimera. However, instead of deploring with Wanda Landowska the multiplicity of choices as a "trap" and an "ambush," we should welcome the chance of varying and enriching the ornamental coloring of Bach's works. Far from being "cruel" to the performer by leaving him a choice of ornamental manipulation, Bach paid him a compliment by trusting his musical intelligence.

The Italian Trill
1710-1760

THEORETICAL DOCUMENTS

In matters of the trill, Tosi has been incorrectly served by Galliard and Agricola, his English and German translators.[1] Though their textual renditions leave little to be desired, the same cannot be said of the many musical illustrations into which these writers transcribed, in mid-18th century, Tosi's exclusively verbal explanations. The transcriptions for the trill were fashioned by the allegiance of both writers to the upper-note-on-the-beat principle. Though Tosi is sometimes vague and therefore vulnerable to arbitrary interpretation, several things he says about the trill make it unequivocally clear that his translators were wrong in bringing him in line with their own preferences.

Tosi distinguishes eight types of trills, but the basic form "from which all others are derived" is the *trillo maggiore*, the trill with a whole step. It consists, he says, in the fast alternation of two tones, "one of which deserves the name of master tone because it occupies *with greater forcefulness* the site of the note which is to be trilled; the other sound, notwithstanding its higher location, plays no other part than that of a helper"[2] (italics mine). This passage alone disowns its illustration by both Agricola (Ex. 30.1a) and Galliard (Ex. b). With the "master" sound of the main note exerting greater forcefulness, according to Tosi's description, there is no basis for an interpretation which places the helper in the role of the master. Not a word was said by Tosi about starting the unprepared trill with the upper note.

a. Agricola (1757)   *b.* Galliard (1742)

Ex. 30.1.

This reasoning is confirmed in the next paragraph (p. 26) where Tosi discusses the *trillo minore*, the trill with the half-tone. With singers, Tosi says, it is difficult to discern the difference between the two trills (the whole-tone and the half-tone type), "even though they are a half-tone apart, because the auxiliary, due to its weakness, has difficulty in making itself heard."[3] An emphasized aux-

[1] Tosi, *Opinioni*; trans. Galliard, *Observations*; trans. Agricola, *Anleitung*.

[2] Tosi, p. 25: "Il primo [i.e. the first of the eight trill types] è il Trillo maggiore, che riconosce il suo essere dal moto violento di due Tuoni vicini, uno de' quali merita il nome di principale, perchè occupa con più padronanza il sito della nota, che lo chiede; L'altro poi ancorchè col suo movimento possegga il luogo della voce superiore, nulladimeno non vi fà altra figura, che di ausiliario." Even Agricola underlines the rank order of the two tones by the words *Gebieter* and *Gehilfe* (Agricola, p. 95) but seems unaware of the contradiction between these characterizations and his own transcription which reverses their order.

[3] Tosi, p. 26: "Se non è facile di scoprir ne' Vocalisti la differenza di questi due Trilli,

iliary could not have such troubles. There can be no doubt that the trill Tosi is talking about is main-note emphasized and starts with the main note on the beat when done without preparation.

Tosi's third type is the *mezzotrillo*, a short and fast trill for lively songs. Derived, we are told, from the first two types, this *mezzotrillo* must have the same characteristics of main-note predominance. Hence, here too Galliard's and Agricola's descriptions of this type as a prall trill, emphasizing the auxiliary, are unjustified.

Types four and five, the *trillo cresciuto* and *trillo calato*, are the unusual patterns of trilled slow glissandi, the first upward, the second downward. This meaning clearly emerges from Tosi's explanation of type four: "raising the voice imperceptibly while trilling from comma to comma so that the rise is not noticeable."[4] Type five is the same in reverse. Tosi rejects these trills as outmoded. The interesting thing about them is their double misrepresentation by Galliard,[5] as shown in Ex. 30.2. Not only is the "imperceptible rise" from comma to comma turned into a chromatic ascent, but by insisting on starting each new step with the upper note, the resulting leaps reach the size of thirds. The rise, and even more so the descent—here every second trill starts not even with the auxiliary (which would involve tone repetition) but with a note above the auxiliary—are obtrusive by their musical illogic and awkwardness. Clearly, Galliard's realization is entirely incompatible with Tosi's text. Agricola, who understood the passage correctly, set these glissando trills apart from the usual rising or falling trill chains.

Ex. 30.2. Galliard

Type six is a slow trill, also disliked by Tosi. Type seven is the *trillo radoppiato*, involving the insertion of a few different tones in the middle of a longer trill. Type eight is the *trillo mordente*, a very fast and very short trill said to be especially useful in *passaggi* and after an appoggiatura. Agricola's interpretation as mordent is most likely erroneous. Agricola himself complains in this connection that the Italians always confuse the mordent with the (fast and short) *Prall-Triller*.

According to Tosi, the trill must often be "prepared," which means a more or less long appoggiatura support. However, "not always is such preparation required, because every so often time or taste would not permit it. However, such preparation is needed in most final cadences and in various other analogous locations."[6]

From his discussion of the many kinds of trills, two types stand out as the fundamental ones: the prepared trill with appoggiatura support, and the unprepared trill, strongly anchored on the main note, which is on the beat and dynamically emphasized.

quantunque sia di mezza voce, se ne attribuisca la cagione alla poca forza che ha l'ausiliario per farsi sentire. . . ."

[4] Ibid.: ". . . far ascendere impercettibilmente la voce trillando di Coma in Coma senza que si conosca l'aumento."

[5] Galliard, plate 4.

[6] Tosi, p. 28: "Il Trillo per sua bellezza vuol esser preparato, però non sempre esige la sua preparazione, poichè alle volte non glie la permetterebbe nè il Tempo, nè il gusto; La chiede ben sì quasi in tutte le Cadenze terminate, e in diversi altri siti congrui. . . ."

Geminiani distinguishes four basic types of trills.[7] The first is the plain shake or *trillo semplice* (symbol: tr) as given in Ex. 30.3a. The second is the turned shake or *trillo composto* (symbol: ᴖ), a trill with suffix (Ex. *b*). Very interesting is type three, which together with type four is given under the label of "holding a note," *trattenimento sopra la nota*. In type three (Ex. *c*) the main note is held at the beginning, in a support symbolized by a horizontal dash preceding the sign for the turned shake —ᴖ. In the second version of this species, trill-type four, the order is reversed, as indicated by the symbol ᴖ—, first the shake, then the hold. Geminiani has an interesting comment about these "holds." "It is necessary," he writes, "to use this [design] often; for were we to make Beats and Shakes continually without sometimes suffering the pure Note to be heard, the Melody would be too much diversified." The word "diversified" is probably to be understood in the sense of blurring or distorting.

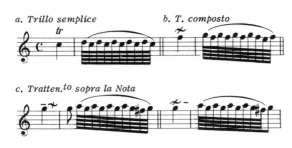

Ex. 30.3. Geminiani (1751)

Also shown are two types of the supported appoggiatura trill, one with, one without, a rest point but both with suffix, as reproduced in Ex. 30.4 (the wedge over the appoggiatura denotes crescendo from a soft start).

Ex. 30.4. Geminiani

From the models, it would appear that Geminiani's basic trill type is the plain appoggiatura style, and that the two chief variants are the supported appoggiatura trill and the supported main-note trill. Musical evidence, to be presented later, will show that Geminiani's trills included also the regular main-note and the grace-note types.

Tartini's works reveal the brilliant use he made of the trill, and his treatise reflects the importance he attaches to this grace. In two long chapters on the trill, Tartini never mentions the need to start with the upper note.[8] On the other hand, the patterns of the treatise do show upper-note start and anchor. This is true of the basic model, given in Ex. 30.5a, as well as of the models of Ex. *b*, which demonstrates gradual acceleration, and Ex. *c*, which shows how acceleration can be combined with a crescendo effect. The start with an appoggiatura

[7] *Treatise*, p. 2 (text), p. 1 (music); *Art*, p. 26, Exx. 18 and 19 and text pertaining to these examples in the preface.
[8] Tartini, *Regole*, facs. ed., pp. 10-15.

support ("con un' appoggiatura sostentata") is shown in à simple model (Ex. *d*) without further clarification. From previous comments about the long appoggiatura, one can derive approximate quarter-note value for the support in this example.

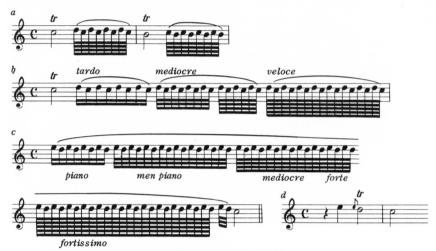

Ex. 30.5. Tartini (c. 1750)

The evidence value of these examples for the basic trill design is strongly qualified by a later document of Tartini's, his famous letter to Signora Maddalena Lombardini.[9] In it he discusses among other matters the trill and advises its practice in gradual acceleration. His model, given in Ex. 30.6, shows main-note start and anchor.[10]

Ex. 30.6. Tartini

It cannot be argued that we have to do here with a pedagogical device of starting with a simpler study pattern before proceeding to a more complex artistic design, because on string instruments the appoggiatura patterns with continuing upper-note anchor are easier than their main-note counterparts.[11]

Further theoretical evidence that the upper note on the beat was not a general principle emerges from a number of illustrations given by Tartini as samples of the "infinite" uses for the trill in both expressive (*cantabile*) and lively (*sonabile*) contexts.

For dotted notes, for instance, "it will make an excellent effect to trill [only] on the dot as shown in the following example" (Ex. 30.7*a*). The design is that of

[9] This letter, dated March 5, 1760, was published after Tartini's death under the title *Lettera del defonto Signor Giuseppe Tartini alla Signora Maddalena Lombardini.* . . .

[10] Beyschlag (p. 145) had already pointed out the contradiction of the two models; he considered the upper-note pattern of the treatise as a theoretical model and the main-note

pattern of the letter as the practical model.

[11] On strings, the lower finger rests to hold the main note, and only the upper finger moves to tap out the alternations of the auxiliary. It is easier to tap *on* the beat and its subdivisions than to do so after the beats, which requires more coordination.

a main-note support. Main-note start is unquestionable also in Tartini's patterns of Ex. *b*.

Ex. 30.7. Tartini

Speaking of trill chains that are "derived from the *portamento* of the voice both in a rising and falling scale," Tartini shows (see Ex. 30.8) how the scale of Ex. *a* is played on the violin *portamento*-style by the second finger alone (or by any other single finger); then, he says, the pattern of Ex. *b* "is done in the same way as the foregoing, with a trill added." A trill superimposed on the sliding movement of a single finger is technically feasible only with a series of main-note starts; also, this procedure is the only one that would match the desired *portamento*, i.e. glissando, effect. On the descending scale of Ex. *c*, the need to start each trill with the main note is even more imperative under the terms described by Tartini.

Ex. 30.8. Tartini

In the chapter on the "short passing appoggiatura," we find a perfect theoretical presentation of the grace-note trill. "Passing appoggiatura" (*di passaggio*) was, as will be remembered, Tartini's term for the anticipated *Vorschlag*. In showing *Vorschläge* before notes of equal value (a pattern he considered particularly conducive to the anticipated species), Tartini gives an illustration (Ex. 30.9) of "its perfect execution." Here the grace note becomes the anticipated auxiliary of a series of very brief trills with suffix.

Ex. 30.9. Tartini

We thus find the full range of trill designs in Tartini's theoretical models, the plain and the supported appoggiatura trill, the plain and the supported main-note trill, and the grace-note trill. Musical evidence to be presented later in this chapter will confirm his routine use of all these species.

Compared to the works of Tosi, Geminiani, and Tartini, the following documents are individually certainly of lesser importance. In one or two cases it was impossible to establish the credentials of the author; however, their unanimous endorsement of the main-note trill is significant. The documents from the latter part of the century testify to the long survival of the old Italian main-note trill, one hundred years after it was believed to be extinct.

In Vincenzo Panerai's small tract (c. 1750-1780) we find the following transcription of the *trillo*:[12]

Ex. 30.10. Panerai (c. 1775)

Carlo Testori in 1767 provides incidental intelligence.[13] In an important theoretical treatise, he shows ways in which to pass from the fourth degree of the scale to the fifth. In one illustration (Ex. 30.11) the fourth degree has a main-note trill that in both illustration and text is referred to as *trillo*.

Ex. 30.11. Testori (1767)

An important statement from this post-Tartinian era comes from Vincenzo Manfredini who reaffirms in 1775 the old Italian concept of the trill and mordent as each other's inversions: "The trill . . . is done by sounding alternately and as fast as possible two tones—a half or a whole step apart—*in upward direction*; the mordent [is] done in sounding two tones—but only those a half-step apart—in the same manner except *in downward direction*."[14] We easily recognize the old pair of the *tremulus ascendens* and *descendens*. His illustration of the trill is given in Ex. 30.12.

Ex. 30.12. V. Manfredini (1775)

Signoretti, an Italian who wrote in French, is influenced by Geminiani in presenting the models of Ex. 30.13 of a *tremblement* starting with the upper note on the beat (Ex. *a*) and the *tenue* starting with a main-note support (Ex. *b*).[15]

Antonio Lorenzoni in his flute treatise of 1779 writes: "the trill is composed of two tones alternatingly sounded, the actual trill tone and the one which follows it immediately

[12] *Principi di musica*, p. 8.
[13] *La musica ragionata*, p. 143 and plate 20, fig. 103.
[14] *Regole armoniche*, pp. 26-27: "Il *Trillo*, il quale si fa esprimendo alternativamente, e più presto che sia possibile due suoni all' in sù, distanti un tono, o un mezzo tono: il

Mordente, che si fa esprimando nella stessa maniera due suoni; ma all' in giù, e distanti un solo mezzo tono. . . ." Son of the more famous Francesco Manfredini, Vincenzo (1737-1799) was highly regarded as theoretician.
[15] *Méthode . . . de la musique et du violon*, III, 10-11 and plate of illustrations.

Ex. 30.13. Signoretti (1777)

according to tonality. Its symbol is *tr*."[16] This explanation, which contains all the author writes about the trill, implies a main-note start.

Antonio Borghese, an Italian composer who had moved to Paris, discusses the trill in a book which he himself translated from the original Italian into French.[17] After giving the usual explanation of tone alternation and stressing the need for great speed and precision, he presents the revealing "example for studying the trill" given in Ex. 30.14.

Re   mi Re mi Re mi Re   A -   -   -   - men

Ex. 30.14. Borghese (1786)

MUSICAL EVIDENCE

Theorists invariably give too narrow a picture of living performance. A scanning of the works of some important composers shows that wide use was made of the trill's many possible forms.

Bonporti, one of the early users of the little notes in Italy, presents interesting evidence that the notation ⟋ *could* stand for a grace-note trill and may, in fact, have always held such meaning for this master who wrote out in regular notation many supported appoggiatura trills.

In Ex. 30.15*a*, onbeat meaning for the little note is hardly possible. In Ex. *b* the very slow tempo (largo) increases the evidence value of parallels. In Ex. *c* there are no written *Vorschlag* notes for the two trills. Here, the facts that the main notes themselves are appoggiaturas, and that parallel fifths in close succession would result from onbeat auxiliaries suggest that the trills were meant to start with either the main note or the anticipated auxiliary.[18]

Ex. 30.15. Bonporti (c. 1715)

[16] *Saggio per ben sonare il flauto traverso*, p. 61. The book is heavily indebted to Quantz.
[17] *L'art musical*, p. 122, plate I, No. 12.
[18] Francesco Antonio Bonporti, *Concertini, e serenate con arie variate . . . a violino, e violoncello, o cembalo*, Op. 12 (Augsburg, n.d. [c. 1715]).

It is most likely that DOMENICO SCARLATTI's trills are also basically of the main-note type. (As symbols he uses interchangeably tr and ⁓.) Certainly, upper-note start was not understood: too frequent are the cases where an upper *Vorschlag* symbol precedes the trill in places where a support is out of the question or where the musical situation calls for extreme shortness of the *Vorschlag* note, which therefore can indicate nothing more than the start of the alternations with the auxiliary. Thus, in Ex. 30.16 from Sonata K 17, extreme shortness and preferably grace-note performance is suggested by the parallel fifths that a longish onbeat rendition would create in both passages.[19]

Ex. 30.16. D. Scarlatti, Sonata K 17

In Ex. 30.17 the onbeat auxiliary is disqualified by open fifths in two-part writing. Here main-note start is probably preferable to grace-note design, because the tone repetition seems to be of thematic importance.

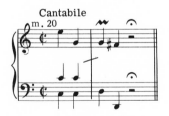

Ex. 30.17. D. Scarlatti, Sonata K 308

A clear case for main-note start of the trill is made in Ex. 30.18*a*, where the theme fragment of three successive a's (indicated in the illustration by a bracket) is insistently repeated four times, landing the last time in the trill. This trill must logically start with its main note.

The same is true of Ex. *b* where a down-rushing scale hits bottom on the main note of a trill. To interrupt the sweep at the moment of its greatest momentum is unthinkable.

In Ex. 30.19*a* we find on a long note the interesting directive, *tremulo di sopra*. This specification does not mean that the trill *starts* from above but that the *tremulo* is to be done with the upper note, not with the lower one. The approximate execution is sketched in Ex. *b*.

That the specification *di sopra* was deemed necessary permits the interesting inference that the *tremulo di sotto*, the old *tremulus descendens* or multiple mordent, was still in use. As a matter of fact, it is most probable that the *di sotto* meaning was implied whenever Scarlatti used the term *tremulo* without specify-

[19] The K numbers refer to Ralph Kirkpatrick's chronological catalogue.

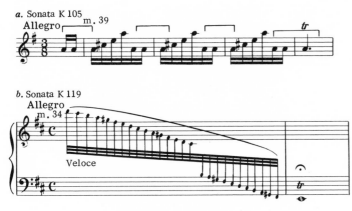

Ex. 30.18. D. Scarlatti

Ex. 30.19. D. Scarlatti, Sonata K 96

ing its direction. It so happens that in the cases where he prescribes *tremulo*, the multiple mordent seems to fit better than the trill. This is the case, for instance, with the four repeated ascending arpeggio figures of Sonata K 132, of which the first is shown in Ex. 30.20a (see also mm. 31, 69, and 71). Its probable intended rendition is sketched in Ex. *b*. In the same sonata, a long-held *tremulo* is preceded by a *Vorschlag* from below (Ex. *c*), which strengthens the supposition for an intended *pincé continu*—the more so since Scarlatti designates a compound trill from below (which would be the only other alternative) with three little notes: (e.g. in Sonata K 260, mm. 82, 87, and parallel spots). In Ex. *d* we see the same combination of a *Vorschlag* from below followed by a *tremulo*.

Moreover, in Ex. *e* we find an arresting passage of eight measures that is full of Scarlatti's famous tone clusters. Each measure starts with a trill indicated alternately with a trill symbol and the word *tremulo*. Since the exact fourfold alternation can hardly be coincidence, it must indicate a difference in rendition. When we see that the four spots marked with *tremulo* all leave ample space below the trilled note in an environment of heavy clusters, whereas the four other trills marked by symbol are thickly set, the likelihood emerges that here the *tremulo* stands for a mordent, the symbols for a trill. It is hardly mere coincidence that the three other times the *tremulo* is marked in the second part of this sonata (in mm. 68, 72, and 76) there is the same apparent concern for sufficient space below.

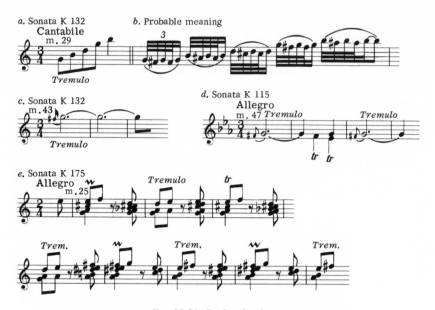

Ex. 30.20. D. Scarlatti

The near certain manifestation in Scarlatti of the old Italian *tremulo* dualism of *di sopra* and *di sotto* leaves us free to speculate that his trill symbols too might on occasion be read as simple or multiple mordents rather than trills. When, for instance, Scarlatti writes a trill with a *Vorschlag* from below (Ex. 30.21a), it is, considering the classical context of a *port de voix et pincé*, very likely that he had a mordent in mind, not a compound trill. The same applies to Ex. *b*. The case for the mordent is particularly strong in Ex. *c*; here, on the last note, mordent interpretation not only makes much better musical sense, but is far easier, since a trill would be extremely awkward technically.[20]

Ex. 30.21. D. Scarlatti

[20] Ralph Kirkpatrick (*Scarlatti*, p. 388) reports that Roseingrave, Scarlatti's friend and admirer, marked in his English edition of Scarlatti sonatas several such spots with the mordent sign: ᴧᴡ . Kirkpatrick counters this revealing evidence with the point that "the sign for a mordent is conspicuously absent in the *Essercizi* and in the Venice and Parma manuscripts." The argument is not convincing, because this French mordent symbol was not used by Italian masters (one more reason why the trill symbol had to do double duty).

If the essayed hypothesis is correct, that Scarlatti's trill symbols (in agreement with Mylius) could stand for a shake in either direction, we shall find many more cases where a mordent will be the more satisfactory interpretation. It seems probable that mordents rather than trills were intended, e.g. at the end of Sonata K 5; at the end of the first section of Sonata K 7; in Sonata K 9, m. 11, as well as at the start of Sonata K 491 and later in m. 22.

We must not be surprised to find the old double-faced nature of the *tremulo* still alive in Scarlatti and probably in many other contemporaries as well. It is not surprising for the echoes of a powerful tradition that dominated the whole 17th century to reverberate for a long time afterward. Relevance of the old traditional trill dualism for Scarlatti would, of course, further support the basic main-note nature of his trills *di sopra*.

Francesco Durante uses the little notes very rarely and may have never used them with trills. Two passages given in Ex. 30.22 suggest the use of main-note trills.[21] In Ex. *a,* the characteristic leap of the diminished seventh and the harmonic dissonance ought to be hit on the beat. In Ex. *b,* where a trill occurs in a fugue theme on every second note of a descending chromatic passage, an appoggiatura would disrupt the melodic line and even a grace note would disturb it.

Ex. 30.22. F. Durante

Vivaldi uses in his Concerto *del gardellino* (F XII No. 9) several interesting trill patterns. Examples 30.23*a* and *b* show the written-out acceleration pattern for a main-note trill; Ex. *c* offers a similar acceleration pattern with anticipated auxiliary.

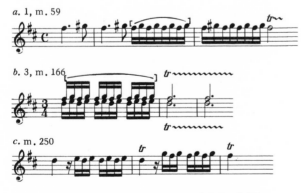

Ex. 30.23. Vivaldi, Concerto del Gardellino

21 *Sonate per cembalo,* MS Bol. EE 173.

Trills with written-out main-note support are given in Ex. 30.24a from a Violin Concerto in A.[22] Example *b* shows the little note before the trill in grace-note meaning, considering that the *Vorschlag* occurs before a syncopated note.[23]

Ex. 30.24. Vivaldi

For reasons stated above, HANDEL will again be included within the Italian school. Beyschlag had already expressed the opinion that most of Handel's trills start with the main note and that a *Vorschlag* note before the trill does not stand for an appoggiatura support but simply indicates the start with the upper note.[24] Beyschlag, however, still assumed that such upper-note start had to fall on the beat, whereas with Handel, too, it often was anticipated. Whether Handel's trills start mostly with the main note is uncertain but probable in view of his Italianate practices; that they often did, can be considered certain.

In the third movement of the *Water Music* (in the usually assumed sequence), the trills of the oboes (Ex. 30.25a) and, later, the violins, assume, in their enforced simplification for the less agile horns, the shape of *Schneller*, written out as seen in Ex. *b*.

Ex. 30.25. Handel, *Water Music*

Example 30.26a shows a main-note trill with acceleration; Ex. *b* has four trills, all of which are placed on appoggiaturas and are therefore ineligible for an additional appoggiatura. Moreover, two of these trills have written-out main-note supports (the mordent before the second of these, which is missing in some manuscript sources, does not alter this fact), and in all four instances the start of the auxiliary on the beat would create unpleasant parallels. For the tied trills (Nos. 1 and 3) either the auxiliary alone or part of the trill has to be anticipated; the other two (Nos. 2 and 4) could start with the main note but will more naturally fall in line with the grace-note style of the others. (See also the analogous patterns of mm. 19-20.)

[22] Foà 30, f. 110r; the beginning of this concerto is missing in the manuscript.

[23] Foá 27, fols. 62r ff.
[24] Beyschlag, p. 108.

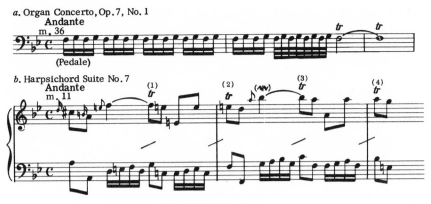

Ex. 30.26. Handel

Occasionally Handel's notation indicates the main-note meaning of the trill proper, for instance in Ex. 30.27a for the two trills. By contrast, on other occasions, e.g. a few measures later in the same movement (Ex. *b*), notation counts on the upper-note start.

Another case where the upper-note start is understood is particularly significant because it shows that what *was* understood was anticipation of the upper note. In the passage given in Ex. *c*, the two little notes—obviously in interbeat space— are clearly intended to slide into the trill via the auxiliary. In this connective function the auxiliary could not be placed on the beat. In his copy of Handel's Suites, in which he added his own ornamental interpretations and additions, Theophil Muffat follows the dictate of musical common sense by spelling out, as shown in Ex. *d*, the prebeat insertion of the auxiliary as part of the slide. Muffat, known for the onbeat patterns of his ornament tables, also clarifies in the same measure the interbeat nature of the little mordent-like grace in the left hand.

Ex. 30.27. Handel

For cadential trills and related occasions, Handel very often writes out an appoggiatura support in regular notes and most often omits the trill symbol (see Ex. 30.28a). That such appoggiatura support can often be legitimately improvised where not indicated cannot be doubted, but not every Handel cadence automatically calls for one. Often the bass figuring reveals that no appoggiatura, or only a short one, was meant to precede a cadential trill. Thus in Ex. *b*, the figure 4, which stands for $\frac{5}{4}$ and not $\frac{6}{4}$, does not favor a *long* support.

Ex. 30.28. Handel

In matters of the trill as well as all other ornaments, small and large, Handel in true Italian manner showed his indifference to matters of detail by delegating most of the executive authority to the performer. For his trills, there is no reason to assume the existence of restrictive rules. In view of the near exclusive Italian vintage of his ornament style, Beyschlag was probably right in placing the main-note design in the center of Handel's practices, but all the other designs can be assumed to have been used too.

The modern performer will probably find the same guidelines useful that were suggested for Bach: testing in a given situation for the suitability of replacing the trill with an appoggiatura or a grace note, or for the unsuitability of any kind of *Vorschlag*, and then selecting the corresponding trill style. Generally, the Handel performer will not often go wrong in choosing a main-note design when the trill is approached from below or from its upper neighbor, a main-note or grace-note design on a repeated note, a grace-note trill on a descending third, and an appoggiatura trill with or without support on a cadence. Suffixes often have to be supplied since Handel practically never indicated them. A performer who is worried about the right way of rendering Handel's trills (or any of his other ornaments) can take comfort from the thought that Handel in his grand manner most likely did not greatly care one way or the other, provided the result was musical and not pedantic, affected, or otherwise in bad taste. Had he greatly cared, he would have been more specific.

Francesco Veracini often writes out the long appoggiatura preparation as shown in Ex. 30.29*a*. At other times, in the same movement for instance, he uses the little note before the trill in the same long appoggiatura meaning, with the intent clarified by the bass figuring (Ex. *b*). Later, we find a semicadential trill (Ex. *c*) where the figuring favors a shorter duration of the *Vorschlag*.[25]

There is greater danger in automatically applying the long appoggiatura formula outside of cadential contexts. In Ex. 30.30, the figuring calls for a major triad on d, favoring a relatively short duration of the *Vorschlag*. The Peters Edition of this work (ed. W. Kolneder) gives the *Vorschlag* quarter-note duration, which in turn necessitates a harmonization at odds with the figuring (and in the process burdens the melody with rhythmic monotony).

For most other contemporaries as well, the long appoggiatura was by no means always understood—not even in cadences—as can be gathered from countless cases. Thus we frequently find, e.g. in Matteo Alberti, the cadential formula of Ex. 30.31, where the figuring favors a shorter than 8th-note appoggiatura.[26]

[25] *Sonate a violino solo e basso*, Op. 1 (Amsterdam, n.d. [c. 1720]; also Dresden, 1721).

[26] *Sonate a violino e basso*, Op. 2 (Bologna, 1721). This master is not to be confused with Domenico Alberti of "Alberti bass" fame.

Ex. 30.29. Veracini

Ex. 30.30. Veracini, Sonata, Op. 1, No. 1, Menuet

Largo e cantabile

Ex. 30.31. G. M. Alberti, Op. 2, No. 2

In Exx. 30.32*a* and *b* from Antonio Caldara, 8th-note meaning of the little note would in both cases result in faulty voice-leading.[27] No doubt, in other contexts the appoggiatura will often be long, but the point is that it does not have to be.

Ex. 30.32. Caldara

The works of Padre Martini, who was revered as an authority in all matters of compositional theory, are filled with examples that are incompatible with

27 *Mitridate* (1728), aut. GMF No. 379; *La pazienza di Socrate, con due moglj*, Scherzo   drammatico . . . (1731), aut. GMF No. 385.

both the upper-note-on-the-beat start as well as the long appoggiatura meaning of the *Vorschlag* symbol before a trilled note.

Of the few but characteristic illustrations shown here, the first, Ex. 30.33a, has a trill which in the transparent two-part writing has to be either a main-note or a grace-note type to avoid unacceptable fifths.[28] In Ex. *b*, a main-note trill is the likeliest means of avoiding octaves with the bass.[29] In Ex. *c*, we find in short sequence four trills on appoggiaturas which, for that reason alone, should not be weakened by an onbeat auxiliary.[30] Moreover, such a start would create open fifths for the third of these trills and hidden fifths for the first and fourth. This faulty voice-leading would be further aggravated by the slow tempo, by the two-part writing, and by the closeness of the trills. Similar circumstances (except for three-part writing this time) prevail in Ex. *d*: here, too, in an Adagio a trill on a written-out appoggiatura would create octaves if done according to the rule. Example *e* offers a further illustration of this point.

Ex. 30.33. G. B. Martini

The very frequent prebeat meaning of Martini's little notes was discussed before in Chapter 17. Hence we can expect that they can signify an anticipated auxiliary when placed before a trill. Such meaning is confirmed in the two passages of Ex. 30.34, where onbeat performance would produce open fifths.[31]

Ex. 30.34. G. B. Martini

[28] *Sonata al Post Communio*, aut. Bol. HH 36.
[29] Aut. Bol. HH 41.
[30] *Sonate d'intavolatura per l'organo, e 'l cembalo* (Amsterdam, 1742) (Exx. *c, d, e*).

[31] *Cantata latina sopra la passione di N.S.G.C.* [Nostro Signore Gesù Cristo], aut. Bol. HH 66 (1745) (Ex. *a*); for source of Ex. *b*, see n. 30 above.

Porpora's written-out main-note supports are shown in Exx. 30.35a and b.[32]

Ex. 30.35. Porpora

The next two illustrations confirm the use of the grace-note trill. In Ex. 30.36a, we see the theme of the violin with its *Vorschlag* before the trill imitated in the bass. Not only is the *Vorschlag* in this exact imitation printed before the bar line, but its onbeat rendition would yield unacceptable fifths. The unquestionable grace-note character of the *Vorschlag* in the bass argues for the same treatment in the violin. In Ex. *b* the little note before the trill is printed clearly before the bar line in a design that recurs several times in the movement.

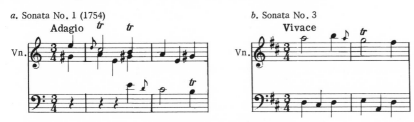

Ex. 30.36. Porpora

An interesting confirmation for Johann Hasse's use of the grace-note trill can be found in Ex. 30.37.[33] The evidence is derived from the typically Italian ornament of an upper prebeat *Vorschlag* plus (written-out) mordent . In the quoted passage it becomes clear that the following trill signs are only an abbreviated notation for the same combined grace. Actually, this grace often substitutes for a trill with suffix where time does not permit the extra alternations that would have completed the trill. Example *b* shows a written-out main-note support.

Ex. 30.37. Hasse, *Leucippo*

In Ex. 30.38 from G. B. Sammartini, the shortness of the trilled note makes on- or prebeat start practically indistinguishable.[34] Interesting here is the fact that the ever-recurring little note was needed to insure a desired upper-note start of the trills.

Ex. 30.38. G. B. Sammartini, Harpsichord Sonata

[32] Cantata *Questo che miri*, from *XII Cantate* (London, 1735); *Sonate XII di violino, e basso* (Vienna, 1754).

[33] *Leucippo, Favola pastorale*, MS AmB 306.
[34] *Sonata per il cembalo*, MS Bol. DD 54.

What Hasse had shown by inference, Locatelli proves directly by adding a trill sign to the *Vorschlag*-mordent pattern (see Ex. 30.39).[35] With the trill over a 32nd-note in a lively movement, the anticipation of the *Vorschlag* is a matter of course.

Ex. 30.39. Locatelli, Concerto No. 12 (1735)

The same diminutive grace-note trill is offered for practice purposes by Leonardo Leo in Ex. 30.40.[36]

Ex. 30.40. Leo, *Solfeggi*

Returning to Geminiani and Tartini, we shall find that their music sheds new light on their theoretical discussions and ornament models by disclosing expanded uses of trill designs. Geminiani's Ex. 30.41*a* shows how a keyboard trill, prepared on the upbeat by its main note, cannot start with the upper note on the beat without producing fifths with the bass.[37] Example *b*, also for the keyboard, shows a trill on an appoggiatura, where a similar start would result in fifths.[38] Example *c* shows the application of the "hold," with the main-note support indicated by the horizontal dash before the trill symbol.[39] Example *d* has a written-out grace-note trill, clarified by the disposition of slurs. In Ex. *e* the same design is clearly indicated with little notes.

Ex. 30.41. Geminiani

[35] *Sei concerti con introduzioni*, Op. 4 (1735) (two sets of 6 concerti each), MS Bol. GG 108. This is a concerto for four solo violins.

[36] *Solfeggi di Leo*, MS Bol. GG 97.

[37] *Pièces de clavecin* (London, 1743). These pieces are transcriptions made by the composer himself from different works for other media.

[38] *The Second Collection of Pieces for the Harpsichord . . .* (London, 1762); this volume contains additional original transcriptions.

[39] *Le prime sonate a violino, e basso*, new corrected edition with addition of ornaments in the Adagio (London, 1739).

The main-note support which Tartini suggests in his treatise for dotted notes is seen in Ex. 30.42a.[40] Examples *b* and *c* reveal that Tartini's basic trill model of the treatise, with its onbeat auxiliary, was not applicable here.[41] In both instances the trill, besides being on top of an appoggiatura, would yield unacceptable parallels.

Ex. 30.42. Tartini

The following illustrations document the anticipation of the little *Vorschlag* note before a trill.[42] In Ex. 30.43a, the first *Vorschlag* would create highly exposed open octaves, the second, hidden fifths if played on the beat. With the entrance of the solo violin, the same pattern is repeated, only the parts reassigned. Later, in the dominant (Ex. *b*), the trills are not written but understood. In Ex. *c* anticipation is necessary to avoid open octaves, especially in the slow tempo. In Ex. *d* the rhythmic design establishes the *Zwischenschlag* character of the little note, sandwiched between an onbeat 16th and a quarter-note trill.[43]

Ex. 30.43. Tartini

[40] This example is from an autograph concerto, the first in a collection of 20 concerti by Tartini (BN MS 9793) some of which are autograph, others contemporary copies.

[41] Sonata 6 from *Sonate a violino e violoncello o cimbalo*, Op. 1 (Paris, n.d.).

[42] The fifth concerto in the above BN collection (see n. 40 above), possibly also autograph.

[43] *Sonate a violino e basso*, Op. 2 (Rome [dedication dated 1745]).

THEORETICAL and musical evidence confirm that the Italian practice ranged over the whole spectrum of the trill. The long appoggiatura preparation was used in many but not all cadences and in other spots where expression and harmony justified it—sometimes written out, sometimes suggested by symbol, sometimes left to the performer's discretion. The main-note trill continued to be used, and in this connection, Tosi was misinterpreted by both of his translators, Galliard and Agricola. For many composers, among them Vivaldi, Domenico Scarlatti, Handel, and probably all other masters of their generation, the main-note design was most likely the basic trill form. The grace-note trill, as revealed by musical evidence and its clear theoretical portrayal by Tartini, flourished simultaneously. That the plain appoggiatura trill was also used can be taken for granted, though it is probable that its use was more frequent toward the later part of the period under consideration. Geminiani's and Tartini's basic models are the chief source for its Italian currency, but the meaning of these documents was strongly qualified by both masters. All in all, the appoggiatura type is at best one among many others that were in use.

We have had several occasions to note how the baroque-*galant* stylistic schism that divided Germany in the Bach era was paralleled by analogous discrepancies of ornamental practice. The trill was no exception. Simultaneously with the freedom claimed for this family of graces by Bach and many other masters of the older school, by resident Italians, and by Italianate Germans, we find new fashions emerging that narrowed the scope for these ornaments and prepared their ultimate hardening by the Berlin disciplinarians.

An early protagonist of the new trend, as noted before, was Theophil Muffat, Georg's son. His most important models for the simple trill are the ones given in Ex. 31.1. We see throughout the upper note on the beat; in Exx. *a*, *b*, *e*, and *f* the upper note also retains its metrical prominence, whereas in Exx. *c* and *d*, where the trill is preceded by a *Vorschlag* symbol, the alternations are main-note anchored.

Ex. 31.1. Th. Muffat (c. 1736)

One of Muffat's non-standard symbols for the trill with suffix (ᴋ) was his father's; another, for the suspension pattern of the *tremblement lié* (ᴌ) was his own. Theophil Muffat's symbols did not find imitators; but his great importance as a representative of a rising trend must be recognized.

A somewhat later advocate of this new orientation was the German-born John Ernest Galliard who translated Tosi's treatise into English in 1742. As mentioned in the preceding chapter in connection with Exx. 30.1*b* and 30.2, he misrepresented Tosi's ideas on the trill by forcing them into the mold of the onbeat-auxiliary fashion.

In 1728, two years after Theophil Muffat's first ornament table, Johann Ludwig Steiner published his treatise,[1] which was characterized as plagiarism of Fuhrmann's *Musikalischer*

[1] Steiner, *Kurz- leicht- und gründtliches Noten-Büchlein*, pp. 66ff. (Cf. ch. 15, n. 22 above.)

Trichter of 1706. Consequently, we find in Steiner's treatise the faithful reproduction of Fuhrmann's *trillo* and *trilletto* patterns with the main-note designs that were shown in Ex. 28.14 above. A plagiarism is not necessarily devoid of evidence value, because the implicit endorsement of the copied document usually bespeaks the continued relevance of the original.[2]

Of three trill models given by the Dutchman Van Blankenburg[3] the first (Ex. 31.2a) stands for a long appoggiatura preparation and a rest point, the second (Ex. *b*) for a similar intent with an added suffix; the third model (Ex. *c*) starts with a main-note support. In the music contained in the *Clavicimbel*, this latter trill design occurs mostly in cases where the trilled note is approached from its lower neighbor, as shown in Ex. *d*, and even in cadences, as seen in Ex. *e*.

Ex. 31.2. Van Blankenburg (1732)

Mattheson, in 1739, calls the grace *trillo*, its short form *trilletto*, and cautions against terminological confusion with the word *tremolo*, which he says should be reserved for the vibrato.[4] He defines the trill as the very fast, sharp, and clear alternation of two neighbor tones, but does not mention how it starts. In Germany, where the start with the upper note was only a fairly recent import that was added to the longstanding main-note tradition, Mattheson's silence on this point would seem to betray a neutral lack of concern in this matter. He tells us that the French singers prefer a rather slow trill which sounds distinct and clean though slightly dull; the Italians by contrast render their regular trills (*gemeine Triller*) very fast, strong, and short, almost like *trillettos*, except when they first hold *either of the two tones*, which they call a *tenuta* and the French a *tenue*.[5] He refers here clearly to either main-note or long appoggiatura support. Moreover, his explanation and illustration of the *ribattuta* (Ex. 31.3a), starting with a dotted pattern which gradually accelerates and "finally ends in a regular trill"

[2] Before we automatically disqualify a plagiarist as a witness, we must realize that many well-known treatises often borrow so massively from previous sources that they are plagiarisms in fact, even if they take the precaution of paraphrase. We would have to eliminate from consideration the better part of L. Mozart's chapters on ornamentation, because they lean so heavily on Tartini, and do likewise with most German treatises of the second half of the 18th century because they copy C.P.E. Bach. As will be remembered, Praetorius borrowed from Bovicelli and Caccini, Herbst and Crüger from Praetorius, Villeneuve from L'Affilard, Cartier from Geminiani, Grassineau from Brossard, etc., etc. Almost always the copyists picked worthy models, but in those times that knew no copyright and no concept of intellectual property, they often did not acknowledge the source.

[3] *Clavicimbel*, Preface.

[4] *Capellmeister*, pt. 2, ch. 3, pars. 27-37. Mattheson takes issue with Printz and Falck for using the terms *tremolo* for trill and *trillo* for tone repetition. Mattheson was obviously not aware that this terminology reached back to Caccini, Diruta, etc., and that it was used by many eminent theorists throughout the 17th century and beyond.

[5] Ibid., par. 33: "ausser dem Fall, wenn etwa auf einem oder andern Ton lange auszuhalten ist . . ."

("sich endlich in ein förmliches langes Trillo endiget"), identifies it as a main-note trill (par. 48).

Further evidence for main-note trills in Mattheson's practice can be found in his description of ascending trill chains.[6] He defines such chains as scalewise ascending notes, each of which carries a trill: "all, however, have to be linked without interruption as if it were only a single [trill] which often continues for six or more degrees."[7] His model is shown in Ex. 31.3b. As pointed out with regard to Tosi's similar description, the effect of a continuous trill can be achieved only by main-note start for each trill inasmuch as upper-note start would involve leaps of a third that break the desired continuity.

Ex. 31.3. Mattheson (1739)

Spiess in 1745 demonstrates how a long-held tone, a *tenuta*, can be enlivened with a *ribattuta* "and may well end with a *trillo*."[8] Example 31.4 gives his illustration, which he adopted from Mattheson; this *trillo*, too, is clearly of the main-note species. When he proceeds on the next page to speak of the *Trillo* and *Mordent*, he feels no need to give an explanation, saying simply that they are known to every musician.

Ex. 31.4. Spiess (1745)

An interesting document showing main-note support in Telemann's practice is taken from a set of flute sonatas (Ex. 31.5) for which he wrote out diminutions along with the simple unadorned setting.[9]

Ex. 31.5. Telemann (1728)

In 1749, Hartung, a clergyman from Gärlsdorf in Swabia, published under the pseudonym "Humanus" a treatise which won high praise from the two eminent contemporary critics Adlung and Hiller.[10] In paragraphs 189 through 192 of his

[6] Mattheson claims credit for the term *cadena di trilli-Trill-Kette* (ibid., par. 37).

[7] Ibid.: ". . . die sich aber alle, ohne Unterbrechung, an einander schliessen müssen, als wäre es nur ein eintziger . . ."

[8] *Tractatus*, pp. 156-157.

[9] *Sonate metodiche à violino solo o flauto traverso*, Op. 13 (Hamburg, 1728); *Continuation des sonates méthodiques . . .* (Hamburg, 1732); Urtext edition, Bärenreiter (Cassel, 1955).

[10] *Musicus theorico-practicus*, p. 26. Adlung, in his *Anleitung zu der musikalischen Gelahrtheit*, quotes Humanus no less than ten times. On p. 246, footnote *k*, he says: "this work is worthy to be read with thoughtful perceptiveness, that is, one ought to reflect well about it." He adds that he could not find out anything about the author. Hiller (as quoted by Carl Ferdinand Becker in his bibliography of 1832) wrote in his *Wöchentliche Nachrichten* (1768, pp. 9 and 27) that Humanus's little volume has more content than many a huge tome.

book, Hartung deals with the trill in a manner reminiscent of Tosi. "The trill," he writes, "sounds the lower note stronger than the upper one; therefore, the lower one must be part of the consonant harmony. . . . Consequently, the following trill is not permitted:

h c h c   c d c d
C   G

because the strongest tone of the trill is in the wrong place." The implications are clear: the trill is a main-note trill with main-note anchor.

C.P.E. BACH

In Book I of the *Versuch* (1753), C.P.E. Bach devotes a long section to the trill.[11] The opening sentence is significant: "The trills animate the melody, and are therefore indispensable."[12] In other words, the trill has the function of enriching the melody; not a word in this section refers to enrichment of the harmony.

Bach established for the keyboard a difference between the *chevron* of three waggles denoting the regular trill, and the shortened symbol of two waggles standing for the very short *Prall-Triller* of two alternations.[13] The symbol for the regular trill is shown in Ex. 31.6a, its realization in Ex. *b*. For long notes, the waggles are extended (Ex. *c*). The regular trill always starts with the auxiliary; therefore, it is not necessary to indicate this circumstance with a little note (Ex. *d*) unless one wishes this note to be held like a [long] *Vorschlag* (par. 5). For other media, he says, the symbols are *tr* or a simple cross (par. 4).

Ex. 31.6. C.P.E. Bach (1753)

Interestingly, Philipp Emanuel stipulates that the regular trill has to be shaken throughout the whole length of the note. Only the short *Prall-Triller* is exempted from this requirement. Bach lists as one of the mistakes that are "as ugly as they are common," the failure to sustain the trill properly: "all types except the *Prall-Triller* have to be shaken for the full value of the note to which the sign belongs."[14] Hence, he rejects the rest point, a prominent feature of both previous and later trill practice that was specifically shown in his father's basic trill model (of the *Explication*), in Couperin's model, in the tables of Georg and Theophil Muffat, of Marpurg, and many others. This is, incidentally, another of a good number of cases that show discrepancies in the ornament practices of father and son.

The shake should be fast and even. "A fast one is always preferable to a slow one" (par. 7). Though one could shake a little more slowly in sad pieces, generally, Philipp Emanuel says, it is the fast trill that serves to highlight a musical

11 *Versuch*, I, ch. 2, sec. 3. The references in the following pages will be to this section unless otherwise specified.

12 "Die Triller beleben den Gesang, und sind also unentbehrlich."

13 Pars. 5 and 30.

14 Par. 21: ". . . wenn man den Triller nicht gehörig aushält, ohngeacht alle Arten davon, biss auf den Prall-Triller, so lange geschlagen werden müssen, als die Geltung der Note, worüber er steht, dauret . . ."

thought. The slower start and the gradual acceleration of Couperin's and Tartini's trills are not mentioned.

In the eyes of Philipp Emanuel, the problem of where to apply unmarked trills seems to have receded considerably, because, he says, composers have formed the habit of marking the trills "almost everywhere" (par. 4). Bach nevertheless voices the usual warning against exaggeration and in this connection makes an interesting point by listing as a mistake the adding of trills in such spots as shown in Ex. 31.7, "although the slurs placed usually over such passages ought to prevent it."[15] A slur apparently was a bar to improvised trills.

Ex. 31.7. C.P.E. Bach

Philipp Emanuel's discussion of the trill's suffix is lengthy (pars. 6, 13-19), but he justifies his prolixity by saying that the discussion is addressed to beginners. The suffix, when rendered as shown in Ex. 31.8a, is often written out (Ex. b) or indicated by a variant of the *chevron* (Ex. c). This latter alternative (used by his father) does not, however, find favor with Philipp Emanuel, because it can so easily be confused with the sign for a multiple mordent.

Ex. 31.8. C.P.E. Bach

Whenever the suffix is prescribed, one only needs to know that it must be rendered as fast as the trill itself (par. 15) and should be connected to the following note with the greatest speed (par. 14). Bach specifies an exception only for dotted notes, where the suffix is to be separated from the following note by a short stretch of main-note sound, a sort of delayed rest point. The only problem is the question of when to add or not to add suffixes that are not indicated, but he sees little difficulty: even a "mediocre ear will always sense where the suffix may be made and where not" (par. 17). Since Philipp Emanuel's rules about use and non-use are generally in accord with the judgment of the modern ear, there is no need to give the details. His teaching in this respect can be summarized by saying that any long note normally requires a suffix; short notes may be, but need not be, given one whenever it is musically justifiable. When the accidentals for both trill and suffix are not marked, they have to be supplied according to the demands of the situation (par. 19).

Philipp Emanuel uses the two-waggle *chevron*: ∿ to indicate a very short, sharp and fast trill which he calls *Prall-Triller*. For its discussion we must turn to the second edition which, in a rare divergence from the first, changes the description of the grace.[16] Accordingly, the illustration of the first edition, shown in Ex. 31.9a ought to be changed to that of Ex. b. Referring to it, Bach says: "Although the upper slur extends from the beginning to the end, all the notes have

---

[15] Par. 20: ". . . ohngeacht die gemeiniglich über diese Passagien gesetzten Bogen dieses verhindern sollten."

[16] I am indebted to Eva and Paul Badura-Skoda for pointing out to me this revision in the second edition.

to be struck except the second *g* and the last *f* which are tied by a slur in such a manner as to remain lying without new articulation. The big slur signifies only the necessary legato rendition."[17]

Ex. 31.9. C.P.E. Bach

The *Prall-Triller* is supposed to be not only the most indispensable and pleasant, but also the most difficult of all ornaments; it is to make the performance "especially vivacious and brilliant" (par. 32). Its only context is said to be stepwise descent within a legato articulation. Moreover, Bach says (par 32) that this trill must truly crackle (*prallen*) and the last of the struck upper trill notes must be *geschnellt*.[18] The directive of being *geschnellt* implies an accent, as indicated in Ex. 31.10*a*. Since an accent seeks the beat, the execution could have sometimes involved partial anticipation as suggested in Ex. 31.10*b*.

Ex. 31.10. C.P.E. Bach

The likelihood of anticipation is supported by the following very interesting passage: "This trill can also . . . occur on a fast note where . . . the trill must be made so fast [that] one is led to believe that the note to which it is applied *loses nothing of its value, but enters with precision at its proper time.* (Italics mine.) Therefore, it must not sound as formidable as it would look if one were to write out all of its notes."[19] If the trill in Ex. 31.11*a* is to give the impression that the trilled note, i.e. the e′, enters exactly on time after the shake is finished, the delayed pattern of the original model has to be modified because it would nearly eliminate the trilled note instead of restoring it to its full value (Ex. *b*). Even the solution proposed by Robert Donington, using a *Schneller* on the beat when speed makes the delayed pattern impractical[20] (Ex. *c*), can hardly meet the terms of Bach's description. In a similar sequence of fast notes, *only anticipation* can achieve the on-time effect for the rest point of the trilled note, as suggested in Ex. *d*.

Ex. 31.11. C.P.E. Bach

[17] Par. 30: "Ohngeachtet sich bey dieser der oberste Bozen vom Anfange biss zu Ende erstreckt, so werden doch alle Noten biss auf das zweyte g und das letzte f angeschlagen, welche durch einen neuen Bogen so gebunden sind, dass sie ohne Anschlag liegen bleiben müssen. Dieser grosse Bogen bedeutet also bloss die nöthige Schleiffung."

[18] The term *geschnellt* (from *schnellen*) means a snap produced by a fast removal of the finger.

[19] Par. 32: "Dieser Triller kan dahero eben so wohl . . . über einer geschwinden Note vorkommen, welche dem ohngeacht nicht verhindern darf, dass dieser Triller desswegen doch so hurtig gemacht werden muss, dass man glauben sollte, die Note, worüber er angebracht wird, verlöhre nicht das geringste hierdurch an ihrer Geltung, sondern träffe auf einen Punct zur rechten Zeit ein. Dahero muss er nicht so fürchterlich klingen, als er aussehen würde, wenn man alle Nötgen von ihm allezeit ausschreiben wollte."

[20] *Interpretation*, p. 252.

Not only is the hypothesis of anticipation for fast notes the only convincing way of explaining the on-time impression, it also explains why the trill would not sound as "formidable" as it would appear when written out on paper according to the onbeat rule.[21] If we add to all this the obvious musical merits of such anticipation, a strong case is built for assuming that this is what Bach actually practiced.

If this hypothesis is correct, it would be delightful proof of what we would like to believe in the first place: that a musician of C.P.E. Bach's eminence was in practice not as rigid and pedantic as he appears to be in theory, and that for him too, musical logic prevailed when it came in conflict with self-proclaimed rules.

Bach discusses the *Schneller* in chapter 2, section 8, to which the following citations will refer. He explains this miniature main-note trill as an inverted simple mordent and marks it: ♩♪. He coined the term in what he wrongly believed to be the first description of this ornament. Numerous instances have been cited where this grace was theoretically demonstrated (among others by Santa Maria, Diruta, Praetorius, Herbst, Crüger, Friderici, Printz, Feyertag) and many other cases shown where it appeared in music examples in regular notation. For convenience's sake we applied the term *Schneller* to all of these graces, even though Bach coined it with special reference to its technical execution on the clavier.

Actually, C.P.E. Bach's use of this grace was more limited than the one envisaged by former theorists, inasmuch as he wanted to confine its appearance to short staccato notes (par. 2). In such contexts, he says, the *Schneller* fulfills the function of a trill without its suffix (par. 3) and is best suited in descending sequences where a suffix would be out of place for short note values. It is interesting that Bach, after mentioning its trill function, sees its difference from the trill not in its main-note start but in its avoidance of a slurred context. However, there is reason to assume that this clearcut difference between the slurred *Prall-Triller*, which normally called for tone suspension, and the staccato *Schneller* could not always be maintained and that the two must have overlapped and fused. As will be seen, Marpurg and others will give the four-note *Prall-Triller* in its use for fast notes the interpretation of the three-note *Schneller*.

MARPURG

In 1749 Marpurg gives the usual explanation of the trill as a rapid alternation of main note and auxiliary, then stresses the need to start with the auxiliary and to stop "on the main note with a certain emphasis on the rest point or stopping point (*point d'arêt*)."[22] This latter stipulation is in disagreement with C.P.E. Bach who rejected the rest point for the ordinary trill.

In Marpurg's models given in Ex. 31.12, we see first (Ex. *a*) what he calls the "free or simple trill" (*der freye oder schlechte Triller*, or *tremblement détaché*). Four different symbols with identical meaning are shown to signify this trill type, and it is interesting to note that the two-waggle and three-waggle *chevrons* are considered to be synonymous. As shown in the example, this trill, when preceded by its upper neighbor, involves a repeat of the upper note and onbeat start. The "slurred trill" (*der gebundene Triller*, *tremblement lié*) of Ex. *b* shows the delayed entrance of the alternations, allowing for upper-note anchor. The next model, the "supported trill" (*der schwebende Triller*, *tremblement appuyé*), shows, after the appoggiatura support, a main-note anchor of the alternations proper (Ex. *c*). Still more striking is the pattern of the *ribattuta* (*der gedehnte oder punctirte Triller*, *tour de gosier*), a main-note trill introduced by the dotted alternation that is started slowly and gradually accelerated (Ex. *d*).

[21] Anticipation finds perhaps some marginal support in the statement from par. 34: "This prall trill can occur only *before* a falling second" (italics mine), considering that the trill occurs not before, but *on* the falling second.
[22] *Crit. Musicus*, p. 57.

Ex. 31.12. Marpurg (1749)

Marpurg's *ribattuta* (like Mattheson's) must not be confused with another pattern found in C.P.E. Bach, Tartini, L. Mozart, and others where the dotted alternation is a prelude to a trill on the next higher note (see Ex. 31.13).

Ex. 31.13.

Marpurg's 1749 model for the suffix shows also four symbols of apparent equivalence which are given in Exx. 31.14*a-d*. The first of these symbols (*a*) is probably derived from D'Anglebert's *tremblement et pincé*, combining the trill symbol with the mordent hook: ᴧᴧ⌐ . Marpurg's symbol is only sporadically found with other masters, Löhlein being one of the few who adopted it. The second symbol (*b*) is Couperin's trill-turn combination; the third (*c*) uses the little notes, the fourth (*d*) regular note values.

The design presented as the transcription of the four symbols is unusual in that it prevents the suffix from exercising a connective function by leading without interruption into the next note. Where such connective function is envisaged, a desired rest point would be more logically inserted *before* not *after* the two-note *Nachschlag*. Certainly, the notation of *c* and *d*, if followed by another tone, would rarely be interpreted in the manner shown.

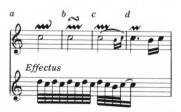

Ex. 31.14. Marpurg (1749)

In 1755 we find in matters of the trill a few changes in the direction of the Berlin School, but also a few continuing deviations from C.P.E. Bach's teachings.[23] New is the frequently quoted definition that "the trill issues from a descending appoggiatura and is consequently nothing else but a series of extremely fast repeated falling appoggiaturas" (p. 53). Gone is the *ribattuta* prepared main-note trill. The design of the supported appoggiatura trill, which he calls *vorbereitet, accentuirt,* or *schwebend,* is shown only in connection with a suffix and the latter's various symbols, as given in Ex. 31.15, but not illustrated in a musical transcription.

Ex. 31.15. Marpurg (1755)

Unchanged and still non-conforming is the continuing rest point for the simple trill, as well as the much more unusual one that follows the trill's suffix. The models of these two designs are practically identical with those shown above in Exx. 31.12a and 31.14.

Marpurg also maintains his independence with regard to the synonymity of the two keyboard symbols ⟆⟆⟆ and ⟆⟆ . He sees only pedantry in the effort of some to have ⟆⟆⟆ signify a long trill and ⟆⟆ a short one. (He uses the word *Subtilität* in a distinctly pejorative sense to characterize such distinction.) There is, he says, no point in making a distinction, since the length of the trill depends on the value of the note. Also unchanged are the models for a trill that follows its upper neighbor. They correspond exactly to the older models shown above in Exx. 31.12a and *b*.

Very interesting is Marpurg's explanation of the way this latter "slurred trill," the *tremblement lié,* can in certain circumstances shed the first note (the tied one) and start "against the rule immediately with the main note," so that a short trill of four notes is reduced to the three notes of the *Schneller.* This "incomplete trill," as he calls it, "can nevertheless in certain cases serve better than the complete trill."[24] The circumstances favoring such substitution are fast descending passages, short notes after a *Vorschlag,* and notes made short by a *Vorschlag.* Key excerpts of his illustrations are given in Ex. 31.16.

Ex. 31.16. Marpurg (1755)

[23] *Anleitung*, pp. 53-58.

[24] Ibid., p. 56: "Wenn . . . wider die Regel des Trillers, sogleich mit dem Haupttone ange-fangen, der Wechselschlag aber abgekürzet und nur auf drey Noten eingeschränket wird: so entsteht zwar daraus ein unvollkommner Triller, der aber nichts desto weniger in gewissen Fällen, besser als der ordentliche voll-kommne Triller gebraucht wird."

Marpurg does expressly equate this three-note "incomplete" trill with C.P.E. Bach's *Prall-Triller*,[25] which increases the likelihood that Bach, as suggested above, may have in a fast tempo yielded to the natural impulse of starting the *Prall-Triller* like a *Schneller* with the main note. After all, in fast tempo, tone repetition can become impractical as can the delayed entry pattern, as Donington convincingly points out.[26] Marpurg probably knew more about C.P.E. Bach's rendition of the *Prall-Triller* than we can today extract from the latter's printed explanations.

Marpurg also introduces the *Schneller* with the illustrations given in Ex. 31.17. His transcriptions do not indicate the staccato articulation specified (though not consistently pursued) by C.P.E. Bach.[27]

Ex. 31.17. Marpurg (1755)

The blurring of the difference between the *Prall-Triller* and the *Schneller* in Marpurg only underlines the futility of the longstanding debate about the correct definition and delineation of these two graces. In view of the confusion that surrounds this terminological dispute, it will be best to call a miniature upper-note trill ◫ a *Pralltriller*, and a miniature main-note trill ◫ a *Schneller*, regardless of melodic context and regardless of articulation.

AGRICOLA

In the previous discussion of Tosi's trills (see Chapter 30), it was pointed out that Agricola, his German translator, had fashioned his added musical illustrations and commentaries in the image of the Berlin School. Agricola presents the basic trill model of Ex. 31.18*a*, which he calls a trill "without *Vorschlag*."[28]

Ex. 31.18. Agricola (1757)

By contrast, a trill "with *Vorschlag*" means one with support, where the upper note is "somewhat sustained" at the start (p. 98). Such a *Vorschlag*, he logically says, must not be made before a trilled note to which, if there were no trill, a

---

[25] Ibid.: "Herr Bach nennet diesen Triller wegen der Schnelligkeit, womit diese drey Noten, und nicht mehrere hervor gebracht werden müssen, einen Pralltriller. . . ."

[26] *Interpretation*, p. 252.

[27] Aldrich (*The Principal Agréments*, p. 373) criticizes Marpurg's use of the "incomplete

trill" (i.e. the *Schneller*) and his equation with C.P.E. Bach's *Prall-Triller*. However, Marpurg was all the more entitled to his opinions when they made such eminently good sense.

[28] *Anleitung*. Chapter 3 (pp. 92-122) is devoted to the trill.

Vorschlag could not be added (p. 109). He also refers to his previous equally rational rule, that an [onbeat] *Vorschlag* must not be superimposed on another *Vorschlag*. Like C.P.E. Bach, he stipulates that the regular trill must be shaken for the whole length of the note, especially in a cadence (p. 110). The suffix, shown above in Ex. 31.18*b*, should follow without a rest in the exact speed of the alternations (pp. 98-99) and be quickly connected to the following note. Agricola restates C.P.E. Bach's exception to this rule for dotted notes (p. 109) in identical terms. Later, Agricola mentions an independent further exception: after a long cadential trill, especially in a slow piece, in which the instruments enter only on the following note, the last note of the suffix can be somewhat sustained, whereupon the following final tone can be briefly anticipated. What he means is obviously this:

Within Agricola's essentially derivative presentation we find nevertheless one surprising element. In demonstrating the best methods for singers to learn a trill, he suggests the technique borrowed from the *ribattuta*, starting with dotted pairs of notes (pp. 97-98). His illustration is given in Ex. 31.19. He advises the singer to practice the pattern in slurred pairs, in which the second, shorter, note must not be weaker than the first, and to gradually accelerate the initially slow tempo, whereupon both the dot and the two-by-two slurs will disappear.[29]

Ex 31.19. Agricola

It is clear that a trill practiced according to these instructions will produce a main-note anchored design. Such a design can, of course, easily be combined with an upper-note support. However, when applied to the trill "without *Vorschlag*," it is likely that singers thus trained will instinctively place the main note on the beat, that is, they will either anticipate the auxiliary or leave it out altogether. Agricola, sensing perhaps the implied contradiction with the prevailing fashion, justifies his teaching method by saying that the lengthening of the main note is to prevent it from being lost or from becoming indistinct; and that the shortening of the equally strong upper note has the purpose of keeping it distinct while preventing it from becoming louder than the main note. Agricola, then, professes to oppose an emphasis on either the auxiliary or the main note, though an emphasis on the latter is what his teaching procedure is likely to produce.

Trill chains in diatonic ascent or descent can have a good effect, Agricola says, especially if in ascending each trill is followed by a suffix. This rendition is at variance with Mattheson's description that such chains should sound like one single trill.

Agricola equates Tosi's "half-trill" with the *Pralltriller* of the instrumentalists (pp. 99-100). For the keyboard, he gives the illustrations of Ex. 31.20 which indicate tone repetition and, like Bach, Agricola says that the *Pralltriller* occurs only before a falling second, regardless of whether occasioned by a *Vorschlag* or a regular note (p. 111).

[29] Ibid., p. 98: "Die Geschwindigkeit des Anschlages beyder Klänge wird es endlich verhindern, dass man weder den Punct zwischen beyden Noten, noch die Schleifung, mehr bemerken könne."

Ex. 31.20. Agricola

QUANTZ

Quantz devotes the whole ninth chapter of his treatise to the trills and, like C.P.E. Bach, states their main purpose in his first sentence: "Trills lend great brilliance to performance."[30] Quantz's basic trill model (Ex. 31.21) affirms the main-note anchor for the alternations and the main-note start of the alternation proper.

Ex. 31.21. Quantz (1752), Table 7, 1

Quantz does say that each trill starts with a *Vorschlag* from either above or below (exceptions to this rule will presently be mentioned) and refers to the treatment of *Vorschlag* in the preceding chapter of his treatise. In this chapter the *Vorschläge*, as will be remembered, were divided into *anschlagende* and *durchgehende*, i.e. long ones that fall on the beat and short ones that are anticipated.

There is no apparent reason why in Quantz's practice both types of *Vorschläge* should not be able to introduce a trill. Quantz says (par. 8): "The *Vorschlag* is sometimes as fast as the other notes of the trill, for instance when after a rest a new theme starts with a trill." In many cases of that type, the anticipated *Vorschlag* (as sketched by me in Ex. 31.22) offers the logical solution of combining a *Vorschlag* (the length of a trill's alternation) with his basic, main-note anchored model.

Ex. 31.22.

An impression to the contrary was created by Dolmetsch, because he made a mistake in translation. The passages just quoted about a *Vorschlag* being as short as a single trill note continues as follows: "This *Vorschlag*, be it long or short, will always be articulated by the tongue: the trill proper with its suffix has to be done in one slur."[31] Dolmetsch translated "mit der Zunge angestossen" as: "This appoggiatura whether long or short, must always be *accented*" (italics mine). An accent would, of course, place the first short *Vorschlag* on the beat. However, the term *anstossen* has no connotation of "accent" and refers simply to the fresh articulation, which can be done as softly or loudly as one chooses.[32]

[30] *Versuch*. In the following pages all references will be to the 9th chapter unless otherwise indicated.

[31] Par. 8: "Dieser Vorschlag mag aber lang oder kurz seyn, so wird er doch allezeit mit der Zunge angestossen: der Triller nebst seinem Nachschlage aber, werden an denselben ge-

schleifet."

[32] Edward R. Reilly in his translation of the treatise (*On Playing the Flute* [London, 1966]) renders this passage as follows: "Whether the appoggiatura is long or short, however, it must always be tipped with the tongue. . . ." For the correct meaning of the term *anstossen*, see also

A specimen of such a grace-note trill can be seen in Ex. 31.23. Since Quantz, as reported above, explained that a *Vorschlag* before a written-out long *Vorschlag* must be anticipated, this rule logically applies to the two trills on the sigh motive.[33]

Ex. 31.23. Quantz, Flute Sonata No. 293

In the frequent instances where a *Vorschlag* symbol before a trill signified a long *Vorschlag*, the grace did, of course, have a harmonic character, but this was due to the appoggiatura and not to the trill proper.

Long appoggiaturas in cadential trills seem to have been written out most frequently in regular notes. A characteristic passage is shown in Ex. 31.24.

Ex. 31.24. Quantz, Sonata No. 99

Quantz himself points out (ch. 8, par. 10) that the *Vorschlag* before a trill that is dissonant with the bass must be very short so that the dissonances are not changed into consonances. His illustration is given in Ex. 31.25. Since even a brief accented onbeat rendition of the consonance would deprive the dissonance of its rhythmical backbone, it is likely that Quantz had unaccented *"durchgehende"* *Vorschläge* in mind here, too.

Ex. 31.25. Quantz

Quantz's illustrations of diminutions and adagio embellishments, together with his concomitant verbal commentaries, offer interesting insights into the treatment of certain trills and their introductory *Vorschläge*. Before longer trills, such as

ch. 8, par. 4: "Man muss die Vorschläge mit der Zunge weich anstossen," i.e. Vorschläge must be *gently articulated* with the tongue (italics mine).

[33] This and the following examples from Quantz's sonatas are from manuscripts at **BB** of the *Königliche Hausbibliothek*.

those on quarter-notes, the *Vorschlag* usually appears to be long and *wachsend*, i.e. starting softly and becoming louder, as shown in Exx. 31.26a and b. (The dynamic markings on the second line of the illustration are not by Quantz but were added according to his written instructions.) In other instances, the *Vorschlag* before the trill is apparently anticipated. Thus in Ex. *c*, the dynamic instructions alone point to the grace-note character of both little notes. They read for the third beat: "D strong, C soft, B strong, A, G, with the trill soft." Moreover, on this third beat, Quantz refers to Fig. 28d of his diminution Table 16, where all patterns of passing notes are shown to be done in anticipation.[34]

In Ex. *d* the *Vorschläge* are supposed to be anticipated in accord with Quantz's rule regarding falling thirds of equal value; moreover, in his instructions concerning this example (ch. 14, par. 42), Quantz says that the eight 16th-notes plus the trill on the e and the following c are to be played strongly and grow in volume; *the four little notes are to be weak* (italics mine), which gives grace-note character to the trill on e.

Ex. 31.26. Quantz

Quantz also describes (ch. 8, par. 14) what he calls a half-trill (*halber Triller*) and says it is one of the graces that can be inserted *between* a Vorschlag and the following main note. His illustrations are shown in Ex. 31.27. Their metrical vagueness suggests that these half-trills probably were used after all types of *Vorschläge*, and in all types of rhythmic designs.

Ex. 31.27. Quantz

In a chapter devoted to the *ripieno* violinists, Quantz mentions a short main-note trill (ch. 17, sec. 2, par. 24). While referring his readers to his main chapter on trills, he adds that "if trills are written over several fast notes, on account of

[34] These references were left out in the music illustrations to keep from cluttering up the text.

the shortness of time, both *Vor-* and *Nachschlag* are not always done; but time and again only a half-trill is being made." A Quantzian trill without a *Vorschlag* is a main-note trill, and, as can be seen from Ex. 31.27, a "half-trill" after the excision of *Vorschlag* and *Nachschlag* is a *Schneller*.

The versatility of Quantz's trill treatment was to be expected from an artist of his demonstrated finesse and flexibility. More surprising is the fact that the one trill design for which no record can be found in Quantz's discussions is the one considered by many the fundamental trill pattern of the century: the series of descending appoggiaturas.

LEOPOLD MOZART

The tenth chapter of Mozart's treatise is devoted to the trill and shows throughout a strong allegiance to the ideas and principles of Tartini; in fact, Mozart borrowed many of Tartini's examples without mentioning the source.[35]

Mozart's basic trill model shows the upper-note start and anchor (Ex. 31.28*a*). The trill is "unprepared" when the alternations start immediately (Ex. *b*) or "prepared" by a more or less long descending appoggiatura (Ex. *c*) or by an *Überwurf* (Ex. *d*), a dotted two-note grace involving a leap of a third that frames the principal note. In this case the alternations have to be main-note anchored. Preparation may also be made by a *ribattuta* on the note below the trill in accord with Tartini's and C.P.E. Bach's pattern (see Ex. 31.13), or the preparation may be with a turn, resulting in a compound trill that will be discussed in a later chapter.

Ex. 31.28. L. Mozart (1756)

Trills of various speeds, according to the character of the piece, as well as those that combine the slow start and acceleration with a gradual crescendo are all described in terms of Tartini's treatise and need not be repeated here.

Mozart seemingly underlines his preferences for the upper-note anchor in the examples showing the way to *practice* a double trill in thirds (par. 27); starting with the main note on the beat, the pattern is reversed with the bow change to an upper-note anchor, as shown in Ex. 31.29. Technical-pedagogical considerations can perhaps best explain the design of this study model with its musically unconvincing reversal of motion; as was pointed out before, a trill on any string instrument is much easier to execute with the upper note *on* instead of *off* the beat. Therefore, Mozart's is a logical practice pattern (and as such it was presented) inasmuch as the doubling in thirds vastly increases the trill's difficulty beyond a certain speed.

"All short trills are played with a fast *Vorschlag* and *Nachschlag*,"[36] says Mozart, and he gives the illustration of Ex. 31.30.

[35] *Violinschule.* All references in the following paragraphs will be to the 10th chapter unless otherwise indicated.

[36] Par. 6: "Mit einem schnellen Vorschlage und Nachschlage spielt man alle kurzen Triller."

Ex. 31.29. L. Mozart

Ex. 31.30. L. Mozart

The "fast" *Vorschlag* is probably identical with the "short" *Vorschlag*, defined by Mozart (ch. 9, par. 9) as the kind in which "the stress is not on the *Vorschlag* but on the principal note. The short *Vorschlag* is played as fast as possible and is rendered not strong but very weak." It is therefore likely that the short *Vorschläge* he mentions for short trills are of the unaccented type which produce a grace-note trill.

More ambiguous is the following sentence. After mentioning the long appoggiatura preparation shown above, he continues: ". . . however, when a passage starts with a trill, the *Vorschlag* is hardly audible and is in such a case nothing but a strong impulse for the trill."[37] He then refers to the illustration given in Ex. 31.31. "Hardly audible" and "strong impulse" are somewhat contradictory. Since he cannot mean a sustained *Vorschlag* of any length, which would be very audible, he presumably had an unlengthened onbeat auxiliary in mind.

Ex. 31.31. L. Mozart

In passing, it should be mentioned that Mozart speaks also of a half-trill (*Halbtriller*) as an adjunct to a long *Vorschlag* (ch. 9, par. 27). His illustrations show that this grace is more in the nature of a turn than of a trill.

In accord with Tartini, Mozart explains in paragraph 19 how a trill on dotted notes can be made on the dot, after sustaining the note proper. The result is a main-note support. Mozart also shows in paragraph 22 the trill chains, following Tartini's pattern of the *portamento* trills. For the same reasons that were stated in connection with Tartini's pattern, these trills have to start with the main note.

This fact is further underlined by Mozart's introduction of an alternate fingering. After showing, as did Tartini, the use of a gliding first or second finger, Mozart remarks that these trills should be also mastered with the alternate use of the first and the second fingers, as shown in Ex. 31.32a. For technical and musical reasons, this fingering eliminates an upper-note start for each trill: in ascending, it would require for every other trill an obtrusive slide of a third (Ex. *b*); in descending, every second trill would involve a tie and the one following would be articulated through a change of finger (Ex. *c*). Musical illogic would be compounded by technical contrariness.

Chromatic trill chains, discussed in paragraph 24 and illustrated as shown in Ex. 31.33, are still more persuasive in their main-note implication. Here Mozart's comment, that the first and second fingers in moving up as well as down have to make the change impercep-

---

[37] Par. 11: "Wenn aber eine Passage mit einem Triller anfängt: so wird der Vorschlag kaum gehört, und er ist in einem solchen Falle nichts denn ein starker Anstoss des Trillers."

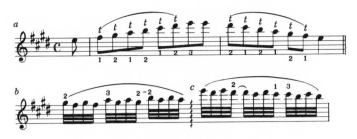

Ex. 31.32. L. Mozart

tively while the shaking finger must continue without interruption, makes technical sense only with main-note start. (The fingerings in the example are not given by Mozart but are indicated as implied by the context.)

Ex. 31.33. L. Mozart

Further evidence for the main-note trill is contained in Mozart's analysis of Tartini's "Devil's trill" which forms an epilogue to Mozart's trill chapter (par. 32). Among other comments, Mozart says: "In the third measure [the first in Ex. 31.34] one must change the finger for the half-note f already on the second 8th and replace the second with the first, as soon as the first d of the lower notes is stopped with the third finger, in order not to hinder the alternation of the upper notes; the same applies to the eleventh measure."[38] To put down the third finger as soon as the first d is sounded implies main-note start for this section, hence for the whole length of the trill.

Ex. 31.34. L. Mozart's analysis of the Devil's Trill

The variety in Mozart's treatment of the trill that could be pieced together from various indications was to be expected in view of the strong Italian and mainly Tartinian influences. Mozart mentions no rule about the start with the upper note. His basic trill model is the only clue for this design, and we have seen with Tartini how misleading such a clue can be.

AFTER midcentury, many, perhaps most, of the German theorists followed the leadership of C.P.E. Bach, though their agreement is rarely if ever total. There were dissidents among theorists and composers. Friedemann Bach, though generally following the latest ornamental fashions, shows a measure of independence when in a sonata movement he has *Vorschläge* written out in front of each of its

[38] Par. 32: "Im dritten Tacte muss man bey der halben Note (f) schon im halben Theile des ersten Viertheils gleich die Finger ändern, und anstatt des zweyten den ersten hinsetzen, so bald die erste (d) Note der unten stehenden Note mit dem dritten Finger ergriffen wird: um den Trillerschlag bey den obern Noten nicht zu hindern; welches auch im eilften Tacte geschieht."

34 trills (see Ex. 31.35*a*). The same thing occurs in a cantata where the trill pattern of Ex. *b* is written out with a little *Vorschlag* note no less than 34 times.[39] Since in fairly fast tempo the difference between onbeat and anticipation can easily be blurred, we can at least gather that the upper-note start of the trill was not taken for granted.

a. Clavier Sonata, Fk. 4, 3

b. Cantata Fk. 88, 5

Ex. 31.35. W. F. Bach (1710-1786)

Löhlein's basic trill pattern, with its suffix before a rest point, follows Marpurg rather than C.P.E. Bach. The model shown in Ex. 31.36*a* from the clavier treatise (1765-1782) is the same in his violin treatise of 1774 and in its above mentioned copy in P 803.[40]

The *Pralltriller* or *Abzug* is shown in Marpurg's form of a *Schneller* (Ex. *b*); another miniature trill with suffix preceded by a long *Vorschlag* is shown as "Abzug mit dem Nachschlage" (Ex. *c*). Both of these patterns are also contained in P 803. In the violin treatise, the *Schneller* design is listed as "der halbe Triller oder Abzug" (Ex. *d*), and the pattern of Ex. *c* is called "der halbe Triller mit dem Nachschlage." It is practically identical with Marpurg's "incomplete trill" (see Ex. 31.16).

a. Clavier treatise (1765-1782) and P 803

b. (1765)

c. (1765)

Der simple Trillo

Der Pralltriller oder Abzug

Der Abzug mit dem Nachschlage

d. Violin treatise (1776)

Der halbe Triller oder Abzug

Ex. 31.36. Löhlein

Kürzinger (1763) mentions nothing about upper-note start in his trill definition (p. 35), and the only model he presents is one that shows the best way to *study* the trill (Ex.

[39] Aut. P 202.

[40] *Clavier-Schule*, ch. 6; *Anweisung zum Violinspielen*, p. 46.

31.37).[41] Main-note start and anchor are here unmistakable (p. 36). The *chevron* over the half-note most likely denotes continuation of the now unmeasured main-note trill, though Kürzinger normally uses the symbol for vibrato. Speaking of trill chains, he reiterates Mattheson's and Tosi's description of singing them as if they were one trill only, thereby confirming their main-note nature.

Ex. 31.37. Kürzinger (1763)

There is an interesting graphic difference between Petri's trill model in the first edition of his treatise (1767) and the one in the second (1782).[42] In the first edition the pattern of the plain trill is written out in metrical notes (Ex. 31.38a); in the second, the trill is indicated in small ornamental notes (Ex. b). A reversed order would have been interpreted as a more precise specification of former vagueness. But when vagueness follows precision, the more probable meaning is the desire to allow for greater rhythmic latitude. The new design seems more suggestive of at least partial anticipation than of straight onbeat rendition.

An unmistakable grace-note trill is illustrated by Deysinger, who explains that the two notes of Ex. c "must be played or sung" as given in Ex. d.[43]

Ex. 31.38.

Hiller, in his three major treatises,[44] follows C.P.E. Bach with scarcely a deviation. One point of some interest is a species of double trill, shown in his second treatise of 1780 (p. 68) which, "used by both singers and instrumentalists" is "worthy of every esteem" ("aller Ehren werth"). This species is closely related to the "Italian double trill" and to C.P.E. Bach's *ribattuta* preparation a tone below the trill, except that in Hiller's model the character of main-note support and trill with main-note anchor is more clearly marked (Ex. 31.39a). In a second version that is to show a still smoother connection, we see a chromatic ascent of the preparatory trill (Ex. b).

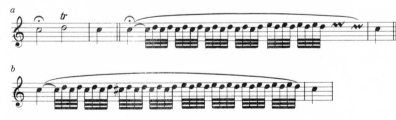

Ex. 31.39. Hiller (1780)

[41] *Getreuer Unterricht*, pp. 35-36.
[42] *Anleitung*, 1st ed., p. 31, 2nd ed., p. 154.
[43] *Compendium musicum*, p. 11 in both 1st and 2nd eds.

[44] *Anweisung z. mus.-richtigen Gesange; Anweisung z. mus.-zierlichen Gesange; Anweisung zum Violinspielen.*

Using the term *Schnelzer*, Vogler illustrates a brief main-note trill with suffix (Ex. 31.40*a*). He describes it as being composed of several (clearly anticipated) *Vorschläge*. His *Triller* is main-note anchored and starts with the tone below.[45]

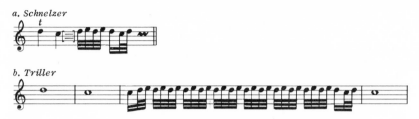

Ex. 31.40. Vogler (1778), Table VI, f. 10

Taking a quick look across the date line staked out for this chapter, it is worthy of note that Türk in 1789 still falls completely in line with C.P.E. Bach, even hardening his attitude on the upper-note start and anchor.[46] Since such a design places the main-note of the trill in a distinctly subservient role, Türk is consistent in suggesting that the name "main note" be discarded and replaced by the term "written note" (ch. 4, sec. 3, par. 27). For similar reasons of principle, he objected, as did Aldrich 150 years later, to Marpurg's, Löhlein's, and other writers' main-note interpretation of the *Pralltriller* (par. 55). However, using examples taken from the works of C.P.E. Bach and E. W. Wolf, he shows how these masters themselves often confused the *Pralltriller* and the *Schneller* (par. 57).

About the same time, a German musician (according to Fétis, his name was *Schwartzendorf*), writing in France under the name of "Martini," seems to use only the main-note trill, even for cadences, though in other matters he leans heavily on Hiller.[47] Example 31.41*a* shows his model of a cadential trill which has an obviously anticipated turn before its main-note start. Example *b* shows a non-cadential trill, Ex. *c* a main-note trill that is approached from below.

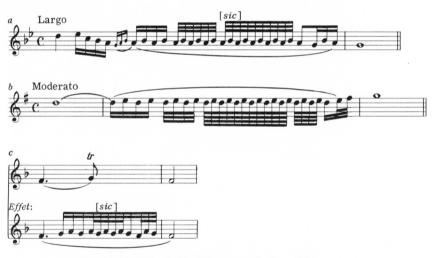

Ex. 31.41. "Martini" (Schwartzendorf, c. 1791)

Another German, J. N. Hüllmandel, composer of note and a student of C.P.E. Bach's, writing in England, has this to say: "The shake begins indiscriminately with either of the two Shaken Notes, or sometimes by a Note under those of the Shake."[48] His models (p. 27) are given in Ex. 31.42.

[45] *Gründe der Kuhrpfälzischen Tonschule in Beispielen*, Table 6.

[46] *Klavierschule*, ch. 4, sec. 3.

[47] *Mélopée moderne*, pp. 13ff.

[48] *Principles of Music*, pp. 16ff. Hüllmandel was an eminent pianist and successful composer whose sonatas were praised by W. A. Mozart.

Ex. 31.42. Hüllmandel (c. 1795)

Tromlitz's chapter on the trill is of considerable interest.[49] In direct contrast to Türk, the term "main note" means to Tromlitz what it says: "there are some who say," he writes, "that one should start the trill with the upper note and consider the auxiliaries in this fast movement as a series of appoggiaturas, hence put the weight on them, while they want to treat the second note which ought to be the main note as the passing one when this is the one which in my opinion ought to carry the weight" (p. 272). Tromlitz rejects the emphasis on the upper note as unnatural, because, he says, the main note has to be heard the same as if there were no trill. When we emphasize the upper note, the real melody note is "displaced and obliterated" ("verdrängt und vertilget"), "the sequence of the melody torn, the proper melody defaced" ("die Folge des guten Gesanges zerrissen, und der eigentliche Gesang unkennlich gemacht"). He makes a particularly convincing case for the main-note anchor of a trill that follows an appoggiatura support. This point has been stressed before in this study, and it is interesting to see how Tromlitz was struck by the illogic of the orthodox execution. Pointing to the phrase given in Ex. 31.43*a*, he says that without a trill it must sound like Ex. *b*, where the second quarter-note is heard distinctly. Hence, a trill placed upon this quarter-note (Ex. *c*) must be of a kind that permits the melody tone to be heard as distinctly as without a trill. Consequently, it has to be played as shown in Ex. *d*. This, he continues, cannot be achieved if one starts from above and places the weight on the upper note, as shown in Ex. *e*, because in this case the quarter-note is only barely audible.[50]

Ex. 31.43. Tromlitz (1791)

Tromlitz's basic trill pattern is identical to Quantz's (Ex. 31.44).

Ex. 31.44. Tromlitz

When it occurs in the middle of a melody, Tromlitz's pattern, like Quantz's, is usually preceded by a *Vorschlag* either from above or below, but not always. A preceding note can take the place of a *Vorschlag* (p. 270). Moreover, at the start of a phrase the trill "may also receive a *Vorschlag* but a very short one [Ex. 31.45*a*], but may also be made without a *Vorschlag*" (see Ex. *b*).[51] Now, a trill without a *Vorschlag* in Tromlitz's as well as in Quantz's terminology means the naked basic trill pattern, hence a main-note trill, while the "short" *Vorschlag* placed before the main-note anchored alternation is most likely a grace-note.

Ex. 31.45. Tromlitz

[49] *Unterricht*, pp. 266ff.

[50] Ibid., p. 273: "Aber wird man das wohl können, wenn man von oben anfängt, und das Gewicht auf die drüber liegende Note legt? und dadurch dieses Viertel verdränget, dass es kaum gehöret wird?"

[51] Ibid., p. 271: "Fängt der Gesang aber mit einem Triller an, es sey im Anfange oder in der Mitte, so kann er auch einen, doch sehr kurzen Vorschlag bekommen, s. 8 [our Ex. *a*] kann aber auch ohne Vorschlag gemachet werden, s. 9 [our Ex. *b*]."

Tromlitz has been dealt with in detail, because it is interesting to see how, by counterbalancing Türk's rigidity, he places the latter's principles into a different perspective. Moreover, Tromlitz's contrasting views should give pause to those who think they can "apply" Türk automatically to Mozart because he happened to be his contemporary.

IN the years around 1715, the Italo-German main-note trill was still very much in evidence and still found, in the next few decades, its theoretical reflection in the treatises of Spiess, "Humanus," and, presumably also, Mattheson. The French upper-note start had been introduced earlier in the century, and among keyboard players it was beginning to gain ground on its way to later ascendancy. The pattern of this development was very irregular, as was to be expected in the random mixture of two traditions. With due allowance for an unavoidable oversimplification, one can roughly distinguish two main streams of development. One was generally linked to the *galant* stylistic tendencies. Its sources were French keyboard models going back to Chambonnières and D'Anglebert. Gradually, these models were rigidified to form a new more specifically German style. This trend can be traced in theoretical models from Theophil Muffat to C.P.E. Bach, Marpurg, and Türk. It is characterized by the onbeat auxiliary and the upper-note anchor ("a series of descending appoggiaturas"). C.P.E. Bach was in the center of this development and drew many theoreticians and performers into his orbit.

The other, older, stream, generally linked to the baroque tradition, issued from the 17th-century Italo-German sources that retained their vital force in spite of having absorbed (after 1700) French admixtures of varying strength. The conservative temper of the baroque masters favored the continued cultivation of the older tradition derived, after all, from the homeland of the baroque style. The followers of this stream, among them Bach and Handel, unbound by any single limiting principle, ranged freely over the field of the combined practices. Even after the final passing of the baroque, some of these freedoms survived among those masters and theorists who had a more cosmopolitan outlook. Although Quantz's trill was fundamentally main-note anchored, he knew, besides the appoggiatura support, the grace-note trill, the preparation with a rising *Vorschlag*, and the main-note trill. Leopold Mozart, in spite of his basic trill model that agreed with C.P.E. Bach, used on occasion all the other starting styles. Other theorists, among them Kürzinger, Vogel, Hüllmandel, and Martini, confirmed the continued use of the main-note trill. Thus, at the end of the century, when we find with Tromlitz a strong case for the main-note anchor and an occasional main-note start, we do not have to do with innovative antecedents of 19th-century practices (so often ascribed to Hummel's "invention") but simply with the same old stream of the Italo-German tradition that never ceased to flow during the 17th and 18th centuries.

PART VI

THE COMPOUND TRILL

Introduction
Turn-Trill, Slide-Trill,
Mordent-Trill

———— •◦• ————

Any grace can join with almost any other grace to form a new combination. Some of these pairings have produced such felicitous designs that their combination has led to semipermanent unions. We have met examples in the mergers of descending *Vorschlag* and trill, trill and suffix, and rising *Vorschlag* and mordent. Three other mergers will be discussed here, because they occupy an important place in the music of Bach and other masters of the period. They are the combination of turn and trill ⨍⨍, slide and trill ⨍⨍, and mordent and trill ⨍⨍. Under the collective designation of "compound trills," I shall refer to them as "turn-trill," "slide-trill," and "mordent-trill." A fourth one of much lesser importance could be called the "Italian double trill" and consists of a—usually cadential—trill that is preceded by a main-note trill a step below: ⨍⨍. The melodic shapes of these graces are sketched in Ex. VI.1 (the number of alternations, of course, *ad libitum*).

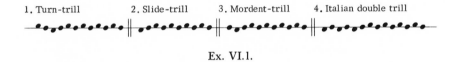

1. Turn-trill   2. Slide-trill   3. Mordent-trill   4. Italian double trill

Ex. VI.1.

The problems specifically related to the compound trill have to do entirely with the rhythmic shape of its start. The usual alternative of prebeat versus onbeat style is complicated here by the number of notes that can be involved in a shift across the line of the beat.

The turn-trill can be rendered on the beat or else three, four, or five notes can be placed before the beat. The respective designs, shown in Ex. VI.2, will be referred to as rhythmic types (= RT) 1 through 4. (The vertical dash indicates the beat.)

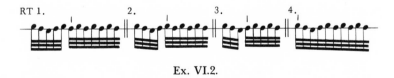

RT 1.   2.   3.   4.

Ex. VI.2.

The logic of a four-note anticipation rests in the clear disposition of the two elements of the grace: the turn *before* the beat, the trill *on* the beat, resulting in RT 2. If the trill is a grace-note design, its anticipated auxiliary joins the four notes of the turn to form RT 1. If the fourth note of the turn merges with the main-note start of the trill, a three-note upbeat results (RT 3). The four-note turn tends to retain its identity within the compound grace, as manifested in its frequent notation with either four regular notes (Ex. VI. 3*a*), four small notes (Ex. *b*), or the usual turn symbol (Ex. *c*). The onbeat placement of the whole grace (RT 4) is the solution generally assumed to be the only authentic one.

Ex. VI.3.

The slide-trill is not a simple inversion of the turn-trill. Only its first note is foreign to a main-note trill, and only the first two notes are foreign to an upper-note trill. The four favored rhythmic designs range from a three-note prebeat to straight onbeat, as shown in Ex. VI.4.

Ex. VI.4.

A prebeat slide preceding an anticipated auxiliary results in the three-note upbeat of RT 1. A prebeat slide leading to an accented auxiliary forms RT 2. When the first note functions as a *Vorschlag* from below and the second note merges with a main-note start of the alternations, we obtain the one-note anticipation of RT 3. Finally, the Lombard pattern of the slide produces the onbeat design of RT 4.

Rhythm types 1 and 3 underline the main note, type 2 the auxiliary. The function of type 4, the onbeat model, is ambiguous. Its only emphasis is on the note below the trill. Although it is the only design for the ascending type that is admitted by the onbeat advocates, it places no emphasis on the auxiliary.

The mordent-trill presents fewer rhythmic problems, since the mordent is mostly written in metric notation and usually anticipated. The alternative of prebeat or onbeat auxiliary of the trill proper (see Ex. VI.5) is the chief question about its execution.

Ex. VI.5.

The Italian double trill, a close relative of the mordent-trill, has its first main-note part usually before the beat. Its two main types are given in Exx. VI.6a and b. The first of these is probably more common.

Ex. VI.6.

The slide-trill may have made its first appearance in England where Christopher Simpson, in one of the oldest known ornament tables (1659), explains a grace called cadent (see Ex. VI.7).

Ex. VI.7. Simpson

In France all three main compound trills appear in Marais's first book of gamba pieces of 1686, and in D'Anglebert's table of 1689 with abstract symbols of his invention. From France, the designs spread to Germany where Bach adopted D'Anglebert's symbols. There is no evidence that the Italians used any of the three main species as standard ornaments. Only the native pattern, the Italian double trill, is recorded by Tartini in mid-18th century. It found some followers in Germany but seems to have played only a small role.

The French Compound Trill
1685-1760

D'Anglebert introduced in his table of 1689 the following patterns, names, and symbols:[1]

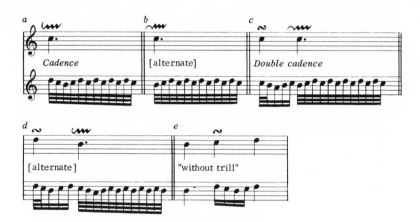

Ex. 32.1. D'Anglebert (1689)

The models indicate onbeat rendition. The first two, Exx. *a* and *b*, which he calls *cadence*, stand for the turn-trill and the slide-trill. Two other models, Exx. *c* and *d*, called *double cadence*, amount to a species of a twice compounded trill in which an older type of turn (the one found in Chambonnières's table) precedes either a slide-trill or a turn-trill.

Although the patterns of Exx. *c* and *d* were used by D'Anglebert in a number of final cadences, they did not become a standard combination. Moreover, they are confusing, because the transcription of the first turn symbol—consisting of five notes that start and end on the main note and reach a third below—is at odds with the meaning given the same symbol in the very next model (Ex. *e*).

A year earlier, André Raison had listed another kind of *double cadence* which consisted of a modern interbeat turn following its main note and leading to a simple trill on the next higher step (see Ex. 32.2).[2] (Interesting in this pattern is the separation of the suffix from the trill, which seems to have been Raison's preferred design since it recurs in the only other two models that contain suffixes.) Raison's pattern is not a turn-trill in our above defined sense, but it is a close relative.

Ex. 32.2. Raison (1688)

---

[1] *Pièces de clavecin.* [2] *Livre d'orgue.*

D'Anglebert's onbeat models were, as far as could be ascertained, the first and the last ones of their kind in France. All the remaining French evidence points to anticipated designs.

In his gamba works, Marin Marais indicated the turn-trill with four little notes preceding the trill symbol (a hook after the note), as shown in Exx. 32.3a and b.[3] Similarly, he marks the slide-trills with two little notes, as shown in Exx. c and d. The mordent-trill is fairly frequent, too, and is usually written out in regular notes (Ex. e). It has been shown before that Marais's little notes, especially those in groups of two or more, were interbeat graces, and the same is quite certainly true of their use in compound trills.

The anticipation of the four-note turn written by little notes is confirmed in a passage given in Ex. f.[4] True, the notation here is inconsistent: the value of each main note is reduced from a quarter to a dotted 8th to accommodate the anticipated turn. However, the ornamental character of the little notes is unmistakable, because they are written with small note heads with their stems upward and their usual three beams; in regular notation they would have needed a fourth beam and be stemmed downward with large note heads. Also, if further confirmation were needed, the second measure of Ex. d shows that here only anticipation would make sense.

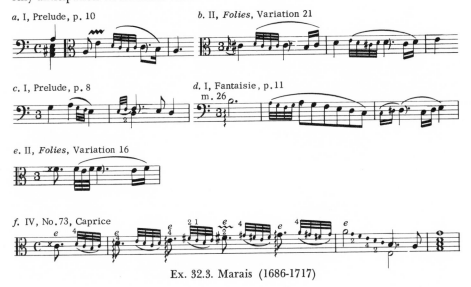

a. I, Prelude, p. 10   b. II, *Folies*, Variation 21

c. I, Prelude, p. 8   d. I, Fantaisie, p. 11
m. 26

e. II, *Folies*, Variation 16

f. IV, No. 73, Caprice

Ex. 32.3. Marais (1686-1717)

Boyvin in 1689 shows in regular notation the prebeat turn-trill of Ex. 32.4a; Grigny in 1699 gives the similar pattern of Ex. b; Le Roux in 1705 writes the prebeat examples of c and d.[5] (In Ex. c the crosses, a common French trill symbol, which do not appear in Le Roux's table, must have been used inadvertently instead of the *chevrons* of Ex. d.)

Dieupart lists a *double cadence* that, like D'Anglebert's, uses Chambonnières's old five-note turn, but here the turn has prebeat character and is followed by a simple, not a compound, trill, as given in Ex. 32.5a.[6] It occurs but rarely in his

[3] See above ch. 9, n. 17. The Roman numerals in the music examples stand for the five volumes.

[4] This example was reproduced with all its details to show the extraordinary care of Marais's editing, which seems two hundred years ahead of his time. The cross stands for

a mordent; the "e" for a crescendo, the horizontal wavy line for a two-finger vibrato, the vertical wavy line for a one-finger vibrato.

[5] Boyvin, *Premier livre d'orgue*; Grigny, *Premier livre d'orgue*; Le Roux, *Pièces de clavessin*.

[6] *Six suittes de clavessin*.

a. Boyvin (1689), *Dessus de Tierce*   b. Grigny (1699), Trio

c. Le Roux (1705), Gavotte   d. Le Roux, Allemande

Ex. 32.4.

pieces. By contrast, we find several times in his book the mordent-trill indicated by small notes but in unmistakable prebeat meaning (Ex. *b*).

a
Double cadence a Shake turn

b. Ouverture in A major

Ex. 32.5. Dieupart (c. 1702)

Hotteterre's *tour de chant* is a mordent-trill (see Ex. 32.6*a*).[7] De la Barre, whose anticipated *Vorschläge* were shown before, has several examples of prebeat compound trills. The illustration of Ex. *b* shows both the mordent-trill and the slide-trill, the latter with prebar notation of the two little notes.[8]

a. Hotteterre (1708)

Tour de chant   *Port de voix*

b. De la Barre (1703), Prelude

Ex. 32.6.

Montéclair gives the name of *tremblement doublé* (symbol: $\hat{t}$) to a variant of the turn-trill which has an interbeat turn introducing the alternations (Ex. 32.7).[9]

t

Tremblement Doublé

Battements   *Tour du gosier*

Ex. 32.7. Montéclair (1736)

[7] *Premier livre de pieces pour la flûte . . . ,*   (Paris, 1703).
2nd ed. (Paris, 1715) (1st ed. 1708).   [9] *Principes,* p. 84.
[8] *Pièces pour la flûte traversiere . . . ,* Op. 4

Once in a while Couperin writes out in regular notes a prebeat turn before a trill—for instance, in the bass of Ex. 32.8a; but much more often he writes the turn with four little notes whose prebeat meaning could hardly be misunderstood, even if it were not verified in such passages as those of Exx. *b* and *c*.[10] The first of these (Ex. *b*) is particularly instructive because it proves the need for full *five*-note anticipation encompassing the trill's auxiliary along with the turn. In the sequence shown, two mordent-trills alternate with two turn-trills. In both turn-trills the onbeat rendition of the turn, and therefore also of the auxiliary, would produce unacceptable fifths. The first measure of the example presents identical proof by way of the rather unusual mordent-turn combination on the first note. Not only does the turn have to precede the following trill, but the auxiliary as well has to be anticipated for the same reasons of voice-leading. (This example is, incidentally, further evidence of Couperin's preference for the grace-note trill.) Hardly less eloquent is Ex. *c*. In the first of three turn-trills that follow one another, the change from f to f sharp in the left hand makes musical sense only if the turn is anticipated. Moreover, it makes *best* sense when the fifth note, the auxiliary, is also anticipated, in order to clarify the chromatic progression.[11]

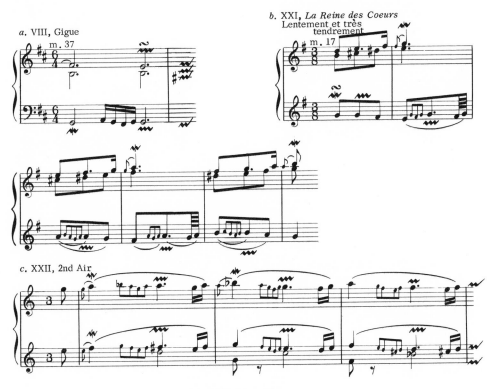

Ex. 32.8. Couperin

The mordent-trill, a favorite of Couperin's, was indicated with little notes in Ex. 32.8b; more often it is written out in regular notes, as shown in Exx. 32.9a and b.[12]

10 As before, the Roman numerals stand for the *ordres* in the four books of harpsichord pieces of 1713, 1716, 1722, and 1730.

11 For further examples of such turn-trills, see XV, *La Régente*, m. 12, and *Prélude* from the first *Concert royal*, m. 3.

12 For further examples, see VIII, *La Raphaéle*, mm. 4 and 7, *Gavotte*, m. 9, and IX, *Le Bavolet flottant*, m. 32.

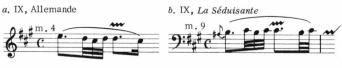

Ex. 32.9. Couperin

The slide-trill appears less frequently in his pieces. Considering the previously demonstrated anticipation of the two-note slide symbol, the slide-trill can also be assumed to fall in line with the interbeat style of the other compound trills. Example 32.10 gives two specimens. Couperin's anticipation of the slide-trill will presently be confirmed by D'Agincour.

Ex. 32.10. Couperin

Nicolas Siret, a contemporary of Couperin and influenced by him uses the anticipated slide-trill with prebar notation in a Sarabande from his first book of harpsichord pieces (Ex. 32.11a). Example b from the second book shows a pre-beat turn-trill indicated by the usual turn symbol.[13]

Ex. 32.11. Siret

D'Agincour, another of Couperin's followers, uses the slide-trill many times in his first harpsichord book of 1733;[14] and when it occurs at the beginning of a measure, the slide is invariably placed before the bar line, as shown in Exx. 32.12a and b. The importance of this revealing evidence is strengthened by D'Agincour's statement concerning his strict adherence to Couperin's practices. In the preface to the book, D'Agincour writes: "I have changed nothing in the use of ornaments or in the manner of playing which Monsieur Couperin has so well formulated and characterized, and which has been adopted by almost all the artists; I can say that we are all infinitely in his obligation for his painstaking explorations of these matters."[15]

Ex. 32.12. D'Agincour

[13] *Pièces de clavecin* (Paris [1716]); *Second livre de pièces de clavecin* (Paris, 1719).

[14] *Pièces de clavecin, Premier Livre* (Paris, 1733).

[15] "Je n'ay rien changé aux agrémens n'y [*sic*] a la maniere de touchér, de celle que M. Couperin a si bien désigné et caractérisée, et dont presque toutes les personnes de l'Art font usage; Je peux dire même que nous lui devons tous sçavoir un gré infini des peines qu'il s'est données d'en faire la recherche." Concerning a misleading ornament table in a modern edition of this work by D'Agincour, see above, ch. 19, n. 12.

The general prebeat meaning of the two little notes when used as a symbol of the slide in France was demonstrated before. Rameau's slide-trill in Ex. 32.13 would result in unlikely fifths if performed on the beat; therefore, it is not far-fetched to assume that he too followed the general French practice and that in similar instances the same prebeat meaning can be expected.[16]

Ex. 32.13. Rameau, *L'Entretien des muses* (1724)

In Ex. 32.14*a* from the *Pièces de clavessin* of 1724, we find a written-out prebeat turn-trill; in Ex. *b* from the *Nouvelles suites*, a similar prebeat turn-trill is indicated by the usual turn symbol.

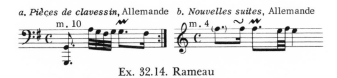

Ex. 32.14. Rameau

Example 32.15 from Royer's book of 1746 clarifies the anticipation of the turn-trill.[17]

Ex. 32.15. Royer (1746), *La Zaïde*

The same is the case for the vocal illustration of Ex. 32.16 from *Pirame et Thisbé* (1726) by Francoeur ("cadet") and Rebel fils.

Ex. 32.16. Francoeur and Rebel, *Pirame et Thisbé* (1726), I, 4

In La Chapelle's treatise of 1736 we meet with one of the rare French theoretical acknowledgments of the turn-trill to be found after D'Anglebert's table.[18] Under the terms of *coulement triple et double triple*, the author shows the pas-

[16] E.g. in *La Coulicam*, m. 9 from the *Pièces de clavecin en concerts*, especially when compared with the written-out prebeat slide of the parallel spot in m. 50.

[17] *Pièces de clavecin, Premier Livre* (Paris, 1746).

[18] *Vrais principes*, II, 14.

sage of Ex. 32.17 where in its first version (Ex. *a*) each note is independently syllabified, hence treated as structural unit. The second version (Ex. *b*) shows how the three 8th-notes of the first measure and the four 16th-notes of the second measure (the turn) can be viewed as ornamental figurations and consequently be pronounced under a single syllable; the third version (Ex. *c*) shows the melismas notated as ornamental small notes. The implied identity of sound of all three versions proves the prebeat rendition of the four little notes.

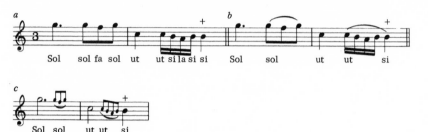

Ex. 32.17. La Chapelle (1736)

THOUGH the three main types of the compound trill were often used by important French masters, the theoretical documentation is very meager. The turn-trill and slide-trill appeared in D'Anglebert's table; only the turn-trill was given in Dieupart's treatise. Some 75 years later the turn-trill appeared in La Chapelle's treatise, and that may be all. D'Anglebert showed the onbeat pattern for these two graces. On the other hand, the musical evidence for the following 75 years indicates prebeat designs, as do the theoretical documents of Dieupart and La Chapelle. In this connection it is interesting to note that as far as could be ascertained, no *French* composer adopted D'Anglebert's symbols for these graces; this may be no coincidence in view of the fact that no one seems to have adopted his designs either. With the exception of D'Anglebert, the vast majority of French masters favored the prebeat rendition of the compound trills. This assumption will find further collaboration in the prebeat compound trills of Marpurg's first essay on ornaments of 1749 which shows strong French influence.

———◆◆———

The compound trills entered Germany with the French ornamental influx in the early years of the 18th century. Prior to that time, no evidence of these ornaments could be found in either Germany or Italy, except for a few isolated occurrences such as those shown in Exx. 33.1*a* and *b*. Here in compositions by Pachelbel and Buxtehude we see slide-trills with anticipated auxiliary; there are also eleven such trills in Georg Muffat's *Apparatus musico-organicus*, Introduction to *Toccata secunda*.

a. Pachelbel, *Hexacordum Appolinis* (1679), Aria   *b.* Buxtehude, Chorale Prelude *Auf meinen lieben Gott*

Ex. 33.1.

Bach was one of the first Germans to use these French graces systematically. By adopting D'Anglebert's symbols for slide- and turn-trill (⟋ᴡᴠᴠ and ⟍ᴡᴠᴠ), he may have actually been solely responsible for their continued, if limited, use in Germany.

In his *Explication*, Bach reproduced D'Anglebert's models under the name of *Doppelt-cadence* (Ex. 33.2).

Ex. 33.2.

These are again strictly keyboard symbols. For other instruments, Bach writes the turn-trill most often in regular notes (Ex. 33.3*a*). The slide-trill occasionally is written similarly (Exx. *b* and *c*), but more frequently he notates it in any of the ways given in Exx. *d*, *e*, and *f*.

Ex. 33.3.

A special problem connected with Bach's compound trills marked by symbols resides in the frequent ambiguity of the sources. The main trouble stems from the confusion of ⟍ᴡᴠᴠ with ⟍ᴡᴠᴠ; also, the simple trill symbol ᴡᴠᴠ is occasionally confused with either of the foregoing two. For example, the London autograph of Prelude 13 (*WC* II), m. 44, reads as shown in Ex. 33.4*a*. In Altnikol's copy of 1744 it reads like Ex. *b*, with a little *Vorschlag* note inserted before the c double-sharp and Bach's clear symbol ⋌⋌⋌ changed to (⋌⋌⋌ . In Altnikol's later copy of 1755, we find the measure written as given in Ex. *c*.

Ex. 33.4. BWV 882, 1

Another illustration of notational problems is found in the Gigue from the 5th Partita. Its chief source is the poorly engraved original print in the *Clavier-Übung* of 1731. In the second part of this Gigue, the *BG* edition interpreted no less than 21 of the symbols as turn-trills. In the original print the symbols are all very small and dainty; their first stroke is distinctly longer, but it is neither vertical to suggest an upper-note start, nor is it the hook that is required for the turn-trill symbol. Instead, it is oblique and nearly always straight; only in a few cases is there a slight intimation of a curve. Musically the most likely choice is a grace-note trill. This design is also suggested by the spot in m. 53 where, as shown in Ex. 33.5, an onbeat auxiliary or an onbeat turn would produce parallel fifths. It is probable that all these trill signs were meant to be plain, as Bach is not known to have ever used either of the compound symbols in such extraordinary profusion.

Ex. 33.5. BWV 829, 7

The many compound trill symbols in the English Suites, for which the autograph has not survived, present problems because few are the cases where the main sources agree. On the other hand, we are probably not far off in assuming that the differences among the sources reflect the feeling within Bach's circle that often it did not greatly matter which type of trill was chosen.

The mordent-trill with its explicit prebeat notation presents no special difficulties. Its problem of prebeat or onbeat auxiliary is not different from that of the regular trill. Example 33.6 shows Bach's use of the mordent-trill for the organ.

Ex. 33.6. BWV 652

There are good reasons for assuming that Bach's practice with regard to the turn-trill and the slide-trill ranged beyond the literalness of the models of the *Explication* and included prebeat along with onbeat designs. One of the reasons for this assumption is the evidence from non-keyboard music where Bach did not use symbols and had to resort to explicit notation. It so happens that all the turns of turn-trills and many slides of slide-trills that could be located were anticipated. Specimens of such turn-trills are given in Ex. 33.7. In Ex. *e*, a keyboard work, the spelling out of the turn-trill can be easily explained by its transcription from a lost violin original.

Ex. 33.7.

There are also a few instances where anticipation is necessary to avoid jarring parallels. Example 33.8 shows a passage from the F major Organ Fugue where onbeat execution of the turn would be singularly offensive. (In one of its sources, P 803, written by J. L. Krebs, the symbol may denote a simple trill. In either case, onbeat start with the auxiliary is most unlikely.)

Ex. 33.8. BWV 540, 2

The above quoted example from the 5th Partita (Ex. 33.5) would belong here too, in case its turn-trill should be authentic.

The slide-trill is not written out too often in regular notes, but a few interesting examples are available. In the opening chorus of the *Christmas Oratorio*, the formula of Ex. 33.9a with its anticipated slide recurs many times.

Another prebeat specimen from the keyboard with the slide in 32nd-notes is shown in Ex. *b*. In this organ work, Bach's desire for contrapuntal coordination is the probable reason why he did not use a rhythmically ambiguous symbol. The same is presumably the case in the Courante, m. 17, from the 3rd Partita. A similar slide-trill written out after a hold (Ex. *c*) is from the C major Triple Concerto, another transcript from a string work. This rhythm pattern provides a clue to the meaning of the little notes that later in the movement convey the same motive with unquestionably the same rhythm (Ex. *d*). In Ex. *e* from the 1st Brandenburg Concerto, the two written-out slide notes are probably joined before the beat by the trill's auxiliary since an appoggiatura seems out of place here.

Ex. 33.9.

Three-note anticipation is occasionally written out in regular notes, for instance in Cantata 47 where we find the figure shown in Ex. 33.10*a* several times within the violin solo (in the *BG* edition this is wrongly labeled as "organ" solo). In Cantata 63 the autograph oboe part has the figure of Ex. *b* twice, and the same spots appear in the alternate, equally autograph (transposed) organ part, as given in Ex. *c*. In the same oboe and organ parts, another slide-trill is indicated twice in each version (mm. 4 and 24) with a *custos*, as shown in Ex. *d*. Its four-fold rendition in the *NBA* (1, 2, pp. 4, 24, 61, and 62), as shown in Ex. *e*, is mistaken: the slide starts on e″ not on d″ and thus implies the solution of Ex. *f*, not of Ex. *g*.

Ex. 33.10.

In the first movement of Cantata 82, we find in the autograph score m. 39 written as shown in Ex. 33.11a. In the original but not autograph 1st oboe part, it reads as in Ex. b. The *BG* (like the *NBA* in Cantata 63), reproduces the slide incorrectly, as shown in Ex. c. In a flute part written in E minor, which takes the place of the oboe in a transposed version, the measure reads in full analogy, as given in Ex. d. An analogous misinterpretation of the slide-trill occurs in Cantata 100,3, m. 54: the autograph flute part (St 97) has the *custos* before the trill on f sharp, whereas the *BG* lowers it to e.

Ex. 33.11. BWV 82, 1

Perhaps the most revealing cases of three-note anticipation occur in the Trio Sonata from the *Musical Offering*. In three out of four slide-trills, written with little notes, onbeat execution would produce the offensive parallel fifths of Exx. 33.12a and b (see also m. 26). Hence we can be reasonably sure that their anticipation was intended.

Ex. 33.12. BWV 1079, 8

Musical evidence combined with the amply demonstrated need for very flexible interpretation of the models in the *Explication* should suffice to suggest the use of prebeat along with onbeat patterns. Further, if we keep in mind that these French-imported graces were overwhelmingly done before the beat in France, and that even Marpurg in 1749 unequivocally advocates the prebeat design for all compound trills, then little doubt should remain that these symbols need not be limited to onbeat interpretation.

A few examples will illustrate this idea. In the Organ Chorale of Ex. 33.13a, onbeat rendition is indicated. The turn-trill is preceded by a plain trill with, at its end, a connective turn that is meant to lead into the downbeat. Onbeat rendition will also probably fit best in Ex. b from the 16th *Goldberg Variation*, where the rhythmic-harmonic emphasis on the auxiliary is favored by the cadential setting.

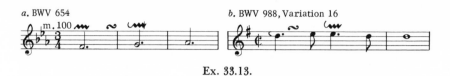

Ex. 33.13.

In the C minor Fantasy, the turn-trill on the fourth beats of mm. 1 and 2, and its parallel spots, might profit by three- (or even five-) note anticipation (Ex. 33.14). On the harpsichord, the accent-implying onbeat rendition would place a wrong emphasis on what is, in both meter and phrasing, an anacrusis to the sequential restatement of the vigorous theme.

Ex. 33.14. BWV 906

In Ex. 33.15a from the theme of the *Goldberg Variations*, the usual rendition of the turn-trill in m. 3, as indicated in Ex. *b*, has the disadvantage of obscuring the thematically essential tone repetition, and of investing the second tone with an appoggiatura quality where an appoggiatura is out of place. Three-note anticipation, as suggested in Ex. *c*, will offer a solution that graces the melody without impinging on its essence.

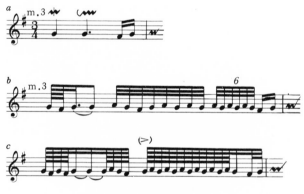

Ex. 33.15. BWV 988, Aria

In Ex. 33.16 from the 1st English Suite, a clash of ornaments—turn-trill and simultaneous mordent—provides the usual problems. Onbeat rendition of both is unsatisfactory, because it deprives each ornament of its individuality. Two other solutions seem preferable: either the mordent is anticipated and the turn played on the beat, or three turn-notes are done *before* the beat and the mordent *on* the beat.

Ex. 33.16. BWV 806 (P 1072), Sarabande

In connection with Bach's compound trills it is relevant to show a passage from the autograph suite collection by Heinrich Nicolaus Gerber (Ex. 33.17). Dated July 1727, when Gerber was still part of Bach's inner circle, the passage, from the *Courente* [*sic*] of the 1st Suite, has in transparent two-part writing a slide-trill whose onbeat start would result in objectionable fifths.

Ex. 33.17. H. N. Gerber (1727), Suite 1, Courente

As to Bach's own compound trills, it should have become clear again that no rules can be given and that the performer has to exercise his judgment in choosing fitting solutions.

The Italian and
German Compound Trill
1715-1780

THE ITALIAN SCHOOL

Tosi in 1723 described under the name of *trillo raddoppiato* a compound ornament in which a few notes are inserted in the middle of a trill so as to divide it into three distinct parts.[1] He speaks of three trills taking the place of one, which would mean that the unspecified middle part was somewhat arbitrary but had to be trill-like in character. Agricola attempts an illustration that sandwiches a turn-trill between two slide-trills,[2] but his model is only a guess and an unlikely one, since its upper-note anchored trills were foreign to Tosi. Also, neither the turn-trill nor the slide-trill were standard ornaments in Italy.

A few traces of the slide-trill in its three-note anticipatory design were found in Geminiani and Tartini. The two passages shown in Exx. 34.1a and *b* are by Geminiani.[3] (In the first example, the sign ⤳– stands for a trill with suffix followed by a rest point; the black wedge indicates a crescendo.)

Ex. 34.1. Geminiani (1739)

In Tartini's treatise we find among his "modes" of improvised ornamentation what we called the Italian double trill, a form of an embellished cadential trill.[4] Two of his models are reproduced in Exx. 34.2a and *b*, the second of which overlaps with a mordent-trill.

Ex. 34.2. Tartini (c. 1750)

In the same frame of improvised ornamentation, Tartini also shows at least one specimen of the slide-trill which when executed "con tutta la velocità" becomes a *mordente* (Ex. 34.3). Tartini described his *mordente* as a fast prebeat grace with the stress on the following principal note. No trace could be found here either of the turn-trill, which seems to have been the most typically French among this family of graces.

[1] *Opinioni*, p. 27.
[2] *Anleitung*, p. 102.
[3] Variations for a melody instrument and

bass. Facs. in Schmitz, pp. 72ff.
[4] *Regole*, facs. ed., p. 34.

Ex. 34.3. Tartini

In Bonporti's *Concertini* (Op. 12) we find a slide leading to a trill from a third below, as shown in Ex. 34.4. Here, incidentally, we find again the anticipation of the slide clarified by the need to avoid parallel octaves with the bass.

Ex. 34.4. Bonporti, Aria variata (c. 1715)

Handel, following Italian procedures, rarely shows any compound trills, and it is understandable that the few we do find are in his French-oriented harpsichord pieces. The Sarabande from the B flat Suite of the second volume is particularly rich in compound (mainly slide-) trills, many of which would profit by prebeat rendition. Example 34.5*a* shows a turn-trill, presumably done in at least partial anticipation; Ex. *b* gives a spelled-out three-note anticipated slide before a trill.

Ex. 34.5. Handel, Suite No. 13, Sarabande

In the first movement of the 2nd Suite we find prebeat slide-trills written out in regular notes (Ex. 34.6*a*), along with the onbeat slide-trill of Ex. *b*. Similarly, we find both styles represented in the Air from the 3rd Suite; the prebeat types are shown in Exx. *c* and *d*, and an onbeat design in Ex. *e*. Clearly, Handel, like Bach, did not limit himself to one design.

Ex. 34.6. Handel

Theophil Muffat includes in his extensive table (c. 1736) only the slide-trill, which is given in onbeat style (Ex. 34.7).[5] The oblique line at the beginning of the symbol is obviously a graphic representation of the ascending slide and probably not derived from D'Anglebert's hook.

Ex. 34.7. Th. Muffat (c. 1736)

Of special interest is the metamorphosis of Marpurg's compound trills that took place between 1749 and 1755.[6] In 1749, Marpurg presents under the terms of *Der gezogene oder geschleifte Triller* or *cadence coulée ou portée,* four types of compound trills, all indicated by the same symbol ⁀ẘ (the one used by D'Anglebert and Bach for the slide-trill only). We recognize among the four models given in Ex. 34.8 the slide-trill in the first and the turn-trill in the fourth one. That the little notes in these patterns were meant to be anticipated is already evident from their notation. However, Marpurg dispels any doubt by explaining the ornaments as types "where, *before the beat starts,* a few neighboring notes are quickly touched. This may be done in various ways, as the context suggests" [italics mine].[7]

Ex. 34.8. Marpurg (1749), *Critischer Musicus,* Table 2

Agricola, in his previously quoted polemical pamphlet of 1749, criticized Marpurg's indiscriminate use of the single symbol. He derided in particular the second and third patterns as designs that "would hardly be used by any person of good taste."[8] Agricola adds that one finds these symbols in the clavier works of J. S. Bach. It may be significant that Agricola, while obviously searching for any weak spot, does not object to Marpurg's prebeat definition.

In 1755, Marpurg's models of the compound trill fully conform to the principles of C.P.E. Bach. Numbers two and three have been dropped, and whereas before one symbol had different meanings, he now presents no less than six dif-

[5] *Componimenti musicali.*
[6] *Crit. Musicus,* I, 58ff. and Table 2, fig. 7; *Anleitung* (1755), p. 57 and Table 5, figs. 9 and 10.
[7] *Crit. Musicus,* p. 58: ". . . wenn man, bevor der Schlag beginnt, einige benachbarte Klänge geschwinde vorher berühret. Es kann derselbe

[i.e. the compound trill] auf allerhand Art gemacht werden, nachdem es die Gelegenheit an die Hand giebt."
[8] *Schreiben an Herrn . . . ,* p. 49: ". . . werden wohl schwerlich von Leuten von gutem Geschmack angebracht werden."

ferent symbols with identical meanings for each of the two main types. Also, both slide- and turn-trills are now placed on the beat, as shown in Ex. 34.9.

Ex. 34.9. Marpurg (1755), *Anleitung*, Table 5

Philipp Emanuel calls the slide-trill the "trill from below" (*Triller von unten*) and the turn-trill the "trill from above" (*Triller von oben*).[9] The keyboard symbols and their translations, as shown in Exx. 34.10*a* and *d*, are the familiar ones from the *Explication*, except that they are slightly unmetrical. For media other than the keyboard, he gives for the slide-trill the two alternate symbols of Exx. *b* and *c* and shows the notation for the turn-trill in the musical illustration of Ex. *e*.

Ex. 34.10. C.P.E. Bach (1753), Table 4

Philipp Emanuel definitely had for those graces, at least on the keyboard, the onbeat in mind. After reemphasizing that ornaments must not impinge on the purity of voice-leading, he points out that in Ex. 34.11 either a turn-trill or a regular trill should be used, and not a slide-trill, because the latter would cause forbidden parallels.[10] Anticipation, which would avoid such parallels, was obviously unacceptable.

Ex. 34.11. C.P.E. Bach

[9] *Versuch*, 1, ch. 2, sec. 3, pars. 22-29, deal with the compound trills.

[10] Ibid., par. 29: ". . . man überhaupt bey

Anbringung der Manieren besonders acht haben müsse, dass man der Reinigkeit der Harmonie keinen Schaden thue. . . ."

Agricola calls the two types *Doppeltriller* or *verdoppelter Triller*, and gives the patterns of Exx. 34.12a and b. Limiting the symbols ⌒w ⌒w as usual to the keyboard, he tells us that the patterns are very rare in the vocal medium, for which he gives C.P.E. Bach's above notation of Ex. 34.10e (p. 112).[11]

Ex. 34.12. Agricola (1757)

In his clavier treatise of 1765, Löhlein shows a slide-trill (*Trillo von unten herauf*; Ex. 34.13a), with unmistakable anticipation of the slide in the sense of Marpurg's 1749 models, and an onbeat turn-trill (*Trillo von oben herein*, Ex. b). Both types are shown with a suffix prior to their rest point.[12] The patterns remain the same through the fourth edition of 1782. In his violin treatise of 1774, he expresses regret that in non-keyboard music only the symbol *tr* is used to cover various possibilities of trill designs.[13] He therefore illustrates the keyboard patterns; but of the compound trills, he shows only the anticipated slide-trill in a model (Ex. c) that is almost identical to that given in the keyboard treatise; for the violin, he leaves out the turn-trill.

Ex. 34.13. Löhlein

Petri speaks of the slide-trill, which he calls *Doppeltriller*, only in the second edition (1782) of his treatise.[14] His freer attitude toward the trill in the second edition, as compared with the first of 1767, has been commented upon before. The slide-trill, indicated by the usual symbol, is again portrayed in the less regimental little notes (Ex. 34.14a), and their graphic disposition in groups of two-four-two, set apart by the alternating direction of the stems, seems to suggest the prebeat nature of the first two notes. Had he had an onbeat design in mind, he would have most probably used regular notes and beamed them all together.

A few years later, Türk once again follows C.P.E. Bach, except for a significant prebeat model (Ex. b), which, he says, is "not unusual." He ascribes it to the Lombard style in which "*Vorschläge* are usually turned into *Nachschläge*."[15] This remark is particularly interesting because it points to the widespread ("usual") North Italian prebeat practices.

[11] *Anleitung*, pp. 101-102, 112-113.
[12] *Clavier-Schule*, pt. 1, ch. 6, par. 4.
[13] *Anweisung*, p. 46.
[14] *Anleitung*, 2nd ed., p. 155.
[15] *Klavierschule*, ch. 4, sec. 3, par. 52.

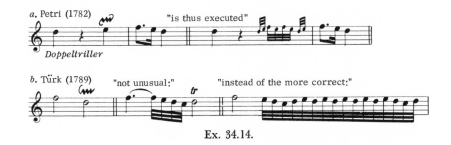

a. Petri (1782)

Doppeltriller

"is thus executed"

b. Türk (1789)

"not unusual:"

"instead of the more correct:"

Ex. 34.14.

Tosi's compound trill has the variable and indetermined "compound" element in the middle rather than at the start of the trill and therefore falls outside the categories under discussion here. Apart from such improvisatory designs, the Italians developed a more nearly standardized form of a compound trill (the "Italian double trill"), as described by Tartini: a cadential trill preceded by a main-note trill a step below. The form was adopted in Germany but apparently unknown in France. Of the compound trills derived from the French, the turn-trill could not be traced in Italy, whereas the slide-trill was found once in a while in its three-note prebeat form.

Handel, as evidenced by his written-out designs, used in his harpsichord works both the prebeat and onbeat forms of the slide-trill, as well as the prebeat designs for the turn-trill. In Germany, C.P.E. Bach's onbeat patterns were widely adopted by his followers on the keyboard and found their last theoretical reflection in Türk's treatise of 1789 but qualified by a significant prebeat model traced to the Lombard style. Other prebeat patterns of both slide- and turn-trills were still theoretically vouched for by Marpurg in 1749, and at least for the slide-trill, by Löhlein and almost certainly also by Petri until 1782, at which time the designs were well on the way to disappearing as standard graces.

PART VII
THE MORDENT

Introduction

Types and Designs

The mordent in its most common form is an oscillation of the principal note with its lower neighbor.

In the second half of the 16th century, the grace, written out in full notation, makes frequent appearances in Claudio Merulo's works, where we find extensive oscillations in both directions, i.e. mordents as well as trills. The duality of upward and downward oscillations was recorded for the one-stroke species by Santa Maria in 1565 (see Exx. 24.1*b* and *c*) and for the multiple oscillation types by Elias Nicolaus Ammerbach in 1571.[1] Ammerbach called both types, the upward and the downward oscillations, *Mordant*. He writes: "*Mordants* are done by mingling a note with its neighbor, and if properly used give grace and sweetness to the song. They are of two kinds, rising and falling. . . ."[2] He continues to explain what is clarified by his illustration (see Ex. VII.1), that on a rising tone the oscillation is done with the lower note, on a falling tone with the upper one. This tendency is rooted in melodic logic and asserted its strength throughout the baroque era.

Ex. VII.1. Ammerbach (1571, 1583), *Mordant*

As was shown in Chapter 28 above, the oscillation with the lower neighbor became in Italy and Germany a steady counterpart to the oscillation with the upper neighbor; throughout the 17th century and beyond, this mirror-image dualism prevailed under the names of *tremulus ascendens* and *descendens*.

In France the mordent was probably first used by lute players; this would explain the frequently used terms of *pincé* or *pincement* which are descriptive of the part played by the "pinching" of the string with a left-hand pizzicato.

The basic type of mordent, which could be called "plain" or "unprepared," will normally start and end with the principal note. Its melodic design will vary according to the number of alternations, which can range from a single one to an indefinite number, as shown in the model VII.2.

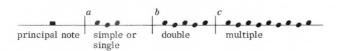

Ex. VII.2.

[1] *Orgel-oder Instrument-Tabulatur*, quoted by Johannes Wolf, *Handbuch der Notations-kunde*, II, 29.

[2] Ibid.: "Mordanten sind, wenn ein Clauis mit dem Nechsten nebem ihm gerürt wird/ dienen viel zur zierd vnnd liebligkeit des gesangs/ wenn sie recht gebraucht werden."

The one-alternation mordent of model *a,* the mirror image of the *Schneller,* is sometimes referred to as a simple or single mordent. The two-alternation species (*b*) was called by some the double mordent, a term, occasionally and not too fittingly, applied also to the multialternation type which would better be called the multiple mordent (*c*).

The simple one-alternation mordent will often strike on the beat with its first note and follow with a fast alternation that produces a sharp, "biting" accent effect. Its notational equivalent will vary with the tempo and with the length of the note. For a quarter-note, its approximate range is shown in Ex. VII.3.

Ex. VII.3.

Often, however even the simple mordent will not "bite" but have a melodic-connective rather than rhythmic-accentual function. It then becomes independent from the beat, which it can anticipate (Ex. VII.4*a*), straddle (Ex. *b*), or avoid altogether by delayed entrance (Ex. *c*). In other cases it can avoid the metrical stress (Ex. *d*) or somewhat slow the alternation into a gentle melodic inflection (Ex. *e*).

Ex. VII.4.

The double mordent, in addition to its "bite," may have a connective and melodic function, in which case it need neither be accented nor start exactly on the beat. Hence the designs of Exx. VII.5*a-f* can be assumed to fit appropriate circumstances.

Ex. VII.5.

The greater the number of the alternations, the more trill-like the mordent becomes, thereby assuming a function of intensifying the melody rather than the rhythm. Couperin coined the term *pincé continu* for such extended mordents. The note sustained by such a mordent will be the principal one, and consequently, the multiple mordent will normally be main-note anchored and not have any harmonic implications. Occasionally, however, we encounter a variant— a borderline case of the *port de voix et pincé*—that starts with the auxiliary instead of the principal note. If placed on the beat, the auxiliary can make an harmonic impact analogous to that of an unsupported appoggiatura trill (see below, Ex. 35.3).

Like the trill, the mordent is often linked with a *Vorschlag* in such close union that a true compound ornament results. In France the link was almost exclusively that of the *port de voix et pincé*, i.e. the *Vorschlag* from below plus the mordent.

The link was far stronger from the side of the *port de voix* than it was from the side of the mordent: the latter occurred countless times by itself in its plain form, but the *port de voix*—especially, but not exclusively, its long onbeat type—was almost routinely followed, offbeat, by a simple mordent. Because of this intimate connection, the combination grace was discussed in relation to the *port de voix* (in Chapter 8) and the scope of its rhythmic design outlined in Ex. 8.3 as ranging from full anticipation of the combined grace to a long onbeat *port de voix* with, at its extreme end, the *pincé* added like a diminutive loop.

It is noteworthy that in this *port de voix-pincé* combination, the mordent loses most of its bite, its accentual rhythmic energy. The only exception is the pattern where anticipation of the *port de voix* alone permits onbeat emphasis on the *pincé* proper. Here, and here alone, the mordent is the leading partner, the *port de voix* an accessory. In all other instances the mordent is an offbeat, unaccented suffix.

The mordent prepared by an anticipated *Vorschlag* from above is a widely used Italian grace: . Occasionally, time permitting, the accent on the principal note is further sharpened by a short trill: .

Not every grace that is called *mordent* or *mordente* belongs to the category dealt with in this part. The Italians in particular use the term *mordente* rather loosely and apply it to various graces that can produce a "biting" effect.

35

The French Mordent
1630-1715

—◦•◦—

Basset, writing in Mersenne's *Harmonie universelle* of 1636 about the lute and its ornaments, gives a clear description of the multiple mordent with either half-tone or whole-tone alternation.

He calls the grace *martellement*, and though he distinguishes two species for which he invents three symbols ∗, ∧ ∧̄ , the difference between the first two refers only to technical execution (one involving an open, the other a stopped string). The first two symbols indicate a whole-tone mordent; the third sign represents a mordent with a half-tone interval.[1] The symbols were new as Basset himself affirms, but the term *martellement* was apparently current at the time.

The symbols used by the French lutenists of the early 17th century often have to be deciphered from context. The only symbol that was in more or less general use was the comma after the letter (c,), signifying the trill. Frequently, however, we find this symbol in spots that are more congenial to the mordent, and it is probable that for some masters who did not use a separate symbol for the mordent, this grace was indicated by the comma symbol. Ennemond (*le vieux*) Gaultier used the symbol of the slanted cross in what always appears to be mordent meaning. Dufaut (or Dufault), who also flourished in the first half of the 17th century, used the same symbol frequently, but its meaning is uncertain. André Souris, in his edition of Dufaut's works, transcribes the cross symbol sometimes as mordent, sometimes as trill, sometimes as *coulé*.[2]

Denis (*le jeune*) Gaultier, Ennemond's cousin, uses the same cross symbol to indicate what he calls *estoufement* (smothering, silencing) and explains it vaguely: "you strike a letter and place one finger below."[3] However, in a later publication (in which he included pieces by his cousin), Denis Gaultier describes the *étouffement* more clearly as plucking a tone with a finger of the right hand, then using a neighbor finger to stop the vibrations.[4] This time he mentions no symbol, but obviously to him the *étouffement* was no mordent. The comma is explained as *tremblement*, and it is likely that it included the mordent, which is not otherwise marked.

We find other signs such as the ∧ and the ∨ which at least with some masters at some time stood for the mordent. Reflecting French practices, Thomas Mace presents in his treatise the multiple mordent with a specified half-tone interval. He calls it "beate" and marks it with a vertical line before the letter: |c.[5]

The elder Gaultier's most interesting use of letters outside the metrical count (the predecessors of the *notes perdues* in regular notation) was mentioned before. Most often his surplus letters indicate one-note graces, but there is at least one case on record where they are used to indicate a one-alternation mordent. The specimen, from a *Volte* (a dance in triple meter), is shown in Ex. 35.1a in tablature, along with its transcription by André Souris.[6] In this spot, the failure to include the letters in the metrical count and their placement before the rhythm symbol of the dotted 8th, suggest anticipation of the mordent. This indication finds a good measure of confirmation two bars later, where in a nearly identical

[1] *Harmonie universelle, Traité des instrumens à chordes, livre second*, pp. 79-80. Johannes Wolf (in his *HdN*, II, 150) has misunderstood this passage. He believed it described a *Zusammenschlag-acciaccatura*, but Basset's technical directives clearly point to an oscillatory multiple mordent.

[2] *Oeuvres de Dufaut*, ed. and transcribed by André Souris (Paris, 1965).

[3] *Pieces de luth*.

[4] *Livre de tablature*.

[5] *Musick's Monument*, pp. 102 and 105.

[6] *Oeuvres du Vieux Gautier*, ed. and transcribed by André Souris (Paris, 1966), p. 64.

phrase the anticipation of the mordent is spelled out (Ex. *b*). Perrine in his *Pieces de luth* (1680) transcribes the unmetrical letters of Ex. *a* in anticipation (see Ex. *c*). A similar spelled-out prebeat mordent at the start of a Gigue by Dufaut is shown in Ex. *d* (with note values halved).

Ex. 35.1.

In many other cases, mordents were unquestionably performed *on* the beat as well as between beats, or in countless ways that were rhythmically undetermined. The French style of lute playing was permeated with rubato freedoms that occasionally were even reflected in the tablature. They were most tellingly revealed—as far as notation is capable of doing so—in Perrine's transcriptions (of 1680) with their perpetual shifting of note values backward and forward with slight anticipations and delays. In view of this great rhythmic freedom in which even structural notes are constantly removed from the beat, it would be unrealistic to think of *any* lute ornament as having to fit into an exact rhythmic pattern.

From the evidence available, but still more from our certain knowledge about the rhythmic freedom of the *style luthé*, we can assume that the French lutenists and their followers abroad used both the multiple and the single mordent in all possible rhythmic designs.

Nivers describes a grace which he simply calls *agrément*.[7] It is symbolized by a short wavy line, and the illustration (Ex. 35.2) reveals a prepared mordent of the *port de voix et pincé* species.

Ex. 35.2. Nivers (1665), *Agrément*

7 *Livre d'orgue*, Preface.

Nivers's student, Gilles Jullien, presents a grace which he calls either *agrément* or *pincement*.[8] The symbol is the more modern one of Chambonnières, and the realization (Ex. 35.3) shows four equal notes which, if started on the beat, would form the above mentioned mirror image of a short appoggiatura trill.

Ex. 35.3. Jullien (1690)

The link with Nivers is unmistakable. Since the alternate term *pincement* confirms the mordent character, it is perhaps a reasonable guess that the actual execution may have occasionally varied from the literal form in two ways: 1) by a slight lengthening of the first note, to bring out its onbeat *port de voix* function and set it off from the *pincé* annex; and 2) by anticipating the first note in a pattern of prebeat *port de voix* and onbeat mordent.

Saint Lambert in 1702 confirms that Nivers's *agrément* is "nothing else but a mordent, except that it starts with the borrowed note, whereas the others start with the main note."[9]

Chambonnières shows the mordent with a single alternation (Ex. 35.4a), and Le Bègue gives the identical pattern.[10] In 1688 Raison follows suit and states his preference for the chromatic nature of the mordent (Ex. *b*).[11]

Ex. 35.4.

Boyvin in 1689 explains the mordent only in connection with the *port de voix*. The *pincement*, he says, is very short and usually approached from a lower pitch. In his second organ book of 1700, he shows the long onbeat *port de voix* halving the value of a long binary note, as well as an apparently short *port de voix* before a dotted note.[12] The illustrations from both books were shown above in Exx. 10.2*b* and *c*. He gives no illustration of an unprepared mordent.

A previously quoted example from Clérambault's first book of harpsichord pieces of 1704 (Ex. 10.13) showed the prebeat nature of a *port de voix* before the mordent by means of a dotted line that clarified the synchronization.

D'Anglebert presents a simple and a double mordent which he calls *pincé* and for which he introduces the symbol of a hook after the note (see Ex. 35.5a). His *cheute [port de voix] et pincé* (Ex. *d*) is of the long onbeat type.[13] In 1705 Le Roux reproduces these models (see Exx. *b* and *e*), and so does Dieupart about

[8] *Premier livre d'orgue*, Preface.
[9] *Principes du clavecin*, p. 47.
[10] Chambonnières, *Pieces de clavessin*; Le Bègue, *Pieces de clavessin*.

[11] *Livre d'orgue*.
[12] *Premier livre d'orgue*; *Traité abrégé de l'accompagnement*.
[13] *Pieces de clavecin*.

the same time. However, Dieupart shows in his bilingual table only the single mordent which he calls *"pincé, a beat"* (Exx. *c* and *f*).[14]

Ex. 35.5.

In Lully's scores the mordents were not marked but certainly were added freely in the proper places.

Georg Muffat, in his retrospective report on the performance of the "Lullyists," uses the term *pincement* and shows a choice of symbols:  .[15] He describes the grace as being very brief, consisting usually of only one alternation, though in his illustration (Ex. 35.6) he shows the double mordent first. His symbols were anachronistic for Lully, but his designs are probably authentic.

Ex. 35.6. G. Muffat (1698)

D'Ambruis in 1685 uses the symbol ∧ for *flatement*, but does not explain how the grace is done.[16] *Flatement* could conceivably signify a mordent, and its use is illustrated in Ex. 35.7.

Ex. 35.7. D'Ambruis (1685), p. 32

The French gamba school of the late 17th century displays not only frustrating discrepancies in terms and symbols but some ambiguities in their explanations.

For instance, the mordent is called *martellement* by Demachy, *pincé* by Danoville, *batement* by Marais and Caix d'Hervelois; the same term, *batement* (or *battement*), is used

14 Le Roux, *Pièces de clavessin*; Dieupart, *Six suittes.*

15 *Florilegium II*, Preface to sec. v.
16 *Livre d'airs.*

by Rousseau, Danoville and—presumably—Demachy to designate the two-finger vibrato which Marais in turn calls *pincé* or *flatement*. Thus, the terms have been thoroughly entangled, and in order to avoid confusion, we shall in the following simply use the term "mordent." To indicate the mordent, Sainte Colombe and Danoville use the simple cross. Marais and his students (among them his son Roland Marais and Caix d'Hervelois) used the slanting cross. Demachy distinguishes the single mordent by a straight line crossed obliquely and placed after the note (♩); the double (and probably multiple) mordent is notated by adding another oblique line. None of Rousseau's music has survived, but in his treatise he does not use any symbols at all.

It is probable that there was less disagreement in matters of execution than there was in matters of terms and symbols. As was pointed out before, Sainte Colombe used the mordent most often in connection with an anticipated *port de voix*, which he writes out in regular notes (see above, Ex. 9.12).[17] His execution of the mordent proper was described by Danoville in the following words: "the mordent is done with abrupt agitation in returning the finger to the fingerboard; the number of strokes depends on the length of the note; it is indicated with a little cross."[18] On the question of the speed of the alternations, Jean Rousseau is more specific still. He says that the finger that stops the note "beats at first two or three little strokes more closely and more hurriedly ("plus serrez et plus pressez") than for the trill, whereupon it remains on the fingerboard."[19] This explanation indicates that to Rousseau too the double or triple mordent formed the standard design for this grace. When in the next paragraph Rousseau stresses the close connection with the *port de voix* ("The mordent is always inseparable from the *port de voix* because the latter must always end with a mordent"), the inseparability concerns the *port de voix* which needs the mordent sequel. He did not imply that every mordent has to be preceded by a *port de voix*.

Since Rousseau used no symbol, he had to give directives about the improvised uses of this grace. He sees as the most inviting context the second note of a half-tone ascent, especially one from a shorter to a longer note value, as shown (from A to B) in his illustration (see Ex. 35.8). He adds that "provided the 8th-notes are equal" (meaning they are not *inégales*), one ought to play a mordent on the first of a pair in ascending (letter C); where quarter-notes are equal, mordents are in order on the first and third beats (letter D). This interesting comment indicates that mordents do not seem to mix readily with *notes inégales*. A later confirmation of this fact will be mentioned presently.

Ex. 35.8. J. Rousseau (1687)

Marais presents terms and symbols for the repercussive graces—the trill, the mordent (*batement*), and the two-finger vibrato (*pincé* or *flatement*)—but does not explain their meaning, which he took for granted.[20] His symbol for the mordent is the slanted cross: ×♩ .

In his viol works we find a multitude of plain, unprepared mordents in almost every conceivable location: on heavy or light beats and on subdivisions of beats, thus displaying a wider use than that indicated by Rousseau.

---

[17] *Concerts à 2 violes.*

[18] *L'art de toucher*, p. 40. This treatise, as mentioned before, was dedicated to the exposi-

tion of Sainte Colombe's playing methods.

[19] *Traité de la viole*, p. 87.

[20] *Pieces a . . . violes* (1686).

The mordent prepared by an anticipated *port de voix* written out in the manner of Sainte Colombe is apparently not to be found in Marais, but frequently it was intended when the *port de voix* in such a combination was written with the newly invented little notes. (An example of clear prebeat meaning for the *port de voix* in such a combination was shown above in Ex. 9.16a.) In Ex. 35.9, the symbol "e," standing for a crescendo, would not be compatible with a long, emphasized *port de voix*. Shortness and lack of accentuation, whether on or before the beat, would seem advisable, and even a complete anticipation of both the *port de voix* and the mordent, in the sense of L'Affilard, would not be unreasonable.

Ex. 35.9. Marais, V, 112, *La Poitevine*

In cases where the mordent is marked for a unison, onbeat execution with the following effect was probably often intended (in analogy to the lute), but not necessarily always.

Mordents on a weak beat preceded by, and slurred to, an accented note strongly favor offbeat rendition. Such mordents are purely connective graces and can hardly have the meaning of rhythmic intensification. Onbeat placement in such a context (for which Exx. 35.10a and b offer illustrations) would produce a musically unwarranted emphasis. Such cases are functionally almost identical to the conventional *off*beat mordent sequel to an emphasized *on*beat *port de voix*. For this very reason Gordon J. Kinney points to spots like those of Ex. c, where "the mordent must be played with the first two notes *before* the accent to avoid clumsiness and false accentuation of the melodic line."[21]

a. IV, 4th Suite, Gavotte

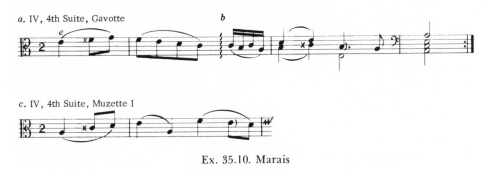

c. IV, 4th Suite, Muzette I

Ex. 35.10. Marais

On the other hand, there are many cases where an indicated rhythmic intensification suggests onbeat execution. Examples 35.11a and b illustrate situations where an onbeat mordent very fittingly solidifies the metrical beat. In the Gigue in particular, an anticipated mordent would weaken the lilt of the dance tune.

a. V, 20, Gigue   *b.* V, 21, Marche à la Turque

Fièrement

Ex. 35.11. Marais

[21] Personal letter.

Like Marais, the flutist Hotteterre calls the mordent *battement*, but he uses the symbol I. The grace is rendered with one or two alternations that are made "as fast as possible."[22] He gives the model of Ex. 35.12 which suggests unstressed execution leaning to anticipation, since for a quarter-note a stressed onbeat intent would have been conveyed more clearly and simply by regular notes.[23]

Ex. 35.12. Hotteterre (1708, 1715)

Hotteterre points to the difficulty of giving rules for the use of the mordent in those places where it is not indicated by symbol; it is, he says, "a matter of taste and practice." By and large, he says, mordents occur more often on short notes, such as quarter-notes in lively tempo, and 8th-notes "in movements where they are even," i.e. not subject to *inégalité*.[24] This passage corroborates Rousseau's indication that mordents are uncongenial to *notes inégales*.

Freillon-Poncein in 1699 uses the terms *battement* and *pincé* for the mordent. He sees the grace as a relative of the *port de voix*, but one that is done with suddenness and great speed.[25] His verbal explanation is inconclusive, but his only illustration (Ex. 35.13) contains three prebeat mordent figures.

Ex. 35.13. Freillon-Poncein (1699)

For the gambists, a multiple alternation of two or three strokes appears to have been the more common design for the accented, onbeat type of a plain mordent or for one that follows a prebeat *port de voix*. The one-stroke mordent was probably more frequently used when there was no time for more alternations, or where the grace was done unaccented off the beat.

In L'Affilard's book, we find the plain mordent (*pincé*) in the context shown in Ex. 35.14a—without a symbol and illustrated by little notes.[26] The mordent appears again as an annex to the *port de voix* (Ex. b). In this model, the anticipation of the *port de voix* is clarified by regular notation, while the metrical position of the mordent proper is still left in doubt.

Ex. 35.14. L'Affilard (1694-1705)

[22] *Principes*, p. 30.
[23] *Premier livre*, Preface.
[24] *Principes*, p. 33.

[25] *La véritable manière*, pp. 20-21.
[26] *Principes* (1694 and 1697), pp. 20-21; (1705 and 1745), pp. 26-27.

An interesting light is shed on this matter by L'Affilard's illustration of a compound ornament called *hélan*, a combination of *port de voix* and *accent*. The passage containing the *hélan*, which, incidentally, is intended to express an *aspiration violente* (roughly the equivalent of a heaving sigh), is the only one in this ornamental demonstration that was substantially changed in the edition of 1705. This very change provides an important clue. In the first two editions (1694 and 1697), the *port de voix et pincé* part of the *hélan* is illustrated as shown in Ex. 35.15a: the *port de voix* in explicit anticipation and the *pincé* in ambiguous little notes. In the 1705 edition, however, both the *port de voix* and the *pincé* are expressed in little notes that are placed before the bar line (Ex. *b*), thus revealing the *anticipation of the mordent* as well. Though this significant model does not prove that L'Affilard's mordent was always anticipated, it does prove that anticipation was in use.

Ex. 35.15. L'Affilard

Loulié, too, sees the mordent as an unaccented, hence essentially offbeat, grace. He calls it *martellement* and marks it with a sign resembling a *V* that stands for a simple mordent with but one alternation.[27] If more alternations are wanted, the *V* is repeated, as seen in the illustration of Ex. 35.16. The anticipatory nature of the mordent is suggested by Loulié's explanation of the grace as "two small, very light [i.e. very soft] sounds in the manner of the *chûte*, one a step below the other which precedes the note on which the mordent is marked."[28] Inasmuch as the terms "small" and "very light" signify together the combination of fastness and softness, and a *chûte* is invariably an offbeat grace which "falls" into the next beat, this definition would seem to establish the prebeat affinity of the grace.

Ex. 35.16. Loulié (1696)

The same can be said of Montéclair. Silent on the mordent in his early treatises, he speaks of it in the *Principes* of 1736 in terms reminiscent of Loulié.[29] Like Jean Rousseau and L'Affilard before him, he uses no symbol. The mordent, he

[27] *Éléments*, p. 72.
[28] Ibid., p. 72: "2 petits Sons fort legers en maniere de Chute d'un degré plus bas l'un de l'autre, lesquels precedent la Notte sur laquelle est marqué le Martellement."
[29] *Principes*, p. 84.

says, is often done when arriving on a strong note (*note forte*) and is realized "by a light pulsation of the throat" ("un battement léger du gosier"). The indicated dynamics favor anticipation, as does Montéclair's explanation that contains no reference to beat or accentuation: "to execute it well, one must first bring the voice up to the pitch of the strong note, then go down one step, whereupon the voice promptly rises again to the strong note, there to come to rest." It will be better understood, he says, by *notes postiches*, as shown in Ex. 35.17. A *pincé*, he says, is always needed as a sequel for the *port de voix*. His illustration with the longer note values for the *port de voix*, suggesting its onbeat start and unaccented *pincé* sequel, was given above in Ex. 9.25.

Pincé Repos

Ex. 35.17. Montéclair (1736)

THE gambists appeared to be very flexible in their use of the plain mordent. They certainly used the onbeat type very often, especially on longer and metrically stressed note values, for which they preferred multiple alternations of two or three very fast and crackling strokes. On the other hand, the single mordent, especially when placed on a light beat and slurred to the preceding note, must have often been anticipated. In the *port de voix et pincé* compound, they generally seem to have favored the anticipation of the *port de voix*. Flutists had similar propensities and presumably so did other wind players about which we did not hear. These conclusions found support from the general theorists as well.

The Mordent of
Couperin and Later Masters
1710-1780

In his ornament table of 1713, Couperin shows three types of plain mordents: the simple, the multiple, and the continuous type.[1]

Ex. 36.1. Couperin

The symbol (✛) itself does not distinguish between mordents with one or more alternations, and the choice is again chiefly dependent on the length of the note. However, when a long note is to be completely filled with alternations, this is indicated by the extension of the wavy line, as shown in the above model and in an actual (rather rare) occurrence (Ex. 36.2). As can be seen in this latter example, Couperin, unlike Bach and most other contemporaries, indicates a desired chromatic alteration of the auxiliary.

Ex. 36.2. Couperin, IX, *L'Insinuante*

In his treatise of 1716/1717, Couperin restates the first two models in nearly identical form (using little 8th-notes instead of 16ths) and adds: "Every mordent is attached to the note on which it is placed . . . the alternations and the tone on which they end must be comprised in the value of the principal note."[2] The statement implies that the plain mordent starts with its main note on the beat, and most of Couperin's plain mordents probably followed this rule. However, exceptions can be expected for such cases where the function of the mordent is connective rather than intensifying and where offbeat rendition yields musical benefits. A typical case that favors such treatment is the one cited for Marais, where a mordent on a light beat is slurred to its preceding metrically emphasized neighbor. With the preceding note acting as a preparation to the mordent, the latter's slightly anticipated or sometimes slightly delayed interbeat rendition will

---

[1] *Piéces de clavecin*, 1st book.

[2] *L'art*, p. 19: "Tout pincé doit être fixé sur la note oû il est posé . . . les batemens, et la note oû l'on s'arête doivent tous être compris dans la valeur de la note èssentièlle."

often produce a more elegant and more logical melodic line. For a rationale, it is well to remember Rameau's principle that every note slurred to an ornament functions as its preparation; this in turn means that preparation and ornament have to be conceived as a unit with no strict dividing line. Examples 36.3a and b well illustrate the point.[3]

Ex. 36.3. Couperin

Another context for such treatment is shown in Ex. 36.4, where the fluidity of the 8th-note movement would seem to be better served by anticipation of both mordents and trills. The same considerations could well apply to *La Bandoline* (V).

Ex. 36.4. Couperin, II, *Double des Canaries*

In pieces like *Matelotes Provençales* (III), *Les Lis naissans* (XIII), and *La Juillet* (XIV), where mordents occur in extraordinary density, occasional use of anticipation will provide some desirable variety. In Ex. 36.5, the opening phrase with a mordent and a simultaneous *tremblement lié* occurs so often that here too varying renditions will be welcome. Anticipation of the mordent alone, or simultaneous anticipation of both mordent and trill (with the trill starting on the main note) could be alternatives to onbeat synchronization of both graces.

Ex. 36.5. Couperin, II, Rigaudon

On a previous page, anticipation was suggested for the mordents in *Le Moucheron* (VI) (see Ex. 25.12a). In the passage given in Ex. 36.6, where exquisite tenderness is supposed to be achieved, onbeat execution of every mordent would sound graceless and awkward. It so happens that in a footnote to this piece (a variant of *Le Rossignol-en-Amour*) Couperin has this to say: "In the above *Double* one must not observe the beat too precisely, everything must be sacrificed to sensitivity [literally: taste], to the proper expression of

[3] The Roman numerals denote the *ordres* in the four books of harpsichord pieces.

all passages, and care be taken to mollify the inflections marked by mordents."[4] How else can the inflections be mollified than by removing the mordents from the confines of a beat (which is to be unnoticeable to begin with)?

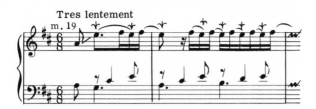

Ex. 36.6. Couperin, XIV, *Double du Rossignol*

Skeptics who will question such license may, in addition to the theorists just cited, be referred to Couperin's several statements about freedom of performance which were quoted before. It will be particularly fitting to recall his felicitous analogy of the difference between grammar and declamation on the one hand, and the difference between musical notation and artistic performance on the other.[5] Any rule he gives, whether for the mordent, the *coulé* and *port de voix*, or the trill, certainly partakes of "grammar" and, according to his own words, has to be adapted to the ever-changing demands of convincing "declamation."

Without an assumed flexibility of Couperin's mordent, it would be hard to explain its omnipresence in his works. A systematic onbeat execution of all of Couperin's mordents according to orthodox precepts would inject into his music a rigidity foreign to its delicate spirit.

Rameau shows in both of his ornament tables of 1706 and 1724[6] the mordent only in its multiple style, as given in Exx. 36.7a and *b*. A difference can be observed in the patterns of the *port de voix et pincé* shown in the two tables: in the first one, the notes of the *port de voix* and the *pincé* are of equal length (a design resembling Nivers's *agrément*); the second, more common design, shows the *port de voix* slightly sustained, marking it as the principal grace and the mordent as annex.

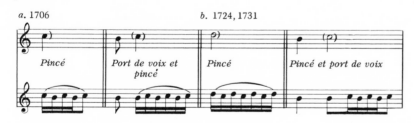

Ex. 36.7. Rameau

Rameau used, for the keyboard only, the symbol of the hook behind the note (which he adopted from D'Anglebert). In his stage works, judging from a few extant autographs

[4] "Il ne faut pas s'attacher trop précisément à la mesure dans le Double cy-dessus, il faut tout sacrificier au goût à la propreté des passages et à bien attendrir les accens marqués par des pincés." The word *accent* did not at the time imply an emphasis (as can be gathered from the use of the term for the com-pletely unemphasized *Nachschlag*). "Inflection" seems to come closest to its meaning in this sentence.

[5] See above, ch. 3, n. 4.

[6] *Premier livre* (1706); *Pièces de clavecin* (1724).

such as *Daphnis et Eglée* (Opéra Rés. 208), *Nélée et Mirthis,* and *Zéphire* (both BN, Cons. MS 372), Rameau used Couperin's trill and mordent symbols in reverse: ∿ stands for the trill and ∿ for the mordent. In the early motet *In convertendo,* the autograph (BN, Rés. Vma 248) shows the more common plain cross as the symbol for the trill and the *chevron* for the mordent.

The onbeat indications in the tables for the mordent and the *port de voix et pincé* combination have to be taken with the usual qualifications. There is evidence that points to the occasional prebeat design of the single mordent, and the *port de voix* in the compound ornament.

In some cases, for instance in Ex. 36.8*a* from the Allemande (1724), the pressure of time alone must have pushed the *port de voix* ahead of the beat. It only stands to reason that a model given for a half-note cannot be expected to be fully applicable to any 16th-note as well. In other cases, different circumstances point to similar deviating solutions. In Ex. *b* from the 5th *Concert* (only the harpsichord part is given), the *ports de voix et pincés* at numbers 1) and 3) coincide with plain mordents in the left hand.[7] Their simultaneous start would produce a confusing effect that most likely was not intended. Two alternative solutions are possible: either the *port de voix* is anticipated and both mordents are synchronized, or the combined grace is anticipated while the plain mordent is done on the beat. This latter solution receives some support from number 2) in the same example, where a simultaneous mordent in parallel fifths is an unlikely intention; here a possible solution would be anticipation of the upper mordent and onbeat execution for the lower one. The same applies to Ex. *c* from the same collection, with its mordent in parallel fifths which recurs in mm. 8, 45, and 47, since in mm. 45 and 47 the lower mordent is unquestionably to be done with g natural not g sharp. In Ex. *d* from the *Nouvelles suites,*[8] onbeat placement would be extremely awkward for the two *ports de voix et pincés* in the right hand, especially the second one which coincides with a trill; the plain mordent sandwiched between the two would form parallel octaves with the mordent in the middle voice when taken on the beat. Here too a solution similar to the one above would seem to be advisable.

Ex. 36.8. Rameau

In Rameau's music and probably that of many other French masters as well, it is not unreasonable to assume that long notes usually called for onbeat rendi-

___

[7] *Pièces de clavecin en concerts.*

[8] *Nouvelles suites de pièces de clavecin* (c. 1728).

tion and multiple alternations, and that the single-oscillation mordent for short note values was occasionally anticipated, either to provide a better melodic-rhythmic continuity, greater clarity in the interplay of the voices, or simply more flexibility.

Siret's *port de voix et pincé* patterns, with the little notes of the *port de voix* written before the bar line, were shown above in Exx. 12.4*a* and *b*. They suggested an analogous prebeat rhythm whenever the *port de voix* occurred in midmeasure.

Siret's plain mordent was certainly often done on the beat, but occasionally it must have been anticipated. In Ex. 36.9 for instance, the simultaneous mordent and slide on the fourth beat of the measure may have been anticipated to avoid crowding and to safeguard the integrity of the second voice in both hands.[9] In the mordent and trill combination of the preceding beat, the trill was presumably anticipated for similar reasons, while the mordent may have been played on the beat.

Ex. 36.9. Siret, Allemande *Le Bouquet*

Dandrieu in his tables of 1724 and 1739 shows a *pincé simple* which in spite of its name is a multiple mordent (Ex. 36.10).[10] His *pincé et port de voix* with the latter's anticipation was shown above (Ex. 12.6).

David in 1737 gives the model of the *pincé* shown in Ex. 36.11*a*; it contains a misprint and should read as shown in Ex. *b*.[11] The symbol  is that found in

Explication

Ex. 36.10. Dandrieu (1724, 1739)

Rameau's theatrical works. As is apparent from the model, David's mordent has only a single alternation. The simultaneous presence of realization and symbol in the demonstration is a feature often encountered in old tables and must not confuse the reader. Here, for instance, it does not imply a multiple alternation. The unaccented, hence offbeat-leaning, nature of the mordent emerges from David's description of the *martellement* as being *feint et precipité: feint* indicates

Ex. 36.11. David (1737), *Pincé*

9 *Pièces de clavecin* [1716]. *Premier livre de pièces d'orgue* (1739).
10 *Premier livre de pièces de clavecin* (1724); 11 *Méthode*, p. 136.

great delicacy, of something only hinted at (like the *tremblement feint* which had only one alternation at the end of a tapering sound).

Michel Corrette in his flute treatise of 1735 has the mordent (*martellement*) always started with a *port de voix*.[12] For the mordent proper, Corrette repeats almost verbatim Jean Rousseau's instruction to beat two or three little strokes "narrower and faster than those of a trill," alternating with the lower note.[13] Corrette's "Italian mordent" was given above in Ex. 12.9. In his harpsichord pieces from 1734, Corrette shows in a table the one-stroke onbeat pattern of Ex. 36.12a.[14] In his cello treatise of 1741, Corrette remarks on the lack of mordent symbol for the cello and illustrates its impromptu execution, as shown in Ex. *b*, with little notes.[15]

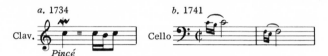

Ex. 36.12. Corrette

Daquin's delayed entry of the *port de voix et pincé* from his book of 1735 was shown before (Ex. 12.11). Foucquet tries to differentiate, through the use of two symbols, between the simple mordent (+) and the double one (⁑), but he is not consistent about it (Ex. 36.13).[16] His models show the grace on the beat and, as mentioned before, his *port de voix et pincé* pattern, like Dandrieu's, keeps the mordent in place on the beat and has the *port de voix* anticipated.

Ex. 36.13. Foucquet (c. 1750)

Lécuyer, speaking of the voice, introduces for the mordent (*martellement*) a new symbol: ⊹ . He explains the grace as "a sort of whiplash which renders the note more brilliant" and offers the illustration of Ex. 36.14.[17] The term "whiplash" suggests fastness and accentuation, hence a tendency to onbeat style.

Ex. 36.14. Lécuyer (1764)

Another singer, Lacassagne, assigns in his important treatise of 1766 a wider range of expression to the mordent (*martellement*), which, he says, "is more or less long or short, more or less tender or lively."[18] He uses no symbol and his

---

[12] *Méthode . . . de la flute*, pp. 34-35.

[13] Ibid., p. 34: ". . . il faut . . . battre . . . deux ou trois petits coups plus serrez et plus pressez que pour faire la cadence. . . ."

[14] *Premier livre de pièces de clavecin* (Paris, 1734).

[15] *Méthode pour . . . le violoncelle*, p. 36.

[16] *Les caractères (Méthode . . . des agréments)*.

[17] *Principes*, p. 17.

[18] *Traité général*, p. 65.

illustration, given in Ex. 36.15, indicates full anticipation of the double mordent, inasmuch as the alternations belong to the following note d″. (The wavy line over the whole note does not stand for a trill; rather, it indicates another type of *martellement* whose oscillations Lacassagne describes as being "so imperceptible that one ought to consider them as simple vibrations or tremors on the same tone."[19] He probably had a vibrato in mind.)

Ex. 36.15. Lacassagne (1766)

Using the term *port de voix réel*, Lacassagne describes an interesting variant of the usual *port de voix et pincé*, one that is to be used for "fondling the notes in tender songs" ("flatter les Notes dans les Airs tendres"). The pattern, shown in Ex. 36.16, can be applied, he says, not only in stepwise ascent but also in upward leaps. In this design, the *port de voix*, after repeating the preceding note, rises to the level of the following note and carries out "a little undulation of the voice" [i.e. the mordent proper] before settling on the principal tone. The latter is then to be gradually swelled, then diminished (*on file [le son]*) and ended with an accent.[20] Explanation, notation, and placement in front of the delicately starting *son filé* imply the unaccented nature of the entire combined grace.

Ex. 36.16. Lacassagne

A similar combined grace, rising by step or by leap, is shown by Abbé Duval in his treatise of 1764 under the term *martellement*.[21] Its design, given in Ex. 36.17, is unusual in that the first note of the mordent proper is lengthened. Duval characterizes the three notes which are thus inserted before a long note as *notes passagères* and adds that in fast and lively pieces the first of the three notes may be left out. Duval's illustration is given in its entirety to show his curious sixfold notational choice for this grace: five different symbols or none at all. All these symbols have to do double duty also for the *port de voix* (on the beat) with *pincé* annex.

Ex. 36.17. L'abbé Duval (1764)

Bérard and Blanchet do not mention a mordent as such but describe a mordent-like grace (which they call *flatté* or *balancé*), involving what may be microtones rather than

---

[19] Ibid.: "Il y a aussi des Martellemens si insensibles, qu'on doit seulement les regarder comme de simples Vibrations ou frémissemens sur le même Ton; et alors on peut les marquer ainsi 〰 ."

[20] The term *filer le son* is usually the equivalent of the Italian *mesa di voce*, the gradual swelling and diminishing of a long-held note. The *accent* is the slight *Nachschlag*.

[21] *Principes*, p. 54.

half-steps. They speak of an almost inaudible inflection of the voice rapidly touching a note below twice.[22]

About 1769, Dard shows two alternate symbols (see Ex. 36.18) for the *martellement*: ▼ or ⌄ for which he allows only one alternation ("un seul coup de gosier").[23]

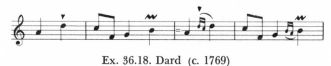

Ex. 36.18. Dard (c. 1769)

Francoeur ("neveu"), in the autograph additions to his treatise of 1772, gives for the single mordent the terms *martellement* and *flaté* as synonyms and uses the symbol of a vertical dash: ╎ .[24] In his models (Ex. 36.19) the suggestion of offbeat intention is strengthened by a comparison with his explicit onbeat realizations of the *coulé* and the *port de voix* (see Ex. 12.22). The term *flaté* meaning flattered, suggests delicacy and tenderness.

Ex. 36.19. Francoeur ("neveu") (1772)

Duval in his vocal treatise of 1775 points to the lack of a mordent symbol for the voice. He shows the grace (*martellement*) as a single alternation on the beat (Ex. 36.20); yet, by defining it as a "light inflection of the throat" ("un léger coup de gosier") that precedes a long note, he suggests a lack of dynamic emphasis.[25]

As mentioned before, Duval shows another grace, which he calls *flatté*; he describes it as a stepwise inflection with usually the upper, occasionally the lower note.[26] In Ex. 21.21*d* above, the first specimen is presumably an anticipated *port de voix et pincé*, the second one a *Schneller*.

Ex. 36.20. Duval (1775)

Levesque and Bêche describe a *flatté* as being slower than the *martellement* which is lively and gay.[27] Their model (Ex. 36.21), which shows the symbol of the vertical dash, is rhythmically noncommittal.

Ex. 36.21. Levesque and Bêche

[22] Bérard, *L'art*, p. 119; Blanchet, *L'art*, p. 116.

[23] *Nouveux principes*, p. 17.

[24] *Diapason*, aut. supplement.

[25] *Méthode agréable*, p. 11.

[26] *Ibid.*, p. 11: "Le Flatté consiste à donner un léger coup de gosier qui joint ensemble deux notes diatoniques, en montant et quelquefois en descendant."

[27] *Solfèges*, p. 6.

De Lusse, in his flute treatise (c. 1760), shows a multiple mordent (*pincé*) starting on the lower note (Ex. 36.22a).[28] This grace, like Nivers's *agrément*, is a variant of the *port de voix et pincé* idea (see also Rameau's early pattern of Ex. 36.7a). Another of De Lusse's patterns, a *tremblement composé inférieur*, shows an anticipated *port de voix* with an onbeat multiple mordent followed by a turn (Ex. *b*).

Ex. 36.22. De Lusse (c. 1760)

THE French mordent seems to have changed only slightly in the course of a century. The variety of the forms and the rhythmic-dynamic designs found in the 17th century were still found in the mid-18th century and after. By and large, the onbeat style for the simple mordent was more at home on the keyboard because it could thus serve as a substitute for the unavailable dynamic accent that clarifies meter and rhythm. It is hardly a coincidence that outside of the keyboard practically all models were given in the noncommittal *notes postiches*. Corrette spells out the downbeat in his clavier treatise but uses the little notes for his cello, flute, and voice treatises. The singers were mostly inclined to unaccented rendition, which in turn is generally attracted to interbeat space. Here again, as with the one-note graces, the unaccented French diction presumably had much to do with this tendency. As will be seen below, the basically unaccented nature of the French mordent finds further confirmation in L. Mozart's treatise.

[28] Charles de Lusse, *L'art de la flûte traversière*.

The Italo-German Mordent
1600-1715

Diruta's model of 1593, given in Ex. 37.1, shows how some players (he mentioned in particular Claudio Merulo) use certain *tremoletti* on stepwise descending notes.[1] The ornament for the first quarter-note is a main-note trill, the next is a double mordent, the third and fourth could be considered either as mordent-related graces or as anticipated trills belonging to the following note.

Ex. 37.1. Diruta (1593, 1597)

After Diruta, no theoretical source for the mordent was found in Italy for almost a century and a half, so here again we have to turn for information to the German exponents of Italian practices.

The German and Italian mordents of this era were so closely tied to the trill that numerous mordent illustrations had to be given in Chapter 28 above. In order to avoid the repetition of most of these illustrations, the reader's indulgence is solicited for a number of back references to Chapter 28, as well as for a few restatements of some key documents.

In Germany, Praetorius, following Ammerbach's lead, sets the pattern for the whole 17th century by juxtaposing the *tremulus ascendens*, the main-note trill, with its inversion, the *tremulus descendens*, the multiple mordent.[2] Noteworthy in his model (Ex. 37.2) is the raised auxiliary for the mordent which reflects the affinity of this grace for half-tone oscillations. In the majority of the models by 17th-century theorists, the mordent is either shown in a natural half-tone setting or has its auxiliary raised.

Ex. 37.2. Praetorius (1619), Herbst (1642), Crüger (1654, 1660)

As mentioned before, Praetorius considers the mordent somewhat inferior to the trill. It may be no coincidence that among his *tremoletti*, his small trills, he gives no mordent patterns.

Herbst in 1642 and 1658, copying Praetorius extensively, gives the identical *tremulus* pattern of Ex. 37.2 but varies some of the older master's *tremoletti* patterns (see above Ex. 28.2) by introducing as counterpart to Praetorius's *Schneller* the single mordent in a context of stepwise ascending notes (Ex. 37.3).[3]

---

[1] *Transylvano*, I (1593), f. 11r (1597), p. 20. [3] *Musica practica* (1642), p. 7.
[2] *Syntagma*, III, 235.

Ex. 37.3. Herbst (1642)

Crüger in 1654 and 1660 follows Praetorius's Ex. 37.2 and also omits mordent patterns for *tremoletti*.[4] Mylius in 1685 shows the usual pair of *tremuli* (see above Ex. 28.6*c*).[5] Like Praetorius, he prefers the ascending *tremulus* to the descending one. Mylius also shows the analogous pair of trill and mordent for the voice, this time using the term *trillo* (see above Exx. 28.6*a* and *b*). Each starts with a support on the main note, presumably to help focus the pitch.

The important illustration of Ex. 28.6*a* significantly proved what was to be expected from the dual nature of the grace, that the *tr* symbol *can stand for mordent as well as for trill*.

Strangely enough, and probably due to an oversight, Mylius expresses preference for the descending *trillo*, which he calls the best and most agreeable, because the ascending type "though also good" carries with it the danger of flattening ("mit der Stimme verfallen"). One might expect such an effect rather from the descending *trillo*; also, in line with his predecessors, he had expressed his preference for the ascending *tremulus* for instruments.

Printz in 1678 shows single mordents and *Schnellers* as two of many simple diminution patterns (*Figuren*) that can vary a single note. Using the term *tremolo*, he shows their multialternation ascending or descending counterparts.[6] For his models, see above Exx. 28.9*a*, *b*, *c*, and *d*.

Falck in 1688 offers the usual *tremulus ascendens* and *descendens* (see above Ex. 28.10) and significantly specifies that his multiple mordent is to use only a half-step, whereas the trill can use half- or whole step.[7]

In 1695 Feyertag describes a single mordent, which he calls *accentus circumflexo remittens*, as a counterpart of the *Schneller*; both may have had prebeat character (see above Ex. 28.11*f*).[8] His ascending and descending multialternation *tremulus* (see above Exx. 28.11*a* and *b*) has the raised auxiliary for the mordent.

The same mirror image is also clearly expressed by Kuhnau who writes in 1689 that the *"Mordant"* (which he indicates by two little oblique lines before the note) "almost equals the trill except that the former makes a short but rather fast [literally: strong] shake with the whole or half-tone below."[9]

Though Kuhnau's mordents probably were done mainly on the beat, there are contexts that suggest prebeat rendition. In Ex. 37.4*a*, the mordent preceding a (main-note) trill would be confusing on the beat, and its probable rendition is sketched in Ex. *b* in the usual style of a mordent-trill. In Ex. *c*, simultaneous execution of the mordent and rising *Vorschlag* would be unnecessarily awkward.[10] Here it might be best to anticipate the *Vorschlag* and play the mordent on the beat, in which case the mordent on the 8th-note of the preceding beat might more fittingly be anticipated. In many a Gigue, a proliferation of mordents and *Vorschläge* on offbeat notes could obscure the characteristic rhythm, unless some of the graces are anticipated (see e.g. the Gigues from the 2nd, 4th, and 6th *Partie* of the *Clavier-Übung*, I).

[4] *Synopsis* (1654), p. 194; *Praecepta* (1660), p. 25.
[5] *Rudimenta* (no pagin.), ch. 5.
[6] *Musica modulatoria*, pp. 45, 47, 54.

[7] *Idea*, p. 100.
[8] *Syntaxis*, pp. 206, 220-221.
[9] *Clavier-Übung Erster Theil*, Preface.
[10] *Clavier-Übung Andrer Theil* (1692).

Ex. 37.4. Kuhnau

Beyer in 1703 shows the usual pair of rising and falling alternations which, like Mylius, he calls *trillo* in a vocal setting. His mordent auxiliary is raised. (See above Ex. 28.12.) In the second edition of his treatise, he limits the use of the multiple mordent to instruments, because in vocal music this grace would render the voice "too lazy and sluggish" ("zu faul und träge").[11]

Murschhauser in 1703 illustrates the symbol *m* as a double mordent, in the usual manner as inversion of an analogous main-note trill, as was shown above in Ex. 28.13.[12] Fuhrmann in 1706 describes a multiple half-tone mordent under the name of *Tremolo* or *Mordant* (symbol: +). It is, he says, "an oscillation of the voice with the half-tone under the note that is to be shaken."[13] Stressing the usual mirror-image relationship, he defines the *tremolo* as an "inverted *trilletto*," in that the *trilletto* "oscillates with the half-tone above, the *tremolo* touches the half-tone below." His illustration was shown above in Ex. 28.14*e*.

Heinichen, in his first treatise on the thorough bass (1711), shows a symbol of two vertical bars preceding the note head for the *Mordant*. He says that it can be used not only as all other graces, in the upper voice of the accompaniment, but "even by beginners" any time in the middle voices.[14] In the much enlarged later version of his treatise (1728), he is more specific and describes three types of mordents on the chosen note c.[15] The first of these three types is one where the b is struck first, then almost simultaneously the c, whereupon the b is released. This, Heinichen says, is how Gasparini describes this grace. Such mordents, Heinichen continues, can be made in all voices of the accompaniment. When the mordent is done in the same fashion but with a whole tone instead of a half-tone, Heinichen, in alleged agreement with Gasparini, calls it *acciaccatura*.[16] The second type is a very fast, single mordent: sounding c b c "with such speed that all three strikes give the c, so-to-speak, a single accent." The third type is a multiple mordent of two to three such alternations that can be applied to long notes.

The sources so far quoted have all issued from the Italo-German tradition. In 1696, Johann Caspar Fischer, in what may be the first French-oriented ornament table in Germany, shows Chambonnières's symbol (⟋) as well as the latter's single-alternation model[17] (Ex. 37.5), which he calls a *semi tremulus* or *mordant*.

[11] *Primae lineae*, 1703, p. 58; 1730, pp. 38-39.

[12] *Prototypon*, Preface.

[13] *Trichter*, p. 66.

[14] *Anweisung*, ch. 5, par. 21.

[15] *Generalbass*, p. 530.

[16] Ibid., footnote on p. 534. More about this in ch. 43.

[17] *Blumen Büschlein*, Preface.

[signum] semi tremuli
vulgo mordant

Ex. 37.5. Fischer (1696)

Twelve years after Fischer's document, J. G. Walther in his early treatise of 1708 shows the French symbol (⁕) alongside another one: ℔ (which he probably derived from Georg Muffat).[18] In his music, Walther uses only the French sign. It appears in the illustration given above in Ex. 15.25*b* which shows a plain single mordent for a quarter-note, whereas the two mordents for 8th-notes are preceded by *ports de voix*. In discussing this illustration, it was pointed out that the *ports de voix* had to be anticipated to safeguard the integrity of the mordent and its basic identity with the unprepared grace on the quarter-note.

In his Lexicon of 1732, Walther lists the *Mordant* as an instrumental grace, and though he does not specify its rhythmic design, his simile—"as if something hard, e.g. a nut, were to be bitten in two"—suggests a single, fast, crackling onbeat alternation. However, certain passages in his works point to flexible rhythmic interpretation.

For example, in the illustrations of Exx. 37.6*a* and *b*, we see the coincidence of mordents and trills. To avoid confusion, the two graces could be synchronized in exact mirror image (the trills starting either on the main note or with anticipated auxiliary), or one of the graces, probably the mordent, could be played before the beat.

Under the title of *Martellement*, Walther refers in his *Lexicon* to Loulié's use of this term and reproduces the latter's models which were given above in Ex. 35.16.

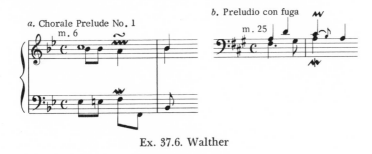

a. Chorale Prelude No. 1   *b.* Preludio con fuga

Ex. 37.6. Walther

DURING the entire Italian-dominated 17th century, the German theorists showed a remarkable measure of agreement on the duality of trill and mordent as twin manifestations of the same grace, the *tremulus.* Some writers carried the idea well into the 18th century. It is only consistent that Mylius's symbol *tr* could signify a mordent as well as a trill. This double meaning, probably common throughout the 17th century, was still to be found in Domenico Scarlatti (as pointed out above in Chapter 30).

Whereas the trill was equally at home with half-tone or whole-tone oscillation, the mordent showed a definite preference for half-tone oscillation. The main form of the mordent was the multiple alternation type. The one-stroke mordent

[18] *Praecepta*, I, ch. 8, par. 6.

appeared chiefly for short note values or, as witnessed by Printz's models, as a simple diminution that as such had no definite rhythmic design.

The one-stroke mordent makes its first appearance as a specific, symbol-indicated ornament in Fischer's French-oriented table of 1696. Walther described the French grace in 1708. (Bach used the French symbol in some of the early keyboard works that could be dated around 1704.) In Germany during the early years of the 18th century, the mixture of the freely improvised Italo-German and the flexible French mordent types must have yielded varied results from one individual artist to another. However, one inheritance can be safely assumed because it was common to both streams of tradition: the important role of the multiple mordent.

J. S. Bach's Mordent

Bach prescribed mordents only for the keyboard and used the French symbol (⋔), which he transcribed in his *Explication* as follows:

Ex. 38.1. *Explication*

Once in a while he extends the wavy line to three or even more waggles, which signifies multiple alternations (without limiting the two-waggle sign to a single-stroke mordent). As with his trill, he does not qualify the symbol with accidentals to indicate a required alteration of the auxiliary. When making the desirable adjustment on his own, the performer will have to be alert to the mordent's strong penchant for half-tone oscillations.

By not using a mordent symbol for other instruments, Bach significantly deviates from French practices. The gambists, as will be remembered, used the mordent symbol lavishly; Couperin prescribed it for other instruments as well; Rameau and others, who used D'Anglebert's hook sign for the keyboard, turned to different symbols for the orchestra, but their meaning was identical.

The limitation of the symbol to the keyboard does not imply an absence of mordents in other media, but it does reflect the more extensive use on the keyboard than elsewhere. In this we can probably detect a trait of the Italo-German tradition in which the *tremulus descendens* was considered less appropriate for the voice (and presumably for melody instruments) than for the keyboard.

Another, stronger Italo-German strain in Bach's mordents can be found in the way he uses the grace: he does so overwhelmingly on the rise from the preceding note, fairly often on repeated notes, but exceedingly rarely on descent.[1] In this he differs from, say, Couperin who used the mordent ubiquitously in any melodic

[1] Among these rare cases are the mordents in the Allemande of the 5th French Suite (mm. 14 and 15) or the one in m. 37 of the C minor harpsichord Phantasy (BWV 906), all of which occur after a downward leap of a fifth. The 20 mordents—18 of which occur upon descent—as given in the BG edition of the Sarabande from the 3rd harpsichord Partita, cannot all be authentic because of their massive incongruence with Bach's usage. The original print of this piece—its primary source—is reproduced in NBA V/1, p. xi with the speculative comment that two different engravers shared in the design of the ornaments. The latter's design is poor throughout and hence, from a purely graphical point of view, the BG interpretation was excusable. However, a few of the symbols, e.g. those on the second note and in mm. 2, 3, 10, 18, do show an extra waggle preceding the one with the mordent slash, thus suggesting the meaning of a trill with suffix (Bach's *trillo und mordant*) though Bach used always four to five waggles for this particular symbol. The notation in the print is, alas, very inconsistent and often obscure. The editor, Richard Douglas Jones, attempted to bring order into the chaos 1) by giving an—abbreviated—trill-plus-suffix symbol for the many appearances of the three-note opening motive (though the print shows rather clearly mordents in mm. 16, 22, 24, 26, some of which are displaced); 2) by giving the mordent symbol upon ascent (mm. 10, 25) and after the downward leaps in mm. 1, 9, 11, 27 (though in m. 9 the print shows a trill).

context. Bach uses the mordent less as an independent grace in the French manner; rather, he applies it as the Italo-German mirror image of the main-note trill, which was favored on melodic descent. The previously shown start of the Organ Chorale, BWV 718 (see above Ex. 29.29*b*), offers a graphic illustration of this characteristic use.[2] It was explained at the time why the graces in the example should be rendered as *Schneller* and one-stroke mordents respectively, and why they all ought to be done in anticipation. The reference to this example may serve as a fitting introduction to some of the difficulties we face with Bach's mordents. Many modern scholars, editors, and performers accept the model from the *Explication* as a definitive formula; accordingly, Bach's mordents are thought of as consisting of one onbeat alternation only. However, the mordent cannot be limited to the literal replica of its model. If we combine the lessons from Bach's Italo-German and the French legacies, we have good reason to assume that his mordent was changeable in both melic and rhythmic design; that it could accommodate multiple alternations, and that on other occasions the mordent, especially the single-stroke type, could be anticipated, as in the example just referred to.

The single onbeat mordent, as pictured in the *Explication*, may well be the design most frequently used. It is usually indicated whenever its rhythm-reinforcing, accent-implying effect is called for. The illustrations of Ex. 38.2 give two specimens that might favor the single-stroke onbeat mordent. (See also the 3rd French Suite, Allemande, m. 1, and the C major Organ Prelude, BWV 547, m. 2.) A clear-cut decision is often not possible; in BWV 547, for instance, double mordents are not out of place if the piece is taken at a leisurely tempo.

Ex. 38.2.

The sustained mordent type, filling the whole length of a note (Couperin's *pincé continu*), may be infrequent in Bach, but occur it does. Thus we do find it explicitly marked by a long wavy line in the autograph of the Clavier Concerto in D major (a transcription from the Violin Concerto in E major). For this mordent, an E sharp auxiliary was most likely intended. Example 38.3 shows both the original and the transcription.

A very interesting and revealing case is reported by Alfred Kreutz and endorsed by Walter Emery.[3] In the Gigue of the 6th English Suite, the thematic material of the first part is inverted in the second. In keeping with this procedure, the long-held trills of the first part are inverted into long-sustained mordents (Exx.

The editor may have guessed right, yet after the downward leaps, trills with suffix are a possible alternative.

[2] According to *NBA*, IV, 3, *KB*, the ornaments to this early Bach work were entered in Leipzig by Kittel on Bach's instructions. A strikingly similar passage occurs in the following opening of Böhm's Chorale Prelude *Vater unser* (Versus 1):

Böhm, *Vater unser*, Versus 1 (P 802)

[3] Kreutz, p. 7; Emery, pp. 146-147.

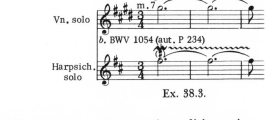

Ex. 38.3.

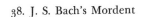
38.4*a* and *b*). The *BG* and most other editions give trills throughout. However, the oldest and most important source (P 1072) has unmistakable mordents throughout the second half.[4] Such a reading makes perfect sense in the frame of the exact inversion. Moreover, as both Kreutz and Emery point out, this very inversion established the main-note character of the trills in the first half of the Gigue. A raised auxiliary for the mordents is again almost mandatory.

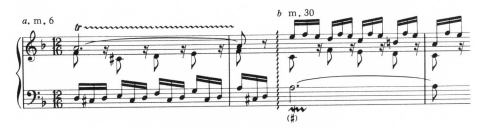

Ex. 38.4. BWV 811 (P 1072), Gigue

Another case is that of the delightful snare-drum effect in the Gavotte from the 3rd English Suite; this passage is also erroneously rendered in the *BG* and most other editions. In the oldest source for these suites (P 1072), the passage reads as given in Ex. 38.5*a*. Two other, much later sources (P 419, Michel, c. 1770 and P 291, anon., c. 1760) give the passage as shown in Ex. *b*. This agreement, as well as the logic of the repeated mordents on an insistent tone repetition with an obvious drum effect, should establish the mordent reading for the whole note with the alternations perhaps persisting into the next measure. The need for an f sharp auxiliary is obvious throughout. (The *BG* version is shown in Ex. *c*.)

Ex. 38.5. BWV 808, Gavotte

[4] The mordent-meaning in the inverted parts is indubitable even though the scribe carelessly placed the mordent dash a few times too far back in a multiple waggle: ꟾ; in m. 35, however, the intent is unmistakable: ꟾ. It is precisely the danger of such misplacement of the dash with the resulting confusion of meaning which prompted C.P.E. Bach and Marpurg to caution against the use of the symbol ꟾ for indicating a trill with suffix (J. S. Bach's *trillo und mordant*).

Apart from such cases of sustained mordents, there are many more places where a multiple mordent of two or three alternations will be desirable. Emery points with good reason to the slow movement from the Italian Concerto where the start of the melody (Ex. 38.6a) might be played as shown in Ex. b.

Ex. 38.6. BWV 971, 2

Such double or triple mordents would seem most appropriate on a note that is long enough to accommodate them and still allow time for a rest point and in contexts where the mordent is used neither to sustain a long note nor to provide a sharp biting accent substitute, but to add emphasis in the vein of a *rinforzando*. Often we shall find proper places at the start of the piece, as already shown in the last example.

The beginning of the D minor Toccata and Fugue (Ex. 38.7) is another such place. Here the opening mordent could possibly have two or three alternations (with the first note perhaps ever so imperceptively sustained) to generate enough energy for this powerful opening. The second and third mordents might then also be doubled.

Ex. 38.7. BWV 565

Double strokes could be applied to advantage in the G minor Organ Prelude ("Fantasy"), BWV 542, for the starting note, which in this rhapsodic setting could well be treated like a small hold (Ex. 38.8). Here, a half-tone auxiliary is certainly required.

Ex. 38.8. BWV 542

Double strokes will make a good effect in the passage from the French Overture given in Ex. 38.9, as well as in other similar contexts.

Ex. 38.9. BWV 831

Mordents on final notes will often gain by multiple alternations. In Ex. 38.10*a* from the Organ Chorale *Komm, heiliger Geist,* the case for a double or even triple mordent is strengthened by the need for the unremitting linear drive of the preceding measures to come to a less precipitate ending. For similar reasons the mordent in m. 194 of the same piece will also best be done with more than one alternation.

Ex. 38.10. BWV 652

The rhythmic displacement of the mordent on or off the beat does not affect voice-leading. What is correct on the beat is correct off the beat and vice versa. Therefore, in contrast to the *Vorschlag,* there can be no evidence that would require one or the other design on the basis of the rules governing parallels. There is, however, other evidence to support Bach's use of anticipation which certainly at that time was alive in both the French and the Italo-German traditions. In the first place, there are many passages similar to the one shown above in Ex. 29.29*b* where an onbeat rendition produces an effect of stiffness if not outright clumsiness; anticipation transforms this awkward effect into one of grace and elegance. Such will usually be the case where the mordent is placed on a note that is to be graced but not weighted, where the mordent consequently serves as a connective, not an accentual or intensifying ornament. Another such example is shown in the illustration of Ex. 38.11*a,* taken from the opening of the very early (1704) *Capriccio sopra la lontananza,* a programatic piece for the departure "of his beloved brother." The mood of this particular section is spelled out in the rare descriptive indication: "it is a cajoling of friends trying to keep him from taking the trip" ("Eine Schmeichelung . . ."). What is suggested by the slow tempo and by the character and contour of the phrase alone—that the graces should be of an insinuating, caressing nature—is strongly confirmed by the professed aim of expressing cajolery. To achieve such effect, both mordents, even the second one which falls on the heaviest beat, might best be anticipated, and the same treatment could be accorded the *Vorschläge,* so that the passage would be rendered approximately as shown in Ex. *b* (with all little notes understood to be in anticipation).[5]

Another context frequently encountered in Bach's works in which anticipation of the mordent will usually be indicated is that of the *port de voix et pincé* in which a long *port de voix* on the beat is written out in regular notes. In this compound grace, as said before, the protagonist is the long *Vorschlag* from below. It takes the beat, it takes the accentual, harmonic, and expressive emphasis; the

[5] According to the *Möllersche Handschrift,* the chief source for this piece (BB Mus. MS 40644, f. 63r), the four ornaments in m. 5 are erroneously rendered in the *BG* edition: the first two should be mordents, not trills, the fourth one a trill, not a mordent, which makes much better musical sense.

Ex. 38.11. BWV 992

446

mordent is an annex whose little loop gracefully eases the transition from the *Vorschlag* to its resolution into the upper neighbor note. Since the mordent sequel, in order to fulfill this auxiliary function, is to be slurred on lightly and unobtrusively, it finds its proper place not on a beat, but either before or after it. This circumstance was mentioned before, but it is important to recall it in connection with Bach who usually wrote out the long *port de voix* for reasons amply discussed before. However, writing out the *Vorschlag* conceals the true nature of the compound ornament. To the unwary, the mordent in such a notation looks like an independent ornament, when in fact it is only the very junior partner in a combination grace. Thus, when Bach writes in the D major Invention the pattern shown in Ex. 38.12a, some Frenchmen and some later Germans might have written it as shown in Ex. *b*; this would have clarified the compound nature of the grace but left its rendition open to a wide range of rhythmic interpretations. Here, as in other similar places, Bach's notation disguises but does not change the nature of the mordent as a simple suffix that finds its place more properly off the beat. In other words, it will best be played as suggested in Ex. *c* rather than in Ex. *d*.

Ex. 38.12. BWV 774

The same analysis applies to the theme of the *Goldberg Variations* (Ex. 38.13a). The tie clarifies the *port de voix et pincé* character; hence, here too an offbeat rendition of the *pincé* suffix, as indicated in Ex. *b*, would seem to be the logical solution.

Ex. 38.13. BWV 988, Aria

Another illustration may be chosen from the 3rd Organ Sonata where a *port de voix et pincé* occurs several times in both left and right hands (Ex. 38.14). Though the slur to the mordent is frequently omitted in this sparsely articulated work (it does appear in the final measure), the harmonic context of a prepared dissonance resolving into the upper neighbor leaves no doubt about the identity of the compound grace. Anticipation is indicated here too.

accent und
mordant

Ex. 38.14. BWV 527, 2   Ex. 38.15. *Explication*

When Bach indicates the *port de voix et pincé* through a combination of the two symbols, with either   or   we face, of course, the sum of their individual ambiguities. The formula of the *Explication* (Ex. 38.15) is certainly not exclusive. Moreover, we see the mordent here in an unstressed offbeat design.

What has been said about the analogous combination of *Vorschlag* and trill symbol applies here too. The hook, or the little note, has a wide range of meanings, from a long *Vorschlag*, as pictured in the *Explication*, to an anticipated one, with corresponding effect on the placement of the mordent proper. Thus, the mordent can fall on the beat with the *port de voix* in anticipation, and there can even be occasions where, in the manner revealed by L'Affilard, the entire combined grace will best be taken before the beat. An onbeat placement of the *port de voix* will occur frequently, but, for reasons given before, its extension beyond the duration of an 8th-note value will be very rare. Thus, when Bach writes in the eighth measure of the Aria from the *Goldberg Variations* the two mordents shown in Ex. 38.16a, the frequently heard interpretation (Ex. *b*) of a quarter-note *port de voix* that permits the synchronization of the two mordents is highly questionable. Bach, as mentioned before, was usually very precise when he was concerned with the synchronization of voices, and he would hardly have left such intended concordance of mordents to chance (especially since in the immediate neighborhood, in mm. 1, 5, and 9 where *no* synchronization was at stake, he wrote out the quarter-note *ports de voix*). The physical separation of the two mordents suggests their corresponding separation in sound. A design approximating the illustration of Ex. *c* will be a much likelier solution.

Ex. 38.16. BWV 988, Aria

The most congenial locations for a long-sustained *port de voix* preceding a mordent will be in holds, in cadences (especially final ones), and on long notes on a heavy beat that are not set against a fast-moving counterpoint. Example 38.17a from the Chorale *Allein Gott* offers an illustration with its suggested rendition (Ex. *b*).

Ex. 38.17. BWV 662

The Chorale Prelude *Wenn wir in höchsten Nöthen sein* has several interesting *ports de voix et pincés*, all in different contexts. The one in the first measure (Ex. 38.18a) is placed on a note long enough to provide comfortable space for a sustained *Vorschlag*, and there are no polyphonic complications that might prejudice its use. Thus, a solution close to the model of the *Explication* seems indicated, as sketched in Ex. *b*. In the passage from the last measure (Ex. *c*), the short amount of time and the 16th-note-movement in the tenor make it advisable to execute the grace quickly and strike the principal note on the first 16th, in order to permit the resolution of the *Vorschlag* into a consonance before the harmony changes (see Ex. *d*). In Ex. *e* from the third measure lack of time favors a prebeat *Vorschlag* (Ex. *f*).

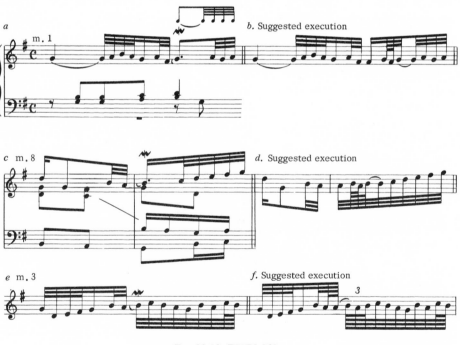

Ex. 38.18. BWV 641

D'Anglebert referred to the trill with suffix as *tremblement et pincé* and notated it with the combination of his symbols for trill and mordent (see above Ex. 24.25e). In the *Explication*, Bach adopted D'Anglebert's model and called it *trillo und mordant*, as shown in Ex. 38.19, but he adjusted the symbol to his own mordent sign. In so doing, he may have been the first to use the extended *chevron* with a mordent bar through its last waggle: ⌁ .

Ex. 38.19. *Explication*

It should be pointed out that to call the trill's suffix a mordent is more a matter of notational convenience than of ornamental logic. The last three notes of the model do look like a mordent. However, since the trill ends on the main note, it is more logical to analyze the suffix as the usual two-note suffix ⌁ — or as a one-note *Nachschlag* ⌁ if the movement comes to a stop on the main note (as in Dieupart's design), than as a three-note mordent annex: ⌁ . Bach's *trillo und mordant* symbol, again strictly confined to the keyboard, was adopted by some of his students and followers. Marpurg and C.P.E. Bach record it but do not recommend its use because it can so easily be confused with the sign for a multiple mordent.

Since Bach uses mordent signs only for the keyboard, the question arises whether non-keyboard performers were expected to add mordents on their own with a frequency comparable to the prescribed specimens on the keyboard. Most likely this was not so. Bach's mordent had a stronger link to the keyboard than to other instruments because the rigid sounds of the former were in need of the plasticity which this grace could impart by its suggestion of inflections, accents, or intensifications. Other instruments were in lesser need of the effects provided by this grace, and therefore the less frequent occurrences could be handled by regular notation.

There are many instances where Bach wrote out mordents in regular notation, and many of these offer interesting insights into his use of this grace. In trying to derive such insights, we must determine when the sequence of three pitches: ⌁ is a mordent and when it is not. The alternative is one between a structural and ornamental figure. In making this distinction we must decide whether the notated rhythm of the mordent pattern must be adhered to strictly or whether it can be modified and also, whether the needed slur is either marked or understood. The tempo will be another factor since, generally, a mordent has to be executed swiftly.

In Ex. 38.20*a* from the 3rd Gamba Sonata, the structural character of the pattern is documented by its necessary rhythmic strictness in its many contrapuntal combinations with other 16th-notes.[6] The innumerable cases in which a fairly slow mordent-like pattern occurs in the bass line, such as the one shown in Ex. *b*, will most often belong to the structural category.

By contrast, Ex. *c* from Cantata 6 will strike the listener simply as an ornamental intensification for the repeat of the imploration *bleibe*. Also, mordent

[6] For similar cases, see the fugue themes of the Sonatas in G minor and A minor for Un- accompanied Violin (BWV 1001,2 and 1003,2).

character may be seen in the continuo figure of Ex. *d* from the *Magnificat*, with its faster speed and implied legato articulation.

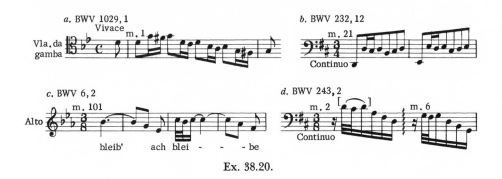

Ex. 38.20.

Other specimens that lean strongly toward mordent characteristics are shown in Ex. 38.21 from Cantatas 185 and 146.

Ex. 38.21.

Further cases are represented by Ex. 38.22*a* from the Sonata in C major for Unaccompanied Violin (marked by an asterisk) and perhaps most tellingly by Ex. *b* from Cantata 187.

Ex. 38.22.

THIS look at Bach's written-out mordents has revealed a marked frequency of the prebeat design. This does not by any means imply that the majority of keyboard mordents were meant to be played in anticipation, because on the keyboard the mordent fulfilled different functions. But the findings do throw an additional light on the fact that Bach did indeed use the mordent as a connective, interbeat grace. This fact is supported by the older French and Italo-German practices and by a number of examples from Bach's keyboard music that could be fitted into the onbeat pattern only with unornamental clumsiness. Thus, the non-keyboard patterns furnish subsidiary evidence that Bach's mordent had a wider range of rhythmic designs than is usually assumed. Consequently, the performer will have to decide whether a given phrase is best served by the accentuating and intensifying effect of the onbeat, or by the connective qualities of the prebeat style; whether single or multiple alternations seem more fitting; and, very importantly, whether there is a reason for not raising the auxiliary to a half-tone distance.

The Italian Mordent
1710-1760

The question of the Italian mordent is complicated by a semantic confusion regarding the term *mordente* which often deviates from the common meaning of the term "mordent."

To Gasparini in 1708, the *mordente* is a note added a half-step under the tone of a quickly arpeggiated chord, struck simultaneously or slightly before the beat, and immediately released.[1] To Tosi in 1723, the *trillo mordente* is no mordent, but a miniature trill.[2] This usage prompted Agricola's lament that the Italians always confuse the mordent with the *Pralltriller*.[3] Tartini's *mordente* (as will be seen presently) was often a prebeat turn.

Geminiani in his ornament tables of 1749 and 1751 gives as principal model a multiple mordent that, as shown in Ex. 39.1a, is unmistakably the old *tremulus descendens* or *tremulo di sotto*, and he does call it *mordente*.[4]

In the corresponding English text he calls it "Beat" and comments on its variable shape and diverse effect, an effect, he says, that ranges from affection and pleasure to grief and horror. His symbol of two oblique lines is an old English one with varying and occasionally unidentified meaning.[5] Other Italian visitors and residents in England adopted it too, but some, Matteis for example, used it to designate the trill, not the mordent.

Under the term *anticipatione*, we find several models, one of which is a mordent on a *Nachschlag* (Ex. *b*). As the term implies, it does have an effect akin to a prebeat mordent. A similar mordent on a *Nachschlag* is presented under the term *separassione* (Ex. *c*).

Ex. 39.1. Geminiani (1749, 1751)

Geminiani offers further varieties, as well as models for combining the mordent with other graces.[6] Among them we find a pattern of a sustained main note, a sort of main-note support before the alternations start (Ex. 39.2a); a mordent-trill (Ex. *b*), and other related mixtures.

Ex. 39.2. Geminiani

In the music examples of Geminiani's violin treatise are found specimens of a *port de voix et pincé* with, presumably, a long onbeat *port de voix* (Ex. 39.3a)

---

[1] *L'armonico pratico al cimbalo*, p. 91.
[2] *Opinioni*, pp. 27-28.
[3] *Anleitung*, p. 103.
[4] References in the following will be to *The Art*, where the mordents are illustrated on p. 26.

[5] The resemblance to Kuhnau's mordent symbol, which is placed *in front* of the note, is most likely accidental (see also above ch. 17, n. 5).
[6] *Essempio* 19, p. 26.

and others with, presumably, anticipated *Vorschläge* (Exx. *b* and *c* from *Composizione* I^a).

Ex. 39.3. Geminiani

Tartini introduces in his treatise (c. 1750) two species of graces which he calls *mordente*.[7] The first of these has the melodic form of a turn; the second is the genuine mordent, which ranges from one to three alternations. It will be well to report on the first type, in spite of its alien melic design, because it sheds light on the rendition of the mordent proper.

The first species of the *mordente* consists of three scalewise notes that are centered on and precede the principal note.[8] This species has two styles: one descending, the other ascending (Exx. 39.4a and *b*). Tartini prefers the first of these, which he considers the more natural one.

Ex. 39.4. Tartini (c. 1750)

The best execution, he says, is one which renders the three little notes with utmost speed. One should not perceive these notes individually but only hear the total effect which imparts vivacity, boldness, and great spirit to the principal note.[9] Therefore, he continues, this *mordente* is generally more fitting for animated than for songful passages, and it should be used in songful passages only in those cases where a spirited expression is desired. By the same token, its use is out of place in solemn, sustained, or sad melodies. Tartini adds the significant comment that in rendering this *mordente*, the accent "does not fall on the three added notes, but on the principal written note of the melody, so that the three added notes are sung or played piano, the principal note forte."[10] This dynamic design will spontaneously lead to anticipation of the grace. Since this *mordente* has the nature of an accent, it should, Tartini adds, be used only on notes where an accent is in order.

At the end of the chapter, Tartini introduces the second species—the regular mordent with single, double, or triple alternations, the number depending on the speed of the passage (Ex. 39.5a).[11] Further illustrations of its use are reproduced in Exx. *b* and *c*.

[7] *Regole*, facs. ed., pp. 17-19.

[8] Ibid., p. 27.

[9] Ibid., p. 17: ". . . non si devono capire le tre note aggiunte, ma solamente sentirne l'affetto, ch'è di render la nota vivace, ardita, e piana di spirito. . . ."

[10] Ibid.: ". . . la forza della voce, o del Suono non cada sopra le tre note aggiunte, ma sopra la nota scritta della cantilena, cosiché le tre note aggiunte siano nel Piano, e la nota scritta nel Forte della voce, o del Suono."

[11] Ibid., p. 19: "Questo Mordente si può fare in due Note, in quattro, in sei, seconda la velocità maggiore, o minore, come si vedrà dagl'Esempj qui annessi." Obviously what is meant here is the speed of the passage as it affects the time available for single or multiple strokes, and not the speed of the finger, i.e. of the alternations, as erroneously rendered in the old French translation which was the basis of the modern trilingual edition.

Ex. 39.5. Tartini

After explaining the trill-like alternations with the lower neighbor, Tartini adds the important directive that the grace is to be rendered "with the expression of the above mentioned [i.e. the first species of the] *mordente.*"[12] This implies that it is to be done piano, with the utmost speed, and with the accent falling on the principal note; in other words, it too is to be done in anticipation. That this is the way in which Tartini conceived the basic nature of this true mordent—undoubtedly with occasional deviations—can also be deduced from Exx. 39.5*b* and *c*. The reader might remember that Tartini, speaking of the appoggiatura, asks for the use of the anticipated types in contexts of even notes, in order not to impinge on the composer's rhythmic intentions. *A fortiori* this would have to apply even more decisively to a two-, four-, or six-note intrusion into the intended evenness of rhythm. Further weighty evidence in support of this inference will be found in the corresponding directives of L. Mozart who, in matters of ornamentation, follows Tartini closely, often to the point of plagiarism. Thus, we can be reasonably sure that for the true mordent, which is also described as being best fitted for gay and spirited passages, Tartini's primary rhythmic design was that of anticipation, with the accent falling on the principal note.

As late as 1775, Vincenzo Manfredini speaks of the trill and mordent as counterparts in the sense of the old mirror image of *tremulus ascendens* and *descendens.*[13] It will be well to recall here his interesting qualification, voiced before by a number of other theorists, that whereas the trill can be made with half-tone or whole tone, the mordent is done with half-tone only. His models are given in Ex. 39.6; here we see his use of the French keyboard symbol—not surprising at this late date—and, in the last measure, the automatically raised auxiliary.

Ex. 39.6. Manfredini (1775)

Musical evidence, hampered by the general absence of a mordent symbol, is not very plentiful on some aspects of the ornament. Important findings in this regard concerned Domenico Scarlatti and were dealt with above in Chapter 30. There, in connection with Exx. 30.19-20, the assumption was strongly supported

12 Ibid.: ". . . con l'espressione del Mordente summentovato."

13 *Regole armoniche*, p. 26.

that not only this master's use of the term *tremulo* referred to the *tremulo di sotto* (the multiple mordent), but also that his usual trill symbol of either *t* or ∿ did signify at times the mordent rather than the trill. It is most likely that Scarlatti would not have resorted to such notation had its ambivalence (in the sense expressed by Mylius) not been widely understood. Hence it is probable that an analogous usage on the part of other masters will be confirmed by further research.

Written-out plain mordents, i.e. mordents not preceded by a *Vorschlag* from above, seem to be rare. Two specimens from Domenico Scarlatti are shown in Ex. 39.7. In Ex. *b*, the omission of the *Vorschlag* after the first beat is probably due more to technical than to musical considerations; but whatever the motive for the omission, the rather obvious need for rhythmical unity reconfirms the anticipation of the *Vorschlag* in this pattern that was previously referred to as typically Italian.

Ex. 39.7. D. Scarlatti

THE old *tremulo* pair of trill and mordent in mutual inversion carried over into the 18th century where distinct traces were found in the harpsichord works of Domenico Scarlatti, as well as in theoretical acknowledgments dating as late as 1775. Tartini comes closest to certain French practices by seeming to limit the mordent to one, two, or three alternations, but above all, by using it essentially in anticipation. Moreover, the Italians developed a mordent design that is typically theirs, the one-stroke mordent preceded by a prebeat descending *Vorschlag*:

Thus we gain a picture of practices that range from the upbeat—even for the triple mordent, so it seems!—to the downbeat, from single to multiple alternations, from plain to *Vorschlag*-adorned designs, from very fast to more moderate speeds. It appears, however, that the unadorned single-stroke mordent was used less frequently in Italy than it was in France or Germany.

The German Mordent

1715-1765

Theopil Muffat lists in his table of c. 1736 the single and double mordent under the same French symbol: ⤳ ; their choice, he says, depends on the length of the note (Exx. 40.1*a* and *b*).[1] The table shows an analogous pair of, unnamed, *ports de voix et pincés* with long onbeat *ports de voix* and either single or double alternations (Exx. *c* and *d*).

Ex. 40.1. Th. Muffat (c. 1736)

Except for Walther's brief article in his dictionary, the next important theoretical source may be the few paragraphs which Mattheson devotes to the mordent in 1739.[2] This master ridicules previous attempts of likening the mordent's effect with the cracking of a nut by the teeth (such as reported by Walther) or with similar comparisons suggesting violence. Although Mattheson tolerates Gasparini's imagery of a small animal's bite and immediate release without wounding, he favors the simile of an amorous kiss. Presumably, he thereby suggests a gentle rather than energetic character for the grace. The mordent, he continues, is not limited to instruments as most, if not all, writers wrongly claim (par. 55). For instruments, though, the mordent has a greater variety of shapes; for the voice he acknowledges only one type: a single-stroke alternation done with such speed that the three tones seem to fuse into one sound (par. 55). He also mentions the *port de voix et pincé*, saying that in vocal music a *Vorschlag* made from below is usually followed by a small mordent. The illustration of Ex. 40.2 shows the shape of the grace only "quite imperfectly," and he adds that the 64th-notes, because of their shortness, are not divided into the measure.[3]

Ex. 40.2. Mattheson (1739)

[1] *Componimenti*, Appendix.
[2] *Capellmeister*, pt. 2, ch. 3, pars. 53-59.
[3] In the first example (lower line), a bar through the C of the meter signature and a *Vorschlag* symbol on d' at the start of the measure are misprints.

Unmetrical notation and the doubly made proviso of being "imperfect" and "approximate" suggest a flexibility of rhythmic rendition that is reinforced by the implied gentleness of the "kiss" simile. For instrumental music, Mattheson's above mentioned greater diversity of designs would indicate a wide range of styles.

Spiess in 1745 considers it unnecessary to discuss the mordent, which, along with the trill, is "known to all musicians."[4]

Marpurg in 1749 adds to the terminological confusion by calling the mordent "*Vorschlag*" and by calling a multiple mordent (see Ex. 40.3a) *einfacher Vorschlag* or *pincé simple*, following Dandrieu rather than Couperin in the use of the term.[5] Like Dandrieu, Marpurg calls it *einfach* (i.e. single or simple), in contrast to the *port de voix et pincé* design, which he calls *doppelter oder accentuirter Vorschlag* (Ex. *b*). The elongated symbol with three or more waggles ( ) is presented as synonymous with the short one ( ).

Ex. 40.3. Marpurg (1749-1750)

The misnomer of the mordent as *Vorschlag* was one of the points criticized by Agricola ("Olibrio") in his pamphlet.[6] Five years later, in his harpsichord treatise of 1755, Marpurg adopts the more usual terms and shows in his models (Exx. 40.4a-d) a one-stroke and a two-stroke mordent.[7] The multiple alternations of the earlier table are gone, but the short and the elongated symbols are still shown to be identical in meaning. All the examples indicate the onbeat placement of either type.

Ex. 40.4. Marpurg (1755)

C.P.E. Bach sees the main function of the mordent in connecting notes, in filling them out, and in rendering them brilliant.[8] The mordent can be multiple, with two or more alternations and a three-waggle symbol, or simple (*kurtz*), with a two-waggle symbol, as shown in Ex. 40.5a. As a third species he shows the

---

[4] *Tractatus*, p. 157.

[5] *Crit. Musicus*, p. 65. Marpurg does mention the "usual" (*insgemein*) term of *Mordant*. Maichelbeck, before him, had unwisely called the *Vorschlag Mordant* (*Caecilia*, p. 38).

[6] Cf. above ch. 18, n. 12.

[7] *Anleitung*, Table V, fig. 11.

[8] *Versuch*, I, ch. 2, sec. 5. References will be to this section.

Zusammenschlag, which will be discussed in a later chapter. The contexts most favorable for the mordent are ascending or upward leaping notes. The mordent, he says, is rare in downward leaps and never occurs in descending seconds (par. 4). In the next paragraphs and in a profusion of illustrations, Bach demonstrates the great versatility of the mordent in all situations (except in descent). He mentions the mordent as the one ornament most frequently used impromptu in the bass (par. 10).

A muliple mordent used to fill out a note must come to a definite rest before the note is over and unlike the trill must not carry the alternations straight into the next note (par. 8). In a *port de voix et pincé* (*Der Mordent nach einem Vorschlage*), the mordent is slurred softly to the preceding *Vorschlag,* according to "the rules for the appoggiatura" (**Ex.** *c*). Accidentals where not indicated have to be added according to context (par. 11). In his illustration (**Ex.** 40.5*b*) and often, but not consistently, in his compositions, he indicates the chromatic alteration above the symbol.

Ex. 40.5. C.P.E. Bach (1753)

Agricola has little to say about the mordent. For the "mordent proper," he shows the single-stroke form (**Ex.** 40.6*a*), as well as the usual pattern for the long *port de voix et pincé* (**Ex.** *b*). He sees the main use for the mordent on keyboard instruments "which can not swell the tone"; in singing where there is less need for it, the most frequent use of the grace occurs after an ascending *Vorschlag.*[9] The mordent, Agricola says, should be done like the *Pralltriller,* with the utmost speed. Significant is his comment that the mordent, for the sake of greater sharpness, is frequently done with the half-tone, even where the key would call for a whole tone. This is interesting further confirmation for the continued tendency to raise the auxiliary.

Ex. 40.6. Agricola (1757)

Quantz in his treatise deals with the mordent only briefly[10] and, unfortunately, his comments are not very clear. First he speaks of the mordent (calling it *Pincé*) as an adjunct to the *Vorschlag,* i.e. as *port de voix et pincé.* In this capacity Quantz

[9] *Anleitung,* pp. 103, 113-114.   29, 30, 32, 33.
[10] *Versuch,* ch. 8, pars. 14-15; Table 6, figs.

distinguishes two kinds, which he illustrates—perhaps significantly—on an upbeat figure, as shown in Exx. 40.7a and b.

a. Fig. 29   *b.* Fig. 30

Pincé

Ex. 40.7. Quantz (1752)

The first model has a double, the second a quadruple alternation. Their rhythmic intention is uncertain and probably variable. For his first pattern, the *Vorschlag* could be *anschlagend* and the mordent the unaccented sequel, though the placement of the *port de voix et pincé* on an anacrusis does not favor such interpretation. In the second pattern, the mordent is too long to admit such design. Here, the *Vorschlag* will have to be quite short to leave sufficient time for the alternations, and Quantz most likely had here (and probably for the first model too) an anticipated *durchgehend Vorschlag* in mind.

In the next paragraph Quantz speaks of *battemens*, a separate grace to be used in leaping notes that do not take a *Vorschlag*. His models show two distinct types. The first, given in Ex. 40.8a, is a regular single-stroke mordent; the second (Ex. *b*) is a multialternation type that starts with the auxiliary. Their rhythmic shape is undetermined.

One way to bring these two contrasting designs under one hat would be the assumption of an unaccented start. Such a start would obscure the differences of design, whereas an accented onbeat start would emphasize the contrast. This tentative suggestion finds support from two quarters. The first is the fact that the closely related three-note grace ♪ (Tartini's type 1 *mordente*) was described also by Quantz as being done softly, with the sound beginning to grow only on the principal note (see below Chapter 41, Ex. 41.33c); the second is the light shed on this matter by a kindred spirit, Leopold Mozart.

a   *b*

Battemens

Ex. 40.8. Quantz

Leopold Mozart's illuminating ideas about the mordent have to be dealt with in some detail.[11] Writing in the spirit of Tartini, Mozart defines the mordent as two or three little notes "which very fast and softly grab hold, so to speak, of the principal note, but disappear immediately so that the principal note alone is heard strongly."[12] The crucial point in this statement is the softness of the mordent and the accentuation of the principal note, a circumstance conducive to prebeat rendition. In paragraph 13 this dynamic pattern is presented as being of the essence: "In general one must use the mordent only if one wishes to give special emphasis to a note; for the loudness of the tone falls on the note itself: the mordent by contrast is slurred to the latter very softly and very fast; or else

11 *Violinschule*, ch. 11, pars. 8-16. References in the text will be to this chapter.

12 Ibid., par 8: "Den Mordente nennet man die 2, 3 und mehr kleine Nötchen, die ganz

schnell und still die Hauptnote, so zu reden, anpacken; sich aber augenblicklich verlieren, dass man die Hauptnote nur allein stark klingen höret."

it would not be called a mordent. It confers vivacity on the note, it distinguishes it from the others and gives the execution a different physiognomy."[13]

Where Tartini had presented two types of mordents, Mozart lists three. They include, as shown in Ex. 40.9, both of Tartini's types—the regular mordent in its one-stroke and two-stroke style (Ex. *a*) and the three-note pattern of the anticipated turn taken either upward or downward (Ex. *b*). Added to these is a two-note grace (Ex. *c*) that frames the principal note and was in the second half of the 18th century more commonly called the *Anschlag*. To justify the inclusion of this latter type, Mozart argues that it has the mordent qualities of soft seizure and immediate release, even though the pattern is somewhat more gentle than the species with three or more notes and could be said to consist of "polite nibblers" ("die höflichen Anbeisser"). On the other hand, Mozart points out, the first type, i.e. the regular mordent, if done with only two notes will also have a much more gentle effect than the types involving more notes. "Does that make it less of a mordent?" Mozart asks.

Ex. 40.9. L. Mozart (1756)

These comments confirm that for all three of Mozart's types softness of the grace and accent on the principal note were of the essence. It is, in fact, this common denominator that allows Mozart to see in these three types embodiments of the same ornamental principle and to join them under the same term of "mordent." There is also little doubt that this common denominator generally favored the prebeat placement for these graces.[14]

Mozart's explicitness in these matters adds weight to the prebeat meaning for Tartini's second type, the regular mordent. The Italian master had implied such meaning ("with the same expression . . .") without spelling it out again. Furthermore, it is likely that Mozart's discussion illuminates Quantz's ambiguity in this respect. Finally, it is noteworthy that Mozart sees the French *pincé* as falling into the same prebeat-favoring dynamic pattern. Speaking about the semantic implications of the word *Mordant*, he says, "I may say . . . that the mordent or the so-called French *pincé* approaches the principal note very softly and quickly, quasi-

[13] Ibid., par. 13: "Uberhaupts muss man den *Mordente* nur brauchen, wenn man einer Note einen besondern Nachdruck geben will. Denn die Stärke des Tones fällt auf die Note selbst: der *Mordant* hingegen wird ganz schwach und recht geschwind an die Hauptnote angeschliffen; sonst würde er kein *Mordant* mehr heissen. Er macht die Note lebhaft; er unterscheidet sie von den übrigen, und giebt dem ganzen Vortrage ein anderes Ansehen."

[14] W. A. Mozart's enchanting use of the three-note *mordente* in the repeated interjections of the oboes and bassoons in Figaro's Wedding March: loses its delightful grace through many a conductor's misguided insistence on accented on-beat rendition instead of unaccented placement before the beat.

nibbling, pinching, or picking the latter: but immediately letting go."[15] Again the key word is "softly."

Set apart from the three "mordent" types is the *batement*, which Mozart illustrates as shown in Ex. 40.10 (in analogy to Quantz's model of Ex. 40.8*b*). This grace, he says, is used in gay pieces in place of *Vorschläge* or mordents; it is always done with the semitone below and apparently with multiple alternations. However, its intended rendition is not quite clear. Presumably, like Quantz's analogous pattern, it was variable, and since this discussion follows closely on the heels of the three unaccented prebeat mordent types, it seems probable that unaccented start was in order.

Ex. 40.10. L. Mozart

Little of consequence could be found in theoretical sources after these important mid-century treatises. Kürzinger, though, in 1763 makes an interesting comment. He groups both the one-stroke mordent and its mirror image the *Schneller* under the term *Mordant*, and says that the grace cannot be accurately described and must be learned through demonstration.[16] This clearly indicates that he felt there was more than one literal shape for each of the two "mordents."

Hiller sees the main use of the mordent for notes that follow a long *Vorschlag* from below, i.e. in the *port de voix et pincé* pattern. The multiple mordent, he says, is more proper for instruments than for singers.[17]

Löhlein in his violin treatise shows the mordent only in its one-stroke onbeat style (Ex. 40.11) except where it follows a long *Vorschlag* from below.[18]

Ex. 40.11. Löhlein (1774)

THE mordent was used in a variety of shapes. We find both the single- and the multiple-alternation types mentioned in almost every source, and their continued widespread coexistence is unquestionable. C.P.E. Bach and others after him tried to differentiate the symbol in order to specify one or the other design, but others made no such effort and left the decision to the performer. C.P.E. Bach and some of his followers, such as Agricola and probably Marpurg, can be assumed to have meant their onbeat patterns in a strictly literal sense. Whether we can make the same assumption for, say, Theophil Muffat is less certain. Kürzinger, for one, makes it clear that there is more to the mordent than meets the eye in the simple

[15] *Violinschule*, footnote to par. 8: ". . . so darf ich vom französischen *pincé*, welches Zwicken, Zupfen oder Pfetzen heisst, wohl sagen: dass der *Mordant* oder das französische so genannte *Pincé* ganz still und geschwind sich an die Hauptnote machet, selbe ungefehr anbeisset, zwicket oder pfetzet; gleich aber wieder auslässt."

[16] *Getreuer Unterricht*, p. 39.

[17] *Musikalisch-zierlicher Gesang*, pp. 70-71.

[18] *Anweisung*, p. 50.

onbeat pattern which he himself presents. Most likely, he was alluding to rhythmic variants since multialternation variants could have been easily presented. Mattheson's mordents, too, were certainly more flexible and variable than those of C.P.E. Bach and his followers. Mattheson's models were rhythmically ambiguous to start with, and more than once he stressed their vagueness. Also, he indicated the gentle character of the grace ("kiss"). Leopold Mozart, following Tartini's lead, extends the mordent concept beyond the usual alternation with the lower neighbor to include not only Tartini's three-note anticipated turn but also the two-note *Anschlag*. The rationale was the nearly identical effect achieved by the unifying bond of fast and soft, hence essentially prebeat-oriented, execution. There is good reason to believe that Quantz followed the same ideas, though his explanations and models are ambiguous.

The mordent is usually viewed as an accented onbeat ornament par excellence. Therefore, the evidence found in midcentury Germany about important unaccented prebeat practices, notably outside of the keyboard, is extremely interesting.

PART VIII

OTHER SMALL ORNAMENTS

The Turn

"Turn" is a collective name for a group of graces that is related to one principal design, to be called the "standard turn," in which three ornamental notes start on the upper neighbor of the parent note and move scalewise to the lower one. The standard turn either 1) precedes its principal note, in which case it is "intensifying," or 2) is embedded in the middle of the principal note, in which case it is usually "connective." The two species will be referred to as Types 1 and 2. Their melic designs are shown in Exx. 41.1*a* and *b* (in Ex. *b* the bracket indicates the continuity of the principal note). Less frequently, the turn is done in inversion by starting from below (Exx. *c* and *d*). Another variant which was used by only a few French masters before and around 1700 has the grace start on the main note and reach a third below, as shown in Ex. *e*. In a form characteristic of Italian 17th-century diminution practice, the standard turn is preceded by a trill-like alternation with the upper neighbor, as shown in Exx. *f* and *g*.

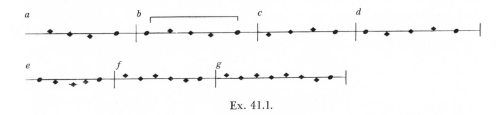

Ex. 41.1.

The rhythmic dispositions for Type 1 (for an assumed quarter-note parent) are sketched in Ex. 41.2. The patterns of *a-c* show the very common onbeat start with the design adapted to tempi varying from slow to fast. Example *d* shows the fairly frequent anticipated entrance, with the dash indicating the location of the beat; Ex. *e* gives the fairly rare delayed entrance, and Ex. *f* the occasional start with the principal note. The designs apply in analogy to the inverted species.

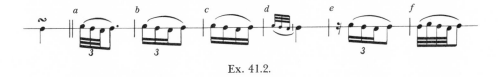

Ex. 41.2.

The rhythmic disposition for the "embedded" Type 2 can vary extensively depending on tempo, length of principal note, affect, and melodic and rhythmic context. The few models of Ex. 41.3 try to intimate the many possibilities for either a binary note (Exx. *a-f*) or a dotted one (Exx. *g-l*). Because the grace is of the connective kind, a succeeding neighbor, arbitrarily chosen, was added for greater clarity.

The rhythmic disposition of the rare French species (of Ex. 41.1*e*) probably ranged mainly from the pattern of Ex. 41.4*a* to that of Ex. *c*. The *groppo* species

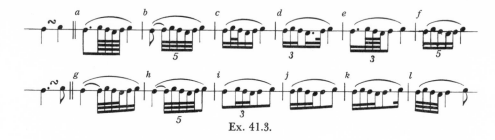

Ex. 41.3.

of Exx. 41.1*f* and *g* was usually rhythmically even, as indicated in Exx. 41.4*d-f*. Such a *groppo* design is distinguished from a regular trill with suffix by the generally slower speed of the alternations and the sharper, usually non-legato articulation.

Ex. 41.4.

In France during the 17th century, the turn, either by itself or when linked with a trill, was most commonly called a *double cadence*. In the 18th century the terms *double* or *doublé* are frequently used, but singers and even some instrumentalists called the grace a *tour de gozier* (turn of the throat). In Italy and Germany during the 17th century, the turn was a formula of improvisation and as such was called *gruppo*, or *groppo*, or a *circolo mezzo*, though these terms covered a somewhat wider field and included several related designs. Bach in his *Explication* called the standard turn *cadence*, and later its usual German name became *Doppelschlag*. Tartini in mid-18th century used the term *mordente* for an anticipated turn from either above or below.

As usual, the terms are confusing, but for once there is considerable agreement on the symbols. The most common sign graphically evokes the melic twist of the grace: ∿ . It originated in France, was adopted in Germany in the first half of the 18th century, and reached Italy in the second half. C.P.E. Bach introduced the reversed sign ∾ to specify the inverted pattern, but not all later masters were consistent in keeping the two signs properly apart.

When the symbol is placed on top of the note, it generally signifies Type 1, and consequently the turn starts immediately with the upper note. When the symbol is placed to the right of the parent note, that is, anywhere between the latter and its right neighbor, it signifies Type 2, the "embedded" species. There are exceptions, however, and a turn with the symbol above the note will sometimes start with the principal note without dwelling on it (as sketched in Ex. 41.2*f*).

The French School

Before turning to the French masters, brief mention should again be made of the Spaniard Tomás de Santa Maria whose treatise of 1565, as surmised before, may have been influenced by French practices. We find in it the anticipated turn pattern of Ex. 41.5*a*, which the author presents as a subspecies of the small trill.[1]

[1] *Arte*, f. 47r.

In a modern transcription, the note values should be at least halved to read as shown in Ex. *b*.

Ex. 41.5. Santa Maria (1565)

A hundred years later, in 1670, Chambonnières may have been the first to introduce the standard symbol. He calls the turn *double cadence* and in an unmetrical model (Ex. 41.6*a*) gives the pattern that moves two steps down and then up.[2]

D'Anglebert in 1689 adopts the same patterns followed by a compound trill and uses the term *double cadence* for the whole tri-ornamental cluster (Ex. *b*). When the turn is not followed by a trill, he offers the standard design (Ex. *c*); when it is done on the lower note of a third, the turn proper starts with a slight delay (Ex. *d*).[3]

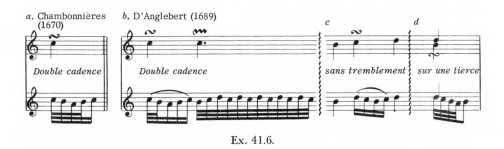

Ex. 41.6.

Saint Lambert in 1702 shows the same turn model while illustrating a new idea of ornament notation. Proposing to draw lines on the staff that correspond exactly to the successive pitches of an ornament, he shows how a *V*-shaped sign drawn from the fourth to the third and back to the fourth line will signify the *double cadence* of Ex. 41.7*a*.[4]

Dieupart in c. 1702 may have been among the last to use the same type of turn, and in combination with a trill he too calls it *double cadence* (Ex. *b*).[5]

Ex. 41.7.

[2] *Pieces de clavessin*, Preface. In the original edition, perhaps by engraver's mistake, the symbol in a few instances is reversed (∾) without apparent difference in meaning.

[3] *Pièces de clavecin*, Preface.
[4] *Principes*, p. 53.
[5] *Six suittes, Explication des marques*.

What Raison in 1687 calls a *double cadence* is a combination of a Type 2 embedded turn and a trill with a detached suffix (see Ex. 41.8a).[6] Le Roux in 1705 shows under the same term only the standard form of Type 1 (Ex. *b*).[7]

Ex. 41.8.

Jean Rousseau in his viol treatise of 1687 presents the *double cadence* as a term for a variety of turn-related designs.[8] He differentiates *double cadences* that fall or rise to the following note, and for either category he distinguishes patterns that are "more double" or "less double," depending on the greater or lesser number of notes involved. His "falling" turn (*en descendant*) is shown in Exx. 41.9*a-c*; Ex. *b* is "less" while Exx. *a* and *c* are "more double." The "rising" type is shown in Exx. *d* and *e*; Ex. *d*, the "less double," is simply a suffix after a trill, but Ex. *e* shows an extended figure of special interest. On first glance this pattern might look like an appoggiatura trill with turned ending. However, closer examination reveals that the whole figure is *not* a trill. Not only would the 16th-notes in C meter, with its slow beat, be too slow for a trill, but Rousseau specifies a detached execution for its use in solo and harmony parts, "with as many bow-strokes as there are notes" ("par autant de coups d'Archet qu'il y a de Notes qui la composent"). It is, consequently, the only pattern that has no slur marks. The resulting non-legato articulation disqualifies it as a trill. Instead, it is clearly related to the Italo-German *groppo* types which were also done more slowly and with sharper articulation than the trill.

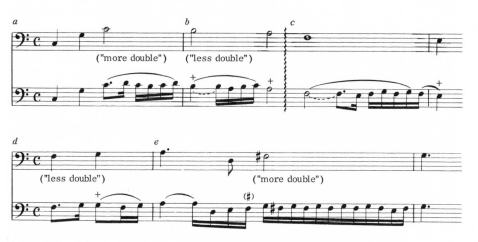

Ex. 41.9. J. Rousseau (1687), *Double cadence*

6 *Livre d'orgue*, Preface.
7 *Pièces de clavessin*, Preface.

8 *Traité*, pp. 97-100.

Rousseau's example and explanation shed a revealing light on certain trill-like figures we find in Marin Marais, a few of which are shown in Ex. 41.10.[9] Like Rousseau's pattern of Ex. 41.9e, they look like appoggiatura trills with a turned ending, but again, like Rousseau's example, none of them has a slur mark.

With almost any other composer one could have assumed that a slur was intended, but not with Marais. The extraordinary care he took in editing his viol works was mentioned before, but in particular, the painstaking precision with which he marked all bowings eliminates the likelihood that the *consistent* absence of intended slurs in any of these figures could have been due to oversight. Rousseau's explanation that such figures—contrary to what our present-day musical instincts may suggest—were actually done with detached bowings provides a decisive clue which makes everything about Marais's passages fall into place.

Clearly we have to do here with Rousseau's *double cadence en montant* done with separate strokes for each tone, and not with a demonstration of how a trill should be played.

a. II, *Folies d'Espagne*, Variation 25

b. I, Double of Gigue, p. 22

c. I, *Fantaisie*, p. 34

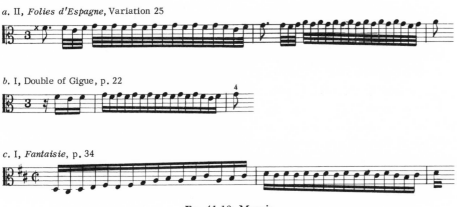

Ex. 41.10. Marais

Bacilly speaks of the *tour de gozier* (sometimes spelled *gosier*) of the French singers in connection with the *double cadence* and declares it to be more a matter of practice than of theory.[10] Unfortunately, his explanations are too vague for an attempted transcription. Loulié in 1696 also calls the turn *tour de gosier* and uses the inverted ∽ symbol (which makes better sense graphically for the turn that starts from above). His illustrations are shown in Exx. 41.11a and b.[11] L'Affilard in 1694 and 1697 shows a model of the Type 2 turn without symbol, hence as an improvised addition in a passage to which he refers as *double cadence coupée* (Ex. c).[12] Montéclair uses for his *tour de gosier* the regular symbol, and although he places it on top of the note, he indicates it should be executed as if it had been placed between the notes (Ex. d). As an added touch, he inserts on the second of the three ornamental notes a miniature trill. The grace is difficult to sing, he says, and difficult to explain; he likens it to a *tremblement feint*.[13]

We find the same vocal term, *tour de gosier*, used for melody instruments, e.g. with Hotterre, who gives the pattern of Ex. 41.12.[14]

[9] *Pièces de violes* [vol. 1], 1686; *Pièces de violes* [vol. 2], 1701.
[10] *Remarques curieuses*, p. 187.
[11] *Éléments*, pp. 73-74 and 92.
[12] *Principes*, pp. 20-21.
[13] *Principes*, pp. 85-86.
[14] *Premier livre*, Preface.

Ex. 41.11.

Ex. 41.12. Hotteterre, *Premier livre* (1708, 1715), *Tour de gosier*

Couperin calls the turn *double* and gives the model of Ex. 41.13a.[15] When he uses the turn as Type 1, with the symbols written above the note according to his model, he does so predominantly—and perhaps exclusively—on a light subdivision of the beat, as illustrated in Exx. *b* and *c*. He also places the symbol fairly often between the notes, as Type 2, as shown in Exx. *d* and *e*. His frequent use of the turn as sequel to the trill, with the symbol $\approx$, has been discussed above. Rameau, using the term *doublé*, gives the same model (Ex. *f*). He uses the turn very rarely and seems to limit it, like Couperin, mostly to the light beats, as shown in the passage of Ex. *g*.[16]

Ex. 41.13.

[15] *Premier livre* (1713).   [16] *Pièces de clavecin* (1724, 1731).

Foucquet calls the turn *redoublé* and gives the designs of Ex. 41.14 for Types 1 and 2.[17]

Ex. 41.14. Foucquet (c. 1750)

A very interesting document showing anticipation of the turn in the sense of Tartini's *mordente* is found in Bedos de Celles's book in the section on mechanical organs that was prepared by Engramelle. There we are shown two forms of *doublés*, the first *on* the beat with the first note lengthened (Ex. 41.15*a*), the second listed as "another *doublée*" with the turn anticipated (Ex. *b*).[18]

Ex. 41.15. Engramelle (Bedos de Celles) (1778)

In the Italo-German realm, the turn and turn-like designs appeared, of course, in diminutions. As we have seen above in connection with the trill, such characteristic cadential formulas:
which were played more slowly and articulated more sharply than trills, were thought of as *groppi*, a form of the turn, and not as trills. We have encountered them in the treatises of Ganassi, Bassano, Dalla Casa, and other theorists, and we have seen them written out by many keyboard masters. Other patterns of the *groppo*, called *circolo mezzo*, which include but are not limited to the standard turn, will be discussed below in connection with free ornamentation.

Stierlein in 1691 presents interesting models under the name of *doppelter Accent*. His illustrations show the turn from below in two styles: one with delayed entrance, the other *on* the beat (Ex. 41.16).[19]

Ex. 41.16. Stierlein (1691)

The model of an anticipated turn that Janowka presented in 1701 was mentioned before because of its affinity to a prebeat slide (Ex. 41.17). He calls it

---

[17] *Les caractères*, Preface.
[18] *L'art*, IV, Planche 109.

[19] *Trifolium*, p. 16.

circuitus and introduces (or reproduces) the symbol *C* with a dot either on top or at the bottom to indicate the direction of the turn.[20] This pattern is repeated in Walther's treatise of 1708 under the name of *halber Circul*. Walther considers it a species of the slide and clarifies its anticipation by adding that "at all times the note after which the slide occurs loses some of its value to permit the following note to enter exactly on time."[21]

Ex. 41.17. Janowka (1701)

J. S. BACH

Bach wrote out in regular notes turns in all rhythmic designs. Example 41.18 from Cantata 179 shows a rare case where he uses the three little notes to indicate an inverted turn that illuminates the word *gleissen* (to glitter).

Ex. 41.18. BWV 179, 3 (aut. P 146)

Bach wrote the symbol both obliquely and vertically, and used it almost exclusively for the keyboard. Rare exceptions occur in late vocal music, e.g. in Cantata 140, movement 3. Even on the keyboard, Bach used the symbol sparingly. On the whole, the connective type written after the notes is more frequent and presents no problems that the instinct of the performer cannot easily solve. Tempo, "affect," length of the principal note, what precedes, what follows, and above all what is happening at the same time in other voices, will influence the choice of the rhythmic design, and there will be a wide latitude of legitimate possibilities.

For instance, in the Organ Chorale *Komm, heiliger Geist,* the connective turn following the mordent in Ex. 41.19*a* cannot be rendered as given in Ex. *b* because it would create fifths with the alto; Exx. *c, d,* and *e* show three possibilities among others.

Ex. 41.19. BWV 652

The turn written *above* the note occurs most often over fairly short note values, such as 8ths or 16ths, and in most cases onbeat execution, according to the basic model, will be indicated. Here too, of course, the context will influence the design and will on occasion suggest a short delay or anticipation.

[20] *Clavis,* s.v. *circuitus.*   [21] *Praecepta,* p. 37.

In Ex. 41.20a from the Organ Chorale *Allein Gott*, Walter Emery suggests a tie to the initial turn note (see Ex. *b*).[22] Probably he wished to avoid an excessive cluster of A sounds. Musically the solution certainly has merit, but whether a contemporary player would have interpreted a turn symbol as a mordent is somewhat doubtful. Perhaps the answer is a slight delay of the turn (Ex. *c*) since it takes the edge off the repeated sound, but melodically more convincing would be to start the turn on the principal note (Ex. *d*). The interpretation given in Ex. *e* is also possible.

Ex. 41.20. BWV 662

A definite onbeat rendition seems indicated in such spots as shown in Ex. 41.21a from the E Minor Prelude (*WC* II). Walter Emery had indicated the two solutions given in Ex. *b*.[23] Later (in a personal communication) he expressed his preference for the first version because the second one would not work in the bass at m. 58.

Ex. 41.21. BWV 879

With reference to D'Anglebert's above noted delayed pattern, Emery sees such delayed entrance as an occasional possibility for Bach. He demonstrates it in the case of a turn that was added along with other ornaments to the autograph of the 5th Sinfonia at a later date. Example 41.22 shows the spot and Emery's suggestion.[24]

Ex. 41.22. BWV 791

D'Anglebert's authority is not needed as long as the solution is more pleasing than the one *on* the beat; anticipation may perhaps work even better, and onbeat start on the *principal* note is another possibility.

Anticipation might be advisable in the passage from the Allemande of the E flat major Suite (Ex. 41.23) in order to preserve the pervasive evenness of the 16th-note rhythm.

Ex. 41.23. BWV 819, 1

22 Emery, Ex. 41.
23 Ibid., Exx. 37-38.

24 Ibid., Ex. 40.

Very interesting are two turns which, along with a few others, were added to the autograph of the D major Invention in different ink but quite certainly in Bach's hand. The first of these turns in m. 11 reads in the autograph as shown in Ex. 41.24a, the other, in m. 53, is written in the same manner. In modern editions the obsolete dot across the bar line is replaced by a tie (Ex. *b*). Normally this would be simply a matter of clearer notation, but here it makes the turn appear to be of the onbeat Type 1, placed as it is on top of the note, whereas the very old-fashioned way of using the dot helps to show that the turn belongs not to the downbeat as an intensifying grace, but to the preceding principal note as a connective grace, a turn written *after* the note. Two logical alternatives would be either to play the turn in anticipation (Ex. *c*) or, probably better, with a slight delay (Ex. *d*).

Ex. 41.24. BWV 774 (aut. P 610)

The special importance of Tartini has been in part demonstrated in Chapter 39, where it was necessary to anticipate his treatment of the turn because it shed light on his prebeat patterns for the mordent. There it was shown that one of the designs he called *mordente* and wrote with small 32nd-notes: was a turn and why his explanation placed the grace before the beat. In another spot, Tartini returns to the same three-note figure, this time written in 16th-notes, and reveals the rhythmic ambivalence of these notes. He says, "When [the 16th-notes] are played with great speed they become a *mordente*; when the first of the three is sustained, it becomes a *modo naturale*."[25] His illustration, given in Ex. 41.25, shows under *a* the slow expressive and dactylic resolution of the *modo naturale* and under *b* the fast anticipated *mordente*.[26]

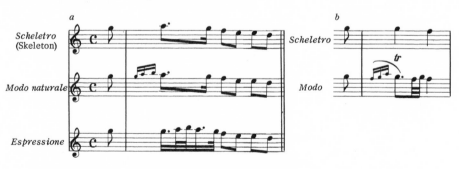

Ex. 41.25. Tartini

[25] *Regole*, p. 27 of facsimile: "Vi un altro modo espresso in Note, come il Mordente, quando le sudette Note si eseguissono con tutta la velocità diventano Mordente, quando si sostenta la prima delle trè, diventa modo naturale."

[26] The French translation of Tartini's *Regole*, until recently the only available source, gives an incorrect account of the two types of turns.

In the Berkeley manuscript collection of the Tartini school, we find many instances of obviously anticipated turns that are written with little notes. Example 41.26 from Carlo Antonio Campioni's Sonata in A major may serve as a representative illustration.[27]

Ex. 41.26. Campioni, Sonata à tre

Marpurg offers in 1749 a variety of interesting melodic designs for the turn (*Doppelschlag*); among them are two models of delay (Exx. 41.27*a* and *b*) that may be derived from D'Anglebert's pattern *sur une tierce*. Examples *c-f* give four different interpretations of the symbol on top of the note. Example *c* shows the standard onbeat design; in model *d* we find the start with the slightly sustained principal note. Marpurg explains that often one sounds the principal note before the turn and that on occasion one even precedes it with a *Vorschlag (accentuiren)*, as shown in Ex. *e* or *f*.[28]

Ex. 41.27. Marpurg (1749)

In 1755, Marpurg devotes a brief section to the turn (still called *Doppelschlag*). He now adopts C.P.E. Bach's dual symbols: ∿ for the standard turn and ∾ for the inverted one (see Ex. 41.28*a*). He explains how the turn may be represented by little notes which are now all strictly rendered on the beat. Furthermore, he presents a turn slurred to its upper neighbor in which the first note of the turn is not articulated (Ex. *b*.)[29]

Ex. 41.28. Marpurg (1755)

[27] Berk. No. 117. Campioni was maestro di capella in Florence.

[28] *Crit. Musicus*, p. 67; Table 2, Nos. 20-22.

[29] *Anleitung* (1755), pp. 52-53, Table 4, figs. 22-24, Table 6, figs. 5, 6, 9.

C.P.E. Bach treats the turn (*Doppelschlag*) with a thoroughness that is commensurate with the great role this grace plays in his music, and only the most salient points need to be recorded here.[30] Speaking of the standard turn whose symbol is placed above the note, he stresses its usual fast execution. Its rhythmic design varies according to tempo, as shown in Ex. 41.29.

Ex. 41.29. C.P.E. Bach (1753)

He extols the versatility of the grace, but says that this very versatility leads to occasional abuse (pars. 6-7). He also points to the turn's frequent function as a substitute for a trill with suffix (par. 9). Another very interesting trill substitute, this time for a main-note trill with suffix, is provided by what C.P.E. Bach calls the *geschnellter Doppelschlag*, which is a turn preceded by the principal note. (Löhlein later called it the "augmented" turn, *der vermehrte Doppelschlag*.) Notated with a little 32nd-note on the same pitch, its transcription is shown in Ex. 41.30*a* (par. 33). This is indeed a *Schneller* with a suffix.

It is to be used whenever a turn is to be made on detached notes (par. 33). It has a wide range of application because it can appear "at the start or in the middle" of a piece, and the only place from which it is seemingly barred is a final note (par. 34). On fast notes, Bach says, this grace is "more convenient than the trill." In the first edition of 1753, we find it in the setting of Ex. *b* (in which C.P.E. Bach contrasted it [in par. 36] with a "simple turn" that occurs *after* a note and has the first note sustained [see Ex. *c*]). In the third edition he goes a step further by showing that "this grace [the *geschnellter Doppelschlag*] can be used also in slurred notes for the rising second," as illustrated in Ex. *d*.[31]

Ex. 41.30. C.P.E. Bach

C.P.E. Bach does not limit the use of this, theoretically compound, grace to the cases specified by notation. On the keyboard, he says, the plain turn symbol (when placed above the note) may be rendered as a *geschnellter Doppelschlag*, and in instruments other than the keyboard which do not use the turn symbol, the trill sign may be given the same interpretation.[32] In other words, C.P.E. makes it clear that ⌒ may stand for ♪♪♪♪ and that any non-keyboard trill on short

30 *Versuch*, I, ch. 2, sec. 4, Table 5, figs. 50-71.

31 Ibid., 3rd ed. (1787), p. 72.

32 *Versuch*, I, ch. 2, sec. 4, par. 34: "Man kan hierbey mit anmercken, dass bey diesen Exempeln ausser dem Claviere das Zeichen des Trillers und bey den Clavier-Sachen das einfache Zeichen des Doppelschlags zu stehen pflegt."

notes may be played as a *Schneller* plus suffix. In this revealing section of the chapter, another surprise is the illustration, given in Ex. 41.31, of an actual anticipation of the turn due to overcrowding (par. 24).

Ex. 41.31. C.P.E. Bach

In the section devoted to the slide, C.P.E. describes the inverted turn under the name of "three-note slide" (*Schleiffer von dreyen Nötgen*) and is the first (so he claims) to introduce the reversed turn symbol of Ex. 41.32.[33]

Ex. 41.32. C.P.E. Bach

Quantz does not formally deal with the turn in his treatise, but we find incidental information on his use of the grace. In one of his tables that demonstrates the practice of diminutions, he gives, using the pattern of Ex. 41.33*a* as a basic motive, the sequence of Ex. *b* with three successive turns as one among many forms of embellishment. In the verbal commentary on this example, he explains its rendition: "the 32nds weak, the quarter-notes C, C, C, growing."[34] Whereas Tartini, who specified for the same design fastness and softness for the grace and immediate loudness for the principal note, left little doubt about the prebeat nature of this figure, Quantz's crescendo on the principal note admits a more flexible rhythmic disposition. Nevertheless, the dynamic design, as outlined in Ex. *c*, still favors the prebeat style with the softness of the grace and the need for enough space to swell the principal note. Certainly, the resulting pattern is the complete opposite of what modern doctrine requires: an accented onbeat placement of the first ornamental note and a consequent tapering of the sound, as indicated in Ex. *d*.

Ex. 41.33. Quantz (1752)

33 Ibid., ch. 2, sec. 7, pars. 5-7; Table 6, figs. 89, a, b.
34 *Versuch*, Table 9, fig. 1; commentary in ch. 14, par. 26.

Leopold Mozart, as shown in the preceding chapter, sees in the turn a species of the mordent and, in full accord with Tartini's prebeat style, has it done soft and fast with the accent falling on the principal note.[35]

I have been unable to find any theoretical German source published after Mozart's treatise that has something new to say about the turn, and therefore, it is not necessary to record the respective statements of Agricola, Löhlein, and Türk who, along with others, simply followed C.P.E. Bach's lead.[36]

Outside of the keyboard, the symbol was (with rare exceptions) not used until the latter part of the century; hence, a desired turn had to be written with the small notes of Tartini, Quantz, and L. Mozart or had to be fully spelled out in regular notation.[37] Certainly, it was a frequent impromptu addition in the vein of the *circolo mezzo*, and we have, moreover, C.P.E. Bach's testimony about its use in response to a trill sign in both its standard form and its "augmented" one that starts with the principal note.

OF the various turn species encountered in this chapter, the old French pattern of Chambonnières did not last long, and by the early years of the 18th century, it seems to have been generally superseded by the standard design. Around the same time, the Italian *groppo type*—a turn preceded by fairly slow, usually non-legato alternations—was gradually merging with the trill-plus-suffix.

Of the two types of the standard turn, the second, the "embedded" species (which is in use to the present day), never presented any particular problems which a sound musical instinct could not solve. There have been no striking developments with regard to Type 1 since it was first established in France at the end of the 17th century with its symbol placed above the note. Generally, its keyboard interpretation favored the start with the upper note on the beat. The anticipated patterns of Tartini, Mozart, and Quantz were more often connected with non-keyboard media and with the little notes rather than the abstract symbol. But he who would, in the rendition of the keyboard symbol, blindly rely on the textbook formula without determining in each case whether anticipation or delay might be musically preferable would run the risk of unmusical execution. (After all, even C.P.E. Bach had an anticipated model!) There was, moreover, the design with the start with the principal note on the beat which Marpurg and C.P.E. Bach admit as an alternative. Whether such rendition was legitimate for J. S. Bach and other older masters is not certain, but the likelihood is great that it *was*, whenever it made musical sense.

---

[35] *Violinschule*, ch. 11, pars. 8-14; see also above, Exx. 40.9-10.

[36] Agricola, *Anleitung*, pp. 114-121; Löhlein, *Clavier-Schule*, p. 15; Türk, *Klavierschule*, ch. 4, pars. 71-86. Türk, though, is more rigid than C.P.E. Bach and in contrast to the latter does not approve of using the main-note start unless specifically prescribed.

[37] Löhlein, *Anweisung*, p. 46, expresses regret that for music written for instruments other than the clavier no symbol is used except the trill sign, and he therefore tries to introduce to the violinist the "clavier graces," including the turn.

If simultaneously with a regular tone (i.e. one that is either written or indicated by the thorough bass) we sound an unharmonic pitch that is neither prepared nor resolved, the resulting clash will be referred to as *Zusammenschlag*.

The term is cumbersome but was chosen in preference to the more familiar one of *acciaccatura* because the latter is ambiguous: in addition to its meaning as *Zusammenschlag*, it is also often used to designate the figurate arpeggio in which the inserted note is played melodically as a passing tone within the arpeggio sequence and is consequently perceived horizontally and not vertically as part of the chord.

Characteristically—but not exclusively—the *Zusammenschlag* was used in thorough bass accompaniment and more specifically in recitatives. It consisted of the insertion of one or more pitches in the intervals between chordal tones. Sometimes after sounding together, these notes were quickly released again to permit the chord to be heard without its ornamental additions; sometimes the inserts were held for the whole duration of the note or notes.

Clashes thus defined constitute a *Zusammenschlag* in the proper, narrower sense of the word. We must distinguish them from related musical effects that result when a *Vorschlag* is taken on the beat and played simultaneously with its resolution on another string of the same instrument or in another voice of an ensemble. Such clashes where the dissonance is properly resolved and often properly prepared are very frequent, but they fulfill a different musical function and can only in a wider sense be related to the percussive clusters of keyboard accompaniment.

The *Zusammenschlag* is very old. Johannes Wolf quotes the 13th-century source, Hieronimus de Moravia, who describes a related ornament under the term *flos harmonicus*: to a long-held tone on the organ one adds its upper neighbor "vibrating."[1] The term "vibrating" obviously refers to the repeated striking and quick release of the ornamental tone, approximately like this: ♪♪ ♪♪ ♪♪ ♪♪ with a resulting trill-like effect. Around 1500, the term *mordent* (or *murdent*) can be found in numerous sources, referring to a similar grace using now the lower instead of the upper neighbor. The frequency of mention would seem to betoken longstanding use.

Hans Buchner (1483-1538), who was identified by Paesler as the author of the *Fundamentbuch von Hans von Constanz*, gives a graphic description of this *Zusammenschlag*, which he indicates with a symbol.[2] Commenting on a music example, Buchner writes: "In this example you see certain notes on the staff with a downward line; some of these notes have a curved tail like this: ♪ , others are crossed in this manner: ♪ ; keep in mind that the notes with curved lines are called *mordents* and observe that always two notes have to be struck simultaneously, namely the one marked by the curved line with the middle finger, its lower neighbor with the index which, however, as in a tremor must be quickly withdrawn. The obliquely crossed line indicates the half-tone [i.e. chromatic

---

[1] Wolf, *Handbuch der Notationskunde*, II, 8: "Est autem flos armonicus decora vocis sive soni celerrima procellarisque vibratio. . . ." Three different styles are mentioned: 1) the *flos longus* with the half-tone added in slow vibration; 2) the *flos subitus* with the same

half-tone in a slowly starting vibration that accelerates to very fast speed; and 3) the *flos apertus* with the whole tone instead of the half-tone.

[2] Paesler, "Fundamentbuch von Hans von Constanz," *VfMw*, vol. 5, pp. 1-192.

alteration]."[3] According to Paesler, we find in the *Buxheim Organ Book* the closely related symbols ↓ and ⌀, as well as the compounded signs for a chromatically altered mordent, ⌁ and ⌂.[4]

Paesler thinks that these mordents—like the *flos harmonicus*—involved the *repeated* striking and release of the ornamented tone. However, the passage from Buchner does not seem to call for such multiple alternations.

The best known discussion of the *Zusammenschlag* is contained in Francesco Gasparini's treatise on the thorough bass (1708) in the chapter dealing with the accompaniment of the recitative.[5] Unfortunately, the chapter is far from clear.

In the recitative, Gasparini says (p. 91), one should deploy the chords in arpeggio fashion ("si deve distender le consonanze quasi arpeggiando"), then while thus arpeggiating the full chord, one can fleetingly touch the half-step below a chordal tone, striking this inserted grace "adroitly together with . . . or rather slightly before" the principal note ("toccandole con certa destrezza nel medemo tempo . . . anzi un poco prima"), then immediately releasing the former, to add charm without offending the ear. "That is why it is called *mordente*, resembling the bite of a little animal that, having barely bitten, immediately lets go and does not hurt" (p. 91).

Generally, Gasparini says, the *mordente* will be best for the minor third, the octave, and the sixth, but one has to use it judiciously: placed on an augmented fifth, for instance, it would be insufferable. Example 42.1 gives some of his illustrations for the *mordente* which reflect even graphically the arpeggio idea. An ambiguity seems to arise when Gasparini declares that the notes between the bar lines are to be played together in a single stroke ("per un sol colpo . . . tutte insieme"). However, in view of the preceding stress on arpeggiation, this directive can be taken to mean that the notes are to be held like a chord, not played successively like a melody.

Ex. 42.1. Gasparini (1708), *Mordente*

The *mordente*, always a half-tone below its parent note, is done in the framework of an arpeggiated chord, mostly, so it seems, as a mere *Zwischenschlag* between chordal notes, hence as a figurate arpeggio. Occasionally, when touched simultaneously or held over slightly, it may be done as a brief *Zusammenschlag*, apparently admitting the following chief forms (Ex. 42.2):

Ex. 42.2.

[3] Ibid., pp. 32-33: ". . . Memineris igitur eas notas quae curvatas habent lineas vocari mordentes, ubi observandum semper duas esse simul tangendas, ea videlicet quae per lineam curvatam signatur medio digito, proxime vero inferiorque indice digito, qui tamen tremebundus mox est subducendus."

[4] Ibid., p. 33, n. 3.

[5] *L'armonico pratico al cimbalo*, ch. 9.

Gasparini then speaks of sometimes using a dissonance "consisting of an *acciaccatura* of two, three, or four notes combined one next to the other."[6] He had first mentioned the term *acciaccatura* in Chapter 6 (p. 49) as a current designation ("come molti suonatori dicono") for certain harmonic clashes.

In that spot Gasparini referred specifically to a cadential $\begin{smallmatrix}6\\4\end{smallmatrix}\ \begin{smallmatrix}5\\3\end{smallmatrix}$ progression in which the sixth and the fourth are doubled in the left hand with the fourth left lying, while in the right hand it resolves to the third. This, he says, creates a pleasant harmony on the harpsichord, but should be avoided on the organ except in a heavily set context. Example 42.3 attempts to transcribe Gasparini's purely verbal description.

Ex. 42.3.

Returning to the recitative chapter, we find that Gasparini unfortunately does not explain the execution of the *acciaccatura* other than by giving models which show this grace interspersed with specimens of the *mordente* (Exx. 42.4a and b). Here too the graphic disposition of the chords indicates their arpeggio character. The models given show, furthermore, that the *acciaccatura* is almost always placed at a whole-tone distance from its upper neighbor (for an exception see Ex. *b* where in the bass of the second measure the distance is a half-step).

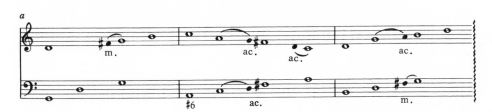

Ex. 42.4. Gasparini

However, for these reasons there must be a greater difference between the two types than the distance from the upper note: the reference to the *acciaccatura* as dissonance (*falsa*); the first introduction of the *acciaccatura* as a sharp cadential clash; the failure to mention its release; the statement that occasionally one has to strike two notes with the same finger (p. 94), a procedure that favors continu-

[6] Ibid., p. 93: "Si usa alcune volte qualche falsa, che sarà con acciaccatura di due, tre, o quattro tasti uniti uno appresso l'altro . . . fanne mirabile effetto. . . ."

ance more than release; the model of Ex. 42.4*b* above whose first measure shows two inserted notes next to each other; another model (Exx. 42.5*a* and *b*) with a fourfold *acciaccatura* which is not even differentiated in print; finally, a remark (p. 95) that after the dissonance of the *acciaccatura* of Ex. *c*, the following *mordente* "remains sweet" ("dopo questa falsa restera dolce il mordente alla Sesta"). All these considerations point to a difference in kind, to a greater harshness, a more definite *Zusammenschlag* character of the *acciaccatura* as compared to the *mordente*. Thus, even when the *acciaccatura* was struck *arpeggiando*, it must have been held longer than the *mordente* and may have been at times fully sustained.

An interesting piece of evidence to that effect—antedating Gasparini by about 30 years and communicated to me by Richard Sherr—is contained in a contemporary manuscript of Stradella's *Il Corispero*; there, in Act I, Scene 1 (and only there), we find the written-out and held-out *acciaccatura* of Ex. 42.5*d*.

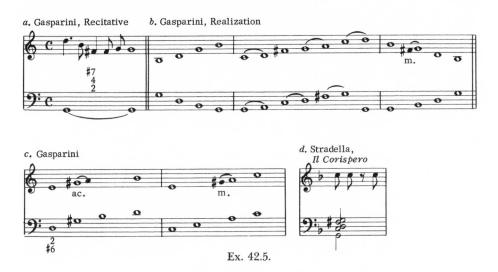

Ex. 42.5.

A manuscript by an anonymous author in the Biblioteca Corsini in Rome, "Regole per accompagnar sopra la parte," deals with the question of the *acciaccatura* and the *mordente* in a manner related to Gasparini and presumably was written about the same time. Ludwig Landshoff was the first to draw attention to this manuscript, which he tentatively dates around 1700.[7] The following comments are based solely on Landshoff's presentation.

In this manuscript we meet again the duality of terms, *mordente* and *acciaccatura*, without a clear delineation of their differences. The anonymous author demonstrates the use of the graces in an arietta with both plain and fully realized bass. In this piece, which Landshoff reproduces in its entirety,[8] we find many dissonant pitches that are written in shorter note values followed by corresponding rests, but as many, if not more, that are written out in the full value of the principal chordal notes. The difference between the two types can be seen in the brief excerpt of Ex. 42.6. On the face of it, the two notational styles suggest the contrast of *mordente* and *acciaccatura*. According to Landshoff, the author does have the shortened note values in mind when he speaks of the *mordente*, in terms almost identical to those of Gasparini: "within chords I place sometimes certain dissonances, touching and releasing them immediately, and call them *mordente* because . . . [here follows Gasparini's simile of the little animal's bite]." Then, however, the

7 "Über das vielstimmige Accompagnement," pp. 189-208.

8 A facsimile of its first page was printed in

an article by Sven Hostrup Hansell, "The Cadence in 18th Century Recitative," *MQ*, vol. 54 (1968), pp. 228-248.

Ex. 42.6. Anon. (c. 1700)

author significantly adds: "should anyone prefer to hold rather than to release the dissonances, he may follow his judgment."[9] The player who decides to hold such a dissonance will apparently turn an incipient *mordente* into a genuine *acciaccatura*, with its longer and sharper clash. That last quoted sentence alone confirms that there is, or can be, much more to the *acciaccatura* than a dissonance touched and immediately released. The remark also proves that the full-value notation of the dissonant tones was meant to signal a greater emphasis on the harmonic clash. This additional evidence will help us see Heinichen's discussion of this matter in a different perspective.

In 1728, Heinichen reports Gasparini's principles at some length, "because especially on the harpsichord his manner is highly effective."[10] Speaking of the unproblematical *mordente*, Heinichen lists its mild arpeggio, the half-tone distance, and immediate release. Instead of the *mordente*, he says, the *acciaccatura* is used when the context suggests that instead of a half-tone "one strikes a whole tone or on occasion three or four neighboring pitches in a mild arpeggio, almost simultaneously, but lets go of the false pitches which do not belong to the chord."[11] Clearly, Heinichen sees no difference in the execution of a *mordente*

[9] Quoted by Landschoff in "Über das vielstimmige Accompagnement": ". . . se ad alcuno piacesse più tenere, che levare le dissonance, starà in suo arbitrio."

[10] *Generalbass*, pp. 534-542. Heinichen tells about reading the book in a footnote on p. 91. It is also likely that he had heard Gasparini perform in Venice.

[11] Ibid., pp. 534-535: "Eine Acciaccatura hingegen nennet er [i.e. Gasparini], wenn man wegen des Ambitus modi statt des Semitonii einen gantzen Ton drunter, oder auch gleichwohl nach Gelegenheit 3-, 4- neben einander liegende Claves in einem gelinden Arpeggio fast zugleich niederschläget, jedoch die falschen, oder nicht zum Accord gehörigen Claves alleine wieder fahren lässet."

and an *acciaccatura*. In particular, the release of the dissonant pitches is a matter of great concern to him, and for this reason he disapproves of striking two keys with one finger "since one could not let go easily of the *acciaccature* as it ought to be done."[12] He recommends the use of *acciaccature* only if one has a free finger, and then, one must not do so often, or else "unclean" accompaniment will result. Only rarely, he says, should three or four neighbor notes be involved, and reminding the reader again of the mild arpeggio, he restates, for the fourth time, the need to release the dissonances (p. 541). In a later reference, after discussing the "extravagant recitative," he declares the latter to be the proper place for *acciaccature*, because the slowly moving bass most easily admits such graces (p. 796).

In equating the *mordente* and the *acciaccatura*, Heinichen both oversimplified and misrepresented Gasparini. His open dissent about striking two keys with one finger is a significant case in point. Unfortunately, Heinichen's interpretation of Gasparini has been accepted as authoritative by many modern scholars who keep echoing the idea that nothing differentiates the *mordente* and the *acciaccatura* except their respective distance from their upper neighbor.

Heinichen believes that the term *acciaccatura* derives from *acciaccare*, i.e. to crush, and reflects the violent collision of non-related pitches (p. 535, n. *d*).

Walther, in 1732, disagrees with Heinichen's etymology (which he reports) and derives the term *acciaccatura* from *acciacco*, meaning "superfluous." As an example of an *acciaccatura*, he gives a g chord where, next to b g d, the f sharp is also sounded. Walther also cites Gasparini's example of the cadential clash.[13]

In 1739, Mattheson, in his discussion of the *mordente*, mentions the *acciaccatura*, on which, he says, Gasparini and Heinichen have bestowed more attention than it is worth. Exclusively used in heavily set thorough bass accompaniments, this grace, he says, is the cause of much impure harmony. He derides the etymological dispute of Heinichen and Walther and the "shallow semantic researches," but does not hesitate to offer another version himself: *accia* means thread, he says, and *acciaccatura* refers to a better connection for the full-voiced chords. Reaffirming his lack of sympathy for the grace itself, he insists that all these "trinkets" contain much that is superfluous and not little that is defective.[14]

C.P.E. Bach lists (without a term) the *Zusammenschlag* in a somewhat different sense—as a species of the regular mordent.[15] Where a very fast mordent is needed, he says, both notes are struck simultaneously, but the grace is lifted almost immediately, as shown in Ex. 42.7*a*. He adds that this design, which occurs *ex abrupto* and not in a connective situation, is "not to be rejected," provided it is used less frequently than the regular mordent. He uses the term *acciaccatura* only in the meaning of the genuine figurate arpeggio, as will be reported in a later chapter.

Marpurg in 1749 does not mention the *Zusammenschlag*, but like C.P.E. Bach lists the term *acciaccatura* as the equivalent of *harpégement figuré*.[16]

In 1755 he presents, as does C.P.E. Bach, the *Zusammenschlag* as a species of the regular mordent and gives the identical illustration (Ex. 42.7*b*), referring to this mordent type as *abgeschnappt* (clipped).[17] It is effective, he says, in a transition from piano to forte and is particularly useful on the organ. Moreover, in the chapter on the arpeggio, Marpurg lists as a subspecies of the figurate arpeggio a genuine *Zusammenschlag*: instead of inserting notes alien to the chord, like

---

12 Ibid., p. 542: "so könte man doch diese Acciaccatur nicht bequem wieder fallen lassen, wie es seyn soll."

13 *Lexicon*, s.v. *acciaccatura*.

14 *Capellmeister*, pt. 2, ch. 3, pars. 57-60.

15 *Versuch*, I, ch. 2, sec. 5, par. 3.

16 *Crit. Musicus*, p. 68.

17 *Anleitung*, pp. 58-59.

Zwischenschläge during arpeggiation, they may be struck simultaneously with the unbroken chord, then quickly released, as shown in Ex. 42.7c.

Ex. 42.7.

A few years later, in 1762, he uses for this grace the term *Zusammenschlag* and lists for it the Italian equivalent of *acciaccatura* and the French of *pincé étouffé*.[18] He now suggests for a symbol a crossed *Vorschlag* note: ♪ .

Late in the century we hear once more from Türk, who speaks of the *Zusammenschlag* and indicates its rarity by referring to it in a footnote as a "not very well-known ornament." His explanation and illustration are the same as C.P.E. Bach's. He says that since the grace causes some harshness, it will best be used in "fiery, quasi-defiant passages."[19]

Returning to the Italians, we find a significant piece of documentation in Geminiani's treatise of 1749.[20] Like Gasparini, he discusses the accompaniment and distinguishes two types of inserted notes. The first he calls *tatto* (spelled *tacto* in the heading to the music examples), "which is performed by touching the Key lightly, and quitting it with such a Spring as if it was Fire." This description, as well as the fact that in his extended music example the *tatto* is always placed at semitone distance from the upper note and appears only singly, make it an exact equivalent of Gasparini's *mordente*. The other grace, the *acciaccatura*, "is a Composition of such Chords as are dissonant with Respect to the fundamental Laws of Harmony; and yet when disposed in their proper Place produce that very effect which it might be expected they would destroy." It has been used, he adds, for over a hundred years. Again in analogy to Gasparini, we see in the examples (a brief excerpt is given in Ex. 42.8) that the *acciaccatura* is at a whole-tone distance from the upper note, and that in contrast to the *tatto* there can be as many as four *acciaccature* per chord. Furthermore, Geminiani brings the difference between the two types of graces into clear graphic relief by printing the *tatto* with a small note head, the *acciaccatura* with a regular one. If to this we add the contrast in Geminiani's definitions which stresses the extreme fastness of the *tatto* and the dissonance of the *acciaccatura*, we can see the analogy to Gasparini's *mordente-acciaccatura* pair with its substantial dissimilarities.

Musical evidence regarding the *Zusammenschlag* is difficult to find because the absence of a symbol and the failure to include the *Zusammenschläge* in the figures of the bass left their use entirely to improvisation. On the other hand, modern writers will often think of tone clusters that defy conventional analysis in terms of *acciaccature*. The danger in using this term lies in the usually implied under-

[18] *Die Kunst*, 4th ed. (1762), p. 23. The reference to the French equivalent of *pincé étouffé*, which was later repeated by Türk, is most likely a misunderstanding. The term *pincé étouffé* derives from Couperin's *L'art de toucher le clavecin*, where on p. 71 he explains how two mordents at the start of XII, *Les Jumèles*, which are written a step above a tied note, have to be simulated (literally: stifled) to preserve the tie ("il faut que les deux pincés . . . soient, en quelque façon étoufés . . ."). There is no resemblance to a *Zusammenschlag*.

[19] *Klavierschule*, ch. 4, pars. 66-67.

[20] *Treatise of Good Taste*, Preface and examples on first (unnumbered) page of music.

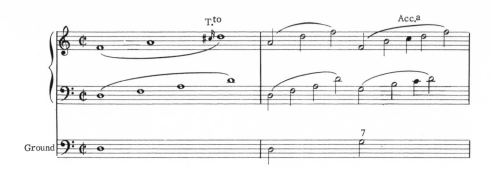

Ground

Ex. 42.8. Geminiani (1749)

standing that the non-chordal tones that are so labeled were meant to be released immediately upon striking, as was the *abgeschnappt* mordent of Marpurg and C.P.E. Bach. However, this meaning frequently is not implied; it certainly is not with Domenico Scarlatti's spectacular dissonances. Some editors, Longo among them, have expurgated such would-be offensive impurities. Others took comfort from the idea of instantaneous release. There is, however, sufficient evidence that Scarlatti's dissonances were not a matter of a momentary clash that quickly disappeared but were meant to be held for the full value of the chord as integral parts of its structure. First, we find extraordinary "20th-century" dissonances in spots that could not possibly be explained in terms of *acciaccature* (see e.g. the sonatas K 96, mm. 65-68 and K 132, m. 25). Moreover, there are numerous passages where the clusters are repeated at such brief intervals that not only is an early release technically impossible, but relentless pounding of the dissonance is the clear artistic intention. See the characteristic Ex. 42.9.

Ex. 42.9. D. Scarlatti, Sonata K 119

Ralph Kirkpatrick does refer to the clusters as *acciaccature*,[21] but he makes it clear that they represent extraordinarily bold harmonic thinking and were not meant to be sugar-coated by the immediate release of the harsh notes.

21 *Scarlatti*, p. 231.

Though such chords cannot be fully equated with the thorough bass *acciaccature* of Gasparini or Geminiani, it is likely that Scarlatti's harmonic fantasy could not have taken such daring flights had his ear not been conditioned by the astringent sounds of the genuine *acciaccature* in thorough bass practice.

THE extent to which the *Zusammenschlag* (in the narrower sense) has been used is very difficult to appraise. It seems to have had its chief home in Italy where, according to Geminiani, in mid-18th century it had been in use for over a hundred years. It seems to have been used mainly in accompaniment (especially of the recitative). The Italians were fond of experimenting with harmonic clashes, notably in cadences (the "Corelli clash" being an example), to intensify the feeling of both tension and release and to add some percussive spice to otherwise boring recitatives. Gasparini referred to the great incidence of such cadential clashes for which, he writes, the word *acciaccatura* was used by many players. Sharp dissonances of this kind prepared the soil from which was to sprout the luxuriant harmonic imagination of Domenico Scarlatti.

It is likely that the *Zusammenschlag* was not common in France, since not a single reference to it was found in French sources.[22] Even the Germans were reluctant to follow completely an Italian thorough bass practice that must have struck them as extravagant. Thus, Heinichen watered down the harsh Italian clashes by insisting on arpeggiation and quick release; moreover, he advises sparing use, limited chiefly to recitatives. We also have Mattheson's testimony that the *acciaccatura* was used exclusively in the accompaniment. He disapproved of the impurities it introduced into the realization of the bass.

A closely related grace for use in places other than the accompaniment is described by C.P.E. Bach and Marpurg; located a half-step below the principal note, it is struck simultaneously and immediately released. Within a chord, Marpurg presents it as an alternative for the figurate arpeggio.

The use of the *Zusammenschlag* for Bach is questionable. A single specimen from the Scherzo of the A minor Partita is presented by Dolmetsch and later by the *Harvard Dictionary*,[23] but the would-be *acciaccatura* is simply an inverted seventh chord of a kind that is commonplace in Bach's harmony. It is certainly possible that Bach and other masters may have occasionally improvised *Zusammenschläge* or used them as alternates to certain short *Vorschläge*. A likely context for such usage could be seen in Ex. 44.28f below for the *Vorschlag* at the start of the measure. This possibility was mentioned above in Chapter 16 where it was also pointed out that we have thus far no documentation on this matter.

---

[22] Peter Williams, in an article "The Harpsichord Acciaccatura," tried to prove the international currency of the *Zusammenschlag* but was misled by the double meaning of the word *acciaccatura*. What he calls the "passing acciaccatura," e.g. Gasparini's *mordente*, was certainly practiced everywhere and was particularly at home with the French clavecinists as *arpégé figuré*. Also, the kinds of clashes that an onbeat *Vorschlag* produces with its resolution in another voice were common in all countries. But the *Zusammenschlag* in the narrower sense, one that enters unprepared and exits unresolved, was an entirely different matter. The irrationality of this practice, which even estranged the German admirers of Italian ways,

would have offended the French ideals of clarity and logic. In the absence of any theoretical mention, Williams's quote of a single example of clusters, not in accompaniment but in a lute piece of the Elder Gaultier (in a late manuscript of very questionable reliability), is hardly evidence enough to establish a French habitat for the "simultaneous *acciaccatura*." Moreover, the term *pincé étouffé* given by Marpurg as the French equivalent for the *Zusammenschlag*, which would imply French usage, was shown to be based on a misunderstanding.

[23] Dolmetsch, p. 301; *Harvard Dictionary of Music*, 2nd ed. (Cambridge, Mass., 1969), s.v. *acciaccatura*.

The *Anschlag*, also known as *Doppelvorschlag*, is a grace of the German *galant* style. Little used outside of Germany, it had no contemporary French or Italian equivalents, and the translation, "double appoggiatura," is a modern coinage. The grace consists of two notes which precede and melodically straddle the principal note. In the most common form of its melic design, its sequence is lower neighbor, upper neighbor, principal note, as indicated (in the usual way) in Ex. 43.1a. Occasionally, however, the straddling interval is larger than a third, though the second ornamental note will always descend stepwise to the principal one. Examples *b* and *c* are illustrations, but other intervals are possible too. Much rarer are the inverted designs starting from above (Exx. *d* and *e*).

Ex. 43.1.

With regard to the rhythmic disposition, there is the usual alternative of pre-beat and onbeat (Exx. 43.2*a* and *b*), and various mixtures of these. Also, there is a dactylic pattern that will normally fall on the beat (Exx. *c* and *d*).

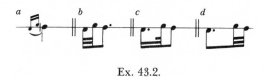

Ex. 43.2.

There is no symbol other than the little notes: and where the dactylic design is intended, the little notes have to be dotted: .

Before the *galant* era, we find the *Anschlag* pattern in chance occurrences only, such as in Bach's E major Clavier Concerto (Ex. 43.3*a*) or, according to an important but non-autograph early manuscript (P 418), in the 3rd French Suite (Ex. *b*).

Ex. 43.3.

Quantz may have been the first to have acknowledged and described the *Anschlag* under this term.[1] He limits the term to the lower-upper neighbor design

---

[1] *Versuch*, ch. 13, par. 41; Table 16, fig. 26. In the Index, Quantz refers to the *Anschlag* as an "arbitrary" ornament, which would exclude its prescription by symbol. This was certainly an oversight.

and shows its application for all intervallic progressions from the rising second to the octave; but he finds the following three examples more graceful than the rest:

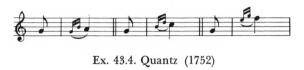

Ex. 43.4. Quantz (1752)

Singers, he says, use the grace for large leaps in order to hit the high tones more securely. It may be used before long notes on either strong or weak beats where no other grace would be appropriate. Revealing are his instructions that the grace must be tied *very fast but weak* to the principal note which is a little stronger. The combination of fastness and softness compared to the principal note, plus the remark that singers use it in a subservient role as an aid to vocal marksmanship, suggest the potential prebeat character of the grace in Quantz's usage.

C.P.E. Bach writes about the *Anschlag* at considerable length.[2] In addition to Quantz's type with its unchanging spread of a third, Philipp Emanuel shows the possibility of a larger spread, in which case, however, the first of the two notes repeats the preceding tone and the second is the upper neighbor of the principal note. This latter type, he says, is done more slowly than the other, but for both he confirms Quantz's rule that the two little notes are "always played softer than the principal note" (par. 3).

His models show the grace *on* the beat in conformance with his principles (Exs. 43.5*a* and *b*). However, since the beat attracts the accent and vice versa, C.P.E.'s solutions form a highly unstable compound that is unlikely to have asserted itself on every occasion. Once in a while, as pointed out before, such a rendition that is at odds with the usual metric-dynamic pattern has the rubato charm of a delayed entrance, but as a routine formula repeated over and over it has the flavor of a manneristic affectation.

In expressive (*affecktuösen*) passages of slow pieces, the *Anschlag* may also appear in a dotted form (Ex. *c*). For this pattern, the first note is loud, the second and the principal notes soft and all three are slurred (par. 10). The more expressive the passage and the slower the tempo, the longer the dot will be held (par. 11).

Ex. 43.5. C.P.E. Bach (1753)

By the time of the third edition (1787), Philipp Emanuel had hardened his stance still further on the downbeat. He shows a changed notation (without a

[2] *Versuch*, I, ch. 2, sec. 6, pars. 1-11.

dot) and a changed execution which manages to place both the first *and* the second note on a beat (p. 79)! He now gives the following "correct" and "incorrect" versions together with the execution:[3]

Ex. 43.6. C.P.E. Bach (1787)

Marpurg made no mention of the *Anschlag* in 1749 but speaks of *Doppelvorschlag* in 1755.[4] He quotes C.P.E. Bach and follows him in describing the three types: the spread of a third (Ex. 43.7*a*), the longer leap with the first note repeating the preceding tone (Ex. *b*), and the dotted pattern (Ex. *c*). The latter, he feels, ought to be written out in order to spare the performer confusion (par. 3). He does not mention dynamic shadings but shows the onbeat execution and also introduces the inverted pattern of Ex. *d*.

Ex. 43.7. Marpurg (1755)

Agricola explains the *Anschlag* as a combination of a *Vorschlag* from below and a *Nachschlag* one step above the principal note.[5] In matters of execution he follows C.P.E. Bach by showing the same melodic and rhythmic types and giving the same instructions regarding dynamics.

Leopold Mozart saw in the *Anschlag* a form of the mordent, as illustrated above in Ex. 40.9*c*, and implied in the text its unaccented prebeat character.

Löhlein in his harpsichord treatise shows only the spread of a third and distinguishes the "short" and the "long" *Anschlag*, the long being dotted (Exx. 43.8*a* and *b*).[6] Hiller calls the grace *Doppel Vorschlag* and shows only the even thirds.[7] Petri, also using the term *Doppelvorschlag*, gives only an example without resolution (Ex. *c*); but by stressing that the little notes are to be done more softly than the principal notes, he too may have implied the prebeat style.[8]

Ex. 43.8.

[3] W. J. Mitchell in his English edition considers the "correct" symbol to be a misprint, because it disagrees with the earlier dotted one. However, not only the symbol has changed, but the execution has changed to the double onbeat design.

[4] *Anleitung*, p. 51.
[5] *Anleitung*, pp. 85-87.
[6] *Clavier-Schule*, p. 15. (The models are identical in all four editions.)
[7] *Anweisung z. mus. richtigen Ges.*, p. 166.
[8] *Anleitung*, 2nd ed., p. 152.

When, near the end of the century, Türk deals with the *Anschlag* as one of the "essential" graces,[9] he follows, as usual, the lead of C.P.E. Bach. Hence, he shows in his models the onbeat placement of the grace but its piano start with a delayed forte on the principal note. He seems to sense some inconsistency in the contrasting rules for the *Vorschläge* which, be they short or long, are to be loud and the *Anschlag* which is to be soft. He tries to resolve the contradiction by seeing in the softness of the *Anschlag* a further proof that the short (*unveränderlich*) *Vorschlag*, too, may be played softly.[10] Of course, in actual practice this dynamic pattern would lead to anticipation in the vast majority of cases.

Tromlitz, speaking of the *Anschlag*, places it on the beat but gives no dynamic instructions.[11] An illustration of an Italian use of the grace is given in Ex. 43.9 from D. Alberti, a pioneer of the homophonic clavier style who died around 1740.[12] The passage shows the anticipation of the grace by its prebar notation at the end of the second measure. Two measures later, the sequence is repeated with the identical prebar notation.

Ex. 43.9. D. Alberti, Sonata No. 8

In its written-out form this grace had many later applications. In its wittiest and most unforgettable use, it permeates Don Giovanni's aria "Metà di voi" as chuckling comment of the orchestra while the Don outwits the vengeance-seeking simpleton Masetto and his companions:

Ex. 43.10. Mozart, *Don Giovanni*

[9] *Klavierschule*, ch. 4, sec. 2, pars. 12-17.
[10] Ibid., par. 13, footnote, which also refers to his previous (ch. 3, sec. 2, par. 19) arguments for softness of the *unveränderlich* [i.e. the short] *Vorschlag* and dynamic emphasis on the principal note, as reported above in our ch. 18.

[11] *Unterricht*, p. 253.
[12] Domenico Alberti, *8 sonate per cembalo*, Op. 1 (London, n.d.). A copy at the BN (L 377) lists the work under *Matteo* Alberti's name.

The Arpeggio

The essence of the arpeggio idea is the successive sounding of a chordally conceived group of pitches. The idea finds its realization in two different ways which will be referred to as 1) the *chordal* and 2) the *linear* arpeggio. In the chordal arpeggio the pitches are announced in very close succession, *without* any specified rhythm, and are sustained to form the sound of the full chord. In the linear arpeggio the pitches are strung up melodically in a *definite* rhythm, without being sustained (though not excluding occasional pedal effects).

THE CHORDAL ARPEGGIO

The chordal arpeggio is limited to a few media only. In addition to the harp, which gave it its name, it is equally native to the lute, and from the lute it probably found its way to harpsichord and clavichord. It has only a marginal and well-nigh negligible significance for the organ.[1] With some modifications, the arpeggio occupies an important place with the strings, though often as a technical makeshift for chords that cannot be sustained in their entirety.

The chordal arpeggio falls into two distinct types: the *plain* and the *figurate* (*arpégé*, or *harpégé figuré*). In the plain type, only the pitches of the chord are involved and are "broken" either upward or, more rarely, downward, as shown in Exx. 44.1*a* and *b*.[2] (A subspecies involving only two pitches will be referred to as an *intervallic arpeggio*, as shown in Ex. *c*.) In the figurate arpeggio, nonchordal pitches are inserted in the manner of *Zwischenschläge*, but not sustained (Ex. *d*).

Ex. 44.1.

Modern doctrine generally extends the onbeat rule to the chordal arpeggio, but no explicit formulation of such a rule has so far been found in any historical document. Not even C.P.E. Bach's authority can be invoked, since he limited his sweeping onbeat rule to "those graces that are indicated by little notes."[3] The only authority for encompassing the arpeggio in the onbeat rule can be found in the literal interpretation of certain ornament tables. As will be presently shown, the reservations concerning this type of evidence have to be raised another degree for the arpeggio.

[1] Boyvin says in the preface to his *Premier livre d'orgue*: "One hardly uses the arpeggio on the organ"; Saint Lambert, in his *Nouveau traité de l'accompagnement . . .* (Paris, 1707), p. 63, writes: "On the organ one never restrikes a chord and one hardly ever uses arpeggios"; for an analogous statement, see also David Kellner, *Treulicher Unterricht im General Bass*, 3rd ed. (Hamburg, 1743), p. 20.

[2] Whenever in this section the term "arpeggio" is used by itself, it will refer to the plain chordal type.

[3] *Versuch*, I, ch. 2, sec. 1, par. 23.

There are certainly many situations where onbeat start is fitting. Foremost among them are cases where the lowest tone of an upward arpeggio is part of the main melody (for example, see the Sarabande from Bach's 4th French Suite, mm. 3-4). Other contexts can be found in accompaniment where the bass pitch and bass rhythm are generally more important than what happens at the other end of the arpeggiated chord. Another situation might arise in soloistic playing when, in absence of a distinct melody, the musical essense of a passage resides in a succession of chords. Here, onbeat start can often be a valid alternative to prebeat start.

The situation is altogether different if in a solo part the arpeggio serves a dominant melody by ending on one of the latter's notes. Example 44.2 from Bach's 5th Partita might serve as an illustration.

Ex. 44.2. BWV 829, Allemande

Here, the arpeggio for the three-note chord of the right hand is clearly of very minor importance. By its omission we would lose no more than a shade of plasticity. What *is* of the essence in this passage is the melody with its characteristic Allemande rhythm at the start. Does it not stand to reason that we should not sacrifice the essential to the unimportant? The start of the arpeggio on the beat would produce two incongruous results. The Allemande pattern of the short upbeat on the pitch of the long downbeat tone: ♪♩· would be distorted to approximately: ♪♩ and the b', which is only a *harmonic* fill note, would be pushed into the spotlight of the downbeat as if it were of the *melodic* essence. Hence we can assume that the indicated execution is the one shown in Ex. 44.3 with the arpeggio in anticipation. This solution has the obvious musical merit of gracing the melody without making it pay an undue price.

Ex. 44.3.

Another revealing case is the arpeggio in the Aria from the *Goldberg Variations*. The thematic motive of the repeated tone with which the aria starts is on its return in m. 11 supported by an arpeggiated chord. The need for the entrance of the first note on the beat is rather obvious, and Ralph Kirkpatrick in his edition of the work could not escape this cogency.[4] However, firmly believing at that time (1938) in the onbeat doctrine (a stance he has since modified), he was faced with a dilemma which he tried to solve by making the arpeggio from above (Ex. 44.4a). This solution sounds somewhat contrived, because the arpeggio more properly ends, not starts, on the *melody* note it supports, hence the final arpeggio note g could be misunderstood as part of the melody. Moreover, Bach's wavy symbol was in all probability generally meant in an upward direction. The simplest solution is anticipation of the upward arpeggio as sketched in Ex. *b*, which adds both grace and emphasis to the melody without impairing its characteristic rhythm.

Ex. 44.4. BWV 988, Aria

Certainly there will be cases where an arpeggio in support of a melody note may be done on or astride the beat, but this would happen in the frame of an intended rubato delay and should not happen in mechanical obedience to a would-be rule. These two examples were shown in order to place the following theoretical documents into clearer perspective.

Early documents about the arpeggio come chiefly, perhaps exclusively, from France. English virginalists probably used the arpeggio but left us no traces of this practice. French lutenists in the first half of the 17th century used symbols for arpeggiation, the most common being the oblique dash between the vertically aligned letters of a chord: $\frac{c}{a}$. This symbol was later adopted by some clavier players and gambists.

The French harpsichordists, beginning with Chambonnières, used and explained arpeggio symbols which were mostly of two kinds. One is the vertical wavy line; the other is the lutenist's oblique bar through the stem of the note whose slant indicates rise or fall. Most of the documentation is embodied in ornament tables, and the more important ones that indicate the onbeat start are given in Exx. 44.5*a-f*, from the works of Chambonnières, Le Bègue, D'Anglebert, Le Roux, Raison, Dieupart, and Rameau.[5]

These models aim at conveying the idea of "breaking" the chord by the principle of successiveness. Out of context, the simplest way of so doing is, as usual, within the metrical value of the principal note, because an overflow could only be considered with reference to a specific musical situation. All models do show the arpeggio in the abstract, none show it in a setting in which a single arpeggiated chord forms a pillar for a melody note. However, in the solo literature with which we are primarily concerned, this happens to be the most frequent and most important setting for the single arpeggio. We need only look at the four-note model of D'Anglebert, Le Roux, or Dieupart to realize that it could not be used in support of a melody in the upper voice that starts on the beat. The masters who wrote these patterns did not have to worry about their neces-

[4] G. Schirmer, New York, 1938.

[5] Chambonnières, *Pieces de clavessin*; Le Bègue, *Pieces de clavessin*; D'Anglebert, *Pieces de clavecin*; Le Roux, *Pièces de clavecin*; Raison, *Livre d'orgue*; Dieupart, *Six suittes*; Rameau, *Pièces de clavessin* [1724].

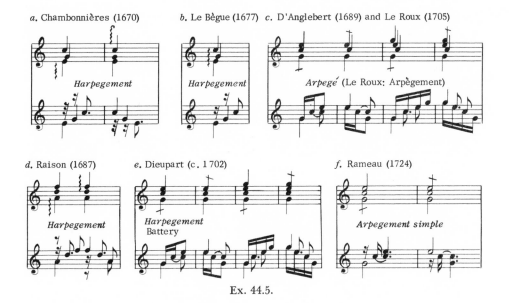

a. Chambonnières (1670) b. Le Bègue (1677) c. D'Anglebert (1689) and Le Roux (1705)

Harpegement   *Harpegement*   *Arpegé* (Le Roux: Arpègement)

d. Raison (1687)   e. Dieupart (c. 1702)   f. Rameau (1724)

Harpegement   *Harpegement*   *Arpegement simple*
Battery

Ex. 44.5.

sary rhythmic adaptation to changing musical needs because to their contemporaries such adaptation was a matter of course.

Interesting are the comments of Saint Lambert, who devotes in his treatise of 1702 a whole chapter to the arpeggio.[6] He distinguishes the *harpégé simple* (i.e. the "plain" one in our terminology) from the *harpégé figuré*. The placement of the wavy line near the top or bottom of the note indicates the direction of the arpeggio; if it appears near the top, the arpeggio is downward, if near the bottom, it is upward.

His models of the *simple* arpeggio, as shown in Ex. 44.6, are rhythmically noncommittal in using the graphic device of a slight shift to the right which suggests successiveness without indicating the location of the beat. Saint Lambert adds the following explanation: "In the arpeggio, be it plain or figurate, the fingers must move on the keys with such agility that there appears between the notes no recognizable time interval that would alter or interrupt the rhythm of the piece."[7] Both model and explanation point to rhythmic flexibility that can accommodate the prebeat along with the onbeat design.

"on two notes"   "on three notes"

Ex. 44.6. Saint Lambert (1702), *Harpegé simple*

Couperin, a decade later, illustrates in his Table of 1713 the arpeggio both upward and downward with comparable rhythmic vagueness.[8] His models are

---

[6] *Principes*, ch. 26.
[7] Ibid., p. 55.

[8] *Piéces de clavecin*, 1st book.

given in Ex. 44.7a. In midcentury, Foucquet offers the nearly identical models of Ex. *b*, but there are no symbols to indicate upward or downward motion.

a. Couperin (1713)   *b.* Foucquet (c. 1750)

Arpègement en montant   *Arpègement en descendant*

Ex. 44.7.

Italian harpsichordists certainly used the arpeggio throughout the 17th century, but they developed no symbol for it.[9] After the introduction of the little notes, we find them occasionally in the service of an arpeggio. Domenico Scarlatti had recourse to them as shown in Ex. 44.8, in which the arpeggio—at least in the right hand—would make best musical sense in anticipation.

Ex. 44.8. D. Scarlatti, Sonata K 394

In Germany, the French oblique dash perhaps preceded the vertical wavy-line symbol. We find the dash in instrumental works of Christian Ritter (c. 1645-1725), as shown in Ex. 44.9.[10]

Ex. 44.9. C. Ritter, Sonatina *(ABB)*

J. S. Bach may have been one of the first Germans to adopt the wavy line for the plain arpeggio. He uses only one symbol, which—to judge from its contexts with regard to melody—seems to signify upward direction only. Earlier in this chapter, two illustrations were shown where the arpeggio in support of a melody note would best be done in anticipation. Similar examples abound in Bach's harpsichord works.

Two arpeggios in the early *Capriccio sopra la lontananza*, both taken from the second, fugal section of the piece, offer an interesting study in contrasts.[11] The first of these arpeggios (Ex. 44.10a) precedes the restatement of the theme in the soprano after four regular

[9] Its place, at least in the accompaniment, was documented by Lorenzo Penna, *Li primi albori* (1672), book 3, ch. 20, rule 19; and, as mentioned above in our ch. 42, by Gasparini in 1708 and Geminiani in 1749.

[10] From the Sonatina's only source, the *ABB*.
[11] They are quoted according to the main source, the *Möllersche Handschrift*, while the *BG* edition differs.

fugal entrances. The theme itself has a clear rhythmic definition, and in its first statement the onbeat start of the first note is further emphasized by a mordent. Hence, on its reentry in m. 6, its decisive onbeat placement is important, therefore requiring the prebeat start of the arpeggio. On the other hand, in Ex. *b* we find simply a cadential formula and no melody with a vested interest in rhythmic integrity. Whether the arpeggio starts here on or before the beat matters little; besides, the location of the beat may have been blurred by now with a cadential retard.

In Bach's organ works, the incidence of the arpeggio is negligible. One of the rare instances can be found in the Weimar version of the Chorale Prelude *Nun komm, der Heiden Heiland* in m. 15 and at the end, as shown below in Ex. *c*. In the final, late autograph version (also in P 271) both arpeggios are omitted. Another specimen can be found at the start of the Organ Chorale *Liebster Jesu* (BWV 633, aut. P 283).

Ex. 44.10.

In 1749, Marpurg gives the German term of *Griffbrechen* in addition to arpeggio and *harpégement* and shows onbeat start in his patterns of Ex. 44.11. He places the slanted stroke symbol *under* the note for the rising type and *above* it for the descending type; the direction of the slant is—surprisingly—immaterial. The same model is repeated in 1755 when he calls the grace *Zergliederung* or *Brechung*.[12]

Ex. 44.11. Marpurg (1749, 1755)

C.P.E. Bach does not include the arpeggio among the ornaments and mentions it only briefly in his chapter on performance. Calling it "broken harmony" (*gebrochene Harmonie*), he offers the models of Exx. 44.12*a-d*. They show the wavy line for the rising arpeggio only. He also gives a new symbol (perhaps of

[12] *Crit. Musicus*, p. 68; *Anleitung* (1755), pp. 59-60, and Table 5, figs. 16, 17.

his own invention), a vertical line with a small bend at the bottom or top as equivalent of the wavy line. If the bend is at the bottom, it signifies a rising arpeggio; if it is at the top, the arpeggio is descending. Moreover, he introduces another type of arpeggio with only the first note held down (Exx. *b* and *d*).[13] A connection may possibly exist between the exclusive ascending meaning of the wavy line for C.P.E. Bach and the—presumably—identical meaning for his father.

Ex. 44.12. C.P.E. Bach (1753)

Löhlein, in his clavier treatise of 1765-1782, gives no model for the arpeggio but explains it verbally and stresses fastness of execution. Later in the century, Türk, in 1789, adopts C.P.E. Bach's symbols and gives almost identical realizations.[14]

THE INTERVALLIC ARPEGGIO

When only two pitches are involved, one could speak of an intervallic arpeggio and justify this terminological distinction, because this type will often serve a different musical function. Such will notably be the case when several intervallic arpeggios follow one another. In the resulting pattern of repeat, the delay of the second note will be measured and regular, forming a distinct rhythmic design that can assume structural characteristics. Perhaps nothing illuminates the difference between the rhythmically regulated intervallic arpeggio and the chordal type better than the frequency with which the organ uses the former and rarely tolerates the latter.

Many times we find the intervallic type written out in regular notation, for instance in Bach's D minor Organ Toccata, mm. 12-15, in the 23rd *Goldberg Variation*, mm. 27-30, or in D. Scarlatti's Sonata K 84, mm. 9-11. Often it is indicated by symbol, sometimes by verbal direction.

In France, Perrine, in his transcription of various lute works from tablature to regular staff (1680), uses the oblique stroke and gives for the two-note arpeggio the resolutions of Ex. 44.13*a*.[15] Le Roux and Dieupart use the same symbol. Le Roux calls the pattern *separez* and like Perrine places the slanted stroke between the note heads (Ex. *b*), but by doing so he confused matters, because most other Frenchmen as well as many Germans understood this symbol (especially between thirds) to mean an inserted middle note. Dieupart places the stroke externally (Ex. *c*).[16]

[13] *Versuch*, I, ch. 3, par. 26.

[14] Löhlein, *Clavier-Schule*, ch. 1, sec. 9; Türk, *Klavierschule*, ch. 4, sec. 4, pars. 89-90.

[15] *Pieces de luth*, p. 7.

[16] Le Roux, *Pièces de clavecin*; Dieupart, *Six suittes.*

a. Perrine (1680)   *b.* Le Roux (1705)   *c.* Dieupart (c. 1702)

separez

Ex. 44.13.

Saint Lambert in 1702 makes a special point in stressing the difference between the intervallic and chordal arpeggio. Whereas the chordal type was to be done with great speed, one has, he says, to exempt from this rule "the type of arpeggio which is done on a two-note basis: for, if several appear in sequence, the notes sound more graceful when separated distinctly even to the point where the second [notes] are reduced to half their value."[17] His illustration is given in Ex. 44.14.

Ex. 44.14. Saint Lambert

Couperin uses his wavy-line arpeggio symbol for two-note intervals as well as for chords, and it is likely that he intended no difference of execution. In *Les Pavots* (XXVII) after m. 17, several such arpeggios appear, ranging from thirds to sixths. Their rhythm is not determined and probably varies from anticipation to onbeat.

In Germany the symbolized use of the intervallic arpeggio seems to have been rare. We find, among others, the passage from Buxtehude's C minor Ciaccone [*sic*] as it appears in the *Andreas Bach Buch* with the verbal specification of *arpeggiando* (Ex. 44.15*a*). Its transcription to the pattern of Ex. *b*, as found in modern editions, seems justified.

Arpeggiando

Ex. 44.15. Buxtehude, Ciaccone

Bach used the slanted stroke symbol once in a while, and seemingly only in early works, for the intervallic type. We find in the primary source of the *Capriccio sopra la lontananza* the passage of Ex. 44.16*a*.[18] The intended rhythm is impossible to determine and probably mattered little. We find this same symbol in the *Aria variata* of 1709 (Ex. *b*). Here the melody is distinctly in the soprano and this would favor anticipation of the lower notes. In later works this symbol will usually stand for the figurate type.

[17] *Principes*, p. 55.   [18] *Möllersche Handschrift.*

Ex. 44.16.

A fairly clear case of anticipated two- and three-note arpeggios from Bach's inner circle can be found in a passage from the *Andreas Bach Buch* taken from an edited version of Kuhnau's 5th Sonata (Ex. 44.17). The prebeat *Vorschlag* written before the bar line at the beginning of the passage transfers its meaning in clear analogy to the start of the next measure where the same theme is repeated a third higher, but where the arpeggio-like *Vorschlag* is now notated with an oblique stroke. Moreover, these two-note arpeggios will logically suggest the prebeat style for the three-note arpeggio in the first measure.

Ex. 44.17. Kuhnau (in *ABB*), Sonata No. 5

THE CHORDAL ARPEGGIO ON STRING INSTRUMENTS

On string instruments the arpeggiation of a single chord is in most cases more a matter of technical necessity than of ornamental choice. The degree to which real or quasi-simultaneity can be achieved for chords varies with circumstances. Viols with the lesser angle between their six strings can sustain chords better than the members of the violin family, and the violin of the period had an advantage over the modern one, not because of the so-called "Bach bow,"[19] but because its shorter and thinner strings had less tension and could be depressed more easily.

An important insight that bears on the matter of freedom of choice between arpeggiated· and non-arpeggiated execution is provided by Marin Marais. In his third book of gamba pieces, he introduces the oblique dash symbol to signify *harpégement* (or arpeggio) and explains it by saying that one should play the notes separately, starting from the bass and continuing to the top note.[20] Later, in the fifth book, he introduces the term *en plein* written under chords, "which

---

[19] The idea of the "Bach bow" which allegedly could sustain tones on all four strings at the same time and permit the playing of Bach's solo sonatas and suites "as written" was originally conceived by Schering and Schweitzer through misinterpretation of an old treatise. Schering recanted, but Schweitzer kept faith in this idea. The polemics on this question should be permanently put to rest by David D. Boyden's conclusive refutation of the theory in his *History of Violin Playing from its Beginnings to 1761* (London, 1965), pp. 431ff.

[20] *Pièces de violes*, 3rd book (1711), Preface: "Cet autre signe qui se trouve a côté des accords, marque qu'il fault les séparer en com-

mençant par la basse et continuant jusques à la partie superieure, ce que l'on peut encore appeller harpégement."

Thomas Mace's *Musick's Monument* of 1676, which was previously quoted in connection with the French lute school, contains a brief section on the gamba. In one passage (p. 249) he complains that some players leave out the bass note when executing a chord. For the playing of final chords ("Full Stop") he recommends that the performer start with the lowest string alone and give it a good share of the bow and some emphasis before leaving it for the other notes.

one usually arpeggiates from the bass to the melody note," to indicate that "one must sound all the tones at the same time instead of separating them."[21]

The two extremes of *en plein* and full separation are not the only available alternatives, and many transitional patterns can be used and undoubtedly were used by string players of the period. Thus the chords can be broken not only one by one, but by twos and threes, forming arpeggiated designs of which only a sampling is shown in Ex. 44.18.

Ex. 44.18.

The choice among the designs will depend on various circumstances. For a genuinely ornamental purpose, the full separation of Ex. *b* above will usually be indicated. On the other hand, when the arpeggio is a simple technical makeshift for a chord that should be sustained, there is no reason why the arpeggiation ought to be limited to the one-note style. Any surrogate aspires to approach as closely as practicable to the unreachable ideal. Therefore, the breaking of such a chord will proceed by twos and threes and not by ones. In each case the desirable execution will depend on the character of the chord, whether it represents pure harmony or whether it is the result of polyphonic voice-leading. If the former, then greatest fullness should be the aim; if the latter, the first concern should then be to clarify the linear relationships of the individual chordal pitches.

A case of pure harmony can be found in the Prelude of Bach's D minor Cello Suite (Ex. 44.19) where the nearly incessant motion of the piece comes to a final rest in five cadential chords. Desirable here is the richest possible resonance.[22]

Ex. 44.19. BWV 1008, Prelude

An instructive contrast between harmonic and polyphonic chords is provided by the opening measures of the Sonatas in G minor and A minor for Unaccompanied Violin. In the first of these (Ex. 44.20a) we find a homophonic setting in which the chords support a single melody. The bass moves mostly from root to root and has no melodic interest. We can therefore aim at rich resonance, provided we see to it that the melody, when it passes through the middle of the chords, is clarified by subtle dynamic emphases. In the first

[21] *Pièces de violes*, 5th book (1725), Preface: "Pour ce qui est des accords qu'on harpege ordinairement en montant de la basse au sujet, et ou j'ay marqué dessous 'en plein,' cela veut dire qu'il faut faire entendre tous les sons a la fois, au lieu de les separer."

[22] There is, on the other hand, no justification in the procedure of some editors and players who dissolve the chords into a figuration patterned after that of the preceding measure.

If, and only if, that last measure had contained an obvious arpeggio formula, its continued application to the chords might have been assumed. However, the melody in that measure does not even resemble an arpeggio and besides, as it stands it is not readily applicable to the following chords. There can be little doubt that the chords were meant to be played as written.

chord, the melody note is on top and its preferred claim to onbeat placement suggests anticipation of the arpeggio, as sketched in Ex. *b*. At the arpeggio's end, the premature release of the alto part is advisable lest it be misunderstood as the new bass. Examples *c*, *d*, and *e* show several possibilities for the rendition of the next three chords. In the last of these, the soprano should be released before the alto to clarify the melody move from a′ to b′ flat.

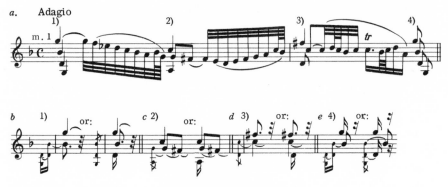

Ex. 44.20. BWV 1001

By contrast, the second sonata (Ex. 44.21*a*) has at its start *two* melody lines whose polyphonic interplay is sketched in Ex. *b* as it would appear when freed from the limitations of the instrument. In order to get this relationship across to the listener, the bass note must first be sounded alone (as suggested in Ex. *c*) to permit its being heard as the start of a line rather than as the foundation of the chord.

Ex. 44.21. BWV 1003

Matters of intelligent execution are still more complicated in the three fugues for solo violin, where often all three or four notes of a chord are generated polyphonically. The clarification of all melody lines often becomes impossible and only compromise solutions can be attempted.

Two mid-18th-century documents confirm the aforementioned idea that in the playing of chords, arpeggiating will tend to approach as nearly as possible the ideal of full simultaneity.

Leopold Mozart stresses the need to play chords "fast and together" ("schnell und zugleich") and gives the illustration shown in Ex. 44.22*a*.[23] In the section addressed to orchestra violinists, Quantz devotes a paragraph to the playing of chords. He makes a difference between short chords followed by rests (Ex. *b*), which require the bow to be

23 *Violinschule*, ch. 12, par. 21.

lifted and reset, and chords not followed by a rest, where the bow remains on the top note (Ex. *c*). "For both types the lowest [strings] must not be sustained, be it in slow or fast tempo, but touched fast and successively: in order not to sound as if they were triplets running through a broken chord."[24] He meant, presumably, that the chord must not be played like Ex. *d*, i.e. in single arpeggiation, but by twos and threes instead.[25] This interpretation is confirmed by the next sentence: "And because these chords are used to surprise the ear unexpectedly with vehemence, those [chords] followed by rests must be played very curtly and with the greatest force of bow, using its lowest part. . . ."[26] Expression of vehemence, application of the greatest force of the bow, and the use of its lowest part leave no doubt about the execution. The one-by-one style would not only be incapable of expressing vehemence, but its execution in the manner described would be violinistically incongruous because it would crush the sound.

Ex. 44.22.

The full-toned breaking of chords within the frame of musical logic and technical feasibility was as much part of Quantz's and L. Mozart's musical practice as it was of Marais's and, as can be reasonably assumed, of other string players and composers, including J. S. Bach.

THE FIGURATE ARPEGGIO (*Arpégé figuré*)

In the figurate arpeggio, pitches alien to the chord are inserted in *Zwischenschlag* fashion, i.e. without being held. We have encountered similar inserts in thorough bass practice in the form of Gasparini's *mordenti* (see above Chapter 42). On the other hand, it is important not to confuse the figurate arpeggio with the Italian *acciaccatura*, as is so often done, because unfortunately several German writers, among them Marpurg and C.P.E. Bach, used the term *acciaccatura* to designate the inserts of the figurate arpeggio. It will be best to speak of these inserts as *Zwischenschläge* and reserve the term *acciaccatura* for its authentic Italian significance.

The simplest form of the figurate arpeggio, which will be discussed first, is the arpeggiated interval of a third with the middle note momentarily sounded as a *Zwischenschlag*. Like the slide to which it is related, this form is much more common upward than downward.

Chambonnières formulates in 1670 the ascending type as a standard ornament, calls it *coulé*, and marks it with an oblique dash between the two note heads, and so does Le Bègue in 1677 (see Ex. 44.23*a*). In 1687, Raison adopts the same sym-

---

[24] *Versuch*, ch. 17, sec. 2, par. 18: "Bey beyden Arten müssen die untersten [Saiten], so wohl im langsamen als geschwinden Tempo, nicht angehalten, sondern geschwind nach einander berühret werden: damit es nicht klinge, als wenn es durch einen Accord gebrochene Triolen wären."

[25] Edward R. Reilly, in his translation of Quantz's treatise, seems to have misunderstood this passage.

[26] *Versuch*, ch. 17, sec. 2, par. 18: "Und weil diese Accorde gebrauchet werden, das Gehör unvermuthet durch eine Heftigkeit zu überraschen; so müssen diejenigen [Accorde], auf welche Pausen folgen, ganz kurz, und mit der grössesten Stärke des Bogens, nämlich mit seinem untersten Theile, gespielet werden. . . ."

bol, term, and model for the organ (Ex. *b*); Jullien's model of 1690 (Ex. *c*) is
rhythmically ambiguous.[27]

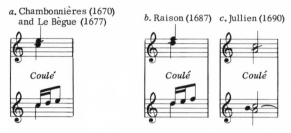

Ex. 44.23.

D'Anglebert (1689) speaks of a *coulé sur une tierce*, introduces a clamp-like
symbol, and shows both upward and downward designs (Ex. 44.24*a*). Le Roux
(1705) copied both models exactly. Dieupart (c. 1702) also follows D'Anglebert
and uses his hook symbol as well as the term *coulé*, for which he gives the English
equivalent of "slur" (Ex. *b*).[28]

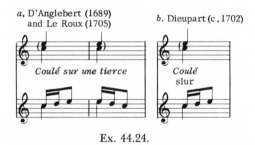

Ex. 44.24.

Couperin's model for what he calls *tierce coulée* is rhythmically ambiguous,
possibly leaning toward anticipation (Ex. 44.25*a*).[29]

Ex. 44.25. Couperin (1713)

The use of the term *coulé* or *tierce coulée* for this form of the figurate arpeggio might
seem confusing, yet there is logic in it. The grace is in fact a compound ornament: a
combination of arpeggio and the very kind of *Zwischenschlag* that was so characteristic
of the filling in of thirds by an interbeat *coulé* or *port de voix* in a purely melodic context.
It must be kept in mind that whether the first principal note is placed on or off the beat,
the true ornamental addition, the middle note, is always done *off* the beat. Yet, though

<hr>

[27] Chambonnières, *Pieces de clavessin*; Le
Bègue, *Pieces de clavessin*; Raison, *Livre
d'orgue*; Jullien, *Premier livre d'orgue*.

[28] D'Anglebert, *Pieces de clavecin*; Le Roux,
Pièces de clavecin; Dieupart, *Six suittes*.
[29] *Pièces de clavecin*, 1st Book.

the onbeat *start* for these filled-in thirds is often, perhaps mostly, intended, it is not a foregone conclusion. The same considerations adduced for the plain arpeggio are operative here too: when the final note is melodically-rhythmically prominent, a prebeat start is indicated.

When such a third with the *figuré* symbol appears as part of a larger chord, the meaning is, of course, the same. Occasionally, two or even more inserted notes are embedded in a single chord. In cases where the interval is larger than a third, the symbol most often calls for a *Zwischenschlag* a step or half-step below the upper note in ascending and above the lower note in descending.

D'Anglebert speaks of the *figuré* pattern within a regular chord as *cheute sur une notte*, or with two inserts (indicated by two hooks), as *cheute sur deux nottes* (Ex. 44.26a). Le Roux adopts D'Anglebert's first model, but places the hook more efficiently between the notes that are linked by the insert; moreover, he gives a descending model (Ex. *b*).[30]

Saint Lambert shows what he calls the *harpegé figuré* with a model (Ex. *c*) that is again rhythmically noncommittal with its intact quarter-notes at the end. He uses D'Anglebert's symbol of a hook and shows examples for one as well as for two inserts. The *figuré*, he says, is almost always done in rising. A desire to have it done in falling has to be indicated by a slanted stroke across the stem of the top note (Ex. *d*).[31]

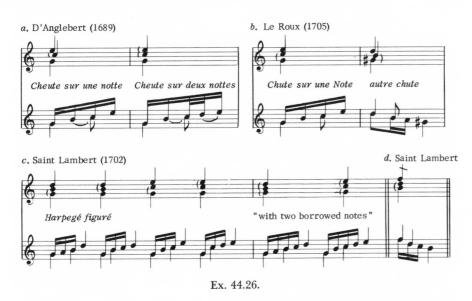

Ex. 44.26.

In Germany, Bach indicates the figurate arpeggio with Chambonnières's oblique dash symbol between the note heads, and uses it in ascending only. The grace does not appear often in his scores but may, of course, have been more frequently improvised. (The early—and apparently later abandoned—use of the same symbol to indicate the plain intervallic arpeggio was mentioned above.) Once in a while, Bach writes the figurate type in regular notes. Examples 44.27*a* and *b* give two such passages from the A minor and E minor Partitas. The first of these shows onbeat start which is logical because the bottom note of the arpeggio is part of the melody; the second example shows anticipation.

Marked by the symbol, the figurate arpeggio occurs in several movements of the English Suites, according to the oldest and most important source (P 1072). Filled-in thirds from the Courante I of the A major Suite are shown in Ex. 44.28*a*;

[30] See n. 28 above.　　　　　[31] *Principes*, p. 55.

Ex. 44.27.

they should start on the beat to underscore the bass melody (Ex. *b*). A fuller chord from the Sarabande is shown in Ex. *c* and its suggested execution in Ex. *d*; here, anticipation seems advisable to safeguard the rhythm of the melody. In Ex. *e* from the ornamented version of the Sarabande in G minor, the same considerations apply. In some of the partitas we find the symbol in the early autograph version of Anna Magdalena's Note Book but not in the later engraved edition. Example *f* shows two passages from the Sarabande of the E minor Partita. Here too it is difficult to find in the usually proposed onbeat start an advantage that would compensate for the loss of the melody's original rhythm.

Ex. 44.28.

Marpurg in 1749 lists *acciaccatura* as the Italian equivalent for the figurate arpeggio; for a symbol he uses a clamp-like hook which is rather confusing because it neither shows where the insertion is to be made nor does it differentiate between a one-note and a two-note insertion. Realizing these shortcomings, he improved these models in 1755 to the ones shown in Ex. 44.29. He now uses the terms *accentuirte Zergliederung* or *accentuirte Brechung*.[32]

[32] *Crit. Musicus*, p. 68; *Anleitung*, p. 60 and Table 5, figs. 18-21.

Ex. 44.29. Marpurg (1755)

Noteworthy are some added models of combined graces that suggest the prebeat start where the arpeggio proper is preceded by either a *Vorschlag* (Ex. 44.30*a*), a mordent (Ex. *b*), a three-note slide (Ex. *c*), or a turn (Ex. *d*).[33] Previously mentioned were interesting models of genuine *Zusammenschläge* of one or two notes within a chord, which Marpurg lists as a species of the figurate arpeggio (see above Exx. 42.7*b* and *c*).

Ex. 44.30. Marpurg (1755)

C.P.E. Bach (1753) devotes only one brief sentence to the figurate arpeggio. He refers to the inserted notes as *acciaccature* and in a single model shows the slanted stroke between note heads. Löhlein (1765) and Türk (1789) use the same term and the same symbol.[34]

THE LINEAR ARPEGGIO

In the linear arpeggio the chord loses its vertical substance and is dissolved into continuous movement. The chordal tones are strung up, one by one, usually throughout the whole time-span allotted to the harmony. For shorter chords, each pitch may be sounded only once (Ex. 44.31*a*); for longer ones they may be restrung many times, be it by continuous repeat (Ex. *b*), by moving up and down in the proper ascending and descending order of the pitches (Ex. *c*), or in all manners of irregular sequence patterns such as the one given in Ex. *d*.

When nothing but pure harmony is involved, the arpeggio character of the linear type will be unmistakable. Sometimes, however, a broken chord may be a genuine melody that happens to be based on the tones of a chord. There are countless shades between the polar contrasts in which the characteristics of both types will blur.

The linear arpeggio is at home in many instrumental media, including the organ, but it plays a particularly characteristic role with those instruments which, like the harpsichord, clavichord, or strings, cannot long sustain the sound of chords. The linear arpeggio is thus a means of keeping the chordal energy alive for any desired length.

---

[33] *Anleitung*, p. 60 and figs. 23-25.
[34] C.P.E. Bach, *Versuch*, I, ch. 3, par. 26;

Löhlein, *Clavier-Schule*, pt. I, ch. 9, par. 9;
Türk, *Klavierschule*, ch. 4, sec. 4, par. 92.

Ex. 44.31.

As long as such arpeggios are written out, they present no particular problem. Problems start when the composer uses an abbreviated notation to signify or imply his wish for arpeggiation but expects the performer to choose both design and articulation.

Occasionally the composer provides guidance by a sample. Example 44.32 shows such instances in passages from Bach's Cantata 74 (Ex. *a*), Cantata 86 (Ex. *b*), and the Ciaccona for Unaccompanied Violin (Ex. *c*). In Ex. *a*, the pattern has to be done for technical reasons with detached bowstrokes. For Ex. *b* the idiomatic rendition will be: ♩♩♩♩♩♩ .

In Ex. *c* the melodic model, determined by a technical consideration, changes automatically in the third measure to the one shown in Ex. *d*.

Ex. 44.32.

Another problem arises when a model given by the composer at the outset of a lengthy arpeggio passage ceases to fit later chords, either because their rhythm has changed or because new melodic elements have been introduced into the chordal texture. In such cases the solution is rarely obvious and the performer has to exercise his judgment.

In the famous arpeggio passage from the Chromatic Fantasy, Bach does give initially the simple up-and-down model of Ex. 44.33*a*, but soon it ceases to be applicable. Example *b* sketches one of various ways in which the arpeggio might be done in mm. 33, 40, and 47-49.

In the Prelude to Handel's 1st Harpsichord Suite, no model is given for the arpeggio and, to complicate matters, melodic passages are interwoven with the

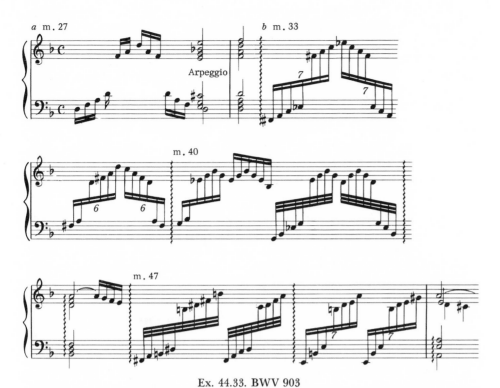

Ex. 44.33. BWV 903

chordal ones. Example 44.34*a* gives the text of mm. 3 and 4, and Ex. *b* outlines a possible execution. A still simpler, straight up-and-down version is suggested by Beyschlag who transcribed the whole Prelude.[35] In mm. 12, 14, and 18, Beyschlag, with good reason, interprets the little notes in the sense of figurate inserts.

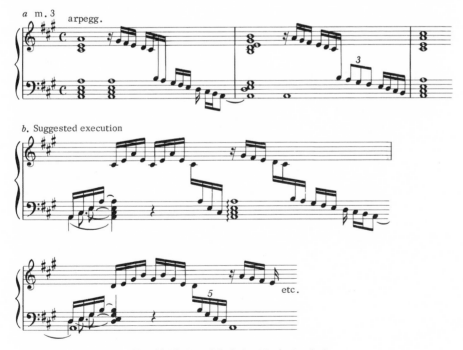

Ex. 44.34. Handel, Suite No. 1, Prelude

[35] Beyschlag, pp. 111-114.

Whenever we have no guidance from the composer, it will generally be advisable to aim at simple, not fancy, solutions. Where more animation seems desirable, a somewhat richer elaboration can be chosen but care should be taken to avoid fussiness.

THE widely accepted idea that the chordal arpeggio should always start on the beat has no historic justification. No rule to such effect has been formulated by any known theoretical source, and those ornament tables which showed the execution within the metrical value of the principal note demonstrated the principle of "breaking" the chord in simple abstraction with no reference to any concrete musical situation. There are many cases where onbeat rendition is fitting, but there are many where it is *not*, because it would upset the priorities of musical logic. Particularly in those contexts where the arpeggio is used to grace a single melody note it is the latter which has the decisive claim to rhythmic integrity. Consequently, where the melody note is intended for the beat, the arpeggio ought to be anticipated.[36] In their functional relationship, the melody note should be the independent, the arpeggio the dependent variable, which means that the arpeggio has to be treated with a flexibility that permits its ready adaptation to any situation, including occasional rubato intents. The same principle applies, of course, also to the figurate arpeggio, in which non-chordal pitches are inserted but not sustained.

The linear arpeggio poses problems only in instances of incomplete notation in which cases a simple realization will generally be preferable to an elaborate one.

[36] Arthur Mendel, who agrees with the need to anticipate the arpeggio in such contexts, brought to my attention an interesting analogy in vocal declamation. Whenever a word starts with one or more consonants, these consonants have to be anticipated, because the beat has to fall on the vowel: credo, strong, or glory. Moreover, the consonants should be sounded at the pitch of the preceding, not the following, vowel, which further strengthens the analogy to the arpeggio. Professor Mendel learned these principles from the late Carl Deis.

The vibrato is a means of enriching the musical tone. During the baroque period the vibrato was looked upon as an ornament sometimes prescribed by symbol, but most often it was freely added.

The vibrato consists of fast, regular fluctuations of pitch, loudness, or timbre, or a combination of these. Its effect rests on the physio-psychological phenomenon of *sonance*, i.e. the fusion of the vibrato oscillations above a definite threshold of speed into the sensation of a richer tone, while the perception of the oscillations is minimized or disappears altogether. The phenomenon is closely akin to the stereophonic merger of slightly different sound impressions into a single one with added depth.

Vocal vibrato must be ageless, and even instrumental vibrato might be as old as many instruments themselves. Haas speaks of a vibrato effect in classical Greece through the use of a plectron in kithara playing. He mentions the use in the Middle Ages of specific ornamental neumes, the *Bistropha* and *Tristropha*, which prescribed a pulsation of the voice.[1]

THE VIBRATO IN FRANCE

Basset, writing in Mersenne's *Harmonie universelle* of 1636, calls the lute vibrato *verre cassé* and introduces the symbol of a comma followed by a dot (the comma by itself signified a trill).[2] Basset speaks of moving the left hand violently while not allowing the finger tip to leave the string. To give still more freedom to the swing, he advises the player to disengage the thumb from the neck of the instrument. Very interesting is his remark that at the time of writing the vibrato was used infrequently as a reaction against its overuse by the older generation. Basset considers both extremes deplorable and recommends a golden mean. Mersenne, speaking of the violin, refers in matters of ornamentation to the chapters on the lute, implying that the same graces, including therefore the vibrato, were to be practiced on the violin as well.[3]

Thomas Mace, speaking in 1676 for the French lute school, describes the vibrato, calls it "sting," and shows the symbol of a wavy line. He says it is "pretty and neat but not modish in these days." Nevertheless, he finds it "very excellent for certain Humours." These are his instructions: "Hold your finger (but not too hard) stopt upon the Place (letting your thumb loose) & wave your hand. . . ."[4] Mary Burwell, also a product of the French lute school, writes in c. 1670 that "the sting is no more in use; it is made by stopping the little finger upon a string and swinging the hand upon it."[5] Miss Burwell obviously overstates the demise of the vibrato, but unquestionably its use declined in those years in which the French lute school was rapidly approaching its end.

Toward the end of the century, we have ample documents about the gambists' use of the vibrato. They knew two types to which they gave distinct symbols and names. The originally preferred type was done with two fingers: the lower finger was firmly placed on the string and the upper finger was pressed tightly against

---

[1] Haas, pp. 25, 42.
[2] *Traité des instrumens à chordes*, pp. 80-81.
[3] Ibid., p. 182.
[4] *Monument*, p. 109.

[5] Thurston Dart, "Miss Mary Burwell's Instruction Book for the Lute," *Galpin Soc. Jour.*, No. 9 (May 1958), pp. 3-62.

the lower one; a shaking of the hand brought the upper finger into gentle repercussive contact with the string.[6] Such action resulted in a trill-like oscillation with a microtone.

The English speak fittingly of a "close shake" and some of their theorists, following the lead of Christopher Simpson, cleverly indicate its character by means of a trill design that remains within the confines of one space on the staff (Ex. 45.1).[7]

Ex. 45.1. Simpson (1659)

Such a trill-type technique was, of course, possible only with the lower three fingers. When the little finger was on the string, the gambists had to resort to what originally appeared to be their second choice: the shaking of the stopping finger itself. After about 1700, however, Marais and other players, realizing the different—and wider—color potentials of the one-finger vibrato, extended its use to the other fingers as well, without abandoning the two-finger type. Terms and symbols vary from one master to another; therefore, the two types will in the following simply be designated as the "one-finger," and the "two-finger" vibrato.

Demachy calls the two-finger vibrato the *tremblement sans appuyer* and marks it with a comma above or below the note head; he calls the one-finger vibrato *aspiration* or *plainte* and indicates it with a wavy line after the note (Ex. 45.2*a*). (Some people, he says, want to call it "mewing" [*miaullement*].)[8]

Danoville's term for the two-finger vibrato is *battement*, his symbol a long wavy line. He specifies that the tone should be started before the tightly squeezed upper finger initiates its fast oscillation and that this oscillation should stop before the bow ends its stroke. The grace, he says, "fills the ear with languishing sweetness."[9] His term for the one-finger vibrato is *balancement de main*. He stresses its close kinship to the *battement* and the fact that it is done with the fourth finger by a "small rocking of the hand." For symbol he uses—as he does for the trill—the comma after the note (Ex. *b*).

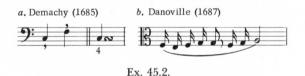

a. Demachy (1685)   *b*. Danoville (1687)

Ex. 45.2.

Jean Rousseau, like Danoville, calls the two-finger vibrato *batement*; it imitates, he says, a certain gentle agitation of the voice. He adds, interestingly, that one uses it any place ("en toutes rencontres") where the length of the note permits it and that it is done for the full extent of the tone. His term for the one-finger vibrato—"mainly with the fourth finger"—is *langueur*.[10]

Marais describes the one-finger vibrato (with the little finger) as being done

[6] On the violin, such procedure later became known as *Bockstriller*—a derogatory term for a trill substitute, especially in higher positions. On the gamba, with its frets and its far larger spacing of intervals, this technique had an entirely different effect.

[7] *Division-Violist*, 1st ed., p. 9, 2nd ed., p. 12.

John Playford, *An Introduction to the Skill of Musick*, 7th ed., bk. 1, p. 116, has the same model.

[8] *Pieces de violle*, pp. 9, 13.

[9] *L'art*, pp. 41-42, 45.

[10] *Traité*, pp. 100-101.

"by rocking the hand." He calls it *plainte* and marks it with a vertical wavy line. He does not describe the two-finger vibrato, but there is little doubt that this is what he means by his terms *pincé* or *flatement*, which are marked (like Danoville's *battement*) with the horizontal wavy line.

Flatement, meaning "flattering," was a frequent term for the vibrato. *Pincé*, of course, far more commonly, and almost exclusively, denoted the mordent. Marais probably derived the term from the pinching of the upper finger against the lower one. As noted before, he used Danoville's and Rousseau's vibrato term (*batement*) to signify the mordent.[11] To compound the terminological confusion within the French gamba school, Rousseau uses the term *plainte* not for a vibrato, as does Marais, but for a downward glissando. In view of this confusion, terms without explanation become meaningless. For instance, in his song collection of 1685, D'Ambruis introduced a *flatement* (symbol: ∧) and a *plainte ou accent* (symbol: |) and took their meaning for granted.[12] Either of these graces occurs occasionally on notes that appear too short for a vibrato. Their exact meaning is uncertain.

An interesting analogy can be found with the French flutists. When Hotteterre speaks of a *flattement* or *tremblement mineur*, he indicates that it is done with the technique of the trill, but that only the edge of the hole is struck. Thus, instead of the higher microtone used by the gambists, the flute's *flattement* is done with the lower one. When all holes are held and this technique impossible, then, Hotteterre says, one should *shake the flute* in order to imitate the effect of the ordinary *flattement*.[13] In his first book of flute pieces, Hotteterre says that the *flattement* should be done on almost all long notes and that, like the trills and mordents, one must do them slower or faster according to the tempo and character of the piece.[14]

Corrette, in his first flute treatise of 1735, says somewhat cryptically that the *flattement* "is done to swell and diminish the sound,"[15] but he also speaks of a vibrato. He gives the gambist's symbol of the wavy line and says that it is very touching on long notes in tender pieces.

The general theorists have the voice in mind when they speak of a *balancement*, which to them appeared to be a wavering of the voice on a single pitch. L'Affilard shows it in the models of Ex. 45.3a with the wavy line of the gambists.[16] Loulié using a clamp symbol, explains the *balancement* as small, gentle, slow breath strokes ("petites aspirations douces & lentes") which are done on a note without changing its pitch (Ex. b).[17]

Montéclair distinguishes a *flaté* and a *balancement* though they are closely related. Both consist of pulsations of the voice on one long note without allegedly any change of pitch. The pulsations are gentle in the *flaté* (Ex. c), slower and more pronounced (*plus marquées*) in the *balancement* where they produce the effect of the organ's *tremblant* register (Ex. d). He uses the wavy line for both, though for the *flaté* he says that there was no symbol in use.[18]

The vibrato character of the Loulié-Montéclair *balancement* is further confirmed by Corrette. In his voice treatise, he repeats Loulié's definition by speaking of gentle and slow breath strokes on the same note in imitation of the *tremblant doux* of the organ.[19]

[11] *Pièces* (1st book), Preface. Caix d'Hervelois (*Premier livre*) uses the same terms and symbols for the two vibrato types.

[12] *Livre d'airs*, Preface. The *plainte* is most likely the French-type *accent*.

[13] *Principes*, pp. 29-30.

[14] *Premier livre*, Preface.

[15] *Méthode pour la flute*, p. 30.

[16] *Principes* (1st and 2nd eds.), pp. 20-21.

[17] *Éléments*, p. 73.

[18] *Principes*, p. 85.

[19] *Le Parfait maître*, p. 50.

Bérard and Blanchet also speak of a *flatté* or *balancé*. Their reference to "manièrant un peu le Son" points to vibrato meaning since on a previous page the *sons manièrés* are said to contain weak oscillations.[20]

David calls a vibrato-like oscillation *plainte*, which he describes as "son filé et aspiré" and illustrates as shown in Ex. *e*.[21] La Chapelle distinguishes for the voice a prepared and an unprepared *balancement*. In the former (symbol: ⊥) the preparation consists in a gradual crescendo of the voice prior to the start of the oscillations. In the unprepared type (symbol: |) the oscillations start immediately (Ex. *f*).[22]

Ex. 45.3.

Later in the century, Choquel defines *balancement* as voice inflections which do not borrow from any other sound.[23] Lacassagne describes a type of *martellement* that consists of simple "vibrations or tremors on the same pitch" ("de simples vibrations ou frémissements sur le même Ton") and may be marked by the symbol: ⌒ .[24] Raparlier and Bailleux, as usual, simply plagiarize Montéclair.

Brossard, whose dictionary of 1703 is devoted mainly to the explanation of Italian terms and practices, distinguishes the *tremolo* from the *trillo à l'Italienne*.[25] He describes the *tremolo* for strings as a pulsation of the *bow* which enables the

[20] Bérard, *L'art*, pp. 119 and 132; Blanchet, *L'art*, pp. 116 and 126; explanation of *sons manièrés*: Bérard, p. 31.

[21] *Méthode*, p. 136.

[22] *Vrais principes*, II, 16.

[23] *La musique*, p. 173.

[24] *Traité*, p. 65.

[25] *Dictionnaire*, s.v. *tremolo* and *trillo*.

performer to play several notes on the same pitch with one stroke "as if to imitate the *tremblant* of the organ." The same grace, he says, is also often marked for the voice; as an example for both voice and instrument, he cites the *trembleurs* from Lully's opera, *Isis*.

Brossard's bow tremolo is of special interest, because it reaffirms a practice which Ganassi had described 150 years earlier in Italy. With this string or voice *tremolo*, Brossard contrasts the Italian *trillo* with its repeated and accelerated repercussions on the same pitch. The very contradistinction which he makes between the *tremolo* and the *trillo* is additional proof that the *trillo* was not simply a measured vibrato of the *balancement* type, but that its tones were often distinctly articulated.

For the better part of the 18th century there is strangely little mention of the string vibrato in France. Corrette does not refer to it in his *Ecole d'Orphée* of 1738 for the violin, nor in his *Méthode* of 1741 for the cello. It is more surprising that L'Abbé le Fils in his much more substantial treatise of 1761 failed to mention it too; but these omissions must not be taken as an indication that the French violinists and cellists did not use the vibrato. The technique was known and certainly applied. Mersenne had, after all, implied its use for the violin in the early 17th century. Dard, in 1769, using the wavy-line symbol, describes the bow vibrato—"en appuyant [l'archet] peu et beaucoup"—and Signoretti, in 1777, speaks of the vibrato with the left hand. The latter uses the term *balancé* and the symbol of the wavy line.[26] François Joseph Gossec, in his *Messe des Morts* of 1760, lavishly uses the bow undulations (with the same symbol) on repeated notes, with a near-certain concomitant left-hand vibrato.

THE VIBRATO IN ITALY

The first known reference to the string vibrato in Italy is probably the following interesting passage from Ganassi's viol treatise of 1543: "At times one trembles with the bow arm and with the fingers of the hand around the neck in order to achieve an expression appropriate for sad and aggrieved music. . . ."[27] He speaks here clearly of a combination of left- and right-hand vibrato, the latter consisting of bow pulsations which produce intensity oscillations within a continuing sound.

Eighty years later, Carlo Farina, a pioneer of virtuoso violin playing, explains in the preface to his *Capriccio stravagante* (1627) the *tremolo* as being done "by pulsating the hand that carries the bow in the manner of the tremulant of the organ." Cesti in his *Pomo d'oro* of 1666 resorts to such bow tremolo to depict Pallas Athene's trembling with rage after being slighted; he uses the wavy line for all upper strings, as shown in Ex. 45.4.

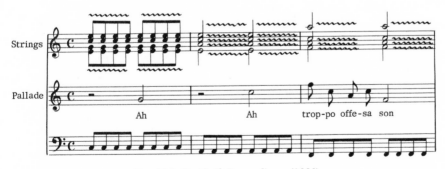

Ex. 45.4. Cesti, *Il Pomo d'oro* (1666)

[26] Dard, *Nouveaux principes*, p. 17; Signoretti, *Méthode*, p. 11.

[27] *Regola Rubertina*, pt. 1, ch. 2.

When Vivaldi writes the passage of accelerated tone repetition given in Ex. 45.5,[28] the slur marks suggest a legato bow pulsation for the violins, while a sharper articulation, the staccato type of the *trillo*, seems intended for the voice. Interesting in the violin parts is the syncopation-like dynamic pattern of piano on the heavy, forte on the light beats (which may have implied a crescendo-decrescendo pattern).

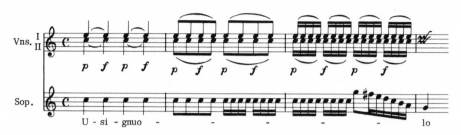

Ex. 45.5. Vivaldi, Cantata *L'Usignuolo*

During the 18th century we still frequently find the wavy-line symbol for strings with vibrato meaning. Practically always the symbol is connected with repeated notes, which suggests an undulation affect of the bow, presumably supplemented by left-hand vibrato. Example 45.6 shows characteristic passages from Padre Martini[29] and Veracini.[30]

Ex. 45.6.

These bow pulsations, indicated by the wavy line, seem to have had an international currency on a much wider scale than generally suspected. In 1659 the Englishman Christopher Simpson describes the bow vibrato and warns against its overuse: "Some also affect a Shake or Tremble with the Bow, like a Shaking-Stop of an Organ, but the frequent use thereof is not (in my opinion) much commendable."[31] Purcell, in *King Arthur*, Act 3, Scene 2, uses the wavy line to indicate first bow oscillations, then the shivering of the voice at the rise of the "Cold Genius." Brossard's definition of the bow tremolo has already been mentioned and a generation later we shall find it described by Mattheson and Walther.

Tartini devotes in his ornamentation treatise a whole chapter to the *tremolo*, referring now with this term solely to the left-hand vibrato.[32] In describing the

[28] *Foà* 28, f. 146.
[29] *D. Chisciotte, Intermezzo secondo,* aut. Bol. HH 37.
[30] Francesco Veracini, *Sonate accademiche,*
[31] *Division-Violist*, p. 9.
[32] *Regole*, facs. ed., pp. 15-16.

Op. 2 (London and Florence, n.d. [1744]).

shaking of the hand which generates the oscillations, he says that the finger should be slightly lifted from the string without losing contact with it ("senza che il dito abbandoni la Corda alzando però un poco il dito della Corda"). The "lifting" without separation implies the kind of periodic pressure changes which add intensity and timbre fluctuation to those of pitch. Tartini shows how the speed of the vibrato can be varied, being even, slow, fast, or accelerating in speed according to the needs of the "affect." In a somewhat obscure sentence he bans the vibrato from the *mesa di voce.*[33]

Tartini clearly reserved the string vibrato for special occasions, treating it as a genuine ornament. He singles out as particularly fitting contexts final notes or sustained notes in syncopated designs such as the ones given in Ex. 45.7. He uses no symbols.

Ex. 45.7. Tartini

Geminiani recommends a much more frequent use of the vibrato which he calls "close shake" in the text and *tremolo* in the musical illustrations; he marks it with the symbol of the wavy line that usually was more commonly associated with the bow vibrato. He mentions strong finger pressure, a slow and even shaking of the wrist, and points to the various affects the vibrato can help produce on long notes. On short notes, it simply "makes their sound more agreeable and for this reason it should be made use of as often as possible."[34] Like Tartini, he does not mention the bow vibrato.

With regard to the voice, the usual pitch vibrato was probably taken for granted in artistic tone production.

Another form of the vibrato, the "legato" style of tone repetition, was used during the 17th century and later. As will be remembered, it coexisted with its staccato counterpart, the regular *trillo*, and merged with the latter in transitional patterns. This legato wavering of the voice seems to be less frequently prescribed than the corresponding wavering of the bow. Interesting examples of an intended tremor of the voice can be seen in Steffani's *Tassilone*, in Gheroldo's aria (No. 14), where they are marked three times with the wavy line on the word *lagrima* (tear).

Theoretical information about these tone oscillations and repetitions (except for Brossard) comes mainly from German sources. Many of them have been quoted before in Chapter 28 and some supplementary information will be offered in the following pages.

THE VIBRATO IN GERMANY

An early mention of the vibrato is made in mid-16th century by Martin Agricola who, speaking of Polish violins (*Polische Geigen*), tells in poetic form how the "trembling" (*zittern frey*) sweetens the melody.[35]

[33] The term *mesa di voce* usually stood for a crescendo-decrescendo phrasing on a long-held note, which seems to favor vibrato use. It is possible, though, that Tartini may have used it in a different meaning, as did Domenico Mazzocchi to whom it meant a simple emphasis. In the preface to his *Madrigale a cinque voci . . .* (Rome, 1638), Mazzocchi uses the V symbol to indicate *sollevatione, o messa di voce,* whereas a C symbol describes the very crescendo-decrescendo which is more commonly associated with the term *mesa di voce.*

[34] *The art,* Preface and p. 26, Ex. 18, fig. 14.

[35] *Musica instrumentalis deudsch* (revised ed., 1545), f. 42.

In the 17th century, when documentation becomes more abundant and Italian ornamental practices dominate the German scene, we find, as we did in Italy, the frequent ambiguity between the staccato and legato types of tone repetition, i.e. between the *trillo* and the *tremolo*. Often it is not easy to say which one is meant, or where one ends and the other begins. For this reason a good part of the documentation bearing on the *tremolo*-vibrato complex had to be presented in Chapter 28 and will only be briefly referred to in the following.

The *trilli* of Praetorius (1619), Herbst (1642), and Crüger (1654) probably leaned toward the staccato style (see above Exx. 28.3c, d, and 28.4d). Printz made a clear distinction between the (staccato) *trillo* and the (legato) *trilletto*. He shed further light on the vibrato nature of the *trilletto* by adding that string instruments achieve the same effect by a fast-recurring pressing down of the finger without its complete release from the strings.[36]

Mylius (1685) mentions the vocal *tremolo*—apparently the legato type—calls it *ardire*, and considers it to be "more a fault than a feat" ("mehr ein Vitium als ein Kunststück").[37] Stierlein's *tremulus* or "Beben in unisono" (1691, Ex. 28.7a) was a measured vibrato. Feyertag's contrasting pair of *trillo* and *trilletto* (1695), like Printz's distinction, corresponded to the staccato and legato types. For Feyertag's model of the *trillo*—he has none for the *trilletto*—see Ex. 28.11d. Beyer's *tremolo* (1703) is illustrated in the manner of Caccini's *trillo* (Ex. 28.12c), but the term alone would seem to point to the legato style, hence to vibrato meaning. A similar ambiguity is manifest in Fuhrmann (1706) who illustrates his *tremoletto* (Ex. 28.14f) with the relatively new staccato dots; yet, as noted before, he explains the grace in unmistakable vibrato terms by a reference to the violin. Sperling (1708) writes that a slur (*Ligatur*) over several notes of the same pitch indicates that they are to be sung with a *Tremolant*. On a later page he describes a *tremolo* or *tremolante* as a micro-trill, where the upper note is either not touched at all or only barely "half-touched" ("fast nur halb berühret werde"). Thus, he says, "a *tremolante* is, so to speak, only a half-trill."[38]

Walther (1732) echoes Brossard by limiting the term *tremolo* for string instruments primarily to bow pulsations, sometimes referred to as *ondeggiando* ("mit einem zitternden Strich") in imitation of the organ tremulant.[39]

Mattheson (1739) stresses the one-pitch nature of the vibrato, which he calls *Tremolo* or *Beben*.[40] It involves, he says, only the very gentlest wavering (*allergelindeste Schwebung*) on a single, definite tone, as produced on instruments "especially lutes, violins and clavichords" by simple pulsation of the fingertip without yielding its place. The tremulant on the organ, he says, has nothing to do with a different pitch, only with oscillating air streams. He adds significantly that such type of pulsation can be produced on the violin with the *bow alone* (par. 28) with no need of a change in pitch. Thus the Ganassi-Brossard bow *tremolo* finds after Walther a second important confirmation in Germany.

Leopold Mozart's discussion of the violin vibrato is completely derived from Tartini, whose examples are bodily taken over.[41] There is no need to report on it except for his revealing remark that there are players who "tremble constantly on every note, as if they had the permanent fever" (par. 3). This remark shows two things: that the incessant vibrato of the present day was practiced at least by some players two hundred years ago; and second, that L. Mozart, in agreement with Tartini, rejected it as being in bad taste.

[36] *Musica modulatoria*, p. 58, repeated in both *Compendium* (1689 ed.), p. 51, and *Phrynis*, II, 63. The description of the violin vibrato (in *Phrynis*) is remarkably similar to that given by Tartini seventy-five years later.

[37] *Rudimenta*, ch. 5 (no pagin.).
[38] *Porta musica*, pp. 68, 84.
[39] *Lexicon*, s.v. *tremolo*.
[40] *Capellmeister*, pt. II, ch. 3, pars. 27-29.
[41] *Violinschule*, ch. 11, pars. 1-7.

J. S. Bach uses the wavy-line symbol with unquestionable vibrato meaning a few times for the voice and for melody instruments. It will be remembered that the symbol has the meaning of an extended trill only for his keyboard works. Example 45.8 shows such passages for the voice taken from the following works: Cantata 66 (Exx. *a* and *b*); Cantata 116 (Ex. *c*); Cantata 87 (Ex. *d*, not in the score, but, as Alfred Dürr assumes, an autograph addition in the original part); the early version of the *Magnificat* (Ex. *e*); the final D major version of the *Magnificat* (Ex. *f*; here the same wavering effect of the voice is indicated by the slur marks over the repeated notes). Examples *g* and *h* are from the *St. John Passion* where they are contained in the original parts, not the score. Example *i* is from the Thomana parts of Cantata 137.

Ex. 45.8.

These vocal examples have a common bond in their chromatic progression and in their connection with words that express a strong affect such as fear (Exx. *c*, *d*, *e*), sorrow (Exx. *a*, *h*, *i*), victory in God (Ex. *b*), or the imploration of God's pity (Ex. *g*). The feeling of gloom and anxiety alone precludes trill meaning for the wavy line. Quite apart from the revealing notation of the example from the *Magnificat*, what would be more incongruous than to have a trill over the words *tot, tot* (dead); what, on the other hand, is more fitting than to dramatize such emotion by a tremor, a wavering of the voice? Vibrato in the sense of intensity fluctuations is the unquestionable meaning of these symbols.

The same meaning can be assumed to apply to the few instances where the symbol occurs for melody instruments. Here too we find the same characteristic chromatic progressions which establish an unmistakable link to the vocal examples. The case of Ex. 45.9*a*, from the Sonata in A minor for Unaccompanied Violin, is particularly intriguing. Editors and performers alike have invariably interpreted the double wavy line as a trill, most often as a double trill, sometimes as a single one. Yet for several reasons both of these interpretations are incorrect. First, Bach's clear *tr* sign over the d sharp by itself excludes trill meaning for the wavy line that precedes it and carefully stops at the second quarter-note. Second, this particular double trill (with two whole tones for a major sixth) was not in the vocabulary of pre-Paganinian violin technique. Third, it makes neither musical nor technical sense to have a double trill on the first sixth, a single trill on the second; fourth, the wavy line was, as pointed out, not a trill symbol outside of the keyboard. There is no doubt that the grace indicated was of the vibrato type. Most likely it implied a *bow tremolando* combined with a left-hand vibrato as approximated in Ex. *b*.[42]

Another case, usually misinterpreted as a trill, occurs in the 5th Brandenburg Concerto (Ex. *c*) where both flute and solo violin have the vibrato sign typically for the *one* measure which ascends chromatically. Here, vibrato, combined with bow oscillations, for the violin and intensity fluctuations for the flute were most likely intended. The third example (Ex. *d*) is from the gamba obbligato in Cantata 76 and a final one (Ex. *e*) from Cantata 8 according to the Thomana autograph parts in the D major version (the part is missing in the equally autograph E major version in Brussels). The vibrato in all these cases is probably intended to underline the emotional coloring which so often is associated with Bach's chromaticism.

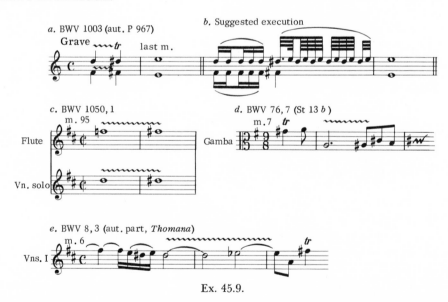

Ex. 45.9.

---

[42] Wladimir Rabey, who discusses this spot in an article "Der Originaltext der Bachschen Soloviolinsonaten und -partiten . . ." (*BJ*, 1963/64, p. 42), sees the possibility of an optional double trill on the first sixth, an obligatory single trill on the d sharp (a rather farfetched idea); however, as an alternative, he proposes the possibility of a left-hand vibrato.

Several authors mention the vibrato on the clavichord. Mattheson, as reported above, had done so in passing. C.P.E. Bach calls it *Bebung* and sees in it one of the special assets of the clavichord over the new pianoforte.[43] In a later chapter he says that a long expressive note can have a *Bebung*, which is done by rocking the key with the finger.[44] The symbol is the following: .

Marpurg distinguishes the *Bebung* from other articulated tone repetitions and describes it as an oscillation with continuing sound. The *Bebung*, he says, is done with the finger on string instruments, with the breath on wind instruments; he feels that only a few clavichords permit its tolerable rendition. His symbol is the same as C.P.E. Bach's, with the number of dots suggesting the number of pulsations.[45]

Türk in 1789 applies the *Bebung*, using the same symbol of dots under a slur, to the *Klavier*, meaning the pianoforte; consequently, he no longer speaks of "rocking" the key, but of reinforcing the tone by repeated gentle pressure.[46] Agricola also describes the *Bebung* for the voice and compares it to the violin vibrato done by rocking the finger. The grace, he says, has good effect in singing too, especially if done toward the end of long notes.[47] Finally, it is interesting that Deysinger confirms the vibrato meaning of the wavy-line symbol (shown in his illustration over four repeated 8th-notes). Speaking of a *signum tremuli*, he says that such notes are to be "played or sung quasi-sobbingly or tremblingly."[48]

"VIBRATO" is a collective term covering oscillations of pitch, intensity, or timbre that singly or in combination serve to enrich the musical sound.

The French gambists preferred at first a vibrato produced by two fingers. After about 1700, the one-finger vibrato, at first a necessity for the fourth finger, was extended as an alternate type to the other fingers as well, while the two-finger species continued to be used. Violinists could use only the one-finger technique. Moreover, all string instruments knew a bow vibrato (documented in Italy, France, Germany, and England), produced by oscillating pressure while continuously drawing the bow. This type of bow tremor, probably done mostly in conjunction with a left-hand vibrato, was apparently intended in most cases where the vibrato was prescribed by the wavy-line symbol.

French flutists also practiced a two-finger microtrill vibrato and, so Hotteterre informs us, resorted to shaking the flute as a substitute, when all the holes were covered.

We can assume that the pitch vibrato was an indispensable ingredient of artistic singing then as it is today. However, when the old theorists speak of oscillations on one pitch, they referred probably to rhythmically controlled intensity fluctuations, the "legato" counterpart of the articulated "staccato" tone repetitions of the *trillo*. These are the wavering oscillations almost certainly intended when Bach uses the wavy-line symbol for the voice (or for melody instruments).

No unified pattern emerged for the use of the vibrato. The bow vibrato and its vocal counterpart, the measured *tremolo*, were probably not often applied unless prescribed by symbol or suggested by slurred notes on the same pitch. The

[43] *Versuch*, I, Introduction, par. 11.
[44] Ibid., ch. 3, par. 20. Since the tangent which strikes the clavichord string remains in touch with it as long as the key is depressed, a certain wiggling of the key will communicate this motion directly to the string.

[45] *Anleitung*, p. 46.
[46] *Klavierschule*, ch. 4, par. 88.
[47] *Anleitung*, pp. 121-122.
[48] *Compendium*, 1st and 2nd eds., p. 11: "[dass man] solche Noten gleichsam hetschend oder zitternd spielet oder singet."

pitch vibrato, on the other hand, was freely used for fitting contexts. Though we do find some theorists who favor its frequent use, other masters advocated discretion. It is interesting that throughout the 19th century the most eminent string players and teachers counseled restraint and considered indiscriminate use of the vibrato in bad taste. It was not until the 20th century that the vibrato spread to engulf every tone. Small wonder then that today the vibrato is no longer considered an ornament.

PART IX

FREE ORNAMENTATION

Introduction

————◆◆————

The small graces prescribed by symbols which have so far occupied our chief attention represent only one wing of the baroque ornamental structure. The other consists of the "free" ornaments not marked in the score but added by the performer on his own initiative, sometimes improvised, sometimes planned in advance. These free ornaments can encompass anything from the briefest one-note grace to the most fanciful flourishes and, in the terminology of some writers, even cadenzas of considerable length.

During the course of this study we have on many occasions touched upon matters of free ornamentation. In turning our full attention to this subject, I shall attempt no more than a sketch in broad outline. Regrettable though this limitation may be in view of the huge role played by free ornamentation in the 17th and 18th centuries, there are several reasons that justify this imbalance.

One reason is the generally less controversial character of the field; the very nature of free ornamentation does not lend itself to the formulation of doctrines. Another reason is the existence of modern studies that discuss many of the known facts in a very satisfying manner.[1] A third reason is the ever-growing availability of *passaggi* written out by composers, as well as of theoretical primary sources in either facsimile or reliable modern editions; in a field where little can be learned by rules and almost everything from example, the ready access to authentic illustrative material is in itself the equivalent to a major study of the subject.

There is clearly no need to duplicate what has been adequately said or illustrated by others—nor for that matter what has been said about free ornamentation above in Chapters 4 through 6. The emphasis of the following chapters will therefore be placed partly on musical documents that are neither familiar nor readily accessible and partly on certain matters that are of considerable interest but have not yet received sufficient attention, such as the question of added ornaments in Bach's music.

[1] Among modern publications with emphasis on actual music examples the two most important ones for our purpose are Ernest T. Ferand, *Die Improvisation in Beispielen . . .* (Cologne, 1956) (hereafter Ferand), and Hans-Peter Schmitz, *Die Kunst der Verzierung im 18. Jahrhundert* (Cassel and Basel, 1955) (hereafter Schmitz). Among general studies, Ferand's *Die Improvisation in der Musik* (Zurich, 1938), is still the foundational one. The same author gives an excellent bibliography in *Aspects of Medieval and Renaissance Music*, ed. Jan La Rue (New York, 1966), pp. 154-172. There is much valuable material from all periods in Haas and many good illustrations in Beyschlag. For the 16th century the finest study is Howard M. Brown, *Embellishing Sixteenth-Century Music.* Max Kuhn, *Die Verzierungs-kunst in der Gesangs-Musik des 16.-17. Jahrhunderts* (1535-1650) (Leipzig, 1902; reprint, Wiesbaden, 1969), in spite of considerable lacunae, is still useful and has some good music examples. For the 17th century, Hugo Goldschmidt, *Die Lehre von der vokalen Ornamentik*, vol. 1 (Charlottenburg, 1907), is a very valuable study with ninety pages of musical illustrations, but out of print at the time of writing. See also the same author's *Die italienische Gesangsmethode des XVII. Jahrhunderts* (Breslau, 1892). For the 18th century, the most important study is the above mentioned book by Schmitz; see also Hans Mersmann, "Beiträge zur Aufführungspraxis der vorklassischen Kammermusik in Deutschland," *Archiv für Musikwissenschaft*, vol. 2 (1920), pp. 99-143.

Free Ornamentation of
the French School

———•◆•———

The flowering of the *air de cour* diminutions during the 17th century was briefly described in Chapter 5 above and illustrated with short examples from the early and middle part of the century (see Exx. 5.1 and 5.2). Supplementing this documentation, Ex. 46.1*a* shows an excerpt from embellishments written out by Estienne Moulinié in his book of *airs de cour* for both second and third couplets of one of his songs.[1] It is the only song in the book for which he provided diminutions, and he was perhaps prompted to do so by his wish to introduce slight variants in both meter and in the lute accompaniment. The illustration reveals that the third couplet is not more elaborate than the second, which tends to suggest that in other *airs*, which often had as many as eight or more couplets, Moulinié improvised new embellishments for each, but made no attempt to raise the degree of ornamental complexity. Interesting, too, is the unmetrical notation (including some unusual dots after certain notes) which exhibits a casualness related to the expected rubato freedoms. Bacilly, as was shown before (Ex. 5.2*b*), used the same notational procedures. Though Michel Lambert and D'Ambruis fitted their diminutions into the meter, unquestionably they executed them with the same rhythmic freedom that naturally belongs to all ornamental figurations.

The juxtaposed brief excerpt from D'Ambruis's late 17th-century collection (Ex. 46.1*b*)[2] is intended to show the progress toward greater refinement of diction which Bacilly was to point to as one of the earmarks of the mature vocal diminution style.

When the D'Ambruis collection came out, diminutions were becoming less popular. Even in Lully's time, and with his strong support, the prevailing aesthetic attitudes had become opposed to elaborate ornamentation and favored the *agréments* over the diminutions.

The ensuing atrophy of the French diminutions is reflected in the works of important theorists. Bacilly devotes the 13th chapter of his treatise to *Passages et Diminutions*.[3] The better part of this chapter is concerned with a defense of the diminutions against the rising wave of criticism. Bacilly speaks of the "considerable" number of detractors who, though outnumbered by the defenders of diminutions, are nevertheless "extremely influential." The critics, so Bacilly tells us, charge the diminutions with irrationality, compare them to a "comedian's patter," and accuse them of destroying true expression and obscuring both melody and words (p. 211). Bacilly tries to disparage some of the critics by casting aspersions on their motives, then answers others by stating that only diminutions that are either poorly invented or wrongly placed have the deplorable effects which the critics try to pin unjustly on all of them. Well-invented and correctly placed

[1] *Airs de cour avec la tablature de la luth et de la guitarre, Troisième Livre* (Paris, 1629).

[2] *Livre d'airs.*

[3] *Remarques curieuses.*

diminutions, so Bacilly claims, will add beauty and expression at no cost whatever to poetry or music. In postulating the principles for the correct use of diminutions, he lays the greatest stress upon the link between diction and ornamentation. Only long syllables, he says, can be legitimate carriers of diminutions.[4]

The bellicose and occasionally venomous tone of Bacilly's polemic reflects the power of the critical blow he was trying to parry. Whether he knew it or not, the handwriting was on the wall. Soon after having reached their highest point of refinement, the vocal diminutions began their inexorable descent and by the turn of the century seem to have been obsolete or drastically reduced in size. They did enjoy a sort of reincarnation in the *doubles* of the clavecinists, though these *doubles* were not improvised but fully written out by the composer.

Thirty years after Bacilly, in Loulié's treatise of 1696, the diminutions have

Ex. 46.1.

b. D'Ambruis (1685)

Ex. 46.1 *cont.*

become more modest.[5] Loulié distinguishes between *coulades* (the scalewise connection between notes) and the *passages* (rhythmically indetermined insertions of several subsidiary pitches between two notes of the melody). He illustrates them (Ex. 46.2*a*) for a simple stepwise progression but points out that any other interval can be similarly varied; he also illustrates what he calls diminutions, the rhythmically measured breaking up of a note into smaller values (Ex. *b*). Though Loulié speaks of notating the *coulades* with little notes, it seems that at least the *passages* were, or could be, improvised.

L'Affilard in 1694 makes no mention of diminutions. In 1736, Montéclair adopts Loulié's terminology and definition of the *coulades*, *passages*, and diminutions.[6] At first he says that the *passages* are indicated by little notes, but he adds that they are arbitrary and that everyone can make them at his pleasure. Examples 46.3 shows one of his several illustrations.

Montéclair obviously disapproves of such embroidery which, he says, is practiced less in vocal than in instrumental music, "especially now when the instru-

5 *Éléments*, pp. 74ff.   6 *Principes*, pp. 86-87.

a. *Passages*

b. *Diminutions*

Ex. 46.2. Loulié (1696)

"Simple melody" "Passages with one breath"

[simple]

Ex. 46.3. Montéclair (1736)

mentalist, wishing to imitate the Italian style, disfigures with frequently ridiculous variations the nobility of simple melodies." Montéclair then confirms in a memorable passage Lully's aversion to diminutions: "the incomparable Lully, this superior genius . . . has preferred the melody, beautiful modulation, pleasing harmony, truthfulness of expression, the naturalness, and finally the noble simplicity to the ridiculousness of the *doubles* and heteroclite strains, whose merit consists only in deviancy, in twisted modulations, in the harshness of chords, in noise and in confusion. All this deceptive luster reveals the aridity of the author's talent, yet never fails to impress ignorant ears."[7] What Montéclair calls diminutions are, as he says, "not arbitrary," for they always exactly double or quadruple the notes. Most likely these were not improvised ornaments but notated variants.

Improvised diminutions were not dead in France, but they had become more and more a marginal phenomenon. On the keyboard hardly a place remained for them; on the violin, where Italian influence was greatest, the vogue of the diminutions was also fast receding. Even the early masters of the sonata, like Aubert, Senallié, or Francoeur "ainé," who looked to Corelli as their master, only

---

[7] Ibid.: "[Les Passages] se pratiquent moins dans la Musique vocale que dans l'instrumentale, sur tout à present que les joüeurs d'instruments, pour imiter le gout des Italiens, defigurent la noblesse des chants simples, par des variations souvent ridicules. . . .

"L'incomparable Lulli, ce génie superieur . . . a preferé la melodie, la belle modulation, l'agréable harmonie, la justesse de l'expression, le naturel et enfin la noble simplicité, au ridicule des Doubles et des musiques heteroclites dont le merite pretendu ne consiste que dans les écarts, dans les modulations detournées, dans la dureté des accords, dans le fracas, et dans la confusion. Tous ces faux brillants decellent la seicheresse du genie de l'autheur, et cependant ils ne laissent pas d'en imposer aux oreilles ignorantes."

rarely wrote Adagios that were so bare that they cried out for diminutions, though some additions were often needed. Leclair, in the preface to his fourth book of violin sonatas of 1738, demands that his performers refrain from adding to songful and expressive pieces "that confusion of notes which serves only to disfigure."[8]

In midcentury we get further confirmation about the absence of free diminutions from Quantz who had studied French practices during an extended stay in Paris. Pieces in the French style, he says, are written in a way "that hardly anything else can be added to what the composer has written" in contrast to works in the Italian style where "much is left to the willfulness and ability of the player." He confirms this statement in a later passage by declaring that the French style suffers no extended passages ("keine weitläuftigen Passagien").[9]

Quantz only verified what could be found in many other sources and what becomes obvious on simple perusal of French music of the period. That the diminution practice lingered on here and there is certain, but since we are not concerned with marginal procedures that are condemned by leading masters and theorists of the period, we can accept the basic proposition that in the French music of the 18th century diminutions in the sense of extended improvised figurations had largely disappeared. Free ornamentation was therefore from now on essentially limited to the domain of the small graces, the *agréments*.

THE whole battery of the French *agréments* had been in improvisatory use in 17th-century France long before symbols were attached to them. After the symbols were introduced by the lutenists, impromptu use of the graces continued to fill actual or imaginary voids left by the composers. The composers themselves differed greatly in the use of the symbols. Some applied them with meticulous precision and with a density that could not be sensibly increased. Others were far more casual and followed the old tradition of relying on the performer to supplement what might be needed. The comparison of two gambists, Marin Marais and Jean Rousseau, both disciples of the same teacher, provides in this respect a revealing contrast.

Marais as early as 1686 provided his viol pieces with extraordinarily precise, varied, and generous ornamental indications. Some of these he declared could be played or left out as the performer wished. On the other hand, there is no need and hardly even space for improvised additions. It would seem that less was acceptable, more not desired. Rousseau's compositions have not been preserved, but in his viol treatise in which he describes the whole array of *agréments*, he had at his disposal only the symbol for the trill (perhaps because the printer lacked the type for others). Hence the other *agréments* had to be added freely. For this reason he went to great length to provide guidelines for the contexts in which each of the graces should and should not be used. Some of the keyboard players of the same generation, D'Anglebert, Le Roux, Dieupart, Grigny, generously sprinkle their music with ornamental symbols; other masters, among them Le Bègue and Louis Couperin, are more sparing in their prescriptions and leave more room for improvised additions. As was briefly mentioned in Chapter 5 above, Saint Lambert proclaimed with regard to ornaments the semblance of a Bill of Rights

---

[8] *Quatrieme livre de sonates à violon seul avec la basse continue* (Paris, n.d. [1738]), Preface: ". . . un point important et sur lequel on ne peut trop insister, c'est d'éviter cette con-fusion de notes que l'on ajoute aux morceaux de chant et d'expression, et qui ne servent qu'à les defigurer."

[9] *Versuch*, ch. 14, pars. 2 and 4.

for the performer: the *agréments*, he says, are extremely free and the composer's symbols represent not firm injunctions but mere suggestions that have no binding authority. The performer, Saint Lambert says, may either 1) play the *agréments* as indicated, 2) leave them out, 3) substitute others for them, or 4) invent entirely new ones in their stead.[10] The "four freedoms," as one could call these principles, seem to have represented widely prevailing conditions of performance. Some composers were not happy with this state of affairs. As mentioned before, Couperin insisted that his pieces were to be played exactly as written with no ornaments left out and none added. Couperin's feelings were probably shared by the masters of his circle, such as Dandrieu, Siret, and D'Agincour, who closely followed him in style and in abundance of ornamental prescriptions. Rameau's ornamental directives, though less profuse than Couperin's, were nevertheless plentiful enough, at least in his keyboard and chamber music works, to obviate the need for free additions. In his operas, occasional insertions of *agréments* will often be admissible though rarely indispensable.

Couperin was ahead of his time when he tried to enforce strict adherence to the letter of the score. Even though the French composers had by that time won the battle against diminutions, quite some time was yet to pass before the "four freedoms" disappeared from the scene; well into the second half of the 18th century, French performers, especially singers, violinists, and flutists, kept improvising *agréments* whenever they felt, rightly or wrongly, that they would thereby improve the composition.

In briefest summary we can say that in post-Lullian music we no longer need to be concerned about diminutions, except in certain violin sonatas and concertos with adagios in semi-skeletal style. For other media, the performer has to assess from case to case whether, in view of the rococo penchant for rich embroidery, judiciously added *agréments* would enhance or detract from the stylistic finish of a given composition.

10 *Principes*, p. 57.

47

Free Ornamentation of the Italo-German School in the 17th Century

The brief sketch of ornamental trends given in Chapters 4 through 6 brought out the differences that developed between the French and Italian attitudes toward free ornamentation. Germany during the 17th century, as was pointed out, followed the Italian lead for the most part.

The diminution treatises that appeared in Italy during the 16th century demonstrated how the melodies of late Renaissance motets and madrigals, as well as their instrumental counterparts, were to be embellished in performance. Example 47.1 gives a few brief illustrations from Zacconi (*a*), Dalla Casa (*b*), Bovicelli (*c*), and several examples (*d-h*) from Francesco Rognoni, author of the last known Italian diminution treatise (1620).[1]

The rhythmic simplicity of Zacconi's example is typical of most of his models. The older Dalla Casa's example is rhythmically more diversified and so is Bovicelli's, whose embellishments of a Palestrina motet start fairly simply, become gradually more luxuriant, and end with the expansive coloratura shown in the second part of the example. Francesco Rognoni is still strongly indebted to his father and other masters of the older generation. However, some modern traits are manifest in the frequent use of the *trillo*-type tone repetition (see Ex. *d*) and the much greater incidence of the "Lombard" rhythms (see Ex. *e*). His highly florid *passaggi* are still within the scope of melodic ornamentation and contain not a single trace of Bovicelli's innovative appoggiaturas, then 25 years old. Genuine onbeat designs are given only for the start of a melody note in the dactylic (nonharmonic) slide pattern familiar from Bovicelli, Diruta, and Banchieri (see above Exx. 20.3*a-e*). Rognoni's start either a third or a fourth below the written note (Ex. *f*) provides these alternative solutions with the express purpose of avoiding a possible dissonance. The integrity of the final note is always preserved with the extremely rare exceptions (no more than two or three among several thousands of examples) where the diminutions slightly spill over into the final note; yet in each of these exceptional occurrences the impulse is linear, not harmonic, as in the case of Ex. *g*. The only intimation of an harmonic implication are the rhythmically (presumably) measured cadential *groppo* patterns familiar from the older treatises (a.o. Ganassi, Bassano, Dalla Casa) which sometimes start with the upper note, sometimes with the slightly lengthened main note. Example *h* offers a characteristic specimen of Rognoni's retrospective floridity.

After the stylistic break that ushered in the early baroque and during the monodic reign, vocal diminutions were temporarily eclipsed and had to yield largely to the demands of affective declamation. As was discussed in greater detail in Chapter 4, rubato devices and dynamic nuances came to the fore, but the *passaggi* still claimed their right in cadences, in support of appropriate verbal clues, and, on a small scale, almost anywhere. The practice thus continued on a

---

[1] Zacconi, *Prattica*, I, ff. 64v, 74v; Dalla Casa, *Vero modo*, I, 40; Bovicelli, *Regole*, pp. 42, 46; Francesco Rognoni, *Selva*. In this latter treatise, except for the first page opposite the *Avvertimenti*, the next 16 pages of the first part as well as pp. 5-35 of the second part are not meant to be read in the usual sequence: each left page is followed by the next left page, each right page by the next right one, and so on. Many other irregularities concerning the numbering of the examples can also easily confuse the unwarned reader.

Ex. 47.1.

Ex. 47.1. *cont.*

lower key, and throughout the period the ability of the singer to invent and perform *passaggi* was considered as much a part of his professional equipment as it must have been in the late Renaissance. Monteverdi, in reporting on singers, judged them characteristically on their ability to sing *gorgie* and *trilli*.[2] Toward midcentury, now largely freed from monodic restrictions, *passaggi* apparently burst into full bloom again. No unified practice could have been expected. Differences developed between cities and regions, some of which were leaning to moderation, while others were more inclined to exuberance.

The absence of treatises during most of the 17th century and a good part of the 18th deprives us of information about the prevailing styles of free embellishment, and our chief clues are such coloraturas that here and there were written out in regular notation. From the early years of the monody we have quoted (Ex. 4.3) a lengthy cadential coloratura by Caccini. The following illustrations (Ex. 47.2), spanning the better part of the century, add specimens from Monte-

[2] Letter to Aless. Striggio, 18 Dec. 1627 (see Arnold and Fortune, *The Monteverdi Com-*   *panion* [New York, 1968], p. 77).

verdi, Luigi Rossi, Cesti, and Albinoni.[3] The Monteverdi example is especially interesting for the way it integrates scale passages, broken chords, the *trillo*, the regular (main-note) trill, the prebeat *Vorschlag*, the *Nachschlag*, and the slide into the coloraturas.

Performers on the violin, viol, cornet, flute, and other melody instruments certainly indulged, like the singers, in improvised embellishments in any soloistic situation. The area of the solo keyboard, however, remained relatively aloof. As was pointed out before, keyboard writing in those styles that would allow exten-

a. Monteverdi (1629), *Exulta filia Sion*

Ex. 47.2.

[3] Monteverdi (Venice, 1629), new ed., *12 composizioni vocali*, ed. W. Osthoff (Milan, 1958); Rossi, quoted by Burney, *History*, IV, 157; Cesti, *DTÖ*, vol. 9; Albinoni, MS, n.d., LC.

Ex. 47.2 *cont.*

sive embellishments embodied in most cases sufficiently florid figuration to remove the need for sizable improvised diminutions. This is true of Frescobaldi, of his students, Michelangelo Rossi, Froberger, and Kerll, of such Italian masters as Strozzi and Starace, and remained true to Domenico Scarlatti and G. B. Martini.

The amount and nature of improvised instrumental ornamentation in ensembles, in church music, and in opera is far more difficult to appraise. Schütz in the preface to his Resurrection Oratorio of 1623 encourages one solo viol to play diminutions in the recitatives of the Evangelist, but apparently not elsewhere.[4] Though the Italians were probably less reserved than their northern disciples, it is questionable whether their indulgence

[4] "Es mag auch etwa eine Viola unter den Hauffen passegiren, wie im falsobordon ge- breuchlichen ist/ und ein guten Effect gibt."

d. Albinoni (1694), *Zenobia*, I, 5

Ex. 47.2 *cont.*

went as far as Robert Donington believes that it did. Donington writes: "Where nothing was provided in writing, the instrumentalist partly prepared and partly improvised in performance the necessary material, which included fully independent melodies as well as chords to fill up the harmony."[5]

A passage from Agazzari of 1607 is the main source for this statement. However, the quotation does not seem to permit such far-reaching conclusions. Having been written in the infancy of the thorough bass, Agazzari's treatise probably still reflects Renaissance ornamental practices which carried over for a while but may not have long survived in the new stylistic climate. Moreover, Agazzari speaks of improvisation, but refers to diminutions, not to independent new melodies. The references he makes to counterpoint do not invalidate this assumption, since theorists frequently spoke of the need for contrapuntal mastery in the playing or singing of diminutions to insure proper voice-leading. Another quotation from Pietro della Valle also clearly speaks of ornaments, hence presumably not of added independent melodies in the vein of the *contrapunto alla mente*.

In Chapter 4 above I cited several composers of operas and church works who, representing the *new* style of the early 17th century, objected categorically to any diminutions of *written* melodies. How can we assume that they welcomed the improvised addition of entirely new melodies? Additional evidence which Professor Donington presents on the basis of an article by Gloria Rose[6] regarding a handful of instrumental sections in operas that were written in the score with only a single bass line still does not seem to support the hypothesis of constant melodic improvisation. Gloria Rose assumes, with good reason, that in the cases where nothing but the bass appeared in the score, the players were furnished with written-out harmonizations from which they could select the part that fitted their instrument. Also, she points to numerous and exacting rehearsals in which there was plenty of time to rehearse and prepare. Such "preparation" may have included the realization of pieces only hastily intimated by the composer, in which case the main improvisatory elements in performance may have been some impromptu embellishments by a few

[5] *Interpretation*, pp. 171-172, 606-609. *JAMS*, vol. 18 (1965), pp. 382-393.
[6] "Agazzari and the Improvising Orchestra,"

selected players. Moreover, not all instruments had to play at all times, and when a composer wrote only a bass line for an instrumental interlude, the continuo instruments alone may have played while the harpsichordist, in the manner of what was later called *partimento*, improvised—or prepared—an appropriate composition. Improvisation by all members of an ensemble would have resulted in chaos.

What we can reasonably be sure of in such situations is that harpsichordists, or whoever played the fundamental instruments, dressed up the harmonies with arpeggios and ornamental flourishes and were ready to step into the breach on their own whenever necessary; that other instruments reinforced the harmony parts; and that a solo instrument here and there added some *passaggi* and an occasional imitative phrase. But beyond that we move into the realm of conjecture.

Among the German commentators and propagators of Italian practices was Praetorius. In 1619 he showed only the simplest patterns of Bovicelli's diminutions, but these were merely a preliminary exposition pending the writing of an extensive treatise on diminution "in Praeceptis und Exemplis."[7] As mentioned before, he died before he could carry out his intention. Herbst, who later in the century (1642 and 1658) based his treatise on Praetorius's work, drew on further Italian models to illustrate proper diminution practice and quotes extensively from Donati, Francesco Rognoni, and Banchieri.[8] In so doing, Herbst confirms that the diminution treatises from around 1600 retained some of their vitality despite the changing style.

The restrictions placed on diminutions by the Italian monodists were also found in Germany. Crüger, in 1654, inveighs against abuse of the *passaggi* and criticizes those who transgress with coloraturas the limits prescribed in song "and obscure the latter to a point where one knows not what they sing and cannot perceive, let alone understand, either the text or the notes as the composer has set them." Instrumentalists, he continues, commit the same offenses, especially on the cornet and the violin. "It would be more praiseworthy and more agreeable to the listener, if on the violin [instead of coloraturas] they would make use of a steady, sustained, long bowstroke together with a fine vibrato" ("mit feinem Tremulanten").[9]

Christoph Bernhard voices (around 1660) a similar appeal for moderation. He distinguishes diminutions from coloraturas: the former remain within the meter, the latter may extend over two or three measures but can be used only on final cadences. Diminutions, he says, should be used only sparingly, otherwise they become difficult for the singer and annoying (*verdriesslich*) for the listener. They must not move too high or too low, not leave the tonality, not create parallel fifths (*Ross-Quint*), octaves (*Küh-Octav*), or unisons, nor destroy the harmony. They should avoid uncomfortable leaps and difficult intervals.[10] In the same vein of conservatism, he also advises that diminutions should return to the written note "in modesty" to avoid false progressions.[11] To do so, he says, is "better and more musical": hence, in embellishing the pattern of Ex. 47.3*a*, the version given in Ex. *b* is "false," and either Exx. *c* or *d* is "better."

---

[7] *Syntagma*, III, 240.

[8] *Musica prattica* (1658), *passim*. Noteworthy among the illustrations are one hundred examples by Banchieri (taken from his *Cartella musicale*) which are unusual in that they do not show the diminution of simply written melodies, but reverse the procedure by extracting the melodic essence from written-out figurations. Pedagogically they served the same purpose by juxtaposing plain and embellished versions, but the very idea of dismantling diminutions was probably unique among historical treatises.

[9] *Synopsis* (1654), p. 189; *Praecepta* (1660), p. 19.

[10] *Singe-Kunst*, pars. 36-39.

[11] This was Ganassi's and Ortiz's basic rule from which, however, these writers admitted numerous exceptions.

Ex. 47.3. Bernhard (c. 1660)

One reason why the Germans were more inclined to moderation in matters of diminution than the Italians is their more complex counterpoint. The denser the texture the less the need for ornamental enrichment and the greater the danger of interference with the basic musical structure. For this reason, some German masters seem to have totally rejected the improvised diminution practice. We owe to Fuhrmann a fascinating glimpse into Buxtehude's performances. In a catalogue of sins committed by performers, Fuhrmann lists as one of them the *vitium multiplicationis*—doubling the number of notes and ornaments indicated in the score. Such procedure he says "messes up" (*verhuntzen*) the counterpoint. Especially when two people sing or play the same part, such things are "patent folly." Whoever disagrees, he says, "ought to hear a performance by the incomparable Buxtehude in Lübeck who has the violin parts played not by two or three but twenty and thirty and even more players; but all these instrumentalists must neither alter a note or a dot, nor bow differently from the way he had prescribed it."[12]

For the small-scale diminutions that reached or crossed the borderline to "small" ornaments, certain stereotyped patterns emerged that were soon identified by specific terms. Before 1600, Italian theorists began to use *accenti* and *trilli* as collective terms, the first standing for many kinds of small melic graces, the second for repercussive graces. More specifically, they used the terms *groppo*, *tremolo*, *trillo*, *tirata*, and a few others which were not as widely accepted. As might be remembered, *tremolo* stood for either trill or mordent, *trillo* mainly for the tone repetition, *tirata* for straight scalewise connection between notes; *groppo* was less clearly defined but most often signified some trill-related alternation with a built-in turn. Other patterns seem to have crystallized later; taught by Italian teachers, they were transmitted to us chiefly by German theorists. Printz may have been the first to combine older and newer patterns in a comprehensive presentation. Starting in 1677 with *Phrynis* (II) and continuing through a series of related treatises, he shows an array of small diminution designs.[13] Some of these designs and terms keep appearing for some one hundred years.

Among them is the *circolo mezzo* (Ex. 47.4*a*), meaning half a circle, a four-note figure of the turn family which can be rising (*intendens*) or falling (*remittens*). In either case the second and fourth tones, which represent the principal note, are the same. The two half-circles can be combined in either sequence to form a *circolo*, a full circle. A closely related figure, with the actual turn either anticipated or delayed, is called *figura suspirans* (Ex. *b*). If this was a standard Italian

12 *Trichter*, p. 78: "Wem dieses missfällt, der höre einmal den unvergleichlichen Herrn Buxtehude zu Lübeck musiciren, der lässt die Violinen nicht 2 oder 3, sondern 20 and 30fach und wol mit mehr Personen besetzen; allein alle diese Instrumentalisten müssen ihm auch

keine Note oder Punct verrücken und anders streichen, als ers ihnen vorgeschrieben. . . ."
13 *Phrynis*, II (1677), chs. 9-12 (no pagin.); *Musica modulatoria* (1678), pp. 48-55; *Compendium* (1689), pp. 48ff.

grace, it was the predecessor of the later Tartinian *mordente*, the fast, anticipated turn. Printz calls a tone repetition *figura bombilans*, or *bombo*, or *Schwärmer* (Ex. *c*). It seems related to the *trillo*, and he shows it in groups of four notes each. The *tirata*, which the Germans call *Pfeil* (arrow), is a straight-line connection between notes (Ex. *d*), and the *figura corta* is a three-note figure whose first or third note is usually twice as long as the other two, except that, as Printz tells us, in a faster tempo they may be equalized as triplets (Ex. *e*).

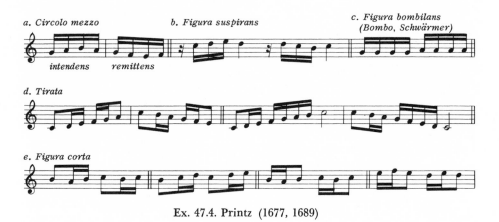

Ex. 47.4. Printz (1677, 1689)

Printz uses the old term *groppo* (or *gruppo*) to describe two different graces. One is the Caccini-Praetorius type of a turn embedded in a trill-like, though slower, alternation formula (Ex. 47.5*a*). The other is either a simple *tierce coulée* (Exx. *b* and *d*) or, more commonly, a four-note turn closely related to the *circolo mezzo*, except that the *groppo* starts with the principal pitch and reiterates it on the third note (Exx. *c* and *e*), whereas the *circolo* started a step below or above. Because in its four-note form this *groppo* seems to roll from one note to another, it was called in German *Kugel* (ball) or *Walze* (roller), terms already used by Herbst in 1642.[14]

Ex. 47.5. Printz

Most, perhaps all, of these patterns were of Italian origin. In 1701 Brossard listed some of them—the *tirata*, the *circolo mezzo*, the *groppo*—as Italian ornaments.[15]

The designs with their labels must have been widely known and used, because

[14] *Musica practica* (1642), p. 7.
[15] *Dictionnaire*, under the respective headings.

nothing else could explain their remarkable longevity. After Printz, we find many of these models with Fuhrmann (1706), Walther (1732), Mattheson (1739), Marpurg (1749 and 1755), L. Mozart (1756), and Türk (1789).[16]

The smallest impromptu ornaments, consisting of one- and two-note graces, were omnipresent in Italy as well as in Germany. Mostly they were prebeat designs in keeping with the general character of diminutions, but there were exceptions.

We have encountered several improvised prebeat styles for the slide (for instance, in Exx. 20.1 and 20.2). On the other hand, there was Bovicelli's favorite dactylic start of a melody a third below the written note (Ex. 20.3*b*); there was Diruta's similar pattern which he called *clamatione* (Ex. 20.3*e*), as well as Banchieri's analogous model (Ex. 20.3*c*) and Francesco Rognoni's two dactylic designs, a third or a fourth below the starting note (Ex. 47.1*f*). For reasons explained before, none of these had harmonic implications.

Christoph Bernhard may have been the first to acquaint us with what he called the "Roman" categories for the one-note graces: the *cercar della nota*, the *anticipatione della nota, anticipatione della syllaba*, and the *accento*. All four of these, according to Bernhard's description, had exclusively prebeat character. The same terms with the same meaning remained alive for a long time and were even recorded by Walther's dictionary of 1732. The only change in meaning was the extension of the *accento* to include onbeat as well as prebeat meaning. This was in keeping with the duality of practice, shown first by Bovicelli and, as documented in Chapter 15, transmitted by Praetorius, Herbst, Crüger, and Printz to their German public. Mylius, Bernhard's student, showed the same duality in 1685 and passed it on to Walther.

The use of the onbeat *accento* brings up the question of when such appoggiaturas developed from an occasional occurrence to the status of a quasi-convention in final cadences and in those recitative formulas that became partially stereotyped in the 18th century. At the moment the question cannot be answered and more research is needed. In arias and the like, the melodic-harmonic context which favors such appoggiaturas is infrequent before the end of the century and is absent in most of the cases where a prebeat *Vorschlag* is written out before the final note. It is this latter iambic treatment of last unaccented syllables which was a true 17th-century convention.

In the recitatives, we do find from the early and middle part of the 17th century falling thirds and fourths in chance appearances, but Jack A. Westrup, who quotes a few such examples, properly cautions against seeing in them precursors of 18th-century practices.[17] He does quote an example from Franceschini's *Arsinoë* (1676) which might be linked to the later convention. (This convention, however, was not nearly as firmly established as is generally believed. The reader might remember that Agricola, as quoted above in Chapter 16, referred to the insertion of an appoggiatura for a falling third as being done "occasionally" and, as shown in our Ex. 16.55, gave illustrations of its non-use.) On the other hand, the use of the appoggiatura was certainly possible in one or the other—or both—falling thirds of Ex. 47.6 from Stradella's *Il Corispero*, which incidentally, like most 17th

[16] Fuhrmann, *Trichter*, pp. 66-70; Walther, *Lexicon*, s.v. *circolo mezzo, groppo, bombo, tremolo, tirata*; Mattheson, *Capellmeister*, pt. II, ch. 3; Marpurg, *Crit. Musicus*, pp. 82ff., *Anleitung* (1755), pp. 39ff.; L. Mozart, *Violin-* schule, ch. 9, pars. 18-22; Türk, *Klavierschule*, pp. 388-390.

[17] Jack Allan Westrup, "The Cadence in Baroque Recitative," pp. 244-246.

century vocal works, is filled with written-out prebeat *Vorschläge* on unaccented syllables.

Ex. 47.6. Stradella, *Il Corispero*, I, 1

Apart from the *Vorschlag*, all the other small graces, on or off the beat, could be added any place where they could make a contribution.

Some German masters communicated their intentions in this respect. Johann Krieger tells in the preface to his *Sechs musicalische Partien . . .* (Nürnberg, 1697) that he leaves all the graces (*Manieren*) to the discretion of the player who, after noting the markings adagio or allegro, should be guided by his own feelings in trying to give pleasure to himself or to an interested listener.[18]

Somewhat unusual is the case of Kuhnau. Generally, composers strove for greater control over the details of performance, and once they made progress in that direction they rarely retreated voluntarily; yet this is exactly what Kuhnau did. In his *Clavier-Übung* (1689 and 1692) he introduced, besides the *t* for the trill, symbols for *Vorschläge, Nachschläge*, mordents, and slides and used them lavishly throughout both volumes. At this time in Germany this was a remarkable pioneering deed in matters of notation. As it turned out, however, he occupied this new ground simply with a view to teaching a lesson. A few years later in the *Frische Clavier Früchte* (1696) he eliminates all the symbols except the one for the trill. In the preface he explains that having demonstrated the use of the graces in his previous works, he now expects the performer to know how to go about it on his own.

FREE ornamentation played an enormous role in the 17th century, yet all that we have are bits and pieces of information surrounded by speculation. We know that even during the lean years of monody, small graces were needed everywhere and that larger ones were admitted on occasion, especially in cadences. We know that later in the century diminutions flourished again and became a necessity in *da capos* and in all slow movements that had a patently skeletal design. But we also know that some composers became exasperated by the excesses of tasteless performers. Much more research is needed to shed light on many dark areas. Among them are the questions of regional differences in matters of ornamental additions, also of individual differences with regard to such important masters as Monteverdi, Cavalli, Cesti, and Stradella, to name but a few. Problematic, too, are the licenses willingly granted to orchestral musicians (not those arrogated against the composer's wishes), the appoggiaturas in late 17th-century recitatives, and other matters as well.

For the modern performer of 17th-century Italian or German music who feels handicapped by the scarcity of historical models, Printz's tabulation of small

[18] "Was aber die Manieren an sich selbst betrifft, so wird es einen verständigen Liebhaber anheim gestellt, wie er nach Anleitung der Clausuln adagio oder allegro spielen soll: indem solches bey dem Affect und der Inclination eines jedweden beruhen muss, der sich oder einen curieusen Zuhörer nach Gelegenheit der Zeit wohl zu vergnügen gedenkt."

diminution formulas may prove very helpful. The patterns listed constitute a basic diminution vocabulary, and in many situations these designs will do by themselves, especially if occasionally extended by sequential treatment of the *circolo mezzo* and the *figura corta*, and if supplemented by the timeless devices of scale passages, in straight or bent lines, by trills, mordents, *trillos*, and generally by the *simpler* smaller designs of late 16th-century diminutions. Many of the latter are timeless and fit the 18th century as well as the 17th or 16th.

47. The Italo-German School
in the 17th Century

543

In defiance of the prevailing convention, Bach wrote out his diminutions in regular notes and did so with a greater measure of consistency than he displayed in almost all other notational matters. Thus, we do not find in his slow movements the look of austerity so typical among Italian masters, where the lack of short note values betrays on first glance the need for ornamental additions. He had good reason to do as he did. As Ludwig Landshoff wisely points out, Bach's music with its richer harmony, its denser texture, and its fast-moving basses presented far greater problems for the proper invention of diminutions than the much simpler fabrics of his Italian contemporaries.[1] Consequently, Bach had a greater need to protect his music from the dangers of inadequate skill and questionable taste on the part of his singers and players.

Since Bach was never totally consistent, we do meet once in a while with an instance where he failed to write out a desired diminution. There is at least one case on record where Bach specifically asks for a brief improvised flourish. In the autograph score of Cantata 99, Bach wrote the word *groppo* at the end of a long trill in the flute (Ex. 48.1a). His copyist for unknown reasons did not enter the word into the flute part, but what Bach had originally in mind may have been on the order of Ex. *b*.

Ex. 48.1. BWV 99, 1 (aut. P 647)

Bach probably expected the performer to add *passaggi* on his own in places where they could not harm the intricate fabric of the music: in rests between phrases, on holds, on cadences. Such *passaggi* are not diminutions, as was explained before, because they are not built on an underlying melody; rather, they are brief cadenzas that can occur in fast movements as well as in slow ones. Bach often writes out such passages, but he does so with lesser regularity than the genuine diminutions, and frequently he leaves striking gaps between phrases that seem to call for an ornamental bridge. Examples of written-out embellishments on specified or implied holds can be found in Preludes 2, 5, and 7 (*WC* I),

[1] *Revisions-Bericht*, p. 31. Bach's habit of writing out all diminutions was one of the reproaches leveled against him in the notorious attack by Johann Adolf Scheibe in 1737 (see David and Mendel, *The Bach Reader*, p. 238).

Bach's inclination for writing out diminutions was shown during his initial intense encounter with Italian music. In Weimar he transcribed, along with Walther, a series of Italian concerti (nine of them by Vivaldi). In these transcriptions he spelled out those diminutions which he felt were indispensable. Two interesting movements from BWV 973,2

(after Vivaldi's Concerto, Op. 7, Book 2, No. 2) and BWV 974,2 (after an oboe concerto by Alessandro Marcello) are reproduced in Schmitz, pp. 99-102; the Marcello piece also appears in Ferand, pp. 128-129. In the Largo of the first of these concerti, Bach did more than just ornament it—he added a polyphonic dimension by inserting throughout a new melodic middle voice. (The original Vivaldi concerto is printed in the Annex to the *BG*, vol. 42, pp. 124ff.) The style of Bach's embellishments is a mixture of Italian diminutions and the more conservative French *double* procedures.

or in the oboe coloratura near the end of the Adagio of the 1st Brandenburg Concerto.

In his autograph harpsichord transcription of the E major Violin Concerto (transposed to D major), Bach supplied some transitional passages that were not contained in the original version, as shown in Exx. 48.2a and b (both given in skeletal score). Note also the *tirata* added in m. 11.

Ex. 48.2.

The comparison of the two versions suggests that such flourishes would be appropriate also for the original. It is hard to imagine a violinist like Pisendel, who was steeped in the Italian manner of improvised embellishments, playing this concerto without *at least* resorting to filling in these empty spaces between phrases.[2] Very probably a violinist of such background would have also filled the gap in the first movement between the written-out "Adagio" cadenza and the *da capo* start of the ritornello, though in the keyboard version no passage work is inserted here.

The D minor Clavier Concerto, also transcribed from the violin and preserved in autograph (P 234), contains several interesting written-out transitional figurations, two of which are shown in Exx. 48.3a and b. Moreover, there is a three-measure cadenza-like solo passage on a fermata in the first movement (mm. 109-112). All of these *passaggi* are so eminently violinistic that it is hard to believe that they were not spelled out in the lost original version.

Ex. 48.3. BWV 1052, 2 (aut. P 234)

[2] According to Willibald Gurlitt (*Johann Sebastian Bach*, p. 82), Bach's Sonatas for Unaccompanied Violin were written for Pisendel. Gurlitt does not cite any evidence for this statement, but there can be little doubt that they were written with a virtuoso player in mind.

Similar connective passages are spelled out in several early Organ Chorales that were written for actual accompaniment of congregational singing. The passages connect verses after a hold (and incidentally seem to disprove the modern theory that the holds in chorales were not meant to be honored).[3] Example 48.4 shows two of these specimens from *Herr Jesu Christ*. For others see BWV 715, 722, and 732.

Ex. 48.4. BWV 726

It is probable that passages of this type were often meant to be improvised to fill in holes left open with a view to such initiative. Foremost among such contexts may have been *da capo* arias where the cadence of the middle part is sometimes separated from the *da capo* by an awkward gap. Once in a while an obbligato instrument might be the likeliest tool for such an ornamental transition, on occasion perhaps the voice (see Ex. 48.5a from Cantata 12 and the suggested approach of Ex. *b*). More often, such responsibility would seem to devolve on the continuo player. Example *c* from Cantata 3, shows a case where there is an obvious need to fill a vacuum with a transitional passage, perhaps of the kind shown in Ex. *d*.

In purely instrumental music, the places where the insertion of small cadenzas appears needed are less frequent, but they do occur. Two passages from the 1st Gamba-Clavier Sonata and the Flute Sonata in E flat (Exx. 48.6a and *c*) illustrate the point, with suggestions for their embellishment given in Exx. *b* and *d*. In the first of the illustrations, the hole, at adagio tempo, is embarrassingly large, and in the second, a trill alone (which is a minimal requirement) seems too bare for the implied ritardando.

There is also the well-known case of the two adagio chords which are inserted between the two fast movements of the 3rd Brandenburg Concerto (Ex. 48.7a).

[3] The main argument against sustaining the holds applies to certain chorale preludes where the hold symbols are written but where the polyphonic setting does not permit them to be held. The argument is not convincing. The holds in these cases were simply a matter of citation, identifying the ends of phrases. In many more chorale preludes, as well as in chorale fantasies in cantatas, the lengthening of the holds is spelled out. (See for instance BWV 647, 649, 651, 654, 668, 689, 694, 711, Cantatas 1,1; 3,1, and many more.)

Ex. 48.5.

Ex. 48.6.

To play the measure as written, as a naked progression· of chords, might have made sense if the chords were meant as a simple harmonic link, say, a modulation, between the two movements. But such is not the case. Both corner movements are in G major, and the chords represent subdominant and dominant of the relative minor; hence they are disconnected at either end. With their demonstrative independence, they have to be treated as a separate entity that provides, in extreme condensation, the contrast of a slow middle movement. To support this musical function, a degree of embellishment is necessary. Example *b* is meant to give no more than a rough idea of what might be done as a very minimum.

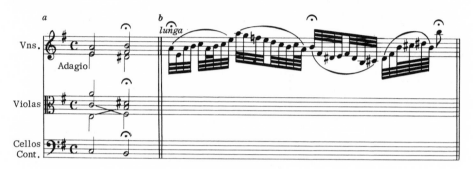

Ex. 48.7. BWV 1048

A different matter are the *doubles* in the English Suites (for the Courante of the 1st, the Sarabandes of the 3rd and 6th). True to their French models, these *doubles* are more in the nature of variations that involve not only the melody but the whole texture. Even in the Sarabande of the 2nd Suite, where the original movement is followed by a version of the top line alone and designated *Les agréments du* [sic] *même Sarabande*, the latter version leans more to free variation than to pure ornament in view of the substantive, expressive quality of the new melody which has a structural ring and lacks the light-weight figuration that could be easily omitted. These considerations are important because they suggest that these specimens from the English Suites are not to be taken as models for free ornamentation in other movements of Bach's instrumental works.[4] Thus, the Sarabande from the 6th Suite never would have appeared in such austere shape had it not been followed by the written-out *double*. A comparable austerity will be very hard to find in any other of Bach's slow movements.

Couperin, as he expressly told us, notated all the ornaments he wanted. Even without his saying so, the profuseness of his graces would have left little doubt on the matter. Bach may have often done the same, but we can rarely be sure, and in many cases we have good reason to assume that his notation was incomplete with regard to small graces and that some judicious additions would be desirable or at least acceptable. The degree of such apparent incompleteness varies greatly from work to work. The most careful and explicit scores are those few which he prepared for publication and certain instrumental works for which he prepared fair copies. At the other end of the line are scores, representing the first draft of cantatas and related works, written very hurriedly when Bach was

4 The *doubles* in the B minor Partita for Unaccompanied Violin are pure variations with hardly an intimation of ornamental character.

understandably concerned with the essence more than with surface niceties. Diminutions were too important a matter to be left out and were taken care of even in hastily written scores, but the notation of small graces is often sketchy, often completely ignored. The omissions of the score were remedied by the editing of the parts that proceeded under Bach's supervision and usually active participation.

The interesting dualism we find in Bach's vocal works between score and original performance parts has a parallel in parodies, in transcriptions and revisions. Frequently, the later version contains more ornaments than the original one. Such discrepancies raise the interesting question whether the earlier version was distinctly under-ornamented and never meant to be performed without added graces. The answer will vary with the circumstances. In the score-parts duality, the editorial addition amounts simply to a filling in of an incomplete notation. Hence it will be necessary to add comparable graces to such ensemble works for which the original parts have been lost.

In the case of parodies for the same medium, such as the transformation of a secular into a sacred cantata, the ornamental additions may spring from second thoughts or from the desire for better textual adaptation. In parodies for a different medium (concerto to chorus, for instance), idiomatic considerations may have played a part in the ornamental additions and care must be taken in evaluating such motives before applying the new graces retroactively to the original.

The problem is still more involved with successive versions of the same piece at different ornamental levels. The Inventions and Sinfonias are cases in point. They come not just in two but in multiple levels of ornamentation. The first version, contained in Friedemann's *Clavierbüchlein* (hereafter *CB*) which was started in 1720, is on the whole, though not in every detail, the simplest with regard to ornaments. In 1723, Bach wrote the famous fair copy (P 610) which in its original form has a few graces added, but some left out (the 7th Invention has more graces in *CB* than in P 610). At a later date, more ornaments were added to P 610 with a distinctly different black ink (Ludwig Landshoff thinks on the basis of a handwriting comparison that they stem from Bach's last years). An example of these additions in P 610 is the shower of some 30 mordents and 10 trills added to the E flat Invention which at first, in both *CB* and P 610, had no ornaments marked other than a single cadential trill (Ex. 48.8).

Ex. 48.8. BWV 776

Another instance of such later entries are the lavish embellishments added in P 610 by Bach to the E flat Sinfonia which originally had nothing marked except the cadential trill in m. 12.

A third source, P 219, though not autograph, is important because it derived in the early 1720's from one of Bach's students to whom we owe several other important manuscripts.[5] P 219 is based on the original version of P 610 prior to the later entries, but it contains a number of new ornaments. To complicate matters, additions in this copy are in various layers: while some were written with the notes, others were entered at various later dates and in part by different writers. A fourth important source is a copy by Gerber. Written in 1725, it also contains later additions which at least in part agree with similar later additions of P 219, thus strengthening the supposition that these entries were based on Bach's own performance or directives. Example 48.9a shows graces added in P 219 to the E minor Sinfonia, and Ex. *b* gives the beginning of the lavish embellishments to the F minor Sinfonia which were later entries in both the Gerber copy and in P 219. In both *CB* and P 610 these pieces remained unembellished.

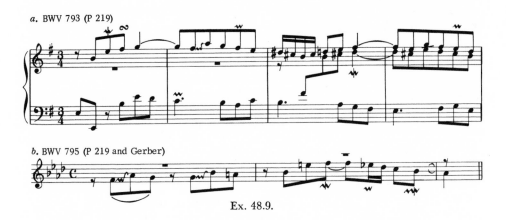

Ex. 48.9.

Such documents raise the following questions: do the earlier versions represent an incomplete notation in analogy to cantata scores, and did Bach never intend to have them rendered without additional graces of the kind shown later? If the answer were in the affirmative, it would imply that other works of comparatively modest level of embellishment were equally in need of impromptu additions. Such a conclusion would add a new dimension to the ornamental problem in Bach's music. Most likely the answer can be found in the concept of an "ornamentation belt," implying that works of the period can be legitimately rendered at different levels of ornamentation, stretching from a desirable minimum to a saturation point. The original versions of the Inventions and Sinfonias may be near the lower border of the belt, but they are not outside of it; they are not underornamented in the sense that they crave embellishment as do the austere Adagios of the Italian school. Though the lavish embellishments in P 219 for several Sinfonias can most likely be traced to Bach, they simply show what may be done on occasion but not necessarily what ought to be done routinely. All this simply means that the later additions to the Inventions and Sinfonias may be used but do not have to be used. Even Bach's own written additions must not be viewed as stringent obligations, because he may well have put them down as alternative choices rather than definite injunctions.

There are, however, cases in all types of Bach's music where additions of small

---

[5] Among them are P 418 for the French Suites, P 1072 for the English Suites, both of which have long been believed to be autograph.

ornaments are practically required, where such graces were not specified simply because they were taken for granted. Trills are most frequently omitted; yet on cadences and certain other contexts they were unquestionably understood. This particular matter was discussed above in Chapter 29, and a number of pertinent examples shown in Ex. 29.55.

On the harpsichord, another routine ornamental addition was probably an arpeggiation on a final chord of certain length. Depending on the tempo and on what happened prior to the final note, this arpeggio may have been done in various styles, singly up or down, or in multiple movement starting or ending in either direction.

The chief problem of ornamental additions for Bach centers on repeats or *da capos*, the classical places where ornamental enrichments had become a widespread convention. The concept *variatio delectat* is, after all, the fountain head of all ornamentation. It is only reasonable to assume that Bach's *da capos* and repeats ought not to be done as exact replicas. Sometimes a different registration on the harpsichord or organ, or a change of dynamics in other media, might be all that is needed to inject the necessary element of diversity. Often, however, it will be advisable to change the level of ornamentation. This can be done in two ways: in sections that are well marked with graces, some or all may perhaps be omitted the first time and rendered only on the repeat; or, where there were few to begin with, new ones may have to be introduced.

Where additions would appear to be advisable, it might be helpful to keep in mind the following patterns which show Bach's characteristic use of various graces. For the one-note graces, a *Zwischenschlag* can always be inserted in descending thirds, and often in ascending ones too. A descending *Vorschlag* may be applied to repeated pitches and to all descending intervals, even to such characteristic ones as a diminished fifth but not as fittingly to an augmented fourth. Great caution is in order before introducing a descending *Vorschlag* before a rising second or third, though once in a while it does occur in such contexts. The stepwise ascending *Vorschlag* will best be used only on stepwise ascent, preferably on a strong beat. On any intervals a fourth or larger, the leaping *Vorschlag* may be used—sparingly—either upward or downward; the *tirata* also may be used occasionally. The trill can be done almost anywhere, on light as well as heavy beats, but it should be avoided at the start of a phrase and is not generally recommended after a rise of a fourth or more. For the rise of a third, the slide-trill will be best, whereas the turn-trill will be better only on descent or on a repeated note. The mordent will fit best on a repeated note or on a rising interval—preferably, but not exclusively, on the beat. It can be used to start a phrase, especially on a strong beat, but should be avoided after a descending interval. The slide can be used on heavy and light beats on a rising interval of a third or more. The turn, indifferent to the place in the measure, fits anywhere where a descending *Vorschlag* is proper. The arpeggio can be applied to many chords but must not interfere with the rhythm of the melody and should not be used so often that it becomes a mannerism.

The rhythmic design of these graces will, of course, best follow the general principles and tendencies inherent in their use as was described before. However, the performer, in improvising graces, will generally do well to favor the prebeat types, because they add the needed variety with no danger of interfering with a harmony, a rhythm, or a linear relationship that Bach might not have wished to be affected. Onbeat graces need not and must not be avoided, but because of their stronger potency greater circumspection is needed for their use. Here too the better part of wisdom will be restraint. The performer should attempt to do what seems necessary and favor the lower over the upper borderline of the "ornamentation belt."

Free Ornamentation of
the Italo-German School
1700-1775

Germany followed the Italian lead during the 17th century in *all* matters of ornamentation, and it continued to do so in the 18th century in matters of diminutions, the "arbitrary ornaments" in Germany terminology. Since the latter constitute the major problem of free ornamentation, it seems justified to continue speaking in this specific field of an Italo-German School for the first two-thirds of the century, years that roughly cover the late baroque and *galant* periods. There were, to be true, considerable differences between masters, but they seemed to be less rooted in national than in individual styles.

In his treatise of 1723, Tosi offers many enlightening comments on free ornamentation, though the lack of musical illustrations is again a strongly felt drawback. He makes what may be the first theoretical statement about the embellishment of the *da capo* aria. In such an aria, he says, the first part should have only a few simple and tasteful ornaments, in order to preserve the integrity of the composition ("affinchè la composizione resti intatta"); the second part should be given a little extra garnish to show more of the singer's ability; in the *da capo*, "whoever cannot vary and thereby improve what he has sung before, is no great luminary" ("non è grand' Uomo").[1]

The embellishments he had in mind were apparently on a relatively modest scale and a far cry from what was being done at the time of his writing by many well-known singers. Tosi, writing at the age of 70, belonged to an older school that believed in restraint and abhorred extravagance. The depth of this feeling shows in the impassioned tone with which he fulminates over and over again against the excesses of the "moderns" and heaps scorn on their offenses against the true art of singing. He reminisces from childhood that his solfège teacher had told him about an ancient (*antichissamente*) vocal style that was insufferable because of its endless *passaggi* which were always of the same kind, "like today," he adds. Eventually, these passages became so odious that they had to be eliminated rather than amended.[2]

True taste, he says, resides not in constant velocity and in a ceaseless and baseless roaming of the voice, but in songfulness, in the sweetness of the *portamento*, the appoggiaturas, in the art and wisdom of the small graces (*passi*), the "unexpected deceptive play with note values within the strict movement of the bass" ("inaspettati inganni con rubamento di Tempo e SUL MOTO DE' BASSI"). Such are, he says, the indispensable qualities of good singing and they are absent in the "extravagant cadenzas."

---

[1] *Opinioni*, pp. 59-60.

[2] Ibid., p. 82. As a castrato, Tosi must have had his basic musical training in his early youth, which would place the reported incident around the year 1660. His reference to a very old happening suggests that the story refers to late Renaissance diminutions and their rejection by the monodists.

His reference to rubato procedures within the strictness of the beat is of particular interest. He contrasts them with the metric arbitrariness that was practiced by "the oldest singers" until, over fifty years ago, [hence around 1670] such procedures began to be rejected by a number of leading artists. He names especially Pistocchi,[3] "the most famous singer of all times," as the one who taught everyone how to apply all the adornments of the art without infringing on the beat ("per aver insegnato a tutti le bellezze dell' Arte senza offendere le misure del Tempo"). Several more times Tosi emphatically reaffirms the integrity of the beat as supreme principle for all ornamental execution. For this reason alone, he generally disapproves of cadenzas. He rejects them unconditionally in the middle of a piece, whereas he finds this "abuse" tolerable at the final cadence. Here, he says, the singer may insert a moderate flourish ("qualque moderato arbitrio") to show that the end is at hand, but must not do so "outside of the regular measure, and without taste, art, or understanding." It becomes intolerable, he adds, when the singer insists on "nauseating intelligent listeners with his tiresome gargling." He ridicules those singers who in a *da capo* aria will sing long *passaggi* at the end of the first section, much longer ones at the end of the second, and colossal ones at the end of the *da capo* (p. 81).

Interesting is Tosi's revelation that most of the *passaggi* were done non-legato. He distinguishes the detached from the slurred types by contrasting *battuto* and *scivolato*, but he declares the detached one to be more frequent. The slur, he says somewhat surprisingly, has only a limited application in singing and should not string together more than four notes. For the detached type, the voice must move with greatest facility; the notes should be articulated with great evenness and with a *moderate* detachment so that the *passaggio* is neither too legato nor too staccato.[4] Tosi, once again, counseling moderation in the use of the *passaggi*, singles out sicilianos as tolerating neither trills nor diminutions.

He names five types of small—improvised—ornaments (*passi*), "the most treasured delight of connoisseurs": the appoggiatura, the trill, the *portamento di voce*, the *scivolo*, and the *strascino* (p. 111). *Scivolo* presumably meant legato and its listing as an ornament seems to confirm further that the basic articulation was non-legato. The *strascino* (literally: dragging) is described in an obscure paragraph (pp. 114-115) from which, nevertheless, emerges the meaning of a rubato within a steady beat. Among other directives for the proper use of the *passi*, Tosi says that they should be rather well spaced from one another and should never be repeated on the same spot. Tosi, as mentioned above, speaks very sharply against the new fashion of indicating appoggiaturas with little notes instead of trusting the singer's judgment for their proper use.

Most significant in Tosi's presentation is the relatively modest scope he allows to the *passaggi* and his almost obsessive insistence on the integrity of the beat. His ideas may have been colored by retrospection, but he was by no means alone in his stand for moderation. Composers had generally little sympathy for the exhibitionism of singers but were often powerless to do much about it. Benedetto Marcello in his famous operatic satire (*Il teatro alla moda*) gives the impression that the star singers always had the upper hand, but as with any caricature, his picture was overdrawn; the situation was not always that one-sided.

---

[3] Concerning Pistocchi and the influence of his school, see Quantz, *Versuch*, ch. 18, par. 56.

[4] *Opinioni*, p. 31: ". . . tutte articolate con egual proporzione, e moderato distaccamento, affinchè il Passaggio no sia, nè troppo attaccato, nè battuto soverchio." A whole chapter is devoted to the *passaggio* (pp. 30-40).

Agostino Steffani, as stated by Hawkins, was extremely strict and must have managed to assert himself: ". . . he would never admit of any divisions, or graces, even on the most plain and simple passages, except what he wrote himself: nor would he, with regard to his duets in particular, even suffer them to be performed by any of those luxuriant singers, who had not sense enough to see the folly of sacrificing to the idle vanity of displaying their extent, or power, of voice, not merely the air, but frequently the very harmony of an author's compositions."[5]

Handel was not nearly as severe, but we have reason to believe that he did not permit excesses. We know from Burney that he ruled his establishment with a strong hand and rehearsed his singers individually and carefully at the keyboard. It is likely that on these occasions he let them know what they could and what they could not do. Also, we have a few documents which point to Handel's preference for, or at least to his satisfaction with, a very modest vocal embellishment style. Beyschlag reproduced Handel's autograph additions to his Italian Cantata *Dolce pur d'amor l'affanno*, which he entered for the benefit of a singer. Of 148 measures, only 14 contained additions written in little notes and they were quite modest.[6] Example 49.1a gives a few excerpts.

James S. and Martin V. Hall report about Handel songs in the Bodleian Library which contain what they consider to be autograph ornamental additions.[7] Again these additions are notably modest, as shown in the two excerpts of Exx. b and c.

Beyschlag takes issue with a piano score of the *Messiah* published in 1902 by Chrysander and Seiffert in which these eminent Handel scholars entered many embellishments with the claim that they represent "absolutely authoritative documents direct from Handel's performance practice." Beyschlag points out that of all the ornamental additions, only the brief cadenza (given here in Ex. d) was in the writing of J. C. Smith, Handel's copyist and assistant, in one of four performance copies prepared by the latter. Beyschlag goes on to say that all other embellishments printed in the piano score were apocryphal or at best of very doubtful authenticity, in that some were based on later entries by an unknown hand of unknown date, some could be traced to the tenor Harrisson who was born a year after Handel's death, and some were composed by Chrysander himself.[8]

William Babell, who was Handel's accompanist for the performance of *Rinaldo*, enjoyed a great reputation for his skill in impromptu ornamentation. He also transcribed many of Handel's overtures and arias for the harpsichord. Babell's version of the famous aria "Lascia ch'io pianga" from *Rinaldo* is reproduced in Schmitz (pp. 104-105) and shows remarkable restraint for the melody proper, which is chiefly embellished only by small graces. We find coloratura runs only to fill in gaps between phrases (which correspond most likely to the accompanist's rather than the singer's improvisation in actual operatic performance) and, understandably, a healthy flourish at the final cadence. From this document we might possibly derive an added suggestion that Handel did not favor the performer's insertion of overly luxuriant diminutions.

Often, however, what may have been frowned upon by the moderate school must have been redeemed by the superb style of a great singer. Farinelli's cadenzas and *passaggi*, some of which have been preserved, would have failed by a wide margin Tosi's severe standards of restraint, but they were universally admired as the epitome of the vocal art. Extensive illustrations can be found

---

[5] Quoted by Donington, p. 156.

[6] Beyschlag, pp. 116-117. The autograph is in the Fitzwilliam Museum in Cambridge (No. 252, pp. 11ff.). Beyschlag did not list the source and I am indebted to Prof. Alfred Mann for the reference and a photocopy of the autograph.

[7] "Handel's Graces," *Händel Jahrbuch* (1957), pp. 25-43.

[8] Beyschlag, pp. 117-118.

a. Cantata *Dolce pur d'amor l'affanno*

(d'a-)mor l'af-fan - no   se, com - pa - gno   del   tor (mènto)   Dol - ce

pur   d'a - mor   l'af-fan - no   se   com - pa - - gno

del   tor - men - to   il   se   le   pe - ne   u -

ni - te van - no   con la   spe - me   e   con   l'af-

fet - to   il di-let-to è poi   mag-gior, il   di-let - to   è   poi mag-gior

b. *Benche mi sia*

in   fi - de   l'al-ma   mi - a

c. *Alla fama*

ve - ro   dim-mi   il   ve-ro

d. *Messiah* cadenza in J.C. Smith's hand

Ex. 49.1. Handel

in Haas (pp. 185-187) and in Schmitz (pp. 76-93). In Exx. 49.2*a-c*, a few brief excerpts from Farinelli and two other virtuoso singers are reproduced from Burney's *General History*, where many more can be found.[9] The illustrations show Farinelli in *Orfeo* (a *pasticcio* of 1736), Moscovita in *Diana and Endymion* (an Italian *serenata* of 1740 by an unnamed composer), and Monticelli in *Alceste* by Lampugnani (1744). (Interesting, in the last of these examples, is the tone repetition of the old *trillo* type.) These were some of the famous singers whom Quantz had in mind when he wrote that in the first three decades of the century the art of singing had reached its highest summit.[10]

Italian singers continued on the whole in the same vein for the rest of the century. Cadenzas which Tosi disliked became an unchallenged institution. As the century progressed, singers, under the spell of rococo engrossment with lavish ornamentation, tended to push their extravagances to ever higher levels. Haas illustrates this point with a remarkable document of a Cherubini rondo of 1784 as sung by Luigi Marchesi.[11]

In Germany, too, the Italian manner continued for the better part of the century. Agricola, Tosi's translator, notes the latter's rejection of cadenzas and speaks out in their defense.[12]

9 *History*, IV, 437-444, 461-462.
10 *Versuch*, ch. 18, par. 56.
11 Haas, pp. 225-230.
12 Agricola, *Anleitung*, p. 196. He echoes Quantz's belief that cadenzas originated be-

tween 1710 and 1716 (*Versuch*, ch. 15, par. 2). The cadenzas, however, are older than both writers assumed and presumably go back to the end of the 17th century.

_a._ Farinelli in _Orfeo_ (1736)

in - a - mo - rar -

più - fi - da - in a - mo - rar

_b._ Moscovita in _Diana and Endymion_ (1740)

A con - so - lar -

_c._ Monticelli in _Alceste_ (1744)

Ex. 49.2.

They are justified, he feels, provided they follow certain principles: they must not occur too often and not be too long; they must conform to the principal mood of the aria ("müssen sich allemal auf den . . . Hauptaffect beziehen") and whenever possible refer to actual musical material. They must not repeat certain figures too often; nor should they be metrically measured or wander off into distant keys (pp. 203-204).

Schmitz reproduces the very lavish embellishments of Frederick the Great to an aria by Hasse, and a richly ornamented aria by Johann Adam Hiller from the latter's treatise of 1780. However, in some areas of the German musical scene, these procedures encountered after midcentury a powerful challenge in the aesthetic attitudes that, issuing from the Enlightenment, were hostile to the arbitrariness of performers.

Gluck was violently opposed to _passaggi_ and cadenzas, and his role in Germany was not unlike the one played by Lully in France one hundred years earlier. He did not, though, make any impact on Italy nor on those Germans who continued to follow the Italian lead. However, with the advent of the high classical style, the freedom of extensive ornamental improvisation was severely curtailed.

About 1715, Estienne Roger published in Amsterdam an edition of the first six of Corelli's Violin Sonatas (Op. 5) with embellishments allegedly written out by Corelli himself.[13] The many long arabesques of this much quoted version surprise

[13] _Sonate a violino e violone o cimbalo . . . Opera quinta, parte prima, troisième édition où l'on a joint les agréments des adagios de cet ouvrage, composez par Mr. Corelli, comme_ _il les joue,_ Roger (Amsterdam, n.d. [c. 1715]). For excerpts, see Schmitz, pp. 55-61, and Ferand, pp. 112-113.

by their luxuriance, and Roger North, an astute and well-informed contemporary observer, bluntly condemned the publication as a fraud: "Upon the bare view of the print any one would wonder how so much vermin could creep into the works of such a master."[14]

Skepticism must have been voiced from various quarters, because Estienne Roger felt compelled to advertise in 1716 an offer to show the Corelli manuscript and correspondence to any interested person. Since Roger, whose business practices were not always above reproach, never to our knowledge produced the documents, some doubts are still in order that the lavishness of the coloraturas, which often create a feeling of imbalance, were a true reflection of Corelli's playing style.[15]

Geminiani's way of playing a Corelli sonata (Op. 5, No. 9) is preserved in a document which shows far greater reserve and a better balance between structural and ornamental elements.[16] Since Geminiani, a student of Corelli's, was (according to Burney) notorious for his wild, undisciplined playing style,[17] the ornamental reserve seems doubly significant. Noteworthy is the discreet simplicity with which the third movement, a brief adagio interlude of eight measures, has been treated. The fast movements show considerable alterations that must have been intended for the repeat; they were variations, not ornaments, and did not involve smaller note values.

Geminiani gave us other instructive examples in dual notation. His Sonatas for Violin and Bass (Op. 1) were published in London in 1716 (and again in an undated edition c. 1732) in the usual plain manner. In 1739, perhaps with regard to an English public less familiar with the Italian style of embellishment, he reissued these sonatas "carefully corrected and with the addition, for the sake of greater ease, of the embellishments for the adagios. . . ."[18] What is truly remarkable about the edition is the lesson it teaches in modesty and the concurrent demonstration of how limited an amount of adornment can satisfy the stylistic requirements.

Because these two versions of the Geminiani sonatas are not readily accessible, brief excerpts are given in Ex. 49.3 which are representative of the whole volume. (In Ex. *a* the dash before the trill sign in mm. 2 and 3 stands for main-note support of the trill.) In his sonatas of Op. 4 and Op. 5, Geminiani conveys the same lesson by indicating all the necessary ornaments. Their style is throughout the same as in Op. 1.

At the other extreme we find a Dresden manuscript showing various versions, all extravagant, of embellishments to a Vivaldi concerto. Arnold Schering speculated in 1905 that Pisendel was the author and that the embellishments might reflect Vivaldian practices.[19]

[14] *Roger North on Music*, p. 161.

[15] Marc Pincherle believes in the authenticity of the document, but his arguments are not totally convincing (*Corelli* [New York, 1956], pp. 111-114). Quantz, who mentions this Roger edition (*Versuch*, ch. 15, par. 2), expresses no suspicion regarding its genuineness; he adds that Nicola Matteis has written other ornaments to the same Adagios. Unfortunately, the Matteis version is lost.

[16] Hawkins, *History* (new ed., 1853), II, 904-907; reprinted in Schmitz, pp. 62-69.

[17] *History*, IV, 641.

[18] *Sonate a violino, violone e cembalo*, Op. 1 (London, 1716); Le prime sonate a violino, e basso, nuovamente ristampate, e con diligenza corrette, aggiuntovi—ancora per maggior facilità le grazie agli adagi . . . (London, 1739).

[19] "Zur instrumentalen Verzierungskunst im 18. Jahrhundert," *SIMG*, vol. 7 (1905-1906), pp. 365-385. Kolneder (*Aufführungspraxis bei Vivaldi*, p. 56) supports Schering's hypothesis as "likely."

Ex. 49.3. Geminiani

Dual notation, or at least differentiation in print of the ornamental additions, provides the best insight into a master's style of embellishment. But much can be learned also from works in which the diminutions are written out in regular notation, provided we properly identify figurations as ornamental in character and are able to "decolor" them. After 1700, such written-out diminutions became more frequent. We have to realize, though, that there are intermediate stages between skeletal notation and fully written-out diminutions. For convenience' sake, we shall speak of "first-degree" and "second-degree" ornamentation which corresponds to budding and fully bloomed diminutions. As a rule of thumb, an Adagio is skeletal if it contains no, or only very few, notes smaller than 8ths; it has "first-degree" diminutions if it contains many 16th-notes; it has "second-degree" diminutions if it contains a wealth of 32nd-notes or smaller values. Generally, the skeletal types were always embellished; the first-degree types were usually further elaborated, notably on repeats. The second-degree designs needed no further enrichment but were probably often still surcharged by some performers with unnecessary and undesirable additions.

We find Vivaldi's notation running the gamut from skeletal to fully written-out diminutions, while most of his slow movements ranged near the first-degree stage. Locatelli's sonatas (Op. 6 of 1732) are fully ornamented throughout and include a number of cadenzas. Many similar second-degree specimens can be found with Bonporti, Veracini, and others. Bach was not alone in writing out his diminutions, he was alone only in being consistent about it.

The original edition of Handel's Harpsichord Suites contains two pieces in which the lavish diminutions were set off against the structural notes by smaller type (though they were metrically divided into the measure). We find this procedure in the first Adagio from the 2nd Suite and in the Air from the 3rd.[20] It would be a mistake, however, to take them as models for embellishing Handel's pieces that are written in skeletal notation. We can gather this from a piece like the second Adagio from the 2nd Suite which seems fully ornamented but on a much more modest scale (reminiscent of the aforementioned documents of restrained vocal embellishments). Here we find an extensive coloratura only at the final cadence, whereas for the rest, the embellishments are even simpler than Geminiani's. We can only surmise that Handel's own improvisatory practices varied with his mood and the type of piece, ranging from discretion to occasional luxuriance.

We find a similar range in Babell; in two volumes of sonatas, he wrote out all the diminutions and set them off in smaller print from the structural notes.[21] His embellishments are on occasion rich, perhaps overly so, but sometimes remarkably restrained. Example 49.4a shows his luxuriant style, reminiscent of the alleged Corellian diminutions, with runs moving scalewise in straight and curved lines. Example b, on the other hand, is a sample of an Adagio with only minimal embellishments. Sometimes we find very long notes completely unadorned, e.g. in the Adagio of Vol. I, Sonata 9, a note is held for three whole measures with no grace added at all. With most masters, and Babell is no exception, it seems that the first Adagio in a sonata was more heavily ornamented than the second one.

[20] A facsimile of these two movements is contained in the Lea Pocket Score edition of the suite (Vol. 86).

[21] William Babell, Part I of Posthumous Works: *12 Solos for a Violin or Hautboy with a Bass, figured for the Harpsichord. With proper Graces adapted to each Adagio by the Author* (London [Walsh], n.d.); Part II of Posthumous Works: *12 Solos for a Violin or German Flute* . . . [as above] (London, n.d.).

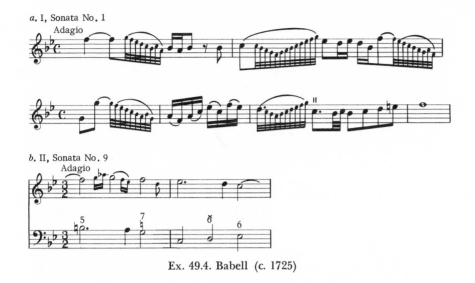

a. I, Sonata No. 1

b. II, Sonata No. 9

Ex. 49.4. Babell (c. 1725)

Tartini devotes more than half of his treatise to the problem of diminutions.[22] He calls them *modi*, and since he also includes under that name improvised small graces, the term here used in translation will be (ornamental) "figuration." Tartini distinguishes "natural" and "artificial figuration" (*modi naturali* and *artifiziali*). The *naturali* are identified as those that may be spontaneously done even by unskilled performers, the *artifiziali* are variants of the melody on a given bass and depend on the mastery of counterpoint. The borderline between the two types is quite vague. Though the *artifiziali* are more sophisticated and can become quite elaborate, their simpler specimens are melodically indistinguishable from the *naturali*. Of the latter, he says that they must not interfere with the melody nor form a discord with the bass ("senza prejudizio della medesima [i.e. cantilena], o discordanza col Basso . . ."). This principle is consistently followed in all examples which reveal, with rarest exceptions, the figuration strictly *between* the skeletal notes, as shown in the two representative models of Ex. 49.5.

"Skeleton"

"Figuration"

Ex. 49.5. Tartini, "Natural Figuration"

Tartini sees a proper place for the *naturali* in half-cadences which do not fully conclude a melody. Among the *naturali*, he presents the dactylic slide, which he says has "infinite use" (see Ex. 49.6a); then he demonstrates the application of the *naturali* to prepared and resolved dissonances (Ex. *b*). Here, he says, the figuration should be placed on the preparatory note, though the dissonance itself

[22] *Regole*, chs. *Modi Naturali, Modi Arti-*   facs. ed., pp. 20-43.
fiziali, Cadenze Naturali, Cadenze Artifiziali;

may receive a modest embellishment too (which in most examples is simply a trill with a suffix).

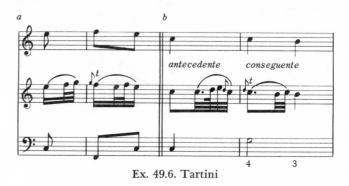

Ex. 49.6. Tartini

Examples 49.7*a* and *b* show the approximate range between the simple and elaborate designs of the more florid *modi artifiziali*. They are, Tartini says, best suited for full cadences. Significantly, they too respect in most cases the integrity of the structural notes and place their flourishes between them; and whenever a skeletal note is replaced, it is most often done by one belonging to the same chord. Rare are the cases of Ex. *c* where for the trilled note an appoggiatura is written out as part of the *modo*.

Ex. 49.7. Tartini, "Artificial Figuration"

Worthy of note is Tartini's formal proposition that *modi artifiziali* cannot and must not be applied whenever the melody or a part thereof is either of such thematic significance or of such specific expression that it cannot be altered and must be rendered as written.[23] It should be mentioned that Tartini deals also

[23] Ibid., facs., p. 29: ". . . li Modi Artifiziali non possono ne devono aver luoco in tutti que' casi, ne' quali il Tema della Composizione, o le parti della medesima siano o a Soggetto, o di tal sentimento specifico, che non possa alterarsi in modo alcuno, ma debba esprimarsi tale quale si trova."

with cadenzas and gives a number of illustrations, all of which are fairly brief and consist of purely virtuoso figurations.

Still more interesting and revealing than Tartini's theoretical discussion are a few examples of whole ornamented movements that are preserved in his autograph. Some of these gain in interest by showing two layers of diminutions, one very simple, one more elaborate. One brief excerpt, shown in Ex. 49.8, is notable for its relative discretion.[24] The graces for the first twelve measures are very simple, and where they become more florid (from the thirteenth measure on), Tartini enters an alternate version of only minimal elaboration, consisting mainly of the addition of a few trills; in fact, whole measures remain unaltered. Numerous performers of the age—among them many of Tartini's own students and followers who lacked the master's taste and sense of proportion—indulged in ornamental exaggerations that often disfigured Tartini's music.[25] Toward the end of the century, such excesses were pushed to a deplorable extreme in an illustration from Cartier's *Ecole de violon* (c. 1798) that shows a Tartinian Adagio with a choice of no less than sixteen versions of embellishments, most of them absurdly overladen.[26] Of such players Quantz says that they "overload

Ex. 49.8. Tartini, autograph embellishments to Sonata, Op. 7, No. 4

[24] A copy of the autograph (from the Capella Antoniana Collection), is found in Berk. B. E. 4 (item 724).

[25] Many immoderate ornamented versions from Tartini students and followers are in the Berkeley collection.

[26] This tour de force is reproduced in Schmitz, pp. 131ff. In the same book we find diminutions of a Nardini sonata also published by Cartier and showing the same questionable exaggerations (pp. 96ff.).

2nd version

Ex. 49.8 *cont.*

an Adagio with so many embellishments and wild runs, that one would mistake it for a gay Allegro, while the qualities of the Adagio are hardly noticeable any more."[27]

In Germany, Telemann left us two collections in dual notation, one of sonatas, one of trios.[28] They represent what might well be the most valuable textbook of late baroque diminution practice, because they strike a happy balance between austerity and luxuriance. They show respect for the structural notes which are not obscured and remain intact in their proper place; in the rare cases where another note takes the place of a structural note, it represents a consonant interval. For obvious reasons, the trio embellishments are much simpler, but their

[27] *Versuch*, ch. 18, par. 60.
[28] *Sonate metodiche* for violon or flute and continuo (Hamburg, 1728); *Continuation des sonates méthodiques* (1732; modern ed. of the complete collection, Cassel, 1955); *3 Trietti metodichi e 3 Scherzi* for two flutes or violins and continuo (1731).

execution must have depended on previous agreement during rehearsal. Interesting is the limitation of the embellishments to first movements only.   The second slow movements are rarely Adagios and either move at a sufficiently lively pace or contain enough small graces to obviate the need for further ornamentation. Since the sonatas are easily accessible, only a brief excerpt is shown in Ex. 49.9*a*. Of the two passages given from the trios (which at the time of writing are out of print), the first (Ex. *b*) throws light on the ornament-structure relationship by showing that all the 8th-notes and all the *first* notes of a pair of 16th-notes remained untouched, whereas some of the second 16th-notes were treated as ornamental additions (first-degree ornaments) and therefore frequently ignored. Example *c* was added for its special interest as a solution of a pattern often encountered in Handel and many Italian masters: a cadence in the form of a few chords separated by rests.

Ex. 49.9. Telemann

Quantz, in his treatise of 1752, deals at great length with diminutions, which he calls *Veränderungen* (variants).[29] Quantz very positively assigns the diminutions to the realm of the Italian style and sees no place for them in French

[29] *Versuch.* Chapters 13 and 14 are devoted to diminutions, ch. 15 to cadenzas. Unless otherwise specified, the references in the text will be to ch. 13.

Ex. 49.9 *cont.*

music in which "essential" ornaments were indicated by symbol and hardly any others meant to be added (par. 2). Outside of France, however, Quantz continues, musicians are not satsified with the "essential" ornaments and want to add diminutions. Because many performers do so in a clumsy manner, Quantz proposes to improve the standards of this practice by his detailed presentation. At first he states a few general principles, the most important of which bears on the integrity of the structural notes that must not be obscured and as a rule ought to remain in place. If occasionally another note is substituted, it must be one "from the harmony of the bass" and the regular note must be sounded immediately afterward (par. 7). We had occasion to note that Telemann's and, by and large, Tartini's practice agreed with these principles. The diminutions, Quantz continues, must not be applied until after the melody has been heard in its simple shape; otherwise, the listener will not be able to identify the diminutions as such (par. 9). A well-written melody, Quantz says, which has sufficient grace as it

Ex. 49.9 *cont.*

stands, must not be further embellished unless one is sure to improve on it, and such a decision, he adds, requires extraordinary insight and experience. Quantz sees a danger that extremely florid diminutions, whose brilliancy might astound the listener, will deprive the melody of its capacity to "move the heart." Therefore, Quantz cautions against indulging too freely in diminutions; instead, he says, players should try to render a simple melody nobly, clearly, and neatly (par. 9).

Quantz presents his material, as some 16th-century theorists had done, first in the abstract, in the form of brief melodic and cadential formulas, and later in a musical context by writing out the embellishment of a whole adagio movement in double notation.

It would not normally be necessary to reproduce here any of Quantz's illustrations since they are easily accessible in at least three modern editions.[30] How-

[30] *Versuch*, facs. ed. (Cassel, 1953); E. R. Reilly's translation (London, 1966); and par- tial reproduction in Schmitz, pp. 110-120.

ever, the music examples as such are incomplete because Quantz supplemented them with verbal comments concerning their dynamic shadings to compensate for the insufficiency of available symbols. Unfortunately, his comments are contained in numerous paragraphs of such forbidding dryness that they must have deterred many readers then as well as now. The instructions are fascinating since they display a highly sophisticated finesse of dynamic nuances and subtle phrasing. Example 49.10 shows a small sample of the embellished Adagio, wherein Quantz's verbal directives are transcribed into modern dynamic symbols.[31]

(Dynamic marks added according
to Quantz's verbal directives)

Ex. 49.10. Quantz (1752)

In Chapter 16, Quantz discusses the dependence of diminutions on the types, or more properly on the texture, of the piece performed: the greatest freedom obviously is available in "solo" settings such as the one shown in the above example. Next in line is the concerto, yet here the soloist has to refrain from diminutions whenever an accompanying part is entrusted with a melodic line

———

[31] The comments on the embellished Adagio are contained in ch. 14, pars. 26-43, while par. 25 contains information on the abbreviated shorthand employed and advice on the judicious interpretation of the directives. Quantz admonishes the player to use, like a painter, not just the extremes but the full range of *mezze tinte*, i.e. of intermediate shades, and also to utilize the diminishing and swelling of sounds.

Ex. 49.10 *cont.*

instead of with pure harmony. In a "trio" (meaning two soloists and continuo), the scope of diminutions is said to be small: they may be applied only to such melodies that are imitated in the second voice which has a chance to hear the embellishment first and follow suit. Melodies in thirds and sixths must not be embellished unless both players have agreed beforehand on what to do. Quantz hardly needed to mention that in a quartet the scope for diminutions is further reduced. Quantz has summed up the technique and principles of *galant* diminutions so thoroughly and so capably that there is little need to dwell in detail on the presentations made by later writers.

C.P.E. Bach gives short shrift to diminutions and explains why they need not be discussed. They depend, he says, on taste and style and are too subject to change; in clavier music they are often written out; besides, in view of the sufficient number of small ornaments, they can easily be omitted.[32] He does devote, though, a few lines and a few illustrations to the embellishment of fermatas.[33] Such embellishments, however, are small cadenzas which, as he himself had said, are improvised compositions not ornaments.

When a few years later, in the preface to his *Sechs Sonaten für Klavier mit veränderten Reprisen*, he speaks of the necessity for variation (*das Verändern*) in the repeat, he has in mind a reshaping of the melody, a true "change," not the insertion of diminutions. It is the type of variant we have seen—for fast movements—in Geminiani's version of the Corelli sonata and shall find again with Benda. In these repeats we find no fragmentation of the melody into smaller note values, the true mark of diminutions. Occasional increases in the number of notes are strictly coincidental and more than compensated for by other instances where the variant has fewer notes than the original.[34]

Leopold Mozart has little use for diminutions, and in this matter he significantly parts company with Tartini, whom he had followed so closely in matters of the small graces. He mentions only the standardized small patterns of the *groppo*, the *circolo mezzo*, the *tirata*, and limits them to solo playing only. In addition, he stipulates that they must be used "in great moderation, at the right time, and *only* for the sake of varying passages which occur several times in succession."[35]

[32] *Versuch*, I, ch. 2, sec. 1, par. 7.
[33] *Ibid.*, sec. 9, pars. 5-6.
[34] One of these sonatas is reprinted in Ferand under No. 37. They are available in a modern edition (Leipzig, 1957).
[35] *Versuch*, ch. 9, pars. 18-22: "Alle diese

Auszierungen brauche man aber nur, wenn man ein Solo spielet; und dort sehr mässig, zur rechten Zeit, und nur zur Abwechslung einiger öfter nach einander kommenden Passagen."

Probably the richest musical source for late *galant* diminution practice in Germany is a huge manuscript volume containing 33 violin sonatas by Franz Benda.[36] Example 49.11 gives a brief illustration. With very few exceptions, all movements of the 33 sonatas are written in two versions: for the slow movements the plain and ornamented lines, for the fast ones the original and the variants for the repeats. The latter variants are not, as Mersmann assumes, ornamentations on a par with the Adagio embellishments, but are, in analogy to C.P.E. Bach's "varied repeats," genuine non-ornamental variations with the melody recast and the note values as often augmented as diminished. In only two movements of the whole volume, the Adagio has two embellished versions, one simpler, one more elaborate. Generally, the diminutions are extremely florid, more so than Quantz's or Tartini's, and represent a late stage of luxuriance.

Ex. 49.11. Benda (1709-1786), Sonata No. 2

[36] BB Mus. MSS 1315/15 (PK). The first of these sonatas is reproduced in Schmitz, pp. 135-139 and part of it also reprinted in Ferand. An analysis of the whole volume and an appraisal of its significance is contained in the article by Hans Mersmann, "Beiträge zur Aufführungspraxis. . . ."

The continuance of the diminution practice into the late part of the 18th century is further attested by the treatises of Hiller (1780), Türk (1789), and Tromlitz (1791). These documents, however, reflected only a section of the German musical scene. As was mentioned before regarding the voice, in the realm of the unfolding classical style, the diminutions were gradually being eliminated. Mozart, as reported by Reinecke, used in his own clavier performances impromptu embellishments on the restatement of themes and occasionally filled out harmonies.[37] I. F. Mosel reports that nothing offended Mozart more than improvised embellishments in his operas. In such cases he invariably said that had he wished it done in this manner he would have written it thus.[38]

In Italy and Germany, especially in the former, diminution practice in some residual forms lingered on well into the 19th century and was not even limited to soloistic playing but continued even in the unlikely medium of orchestral performance. Spohr records with disgust the ornamental antics of Italian orchestra players; but even in mid-19th century German orchestral practice was not entirely free of ornamental arbitrariness.[39] The practice had its deepest roots in Italian opera where the willfulness of the singers must have infected the orchestra. It is of interest to note that Rossini was probably the first Italian opera composer to fight the diminution mania of his singers with the same method that Bach had employed one hundred years earlier for a similar purpose. Beginning about 1815, Rossini began to write out all coloraturas, leaving no room for any additions, and thus managed to protect his music from the encroachment of incompetence and bad taste. His example was not followed by all Italian masters, and for singers, the practice continued and has survived in rudimentary fashion to the present day.[40]

DURING the late baroque and *galant* eras, which are roughly covered by the period under consideration, the diminution practice continued, generally growing in luxuriance and occasionally degenerating into extravagance. In the vocal field, florid embellishments took on a new dimension with the fashion, originating about 1700, of adding cadenzas to many holds and sometimes even to notes that were not meant to be held. Tosi in 1723 asked for moderation in the use of diminutions and disapproved of cadenzas (except for a moderate flourish at the end of an aria), but the virtuoso singers of the era were not willing to accept such limits. In Italy and in its musically conquered territory abroad, the fashion of lavish embellishments lasted with no serious challenge for the entire 18th century and beyond. German singers who emulated the Italian example continued in the same manner for the best part of the century. However, the radiations emanating from the Enlightenment had a restraining effect on ornamental excesses, and Gluck, by vigorously opposing any kind of improvised embellishment, helped prepare the radical restrictions of diminutions that materialized within the classical style.

[37] Quoted by Haas, p. 245.
[38] Quoted by Haas, p. 259.
[39] Haas, p. 255.
[40] There are some recordings extant from the early years of this century that show some grotesque manifestations of singers' willfulness and presumption. Among them is that of a famous prima donna who inserted long cadenzas into both arias of the Queen of the Night. Even the formidable Toscanini could not entirely eradicate this usage. I remember a performance of *Rigoletto* at La Scala (1929) under his direction in which the tenor inserted an exuberant coloratura in "La donna è mobile" that was definitely not in the score.

After 1700, slow movements in the instrumental medium continued to be written in skeletal form and were more or less floridly embellished by the performer; some composers wrote Adagios with less austere lines, embodying in the form of many 16th-notes what we called first-degree ornamentation. In such works, further embellishments in smaller note values (second-degree ornamentation) were usually added, especially on repeats. For instruments too we find the same tendency to growing floridity of the diminutions as well as the insertion of cadenzas in sonatas and concertos.

However, at any given time there were great differences in individual styles, ranging from reserve to abandon. Corelli's highly florid ornaments are of uncertain authenticity, but they certainly document someone's practice in the first years of the 18th century. Geminiani was much more restrained and gives a telling lesson of how little was needed to meet the requirements. Telemann strikes a happy medium, while the styles of Quantz and Tartini tend to greater internal complexity. Yet both of these masters counseled moderation. Tartini's students and followers, however, became engulfed in exaggerations in which a parasitic overgrowth of embellishments totally suffocated the original melody. The absurdity of such excesses was self-defeating: the point of no return was passed and the only exit led to limbo.

In German instrumental music, diminutions persisted generally through the *galant* era and in certain Italian-dominated areas survived longer. But outside of the sphere of direct Italian influence, the aesthetics of the Enlightenment and the temper of the classical style combined in first restricting and finally nearly eliminating all improvised diminutions.

FREE ornamentation is arbitrary and therefore by definition not subject to directives. Consequently, suggestions for its use can be made only in the most general terms. One point to be made is the need to add some embellishments to Adagios that are unmistakably written in skeletal style. In almost all such cases we have to do not with "classical simplicity" but with fragmentary notation which the performer was expected to complete on his own. To play such a movement as written amounts to a misrepresentation. For Adagios notated with many 16th-notes of the first-degree ornamentation type, the decision will depend on the circumstances. In many cases some further embroidery in the shorter note values of second-degree ornamentation will be desirable. Such will be the case particularly where repeats are involved, be it of a theme, of a section, or of the whole piece. In slow *da capo* arias the repeat will practically always call for some ornamental additions, usually including a small cadenza-like flourish for a last hold. The first and second part might also need minor graces if written in an austere melodic style. The same applies to slow non-*da capo* arias as well. Instrumental and vocal duos under similar circumstances ought to be embellished too. Discreet ornaments would have to be prepared in advance to assure coordination and balance between the parts.

The design of the added graces is difficult to discuss in view of the enormously wide range of styles that were employed. The modern performer, unless he combines a gift for melodic invention with a sure sense of historical styles, will generally be best advised to exercise great reserve; in other words, he should search for the lower border of the "ornamentation belt" and not aspire to any degree of luxuriance. The illustrations given above from Handel and Geminiani offer excellent examples of how little is sufficient, but also of what seemed near minimal requirements for a *da capo* or a repeat. The smaller the addition, the smaller the offense if the style is not right. In addition to the illustrations of *moderate* embellishments presented here or referred to in Schmitz and Ferand, a careful study of Telemann's "Methodical Sonatas" is certain to be helpful. Very instructive too will be the reverse procedure of "decoloring" Bach's—or Locatelli's, Vivaldi's, and other masters'—written-out diminutions. Such an attempt to extract the structural essence can be done in two stages: first by paring down "second-degree" diminutions to "first-degree" ones, then by reducing the latter to their skeletal form. Performers who are still at a loss as to what to do should at least have recourse to the "small" graces which, though often not an adequate solution, are preferable to total skeletal austerity which was foreign to the period's style.

Postscript
Historical Research and
Modern Performance

At the end of this long study that was undertaken to provide for today's performers new insights into the ornamental practices of the past, it might be proper to take a brief look at the relationship between historic research and modern performance. In this relationship several controversial issues are involved that touch to various degrees on the matter of ornamentation.

The best known of these issues centers on the alternative of old versus modern instruments. The two schools of thought on this matter could be for the sake of convenience referred to as "purist" and "modernizing." The purists hold that only a performance duplicating the authentic sound will do justice to the spirit of an old composition. The modernizers, though generally concerned about the historic sound, feel that it needs to be adjusted to the sensibilities of today. The purist theory seems vulnerable in its basic proposition that the spirit of an old masterwork is totally at one with its original sound and therefore inseparable from it. It is, however, far from self-evident that a timeless spirit should be indissolubly linked with a time-bound medium. Who would claim that Shakespeare's plays must not be rendered other than as replicas of their original Globe Theater productions—even if we knew all about the latter? As mentioned at the start of this study, the spirit of a composition (or whatever we choose to call the ungraspable, undefinable essence that a work of art communicates to the recipient) was in baroque aesthetics equated with its "affect," i.e. the impression it made on the listener's mind and emotions. This impression is partly dependent on our aural sensitivity, and surely this sensitivity could not remain unaffected by 300 years of spectacular musical development. Therefore, the identical sound will not convey the identical message today as it did then. Hence it could be argued that what matters in the preservation of the "spirit" of a work is not sameness of sound but sameness of the message. In pursuit of this thought, sameness of the message would require adjustment of the sound. This argument does not in the least imply that we should dispense with old instruments, but it does imply that we must not be narrow-minded about *modern* instruments and should realize their frequent potential for enhancement rather than for alleged degradation. To hear the sound of the old instruments is always fascinating and enormously enlightening, and often delightfully gratifying. Often, not always. Some of the old instruments were at least in part inferior to their modern descendants, otherwise they would not have died out. The very "spirit" of a work was occasionally hemmed in by the deficiencies of an old instrument and is permitted to unfold more freely within the wider potential of a modern one. Thus our piano, with its capacity for dynamic shading, can give a plasticity to phrases which on the harpsichord had to remain two-dimensional; the same capacity allows for a more imaginative treatment of ornaments. In ensemble, the modern piano can achieve subtleties of balance which were beyond the reach of its ancestor. Anyone who claims that the dynamic limitations of the harpsichord as a solo instrument are an asset not a drawback only practices self-deception. The harpsichord, however, has its compensations in a better blend with strings and winds and is therefore superior to the piano as a continuo instrument. Also certain works for solo harpsichord are so thoroughly idiomatic, so plainly inspired by the characteristic sound of the instrument, that they lose more from modern tone-coloring than they gain from added dynamic flexibility. The same applies in analogy to some works for certain other old instruments. There will always be two sides to this issue.

Closely connected with the question of instruments, but having a wider implication for all matters of performance, is the issue of the role of musicology. According to some, musicology should be in full control of modern performance: what is found out about the past is automatically turned into rules for the present. (The purist's attitude regarding old instruments is a case in point.) A differing point of view sees the role of musicology limited to historical research, with the application of the gained insight falling into the province of aesthetics— where philosophy and music criticism have their say—and the historically informed artist having the final decision. Such "separation of powers" makes good sense. When a historian has found out what was and why it was, he has reached the limits of his competence and should not venture beyond this line by aspiring to become a lawgiver. Too many complex issues are involved that cannot be handled by the simplistic formula: thus it was, thus it has to be now. Any performance, to be valid and convincing, must be an act of artistry, not of historical demonstration.

Another issue has to do with the concept of a "definitive performance." Some musicologists feel that with the help of rules extracted from treatises they can reconstruct the exact image of *the* authentic performance. They can be heard demonstrating that this is how Bach played this piece and implying that all deviations are historically false. Such claims are unrealistic. There is no such thing as a "definitive" interpretation. Can we reasonably assume that Bach played a piece the same on the organ, on the harpsichord, on the clavichord, the same when transcribed for other media or vice versa; that he played a piece the same way when he was 25 and when he was 60 years old; the same when he was fresh or when he was tired; when he felt exhilarated or depressed; the same regardless of what musical ideas had just been whirling through his head? Which would be the model for the "definitive" performance? We can be sure that all these performances varied, but we can also be reasonably sure that they did not vary wildly and that they had a common denominator of an overall stylistic frame within which many details could change without altering the essence. It is this stylistic essence of a performance which was a reality and which should constitute the chief object of our search for historical interpretation. In this pursuit where much remains to be done and equally much remains to be reviewed and revised, it behooves us to be humble in the awareness of our still-limited knowledge of a field that is at best only incompletely explorable. That we have to search for approximation and not for the non-existing chimera of one definitive performance applies with still greater force to ornaments. On that matter no more needs to be said.

Ornamentation occupies a special place with regard to the interpretation of old music because to date it has been almost totally dominated by the dictates of musicology. Modern performance, with regard to rhythm, phrasing, dynamics, or tempo, has been slower and more hesitant to submit to new doctrines. That in matters of ornamentation the prevailing doctrines have been almost universally accepted was partly due to their seniority: they were the oldest theories in the field and enjoyed a long term of unchallenged supremacy. Another reason lay in the simplicity of the rules which gave the performers "instant authenticity." For many, the "rules" soon became a conditioned reflex, and in the end an acquired taste. However, it is most important to realize that the performers who so honored the rules did so at first not from free artistic choice, but from faith in their rightness. Conformance, though, was not absolute. Deviations of the "modernizing" type show up with artists who bypass the alleged rules, often probably without being aware of it, when they instinctively try to avoid unmusical results.

A more extreme, and so far quite rare, breed of modernizers want to abolish ornaments altogether from a conviction (so it would seem) that they deface or obscure the structural lines. With all due respect to the rights of artistic judgment, great reservations should be made against such willful rejection of a master's clearly expressed musical intentions. Ornaments in baroque music were more than expendable surface glitter, they were a fundamental element of style. To tear out all ornaments would be comparable to the "modernization" of a baroque façade through the removal of all decorative designs. We have to do here not with an adjustment of sound, but with a reworking of the composition not far removed from the jazz arrangements and similar manipulative processes of recent times. All of these may have validity within a certain sphere, but none ought to claim to be a legitimate attempt at interpreting the master's ideas. Moreover, some performers who eliminate the ornaments leave out only those that are written in little notes or indicated by symbol, obviously unaware of the fact that many other ornaments of the same type happen to be written out in regular notation. To be consistent, even the spelled-out diminutions would then have to be "decolored."

In this book I have tried to show that the currently prevailing doctrines about ornaments are largely mistaken and that with the exception of some centers of rigidity that developed in mid-18th century and concerned music of relatively small interest to us ornaments were much freer than generally assumed. It is well to realize that the argument was made not from a "modernizing" point of view that proposes concessions to our present taste, but from findings of historical facts. In case I should have succeeded in making my argument persuasive, I would expect that open-minded artists should be glad to avail themselves of the new areas of freedom staked out by this study. Great baroque music has survived the strong overdose of rigid ornaments which it was administered for all too long, and the question is by no means a matter of artistic life and death. But if we can free Bach and other great masters from the dead weight of ornamental rigorism, the beauty of their music will shine with enhanced radiance.

Appendix
Selective Glossary of Terms
and Symbols

————•◆•————

Abbreviations

E	English		equiv.	equivalent
F	French		*pdv*	*port de voix*
G	German		*pdv & p*	*port de voix et pincé*
It.	Italian		pl	plural
It-G	Italo-German		prob.	probably
L	Latin		sp	spelling
a. o.	among others		syn	synonym
ant	antonym		*tr't*	*tremblement*
appogg.	appoggiatura			

1. TERMS

Different meanings of the same term are listed in the approximate order of their importance. Whenever a working definition was given in the text, this definition is given first and identified by the word "Here." Terms that are derived from treatises, prefaces, and ornament tables carry with themselves the limitations of their sources in that their meanings are sometimes ambiguous and often incomplete.

Whenever it seemed advisable, the plural form of a foreign term is indicated in parentheses. Linguistic origins are listed only in cases that are open to doubt.

An asterisk indicates that the term is defined in a separate entry. The asterisk will, however, be omitted for the following frequently used terms: Appoggiatura, *Coulé*, Mordent, *Nachschlag*, *Port de voix*, Slide, Trill, Turn, *Vorschlag*. The synonyms and antonyms given for a particular term were used *only* by the author (or authors) after whose name they appear.

Abfall: *Nachschlag* anticipating the pitch of the following note (L. Mozart)

Abgeschnappter Mordent: Rudimentary mordent in which the auxiliary is struck simultaneously with the *Principal note but immediately released (Marpurg)

Abruptio: The solo part making the cadence before the bass (Stierlein, Samber)

Abziehen (G verb): Descending *Vorschlag* (Baron, G lute school 18th cent.)

Abzug: 1. The dynamic tapering of a long appogg. into the following *Principal note (Quantz, Marpurg)

    2. *Schneller* (Löhlein)

— *mit Nachschlage*: *Schneller* plus *Two-note suffix (Löhlein)

Accent [F]: 1. Largely French ornament: a *Nachschlag* most commonly rising one step then falling to the next note (Bacilly, L'Affilard, Loulié, Couperin, Hotteterre, Choquel); occasionally we find the pattern inverted by stepwise fall before a rise (Hotteterre whose pattern is two-directional, Dard); or the *accent* may repeat the pitch of the *Principal note (Duval, Lécuyer); syn: *Aspiration*, *Plainte*. To avoid confusion with the other types of *accents*, this grace will in the following be referred to as *French *accent*.

    2. *Vorschlag* (J. S. Bach, Walther)

    3. *Vorschlag* or *French *accent* (Stierlein)

    4. *Accento* 1 (Mylius); see also *Accento, *Accentus*

Accent plaintif: *Pdv* (Basset [Mersenne])

Accent und mordant: *Pdv & p (J. S. Bach)

Accent und trillo: *Supported appogg. trill (J. S. Bach)

Accenti [It. pl]: Generic term for non-repercussive ornaments of from one to about four or five notes (It. around 1600)

Accento(-i): 1. *Vorschlag* or *Nachschlag* (It-G 17th to early 18th cent.; Bernhard, Mylius, Printz, Fuhrmann)

      2. *Vorschlag* (Feyertag)

      3. *French *accent* (Diruta)

      4. *Dactylic slide (Banchieri)

Accento doppio: *Gedoppelter Accent (Walther, who lists also the F and L equiv. of *Accent double* and *Accentus duplex*)

Accentuirte Brechung: *Figurate arpeggio (Marpurg, syn: *Accentuirte Zergliederung*)

Accentuirter Triller: *Supported appogg. trill (Marpurg)

Accentuirter Vorschlag: *Pdv & p (Marpurg 1749)

Accentus: 1. *Vorschlag* stepwise rising or falling (Walther, who specifies the ∼ as *minor* and *major* for half-step or whole-step interval, and *ascendens* and *descendens* for its direction)

      2. *Vorschlag* or *Nachschlag* (Stierlein, Kuhnau)

      3. *French *accent* (Samber)

      4. *Schneller or *Single mordent (Printz)

— *circumflexo intendens*: *Schneller (Feyertag)

— *circumflexo remittens*: *Single mordent (Feyertag)

Accentus musicus: *Vorschlag* (Spiess)

Acciaccatura(-e): 1. Striking non-harmonic tones with a chord and holding them for an indetermined time (Gasparini, Geminiani)

      2. Striking and immediately releasing a non-harmonic tone, a whole step below a regular chordal pitch (Heinichen, Spiess)

      3. The insert(s) of a *Figurate arpeggio (C.P.E. Bach, Marpurg, Löhlein, Türk). (The modern use of the term to signify a *Grace note or short appogg. is unhistorical.)

Afterbeat: In frequent modern usage: *Nachschlag*-type *Suffix following a trill

Agrément: Brief mordent starting with the auxiliary (Nivers, Jullien)

Agréments (pl): Generic term for the French standardized *Small ornaments that lend themselves to indication by symbols, though they were often freely added by the performer (F 17th and 18th cent.)

Anapestic slide: Here: prebeat slide with stress on the principal note

Anschlag: Two ornamental notes which precede and straddle the *Principal note; most commonly first the lower then the upper neighbor (Quantz, C.P.E. Bach, Löhlein)

Anschlagender Vorschlag: Onbeat *Vorschlag* (Quantz, L. Mozart)

Anticipated ornament: Here: an ornament (such as a *Vorschlag*, mordent, trill, etc.) rendered before the notated starting point of its *Parent note

Anticipatio: Premature entry of a note (Spiess, syn: *Prolepsis*; ant: *Retardatio*)

Anticipatione della nota: 1. *Nachschlag* to the pitch of the following note (It-G, 17th to early 18th cent.; Bernhard, Mylius, Walther [1732]).

      2. Prebeat *Vorschlag* (Walther 1708)

Anticipatione della syllaba: Prebeat *Vorschlag* (It-G 17th and early 18th cent.; Bernhard, Mylius, Feyertag, Beyer, Fuhrmann, Walther)

Appoggiatura: Here: *Vorschlag* from either direction that falls on the beat. Old Italian writers, a. o. Tosi, Tartini, Geminiani, used the term for *Vorschläge* of all rhythmic designs (see the next two entries). Geminiani clarifies the direction by distinguishing a "superior" and "inferior" ∼. The all-encompassing use of the term for *Vorschläge* of all rhythmic designs persists in modern literature in It., E, and G as well as in F in the Frenchified form of *l'appoggiature*.

— *breve* or — *di passaggio*: Prebeat *Vorschlag* (Tartini)

— *lunga* or — *sostentata*: Long onbeat *Vorschlag* (Tartini)

Appoggiatura trill: Here: Trill, starting with the auxiliary on the beat

Appui (old sp *appuy*): 1. Here (and most commonly in F): the onbeat sustained first note of a trill, usually the auxiliary, occasionally the main note

   2. Upper-note start of a trill either *on* or *before* the beat (Jean Rousseau, syn: *Support*)

Ardire (It.): Vocal pulsation (It-G 17th cent.; Bernhard, Mylius)

Arpégé or *Arpègement*: *Arpeggio (F 17th and 18th cent.), see also *Harpégé*

Arpeggiando: In arpeggio style (It-G 17th to 18th cent.)

Arpeggio: Successive sounding of a chordally conceived series of pitches

Aspiration [F]: 1. *French *accent* (Bacilly, Jean Rousseau, Saint Lambert, David)

   2. Shortening of note value, equiv. of mild staccato (Couperin)

   3. *One-finger gamba vibrato (Demachy, syn: *Plainte*)

Avant-son: *Vorschlag* (Millet)

Backfall: Descending *Vorschlag* (Dieupart, Mace)

Balancé: 1. *Vibrato (Signoretti)

   2. Prob. vocal pulsations with microtone (Bérard-Blanchet, syn: *Flatté*)

Balancement: Intensity fluctuations of the voice (L'Affilard, Loulié, Corrette, Choquel; Montéclair specifies that the intensity fluctuations of the ∼ are slower and more pronounced than those of the *Flaté*.)

Balancement de main: *One-finger gamba vibrato (Danoville)

Bat(t)ement: 1. Mordent (Marais, Caix d'Hervelois, Hotteterre, Freillon-Poncein, Corrette)

   2. *Two-finger gamba vibrato (Jean Rousseau, Danoville)

   3. *Supported main-note trill (Mercadier de Belesta)

   4. *Main-note trill (Jean Jacques Rousseau [prob. also with main-note support like ∼ 3], possibly also Demachy)

   5. *Multiple mordent with half-step starting with the auxiliary (L. Mozart, Löhlein)

Battuto: Detached articulation (Tosi)

Beat: Mordent (Dieupart)

Beate: Mordent (Mace)

Beben: Instrumental vibrato (Mattheson, syn: *Tremolo*)

Bebung: 1. Clavichord vibrato (Marpurg, C.P.E. Bach)

   2. Vocal vibrato (Agricola); violin vibrato (Löhlein)

   3. *Vibrato in all media (Petri)

Bombo: Tone repetition as diminution pattern (Printz, Marpurg 1749), equiv., *Figura bombilans*, *Schwärmer*

Brechung: *Arpeggio (Marpurg)

Brissé: *Schneller* (Francoeur "neveu")

Broderie(-s) [F]: *Passaggio*

Cadence(-s) [F]: 1. Trill; originally used for cadential trills, then extended to any trill (F 17th and 18th cent.), equiv., *Tremblement*

   2. Turn (J. S. Bach)

   3. *Turn-trill or *Slide-trill (D'Anglebert)

—*achevée*: *Supported appogg. trill with *Suffix (Levesque & Bêche, syn: *Cadence appuyée*)

—*appuyée*: 1. *Supported appogg. trill (Rameau, Corrette, Dandrieu, Dard, Levesque & Bêche)

   2. *Tr't lié (L'Abbé le Fils)

Cadencé aspiré: Prematurely cut-off trill (Foucquet)

Cadence avec appuy or —*avec support*: *Upper-note trill (Jean Rousseau); it can be of two kinds: (1) *par la seule anticipation du son* with the auxiliary *on* the beat, and (2) *avec anticipation de valeur et de son* with the auxiliary *before* the beat.

Cadence brise [sic] or — *finte* [sic]: Brief anticipated trill (Francoeur "neveu")

— *brisée*: 1. *~ *feinte* 1 (Corrette, Lécuyer, Saint Philbert)

      2. [Unsupported] *Appogg. trill (Rodolphe, Levesque & Bêche)

      3. *Upper-note trill (Mercadier de Belesta)

— *coulée*: 1. *~ *feinte* 1 (David); however, when the ~ *coulée* occurs on descent of a fourth or fifth, it becomes a *Main-note supported trill, introduced by a descending slide.

      2. *Compound trill (Marpurg 1749, syn: ~ *portée*)

— *coupée*: 1. Trill with *Rest point (Corrette)

      2. Prob. *Schneller* (Bordet)

      3. Prob. *Main-note trill (La Chapelle)

— *double*: 1. *Unprepared trill with *Two-note suffix (Lécuyer)

      2. *Ribattuta* (Bérard-Blanchet)

— *doublée*: 1. *Double cadence* 1 (Dupont, Duval, L'abbé Duval)

      2. *Supported main-note trill with *Two-note suffix (Brijon)

— *en l'air*: *Main-note trill (Jean Rousseau, prob. also d'Ambruis and Denis)

— *feinte*: 1. Here: very long appogg. preparation and a token trill at the end (Corrette, David, Lécuyer, L'abbé Duval)

      2. Anticipated *Schneller* after stepwise descent (Durieu)

— *fermée*: *Supported appogg. trill with *One-note suffix that, descending stepwise, anticipates the pitch of the following note (Corrette, Dupont)

— *finte* [sic]: Anticipated brief trill (Francoeur "neveu")

— *jet(t)ée*: 1. Unprepared *Main-note trill (Duval, Denis, Brijon, Levesque & Bêche, prob. also Lécuyer)

      2. *Unprepared trill starting with either pitch (Lacassagne)

      3. *Grace-note trill with (slight) main-note support (David [*cadence jettée en descendant*], L'Abbé le Fils)

      4. Anticipated trill detached from the preceding note (Engramelle [Bedos de Celles])

      5. Trill with slightly anticipated start of alternations (David)

— *lente*: *Main-note trill with acceleration (Dellain)

— *liée*: *Tr't lié* (Dupuit)

— *molle*: 1. Trill with very slow but very distinct alternations (Lécuyer, syn: ~ *sanglottante*)

      2. *Main-note trill with very slow but very gentle alternations (Bérard-Blanchet)

— *parfaite*: 1. *Supported appogg. trill (Duval)

      2. *Supported appogg. trill with *Two-note suffix (Lécuyer, Levesque & Bêche)

— *pleine*: 1. *Main-note trill (Mercadier de Belesta)

      2. *Supported main-note trill (Brijon)

      3. *Supported appogg. trill (Duval, syn: ~ *parfaite* or *préparée*)

      4. *Tr't lié* (Jean Jacques Rousseau)

— *pleine à progression*: *Ribattuta* (Lacassagne)

— *portée*: *Compound trill (Marpurg 1749)

— *précipitée*: 1. *Main-note trill (Bérard-Blanchet)

      2. *Unprepared trill (Corrette, syn: ~ *subite*)

— *préparée*: 1. *Supported appogg. trill (David, Duval, Denis, L'abbé Duval, Durieu)

      2. Either *Supported main-note trill or *Supported appogg. trill (Lacassagne)

      3. *Grace-note trill (Rodolphe)

— *sanglottante*: *~ *molle* (Lécuyer)

— *sanglottée*: *~ *feinte* 1 (Denis)

— *sans préparation*: *Main-note trill (Rodolphe)

— *simple*: 1. *Main-note trill (Jean Rousseau)

      2. *Supported appogg. trill (Choquel)

— *soutenue*: *Supported appogg. trill (L'Affilard)

— *subit(t)e*: 1. *Unprepared trill (Corrette, syn: ~ *précipitée*, Bordier, Durieu)

      2. Unprepared *Upper-note trill (Duval, Saint Philbert, prob. also Lécuyer)

3. Unprepared *Main-note trill (L'abbé Duval, Buterne)

4. *Grace-note trill (L'Abbé le Fils)

Cadencé suspendu: Trill with delayed entrance (Foucquet)

Cadence tournée: Trill and *Two-note suffix (L'Abbé le Fils)

— *tremblée*: *Appogg. trill with gradual acceleration (La Chapelle)

Cadenza(-e): Embellishment of a hold, often expanding into sizable free fantasia; intended for improvisation, it was occasionally written out by the composer (It-G late 17th to 18th cent. and beyond)

Cercar della nota: (Literally: "searching for the note"); anticipated stepwise *Vorschlag* from either direction (It-G 17th to early 18th cent.; Bernhard, Mylius, Ahle, Beyer, Fuhrmann, Walther)

Chevron (F): The symbol: ᨠ or ᨠᨠ

Chordal arpeggio: Here: pitches of a chord, sounded in close succession without any defined rhythm, either upward or (less commonly) downward, and sustained to form in the end the sound of the full chord (see *Linear arpeggio)

Chûte (old sp: *Cheute* or *Chute*): 1. Here: falling *Nachschlag* to pitch of the following note (F 17th to 18th cent.)

2. Stepwise descending *Vorschlag* (Jean Rousseau, Dieupart)

Ch(e)ute en descendant: *Chûte 2 (D'Anglebert, Le Roux)

— *en montant*: Stepwise rising *Vorschlag* (D'Anglebert, Le Roux). The surprising use of the term *chûte* which means "fall" for a rising *Vorschlag* can be explained by its lute origin (which is attested to by Demachy) where the *fall* of the upper finger sounds the principal note.

— *et pincé*: *Pdv & p (D'Anglebert, Le Roux)

— *sur une (deux) notte(s)*: Upward *Figurate arpeggio with one (or two) inserted notes (D'Anglebert)

Chute sur une note: *Figurate arpeggio, either up or down (Le Roux)

Circolo(-i): Combination of two *circoli mezzi*, one rising, one falling (It-G 17th to mid-18th cent.)

Circolo mezzo: Turn from either above or below, or a grace of closely related design that moves stepwise first up then down or vice versa (It-G 17th to mid-18th cent.; Printz, Ahle, Brossard, Mattheson, Walther, Spiess)

Circuitus: Anticipated turn-related grace (Janowka, Walther)

Clamatione(-i): Slide-like grace (Diruta)

Close shake: *Vibrato (E 17th to 18th cent.; Geminiani)

Coloratura(-e): *Passaggio

Compound trill: Here: trill preceded without interruption by a turn, slide, mordent, or related figure (see *Turn-trill, *Slide-trill, *Mordent-trill)

Couché du doigt: *Doigt couché (Danoville)

Coulade(s): Scalewise slurred connection between notes (Loulié, Marais, Montéclair)

Coulé(s): 1. Here: stepwise descending *Vorschlag* (L'Affilard, Loulié, Montéclair, Couperin, Rameau)

2. Insertion and immediate release of the middle note in the arpeggiated interval of a third (Chambonnières, Le Bègue, Jullien, Raison, Dieupart)

3. Slurred articulation (F 17th and 18th cent.)

4. Slide (Marpurg 1749)

— *bref*: Prebeat *coulé* (L'Abbé le Fils)

— *de doigt*: Gliding a finger from fret to fret to achieve a *portamento* effect (Danoville, Marais, syn: *Son glissé*)

— *soûtenu*: Onbeat *coulé* (L'Abbé le Fils)

— *sur une tierce*: *Coulé 2 (D'Anglebert)

Coulemen: *Couler les tierces (L'Affilard)

Coulement des notes: Slurred articulation (Nivers)

Couler les tierces: Interbeat stepwise inserts between leaps of thirds; more frequent in descent than ascent (F 17th and 18th cent.)

Coup de gozier or *gosier*: Undefined small grace, such as a *Vorschlag*, **Schneller*, **Single mordent, glissando, *Nachschlag*, etc. (F 17th and 18th cent.)

Curta: **Figura corta* (Vogt, Spiess)

Dactylic slide: Here: onbeat slide with first ornamental note lengthened

Demi-cadence: **Cadence feinte* 1 (Bérard-Blanchet)

Demie cadence appuyée: **Cadence feinte* 1 (Hotteterre)

Demy tremblement: **Tr't feint* (Bacilly, syn: *Tr't étouffé*)

Demy port de voix: 1. **Pdv feint* (Bacilly)
  2. Smoothly (prob. fast) executed, fully anticipated *Pdv* with no, or only a very gentle, *pincé* annex (Bacilly, syn: *Pdv glissé*)

Diminutions: 1. Here and most commonly: embellishments of a written melodic line through figurations of smaller note values; subspecies of the **Passaggi* which is the wider term (see the latter)
  2. Rhythmically measured embellishments involving the exact doubling, quadrupling, etc. of the tones of a written melody (Loulié, Montéclair)

Divisions: **Diminutions* 1 (E 17th and 18th cent.)

Doigt couché: Stopping two or more gamba strings with the same finger (Marais)

Doppelaccent: Twice-sounded *Vorschlag* (Marpurg 1749)

Doppelschlag: Turn (Marpurg, C.P.E. Bach, Petri)

Doppelt-cadence: **Slide-trill or **Turn-trill (J. S. Bach)

Doppelter Accent: Inverted turn (Stierlein)

Doppelter Nachschlag: **Two-note suffix (Hiller)

Doppelter Vorschlag: **Pdv & p* (Marpurg 1749)

Doppeltriller: 1. **Slide-trill and **Suffix (Petri)
  2. **Slide-trill or **Turn-trill (Agricola)
  3. Trill with **Suffix (Marpurg 1749)

Doppelvorschlag: **Anschlag* (Marpurg, Petri, Hiller)

Dopplierung: Twice-sounded *Vorschlag* (Maichelbeck), equiv., **Doppelaccent*

Double(s) [F]: 1. Second couplet of an air with added **Diminutions; in instrumental music, the variation of a piece either through added diminutions or through structural changes of the melody in which case no smaller note values need to be involved; or through a combination of both
  2. Turn (Couperin)

Doublé: Turn (Rameau, Engramelle)

Double cadence: 1. Here: trill and **Two-note suffix (F 17th and 18th cent.)
  2. Turn (Chambonnières)
  3. Combination of **Old French turn and either **Slide-trill or **Turn-trill (D'Anglebert)
  4. Combination of **Old French turn and regular trill (Dieupart)
  5. **Embedded turn, followed by trill with **Two-note suffix (Raison)
  6. Various turn-related designs, including a trill-like oscillation played with detached bow strokes and ending with a turn (Jean Rousseau)
  7. **Ribattuta* (Bérard-Blanchet)
  8. **Old French turn (Saint Lambert)

Double cadence coupée: **Embedded turn (L'Affilard)

Double mordent: Here: mordent with two alternations

Durchgang: Interbeat insertion of middle note between the leap of a third (Heinichen, syn: *Transitus*)

Durchgehender Vorschlag: Prebeat *Vorschlag* (Quantz, L. Mozart, Tromlitz)

Einfacher Vorschlag: **Multiple mordent without *Pdv* prefix (Marpurg 1749)

Einfall: Onbeat *Vorschlag* (Janowka)

Einfallen (G verb): Descending *Vorschlag* (G lute school early 18th cent.; Baron)

Eingang: Normally improvised, occasionally written-out, introductory passage to a new section or phrase (G 18th cent.)

Ellipsis: Replacement of a tied consonant note by a rest (Stierlein). Samber, under the term *Eclypsis*, includes in addition to the foregoing the analogous omission of a dissonant suspension.

Embedded turn: Here: turn sounded in the middle of its *Principal note

Esclamatione [It.] or *Exclamatio* [L]: 1. Dynamic intensification (Caccini, Praetorius, Herbst, Crüger, Falck)

    2. One- or two-note *Nachschlag* (Feyertag)

Figura bombilans: *Bombo* (Printz)

Figura corta: Three-note diminution pattern of various stepwise designs and usually uneven rhythm with either the first or the third note twice as long as the other two but evened out in faster tempo into triplets (Printz)

Figura suspirans: Small diminution pattern related to anticipated or delayed turn (Printz)

Figurate arpeggio: A *Chordal arpeggio with one or more non-chordal pitches inserted (like *Zwischenschläge) but not held

Fioretto(-i): *Passaggio

Fioritura(-e): *Passaggio

Flat(t)é: 1. Gentle intensity fluctuation on a long note (Montéclair)

    2. French *accent* (prob. with microtone) returning to preceding pitch (Corrette)

    3. *Balancé 2 (Bérard-Blanchet)

    4. Mordent (Jean Jacques Rousseau, Francoeur "neveu")

    5. A slower mordent than the *Martellement 1 (Levesque & Bêche)

    6. *Single mordent, *Schneller, or *Pdv & p to connect two stepwise moving notes (Duval)

Flat(t)ement: 1. *Vibrato (Hotteterre, syn: *Tr't mineur*, Corrette)

    2. *Two-finger vibrato (Marais)

    3. ? (d'Ambruis)

Forefall beat: *Pdv & p (Dieupart)

Forefall up: Ascending *Vorschlag* (Dieupart)

French accent: Here: a *Nachschlag*, typically stepwise upward, followed by melodic descent

Freyer Triller: Simple, unprepared trill (Marpurg 1749, syn: *Schlechter Triller* or *Tr't détaché*)

Fusée: *Passaggio consisting of scalewise figures that rise and fall (Lacassagne)

Gebrochene Harmonie: *Arpeggio (C.P.E. Bach)

Gebundener Triller: *Tr't lié in *Suspension pattern (Marpurg)

Gedehnter Triller: *Ribattuta (Marpurg)

Gedoppelter Accent: Nachschlag to pitch of next note (Walther 1708)

Geschleifter Triller: *Compound trill (Marpurg)

Geschnellter Doppelschlag: Turn starting with *Principal note, like a *Schneller with *Suffix (C.P.E. Bach)

Gezogener Triller: *Compound trill (Marpurg)

Gorgia(-ie) or *Gorga* (*Gorghe*): *Passaggio (It. early 17th cent.)

Grace note: Here: prebeat *Vorschlag*

Grace-note trill: Here: trill starting with the auxiliary before the beat

Griffbrechen: *Arpeggio (Marpurg)

Groppetto(-i): Undefined figuration of modest size that usually seems to combine melodic and repercussive elements (Bovicelli)

Groppo(-i) or *Gruppo(-i)*: 1. An ornament related to both the trill and the turn, starting with either the upper note or the slightly held main note and ending with a turn; the alternations are usually slower and more distinct than those of a trill, and in contrast to the latter often rhythmically measured (It-G 17th cent.; Conforto, Caccini, Praetorius, Crüger, Herbst, Printz)

    2. *Groppetto (Diruta)

    3. Interbeat graces filling in intervals, especially thirds, either by single notes

like *Tierces coulées, or by turn-related designs such as:
(Herbst, Crüger, Printz, Ahle, Mattheson)
    4. *Circolo mezzo (Brossard, Printz, Walther)
    5. *Ribattuta (Stierlein)
Groppo di sotto: Mordent-related inversion of Groppo 1 (Conforto)
Groppolo: *Groppo 1 (with main-note start [Cavalieri])

Halb-Circkel or Halbzirkel: *Circolo mezzo (Mattheson, Hiller, E. W. Wolf)
Halber Circul: *Circuitus (Walther)
Halber Triller: 1. A miniature trill related to both the *Schneller and the *Prall-Triller,
    with or without a *One-note suffix (Quantz)
    2. *Schneller (Löhlein)
    3. A fast turn, starting with the main note, inserted between a long appogg.
    and the *Principal note (L. Mozart)
    4. Mordent (Samber)
Half fall: Short appogg. from half-step below (Mace)
Harmonic ornament: Here: ornament whose onbeat placement enriches the harmony by
    changing a consonance into a dissonance or a milder dissonance into a stronger
    one
Harpégé or Harpègement: *Arpeggio (Chambonnières, Le Bègue, Saint Lambert, Raison,
    Marais)
Harpégé figuré: *Figurate arpeggio (Saint Lambert)
Hélan: Vocal Pdv followed by *French accent, prob. sung with intense expressiveness
    (L'Affilard, Villeneuve); see also Sanglot

Intendens [L]: Qualifying participle indicating the rising style of an ornament, e.g. accen-
    tus intendens; ant: remittens
Intervallic arpeggio: Here: the successive sounding of two pitches that are then held
    simultaneously
Intonatio [L] or Intonazione [It.]: The way of starting a vocal phrase with either the
    written note or with a different pitch, such as the second, third, or fourth below
    (Caccini, Praetorius, Falck)
Italian double trill: Here: species of a *Compound trill where a usually cadential appogg.
    trill is preceded by a *Main-note trill a step below. Sometimes the preliminary
    main-note trill is done in *Ribattuta style.

Kugel: (G for "ball"); small turn-related diminution formulas usually repeated sequen-
    tially, hence rolling like a "ball," equiv., Walze, Gruppo 3 (G 17th to early
    18th cent.)

Langueur: *One-finger vibrato (Jean Rousseau)
Läufer: *Tirata (Hiller)
Linear arpeggio: Here: pitches of a chord that are strung up melodically in a definite
    rhythm without being sustained
Lombard rhythm: Here (and generally today): rhythmic design where one or more short
    notes are placed on the beat and are more or less sharply accented, followed
    within the same beat by a longer note
Lombard slide: Here: an onbeat slide with the stress on the first of two equally short
    ornamental notes

Main-note trill: Here: trill starting with the written note
Manier(-en): Ornament(s) (G late 17th and 18th cent.)
Martellement: 1. Mordent (Basset [Mersenne], Demachy, Loulié, Duval, Lacassagne,
    Lécuyer, Levesque & Bêche)
    2. *Supported main-note trill (Choquel)
    3. Vocal vibrato, subspecies of *Multiple mordent (Lacassagne)

Melic: Here: adjective qualifying an ornament as a non-repercussive, hence essentially melodic, grace, ranging from one to an undetermined number of notes

Melodic ornament: Here: ornament, generally placed between the starting points of the structural notes, that embellishes the melodic line with negligible or no impact on the harmony

Mezzo groppo: Short type of *Groppo 1 (Conforto)

Mezzo trillo: Short and fast trill (Tosi)

Modus lubricandi: Coulé 2 (Fischer, syn: *Coulé*)

Monachina: *Multiple mordent (Cavalieri)

Mordant(-en) [G]: 1. Old sp for *Mordent*

    2. Trill or *Multiple mordent (Ammerbach, 16th cent.)

    3. Mordent with half-step (Fuhrmann)

    4. *Vorschlag* (Maichelbeck)

    5. *Schneller* or *Single mordent (Kürzinger)

Mordent: 1. Here: oscillations of *Principal note with its lower neighbor; according to the number of oscillations, we refer here to *single, double,* or *multiple* mordents

    2. *Mordente 3 (Heinichen)

Mordent nach einem Vorschlage: *Pdv & p (C.P.E. Bach)

Mordent-trill: Here: a trill preceded before the beat by a *Single mordent

Mordente(-i) [It.]: 1. Mordent 1 (Geminiani, Tartini)

    2. Prebeat, fast and unaccented turn from either above or below (Tartini)

    3. Non-harmonic tone at half-tone distance below a chordal pitch, struck and quickly released; mostly used in accompaniment (Gasparini)

Multiple mordent: Here: mordent with three or more alternations

Multiplicatio: 1. Tone repetition (Samber)

    2. *Diminution (Fuhrmann)

Nachschlag(-schläge): 1. Here: a single ornamental note that belongs exclusively or predominantly to the preceding *Principal note, to which it is slurred and with which, in vocal music, it shares the same syllable. Some modern writers use the term to designate (not too logically) a prebeat *Vorschlag*.

    2. *Two-note suffix (Marpurg and many later German writers, to the present day)

Notes de goût: Ornaments, whether written out in regular or in small notes (Jean Jacques Rousseau)

Notes perdues or *Notes postiches*: The notes in small type that are not divided into the measure (F 17th to 18th cent.)

Old French turn: Here: a species of the turn, starting on the *Principal note, then moving scalewise, first two steps down then two steps up to the principal note (D'Anglebert, Le Roux, Dieupart)

Onbeat ornaments: Here: ornaments that strike at the prescribed starting points (usually the beat) of the *Parent note whose entrance is thereby delayed

One-finger vibrato: Here: the kind of gamba or lute vibrato that is produced by shaking the playing finger itself, as contrasted to the *Two-finger vibrato

One-note suffix: Here: a *Nachschlag* after a trill on (usually) the pitch a step below the main note, sometimes on the pitch of the auxiliary

Parent note(s): The regular note or notes to which an ornament is attached, syn: Principal note

Partimento: Melodic improvisation over a thorough bass

Passage(s) [F]: *Passaggio*

Passaggio(-ggi): Florid ornamental figurations, often left to improvisation, sometimes written out. In addition to *Diminutions, which are a subspecies of the *passaggi*, the latter also comprise such figurations that have no reference to an underlying melody, e.g. transitional passages between phrases, a freely starting introductory passage leading into a new phrase (see *Eingang*), or the embellishments of a hold (see *Cadenza*).

Passo(-i): *Small ornament (Tosi)

Petit tremblement: Short trill (Demachy)

Petite cadence: *Schneller (Devienne, syn: *Trille*)

Pfeil [G]: *Tirata (G 17th and 18th cent.)

Pincé: 1. Mordent (Danoville, L'Affilard, Freillon-Poncein, Couperin, Rameau)
   2. *Two-finger vibrato (Marais, syn: *Flatement*, Caix d'Hervelois)
   3. Mordent starting with auxiliary (De Lusse, Signoretti)

— *continu*: Long sustained *Multiple mordent (Couperin)

— *étouffé*: Simulated mordent when the auxiliary is held down on the keyboard as a tied-over note (Couperin; the use of the term by Marpurg and other German writers to designate a *Zusammenschlag* is probably due to a misunderstanding)

— *simple*: *Multiple mordent without *Pdv* prefix (Dandrieu, Marpurg)

Pincement: *Pincé 1 (Chambonnières, Boyvin, Raison, Le Roux)

Plain arpeggio: Here: an *Arpeggio consisting only of the chordal notes, in contrast to the *Figurate arpeggio

Plain shake: Unprepared *Upper-note trill (Geminiani)

Plainte: 1. *French *accent* (D'Ambruis, David)
   2. *One-finger vibrato (Marais, Caix d'Hervelois)
   3. Gamba vibrato (Demachy, syn: *Aspiration*)
   4. Vocal pulsations (David)
   5. Downward glissando (Jean Rousseau)

Point d'ar(r)êt or *d'arest*: Sustained main note of a trill after the alternations have stopped (Couperin)

Port de voix: 1. Here: the French ascending *Vorschlag* (Mersenne, Bacilly, Jean Rousseau, Loulié, Montéclair, Couperin, Rameau, L'Abbé le Fils, and most 18th-cent. masters)
   2. *Vorschlag* in both directions (Nivers, Gigault, Chaumont, Saint Lambert, Marais, Danoville; with some exceptions like Choquel, mostly masters of the 17th cent.)

Pdv achevé: 1. Prob. short *Pdv* before a long note (Lécuyer)
   2. Onbeat *Pdv & p (Francoeur "neveu," Marcou)

Pdv appuyé: 1. Onbeat *Pdv* (Lécuyer)
   2. Ascending or descending *Vorschlag* from a note a step apart, touching the latter twice more in anticipation (Saint Lambert)

Pdv coulé: 1. *Pdv* without *pincé* annex (Couperin)
   2. *Demy pdv 2 (Bacilly)

Pdv double or *doublé*: 1. Slide (L'Affilard, Corrette, David, Villeneuve, La Chapelle, Hotteterre)
   2. *Pdv* followed by two-stroke *Pincé (Couperin)

Pdv et pincé: *Pdv* followed by a mordent (Dieupart, Rameau, Dandrieu [the latter two: *pincé et pdv*])

Pdv feint: Very long-held *Pdv*, most often tapering toward the end when the *Principal note is sounded briefly, usually with a delicate *pincé* annex (Duval, Bérard-Blanchet, Lacassagne, L'abbé Duval, Lécuyer)

Pdv finit [sic]: *Pdv & p (Francoeur "neveu")

Pdv glissé: *Demy pdv 2 (Bacilly)

Pdv jetté *Pdv feint with *Pincé* annex (Jean Jacques Rousseau)

Pdv par anticipation de son seulement: Onbeat *Pdv* (Jean Rousseau)

Pdv par anticipation de valeur et de son: Anticipated *Pdv* (Jean Rousseau)

Pdv perdu: *Pdv* with prebeat start, but sustained almost to the end of the *Principal note's value, followed by a delicate *doublement* (i.e. prob. a *Pincé); except for its prebeat start, the equiv. of a *Pdv feint (Bacilly)

Pdv plein or *véritable*: *Pdv* with anticipated sustained start and firmly rendered *doublement* (prob. a *Pincé) with occasional straddling of the beat (Bacilly)

Pdv réel: [Prob. unaccented] *Pdv & p*, not limited to stepwise ascent (Lacassagne)

Pdv simple: 1. *Pdv* followed by one-stroke *Pincé* (Couperin)

  2. Anticipated, stepwise *Vorschlag* from either direction that repeats the preceding note (Saint Lambert)

Prall trill: Here: miniature *Upper-note trill

Prall-Triller or *Pralltriller*: Two-alternation trill starting with the auxiliary on the beat (C.P.E. Bach)

Préoccupation: *Nachschlag* to pitch of following note (G. Muffat), equiv., *Anticipatione della nota*

Principal note: *Parent note

Punctirter Triller: *Ribattuta* (Marpurg)

Quaesitio notae: *Cercar della nota* (Bernhard)

Quiebro reyterado: Trill (Santa Maria)

— *senzillo*: Either *Schneller* or *Single mordent (Santa Maria)

Redoublé: Turn (Foucquet)

Remittens [L]: Qualifying participle: "falling," e.g. *accentus remittens*, syn: *descendens*, ant: *intendens*

Repercussive ornaments: Here: ornaments consisting of the alternation of two pitches a step apart or of articulated tone repetition

Reste du son: *Nachschlag* (Millet)

Rest point: Here: sustained main note after the alternations of a trill; equiv., *Point d'arêt*

Retardatio [L]: 1. Delayed entrance of a note (Spiess)

  2. Ascending suspension appogg. (Stierlein)

Retardatione della syllaba: Brief onbeat *Vorschlag* (Beyer)

Ribattuta (di gola): Originally dotted trill-like design starting on main note (It-G 17th cent.; Caccini, Herbst, Crüger); later, especially in 18th cent., this design usually accelerated while gradually evening out to end in a regular trill (Mattheson, Marpurg, Spiess); among many equiv., *Punctirter Triller*, *Cadence pleine à progression*

Rolle [G]: *Geschnellter Doppelschlag* (Marpurg)

Roulade(s) [F]: 1. *Passaggio* (F 17th to 18th cent.)

  2. A *Passaggio* that does not move in scalewise figures; ant: *Fusée* (Lacassagne)

Rückfall: A descending *Nachschlag* either to the pitch of the following note or to a step above the latter in order to soften the angularity of a big downward leap (L. Mozart); see also *Abfall*

Rückschlag: Stepwise *Nachschlag* between notes of identical pitch (Marpurg 1749)

Sanglot [F]: A heaving sigh on affect-filled exclamations, usually followed by a *French accent or a *Chûte* (Montéclair); see also *Hélan*

Schlechter Triller: *Freyer Triller* (Marpurg 1749)

Schleifender Vorschlag: Long appogg. (Thielo)

Schleif(f)er: Slide (Kuhnau, Walther, Marpurg, C.P.E. Bach, Agricola, Petri)

Schleiffer von dreyen Nötgen: Inverted turn (C.P.E. Bach)

Schneller: One-alternation trill starting and ending with main note (C.P.E. Bach, Marpurg, Petri); referred to by some as "inverted mordent"

Schwärmer: *Bombo* (Printz, Marpurg 1749, Hiller, E. W. Wolf)

Schwebender Triller: *Supported appogg. trill (Marpurg, syn: *Tr't appuyé*)

Scivolato: Legato articulation (Tosi)

Semi tremulus: Mordent (Fischer, Samber)

Séparez: Species of *Intervallic arpeggio on a third (Le Roux)

Setzmanieren (pl): Ornaments written out in regular notation (G 18th cent.)

Single mordent: Here: one-alternation mordent, starting and ending with main note; inversion of *Schneller

Slide: Here: in the strict sense, two ornamental notes moving scalewise to their principal note, mostly from a third below upward, sometimes from a third above downward. In the wider sense, similar scalewise graces of three or more notes.

Slide-trill: Here: type of *Compound trill, consisting of a slide leading into a trill without interruption and mostly with the same speed

Small ornament: Here: *Melic graces from one to four ornamental notes as well as all *Repercussive ornaments

Sollevatione: Dynamic intensification (D. Mazzocchi), prob. equiv., *Esclamatione*

Son coupé: Shortened note (Rameau), syn: *Aspiration* 2 (Couperin)

Son demi-filé: Crescendo on single tone (Bérard-Blanchet)

Son filé: 1. Crescendo-decrescendo on a single, fairly long tone (Bérard-Blanchet, Lacassagne, Lécuyer); equiv., *mesa di voce*

    2. Absolute evenness of a long-held tone (Montéclair)

Son filé et aspiré: Vocal pulsations (David, syn: *plainte*)

Son glissé: Gliding connection between pitches for the voice or the gamba (Montéclair)

Spielmanieren: Ornaments either improvised or indicated by symbol (including the small notes) in contrast to such ornaments (*Setzmanieren*) that ⸱are written out in regular notation (G 18th cent.)

Springer: *French *accent* (Mace, Playford)

Stimm-Einfall: *Vorschlag* (Spiess)

Sting: *Vibrato (Mace)

Strascino: Prob. rubato within a steady beat (Tosi)

Subsumtio: *Cercar della nota* (Walther)

— *postpositiva*: 1. *Nachschlag*, occasionally overlapping with prebeat *Vorschlag* (Bernhard, Samber)

    2. *Nachschlag* of the *Anticipatione della nota* type (Stierlein)

Subsumtio praepositiva: 1. Prebeat *Vorschlag* (Bernhard)

    2. Onbeat *Vorschlag* (Samber)

Suffix: Here: the *Nachschlag*-type one- or two-note sequel to a trill. See also *Trill with suffix.

Superjectio: 1. *Nachschlag* of the *French *accent* type (Bernhard, Heinichen; Spiess, syn: *Überschlag*)

    2. *Accentus* 2 (Stierlein)

Support [E]: Here: sustained appogg. or onbeat main note prior to a trill's alternations

Support [F]: Trill preparation with auxiliary either before or on the beat (Jean Rousseau, syn: *appuy*)

Supported appoggiatura trill: Here: trill prepared by a lengthened descending appogg.

Supported main-note trill: Here: trill prepared by its lengthened main note

Suspension pattern: Here: a *Tr't lié* in which the slurred preceding note is tied over the beat

Tatto or *Tacto*: *Mordente* 3 (Geminiani)

Tenue [F]: 1. *Supported main-note trill (Signoretti, Cartier), equiv., *Trattenimento*

    2. *Supported main-note trill or *Supported appogg. trill (Mattheson)

    3. Keeping a finger on the string until needed again (Marais, Danoville)

Tenuta: *Tenue* 2 (Mattheson)

Terminaison: *Suffix after a trill (Lécuyer)

Tierces coulées: 1. Here: the interbeat insertion of the middle pitch within the leap of a third

    2. Insertion of the middle note in the manner of a *Figurate arpeggio between thirds successively sounded but held out (Couperin, specifying *en montant* or *en descendant*)

Tirata: Scale-like ornamental connection between notes of a fifth or more apart (It-G 17th to 18th cent.), equiv., *Pfeil, *Coulade

Tiret [F]: Short (lute) trill (Demachy)

Tonverziehung: Anticipated or delayed entrance of a tone (Hiller, E. W. Wolf)

Tour de gozier or *gosier*: 1. Turn (Loulié, Hotteterre, Montéclair, Rodolphe)

      2. Small *Melic figure of indetermined design (F 17th and 18th cent.)

      3. *Ribattuta (Marpurg 1749)

Transitus: *Durchgang (Heinichen)

Trattenimento (sopra la nota): *Supported main-note trill (Geminiani)

Tremblant [F]: Pulsating organ register, equiv., *Tremulant*

Tremblement: Trill (F 17th to 18th cent.), equiv., *Cadence

— *appuyé*: *Supported appogg. trill (D'Anglebert, Le Roux, Marpurg)

— *continu*: Long trill with continuous alternations (Couperin)

— *détaché*: 1. Anticipated trill detached from its preceding note (Couperin), equiv.,
      *Cadence jetée 4

      2. *Freyer Triller (Marpurg 1749)

— *doublé*: Variant of *Turn-trill, introduced by main-note *Appui (Montéclair)

— *et pincé*: Trill with *Two-note suffix (D'Anglebert, Le Roux)

— *étouffé*: *Tr't feint (Bacilly, syn: *Demy tr't*)

— *feint*: Very long appogg. support with miniature trill at the end (Duval, Denis, Corrette, Brijon), equiv., *Cadence feinte 1

— *fermé*: Trill with *Two-note suffix, moving stepwise downward (Couperin)

— *lié*: Here: trill slurred to a preceding written-out appogg.

— *lié sans être appuyé*: Anticipated trill slurred to its preceding written-out upper neighbor note (Couperin)

— *mineur*: *Vibrato (Hotteterre)

— *ouvert*: Trill with *Two-note suffix moving upward (Couperin, Foucquet)

— *réfléchissant*: *Supported appogg. trill with *One-note suffix before *Rest point (G. Muffat)

— *roulant*: *Upper-note trill with *Two-note suffix, leading without *Rest point into the following note (G. Muffat)

— *sans appuyer*: *Two-finger gamba vibrato (Demachy)

— *subit*: *Unprepared trill (L'Affilard); see also *Cadence subite 1

Tremolante: *Vibrato (Sperling)

Tremoletto(-i): 1. Main-note miniature trill, incl. *Schneller (Diruta, Praetorius, Herbst, Crüger, Mylius [Herbst includes under this term also the *Single mordent])

      2. Small, very fast *Main-note trill (Feyertag)

      3. *Vibrato (Fuhrmann)

Tremolo(-i) also *Tremulo(-i)*: 1. Trill or *Multiple mordent (It-G 17th cent.; Diruta, Praetorius, Herbst, Crüger, Mylius, Feyertag, Printz; most likely also Dom. Scarlatti and other It. keyboard masters of the 18th cent.)

      2. *Multiple mordent with half-step (Fuhrmann)

      3. *Vibrato (Farina, Tartini, Geminiani, Mattheson, L. Mozart)

      4. Tone repetition (Brossard [incl. bow oscillations], Beyer ["on-pitch oscillations"])

Tremulo di sopra: Prob. extended *Main-note trill (Dom. Scarlatti; without the qualification *di sopra*, his *Tremulo* is most likely a *Multiple mordent; see above *Tremolo 1)

Tremulus: 1. *Tremolo 1 (G 17th cent.), its two aspects mostly distinguished as *ascendens* for the *Main-note trill, *descendens* for the *Multiple mordent (Praetorius, Herbst, Crüger, Mylius, Falck, Reinken)

      2. On-pitch tone oscillation or tone repetition (Stierlein)

      3. *Vibrato (Deysinger)

Trill with suffix: Here: ♩ (two-note) or ♩ ♪ (one-note suffix)

Trille [F]: *Schneller (Devienne, syn: *Petite cadence*)

Triller [G]: Trill (Quantz, C.P.E. Bach, L. Mozart, to present)

— *von oben*: *Turn-trill (C.P.E. Bach)

— *von unten*: *Slide-trill (C.P.E. Bach)

Trilletto: 1. On-pitch oscillation, gently articulated (Printz, Feyertag)

2. Short trill (Mattheson)

3. *Main-note trill with half-step (Fuhrmann)

Trilli [It. pl]: Collective term for various repercussive or semi-repercussive graces (It. around 1600) used mostly in the combination *accenti e trilli*

Trillo: 1. Here: tone repetition varying from clear articulation (referred to as "staccato" style) to gentle "legato" intensity fluctuations (Caccini, Praetorius, Herbst, Crüger, Falck); occasionally started with a *Vorschlag* and ended with a *Suffix (a. o. Conforto)

2. Trill (Cavalieri, Frescobaldi, Trabaci, Tosi, Stierlein, Brossard, J. S. Bach, Mattheson, Geminiani, Tartini)

3. *Supported main-note trill plus *Two-note suffix (Poglietti)

4. Brief undefined melisma that usually contains an element of tone repetition (Praetorius)

5. *Main-note trill with whole step (Fuhrmann)

6. *Tremolo 1 (Beyer)

— *calato*: Trilled glissando (Tosi, syn: *Trillo cresciuto*)

— *composto*: Trill with *Two-note suffix (Geminiani, E equiv., Turned shake)

— *cresciuto*: *Trillo calato* (Tosi)

— *doppio*: 1. Trill plus turn or *Two-note suffix (Trabaci)

2. Combination of descending *Vorschlag*, tone repetition, and *Two-note suffix (Bernhard)

— *gagliardo*: (Meaning: "robust trill") either an appogg. trill. or (more prob.) *Multiple mordent (Poglietti)

— *in unisono*: Gentle ("legato") tone repetition (Falck)

— *maggiore*: Trill with whole step (Tosi)

— *minore*: Trill with half-step (Tosi)

— *mordente*: Fast, very short trill (Tosi)

— *radoppiato*: Trill with an inserted—undefined—figuration in its middle (Tosi)

— *semplice*: Unprepared *Upper-note trill (Geminiani, E equiv., *Plain shake)

— *und mordant*: Trill with *Two-note suffix (J. S. Bach)

— *von unten herauf*: *Slide-trill (Löhlein)

— *von oben herein*: *Turn-trill (Löhlein)

Turn: Here: three ornamental notes starting a step above the principal note, moving scalewise to the note below the principal one and returning to the latter. Referred to as "standard turn" when starting with the upper note on the beat; see also *Embedded turn

Turned shake: Trill with *Two-note suffix (Geminiani)

Turn-trill: Here: type of compound ornament where a turn precedes a trill

Two-finger vibrato: Here: a vibrato type used by French lutenists and gambists: the lower finger firmly placed on the string, the upper finger pressed closely against the lower one and, through the shaking of the hand, brought into gentle repercussive contact with the string

Two-note suffix: Here: *Nachschlag*-type sequel to a trill that mostly serves a connective function with the following note and consists of the pitch below the main note, followed by the latter; see *Suffix

Überschlag: 1. *Superjectio 1 (Spiess)

2. Ascending *Nachschlag* (Wiedeburg)

Überwurf: 1. Ascending *Nachschlag* (L. Mozart)

2. For a trill preparation, the ∼ follows the *Vorschlag* from below (L. Mozart)

Unprepared trill or Unsupported trill: Here: trill starting its alternations immediately, i.e. without sustaining either of its constituent pitches

Unveränderlicher Vorschlag: Very short [literally: "invariable"] appogg. (C.P.E. Bach and followers)

Upper-note trill: Here: trill starting with the auxiliary regardless of the latter's rhythmic placement

Veränderlicher Vorschlag: Long [literally: "variable"] appogg. (C.P.E. Bach and followers)

Verkehrter Doppelschlag: Inverted turn (Löhlein)

Vermehrter Doppelschlag: **Geschnellter Doppelschlag* (Löhlein)

Verre cassé: (Lute) *Vibrato (Basset [Mersenne])

Vibrato: Oscillations of pitch, loudness, timbre, or their combinations

Vorbereiteter Triller: *Supported appogg. trill (Marpurg)

Vorhalt: Term used by some German writers of the 2nd half of the 18th cent. (Petri a. o.) to designate the *long* appogg. while reserving the term *Vorschlag* for a *short* appogg. (and on occasion for a *Grace note)

Vorschlag: 1. Here: a generic term for a single ornamental note that belongs either exclusively or predominantly to the following *Parent note. In instrumental music the ∼ is slurred to the principal note and is more or less clearly detached from the preceding note. In vocal music, the ∼ shares with its *Parent note the same syllable. Rhythmically neutral, the ∼ can fall before, between, on, or after the beat. One of the earliest users of the term may have been Heinichen in 1728. See also **Anschlagender* ∼ and **Durchgehender* ∼, *Accent, *Accento, **Accentus*, **Cercar della nota*, **Anticipatione della syllaba*, **Veränderlicher* ∼, and **Unveränderlicher* ∼)

2. Long appogg. (Heinichen)

3. Mordent (Marpurg 1749)

Walze: *Kugel (G 17th to 18th cent.)

Wesentliche Manieren: (G: "essential ornaments") small standardized ornaments that can be, and often were, prescribed by symbol (Quantz, C.P.E. Bach a. o.), ant: *Willkürliche Manieren*

Whole-fall: Slide (Mace)

Willkürliche Manieren: (G: "arbitrary ornaments") **Passaggi* (Quantz, C.P.E. Bach, Hiller)

Zergliederung: *Arpeggio (Marpurg)

Zimbalo: Dotted alternation with upper note (Cavalieri), syn: **Ribattuta*

Zurückschlag: **Ribattuta* (L. Mozart)

Zusammenschlag: 1. Here: simultaneous sounding of unprepared and unresolved non-harmonic tones within a chord

2. Species of mordent with ornamental note struck simultaneously but immediately released (Marpurg 1762), syn: *Abgeschnappter Mordent*

Zwischenschlag: 1. Here: single ornamental note that belongs equally to the regular note that precedes it and to the one that follows it. In instrumental music it is encompassed within the written or implied slur that connects its two parent notes; in vocal music it shares with both of them the same syllable.

2. Two interbeat ornamental notes that serve a connective purpose (L. Mozart)

2. SYMBOLS

The following tabulation does not include the unmetrical small notes except where they appear in non-standard designs. Whenever the placement of the symbol with regard to the ornamented note is not indicated, its location straight above or below the note is understood. The explanations are generally given in the working terminology used in the text and defined in the preceding Glossary of Terms. Whenever one or more authors listed among the sources uses a specific term, it is listed after the last of the names given; if an author uses the symbol but no specific term, only his name is listed. Different meanings of the same symbol are listed in the approximate order of their importance. Lute tablature letters are arbitrarily chosen.

I. Letters
  A. Capital
  B. Lower case
  C. With additions
II. Dots
III. Straight Lines
  A. Vertical: |
  B. Oblique: / | \
  C. Parallel: ‖ | // | \\
IV. Broken Lines
  A. ∧ shape
  B. ∨ shape
V. Crosses
  A. Straight: +
  B. Slanted: ×
VI. Other Composite Straight Lines
VII. Curved Lines
  A. Commas: ’
  B. Hooks or half-circles: ⊃|⊂ | ⌒ | ⌣
  C. Winding designs: ∼ | ∾ | ∽
VIII. Wavy and Zigzag Lines
  A. Horizontal: ∼ | 〰
  B. Vertical: ⌇
  C. With slash: 〰
  D. With additions: 〰 | 〰 | 〰 | 〰 etc.
IX. Miscellaneous
X. Combinations

I. Letters

A. Capital

A	French *accent* (Diruta: *Accento*)
C	1. Prebeat stepwise *Vorschlag* (Bernhard, Mylius: *Cercar della nota*) 2. Slide-like grace (Diruta: *Clamatione*) 3. Prebeat slide-like grace (Janowka, Walther: *Circuitus*); a dot at the top (C·) indicating descending, a dot at the bottom (C.) indicating ascending design 4. Swelling and tapering a single tone (D. Mazzocchi)
G	Undefined small figurations containing most often some repercussive elements (Diruta: *Groppo*)
M	Diminutions (Diruta: *Minuta*)
N	*Nachschlag* to pitch of following note (Bernhard: *Anticipatione della nota*)
S	Trill with half-step (Ganassi: *Suave*)
T	1. Main-note trill or Multiple mordent (Diruta: *Tremolo*) 2. Trill (Trabaci: *Trillo*)
V	Trill with whole step (Ganassi: *Vivace*)
Greek: Ε (Epsilon)	Gentle vocal pitch oscillation (Bérard: *Balancé* or *Flatté*)
Τ (Tau)	French *accent* (Bérard: *accent*)
Ψ (Psi)	Supported appogg. trill (Bérard: *Cadence appuyée*)
Hebrew: כ (Caph)	Swelling and tapering on long-held note (Bérard: *Son filé entier*)
ד (Daleph)	Swelling on long-held note (Bérard: *Son demi-filé*)

B. Lower Case

c	1. Slide (Murschhauser) 2. Phrasing or breathing mark (L'Affilard: ♩c♩)
e	Swelling of tone (Marais)
g	Trill-like ornament, starting on the main note with turned ending (Cavalieri: *Groppolo*)
h	Phrasing (breathing) mark (Blavet)
m	Mordent (Cavalieri: *Monachina*; Murschhauser)

t 1. Trill (It-G, F, 17th cent. to present)
  2. Trill *or* tone repetition, the latter usually suggested when the symbol is written between two notes of the same pitch: (It-G 17th cent.)
  3. Supported appogg. trill (Montéclair: *tr't appuyé*)

tr 1. Frequent alternative to t (often in the truncated form: t)
  2. Trill *or* (Multiple) mordent (Mylius: *Trillo*; most prob. also Dom. Scarlatti and other It. masters 17th to 18th cent.)
  3. *Schneller* or very short Main-note trill without Suffix (Devienne: *Trille* or *Petite cadence*)

v Fast trill (Ganassi: *vivace*)

z *Ribattuta* (Cavalieri: *Zimbalo*)

C. With Additions

ɯ Mordent (Samber: *Mordant, Semitremulus, Halber Triller*)

t 1. Trill, presumably truncated form of tr (J. S. Bach)

  2. Supported appogg. trill with Suffix and Rest point (G. Muffat: *Tr't réfléchissant*)

  3. Unsupported appogg. trill with Two-note suffix (Th. Muffat)

tɯ Lengthy non-keyboard trill (J. S. Bach [rare])

tɯ Non-keyboard trill with Two-note suffix (J. S. Bach [rare])

tr Mordent (Walther: *Mordant*)

t Mordent (G. Muffat: *Pincement*)

tɯ Unsupported appogg. trill with Two-note suffix and no Rest point (G. Muffat: *Tr't roulant*)

tr~~~ Long sustained trill alternations (Couperin: *Tr't continu*)

t̑ Trill with Suffix (Montéclair: *Tr't doublé*)

t̮ *Tr't lié* with Suspension pattern (Th. Muffat)

t₊ Trill starting with a leap of a third framing the main note (Trabaci)

II. Dots

˙ 1. Non-legato or staccato articulation (ubiquitous)

  2. Cancellation of *notes inégales* (F 17th to 18th cent.)

  3. Dynamic accent on occasional single notes (prob. J. S. Bach a. o.)

  4. Premature entry (Du Phly)

  Optional interbeat graces (Marais)

  Harmonic fill tones between bass and melody to avoid the accidental sounding of wrong tones (Marais)

$\cdot$ $\overset{\cdot}{2}$ $\cdot$
$\cdot$ $\cdot$ $\cdot$ $\Big\}$
$\underset{4}{}$

Number of dots signifies the gamba string on which the numbered finger is to play (Marais)

. d   Lute trill (Mace: Shake)

$\underset{\cdot}{d}$ Index finger plucking (F lutenists, 17th cent., Mace)

$\underset{\cdot\cdot}{d}$ Middle finger plucking (F lutenists, 17th cent., Mace)

$\cdot$ b
$\cdot\cdot$ c $\Big\}$
$\cdot\cdot\cdot$ d
$\cdot\cdot\cdot\cdot$ f

One to four dots before the letter refer to left-hand fingering (Vallet and some F lutenists, 17th cent.)

∴.d   *Vorschlag* from above plus Two-note suffix (Mace: Single relish)

: d   Stopping the string vibration (Mace: Tut)

III. STRAIGHT LINES

A. Vertical

1. Staccato articulation, usually implying greater sharpness than the dot (ubiquitous, including Couperin's *Aspiration* and Rameau's *Son coupé*)

2. On single notes: dynamic accent (a. o. J. S. Bach, Telemann, Quantz)

3. Cancellation of *notes inégales*

4. Two-finger gamba vibrato (Demachy: *Tr't sans appuyer*)

5. Mordent (Francoeur "neveu": *Martellement* or *Flaté*)

6. Slow Multiple mordent (Levesque & Bêche: *Flatté*)

7. Voice pulsation on one pitch (La Chapelle: *Balancement*)

The stepwise ascending *Nachschlag* of the French *accent* (D'Ambruis: *Plainte* or *Accent*; Loulié [his slash is placed above the note], L'Affilard, Montéclair, Denis, Villeneuve: *Accent*)

1. Phrasing mark (Le Bègue, Luc Marchand a. o.)

2. Phrasing mark or sign indicating the end of a specific expression (*Affectûs*) such as softness, fastness, etc. (Sperling: *Virgula* or *Comma*, terms suggesting that the sign may have had the shape of a comma like Couperin's [see below under VII *A*] rather than a slash)

| d   (Lute) Mordent (Mace: Beate)

B. Oblique

1. Rising *Vorschlag* (Fux; Janowka: *Einfall*; Walther: *Accentus*; Montéclair: *Pdv*)

2. Rising *Vorschlag* or *Nachschlag* (Kuhnau: *Accentus*)

3. Slide (Boyvin; Hotteterre: *Pdv doublé*; Montéclair: *Pdv double*)

4. *Nachschlag* to the pitch of the following note (Marpurg)

5. Strong legato with overlapping of the notes (Foucquet: *Liaison en montant*; prob. similar meaning for Couperin)

1. Falling *Vorschlag* (Fux; Janowka: *Einfall*; Walther: *Accentus*)

2. Falling *Vorschlag* or *Nachschlag* (Kuhnau: *Accentus*)

3. Falling *Nachschlag* to pitch of following note (Villeneuve: *Plainte*; Marpurg)

4. Legato with overlapping notes (Foucquet: *Liaison en descendant*; prob. also Couperin)

1. *Pdv* (Loulié, Montéclair [for the latter an alternate to the placement of the dash between the note heads])

2. Rising appogg. stepwise or leaping, but always repeating the pitch of the preceding note (G. Muffat: *Pdv*)

3. Stepwise ascending appogg. (Th. Muffat)

4. Extra legato in stepwise ascent (Nivers)

1. Falling *Nachschlag* to pitch of following note (Loulié: *Chute*)

2. Descending appogg. stepwise or leaping, the grace repeating the pitch of the preceding note (G. Muffat: *Pdv*)

3. Stepwise descending appogg. (Th. Muffat)

4. Extra legato in stepwise descent (Nivers)

Arpeggio upward (D'Anglebert, Le Roux: *Arpégé*; Dieupart: *Arpègement*; Rameau: *Arpègement simple*; Marpurg: *Zergliederung* or *Brechung*). With Marpurg the direction of the slant is immaterial: if slash is above the note, the arpeggio descends, if below, it ascends.

Arpeggio downward (same as above)

Arpeggio (Marais: *Harpègement*)

Intervallic arpeggio (Buxtehude, early J. S. Bach)

1. Figurate insert of middle pitch in ascent: ♫ (Chambonnières, Le Bègue, Raison, Jullien, Fischer: *Coulé*; Couperin: *Tierce coulée en montant*; J. S. Bach; C.P.E. Bach, Löhlein, Türk: *Acciaccatura*)

2. Intervallic arpeggio: ♫ (Le Roux: *Separez*; Fux)

1. Figurate insert of middle pitch in descent: ♫ (Couperin: *Tierce coulée en descendant*)

2. Descending Intervallic arpeggio (Le Roux: *Separez*)

Descending Intervallic arpeggio (Dieupart)

Ascending Intervallic arpeggio (Dieupart)

⁄d — (Lute) *Pdv* from half-step (Mace: Half fall)

d / c / a — Arpeggio (F lutenists, 17th cent.)

C. Parallel

1. Trill (Reincken: *Tremulus*)

2. *Nachschlag* to pitch of following note (Janowka; Walther: *Gedoppelter Accent*)

3. Mordent (Signoretti: *Pincé*)

Mordent (Heinichen 1711)

Onbeat *Vorschlag*, its pitch indicated by the location of the symbol (G. Muffat: *Suraccent* or *Praeaccentus* in descending: ; *Sous-accent* or *Subsumtio* in ascending: ; *Sursaut* or *Insultura* when leaping downward:)

Nachschlag, its pitch indicated by the location of the symbol (G. Muffat: *Accent* or *Accentus* when stepwise ascending: ; *Relâchement* or *Remissio* when stepwise falling: ; *Dispersion* or *Disjectio* when leaping upward: ; *Préoccupation* or *Praeoccupatio* when anticipating the following pitch:). The German and Italian equivalents of all these terms (contained in Muffat's quadrilingual dissertation) are omitted here.

Mordent (Kuhnau: *Mordant*)

1. Trill (Matteis)

2. Mordent (Geminiani: *Mordente*, Beat)

Supported appogg. trill (Blankenburg)

Supported main-note trill (Blankenburg)

IV. Broken Lines

A.

^

1. *Coulé* (Hotteterre: *Coulement*; Bordet [alternate to little notes], Démotz; prob. En. Gaultier)

2. *Pdv* or *Coulé* (Chaumont: *Pdv*)

3. *Pdv feint* (Bérard)

4. Prob. *Pdv* (Denis Gaultier: *accent*)

5. Mordent with whole step; ⊼ , Mordent with half-step (Basset [Mersenne])

6. Prob. trill (Bovicelli: *Tremolo*)

7. *Nachschlag* stepwise downward (Dard: *Accent*)

8. ? perhaps mordent (D'Ambruis: *Flattement*)

Nachschlag stepwise upward between notes of same pitch (Saint Lambert: *Aspiration*; Marpurg records the former use of this symbol and its being superseded by the little note with the reversed flag [see below under IX])

B.

Nachschlag stepwise downward (same as for the preceding entry)

1. *Pdv* (D'Ambruis, Berthet, L'Affilard, Hotteterre, Montéclair, Démotz, David, Bordet, Bérard)

2. Mordent with single stroke (Loulié: *Martellement*)

3. Ascending *Vorschlag* (Murschhauser)

Gamba glissando (Marais: *Coulé de doigt*)

Slide (Blankenburg)

Guidon indicates the placement of the next, occasionally of the preceding, note (F 17th and 18th cent.), equiv. of German *custos* ⌣ which was also used by some Frenchmen.

Descending *Vorschlag* (Murschhauser). The modern meaning of the symbol as dynamic accent originated probably at the very end of the 18th century.

V. CROSSES

A. Straight

+

1. Trill of any design (F mostly non-keyboard, 17th to 18th cent.)

2. Unsupported Upper-note trill, most likely Grace-note trill (Loulié: *Tremblement*; Montéclair: *Tremblement subit*)

3. Unsupported main-note trill (Lécuyer: *Cadence subite*)

4. One-stroke mordent (Foucquet: *Pincé simple*)

5. Multiple mordent (Fuhrmann: *Tremolo* or *Mordant*)

Supported appogg. trill (Loulié: *Tremblement appuyé*; L'Affilard: *Cadence soutenue* or *appuyée*)

Cadence feinte 1 (Hotteterre: *Demie cadence appuyée*)

Unsupported Upper-note trill (Lécuyer: *Cadence jettée*)

1. Mordent (Sainte Colombe; Danoville: *Pincé*; Forqueraye le Père)

2. *Coulé* (Boyvin: *Pdv*)

+d   (Lute) Slide (Mace: Whole-fall)

B. Slanted

×   1. Trill of any design (F 17th to 18th cent.; less frequent alternate to + , mostly non-keyboard)

2. Unsupported Main-note trill (Bérard: *Cadence précipitée* or *jettée*; prob. also D'Ambruis: *Cadence* or *Tr't en l'air*)

3. Mordent (Reincken: *Tremulus*)

ȣ̇   Prob. Supported appogg. trill (D'Ambruis: *Cadence* or *Tr't appuyé(e)*)

×ͱ   (Gamba) Mordent (Marais: *Batement*; Caix d'Hervelois)

×ͱ   Dactylic slide (Heinichen: *Schleifung*)

×d   (Lute) Mordent (En. Gaultier a. o.)

d×   1. (Lute) Trill (Vallet)

2. Stopping the vibration of the lute string (Denis Gaultier: *Étouffement*)

d×   (Lute) Vibrato downward (G 18th cent., Baron)

VI. Other Composite Straight Lines

ᴧ|ᴧᴧ   Mordent with double, resp. triple, alternations (Loulié: *Martellement*)

ͱ   Mordent (Hotteterre: *Battement*)

ɟ+   Single mordent (Demachy: *Martellement*)

ɟ‡   Double and prob. Multiple mordent (Demachy: *Double martellement*)

ͱ   *Hélan*, i.e. *Pdv* followed by French *accent* with dynamic intensification (L'Affilard, Villeneuve)

⋇   *Ribattuta* (Bérard: *Double cadence*)

1   Vocal pulsation on a long note, prepared by a crescendo (La Chapelle: *Balancement préparé*)

▼   Mordent (Dard: *Martellement*) alternate to ᴧᴧ

⌈ᵈ   Arpeggio upward (C.P.E. Bach: *Gebrochene Harmonie*)

⌈ᵈ   Arpeggio downward (same as above)

VII. Curved Lines

A. Commas

♪' 1. *Coulé* (Loulié)

2. Phrasing mark (Couperin)

♪' 1. Short trill, as contrasted to ♪) (Demachy: *Petit tr't*)

2. One-finger gamba vibrato (Danoville: *Balancement de main*)

♪ Two-finger gamba vibrato (Demachy: *Tr't sans appuyer*)

d, 1. (Lute) *Coulé* (Vallet)

2. Trill with half-tone (Basset [Mersenne]), as contrasted to d⸗ : trill with whole tone

3. Trill, and prob. also mordent, where no separate symbol was used for the latter (F lutenists 17th cent.)

4. Vibrato with the 4th finger (Danoville: *Balancement de main*)

d,· Vibrato (Basset [Mersenne]: *Verre cassé*)

,d Descending *Vorschlag* (Mace: Backfall)

B. Hooks or Half-Circles

♪) 1. (Gamba) Trill (Sainte Colombe; Marais, Demachy, Danoville, Caix d'Hervelois: *Tr't*)

2. (Keyboard) Mordent (D'Anglebert, Rameau: *Pincé*)

♪) (D'Anglebert, Le Roux: *Coulé sur une tierce*)

♪) Filled-in interbeat third (Saint Lambert: *Demy pdv*)

ᴕ (Keyboard) *Pdv*, mostly onbeat (D'Anglebert, Le Roux: *Pdv* or *Cheute en montant*; Dieupart: *Pdv* or Forefall up; Rameau: *Pdv*; J. S. Bach: *Accent steigend*)

ᴗ (Keyboard) *Coulé*, mostly onbeat (D'Anglebert, Le Roux: *Pdv* or *Ch(e)ute en descendant*; Dieupart: *Cheute* or Backfall; Rameau: *Coulez*; J. S. Bach: *Accent fallend*)

⸙ Variants of the last two entries. The upper crescent represents a slur mark (J. S. Bach)

✝ᴕ (Anticipated) *Vorschlag* from either direction (Saint Lambert: *Pdv simple*)

✝ᴕ 1. Twice-sounded prebeat *Vorschlag* (Saint Lambert: *Pdv appuyé*)

2. Twice-sounded onbeat *Vorschlag* (Marpurg: *Doppelaccent*)

✝ (D'Anglebert, Le Roux: *Coulé sur une tierce*)

Figurate ascending arpeggio with one insert (D'Anglebert, Le Roux: *Ch(e)ute sur une not(t)e*)

Figurate ascending arpeggio with two inserts (D'Anglebert: *Cheute sur deux nottes*)

Figurate descending arpeggio with one insert (Le Roux: *Chute sur une note*)

Figurate ascending arpeggio, the location of the hook indicating the placement of the inserted note(s), which was not the case in the previous entries (Saint Lambert: *Harpégé figuré*; Marpurg: *Accentuirte Brechung* or *Zergliederung*)

Figurate descending arpeggio (same as above)

Insertion of interbeat *Vorschläge* between the thirds (L'Affilard, Dupont, Villeneuve: *Coulement*). The crescents do not as such imply legato articulation between the principal notes; for the latter, Dupont, for example, indicates changing bow strokes.

Slide (D'Anglebert: *Coulé sur 2 nottes de suite*)

Ascending prebeat *Vorschlag* (Walther 1708: *Accentus ascendens*)

Descending prebeat *Vorschlag* (Walther 1708: *Accentus descendens*)

(Gamba) Glissando (Danoville: *Coulé du doigt*)

(Lute) *Pdv* (En. Gaultier, Baron, prob. also Dufaut)

(Lute) *Coulé* (Baron)

(Keyboard) *Pdv & p* (D'Anglebert, Le Roux: *Ch(e)ute et pincé*; Dieupart: *Pdv et pincé* or forefall beat; Rameau: *Pincé et pdv*)

C. Winding Designs

Mordent starting with the auxiliary (Nivers: *Agrément*)

Pdv (Demachy)

One-finger gamba vibrato (Demachy: *Aspiration*)

1. Turn, mostly four-note standard turn starting with the upper note on the beat (F 17th cent. on, a. o. Raison, D'Anglebert, Le Roux: *Double cadence*; L'Affilard: *Double cadence coupée*; Loulié, Hotteterre, Montéclair: *Tour de gosier*; Couperin: *Double*; Rameau: *Doublé*; Foucquet: *Redoublé*; G 18th cent. on, a. o. J. S. Bach: *Cadence*; C.P.E. Bach, Marpurg: *Doppelschlag*). J. S. Bach usually writes the sign from an oblique position to a vertical one.

2. Five-note turn starting with principal note (C.P.E. Bach: *Geschnellter Doppelschlag*; prob. sometimes J. S. Bach)

3. Old French turn (Chambonnières, D'Anglebert, Dieupart: *Double cadence*)

~ "Embedded" turn sounded in the middle or at the end of the principal notes. (Terms are generally the same as above under 1)

1. Inverted turn (C.P.E. Bach: *Schleiffer von dreyen Nötgen*; Löhlein; *Verkehrter Doppelschlag*; Marpurg; Petri)

2. Turn (Loulié: *Tour de gozier*)

VIII. Wavy and Zigzag Lines

A. *Horizontal*

1. (Keyboard) Trill of indetermined length (F 17th to 18th cent., G late 17th to 18th cent. incl. J. S. Bach: *Trillo*; also Dom. Scarlatti, as alternate to tr)

2. Very brief keyboard trill, *Prall-Triller* (C.P.E. Bach) sometimes *Schneller* (G 18th cent. and later)

3. Mordent (Rameau [orchestra]; David: *Pincé*; Dard: *Martellement*, as alternate to ▼)

1. Trill, equiv. of ⋀ (very common F and G 18th cent.)

2. Long trill as contrasted to short trill of ⋀ (C.P.E. Bach, Agricola a. o.)

3. Trill with Two-note suffix (Nivers: *Double cadence*)

4. Mordent (Murschhauser)
Long sustained trill alternations (a. o. Raison, J. S. Bach); see also above under IC: *tr*⋀⋀

Prob. trill with Two-note suffix (D'Ambruis: *Double cadence*)

Prob. Main-note trill (Demachy: *Battement*)

1. Vocal vibrato or intensity pulsations (F, It., G, E, 17th and 18th cent., including J. S. Bach; L'Affilard, Loulié, Montéclair, Villeneuve: *Balancement*; Lacassagne: species of *Martellement*; Stierlein, Deysinger: *Tremulus*; Sperling, Mattheson: *Tremolo*)

2. Instrumental vibrato including, sometimes, on strings, bow oscillations (It., F, G, E, 16th to 18th cent., incl. J. S. Bach; Tartini, Geminiani, L. Mozart: *Tremolo*; Brossard: *Tremolo* or *Tremulo* or *Tremulante*)

3. Two-finger gamba vibrato (Marais, Caix d'Hervelois: *Pincé* or *Flatement*; Danoville: *Battement*)

B. *Vertical*

1. Arpeggio, mostly upward, occasionally downward (F 17th cent. on, G 18th cent. on)

2. Arpeggio upward only (C.P.E. Bach; most likely also J. S. Bach and many others)

Arpeggio upward (Chambonnières, Raison: *Harpègement*; Saint Lambert: *Harpégé*)

Arpeggio downward (same as above)

Arpeggio upward (Couperin: *Arpègement en montant*)

Arpeggio downward (Couperin: *Arpègement en descendant*)

(Gamba) One-finger vibrato (Marais, Caix d'Hervelois: *Plainte*)

C. With Slash

⋏⋏ (or ⊹)

1. Mordent, single *or* multiple (F 17th to 18th cent., G 18th cent., It. late 18th cent.; a. o. Boyvin, Raison: *Pincement*; Couperin, Fischer: *Pincé*; Walther, J. S. Bach: *Mordant*; Marpurg: *Mordent*)

2. Single-stroke mordent (C.P.E. Bach, Agricola: *Mordent*)

3. Double-stroke mordent (Foucquet: *Pincé double*, distinguished from + for *Pincé simple*)

4. Trill (Rameau in orchestral works)

5. Mordent starting with auxiliary (Jullien: *Agrément* or *Pincement*)

Variant of preceding symbol (Boyvin: *Pincement*)

Multiple mordent (J. S. Bach)

Long-sustained mordent alternations (Couperin: *Pincé continu*; J. S. Bach)

1. Double or Multiple mordent (C.P.E. Bach, Agricola)

2. Single mordent (Chambonnières, Le Bègue: *Pincement*)

3. Miniature trill at the end of a long-held appogg. (Montéclair: *Tr̃'t feint*)

Trill with Two-note suffix (J. S. Bach: *Trillo und mordant*; Fischer: *Tremulo*)

Trill with Two-note suffix (Geminiani: *Trillo composto*)

D. With Additions

Slide (Kuhnau, Walther: *Schleiffer*; J. S. Bach; Marpurg, C.P.E. Bach: *Schleiffer*)

Custos indicating at end of line the location of the next note (G 17th to 18th cent.; a. o. J. S. Bach; less frequent in F)

Descending slide (Kuhnau, Walther: *Schleiffer*)

Descending appogg. (Heinichen: *Vorschlag*)

Ascending appogg. (Heinichen: *Vorschlag*)

1. (Keyboard) Supported appogg. trill (D'Anglebert, Le Roux: *Tr't appuyé*; Rameau, Dandrieu: *Cadence appuyée*)

2. (Keyboard) Upper-note trill ranging from Supported appogg. trill presumably to Grace-note trill (J. S. Bach: *Accent und trillo*)

Supported appogg. trill with Two-note suffix (Marpurg: *Vorbereiteter* or *accentuirter*, or *schwebender Triller*)

(Keyboard) Turn-trill (D'Anglebert: *Cadence*; J. S. Bach: *Doppeltcadence*; C.P.E. Bach: *Triller von oben*; Agricola: *Doppeltriller*; Marpurg: *Gezogener* or *geschleifter Triller*; Löhlein: *Trillo von oben herein*)

Turn-trill with One-note suffix before Rest point (Marpurg 1755: *Gezogener* or *geschleifter Triller*)

1. (Keyboard) Slide-trill (same sources and terms as above)

2. Any type of Compound trill (Marpurg 1749)

1. Slide-trill with One-note suffix before Rest point (Marpurg 1755)

2. Slide-trill with Two-note suffix (Petri: *Doppeltriller*)

Turn-trill with Two-note suffix (J. S. Bach: *Doppelt cadence und mordant*)

Slide-trill with Two-note suffix (same as above)

Slide-trill (Th. Muffat)

Slide-trill with Two-note suffix (Th. Muffat)

Main-note trill preceded by the upper neighbor, as indicated by the *guidon* (Dandrieu: *Tr't lié*)

Trill with Two-note suffix, moving stepwise upward (Dandrieu: *Tr't ouvert*)

Prebeat *Pdv* followed by Multiple mordent (Dandrieu: *Pincé et pdv*)

IX. Miscellaneous

Delayed entry (Couperin, Rameau: *Suspension*)

? (Couperin)

Vocal intensity pulsations (Loulié: *Balancement*). The clamp sign may be an inadequate printer's mark for the commonly used wavy line:

Clavichord vibrato (C.P.E. Bach, Marpurg, Türk: *Bebung*)

Scalewise slurred interbeat inserts between notes (G. Muffat: *Coulement figuré*)

Scalewise detached interbeat connection between notes (G. Muffat: *Tirade*)

⌢⋱	(Onbeat) Slide (Th. Muffat)
⁒	(Onbeat) Slide (G. Muffat: *Exclamation*)
⌒ᵖ	Anticipated *Vorschlag* [inverted flag of little note] (Marpurg, Petri)
ᴘ	*Nachschlag* [inverted flag] (Marpurg: *Angeschlossner Nachschlag*)
♪	Simultaneously struck but immediately released grace (Marpurg 1762: *Zusammenschlag*), not to be confused with either the 18th-cent. South German notation of a single 16th-note, or the 19th-cent. notation of a grace note.
d♯	Lute vibrato made upward (G Baron)

X. COMBINATIONS

⌒ ᵛ̣ᵖ	Slide, anticipated (L'Affilard, Villeneuve: *Pdv doublé*)
⤙ᵖ ⩘	Upper-note trill (J. S. Bach: *Accento und trillo*, as above: ⩘)
⤙ᵖ ⩘	*Pdv & p* (J. S. Bach: *Accent und mordant*)
⁀⁀	Trill with turned ending and occasional Rest point between the trill proper and the turn (Couperin, Walther, C.P.E. Bach a. o.)
⁀+	Trill with Two-note suffix (Hotteterre: *Double cadence*)
⸲ᵖ⸴	Trill with Two-note suffix (Demachy: *Tr't et martellement*)
⸲ᵖᵌ	Short trill (prob. *Schneller*) with Two-note suffix (Demachy: *Petit tr't et martellement*)
⤙ᵈ⸲	*Pdv & p* (Demachy: *Pdv et martellement*)
⊹	Mordent (Lécuyer: *Martellement*)
⌗	1. Slide-trill (Simpson: Cadent)
	2. Lute grace starting on main note, moving two steps up and back again (Mace: Elevation)
⸜⩘ or ⸜⩘ ~	Turn-trill with Two-note suffix (Marpurg: *Gezogener* or *geschleifter Triller*)
⸜⩘ ~	Slide-trill with Two-note suffix (same as above)
⩘⩘	? (Charpentier)
·⩘	? (Charpentier)
⫽	Ascending *Vorschlag* (Balth. Erben in Hintze MS at Yale)
⫽	Descending *Vorschlag* (same as above)
d.ɔ	(Lute) *Pdv* with whole step (Basset [Mersenne]: *Accent plaintif*)
d.ꝗ̄	(Lute) *Pdv* with half-step (same as above)

Selected Bibliography

1. PRIMARY SOURCES: TREATISES AND COMPOSITIONS CONTAINING THEORETICAL DOCUMENTS

Adlung, Jacob. *Anleitung zu der musikalischen Gelahrtheit.* . . . Erfurt, 1758; facs. Cassel, 1953.

Agincour, Francois d'. *Pieces de clavecin . . . premier livre.* Paris, 1733.

Agricola, Johann Friedrich. *Anleitung zur Singkunst,* trans. from P. Tosi's *Opinioni de' cantori,* with extensive commentaries in different print. Berlin, 1757; facs. (ed. Erwin R. Jacob) Celle, 1966.

———. *Schreiben an Herrn.* . . . [sic] *in welchem Flavio Anicio Olibrio sein Schreiben an den critischen Musicus an der Spree vertheidiget.* . . . Berlin, July 6, 1749.

Agricola, Martin. *Musica instrumentalis deudsch . . . ,* revised ed. Wittenberg, 1545. Reprint *Ges. f. Musikforschung,* Jg. 24, vol. 20, Leipzig, 1896.

Ahle, Johann Georg. *Musicalisches Herbst Gespräche.* . . . Mühlhausen, 1699.

Albrecht, Johann Lorenz. *Gründliche Einleitung in die Anfangslehren der Tonkunst.* . . . Langensalza, 1761.

Ambruis, Honoré d'. *Livre d'airs . . . avec les seconds couplets en diminutions.* . . . Paris, 1685.

Ammerbach, Elias Nicolaus. *Orgel-oder Instrument-Tabulatur.* Leipzig, 1571; 2nd ed., 1583.

Anglebert, Jean-Henri d'. *Pieces de clavecin.* Paris, 1689; facs. New York, 1965.

Azaïs, Pierre-Hyacinthe. *Méthode de musique.* . . . Paris [1776].

Bach, Carl Philipp Emanuel. *Versuch über die wahre Art das Clavier zu spielen . . . ,* part 1. Berlin, 1753; 2nd ed., 1759; 3rd enl. ed., Leipzig, 1787. Part 2, Berlin, 1762; 2nd ed., Leipzig, 1797; facs. Leipzig, 1957; English trans. and ed. Wm. J. Mitchell, New York, 1949.

Bacilly, Bénigne de. *Les trois livres d'airs . . . augmentez . . . d'ornemens pour la methode de chanter,* part 1. Paris, 1668.

———. *Remarques curieuses sur l'art de bien chanter.* . . . Paris, 1668; 2nd ed., 1679 with new preface; facs. Geneva, 1971; English trans. and ed. Austin B. Caswell, Brooklyn, 1968.

Bailleux, Antoine. *Méthode pour apprendre facilement la musique.* . . . Paris [1770]. The text of this treatise is a total plagiarism of Montéclair's *Méthode nouvelle* and *Principes.*

Banchieri, Adriano. *Cartella musicale nel canto figurato fermo et contrapunto.* Venice, 1614; facs. Bologna, 1968.

———. *Cartella overo regole utilissime.* . . . Venice, 1601.

———. *Gemelli Armonici.* . . . Venice, 1609.

———. *Vezzo di perle musicale,* Op. 23. Venice, 1610.

Baron, Ernst Gottlieb. *Historisch-theoretisch und practische Untersuchung des Instruments der Lauten.* . . . Nurnberg, 1727; facs. New York, forthcoming.

Bassano, Giovanni. *Ricercate, passaggi et cadentie.* . . . Venice, 1585.

Bêche, *see* Levesque and Bêche.

Bedos de Celles, Dom François. *L'art du facteur d'orgues,* vol. 4. Paris, 1778; facs. Cassel, 1966.

Beer (or Bähr), Johann. *Musicalische Discurse.* . . . Nurnberg, 1719.

Bérard, Jean-Antoine. *L'art du chant.* Paris, 1755; facs. Geneva, 1972 (*see also* Blanchet).

Bernhard, Christoph. (1) *Von der Singe-Kunst oder Manier;* (2) *Tractatus compositionis augmentatus;* (3) *Ausführlicher Bericht vom Gebrauche der Con- und Dissonantien;* all three treatises preserved in MSS, first publ. ed. Joseph Müller-Blattau, Leipzig, 1926; 2nd ed., Cassel, 1963. English tr. in *Music Forum,* vol. III.

Berthet, Pierre. *Leçons de musique . . . pour apprendre à chanter sa partie à livre ouvert.* 2nd ed., Paris, 1695.

Beyer, Johann Samuel. *Primae lineae musicae vocalis.* . . . Freiberg, 1703; 2nd ed. (in question and answer form), Dresden and Freiberg, 1730.

Blanchet, Jean. *L'art ou les principes philosophiques du chant.* Paris, 1756.

Blankenburg, Quirinus van. *Clavicimbel- en Orgelboeck der gereformeerde Psalmen.* . . . The Hague, 1732.

Bononcini Giovanni Maria. *Sonate da chiesa a due violini,* Op. 6. Venice, 1672.

Bordet, Toussaint. *Méthode raisonnée pour apprendre la musique.* . . . Paris [1755].

Bordier, Louis Charles. *Nouvelle méthode de musique.* Paris [c. 1760].

Borghese, Antonio D. R. *L'art musical ramené à ses vrais principes.* . . . Paris, 1786.

Bornet l'ainé. *Nouvelle méthode de violon et de musique.* . . . Paris [1786].

Bovicelli, Giovanni Battista. *Regole, passaggi di musica.* . . . Venice, 1594; facs. ed. N. Bridgman, Cassel, 1957.

Boyvin, Jacques. *Premier livre d'orgue.* . . . Paris, 1689.

———. *Traité abrégé de l'accompagnement pour l'orgue et pour le clavecin.* . . . 2nd ed., Paris, 1705.

Brijon, C. R. *L'Apollon moderne, ou le développement intellectuel par les sons de la musique* . . . , Op. 2. Lyon, 1780.

———. *Réflexions sur la musique et la vraie maniére de l'exécuter sur le violon.* Paris, 1763; facs. Geneva, 1972.

Brossard, Sébastien de. *Catalogue des livres de musique.* . . . Aut. MS 1724, BN Rés. Vm^8 20.

———. *Dictionnaire de musique.* . . . Paris, 1703; facs. Amsterdam, 1964.

Burney, Charles. *A General History of Music* . . . , vol. 4. London, 1789. (Reprint New York, 1957.)

Buterne, Charles. *Méthode pour apprendre la musique vocale et instrumentale.* Paris, Lyon, and Rouen, 1752.

Caccini, Giulio. *Le nuove musiche.* Florence, 1602 (the year 1601 on the copy in Bol. refers to the Florentine calendar and is actually 1602); facs. New York, 1973.

Capirola, Vincenzo. *Compositione di Meser Vicenzo Capirola* (c. 1517), ed. Otto Gombosi. Neuilly sur Seine, 1955.

Cartier, Jean Baptiste. *L'art du violon.* 3rd ed. rev. and corr., Paris [1803]; facs. New York, 1973.

Cavalieri, Emilio de'. *Rappresentatione di anima et di corpo.* Rome, 1600; facs. Bologna, 1967.

Cerone, Pedro. *El melopeo y maestro.* . . . Naples, 1613.

Chambonnières, Jacques Champion de. *Pieces de clavessin.* Paris, 1670; facs. New York, 1967.

Chaumont, Lambert. *Pieces d'orgue sur les 8 tons.* . . . Liège, 1696.

Choquel, Henri-Louis. *La musique rendue sensible par la méchanique.* . . . Paris, 1759 and 1762; 2nd ed. titled *Méthode pour apprendre facilement la musique soi-même.* . . . Paris, 1782; facs. 1762 ed. Geneva, 1972.

Cima, Giovanni Paolo. *Concerti ecclesiastici.* . . . Milan, 1610.

Conforto, Giovanni Luca. *Breve et facile maniera* . . . *a far passaggi.* . . . Rome, 1593 (year partly illegible, could be 1603).

Corrette, Michel. *Les amusements du Parnasse. Méthode* . . . *pour apprendre à toucher le clavecin.* . . . Paris [1749].

———. *L'École d'Orphée, méthode pour apprendre facilement à jouer du violon.* . . . Paris, 1738.

———. *Méthode pour apprendre aisément à joüer de la flute traversière.* . . . Anon. publ. Paris, date of privil., 1735.

———. *Méthode* . . . *pour apprendre en peu de tems le violoncelle.* . . . Paris, 1741; facs. New York, forthcoming.

———. *Le parfait maître à chanter.* . . . Paris, 1758.

Couperin, François. *L'art de toucher le clavecin.* Paris, 1716; enl. ed., 1717; facs. New York, 1969.

———. *Le Parnasse ou l'apothéose de Lully.* Paris, 1725.

————. *Piéces de clavecin*. Paris, 1713.

————. *Troisiéme livre de piéces de clavecin*. Paris, 1722; facs. New York, 1973.

Crüger, Johann. *Musicae practicae praecepta brevia. . . . Der rechte Weg zur Singekunst. . . .* Berlin, 1660.

————. *Praecepta musicae practicae figuralis. . . .* Berlin, 1625.

————. *Synopsis musica. . . .* Berlin, 1654.

Dagincour, *see* Agincour.

Dalla Casa, Girolamo. *Il vero modo di diminuir . . . ,* vols. 1 and 2. Venice, 1584; facs. Bologna, 1970.

Dandrieu, François. *Premier livre de pièces de clavecin.* Paris, 1724.

————. *Premier livre d'orgue.* Paris, 1739.

Danoville. *L'art de toucher le dessus et basse de violle. . . .* Paris, 1687; facs. Geneva, 1972.

Daquin, Louis-Claude. *1er livre de pieces de clavecin. . . .* Paris, 1735.

Dard. *Nouveaux principes de musique. . . .* Paris [1769].

David, François. *Méthode nouvelle ou principes généraux pour apprendre facilement la musique et l'art de chanter.* Paris, 1737.

Dellain, Charles-Henri. *Nouveau manuel musical. . . .* Paris, 1781.

Demachy. *Pieces de violle. . . .* Paris, date of privil., 1685.

[Démo(t)z de la Salle]. *Méthode de musique selon un nouveau système. . . .* Paris, 1728.

Denis, Pierre. *Nouveau système de musique pratique. . . .* Paris, 1747; 2nd ed. rev. and corr. under title *Nouvelle méthode pour apprendre . . . la musique et l'art de chanter. . . .* Paris [c. 1760].

Devienne, François. *Nouvelle méthode théorique et pratique pour la flûte. . . .* Paris, 1794.

Deysinger, Johann Franz Peter. *Compendium musicum oder fundamenta partiturae. . . .* Augsburg, 1763; 2nd ed., Augsburg, 1788.

Dieupart, Charles. *Six suittes de clavessin. . . .* Amsterdam [c. 1702].

Diruta, Girolamo. *Il Transilvano. . . .* Vol. 1, Venice, 1593; vol. 2, Venice, 1609; facs. (of 1622 ed.) Bologna, 1969.

Dupont, Henri Bonaventure [in privilege called "Pierre"]. *Principes de musique par demande et par réponce. . . .* 2nd ed., Paris, 1718.

————. *Principes de violon par demandes et par réponce. . . .* Paris, 1718, 1740 (both editions are practically identical).

Dupuit, Jean Baptiste. *Principes pour toucher de la viele. . . .* Paris [1741].

Durieu. *Nouvelle méthode de musique vocale. . . .* Paris [1793].

Duval. *Méthode agréable et utile pour apprendre facilement à chanter. . . .* Paris [1775]; facs. Geneva, 1972. The author of this treatise, who calls himself "maître de musique et du goût," is not identical with L'abbé Pierre Duval.

Duval, L'abbé Pierre. *Principes de la musique pratique par demandes et par réponses.* Paris, 1764.

Engramelle, Marie-Dominique-Joseph. *La tonotechnie ou l'art de noter les cylindres. . . .* Paris, 1775; facs. Geneva, 1971.

Falck, Georg. *Idea boni cantoris. . . .* Nurnberg, 1688; facs. New York, forthcoming.

Feyertag, Moritz. *Syntaxis minor zur Sing-Kunst. . . .* Duderstadt, 1695.

Finck, Hermann. *Practica musica. . . .* Wittenberg, 1556.

Fiocco, Joseph Hector. *Pièces de clavecin,* Op. 1. Brussels [1730]; modern ed. *MMB,* vol. 3.

Fischer, Johann Caspar. *Musicalisches Blumen-Büschlein . . . ,* Op. 2. Augsburg [1696].

Foucquet, Pierre-Claude. *Les caractères de la paix, pieces de clavecin.* Paris [c. 1750].

Francoeur, Louis-Joseph ("neveu"). *Diapason général de tous les instrumens à vent. . . .* Paris [1772]; autograph additions on ornaments, BN, MS 1843-1844.

Freillon-Poncein, Jean Pierre. *La véritable manière d'apprendre à jouer en perfection du haut-bois, de la flûte et du flageolet. . . .* Paris, 1700; facs. Geneva, 1971.

Frescobaldi, Girolamo. *Toccate e partite d'intavolatura di cimbalo, libro primo.* Rome, 1615-1616.

Fuhrmann, Martin Heinrich. *Musicalischer Trichter.* . . . Berlin ("Frankfurt an der Spree"), 1706. The *Musica vocalis in nuce* . . . (Berlin [1715]) is essentially a 2nd rev. ed. of the *Trichter.*

Gagliano, Marco. *La Dafne.* Florence, 1608; preface reprinted in vol. 1, pp. 264ff. of Emil Vogel, *Bibliothek der gedruckten weltlichen Vocalmusik Italiens.* 2 vols. Berlin, 1892. (Reprint Hildesheim, 1962.)

Galileo, Vicenzo. *Dialogo della musica antica e della moderna.* Venice, 1581; facs. New York, 1967; excerpts trans. in Strunk, *Source Readings,* pp. 302-322.

Galliard, J. E., *see* Tosi.

Ganassi, Sylvestro. *Opera intitulata Fontegara.* . . . Venice, 1535; facs. Milan, 1934; German trans. H. Peter, Berlin, 1956; English trans. (from the German) D. Swainson, Berlin, 1959.

———. *Regola rubertina.* . . . Venice, 1542; facs. Bologna, 1970.

Gasparini, Francesco. *L'armonico pratico al cimbalo.* . . . Venice, 1708; facs. New York, 1967.

Gaultier, Denis. *Livre de tablature des pieces de luth, de Gaultier Sr de Nève et de Mr Gaultier son cousin.* . . . Paris [1672]; facs. in *MdlMa,* vol. 6, ed. André Tessier, Paris, 1931.

———. *Pieces de luth.* . . . Paris [1669 or 1670].

Geminiani, Francesco. *A Treatise of good Taste in the Art of Musick.* London, 1749; facs. ed. R. Donington, New York, 1969.

———. *The Art of playing on the Violin.* . . . London, 1751; facs. ed. D. Boyden, Oxford, n.d.

Gigault, Nicolas. *Livre de musique dédié à la tres Ste. Vierge.* . . . Paris, 1682.

———. *Livre de musique pour l'orgue.* . . . Paris, 1685.

Hartung (or Hartong). *Musicus theoretico-practicus.* . . . Nurnberg, 1749. Publ. under pseud. P. C. Humanus.

Heinichen, Johann David. *Der Generalbass in der Composition.* . . . Dresden, 1728.

———. *Neu erfundene und gründliche Anweisung . . . zu vollkommener Erlernung des Generalbasses.* . . . Hamburg, 1711.

Helmont, Charles-Joseph van. *Pièces de clavecin,* Op. 1. Brussels [1737].

Herbst, Johann Andreas. *Arte prattica et poëtica.* . . . Frankfurt/Main, 1653.

———. *Musica practica.* . . . Nurnberg, 1642; 2nd enl. ed. titled *Musica moderna prattica.* . . . Frankfurt, 1658; facs. (1st ed.) New York, forthcoming.

Hiller, Johann Adam. *Anweisung zum musikalisch-richtigen Gesange.* . . . Leipzig, 1774.

———. *Anweisung zum musikalisch-zierlichen Gesange.* . . . Leipzig, 1780.

———. *Anweisung zum Violinspielen.* . . . Grätz, 1795; facs. New York, forthcoming.

Hotteterre, Jacques (named "Le Romain"). *Méthode pour la musette.* . . . Paris, 1738.

———. *Premier livre de pièces pour la flûte traversière . . . ,* Op. 2. New ed., Paris, 1715.

———. *Principes de la flute traversière.* . . . Paris, 1707; facs. Cassel, 1958.

Hüllmandel, Nicolas Joseph. *Principles of Music, chiefly calculated for the Piano Forte or Harpsichord.* . . . London [c. 1795].

Humanus, P. C., *see* Hartung.

Janowka, Thomas Balthasar. *Clavis ad thesaurum magnae artis musicae.* . . . Prague, 1701. [A musical lexicon.]

Jullien, Gilles. *Premier livre d'orgue.* . . . Paris, 1690.

Kuhnau, Johann. *Frische Clavier Früchte oder sieben Suonaten.* Leipzig, 1696.

———. *Neuer Clavier-Übung Erster Theil.* Leipzig, 1689. Modern ed. together with *Neuer Clavier-Übung Andrer Theil* (1692), *DDT,* ser. 1, vol. 4, ed. Karl Päsler. Leipzig, 1901.

Kürzinger, Ignaz Franz Xaver. *Getreuer Unterricht zum Singen mit Manieren und die Violin zu spielen.* . . . Augsburg, 1763.

Laag, Heinrich. *Anfangsgründe zum Clavier-spielen und Generalbas.* Osnabrück, 1774.

L'Abbé le Fils (Joseph Barnabé Saint-Sevin). *Principes du violon.* . . . Paris, 1761; facs. ed. Aristide Wirsta, Paris, 1961.

Lacassagne, L'abbé Joseph. *Traité général des élemens du chant.* Paris, 1766; facs. Geneva, 1972.

La Chapelle, Jacques-Alexandre de. *Les vrais principes de la musique.* . . . Vol. 1, Paris, 1736; vol. 2, Paris, 1737; vol. 3, Paris, 1739; vol. 4, Paris [1752?].

L'Affilard, Michel. *Principes très-faciles pour bien apprendre la musique.* . . . Paris, 1694; 2nd ed., 1697; 5th ed., 1705.

Lange, Johann Caspar. *Methodus nova et perspicua in artem musicam.* . . . Hildesheim, 1688.

Le Bègue, Nicolas. *Les pieces de clavessin.* Paris, 1677.

———. *Second livre d'orgue.* Paris [c. 1678].

Leclair, Jean-Marie. *Quatrieme livre de sonates à violon seul avec la basse continue.* Paris [1738].

Lécuyer. *Principes de l'art du chant.* . . . Paris, 1769.

Le Menu de Saint Philbert. *Principes de musique courts et faciles.* Paris [1743].

Le Roux, Gaspard. *Pièces de clavessin.* Paris, 1705.

Levesque and Bêche. *Solfèges d'Italie.* Paris [17—].

Löhlein, Georg Simon. *Anweisung zum Violinspielen.* . . . Leipzig and Züllichau, 1774; facs. New York, forthcoming.

———. *Clavier-Schule.* . . . Leipzig and Züllichau, 1765; 2nd ed., 1773; 3rd ed., 1779; 4th ed., 1782; facs. (1765) New York, forthcoming.

Lorenzoni, Antonio. *Saggio per ben sonare il flauto traverso.* . . . Vicenza, 1779.

Loulié, Étienne. *Éléments ou principes de musique.* . . . Paris, 1696; facs. Geneva, 1971; English trans. and ed. Albert Cohen, New York, 1965.

Lusse, Charles de. *L'art de la flûte traversière.* Paris [1760].

Mace, Thomas. *Musick's Monument.* . . . London, 1676; facs. Paris, 2nd ed. 1966 with 2nd vol. of commentary by Jean Jacquot and transcriptions by André Souris.

Maichelbeck, Franz Anton. *Die auf dem Clavier lehrende Caecilia.* . . . Augsburg, 1738.

Manfredini, Vincenzo. *Regole armoniche.* . . . Venice, 1775; facs. New York, 1966.

Marais, Marin. *Pieces a une et a deux violes.* Paris, 1686; *2nd livre de pièces de viole,* Paris, 1701; *3me livre de pièces de viole,* Paris, 1711; *4me livre de pièces a une et a trois violes,* Paris, 1717; *5me livre de pièces de viole,* Paris, 1725.

Marcou, Pierre. *Elémens théoriques et pratiques de musique.* London, 1782.

Marpurg, Friedrich Wilhelm. *Anleitung zum Clavierspielen.* . . . Berlin, 1755; facs. New York, 1966.

———. *Anleitung zur Musik überhaupt, und zur Singkunst besonders.* . . . Berlin, 1763.

———. *Des critischen Musicus an der Spree erster Band.* Berlin, 1750 (collected issues of the journal *Der critische Musicus* 1749-1750).

———. *Die Kunst das Clavier zu spielen.* . . . 4th enl. ed., Berlin, 1762.

———. *Kritische Briefe über die Tonkunst,* vol. 2. Berlin, 1761-1763.

Martini, Jean-Paul-Égide [acc. to Fétis, a pseud. for Schwartzendorf]. *Mélopée moderne ou l'art du chant.* . . . Paris [c. 1791].

Mattheson, Johann. *Critica musica.* . . . Vol. 1, Hamburg, 1722; vol. 2, Hamburg, 1725.

———. *Das neu-eröffnete Orchestre.* . . . Hamburg, 1713.

———. *Der brauchbare Virtuoso.* . . . Hamburg, 1720.

———. *Der vollkommene Capellmeister.* . . . Hamburg, 1739; facs. Cassel, 1954.

Mercadier de Belesta, Jean-Baptiste. *Nouveau système de musique théorique et pratique.* Paris, 1776.

Mersenne, Marin. *Harmonie universelle, contenant la théorie et la pratique de la musique.* . . . Paris, 1636. This work contains eight treatises, each with its separate pagination. Facs. of a copy with the author's annotations (Centre national de la recherche scientifique), Paris, 1965.

Millet, Jean. *La belle méthode ou l'art de bien chanter.* Lyon, 1666; facs. ed. Albert Cohen, New York, 1973.

Montéclair, Michel Pignolet de. *Nouvelle méthode pour aprendre la musique.* . . . Paris, 1709.

Montéclair, Michel Pignolet de. *Petite méthode pour apprendre la musique aux enfans.* . . . Paris [c. 1710-1734].

———. *Principes de musique.* . . . Paris [1736].

Mozart, Leopold. *Versuch einer gründlichen Violinschule.* . . . Augsburg, 1756; 2nd ed., 1769 and 1770; 3rd ed., 1787; facs. (1st ed.) Vienna, 1922; English trans. E. Knocker, London, 1948.

Muffat, Georg. *Florilegium I.* . . . Augsburg, 1695; *Florilegium II.* . . . Passau, 1698; modern ed. *DTÖ*, vol. 1, no. 2 and vol. 2, no. 2 (1895).

Muffat, Gottlieb (Theophil). *Componimenti musicali per il cembalo,* Augsburg [c. 1736]; facs. New York, 1967; modern ed. *DTÖ*, vol. 3, no. 3 (1896).

———. *Versetl sammt 12 Toccaten.* . . . Vienna, 1726; modern ed. *DTÖ*, vol. 29, no. 3 (1922).

Murschhauser, Franz Xaver Anton. *Prototypon longo breve organicum,* part 1. Nurnberg, 1703; modern ed. *DDT*, ser. 2, vol. 18.

Mylius, Wolfgang Michael [published under autogram cluster: W.M.M.M.T.C.M.G.]. *Rudimenta musices, das ist: eine kurtze und grund-richtige Anweisung zur Singe-Kunst.* . . . Mühlhausen, 1685.

Nivers, Guillaume-Gabriel. *Livre d'orgue.* . . . Paris, 1665.

North, Roger. *Roger North on Music: Being a Selection from his Essays written . . . c. 1695-1728,* ed. John Wilson. London, 1959.

Ortiz, Diego. *Trattado de glosas sobra clausulas.* . . . Rome, 1553; modern ed. with German trans. (M. Schneider). Cassel, 1924.

Panerai, Vincenzo. *Principi di musica.* . . . Florence [c. 1750-1780].

Penna, Lorenzo. *Li primi albori musicali.* . . . 3 vols. Bologna, 1672; 5th ed., 1696.

Peri, Jacopo. *Euridice.* Florence, 1600.

Perrine. *Pieces de luth en musique avec des regles pour les toucher parfaitement sur le luth et sur le clavessin.* . . . Paris [1680].

Petri, Johann Samuel. *Anleitung zur practischen Musik.* . . . Lauban, 1767; 2nd enl. ed., Leipzig, 1782; facs. of 2nd ed. Giebing, 1969.

Petschke, Adolf Friedrich. *Versuch eines Unterrichts zum Klavierspielen.* Leipzig, 1785.

Playford, John. *An Introduction to the Skill of Musick.* 7th ed., London, 1674.

Poglietti, Alessandro. *Compendium oder kurzer Begriff und Einführung zur Musica.* . . . Ms Kremsmünster, Benediktinerstift; microfilm *DMA* 1/2241.

Praetorius, Michael. *Syntagma musicum* . . . , vol. 3. Wolfenbüttel, 1619; facs. Cassel, 1958.

Printz, Wolfgang Caspar. *Compendium musicae signatoriae et modulatoriae vocalis.* . . . Dresden, 1689; 2nd ed., Dresden and Leipzig, 1714.

———. *Musica modulatoria vocalis.* . . . Schweidnitz, 1678.

———. *Phrynis Mytilenaeus oder satyrischer Componist.* . . . Quedlinburg, part 1, 1676; part 2, 1677; 2nd ed., Dresden and Leipzig, 1696, identical except for added pagination.

Quantz, Johann Joachim. *Versuch einer Anweisung, die Flöte traversiere zu spielen.* . . . Berlin, 1752; facs. of 3rd ed. (Breslau, 1789), which is identical with the first except for some modernized spelling, Cassel, 1953; French trans. Berlin, 1752; English ed. and trans. Edward R. Reilly, *On Playing the Flute,* London, 1966.

———. [Autobiography] "Herrn Johann Joachim Quantzens Lebenslauf von ihm selbst entworfen" in F. W. Marpurg, *Historisch-kritische Beyträge zur Aufnahme der Musik,* vol. 1, Berlin, 1755, pp. 197-250.

Raison, André. *Livre d'orgue, contenant cinq messes.* . . . Paris, date of priv. 1688.

Rameau, Jean-Philippe. *Code de musique pratique.* . . . Paris, 1760; facs. New York, 1965.

———. *Pièces de clavessin avec une méthode pour la mechanique des doigts.* . . . Paris [1724], republ. 1731; facs. New York, 1967.

———. *Premier livre de pièces de clavecin.* Paris, 1706.

Raparlier. *Principes de musique.* . . . Lille, 1772. Almost entirely a plagiarism of Montéclair.

Reincken, Johann Adam. *Hortus musicus.* . . . Hamburg, 1687.

Rigler, Franz. *Anleitung zum Klavier.* . . . Vienna [1779].

Rodolphe, Jean-Joseph. *Solfége ou nouvelle méthode de musique.* . . . Paris [c. 1784].

Rogniono, Richardo. *Passaggi per potersi essercitare nel diminuire . . .* (part 2 titled *Il vero modo di diminuire . . .*). Venice, 1592.

Rognoni Taegio, Francesco. *Selva de varii passaggi secondo l'uso moderno.* . . . Milan, 1620; facs. Bologna, 1970.

Rousseau, Jean. *Méthode claire, certaine et facile, pour apprendre à chanter la musique.* . . . [2nd ed.], Paris, 1683; the 1st ed. of 1678 is missing; the "4th ed.," revised and enlarged, is identified as 3rd on p. 66, Amsterdam [1700].

———. *Traité de la viole.* . . . Paris, 1687.

Rousseau, Jean Jacques. *Dictionnaire de musique.* Paris, 1768; facs. Hildesheim, 1969.

Roy, Eugène. *Méthode complete pour le flageolet.* Paris, n.d.

Saint Lambert, Michel de. *Les principes du clavecin.* . . . Paris, 1702; facs. Geneva, 1972.

Samber, Johann Baptist. *Continuatio ad manuductionem organicam.* . . . Salzburg, 1707.

———. *Manuductio ad organum.* . . . Salzburg, 1704; facs. New York, forthcoming.

Santa Maria, Tomás de. *Libro llamado arte de tañer fantasia.* . . . Valladolid, 1565; facs. New York, forthcoming.

Schickhardt, Johann Christian (Jean Christien). *Principes de la flûte . . . ,* Op. 12. Amsterdam [c. 1730?].

Severi, Francesco. *Salmi passaggiati.* . . . Rome, 1615.

Signoretti, P. *Méthode contenant les principes de la musique et du violon.* 3 parts. The Hague, 1777.

Simpson, Christopher. *The Division-Violist: or, an Introduction to the Playing of a Ground.* . . . London, 1659.

Sperling, Johann Peter. *Porta musica, das ist: Eingang zur Music.* . . . Görlitz and Leipzig, 1708.

Spiess, Meinrad. *Tractatus musicus compositorio-practicus.* . . . Augsburg, 1745.

Steiner, Johann Ludwig. *Kurz- leicht- und gründtliches Noten-Büchlein.* . . . Zurich, 1728. A plagiarism of Fuhrmann.

Stierlein, Johann Christoph. *Trifolium musicale consistens in musica theorica, practica et poetica.* . . . Stuttgart, 1691.

Tarade, Théodore-Jean. *Traité du violon.* . . . Paris [c. 1774]; facs. Geneva, 1972.

Tartini, Giuseppe. Letter to Maddalena Lombardini, posthumously published: *Lettera del defonto Signor Giuseppe Tartini alla Signora Maddalena Lombardini inserviente ad una importante lezione per i suonatori di violino,* Venice, 1770; English trans. Dr. Burney, London, 1771; French trans. (anon.) Paris, 1773; German trans. A. Hiller, Leipzig, 1784. Original and translations are contained in the modern edition of Tartini's *Regole,* ed. Erwin R. Jacobi.

———. *Regole per arrivare a saper ben suonar il violino, col vero fondamento di saper sicuramente tutto quello, che si fa.* . . . Ms Bol.; facs. as supplement to German-French-English publication *Traité des agréments,* ed. Erwin R. Jacobi, Celle and New York, 1961. French trans. P. Denis, Paris, 1771; German and English translations based on Denis's partially unreliable French version, before the original was discovered c. 1960 in a MS by Tartini's student G. F. Nicolai. German trans. Erwin R. Jacobi and Ruth Cahn-Fridberg, English trans. Cuthbert M. Girdlestone.

Telemann, Georg Philipp. *Vorbericht zu musicalisches Lob Gottes.* Nurnberg, 1744.

Testori, Carlo Giovanni. *La musica ragionata.* . . . Vercelli, 1767.

Thielo (or Thilo), Carl August. *Grund-Regeln wie man . . . die Fundamenta der Music und des Claviers lernen kan.* . . . Copenhagen, 1753. Published anon. under the autogram C.A.T., it is, according to Fétis, an abridged trans. of Thielo's *Tanker og Regler fra Grunden af om Musiken.* . . . Copenhagen, 1746.

Tosi, Pierfrancesco. *Opinioni de' cantori antichi, e moderni o sieno osservazioni sopra il canto figurato.* Bologna, 1723; facs. as supplement to J. F. Agricola, *Anleitung,* facs. ed. Erwin R. Jacobi, Celle, 1966.

Tromlitz, Johann Georg. *Ausführlicher und gründlicher Unterricht, die Flöte zu spielen.* Leipzig, 1791; facs. New York, forthcoming.

Tubel, C. G. *Kurzer Unterricht von der Music.* . . . Amsterdam, 1766. Bilingual ed. in Dutch and German.

Türk, Daniel Gottlieb. *Klavierschule.* . . . Leipzig und Halle, 1789; facs. Cassel, 1962.

Vallet, Nicolas. *Le secret des muses, 1er livre.* Amsterdam, 1615; modern ed. *CdLF*, Paris, 1970.

Viadana, Lodovico. *Cento concerti ecclesiastici.* . . . Venice, 1602.

Villeneuve, Alexandre de. *Nouvelle méthode très courte et très facile . . . pour aprendre la musique et les agréments du chant.* Paris, 1733; the 2nd "enlarged" ed. of 1756 is identical.

Vogler, Georg Joseph, Abbot. *Kuhrpfälzische Tonschule.* Mannheim [1778]. The pertinent music examples are in *Gründe der Kuhrpfälzischen Tonschule in Beispielen.* . . . Mannheim [1778]; also in *Mannheimer Monatsschrift,* vols. 1-3 (1778-1780).

Walther, Johann Gottfried. *Musicalisches Lexicon.* . . . Leipzig, 1732; facs. Cassel, 1953.

———. *Praecepta der musicalischen Composition.* Aut. MS (1708), Landesbibliothek, Weimar; published ed. Peter Benary, Leipzig, 1955.

Wiedeburg, Michael Johann Friedrich. *Der sich selbst informierende Clavierspieler.* . . . 3 vols. Vol. 1, Halle and Leipzig, 1765; vol. 2, Halle, 1767; vol. 3, Halle, 1775.

Wolf, Ernst Wilhelm. *Musikalischer Unterricht.* . . . Dresden, 1788.

Wolf, Georg Friedrich. *Unterricht im Klavierspielen,* part 1. 3rd enl. ed., Halle, 1789.

Zacconi, Lodovico. *Prattica di musica.* . . . Venice, 1592; facs. Bologna, n.d.

———. *Prattica di musica, seconda parte.* . . . Venice, 1622.

2. SECONDARY SOURCES

Aldrich, Putnam. "On the Interpretation of Bach's Trills," *MQ,* vol. 49 (1963), pp. 289-310.

———. *Ornamentation in J. S. Bach's Organ Works.* New York, 1950.

———. "The Principal Agréments of the 17th and 18th Centuries: A Study in Musical Ornamentation," unpubl. diss., Harvard Univ., 1942.

Arger, Jane. *Les agréments et le rythme.* Paris [1921].

Becker, Carl Ferdinand. *Systematisch-chronologische Darstellung der musikalischen Literatur: von der frühesten bis auf die neueste Zeit.* Leipzig, 1836; supplement, Leipzig, 1839; facs. Amsterdam, 1964.

Beyschlag, Adolf. *Die Ornamentik der Musik.* Leipzig, 1908; reprints, Leipzig, 1953 and 1970.

Bodky, Erwin. *The Interpretation of Bach's Keyboard Works.* Cambridge, Mass., 1960.

Borrel, Eugène. *L'interprétation de la musique française (de Lully à la Révolution).* Paris, 1934.

Boyden, David D. *The History of Violin Playing: from its origins to 1761.* . . . London, 1965.

Brown, Howard M. *Embellishing Sixteenth-Century Music.* Oxford University Press, 1976.

Brunold, Paul. *Traité des signes et agréments employés par les clavecinistes français des 17e et 18e siècles.* Lyon, 1925; reprint, Nice, 1965.

Chrysander, Friedrich. "L. Zacconi als Lehrer des Kunstgesanges," part 2, *VfMw,* vol. 9 (1893), pp. 249-310.

Cohen, Albert. "L'Art de bien chanter (1666) of Jean Millet," *MQ,* vol. 55 (1969), pp. 170-179.

Dadelsen, Georg von. "Verzierungen," *MGG,* vol. 13, cols. 1526-1556.

Dannreuther, Edward. *Musical Ornamentation.* 2 vols. London [1893-1895].

Dart, Thurston. *The Interpretation of Music.* London, 1954; reprint, New York, 1963.

David, Hans T. and Mendel, Arthur. *The Bach Reader,* New York, 1945; rev. ed., 1966.

Dolmetsch, Arnold. *The Interpretation of the Music of the 17th and 18th Centuries: Revealed by Contemporary Evidence.* London [1915]; reprint, London [1944].

Dolmetsch, Carl. *Ornaments and Graces in Music of the 17th and 18th Centuries,* record album UWP 2001 with printed and spoken commentary. Seattle, 1973.

Donington, Robert. *The Interpretation of Early Music.* London, 1963; 2nd ed., 1965; New Version, 1974.

———. *A Performer's Guide to Baroque Music.* New York, 1973.

Emery, Walter. *Bach's Ornaments*. London, 1953.

———. "Is your Bach playing authentic?—I," *Musical Times* (May 1971), pp. 483-488.

Ferand, Ernest T. *Die Improvisation in Beispielen aus neun Jahrhunderten abendländischer Musik*. Vol. 12 of *Das Musikwerk*. Cologne, 1956; 2nd rev. ed., 1961.

———. *Die Improvisation in der Musik*. Zurich, 1938.

Germani, Fernando. *Metodo per organo*, vol. 3 (devoted exclusively to ornamentation). Rome, 1951.

Goldschmidt, Hugo. *Die italienische Gesangsmethode des 17. Jahrhunderts*. Breslau, 1890.

———. *Die Lehre von der vokalen Ornamentik*, vol. 1. Charlottenburg, 1907.

Gurlitt, Willibald. *Johann Sebastian Bach: der Meister und sein Werk*. Cassel, 1959.

Haas, Robert M. *Aufführungspraxis der Musik*, HdM, Wildpark-Potsdam, 1931.

Hall, James S. and Hall, Martin V. "Handel's Graces," *Händel Jahrbuch* (1957), pp. 25-43.

Kast, Paul. *Die Bachhandschriften der Berliner Staatsbibliothek*. Trossingen, 1958.

Keller, Hermann. *Die Klavierwerke Bachs*. Leipzig, 1950.

Kinney, Gordon J. "Problems of Melodic Ornamentation in French Viol. Music," *Jl of the Viola da Gamba Soc. of America*, vol. 6 (1968), pp. 34-50.

Kirkpatrick, Ralph. *Domenico Scarlatti*. Princeton, 1953.

———, ed. J. S. Bach, *Goldberg Variations*. New York, 1938.

Kolneder, Walter. *Aufführungspraxis bei Vivaldi*. Leipzig, 1955.

Kreutz, Alfred. *Die Ornamentik in J. S. Bach's Klavierwerken*. Frankfurt, 1950 (annex to the Peters Urtext edition of the English Suites).

Kuhn, Max. *Die Verzierungskunst in der Gesangs-Musik des 16.-17. Jahrhunderts (1535-1650)*. Leipzig, 1902; reprint, Wiesbaden, 1969.

Landowska, Wanda. "Bach und die französische Klaviermusik," *BJ* (1910), pp. 33-44.

Landshoff, Ludwig. *Revisions-Bericht zur Urtextausgabe von J. S. Bach's Inventionen und Sinfonien*. Leipzig, 1933.

———. "Über das vielstimmige Accompagnement und andere Fragen des Generalbass-piels," *Festschrift Adolf Sandberger*. Munich, 1918, pp. 189-208.

Mellers, Wilfrid. *François Couperin and the French Classical Tradition*. London, 1950.

Mendel, *see* David and Mendel.

Mersmann, Hans. "Beiträge zur Aufführungspraxis der vorklassischen Kammermusik in Deutschland," *Archiv für Musikwissenschaft*, vol. 2 (1920), pp. 99-143.

Neumann, Frederick. "Couperin and the Downbeat Doctrine for Appoggiaturas," *AM*, vol. 41 (1969), pp. 71-85.

———. "External Evidence and Uneven Notes," *MQ*, vol. 52 (1966), pp. 448-464.

———. "The Use of Baroque Treatises on Musical Performance," *M & L*, vol. 48 (1967), pp. 315-324.

Paesler, Carl. "Fundamentbuch von Hans von Constanz," *VjMw*, vol. 5 (1889), pp. 1-192.

Rose, Gloria. "Agazzari and the Improvising Orchestra," *JAMS*, vol. 18 (1965), pp. 382-393.

Schering, Arnold. *Aufführungspraxis alter Musik*. Leipzig, 1931; reprint, Wiesbaden, 1969.

———. "Zur instrumentalen Verzierungskunst im 18. Jahrhundert," *SIMG*, vol. 7 (1905-1906), pp. 365-385.

Schmitz, Hans-Peter. *Die Kunst der Verzierung im 18. Jahrhundert*. Cassel, 1955.

Spitta, Philipp. *Johann Sebastian Bach*. 2 vols. Leipzig, 1873, 1880.

Strunk, Oliver. *Source Readings in Music History: From Classical Antiquity through the Romantic Era*. New York, 1950.

Westrup, Jack Allen. "The Cadence in Baroque Recitative," *Natalicia Musicologica Festschrift Knud Jeppesen*. Copenhagen, 1962, pp. 243-252.

Williams, Peter. "The Harpsichord Acciaccatura: Theory and Practice in Harmony, 1650-1750," *MQ*, vol. 54 (1968), pp. 503-523.

Wolf, Johannes. *Handbuch der Notationskunde*. 2 vols. Leipzig, 1913; reprint (Olms), Hildesheim, 1963.

Zietz, Hermann. *Quellenkritische Untersuchungen an den Bach-Handschriften P 801, P 802 und P 803. . . .* Hamburg, 1969.

Index

Page numbers in italic indicate musical examples. The terms for ornaments used in the index are those of the working terminology introduced in the book. For their definitions consult the Glossary. "Bach" without initials refers to Johann Sebastian.

ABBREVIATIONS

appogg.	appoggiatura	orn., orn's	ornament, ornaments
arpg.	arpeggio	*pdv*	*port de voix*
dimin's	diminutions	*pdv & p*	*port de voix et pincé*
E.	English	*pcs de cl*	*pièces de clavecin*
F.	French	*tr't*	*tremblement*
G.	German	*V'g*	*Vorschlag*
It.	Italian	*Zus'g*	*Zusammenschlag*
N'g.	*Nachschlag*	*Zw'g*	*Zwischenschlag*

accent (F.), 92; d'Ambruis, 92; Bacilly, 93; Choquel, 95-96; Corrette, 94; Dard, 95, 96; David, 94; defined, 92; Denis, 94; Duval, 95; L'abbé Duval, 95; Hotteterre, 95; L'Abbé le Fils, 94; Lacassagne, 95; de la Chapelle, 94; L'Affilard, 92, 93; Lécuyer, 95; Loulié, 92, 93; Montéclair, 93; J. Rousseau, 59, 93; J. J. Rousseau, 94; Saint Lambert, 94; symbols for, 92-93; Villeneuve, 84, 94; Walther, 96. *See also N'g*

Accent (G.), Bach, 96; Beyer, 113-114; Marpurg, 186; Mattheson, 180-181; Mylius, 108, 109, 110, 111; Walther, 110, 117. *See also* appogg.; *N'g*; *V'g*

accento, 92; Banchieri (slide), 211-212; Bernhard, 105; Crüger, 103-104; Diruta, 97-98; in final cadences, 541; Fuhrmann, 116; Ganassi, 96; Herbst, 103, 104; shortness of, 128; Viadana, 24; Walther, 113, 118; Zacconi, 22-23, 97, 98. *See also* appogg; *N'g*; *V'g*

accento doppio, 119

accentus: Falck, 212-213; Feyertag, 112-113; Kuhnau, 119-120; Praetorius, 103; Printz, 111; Samber, 115; Stierlein, 111-112. *See also Accent* (G.); *accento*; appogg.; *N'g*; *V'g*

acciaccatura, 48, 92, 479; Gasparini, 481-482; Geminiani, 485-486; Heinichen, 438; D. Scarlatti, 486-487; Williams, 487n. *See also* arpg., figurate; *Zus'g*

Adlung, Jacob, on Mylius, 108n; on Humanus (Hartung), 367n

Agazzari, Adrio, free ornamentation, 537

Agincour, François d', 531; orn. table in modern edition, 208n; slide, 208, 209; slide-trill, 396

agogic accent, 23n

agréments, 34-36; in Bach's keyboard suites, 42-43; freedom of, 531; Loulié, 61-62; Nivers, 258-259; shift to onbeat leanings of, 36. *See also* orn's; ornamentation, free

Agricola, Johann Friedrich, 39, 41, 43, 161, 185, 191, 198, 213-214; *Anschlag*, 490; appogg. in recitative, 159, 541; attack on Marpurg, 186; on cadenzas, 556-557; compound trill, 410; on Marpurg's compound trill, 408; on Marpurg's mordent, 457; mordent, 458, 461; on mordent terminology, 452; *N'g*, 188;

pdv & p, 458; *Pralltriller*, 375; *ribattuta*, 375; slide, 234, 235, 236; *Tactglied* and *Tacttheil*, 235n; on Tosi's compound trill, 406; on Tosi's trill, 345, 346; trill, 374, 375, 376; trill symbols, 186; trill with suffix, 374, 375; turn, 478; vibrato, 521; *V'g*, 131, 187-188, 374-375

Agricola, Martin, vibrato, 517

Ahle, Johann Georg, forbidden parallels, 14

airs de cour, diminutions in, 31, 32-33, 526, 527-528. *See also* d'Ambruis; Bacilly; de Bailly; Lambert; Mersenne; Moulinié

Alberghi, Paolo, slide, 229; *V'g*, 171

Alberti, Domenico, 358n; *Anschlag*, 491

Alberti, Giuseppe Matteo, 491n; appogg.-trill, 358-359

Albinoni, Tomaso, free ornamentation, 535, 537

Albrecht, Johann Lorenz, 197

Aldrich, Putnam, 266, 312, 374n, 384

Altnikol, Johann Christoph, 140, 227n, 335n

Ambruis, Honoré d', 32, 513; *accent*, 92; *coulé*, 53; free ornamentation, 526-527; mordent, 421; *pdv*, 57; trill, 247-248; *V'g*, 52

Ammerbach, Elias Nicolaus, mordent, 415; trill, 415

Andreas Bach Buch, 121n; notation of slide, 215-216, 222

Anfossi, Giovanni, *V'g*, 168

Anglebert, Jean-Henri d', 69, 70, 73, 74, 75, 80, 92, 179, 210, 530; arpg., chordal, 494-495; arpg., figurate, 504-505; Bach's use of orn. table by, 127; compound trills, 391, 392, 393, 398; *coulé*, 68; mordent, 420, 421; orn. symbols, 35; *pdv*, 68; *pdv & p*, 68, 420, 421; slide, 205; studied by Bach, 41; trill, 259, 260, 261; trill with suffix, 448; turn, 392, 467 WORKS: *pcs de cl*, 68, 261

Anschlag, 203, 488; Agricola, 490; D. Alberti, 491; C.P.E. Bach, 489-490; Bach, 488; Hiller, 490; Löhlein, 490; Marpurg, 490; melodic design of, 488; W. J. Mitchell on C.P.E. Bach's, 490n; L. Mozart, 460, 490; W. A. Mozart, 491; Petri, 490; Quantz, 488-489; rhythmic disposition of, 488; Tromlitz, 491; Türk, 491

Anschlagender Vorschlag: Quantz, 189; Tromlitz, 198

Library of Congress Cataloging in Publication Data

Neumann, Frederick.
   Ornamentation in baroque and post-baroque music.

   Bibliography: p.
   Includes index.
   1.   Embellishment (Music)   2.   Bach, Johann
Sebastian, 1685-1750. Works.   I.   Title.
MT80.N48   781.6'7   77-72130
ISBN 0-691-9123-4